Microsoft® Small Business Server 2003 UNLEASHED

Eriq Oliver Neale, et al.

800 East 96th Street, Indianapolis, Indiana 46240

Microsoft Small Business Server 2003 Unleashed

Copyright © 2006 by Sams Publishing

All rights reserved. No part of this book shall be reproduced, stored in a retrieval system, or transmitted by any means, electronic, mechanical, photocopying, recording, or otherwise, without written permission from the publisher. No patent liability is assumed with respect to the use of the information contained herein. Although every precaution has been taken in the preparation of this book, the publisher and author assume no responsibility for errors or omissions. Nor is any liability assumed for damages resulting from the use of the information contained herein.

International Standard Book Number: 0-672-32805-4

Library of Congress Catalog Card Number: 2003111834

Printed in the United States of America

First Printing: December 2005

05 04 03 02 4 3 2 1

Trademarks

All terms mentioned in this book that are known to be trademarks or service marks have been appropriately capitalized. Sams Publishing cannot attest to the accuracy of this information. Use of a term in this book should not be regarded as affecting the validity of any trademark or service mark.

Warning and Disclaimer

Every effort has been made to make this book as complete and as accurate as possible, but no warranty or fitness is implied. The information provided is on an "as is" basis. The authors and the publisher shall have neither liability nor responsibility to any person or entity with respect to any loss or damages arising from the information contained in this book.

Bulk Sales

Sams Publishing offers excellent discounts on this book when ordered in quantity for bulk purchases or special sales. For more information, please contact

U.S. Corporate and Government Sales
1-800-382-3419
corpsales@pearsontechgroup.com

For sales outside the U.S., please contact

International Sales
international@pearsoned.com

Publisher
Paul Boger

Acquisitions Editor
Loretta Yates

Development Editor
Mark Renfrow

Managing Editor
Charlotte Clapp

Project Editor
George Nedeff

Copy Editor
Geneil Breeze

Indexer
Erika Millen

Proofreader
Linda Seifert

Technical Editor
Susan Bradley

Publishing Coordinator
Cindy Teeters

Interior Designer
Gary Adair

Cover Designer
Gary Adair

Page Layout
Michelle Mitchell

Contents at a Glance

Table of Contents

About the Lead Author

Eriq Oliver Neale is an internationally recognized Small Business Server expert in addition to being an accomplished author, musician, blogger, teacher, and all-around geek. He started building PCs from scratch to help pay his way through college and never looked back. In the 17 years he has worked in IT, he has dealt with DOS, VAX/VMS, Novell, Macintosh, all flavors of Windows, and all manner of communication technologies, including email systems and remote access solutions.

Eriq's writing credits include contributions to *The Internet Unleashed 1997* from Sams Publishing, *Windows 2000 Server System Administrator's Handbook, E-mail Virus Protection Handbook,* and several books in both the 2000 and 2003 MCSE exam preparation series. One of his earliest works, an article on MIDI (musical instrument digital interface), is still a frequently referenced document on the Internet.

Eriq spent a year as a support engineer in the Small Business Server team of Microsoft's Product Support Services. In addition to resolving complex support issues, he also developed internal documentation used by other support engineers. He also contributed heavily to the "Connecting Macintosh Clients to a Windows Small Business Server" document released by Microsoft early in 2005.

Eriq makes his home in northern Texas with his wife and pets. His consulting practice provides direct support to small businesses locally, and he consults with other small business IT support firms around the globe. When he is not posting in the newsgroups, participating in email discussion groups, supporting clients domestically and abroad, taping his weekly small business technology radio show, or writing about small business topics in his blogs, Eriq can usually be found in his recording studio, curled up with a good mystery, or relaxing in front of the television.

About the Other Authors

Amy Babinchak holds degrees from Michigan State University in Public Affairs, Natural Resources, and Environmental Economics. In 1995, she made the switch from environmentalist to computer tech after getting tired of applying for grants to do "good works" and ending up as the computer person anyway. At times she has supported Novell 3.12 - 5, Mac OS, Microsoft NT, and everything on up. Amy enjoys learning new things, so when ISA showed up in SBS 2000 she viewed it as a challenge and focused on mastering this new security tool. She started Harbor Computer Services in 2000 to fill an obvious gap in qualified small business support. In 2005, her company was recognized by Microsoft as the first Small Business Specialist in the Detroit, Michigan, area. Recently Amy has begun speaking to user groups and accepting ISA consulting contracts from other firms. When not running her business, blogging, and supporting clients, she can be found on Lake Huron getting away from it all on her sailboat without which she would shrivel up and die.

Timothy Truman Barrett is cleverly disguised as a mild-mannered geek. He actually is a happily married man with his lovely wife of 15 years, Dayna. They have two wonderful daughters, Stephanie and Lauren, who are also lovely. And Tim hates monkeys. A lot.

Obsessed with building things from Lincoln Logs and Tinker Toys almost from birth, Tim finally got his first computer at age 15—an old, used TRS-80 Model I. It had no instructions or manuals, but by trial and error, he figured out how to make it work. He also learned BASIC and spent the entire summer bugging his mother and six siblings by constantly showing them all the "cool" stuff he could do with it.

After studying computer aided drafting (CAD) and physics at Louisville Technical Institute, he went to work in the healthcare industry. As a veritable "jack-of-all-trades," Tim has worked with just about everything: sewing machines, table saws, X-ray machines, IBM mainframes, phone systems, servers, PCs, and the occasional backhoe.

At age 36, Tim is currently a Microsoft Certified Professional, a Microsoft Small Business Specialist, and the founder of the Kentucky Small Business Server User Group (KYSBSUG). His motto is, "No Geek Left Behind." He also has strong religious values as one of Jehovah's Witnesses.

Susan Bradley, SBS MVP, CPA/CITP, MCP, GSEC, also known as the SBS Diva (a nickname given to her by David Coursey from ZDNet), is a geek, blogger (`www.msmvps.com/bradley`), and a CPA/CITP who holds the GSEC security credential. She writes on patch management issues for Brian Livingston's *Windows Secrets* newsletter and has co-authored a book on Small Business Server. She also co-authored an e-book on patch management with Anne Stanton for Ecora Software. She is a Microsoft MVP in the categories of Small Business Server and security, and volunteers for the Center for Internet Security in its benchmark and standard setting processes. She has been an "SBSer" since the 4.0 days (yes, believe it or not, she liked the platform even then).

Past chairman of the Technology Committee for the California Society of CPAs, Susan's been a speaker at past SMB Nation events, AICPA Tech Conferences, and regional CPA Technology Conferences. A firm believer that community involvement is key to keeping all of us safe and secure, you can find Susan most days in the newsgroups or blogging or on the PatchManagement.org listserve. She strongly urges businesses of all shapes and sizes to be more secure. Unless she can figure out a way to service patch her end users, the best things she can do to protect them is to lock down desktops and ensure that patches are installed, firewalls enabled, and install antivirus and antispyware on all computers. Susan believes that the key to protecting client data and identities from the bad guys is to be proactive and not reactive.

Susan started her career in computing with IBM 8088 computers and Compaq "luggable" portables. To this day she is convinced that her right arm is longer than her left arm because she lugged those dang "luggables" for an entire summer at an audit job. Now she practically has an RJ45 connection growing out of her body.

Frank Clark has been involved with IT, directly or indirectly, for more than two decades. Since the late 4.0 days, he has become increasingly involved in Microsoft's Small Business Server product line as a customer, consultant, and evangelist. With a detailed-oriented approach and the desire to tinker and learn more, he has delved further under the hood of SBS than few others and enjoys sharing the tales of exploration. His background in EMS and healthcare along with his experience in the U.S. Army provides unique perspectives and solutions utilizing SBS and other technologies while encompassing a healthy dose of security.

Henry Craven cites curiosity as the force that led him to his 15 years in the IT industry. As a commercial photographer, his initial interest in computing was fired by the potential for cataloging and retrieving images. Based on his considerable business experience, he quickly began to apply the new technology to wider business problems, both for himself and clients. Finding early PC software generally too limited to be of real business use, he began writing software in BASIC, Turbo Pascal, and, later, Paradox. This led to the need for networking and the deployment of his solutions over LANs through Novell, OS/2, and early Windows peer-to-peer networks.

An early adopter of MS Access as the primary desktop database application environment for rapid development of small business applications, Henry soon became an authority in small business data-based application development and contributed generously to the online communities of CompuServe, Deja News, and Microsoft public forums.

Henry's commitment to finding real-world solutions for business problems continued when he set Microsoft Small Business Server as his primary focus. Recognized by Microsoft for two years running as a Small Business Server Most Valuable Professional, Henry continues to participate tirelessly in online peer communities and as an expert speaker. Henry sees SBS as providing a much-needed rich, stable, scalable, and affordable network solution and business application platform for small businesses.

Henry attributes his success to these tenets:

- Listen and learn from all those around you, ceaselessly.
- Regard yourself as a partner with your clients and apply your expertise to help them achieve their goals.
- A good solution should be almost transparent to the client.
- Your client's ability to grow with the technology is a measure of your success.

Javier Gomez is a Microsoft MVP for Small Business Server and an active participant in both online and offline IT communities focusing in the SMB market. Although a chemical engineer by education, he is really an entrepreneur at heart. He strongly believes in using technology not just for the sake of it but as a key business tool to work smarter and faster. As a Microsoft MVP, he has helped hundreds of administrators and end users around the globe to get the most out of their servers. He is a member of several SBS user groups in Maryland; Washington, DC; and Philadelphia. In his free time he enjoys BBQs, movies, beaches, and visiting Puerto Rico.

Chad A. Gross is a Partner and Chief Technology Officer with Mobitech in Omaha, Nebraska, as well as a Microsoft Small Business Server Most Valuable Professional (MVP). Chad earned a Bachelor of Arts degree in Computer Science from Central College in Pella, Iowa; has worked supporting the computing needs of small businesses since 1999, and has worked with Small Business Server since SBS 4.5. In addition to working with SBS, he also helps clients streamline workflows and maximize their IT investment by creating custom Microsoft Office solutions mostly based on Microsoft Access, Microsoft Windows SharePoint Services, and Microsoft SQL Reporting Services. Chad uses his unique combination of technical, accounting, and business administration skills to provide tailored solutions that represent tremendous value to Mobitech's clients. Outside of work, Chad enjoys camping, renovating his home, and walking his dog. Chad lives in Council Bluffs, Iowa.

Anne Stanton specializes in leveraging technology within accounting and consulting professional service firms of all sizes all over the world. As a former executive vice president of an advanced practice management software development company for ten years and now as current president of a professional service consulting firm, she continues to increase lines of revenue, streamline procedures, maximize profit, and expand services for best practicing firms. The Norwich Group services are diversified by both business consulting services and technology consulting services within the company. Technology specialties include Customer Relationship Management solutions, Small Business Server, and process focused line-of-business applications. The Business consulting services include leveraging partner affiliations, increasing "A" level clients while weaning "C" level clients, and helping small service firms meet their business goals.

Anne is one of seven globally recognized Microsoft Most Valuable Professionals for the MS CRM software. She is also an active participant in numerous communities and virtual forums. As the moderator of the International Small Business Server Leader's Group, a community of more than 70 international technology group leaders, she leverages contacts to create positive business solutions for all involved. Anne is also the founder of the NH/VT Upper Valley Technology Consultant's Group. She has helped Top 100 accounting and consulting firms all over the country master the practice management software process and has worked with the smallest firms in her area on utilizing their existing office products more efficiently. Anne dives in, helps when she can, and tells you when The Norwich Group services do not meet your needs.

In the first year of business for The Norwich Group, Anne co-authored two books: *The Complete Guide to Patch Management* and *The AICPA's Guide to the 2004 Top Technologies*. She also is a contributing writer for *Accounting Software 411.com*, the *CPA Technology Advisor, iSixSigma and the AICPA's IT Section Newsletter, InfoTech Update*, as well as other industry-specific journals. Anne is an active speaker and has presented at both technology-specific national conferences (such as SMB Nation) and at accounting industry-specific shows such as The AICPA Technology Conference. She is the editor of the *Information Technology Alliance* (`www.italliance.com`) newsletter and an active participant in numerous events. Anne can be reached at `astanton@thenorwichgroup.com`.

Edward E. Walters is a Microsoft Certified Systems Engineer (MCSE), Microsoft Certified Systems Administrator (MCSA), Cisco Certified Network Associate (CCNA), and Cisco Certified Design Associate (CCDA). Living in Rowlett, Texas, he is an independent contractor specializing in Microsoft Small Business Server 2000 and Microsoft Small Business Server 2003.

Acknowledgments

Anyone who has spent any amount of time working with SBS has come to know the community that exists in support of the product. This community extends well beyond the reach of Microsoft and is championed by the SBS MVPs (Most Valuable Partners). This book is for the SBS community, by the SBS community. The authors who have contributed to this book are consultants, MVPs, and former PSS (Product Support Service) engineers who share one key trait—they are evangelists for the Small Business Server product and want everyone who works with this product to be successful with it.

No single person could have penned this book with the level of detail and expertise that this author group has brought to the table. And to that end, no single person could have adequately done the technical edit either. Key resources in the SBS community were targeted to contribute as authors, reviewers, and editors for this work. Without the help of all of them, this project never could have been completed.

I'd like to thank the following individuals for the help and guidance they provided me for the entire process of putting this book together:

- Susan Bradley, for coordinating the technical edit of the book, writing a chapter, reviewing the original book proposal, and hooking me up with the right contacts when I mentioned that I ought to write a book.
- Marina Roos, for reviewing the original book proposal, doing spot-check reviews on chapters while they were in progress, and keeping me on my toes and deadlines.
- Chad Gross, for contributing a chapter and providing a no-holds-barred review of the original book proposal.
- Loretta Yates, for never giving up on me or the book. You've been amazing to work with, and I look forward to our next project.

Thanks also to all the authors, reviewers, and editors from the SBS community who contributed to this project. Even though some of your names may not appear in the pages that follow, your efforts are recognized and appreciated.

I'd like to thank the development team at Sams for their patience and understanding through this process and all the obstacles that came our way. The editing crew was one of the best I've worked with in years.

I owe a special thanks to my clients who let me put them off temporarily while I worked to meet a deadline.

Finally, I owe the biggest thanks of all to my wife, Anna, who put up with the late nights, high stress, and lack of free weekends while I worked on this project. I could not have done this without your understanding and support.

We Want to Hear from You!

As the reader of this book, *you* are our most important critic and commentator. We value your opinion and want to know what we're doing right, what we could do better, what areas you'd like to see us publish in, and any other words of wisdom you're willing to pass our way.

As a publisher for Sams Publishing, I welcome your comments. You can email or write me directly to let me know what you did or didn't like about this book—as well as what we can do to make our books better.

Please note that I cannot help you with technical problems related to the topic of this book. We do have a User Services group, however, where I will forward specific technical questions related to the book.

When you write, please be sure to include this book's title and author as well as your name, email address, and phone number. I will carefully review your comments and share them with the author and editors who worked on the book.

Email: feedback@samspublishing.com

Mail: Paul Boger
Publisher
Sams Publishing
800 East 96th Street
Indianapolis, IN 46240 USA

For more information about this book or another Sams Publishing title, visit our website at `www.samspublishing.com`. Type the ISBN (excluding hyphens) or the title of a book in the Search field to find the page you're looking for.

Introduction

Microsoft's recent focus on the small business market segment is nowhere more evident than in the development and marketing of the Small Business Server product. For years, while Microsoft pushed the mentality that each of its major product offerings really needed to be installed on separate servers, a small group of developers quietly worked to integrate these enterprise-level technologies into a single-server implementation that worked reliably. But not until the Small Business Server 2003 product did Microsoft really get it right. And with the release of Service Pack 1 for SBS 2003, the product has reached a maturity that equals the demand small businesses have for such a product.

With the announcement of the Small Business Specialist designation in the summer of 2005, Microsoft began a huge marketing push to get existing partners to qualify for the designation as well as to draw new partners into the program. Many larger partners have not had the exposure to the product or the market space and frequently find themselves in a jam when working with the SBS product for the first time. Until now, there has not been a single reliable resource for partners to use to not only get an understanding of the SBS product but also to "go beyond the wizards" and learn the best ways to customize the product.

This book was developed to fit that need. Each chapter in the book covers a technology or implementation issue at several levels. First, the chapter introduces the topic and gives a fairly detailed overview for the reader who has not been exposed to the topic previously. Second, the chapter presents the configuration settings for a default installation, where appropriate, as a reference for the reader. Next, the chapter goes into advanced configuration for the technology, including how-to steps for commonly requested customizations. Finally, the chapter ends with a troubleshooting section that details more than just "rerunning the wizard."

In addition, this book spreads beyond the typical Microsoft publication on a topic by covering aspects of Small Business Server installations that consultants face in the real world. Consultants who have needed to incorporate other operating systems, Macintosh and Linux specifically, into an SBS network now have a set of reference and how-to material that will aid them in quickly including these technologies into the SBS environment.

This text is not the end-all, be-all on the SBS topic, however. Certain topics and issues had to be left out to keep the book at a reasonable size. Technician's toolkits are large enough already without lugging an 80-pound book along with them. For those topics not addressed within these pages, the reader can review the public references found in Appendix A, "SBS Resources," to locate help and reference materials. The SBS community is worldwide, and the majority of community members is more than willing to help out a newcomer when he runs into the first major problem.

Book Overview

- Part I, "Overview of Microsoft Small Business Server 2003," details the history of the product and presents the business case for using SBS in a small office environment.
- Part II, "SBS 2003 Installation," covers the planning and execution of a Small Business Server 2003 new installation.
- Part III, "SBS 2003 Networking," focuses on the networking technologies of SBS, including DHCP, DNS, IIS, remote access, VPN, and Terminal Services.
- Part IV, "Security," takes an in-depth look at security issues facing network administrators at both the server and workstation level.
- Part V, "Exchange," focuses on the email features of SBS at the client and server level and covers Exchange disaster recovery issues as well.
- Part VI, "Web Technologies," looks at two of the most popular innovations of SBS, Remote Web Workplace and Companyweb.
- Part VII, "Client Connectivity," details the management of clients in the SBS network and covers incorporating Macintosh and Linux clients.
- Part VIII, "Administration and Management," takes an in-depth look at the maintenance side of SBS, including the monitoring and reporting tools, backups, group policy, and keeping systems up to date with security patches.
- Part IX, "Internet Security and Acceleration (ISA) Server," looks at ISA 2004 and how it integrates into the SBS environment.

PART I

Overview of Microsoft Small Business Server 2003

IN THIS PART

CHAPTER 1

Understanding SBS Technologies

IN THIS CHAPTER

- The Growth and Maturing of SBS
- Versions of SBS 2003

Businesses are increasingly challenged to perform better, faster, and more economically with fewer resources. This is especially true of smaller companies; strapped for the tools and technology to improve their business, they are often caught between staying with inefficient systems that work or gambling the future of the company on new or unproven technology.

Starting from humble beginnings, Microsoft Small Business Server 2003, known as SBS 2003, provides a comprehensive networking solution for smaller businesses. Including many features such as shared documents and calendars, email, messaging, secure Internet access and data storage, reliable printing and faxing, and remote administration, SBS 2003 has evolved into a proven world-class business platform providing technologies and tools that enable small businesses to be more productive and efficient. SBS 2003 accomplishes this by utilizing several key Microsoft tools and technologies:

- Windows Server 2003
- Windows SharePoint Services
- Exchange Server
- Microsoft Office Outlook
- Microsoft Office FrontPage
- SQL Server
- ISA Server

Listing the included technologies does nothing to explain what SBS is really all about and barely scratches the surface of its potential. Retail copies of SBS can be obtained and can be up and running quickly and easily. SBS 2003 is also available preloaded from many OEM, system builders, and consultants both large and small and can be deployed in minimal time frames. The SBS development team has done a great job and all but eliminated the need for great depths of knowledge and lengthy training by creating wizards to assist with the most common tasks. SBS still does have a learning curve, but this can be overcome relatively easily with time and guidance from those familiar with and knowledgeable about the product. It is still recommended to be well versed in SBS for the planning and deployment of an SBS network and to be available if major problems arise.

Because SBS 2003 has been rolled into the Windows Server 2003 family, the standard interface provides a consistent look and feel across the entire platform. This means that usage and management provide the same experience whether using a desktop computer, working on the SBS server, or even when accessing a member server in the domain. So those familiar with Microsoft's products will spend less time learning the product and more time using the product, while being more productive in the process. The Client Setup Wizard provides a mechanism to migrate user profile settings and data from a peer-to-peer network based on the Windows 2000 or Windows XP operating systems without disruptions to users. Improved wizards, monitoring tools, and usage reports provide simpler administration, greater details of system and network status, and information on utilization.

Because SBS 2003 is truly built on Windows Server 2003, after it is deployed, it will keep your business up and running while minimizing possible data loss. Volume Shadow Copy enables point-in-time backups to assist recovering accidentally deleted files and helping backups run quickly with minimal errors and downtime. The Backup Configuration Wizard guides you through the creation and implementation of a successful data backup strategy reducing the time and effort needed to ensure business continuity.

Another component of data continuity is securing that data while limiting access and restricting the installation or use of software to manipulate the data. Access to critical business data and applications is controlled through secure centralized storage, which ensures that authorized users can access needed information in their computers while also preventing those who have no need for the data from acquiring it. Windows Server 2003, has increased available services by more than 200% while mitigating attacks against the system by 60%. Software restriction policies help prevent unapproved software installations and usage, helping protect against viruses and other attacks. Wizards simplify security settings and help ensure that all the necessary security steps are taken while setting up the network. SBS 2003 includes both internal and external firewall support. This provides a high degree of security for the SBS network.

Not only is it important to increase individual performance, but team performance also improves through enhanced collaboration and data access. Companyweb, a preconfigured internal website based on Microsoft Windows SharePoint Services, allows coworkers to share information, including document libraries, announcements, events, and links. Enhanced Microsoft Outlook Web Access (OWA) enables users to access an Internet version of Microsoft Office Outlook 2003 from the Internet to share files and schedules. Small Business Server 2003, Premium Edition, with SQL Server, provides small businesses the capability to run several business applications in a simple and cost-effective information technology environment to analyze and manage business information with a large selection of line-of-business applications from both Microsoft and third-party vendors. Working with a broad array of Microsoft partners, small business owners have more flexibility in selecting business applications to improve operations, reduce costs, reach more customers, and serve them better, while conducting business in a professional manner and ensuring customers that you are the right choice for their business.

Few businesses operate strictly within the walls of their locations and increasingly find that they need access to crucial data outside the office. Virtualization of companies of all sizes, and the extension of where and how business is conducted, continues to grow the need for remote access and collaboration. Remote access to information from anywhere, at anytime, and on any device is now provided by SBS and associated technologies. Remote Web Workplace (RWW), the new remote portal, allows authorized users to access features using the Internet. Businesses running the Premium Edition can now establish an interactive web presence with an unlimited number of visitors and can run as many business applications as needed.

SBS provides the platform and framework that easily grows with your operations instead of limiting productivity and communications and becomes a platform that you really never outgrow. Because SBS 2003 is part of the Windows Server 2003 family, adding additional Windows servers to your network as a dedicated line-of-business server, a server dedicated to running Windows Terminal Server in application-sharing mode, or other roles is not a problem. If you find you do outgrow the limits of SBS, the Windows Small Business Server Transition Pack removes these limitations while keeping your infrastructure in place and functioning. Before you can continue on to really understanding where SBS is today, it is important to understand where SBS came from and how it got here. At that point you can have a deeper understanding of where SBS is going.

The Growth and Maturing of SBS

SBS has a relatively long and dubious history. Reflecting both Microsoft's technology and business culture, SBS has grown to be one of Microsoft's leading product lines and technologies. But to completely understand this transition, it is necessary to go back to the beginning. Back in the 1990s, Microsoft was riding high on the wave of success with the BackOffice Server product line. Its acceptance in both large and medium business spaces allowed companies to load the suite's products across a many servers for one bundled price. Many companies found the capability to both load all the products they need and disperse them across their network increased productivity. Capitalizing on the success of BackOffice Server, Microsoft was looking for a product to enable the small business market in a similar way.

Despite BackOffice being a great product and a great value, Microsoft kept hearing it was too large, complicated, and expensive for smaller businesses, many looking for their first server solution. At the same time NT Server by itself didn't fit this bill and became even more expensive and unwieldy as other server products were added. From this divide was born BackOffice Small Business Server, providing similar functionality in a one-server solution heralding an era of right-sizing Microsoft solutions to meet the different needs specific to small business. Now, with one piece of software, small business could provide a viable and respected networking solution for this long-neglected segment.

THE LIMITATIONS OF SMALL BUSINESS SERVER

If you listen to people talk about SBS, you will find many supporters and detractors of the product. Additionally, you will find many urban myths on the limitations of how SBS truly works. Many of those who remain unfamiliar with SBS are those who love the product but because of all the included components easily get muddled down. The biggest detractors of SBS are usually those unfamiliar with the product who may have little to no computing experience and expect it to function like a desktop operating system. More often, detractors may be experienced administrators who try to manage the product like any other Microsoft product they are used to and ignore the built-in tools.

One misunderstanding about managing SBS involves the use of the SBS wizards. The SBS community, from the product development and support teams at Microsoft to the SBS MVPs (Most Valuable Partners) to seasoned SBS administrators, strongly recommends using the wizards as the best way to manage an SBS server. The wizards are the first step in making sure that all the parts and pieces that make up SBS are correctly configured to play well together. That does not mean that all management of SBS can be done through the wizards. As you go through the remainder of this book, you will find multiple examples of situations where implementing certain configurations cannot be done through the wizards. You will also see that some of the tasks listed in the Server Management Console do not launch wizards but instead open the individual management consoles, such as Active Directory Users and Computers, to complete the task.

Now to address some of the other issues: SBS is based on the actual server software pieces and the limits imposed on top of that software.

SBS does use its own Client Access Licenses, which are different. These CALs are all-inclusive for those products in the SBS suite and don't require a separate product CAL. This all-inclusive CAL provides cost savings along with ease of administration.

The biggest reason for any restrictions in SBS is to keep it accessible to those companies it is intended to help. Otherwise, the large enterprise businesses of the world would be able to get all their software at substantial savings over list and then string multiple SBS servers together to form their data centers. This is not the intent of Microsoft; SBS is designed as an enabling product for smaller companies or those with limited IT needs and is provided at great savings. Where else can you buy one product and have the rest included along with integrated implementation tools?

Because of that SBS server has the following restrictions, and more details can be found at `http://www.microsoft.com/windowsserver2003/sbs/techinfo/overview/generalfaq.mspx#EIBAA`:

- Only one computer in a domain can be running SBS.
- SBS must be the root of the forest.
- SBS cannot have any external trusts with other domains.

- SBS is limited to a certain number of users based on the version.
- SBS cannot have any child domains.

So SBS is limited to a one-domain solution. What's the big deal? Companies large and small should need only one Windows domain. There are no limitations on sites, and this forces designers to consider the guideline for domain creation and administration from Microsoft.

Additional servers and domain controllers can be added to the SBS domain for redundancy. The only caveat is that each additional server must have its own license and use an SBS CAL.

If you can work within these limitations, SBS may be the solution for you. Everyone can benefit from being more familiar with the limitations and advantages of SBS.

First Release—SBS 4.0

The first iteration of Small Business Server, SBS 4.0 made its debut in late 1997 with little fanfare. Built on top of NT Server 4.0 Service Pack 3, SBS 4.0 was an alphabet soup of solutions addressing the needs of the small business market allowing companies of fewer than 25 users options they had never been able to effectively utilize before. Designed to be easily managed without a dedicated IT manager and attractively priced—less expensive than the sum of its components—SBS 4.0 shipped with five Client Access Licenses (CALs) and was expandable to 25 licenses in packs of five at a time. Other products included Exchange 5.0, Proxy Server, SQL Server 6.5, Modem Sharing service, and Fax service and were the same or similar to the full products but with some restrictions.

Not limited to just the server, client-side applications such as Internet Explorer, Microsoft Outlook, SBS redirectors for modems and faxing, and Proxy Server were included with few restrictions. These restrictions were designed, and still are, to prevent organizations from purchasing multiple copies of SBS and linking them together; as a result, there can only be one SBS server in a domain.

Exchange 5.0 along with the included Outlook 95 provided shared calendaring and messaging along with internal email and integrated external email. This was remarkable; for the first time small firms could have a communication system comparable to those of large multinational corporations in one small package.

Secure web browsing and hosting with web reporting was provided by Proxy Server, the forerunner of ISA Server. The inclusion of IIS 3.0, Active Server Pages, and FrontPage 97 provided tools to build robust internal and external web applications accessible by customers and company personnel.

The inclusion of SQL Server 6.5 was also the tip of the iceberg for a more business-based solution, but the inclusion of Index Server 1.1 and Crystal Reports provided the capability to build robust data collection and reporting tools unseen at this price point before.

The networking package was phenomenal in what it accomplished and had few if any rivals to its features. Remote Access Services (RAS) provided by a dial-up package gave mobile users direct access to the server, providing a way to share files and information remotely before this was as common as it is today. Not to be outdone by remote access, a unique modem sharing server, pooling up to four modems on the server, allocated bandwidth on demand to network users and eliminated the need for each computer to have a dedicated modem line. In many offices, data/fax lines were in short supply or prohibitively expensive, and modem sharing alone many times justified the cost of SBS 4.0.

But what good are all these tools and advances if you have to hire a full-time IT person or spend days administering the network and systems? This is where SBS really excelled. Providing extensive information to both administrators and users by means of the default Intranet page, the SBS Console, server-based wizards for SBS server setup, and the Internet Connection Wizard, along with device and peripheral management, reduced network monitoring needs to hours, not days. Even client deployment was simplified with the Client Setup Wizard and the creation of the client installation disk—that is, the SBS magic disk.

Although the SBS market share was and still is difficult to gauge, Microsoft was pleasantly surprised by the response to SBS. At this point in time, SBS sales were almost exclusively channel driven. Value added resellers (VARs) and consultants typically installed SBS 4.0 to provide a platform for delivery of full-featured software, such as accounting or database. A few hardy companies pursued SBS on their own, but this was more the exception than the rule.

Despite its potential, SBS 4.0 had its problems. To start, Windows 95 and NT Workstation were the only supported clients at the time, leaving out the newer clients such as Windows 98. RAS provided for remote management, but most found that the graphically intense console provided unacceptable performance over a dial-up modem, and, consequently, service providers turned toward other remote control applications. The approved hardware list was restrictive, and if the wizards found unexpected hardware or conditions, the wizards would often break in such a way that the problems created were difficult to correct. A service release (v4.0a) appeared quickly after the initial iteration of SBS to fix many of these problems.

SBS 4.0a

SBS 4.0a was unleashed to the world in late summer 1998 as Service Pack 1 for SBS. Internet Explorer was upgraded to version 4.01 on both the server and clients. This was necessary for the redesigned consoles to work and take advantage of Internet Explorer's new 4.x HTML improvements.

The new and improved consoles fixed many of the bugs, hang-ups, and crashes experienced by SBS 4.0 users. The Internet Mail and News settings were fixed and added to the automatic configurations settings along with fixes to Exchange's maximum message file size error reporting. Improving both the stability and performance, SBS 4.0a showed the viability, responsiveness, and adaptability of the product.

Second Release—SBS 4.5

Summer 1999 saw the second major release of Microsoft BackOffice Small Business Server—version 4.5. Even though the approved hardware compatibility lists (HCL) and recommended system requirements remained virtually unchanged, SBS 4.5 provided many enhancements while further improving stability. If the optional install of Office 2000 was performed, the disk space requirements doubled to a whopping 4GB.

SBS 4.5 provide a more flexible server setup program than SBS 4.0's highly automated inflexible setup program. Despite the increased flexibility, SBS 4.5 required a floppy drive configured as the A: drive and a modem and network card from the HCL. Many times if these last two components weren't on the HCL they would not work, and the server would not load.

The Internet Connection Wizard (ICW) in SBS 4.0 assumed that users were signing up with an ISP for the first time. By the release of SBS 4.5, the ICW provides two options: automated sign-up and manual sign-up. These options let you rapidly create new accounts with an SBS-friendly ISP or configure SBS to use an existing ISP account. The ICW included template forms that could be sent to the ISP or used locally to gather required information. Microsoft customized the templates for the three major supported connectivity options: modem, router, or full-time/broadband. These three templates extend SBS's reach into the realms of the ISDN, asymmetric digital subscriber line (ADSL), and cable modems users. Because port settings in SBS were difficult at best for both end users and administrators, SBS 4.5 provided a new firewall configuration interface to take the guesswork out of properly configuring security; configuration of the proxy settings for Exchange Server, Proxy Server, PPTP, and POP3 were among those available. Another improvement over 4.0, along with the continued rise in DSL, was that modems could be added after installation of SBS, but the configuration of services such as RAS, Proxy Server, Faxing, and others needed to be done by hand if the device wasn't present at install.

After finalizing the hardware installation portion, SBS 4.5 displayed a new and exciting dialog box. This option allowed for the review of disk-space requirements and more importantly the altering of target locations for most of the server applications, allowing you to split SBS components, data directories, a company-shared folder, and users' folders across different physical and logical drives. Other than the requirement of the NT Server and a few other services to be installed on the system drive, the SBS applications could be structured and installed in other locations, allowing even the data folders (for example, Company, Users) to be moved to a nondefault drive or path.

Speaking of the components, many were updated in SBS 4.5. SQL Server 7.0 replaced the buggy SQL Server 6.5, and the database limits were increased from 1GB for all databases to an unlimited number of databases with 10GB per database. IIS 3.0 was replaced by Internet Information Server (IIS) 4.0, as well as Exchange Server 5.5 over Exchange 5.0. Mail and calendaring were drastically improved with Outlook 2000, FrontPage 98 improved web development over its predecessor, and Proxy Server 2.0 was a refresh for the previous version. Although some of these had been available for SBS 4.0, SBS 4.5 integrated these into the server setup.

Like its predecessor, SBS 4.5 allowed the creation of an unlimited number of user accounts but raised the limit for congruent logons from 25 to 50. Client requirements did improve and now supported both the Windows NT and the complete Windows 9x platforms. The Add User Accounts and Set Up Computer Wizards remained mainly the same except for one major change that allowed for the customization of the SBS client disk to push out not only unattended install of the associated SBS client application but also other Microsoft Applications such as Office 2000 along with other third-party applications. Following a reboot on the client machine, the first logon to the domain triggered the unattended installation of the previously selected applications.

The idea of an HTML-based customizable console isn't new to SBS. However, SBS 4.5 added more functionality to the central management console page by including indicators for available and total disk space for each volume. Another section of the console page displayed indicators for any stopped crucial services. Double-clicking on the stopped service would restart the service eliminating the need to visit the Services Control Panel and event logs to find critical stopped services. One drawback of the console, though, was its lack of an autorefresh; it had to be updated often to display the current status information. Also new to SBS 4.5 was the Server Status tool. A windfall for proactive network administrators, it would email or fax status reports and associate log files at scheduled times allowing monitoring of key indicators and logs at a glance.

Remote management in SBS 4.0 was abysmal at best utilizing RAS via a dial-up network connection. The limited bandwidth proved unable to handle the graphically intense console and provided poor performance over analog lines. Realizing this problem, SBS designers retooled the SBS 4.5 remote management capabilities to use the remote desktop features of NetMeeting—version 2.1 at the time—to access the SBS console. Although intended as a security feature, NetMeeting 2.1 required someone to accept the connection at the server. Many found this security mechanism frustrating, but fortunately NetMeeting 3.0 took care of this problem and rectified the problems of remotely managing an SBS server without resorting to third-party solutions.

Microsoft still didn't really understand the small business market share but did realize it had a good thing going. Katy Hunter, SBS product manager at the time, characterized the product as exceeding Microsoft's projections. According to Joshua Feinberg, author of *Building Profitable Solutions with Microsoft BackOffice Small Business Server 4.5* (Microsoft Press, 1999), stated that "SBS sales [remained] almost entirely channel driven." Microsoft VARs continued installing SBS to provide not only the core functionality of SBS but also as a delivery platform for other solutions. OEM SBS 4.5 installation did make an appearance, but was very limited. SBS 4.5 continued the huge strides forward in terms of installation flexibility, ease of deployment, remote administration, proactive management, and stability.

Third Release—SBS 2000

The third release in the product line, Windows Small Business Server 2000, was widely anticipated to be released in the third quarter of 2000 but was delayed waiting for extended release dates of some of its component parts. When SBS 2000 finally debuted to the world in New Jersey, spring 2001, the launch and accompanying webcast were much larger than expected. SBS had finally surpassed the point of critical mass for the product to truly succeed, and by many accounts was the first SBS ready for prime time.

Massive changes took place in the Microsoft platform between NT and Windows 2000 along with great strides in SBS. Loaded full of standard versions of Microsoft newly updated Servers platforms, SBS 2000 delivered Windows 2000 Server, plus Windows 2000 Server-based solutions for email, fax, database, and secure, shared Internet access all in one integrated solution for an exceptional value. This exceptional value gave small business unprecedented tools and resources to compete in the new emerging global economy.

What made Server 2000 products so special and robust? Two words: Active Directory. Active Directory, first implemented in Windows 2000, is Microsoft's implementation of a centralized LDAP-compliant directory. Centralizing and integrating many of the previously divergent technologies and platforms provided amazing benefits in interoperability, usability, and management while reducing the complexity of maintaining the computing environment. All this powerful technology enables unified setup and centralized management across all the component applications and even down to the client level. Coinciding with that, an explosion of new and improved services and applications made the Server 2000 platform so robust and usable. Built on top of that was the SBS 2000 integrated setup experience, remote server administration capabilities, rich server monitoring features, and alert-based reporting of critical server events, setting new standards for ease of installation, use, and administration. Despite remaining at 50 concurrent users, SBS offered far greater value than any other SBS product and understates its true capability.

Many of the nagging problems of the past vanished. Setup was easy, intuitive, and repeatable. The HCL was extensive, but hardware not on the list generally worked without problems. If installation problems did arise or required hardware was installed later, the integrated setup could be rerun to correct the problem.

As in previous releases, SBS 2000 saw refreshes to the latest Microsoft products. NT Server was replaced with Windows Server 2000, and, because the interface had been standard across most products, those familiar with other Windows 2000 products were able to find things in their usual places. SQL Server 7 was replaced with the more robust SQL 2000 with integrated Windows security and functions, allowing better applications with better administration and access controls.

Another leap forward in Microsoft technology and in SBS was the tag out of Exchange 5.5 by Exchange 2000. The first improvement was that Exchange 2000's database was integrated into Active Directory and no longer required its own database for mailbox and contact stores. The email store itself was still separate. This also meant that lookup of email and other contact information could be done through both Active Directory and the Exchange/Outlook combination. Outlook Web Access saw great improvements in Exchange 2000 with an interface that matched Outlook's form and functionality better and was relatively easy to access and deploy.

The other major replacement of SBS 2000 was that Proxy Server 2.0 was replaced with the new and super improved Microsoft Internet Acceleration and Access Server 2000 better known as ISA 2000. Proxy was good, but ISA was really good. Both products provided companywide, shared Internet access, but ISA provided faster and more secure access than before. Greater capability to adjust the limits and retention of cached content made it possible to reclaim bandwidth previously used by repeated access to the same Internet content. Along with this was the ability to manage employee Internet access based on time of day, group membership, and job roles. With the ever-increasing number of

Internet applications, the expanded filtering made it possible to still allow access to the Web while blocking those applications that were not appropriate for that environment. Access and control to the network through virtual private networks (VPNs) were enhanced with ISA 2000; securely accessing the network remotely became easier to implement and manage. And what good would all this functionality be without the monitoring and reporting? That was taken care of too. ISA 2000 provided detailed overviews and reports on all activity through the external interface of the server.

With little change in the price of the product and the major gains in its functionality, SBS 2000 was well worth the price of admission, but the SBS development team was not satisfied to stop there. The small business administration console and wizards were improved and extended. The design of SBS remained to provide ease-of-administration capabilities wherever and whenever possible, and even though administration could be performed outside the wizards the easiest way to keep the system healthy was to follow the wizards. The wizards performed an increasingly complex scripted process that saved many steps.

Internet and email connectivity was accomplished with the new Internet Connection Wizard. User and computer setup wizards were further expanded and improved, and even though the mystical "SBS setup disk" wasn't needed, it still simplified setup. SBS 2000 software installation capabilities included the Add User Wizard or the Define Client Applications link but continued to use Windows installer files and not Group Policy for software deployment. By doing this the need for a Windows 2000-only environment was eliminated and allowed more flexibility in SBS 2000 to customize application installs without direct user intervention.

Shared Fax and Modem Services Fax continued into SBS 2000. Although the shared modem service use declined, the shared fax continued to grow. Furthermore, the wizards created appropriate settings in Windows 2000, ISA Server, and Exchange, and if needed could be rerun to change appropriate settings and configurations.

A new tool emerged from the development team in SBS 2000, the Microsoft Exchange POP3 Connector was designed to fill the gap for those wanting native SMTP service of Exchange while maintaining the identity surrounding their current POP accounts. Even after migrating to SBS, many small businesses were unable to separate themselves from the identity and connectivity they had built around their current accounts. Because of this, the POP3 Connector was designed to translate existing POP3 email into Exchange's Information Store, allowing users to keep their POP3 email accounts while taking advantage of the new features of Exchange Server.

Interestingly, SBS could be configured to support both the POP3 Connector along with the native SMTP capabilities of Exchange 2000. Why would you want to do this? The first reason would be to allow the graceful transition from POP3-based accounts to native SMTP emails over time and without loss of contact. After a reasonable transition period, the old POP3 account could be cancelled and deleted. The other reason for this would be to provide a degree of disaster recovery and redundancy in cases of unavailability of the SBS server. The MX records could be set to provide delivery to an alternative location; thus emails wouldn't be lost in the process. After the return of connectivity or availability of the server, the email could be pulled down from the POP3 server to the Exchange store on the SBS server with no loss of emails in the process. This provided great power in being able to connect and stay connected with customers. Add to this, email aliasing and mail-enabled public folders, and you had solutions that were the envy of larger organizations.

IIS 5.0 along with FrontPage 2000 increased the capability to provide companies with web-enabled presence and solutions giving potential customers increased access to information and products. After SBS 2000 was released, the recommendation of hosting externally oriented websites on SBS was discouraged but could still be done and was a solution for smaller companies looking for their first web presence.

Advances in Microsoft Health Monitor provided more robust monitoring and reporting, providing more advanced warning of potentially critical problems. Terminal Services replaced Net Meeting for not only remote administration but also remote access to the server, allowing unprecedented remote access to the system.

Although the applications on the client side remained relatively unchanged, changes on the server side were remarkable. The majority of the problems that had plagued SBS in the past had disappeared. Installation and setup had become straightforward, stable, and repeatable. The narrow list of acceptable hardware was expanded to easily work with most Windows-compliant hardware. Although SBS 2000 was still mainly deployed by partners and consultants as a first server solution or as a platform for other applications, the number of OEM offers increased significantly. SBS finally became a feasible product for Microsoft and continued on despite the discontinuation of Microsoft BackOffice Server Suite.

Fourth Release—SBS 2003

The fourth iteration of the product, SBS 2003, was again a product born of a new paradigm. The Windows 2000 platform provided great form and function, but at the same time was released with most of its services turned on by default. This had been a friendlier and safer time, but the advent of the Internet also saw an increase in malicious activity. Microsoft came under increasing scrutiny for its vulnerabilities and lax security. The emphasis had been on revolutionary increases in productivity while leaving the security and lockdown of the system to those using the system. This all changed with Microsoft's security lockdown in 2002 along with the beginnings of the trustworthy security initiative. The mantra became secure by design, secure by default, secure by deployment. So, moving forward, products would be shipped to have all but the needed services for core functionality turned off and remote access blocked or secured from malicious access.

In the same time frame, Microsoft and others began to realize that the computing world was approaching the limits of increased productivity and that the individual, even if given better tools, could not provide greater productivity alone. The greater emphasis on collaborative solutions began to emerge. With better collaboration and access to information, teams of individuals could be more productive and waste less time looking for information or re-creating work that had been previously performed.

So into this environment SBS 2003 was born in late 2003 after an extended development and testing process. Whereas SBS 2000 was thought of as the first real release of Small Business Server, SBS 2003 is the follow-up to that and provides leaps in functionality and usability. SBS 2003 is built on Windows 2003, which takes advantage of the stability of Windows 2000 Server and as noted before boots up with none of the server components turned on, reducing the attack surface to minimal levels.

Other improvements in Windows Server 2003 were improvements to Active Directory and the inclusion of the capability to delete classes from the schema, which had been impossible under Windows 2000. Group Policy was improved to help with administration along with improved scripting and command-line tools. Disk management and backup were enhanced, and the inclusion of Volume Shadow Copy now allows backup of open files along with other benefits. Many of these improvements do not directly impact most users but are the technologies on which SBS 2003 are built.

By default SBS 2003 installs Active Directory, Windows SharePoint Services, and Exchange Server. Other services include a robust basic firewall, DHCP server, and NAT routing using two network cards. The interface has been enhanced to assist the new administrator to manage the environment while providing advanced tools for the seasoned SBS professional. Even though designed to be a first server solution for many companies, SBS 2003 is easily expandable to a multiserver solution. A terminal server is often the first additional server deployed within an SBS domain because Terminal Services in Application mode has been removed from SBS 2003. Realizing the increased market for small to medium-sized business and that often companies ran into problems with the previous user limits, Microsoft again raised the user limit, this time to 75 congruent users. Now additional licenses can be added without the need of the licensing disk and can be activated over the Internet.

At SBS 2003's one-year anniversary, Microsoft revealed the fact that in the first four months after its release, SBS 2003 sold more units than were sold in the entire first year after the release of SBS 2000. According to Scott Bekker, "Microsoft announced that it [had] sold 262 percent more Small Business Server licenses in the year since launching SBS 2003 than it did in the 12 months after the launch of SBS 2000." Part of this is due to the new technology mix, but it is probably more because of the continued economic value of SBS. More importantly there has been a shift to the majority of the deployments coming from OEMs and larger system builders. Although consultants are still deploying SBS in record numbers, they are no longer the largest category of deployments for SBS.

Versions of SBS 2003

Another unique feature of SBS is that it is now available in two editions: Standard and Premium. The foundation of both editions remains Windows Server 2003, Windows SharePoint Services, and Microsoft Exchange Server 2003, while benefiting from wizards and prepackaged functionality built around RWW and Windows Shared Fax services. After gathering input from customers and partners, Microsoft found that many were not implementing some of the advanced or premium technologies of SBS. After long thought and further input from other partners and more customers, Microsoft split SBS into a Standard Edition and a Premium Edition.

SBS 2003 Standard Edition

Designed to provide companies with all the technologies needed for a first server solution, SBS 2003 provides a stable, secure, and scalable environment on which to build. Everything from messaging to remote access is included out of the box. Collaboration and secure access are included, and with the improved interface it is easier than ever to set up and extend for any number of different business environments.

Table 1.1 summarizes the features of the two editions of Small Business Server 2003, enabling you to choose the best solution for your company needs.

TABLE 1.1 SBS 2003 Features at a Glance

Feature	Standard Edition	Premium Edition
Windows Server 2003	✔	✔
Windows SharePoint Services	✔	✔
Exchange Server 2003 Technology	✔	✔
Microsoft Office Outlook 2003	✔	✔
Microsoft Shared Fax Service	✔	✔
Routing and Remote Access Services (RRAS)	✔	✔
SQL Server 2000		✔
Microsoft Office FrontPage 2003		✔
ISA Server 2000/2004		✔

SBS 2003 Premium Edition

SBS also released with an enhanced package, the Premium Edition, adding Microsoft SQL Server 2000 and Microsoft Internet Security and Acceleration Server 2000 to the mix. These premium technologies were found to be less used but still desirable by many SBS customers. SQL Server 2000 still provides great value and a stable platform to build other solutions and programs on. Even though SBS 2003 Standard ships with MSDE integrated, some solutions require the expanded capabilities, manageability, and security of SQL Server.

The other additional premium technology not included in the Standard Edition is ISA Server 2000. Often misunderstood and called difficult to implement, ISA provides greater security and reporting than the basic firewall. ISA also provides better remote VPN and monitoring functionality. Access control can be set at a granular level. The ability to create and modify websites is provided by Microsoft Office FrontPage and can be used to modify Windows SharePoint Services sites.

The inclusion of these technologies provide the advanced functionality and granularity that many customers seek.

SBS 2003 SP1

On March 30, 2005, Microsoft released Service Pack 1 for Windows Server 2003. Many improvements are the same updates provided by Windows XP with Service Pack 2. Among the improvements are the Security Configuration Wizard, which allows easy research and changes to security policies; the ability to update DLLs, drivers, and non-kernel patches without rebooting; auditing and tracking of IIS 6.0 metabase; a Windows firewall that allows administrators to more easily manage incoming open ports, assisting in automatically detecting and selecting default roles; and post-setup security updates that configure the firewall to block all incoming connections and direct the user to install updates. These are just a few of a long list of updates provided by Service Pack 1 for Server 2003. It's worthwhile and beneficial to check out the full list of updates on the Microsoft website. The full list can be viewed in Microsoft KB article 824721 (`http://support.microsoft.com/kb/824721`).

Do not install Windows Server 2003 SP1 on SBS 2003 until you are ready to complete the full SBS 2003 SP1 installation process. Doing so will break many of the wizards for SBS.

NOTE

One of the additions in Windows Server 2003 SP1 is the Security Configuration Wizard. Normally, this wizard appears as a shortcut on the desktop of the server after the service pack has been installed. When all of SBS 2003 SP1 has been installed, however, this shortcut will not appear.

Running the Security Configuration Wizard on an SBS server will not break anything on the SBS server, but it will not harden the security on the server. In fact, it will make the server less secure in some ways. This wizard must be run on all Windows Server 2003 member servers in the SBS domain but not on the SBS server itself. You will not kill the server, but you will not help it, either.

The SBS development team told the SBS community to be patient and that Service Pack 1 would be out within 60 days of SP1 for Server, and as promised Service Pack 1 for SBS was released June 2005. To receive all the included updates for SBS, you should download and review a copy of "What's New for Windows SBS 2003 with Service Pack 1" `http://www.microsoft.com/downloads/details.aspx?familyid=B5846A14-F306-41F0-9D1F-97F615E62ADF&displaylang=en`.

Not only does the Service Pack include SP1 for Server, but also specific fixes for SBS 2003. Windows SharePoint Services SP1 and Exchange SP1 are also included, but one of the big benefits of SBS SP1 is that those with SBS 2003 are entitled to receive a copy of ISA 2004, and again this is more than merely an update to the product but a major upgrade to the product line. Information on Service Pack 1 for SBS can be found at the Microsoft website at `http://www.microsoft.com/windowsserver2003/sbs/downloads/sp1/default.mspx`.

If you have a simple install of SBS, you should be okay with the Service Pack, but if you have moved folders around or have done much customization, you will want to review your setup to make sure that all settings for file folders are pointing to the correct place and haven't been relocated.

Summary

To meet the challenge of performing better, faster, and more economically with fewer resources, businesses have increasingly turned to Microsoft Small Business Server 2003 to provide a stable, proven solution. Including several proven technologies such as Windows Server 2003, Exchange 2003, SQL Server 2000, Windows SharePoint Services, and ISA Server, SBS 2003 provides a great collaboration and communication platform.

The history of SBS started in late 1997 with the release of SBS 4.0 with many great features and functions for small businesses. Based on NT Server 4.0, SBS 4.0 allowed up to 25 users and provided a full range of solutions with the included components. Showing some problems, SBS was quickly upgraded to 4.0a providing more stability and function.

SBS 4.5 burst on the scene in summer 1999, still based on NT 4.0 Server, and had a refresh of the included technology SQL Server 7.0, Exchange 5.5, and Proxy 2.0. Stability was increased by expanding the list of supported hardware. Fixes to the wizards made SBS 4.5 more usable and eliminated the problem of not being able to recover the system if it became broken.

Delayed by some of the component parts, SBS 2000 was released in early 2001 to jubilation and accolades. Windows 2000 was a world of difference from NT, and SBS 2000 reflected these changes. All the components were upgraded to the Windows 2000 integrated products. The installation process was greatly improved. With all the focus on adding products to the HCL and plug-and-play support in the OS, you could build the server without worrying about having all the hardware components present for the initial installation. Monitoring and status reports were greatly improved. Overall, it just worked.

SBS 2003, launched with great fanfare in Fall 2003, is the latest in the family and brings many unique and useful features to the small business—not only to improve individual productivity but also to improve on group productivity. SBS 2003 is the first to come in two flavors: Standard, for those seeking a budget-conscience solution to build their network on, and Premium, which includes SQL Server 2000, FrontPage 2003, and ISA 2000 (replaced by ISA Server 2004 with SP1).

Service Pack 1 for SBS provides a technology refresh to SBS and provides new features and improvements to the platform. Although the updates to SharePoint and Exchange could be applied separately prior to SP1, for SBS some of the new components such as SP1 for Server and ISA 2004 could not be applied because doing so would have broken the box. Also new is SP4 for SQL 2000/MSDE 2000.

Despite its limitations, which were put in place to prevent enterprise-level companies from stringing a number of SBS servers together, SBS provides a robust and manageable platform and encourages the use of solutions that Microsoft in many ways recommends for domain management. These limitations can be its strength.

CHAPTER 2

Making the Business Case for SBS

IN THIS CHAPTER

- Definition of a Small Business
- Overlapping Needs of Enterprise and Small Business
- Unique Tendencies
- Prioritized List of Needs
- SBS in the Field—Case Studies
- Specific Small Business Niches

There's no question that effectively simplifying tasks has become a global business issue and worldwide goal, particularly with the development of technology and the maturity of software tools. Nowhere is this more evident than in the small business niche with all its (necessary) attention to detail, multifunction demands on human resources, and volumes of paperwork. For businesses in the small to midsize niche, there is a real need to concentrate on business and related practice issues, not technology and software. Although the technical resource people available solve problems and perhaps do training, there always seems to be a need for more! Without the luxury of a full- or part-time technology staff involved with the management of the business, what are the options for the small business owner?

Small Business Server (SBS) was designed with the goal of being a perfectly bundled solution for the smaller business. The license model for SBS is set to any firm between 1 and 75 people; however, depending on whom you ask, small businesses have a number of different definitions and different priorities and needs. Small businesses are in a position to need to balance cost and available resources (both human and monetary) versus solutions such as triple redundancy and dedicated staff. What are some of the issues for a small business? You first need to understand the model.

Definition of a Small Business

A small business can be defined differently depending on a number of factors, including the audience, whom you ask, revenue flow, and the existing serviced population. A small business can range in size from 1 to more than 200 people or from more than a $100,000 to millions in revenue. If you are working in the world of enterprise and your standard prospect or customer is more than a few thousand people, a 200-person firm is a small business. On the other hand, if all your customers are 5- to 10-person firms, a 200-person firm would definitely be considered large in comparison. Take for example this recent California legislation that defines a micro business: "In 2001, AB 1084 established the definition of a micro business as a subset category of a small business. It's the state's intent that micro businesses are afforded the same entitlements and business participation benefits as a small business. A micro business is: A small business that, together with affiliates, has an average annual gross receipts of two million five hundred thousand dollars ($2,500,000) or less over the previous three years, or is a small business manufacturer with 25 or fewer employees." (State of California, 2004) Does this not immediately point out the wide range of opinions on what a small business is? This perception causes trouble when listening to vendors working on solving the needs of the "small" business niche. Take for example a software product; is this product crafted for the correct "S" (of SMB—the small and medium business) audience, or is the vendor taking an enterprise-level product and rebranding it for the small or micro firm niche? Does it matter? We will explore this after looking at two other subsets of small business.

Definition of a Micro Business (a Subset of Small)

The term micro business tends to better describe the smallest niche within the small business world. A micro business is, in general, fewer than 10 people and includes some unique needs to that space. The president of a micro business must be a master at managing, in addition to a master at each task required by the business. She must be good at defining process and following process, while also being reactive. Many businesses have their own personality, but a micro business is impacted by the personality of the president of the firm. The quirks and idiosyncrasies of the president or possibly the vice president quickly get incorporated into the world of a micro business. In addition to the general culture, the risk factors for a micro business can be significantly higher with regards to the loss of one of the key players. Vulnerabilities are a key factor to pay attention to when it comes to business continuity and stability for the micro business. Micro business is a key niche to keep in mind in today's economy and a field that is quickly starting to gain enterprise attention. There are even many new state programs, such as the new state program MicroWorks, which is one of a number of programs in Appalachia that offer a combination of small loans and extensive technical assistance to stimulate the growth of new and existing micro businesses.[1] Colorado also has a program called the Micro Business Development Corporation, which was formed to stimulate and support micro enterprise by creating economic opportunity and business growth by providing access to knowledge, resources, and business capital to underserved populations. Finally, the United States Small Business Association supports small and micro businesses around the USA.

1 Baldwin, F (1999) A Factory without Walls: Microbusinesses in Appalachia Appalachia, September–December 1999 retrieved May 25, 2005 from `http://www.arc.gov/index.do?nodeId=1058`.

The Sole Proprietary

The *sole proprietary* is the smallest company within the small business community. The president of a one-person business must not only have vision, such as a larger enterprise CEO, but he also must also know how to get things done. He must wear the hat of the salesperson, the marketing person, the information technology liaison, and the financial manager. He must be good at planning and often is a master of business alliances and partnerships. A sole proprietor must consider not only his business needs but also the vulnerabilities to his family relations and infrastructure. The sole proprietorship is a multisided diamond resting on the shoulders of one person.

Overlapping Needs of Enterprise and Small Business

There are similar needs and demands between the world of enterprise and the world of a small business. If you consider that an enterprise is often broken down into multiple divisions and within those divisions multiple departments, each department could be considered similar to a small business. Each department has a budget to prepare and financial responsibilities, specific goals to reach, and tasks and roles required to meet those goals. In some enterprises, each department has enough empowerment that it also determines the vision and direction for its group and chooses the technology tools to meet those goals. These department requirements overlap with similar demands in the small business but are also unique in their own right. In an enterprise, SBS can be deployed, but when it is, the software tends to be a department-specific solution detached from the overall infrastructure of the firm. SBS is not designed to be part of a bigger infrastructure solution; although, it can work with proper configuration in that model. The key to remember about SBS in an enterprise is that SBS is a round peg in a square hole when used as a solution for the much larger firms, and this creates problems that result in customizations to make it work. For the large enterprise it makes more sense to deploy a different solution.

Unique Tendencies

According to the National Association for the Self Employed (NASE) one of the most intimidating aspects of starting and owning a micro business is the record keeping required to produce the accounting information necessary to evaluate business goals, provide financial statements to lenders, and accumulate the appropriate information to prepare a tax return. Another key issue for the small business owner is getting all the jobs done with limited human resources. This includes marketing, sales, finance, technology utilization, administration, and product development. We must also consider that a small business owner might not have the flexibility to leave a store untended or have backup resources if a computer or product is unavailable. The following sections look at each role in a little more depth.

Marketing Within the World of the Small Business

Marketing in the micro business culture often takes the title of "grassroots." The business owner uses her creative energy to come up with every possible avenue for word-of-mouth marketing and low-cost advertisement that she can muster, while also staying within the business's vision. A small business often invests in professional business cards, brochures, and a web page (hopefully), but rarely has the budget to invest one-third of its profits to increase sales through marketing. SBS offers the marketing niche of a small business the capability to integrate the power and affordability of the Internet with the marketing plan. SBS features that might appeal to the small marketing team include the capability to send and capture faxes remotely and the capability to send and receive emails through a specially defined email address or path. Additionally, Microsoft Office and the Microsoft free templates significantly increase the marketing power of the small business. When thinking about meeting the marketing needs for the small business owner, remember to mention items such as Microsoft Publisher and the Microsoft website of standard templates located easily through the Office software or through the office.microsoft.com website. The direct link is `http://office.microsoft.com/en-us/templates/default.aspx?Application=OF&Ver=11`.

The Sales Impact in the World of Small Business

In a micro business, with a sales team of one or two, which often includes the business owner, a small firm must stay organized. Each member of the team must handle more responsibility than just sales while also efficiently communicating to the other multitasking members about who has been talked to when and what was said. Utilization of the public folders within Outlook and Exchange can significantly help keep a small firm organized. Collaborative calendars, an incoming email address defined as "sales," and joint task lists can be used to increase communication and documentation of best practice process. The sales team and process in a micro business also include referrals and business alliance partners who need access to critical proprietary information. A SharePoint partner page available to a few selected partners can increase the reliability of consistent messages going out to prospects. A SharePoint site also allows other documents, key to good business alliances, to be stored and shared in this manner; including signed contracts, letters of agreement, price lists, and project plans.

Technology and the Small Business Owner

As much as the small business owner would love the luxury of a full-time information technology specialist onsite, he often must depend on an outside IT consultant for support needs. Today's IT support billing model is by the hour, and every hour of support that can be saved means a smaller impact to the bottom line for a small business. SBS helps with this issue by specifically targeting the best practice of a remote support model. In fact most of the time SBS does not require that a technician be onsite for support and support can be supplied on a running basis from anywhere in the world utilizing the remote control features of SBS. This increases the technology resources available to the small business owner without increasing the costs. This increases the funds available for the small business owner to invest in training and higher utilization of the technology tools he has purchased. When support is not draining all the resources of the small business, more resources can be invested in leveraging technology as a competitive advantage.

Finance and Cash Flow for the Managers of Small Business

The small business niche has unique financial needs that center on cash flow. The lack of cash flow within a small business can almost always kill a potential sale, and the variable can change significantly from one day to the next. It is important to understand not only that the small business can be cash flow sensitive but also that each industry niche can impact the area of finance differently. For example, if you look at the Accounting firm niche, you would find that most purchases are made in May and June. This comes from two variables. The first is that individual tax season is over as of April 15, and the second is that the billing and receivables for those completed tax returns are received in May and June.

The small business owner specializing in a specific product or service must continually consider the financial requirements offered and must deal with new unfamiliar terms and new ways to do things. The small business owner must deal with decisions about complex accounting situations. In medium size or large enterprise firms, a CFO or Accounting Department, trained in the intricacies of finance, handles this organizational need. If we also consider the tax requirements, we can easily categorize finance as a unique beast within the small business niche. When it comes to the IRS and taxpayers, there is a special group called the *self-employed small business owner*. The tax return of the self-employed contains schedules and forms not required by other working Americans and in many respects is more complicated and expensive to prepare, and yet the small business owner also has another limiting factor: Their choices are often significantly limited by their available budgets and cash flow.

Prioritized List of Needs

All businesses have needs, but small businesses have some critical needs that if addressed can easily make a big difference to their bottom line. When selling to a small business focus on specific needs to ensure that the business owner or decision maker is satisfied on key points. Focus also helps teams and consultants stay on task and keep billable time to a minimum. The following are key points to consider when thinking about the prioritized list of needs for a small business:

- Access to data anywhere, anytime
- Easy systems for communicating with customers and prospects
- Storage, management, and backup of communication with customers and prospects
- Reliable automatic backups to reduce risk and downtime
- Redundancy of data from laptop machines to a central repository to reduce the risk when equipment is lost
- Collaborative tools for small teams, partner firms, and relations
- Low-cost alternatives to enterprise-level options and features
- Organized electronic document management
- PDA mobility integration

- The ability to store retrievable tidbits needed in the daily running of the business
- Templates for best practice methodology documentation, marketing material, and contracts

How SBS Meets These Needs

SBS meets the list of prioritized needs specifically with key core features including remote access, mail hosting, and Companyweb, which is an intranet. Table 2.1 illustrates how SBS meets needs.

TABLE 2.1 Small Business Needs Met by SBS

Small Business Need	SBS Feature
Access to data anywhere, anytime	SBS includes Remote Web Workplace (RWW) and Outlook Web Access (OWA) both of which meet this need.
Easy systems for communicating with customers and prospects	SBS contains Exchange and Outlook email, SharePoint intranet, and Electronic Fax Services.
The ability to store retrievable tidbits needed in the daily running of the business	SBS contains the MSDE database, SharePoint, and Outlook.
Storage, management, and backup of communication with customers and prospects	SBS includes advanced mail servicing using MS Exchange as a solution that ensures that large quantities of mail are efficiently managed and backed up.
PDA mobility integration	SBS integrates and synchronizes to numerous personal data assistants (PDAs) offering mail history and Internet access to the server through RWW.
Reliable automatic backups to reduce risk and downtime	SBS has built-in backup routines.
Redundancy of data from laptop machines to a central repository to reduce the risk when equipment is lost	SBS offers a full server environment where the central server manages the networked machines.
Collaborative tools for small teams	SBS contains SharePoint and Companyweb for collaboration and supports more MS applications such as Live Meeting.
Collaborative tools for partner firms and relations	An SBS intranet can be set up for sharing data with partners and relations.
Templates for best practice methodology documentation, marketing material, and contracts	The SBS methodology includes easy walk-through documentation and templates.
Low-cost alternatives to enterprise-level options and features	Priced significantly below what purchasing all the components separately would cost, the SBS bundle is positioned for the small business.
Organized electronic document management	SBS includes document management through the SharePoint intranet features.

SBS in the Field—Case Studies

One of the best ways to understand the impact of SBS on a small business is to read about how SBS is being used at a few different small businesses. The following case studies give a bit of overview on a company and the main features that meet the needs of that business.

Calvert Technologies

Since 1995 Calvert Technologies has been one of Adelaide, Australia's, leading network infrastructure specialists, implementing and supporting IT solutions for the small to medium business space throughout South Australia. At Calvert Technologies staff members can spend several days at a time out of the office, providing services to clients all over the city. In addition, Dean Calvert, managing director, often travels interstate and overseas, which is only possible if he can keep in touch with fellow staff members, clients, and company information efficiently. The implementation of Microsoft Small Business Server 2003 Premium in early 2004 provided the staff of Calvert Technologies with all the right pieces to be able to keep in touch with each other and their clients efficiently. Calvert Technologies uses Outlook Web Access (OWA) for email, which is securely and readily available, whereas outside the office Outlook Mobile Access and the RCP/HTTPS features that SBS 2003 provide are used. This means, no matter where in the city, country, or world staff members happen to be, they can communicate with clients as simply as if they were in the office. The Remote Web Workplace (RWW) feature means secure and simple access to the company's terminal services server, providing access to key company applications from almost anywhere. The end result is seamless communication and access to the data necessary to provide award winning support to clients and business partners. It also serves as a great testimony to their clients that Calvert Technologies "eat their own dog food."

Needs Met by SBS:

- Access to data anywhere, anytime
- Mobility

HeadNETWORKS, LLC

HeadNETWORKS, LLC, offers Telco and PBX engineering, voice and data convergence, project management, and independent consulting services for designing, implementing, and managing high-bandwidth, state-of-the-art, and voice and data telecommunications networks. HeadNETWORKS specializes in the converging telecommunications industry and works with many independent telephone companies and associations around New England. In addition to client work, the president of HeadNETWORKS, LLC, Steve Head, is involved in numerous associations including the Maine Telecomm Association (MTUG).

An advantage for HeadNETWORKS in using SBS is the provided consolidation of files and collaborative services that allows the teams to share files in an organized manner. Another big advantage of SBS for HeadNETWORKS is added protection and disaster recovery. HeadNETWORKS offers disaster recovery services for its clients, and being able to have a good internal disaster recovery system using SBS is important. If a team member has a laptop in the field and it crashes or is compromised, having all the data available on the server for a quick recovery saves time. Having the data on a common server that adheres to a strict backup policy becomes one of the key assets for HeadNETWORKS. SBS also provides HeadNETWORKS with a layered set of security and firewall protection for the internal network. Having SBS collect all emails for the team and then building an email retention policy keeps the file sizes to a manageable level.

Needs Met by SBS:

- Access to data anywhere, anytime
- Mobility
- Redundancy of data from laptop machines to a central repository to reduce the risk when equipment is lost
- Organized electronic document management
- Collaborative tools for small teams

Interprom Computer Technologies

Interprom utilizes specialized skills to serve small to medium-sized organizations that depend on reliable technology to perform. Customers benefit from strategically designed and supported technology solutions that help them succeed. Interprom Computer Technologies is the trusted Business Technology Department for hundreds of people. SBS 2003 has enabled Interprom to move from a disorganized ad hoc method of working, into a well-organized, efficient workflow process that enables Interprom to get more done with less wasted effort, expense, and difficulty.

Before SBS, Interprom had to rely on printed paper, the office support staff, and phone calls to stay in touch, manage schedules, and access information. If something was forgotten at the office or needed to be modified, the staff of Interprom could nobly rely on trips back to the office or a courier, which were both expensive and inefficient. Today, thanks to SBS, the Interprom staff has simple secure access to all the company information where and when they need it. RWW provides a secure easy portal that, from almost any Internet browser in the world, provides access to real-time email, schedules, private and company shared contacts, documents, and the company intranet. It also provides the ability to work directly on the desktops from outside the office.

Mobile technology such as Pocket PC and Smartphones coupled with a wireless account from a wireless service provider enable access to all the information mentioned previously even when not hard-wired to the Internet. The staff and president of Interprom, Gavin Steiner, can literally pull over in their cars, turn on their PDAs or Smartphones, and access any information back at the office instantly. Mobility features built into SBS 2003 make providing up-to-date information to a client or prospect not only possible but also impressive. Interprom clients want to deal with a company that can prove it is "on the ball," and SBS 2003 allows Interprom to be that company.

Needs Met by SBS:

- Access to data anywhere, anytime
- Mobility
- Collaborative tools for small teams

Rehab Designs, Inc.

Rehab Designs, Inc., is a 14-year old medical equipment company that specializes in custom wheelchairs for the disabled. The wheelchair designs range from titanium three-wheeled tennis chairs, to pediatric tilt-in-space frames, to $20,000 power wheelchairs that stand up. Processing the necessary documentation to order, build, and get paid for these wheelchairs requires an enormous amount of information. Because Rehab Designs purchases frames, materials, and seating components from more than 120 different manufacturers, it has more than 1,000 price lists and order forms that must be accessible to all employees. These documents must also be kept up-to-date through price changes or coding updates, which may occur several times each year.

Before SBS, each time one of the distributors or manufacturers had a price change or order form update, copies would have to be mailed or faxed to the company, distributed to each employee, and placed in a binder; then the outdated versions would need to be destroyed. Invariably, outdated pricing or specification information would creep back into the system from time to time, and often employees would accidentally mark up an original order form in their binder, so keeping the binders complete was a challenge.

During the installation and configuration of SBS, special folders were created for each manufacturer on the company intranet via Windows SharePoint Services. These folders, called *document libraries*, were then populated with electronic PDF copies of the order forms and price lists. As changes and updates occur, a company employee can easily remove the outdated documents and upload the new ones. There is no need to contact a computer vendor or programmer to make these changes, and all updates are handled through a regular web browser. Now every employee in the company can access the most up-to-date price lists, wheelchair specifications, and medical coding information from any computer, and hard copies are just a mouse click away.

The result is companywide access to the most accurate information. This reduces delays, confusion, and waste. It also provides a cost savings from the reduced administrative burden, as well as paper and postage costs. The customers, managers, and employees all benefit from this streamlined process, thanks to the technology included in SBS.

Needs Met by SBS:

- Access to data anywhere, anytime
- Electronic document organization

Correct Solutions Pty Ltd.

Wayne Small, president of Correct Solutions Pty Ltd., not only sells SBS solutions, but also uses SBS to run the business and benefits in numerous ways. The first feature critical to the success of Correct Solutions Pty Ltd. is RWW, which is a standard feature of all versions of SBS. According to Wayne, the RWW feature is by far the killer feature for Correct Solutions because it allows the engineers full access to resources in the office anywhere, anytime. Wayne says, "The ability to get to a Terminal Services session is critical and is one of the key features we use." Wayne also indicates that second to RWW is the intranet using the Companyweb feature of SBS. This intranet is used to track information about customers and works lists via a SharePoint document library. The versioning feature within SharePoint helps the firm track changes to the documents over time and allows them to look at the history of tasks. These task lists allow Correct Solutions to track and assign specific tasks to group members. The access to information is one of the key ways SBS offers a competitive edge over any firm not using the software. Another killer SBS feature includes Correct Solutions PDA integration to email and the ability to synchronize email over GPRS or wireless. This means that staff can be on the road and still be aware of calendar changes, email changes, and phone messages.

Recently, Wayne was onsite with a customer. Wayne had his tablet PC with an iBurst wireless broadband modem, and as he was walking around the office, he was connected via DSL speeds to the Internet. As meetings and required phone calls occurred, Wayne was able to use Outlook over HTTP to quickly retrieve email required for his discussions; furthermore, when onsite it gave Wayne the chance to download drivers for a network card for a server when the server could not connect to the Internet.

Needs Meet by SBS:

- Access to data anywhere, anytime
- PDA mobility integration
- Collaborative tools for small teams
- Organized electronic document management

JD Fogg Technology

JD Fogg Technology is a two-year old technology consultancy supporting both enterprise and small to medium-sized business (SMB) customers with its information infrastructure, networking, and IP telephony needs. The mission of the company is to bring the enterprise computing experience to small and medium-sized businesses. JD Fogg Technology serves clients as large as Fortune 500 members and as small as 10 users and has clients in six states on both coasts.

Although JD Fogg Technology supports UNIX and Linux networks, it also supports the full Microsoft product line. The decision to become a Microsoft partner brought with it access to Microsoft products for the company's own internal use. Because JD Fogg Technology needed to become more comfortable with the SMB market, it chose to install and use Microsoft's SBS as the core business system, replacing several UNIX servers and storage systems the company had been using.

JD Fogg Technology knew that it would have been easy to install separate Microsoft servers and applications, but SBS had a compelling bundle of capabilities, some unique to SBS. For JD Fogg Technology, installation and configuration of SBS was without surprise, and yet the company was amazed with the changes the business experienced after implementation. As a small company using "virtual" offices and working with other consultancies, JD Fogg faced the daily struggle of scheduling, communication, document management, and collaboration that haunts many companies both large and small. Microsoft Exchange was the first big improvement. It brought scheduling, file sharing, and simple contact management where Sendmail provided only messaging.

Another important feature of SBS to the company is the ability to store email in a central location and back it up easily. Additionally, Exchange Outlook Web Access (OWA) has made a big difference when people are on the road. Microsoft Internet Mail Filter has also solved many of the spam problems. After learning how to get the most from Exchange/Outlook, James Fogg, President of JD Fogg Technology, began to explore SharePoint. Its value as a central document store and collaboration tool was of interest and has turned out to be great. By allowing everyone involved in a project to see and modify all related documents, project management has become faster and easier. Everyone now knows all the job notes, work orders, and documents regardless of who created them. By authenticating SharePoint users and using Windows security, JD Fogg Technology can decide who should be able to access documents. Integrating Exchange and SharePoint into the business has also greatly improved data management and communications and leaves more time to serve customers. Other capabilities of SBS, such as RWW and monitoring and reporting have also made life easier.

Needs met by SBS:

- Organized electronic document management
- Access to data anywhere, anytime
- PDA mobility integration
- Collaborative tools for small teams

The Norwich Group

The Norwich Group is a business consulting firm offering business and technology services to accounting and information technology firms around the world. Travel is a requirement for Anne Stanton, president of The Norwich Group, and access to information is paramount for success. The Norwich Group used to get the job done without SBS, but the risks and the vulnerabilities to the company were higher. SBS has offered data redundancy from the traveling laptops to the office server and secure access to email via Outlook Web Access. Furthermore, business alliance relationships around the world have allowed The Norwich Group to get remote advanced SBS support from some of the premier SBS specialists available within their network.

Needs Met by SBS:

- Access to data anywhere, anytime
- Electronic document organization

Specific Small Business Niches

SBS not only meets the general needs of small business, it can also meet the unique needs of a specific industry niche within the world of small to medium-sized businesses (SMB). As an outside observer of numerous businesses, you have the unique ability to find these specific industry niche needs that SBS meets and then to leverage these needs to successfully close the sale. It is always beneficial to point these out and how they are met by the product.

Medical Offices

Critical items to medical offices include scheduling, patient record retention, record retrieval, security, and insurance billing. A medical office needs a secure stable platform that can run industry-specific software and support the small office staff. Secure remote access to records is also convenient to the doctors on call during off hours. The office staff needs to share printers, copiers, and fax services. Use SBS to configure a digital process for sharing and utilizing the hardware in a small office efficiently. Offer the doctors remote access when on call to do their job more efficiently and the nurses and office staff easy access to the Internet for research.

Professional Services

Professional service firms are focused on efficiency and billable time. Their biggest pain point is mobility, because they need to capture billable time on the road, in the office, or at home. Work with the professional service firm on the mobility features and the remote access features of SBS. The professional service firm also uses standard forms and templates for services. The SharePoint intranet offers the central repository and library for critical documents for the professional services firm.

Law Firms

A law firm needs to keep careful records, has a huge number of documents, and is sensitive to security. Emphasizing the core security strength built into SBS can be a good angle for discussion. You can talk generically, but it might be even more impressive to the lawyer to explain exactly how the security tunnels of OWA work. You might also want to discuss ISA 2004, which can completely eliminate the need for a hardware firewall solution. There are significant differences between offering ISA 2000 with SBS 2003 and ISA 2004 with SBS 2003.

CPA Firms

A CPA firm's priority, after agreement is met that a product meets the need, is cost. A carefully designed Return on Investment (ROI) is one of the best tools that you can use when selling SBS to a CPA firm. The bundle of software within SBS and the price model far exceed collecting and installing each of the software packages separately and makes for a good selling point.

Consulting Firms

Consulting firms are also concerned with cost, but they have numerous best practice templates and documents that need to be shared among the members of the team. These documents can easily be housed and kept current in a central repository using SharePoint on SBS. The consultant also needs remote access to email and files for she is often at client sites where access to information is critical to the success and acceptance of the consultant's recommendations.

Business Valuation

The business of valuation requires numerous documents reviewed by the customer, accountant, lawyers, and any number of partners if merger and acquisition are on the table. SBS can be used to significantly reduce the number of documents being emailed and the loss of version control that happens so easily when dealing with this business need.

Retail

The retail world centers on the doors opening in the morning and closing at night. A busy retail owner must often do paperwork late into the evening, because customers' demands during the day mean no time for doing the books. Remote access to the office is a key selling feature to the CEO of a retail business. Additionally, retail requires a yearly physical inventory and in today's world the mobility tools for inventory can easily be linked to the SBS framework. SBS mobility features can be a selling point for some pieces of the retail business.

Summary

Small Business Server (SBS) is not just another upgrade or bundle that should be purchased to be more secure or to stay current. At eight years old, SBS 2003 is a proven competitive distinguisher to thousands of small businesses around the world. SBS provides the small business owner and the teams with access to company data anywhere and anytime; extremely easy systems for communicating with customers and prospects; the ability to store retrievable tidbits needed in the daily running of the business; the storage, management, and backup of communication with customers and prospects; PDA mobility integration; reliable automatic backups to reduce risk and downtime; redundancy of data from laptop machines to a central repository to reduce the risk when equipment is lost; collaborative tools for small teams, partner firms, and relations; templates for best practice methodology documentation, marketing material, and contracts; low-cost alternatives to enterprise-level options and features; and organized electronic document management.

Gone are the days when business owners needed to fight with complex backup routines that do not capture all the data on individual machines. Nor does the small business owner have to tolerate high levels of data loss and high levels of risk with the redundancy a server environment offers. SBS enables small businesses to use the core key pieces of technology that help them solve their most critical needs while remaining easy to support, install, and manage.

PART II

SBS 2003 Installation

IN THIS PART

CHAPTER 3

Planning a New SBS Installation

IN THIS CHAPTER

- Knowing the Client Base
- Planning for Correct Licensing
- Planning the Network
- Planning the Storage Layout

The ideal situation for an SBS installation is bringing a new server into a non-networked environment, or at least an environment without an existing server. Although comparatively few SBS installations match this scenario, it's not as uncommon as you might think. Plus, there are other situations where a fresh installation of SBS, as opposed to an upgrade or migration, might be the best scenario. Regardless of the actual installation approach you may choose, many aspects of the customer's network environment must be considered when bringing SBS into the mix. This chapter focuses on gathering the information necessary to successfully bring the SBS product into any environment. Based on the information covered in this chapter, a small business consultant or internal IT support professional should be able to build a proposal to outline how the network and server will be configured.

Knowing the Client Base

The biggest mistake many new consultants and IT professionals can make is proposing a solution that does not meet the needs of the client. I have seen far too many instances where a technologist implemented a solution that she was comfortable with that just didn't match the business environment. Chapter 2, "Making the Business Case for SBS," discussed the business aspects of determining whether SBS was a fit for a particular instance. Operating on the assumption that the SBS technology makes business sense, let's now take a look at the technical side of the puzzle.

Before acquiring equipment and starting the installation, you need to collect some technical information related to the existing and desired infrastructure. The more information you can collect up front, the smoother the installation and configuration process will be down the road. The following are some basic questions you will likely need answered. A more detailed examination of other aspects of the installation follows. Questions that should be asked before attempting an SBS installation include

- How many users are in the organization?
- How many devices are in the organization?
- What is the geographic layout of the organization (one site, multiple sites, and so on)?
- What desktop technologies are being used? (Windows XP, Windows 2000, Windows 98, Mac OS X, Mac OS 9, Linux, and so on)
- What is the connection to the Internet?
- Does the organization have an existing domain name for the Web?
- Does the organization have an existing email domain name and provider?
- Does the organization have users who want to work remotely, either from home or while traveling for business?
- Does the organization want to restrict or track access to external websites?
- How many printers are in the organization? How many of them need to be shared?
- Does the organization have a FAX machine? Will the organization be using the FAX services of SBS?
- Does the organization have or need a terminal server?

Planning for Correct Licensing

Licensing with SBS is one of the simplest pieces of the installation and maintenance of a system, yet it leads to the most confusion on the part of business owners and consultants alike. You do not have to be a licensing guru to be able to procure the correct number and types of licenses for SBS. Microsoft does offer multiple licensing programs, however, and an explanation of those programs and how they apply to your installation is beyond the scope of this book.

First, SBS uses a different type of Client Access License (CAL) than the standard Windows Server product. The SBS CALs cover access to all the technologies included with SBS—Windows Server, Exchange, SQL, and so on. These CALs are divided into two types: user and device. Depending on the makeup of the organization you may use one type or the other, possibly both.

When to Use User CALs

User CALs are associated with a particular user—not a user account, not a login name, but the actual human being who will be logging in to the server. The User CAL allows the user to access the server from any number of different devices, even multiple devices at the same time. This is the type of CAL that would be allocated to the system administrator—he will be accessing the server from multiple locations, probably even from home. Other users who would likely need a User CAL is a company executive who travels and may access his email from web terminals at airports, coffee shops, or trade shows. If this person also has more than one system that he uses regularly—for example, a desktop at the office and a laptop for travel or home use—that person would need a User CAL.

NOTE

A question that comes up regularly in the newsgroups dealing with User CALs is "How many CALs are needed if multiple individuals use the same logon account to access the server?" Because the CAL is tied to the actual person and not an account, each person who uses that account would need a CAL. See the following discussion about Device CALs to discover the one scenario where this would not apply.

When to Use Device CALs

Device CALs are associated with a particular device—a PC, laptop, or PDA. Assigning a Device CAL to a particular computer is really only needed in one scenario: A shipping company has a warehouse staffed 24 hours a day. Three employees who work in shifts use a single computer terminal over the course of the day: one from 8:00 a.m. to 4:00 p.m., one from 4:00 p.m. to midnight, and the other from midnight to 8:00 a.m. In this case, assigning a Device CAL to the PC that all three employees use makes the most sense because you will need only one Device CAL rather than three User CALs to account for the use on that computer. On the other hand, if any of those employees uses another computer on the network that is not covered by a Device CAL, that person should have a User CAL assigned instead.

BEST PRACTICE—DETERMINING THE NUMBER AND TYPE OF CALS NEEDED

In practice, unless an organization has a dedicated service area staffed only by shift employees who will only be accessing one specific terminal during their shift, your best bet is to purchase User CALs to cover the number of employees who will be accessing the server.

Think of a CAL as a yellow dot sticker. Each sticker must be placed on a person's forehead or device. A person can only log in to the network if she has a yellow dot stuck to her forehead or she logs in on a computer that has a yellow dot on it. If a person with no yellow dot on her forehead tries to access a computer that does not have a yellow dot on it, that person is accessing the network in violation of the license.

Using this analogy, understanding how the transfer of CALs works is simple. If a user who is assigned a User CAL (has a yellow dot on his forehead) leaves the company, he surrenders the CAL. That CAL can then be assigned to another user, his replacement for example, and then the CAL belongs to her (the yellow dot goes on her forehead). Device CALs work the same way. When a PC with a Device CAL is retired, the yellow dot is removed from the old PC and stuck on the new one.

Terminal Server CALs

Now that you have a solid understanding of how CALs work, let's add a twist to the mix—terminal server. To access a terminal server on a network, you need to have a Terminal Server CAL (TSCAL) in addition to a User or Device CAL. The type of TSCAL you need depends on the operating system running on the terminal server.

As discussed in Chapter 1, "Understanding SBS Technologies," SBS 2003 cannot run Terminal Services in Application mode. Therefore, you do not need to purchase any TSCALs to access the server through a remote connection.

> **NOTE**
>
> Another frequently asked question in the newsgroups is "Can I increase the number of remote connections to the server by purchasing addition Terminal Server CALs?" The answer is always "no" because Terminal Server Remote Administration mode, which is the only type of remote connection supported by SBS, has a maximum number of concurrent connections set at two. That number can be reduced but not increased.

If the terminal server is running Windows 2000, no additional TSCALs are needed for workstations running Windows 2000 Professional or Windows XP Professional. When those clients connect, the Windows 2000 terminal server issues a license from its built-in license pool. All other clients connecting to the terminal server require a separate TSCAL to be installed into the Terminal Server Licensing server.

With Windows Server 2003, Microsoft changed the terminal server licensing requirements. Each terminal server connection still requires a TSCAL, but now TSCALs are divided into Per-User and Per-Device categories. The Per-User and Per-Device designations are similar to the User and Device categories for SBS CALs in that a TSCAL can be assigned to an individual or a particular workstation. In addition, Microsoft has removed the "operating system equivalency" feature that allowed Windows 2000 Professional and Windows XP Professional workstations to connect to a Windows 2000 terminal server without a separate CAL. Microsoft does offer a Terminal Server CAL Transition plan for organizations that had rights to run Windows XP on or before April 24, 2003. Under this plan, every eligible Windows XP Professional workstation can acquire a single Per-User or Per-Device TSCAL at no additional cost from Microsoft. More information about this program can be found at `http://www.microsoft.com/windowsserver2003/howtobuy/licensing/tscaltransfaq.mspx`, including the scheduled end date of this program, which is currently December 31, 2005.

> **NOTE**
>
> The TSCAL covers only connectivity to the server. It does not cover the use of any applications that may be installed on the terminal server. Consult the product's licensing to determine how to acquire the correct licenses to run the application on a terminal server.

BEST PRACTICE—IMPLEMENTING TERMINAL SERVICES IN A SMALL BUSINESS SERVER NETWORK

When SBS 2003 was initially released, there was a great uproar from the SBS community regarding the removal of support for Terminal Server in Application Mode on the SBS server itself. Even though Microsoft noted in the product documentation that TS in App Mode had been removed from the product, many SBS consultants initially sold the upgrade to SBS 2003 from SBS 2000 as a feature-for-feature match, only to get burned when they could not have more than two users access the "terminal server" at one time.

Two years after the initial product release, the SBS community is more familiar with the Terminal Server restrictions on SBS 2003, but some are still trying to find ways around the limitations. For anyone to access the SBS server remotely, the user can only log in to the server with an account that has domain administrator privileges. This is a significant security risk to the server and a practice that should be avoided at all cost.

The bottom line is this: If users in the SBS network need to access network resources through a Terminal Server type setup, you must install a separate server running Windows 2000 Server or Windows Server 2003 with Terminal Server in Application Mode configured, and you must have the appropriate TS licenses available.

Planning the Network

After you have the licensing counts established, you can focus on the network implementation. This aspect of the installation covers a number of networking issues, from connecting to the Internet to internal IP address schemes to internal and external domain names. Each piece of this puzzle has a significant impact on the way the server will be set up, and because some networking changes are difficult to impossible to change down the line, it's best to spend some quality time in this area to make sure that you can get it right the first time.

Connection to the Internet

Many small businesses these days have some form of high-speed connection to the Internet, whether by DSL, cable modem, or one of many types of dedicated connections. With the lower-cost solutions, it is common for the ISP to require some form of authentication (PPPoE, for example) when connecting to its network. Others may tie your network connection to a specific MAC address from a network card. Some may require no authentication at all for basic network access.

No matter what the ISP requires for connecting to its network, a growing number of small business consultants strongly recommend placing some type of router/firewall device between the ISP's connection and the rest of the network. In some cases, this is required by the ISP, but the practice is becoming a best practice for small businesses because it adds a layer of protection from the Internet in addition to the protection provided by both editions of SBS 2003.

One NIC or Two

For many experts in the SBS field, this is not really an option. The SBS community strongly recommends the use of two network cards in every SBS server—one to connect to the Internet, one to connect to the internal network. As shown in Figure 3.1, the external NIC in the server is attached to the ISP's network through a DSL or cable modem or some sort of router. The other NIC connects to a hub or switch internally, which then connects to the other workstations and printers on the internal network.

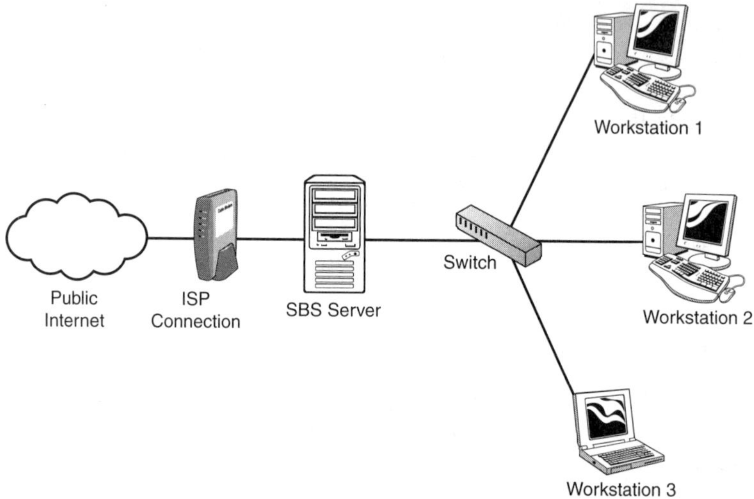

FIGURE 3.1 Network diagram featuring a dual-NIC SBS configuration with the SBS server between the Internet connection and the internal workstations.

Why is this a good idea? There are many reasons, but the main one is that this layout physically separates the organization's computers from the Internet. Like adding a router/firewall between your company's network and the Internet, putting the SBS server between the router and your internal network adds another layer of protection from the Internet for your client computers. The built-in firewall included with SBS 2003 Standard Edition does a fine job of helping block malignant traffic from getting into your network. For even more robust protection, as well as limiting or tracking external network traffic from the client workstations, server administrators can install ISA 2000 (ISA 2004 with SP1) from the Premium Installation, which all but requires two network cards in the server.

Are there downsides to the dual-NIC arrangement? Yes there are, but they are relatively few and relatively insignificant. The first response that many people have to this suggestion is that it represents a single point of failure. True, it does, but then so does your ISP. The other related concern is that in a dual-NIC setup, when the SBS server goes down, no one can get out to the Internet. In a correctly configured SBS setup, which will be detailed later, even if the server is configured with only a single network card, users will have difficulty getting out to the Internet. The reality is, though, that if the SBS server is built correctly and maintained properly, the chances of it going offline for any length of time are minimal.

One problem that can arise in a dual-NIC configuration is the use of a network-aware device behind the SBS server that may not be compatible with ISA. Some devices, such as network-aware cameras or voice over IP (VoIP) phone systems, require direct access to the network without a proxy. In those cases, SBS could be configured with a single NIC and connect to a switch along with the remainder of the workstations and network-aware devices, as shown in Figure 3.2. Alternatively, the network-aware device could be attached directly to the router/firewall along with the external NIC of the SBS server, and the remainder of the workstations would be attached to a switch that connects to the internal NIC of the server, as shown in Figure 3.3.

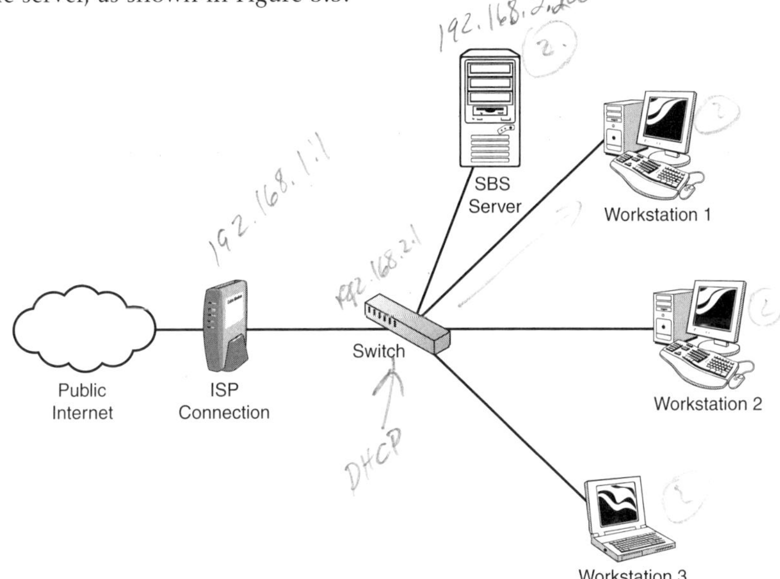

FIGURE 3.2 Network diagram featuring a single-NIC configuration where the server and all workstations connect to a switch, which is behind a hardware firewall.

Although it is possible to configure more than two NICs in an SBS server, this is not recommended. The network configuration wizards in SBS 2003 assume that there will be one or two NICs and will not function as expected if there are more than two present and active in the server. Why would more than two network cards be needed in a server? One reason would be for connecting multiple physical network segments or more than one logical network. Although SBS could be configured to act as a network router in this configuration, would the benefits gained by doing so outweigh the costs of losing the ability to use the SBS wizards to configure the network? If this type of configuration was necessary, the use of a dedicated network router should be considered instead.

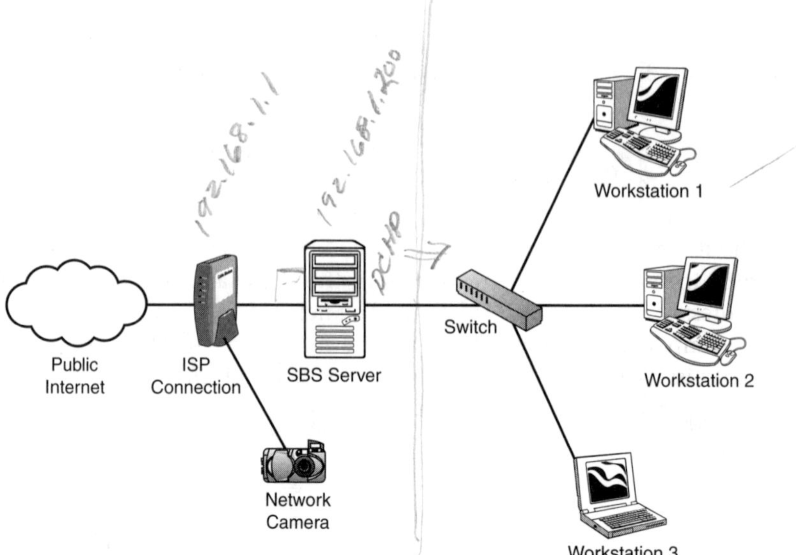

FIGURE 3.3 Network diagram featuring a dual-NIC configuration with a network-aware device behind the hardware firewall but in front of the SBS server.

Another reason people give for wanting to add more than two network cards in an SBS server is to improve network performance for transactions to and from the server. The thought is that by adding an additional NIC on the internal network, the server doubles its network bandwidth on that network. Simply adding another NIC on the same physical network will not achieve this. Certain network cards can be configured in a *teaming NIC* setup, where both NICs act as a single network interface as far as the server OS is concerned. In a small business network environment, chances are that a single network card on the internal network is going to be more than able to handle the network traffic on the internal subnet. If network bandwidth at the server is a bottleneck, upgrading all the devices on the network to a higher-bandwidth interface (such as moving from 100MB to Gigabit) will actually have more impact on network performance than adding another NIC on the internal network.

BEST PRACTICE—PROTECTING THE NETWORK

Let's face it—no system is perfect. All major software companies release updates to their software and then problems are found and fixed. Network devices are the same way. Most network device manufacturers release firmware or other updates after the initial release of the product either to improve performance, add features, or patch holes in the product.

The ideal network setup for an SBS configuration would be as follows: A router/firewall is attached to the ISP's Internet connection. One NIC of the SBS server connects to the router/firewall, and the other to a switch. The remainder of the workstations connect to the switch. In this scenario, if the router/firewall is somehow compromised (bad passwords, security flaw, misconfiguration, and so on), a malicious user on the Internet might be able to get past the router/firewall, but then would have to figure out how to get past the SBS server before actually getting his hands on a workstation.

In a single NIC SBS configuration where the server connects to the same switch as all the workstations, if the router/firewall is compromised, a malicious user now has direct access to all the devices on the network, not just the external interface of the SBS server.

IP Address Ranges

When using SBS in the preferred dual-NIC configuration, the server needs to have two separate IP address ranges, one for each network card. Selecting the appropriate address ranges to use is important because a misconfigured network can cause many performance and connectivity issues.

By default, SBS 2003 designates an IP address of 192.168.16.2 for its internal NIC with a subnet mask of 255.255.255.0. This gives the internal network an address range of 192.168.16.1-192.168.16.255. In a single-site small business installation, this address range should more than cover the number of devices connected to the server. During installation, this address range can be modified, but the IP address of the internal NIC must be a static address.

PRIVATE IP ADDRESS RANGES 10.X.X.X 172.16.X.X 192.168.X.X

Almost every SBS installation uses private IP addresses on the internal network. This is done not only to prevent machines on the Internet from contacting an internal computer directly but also for the simple fact that there are many more networked computers than there are public IP addresses available.

Three ranges of IP addresses have been identified as private and will not be routed across the Internet. Table 3.1 lists the three private address ranges and their subnet masks.

TABLE 3.1 Private IP Address Ranges

Class	Starting Address	Ending Address	Subnet Mask
A	10.0.0.0	10.255.255.255	255.0.0.0
B	172.16.0.0	172.31.255.255	255.255.0.0
C	192.168.0.0	192.168.255.255	255.255.255.0

Most small businesses do not need more than 250 addresses on a single logical network, so most would be able to select one of the subnets in the 192.168.x.x address space and be fine. Others may choose to use addresses from the 10.x.x.x or 172.16.x.x ranges for other reasons. Previous versions of SBS used addresses in the 10.x.x.x address space.

Which address range you use is entirely up to you. Just make sure that the address range you choose for your internal network is different from your external network.

NOTE

Why 192.168.16.x? Because many consumer-grade firewalls use 192.168.1.x for their internal address range. The 192.168.16.x range was selected so it would not conflict with these devices for an out-of-the-box configuration.

The IP address assigned to the external NIC varies depending on a number of factors. In cases where an ISP provides a router to connect to its network, the ISP may configure the router so that it provides a DHCP address to devices that connect to it. The external NIC can be configured to get a DHCP address from the Internet router in this case, or it could be configured with a static IP address within the range of addresses allowed by the ISP router. When possible, the external NIC of the server should be given a static IP address. This is not required, however, unlike the address assigned to the internal NIC.

The most important factor in specifying the IP address ranges for the external and internal networks is making sure that the two network cards do not have addresses in the same IP range. If the internal NIC uses the default 192.168.16.2 address, the external NIC cannot have an address on the 192.168.16.x range. An address in any 192.168.x.x address space other than 192.168.16.x is fine. Some administrators use a 10.x.x.x or 172.16.x.x address range to help avoid confusion as to which network is which when troubleshooting down the line.

The reason for having the internal and external NICs on different IP subnets has to do with IP routing. Suppose that you have a server with two NICs, both on the 192.168.1.x subnet. The external NIC has an address of 192.168.1.2, and the internal NIC has an address of 192.168.1.3. Workstations connected to the internal network have IP addresses starting with 192.168.1.10 and higher. The external NIC connects to a firewall/router with an IP address of 192.168.1.1. The internal NIC is set as the primary network card. If an internal workstation needs to connect to the firewall/router to configure it, the workstation will send a request to 192.168.1.1. That request will be heard by the internal NIC of the SBS server, but the server will ignore it, because the request is for an address on the internal network. The workstation will never be able to make a connection to the device at 192.168.1.1. In the same way, if a user on the server attempts to open a connection to 192.168.1.1, the request will be broadcast on the internal NIC, because that is the primary network interface, and it is on the same subnet. That request will also never get routed to the external NIC, even though 192.168.1.1 would be assigned as the default gateway on the external NIC.

DHCP Configuration

By default, the SBS installation attempts to install DHCP (Dynamic Host Configuration Protocol) services on the SBS server. This allows the SBS server to provide IP configuration information to workstations on the internal network that do not have static IP addresses. In most SBS installations, this is the recommended configuration.

BEST PRACTICE—USE SBS AS THE DHCP SERVER FOR THE NETWORK

In cases where an SBS server is being introduced to an existing network, there may already be a functioning DHCP server on the LAN. Any devices that are providing DHCP services should have the DHCP function disabled so that the SBS server is the only device that provides dynamic network configuration information to the workstations.

The reasoning behind this is simple. When the SBS server is configured using the setup wizards, the proper network configuration information is put into the DHCP server settings and provided to the clients. When the SBS server is not allowed to serve DHCP, it falls on the network administrator to manually configure the DHCP server settings on the device. Chapter 5, "DNS, DHCP, and Active Directory Integration," covers the default DHCP settings for an SBS network in greater detail. However, when planning a new SBS implementation, the plan should include using the SBS server's DHCP services in place of any other DHCP services on the internal network.

Public and Private Domain Names

Selecting an appropriate internal domain name is just as important as selecting the correct IP address range during setup. Active Directory depends on the domain name used during setup, and Microsoft has long recommended against the use of publicly routable domain names for the Active Directory name space. In other words, if your company uses the public domain name `smallbizco.net`, you would not want to use `smallbizco.net` as your internal domain name. Instead, Microsoft would recommend that you use `smallbizco.local` as your internal domain name.

Why not use `smallbizco.net` for the internal domain name? In Active Directory, the internal DNS server acts as the authoritative server for the internal domain, so the SBS DNS server would be the only place internal machines would look for any DNS request on the `smallbizco.net` domain. If the public website `www.smallbizco.net` is hosted with an external web service provider, its DNS record will be managed on public DNS servers, not on the SBS DNS server. If an internal workstation attempted to browse to `www.smallbizco.net`, it would ask the SBS DNS server to look up the address. The SBS DNS server, seeing that the hostname lies within the internal domain namespace, would look at its internal tables for an A record for www. If no record is found, it tells the requesting workstation that no record exists, even though the record actually does exist on the public Internet. The system administrator could add an A record for the www site and give it the public IP address, but then it becomes the system administrator's job to monitor the external web provider for changes to the IP address used to host `www.smallbizco.net` and make changes to the internal DNS whenever the public IP address changes. So the recommendation is to use a separate domain name scheme for internal domain records.

Despite Microsoft recommendations, a growing number of SBS experts recommend the use of a name other than `.local` for the internal domain name. The primary reason for this is the growing number of Macintosh computers in the small business space. With the release of Mac OS X 10.2, Apple introduced a peer-to-peer network discovery technology called Rendezvous, which uses the `.local` namespace for name resolution. This implementation prevents Macintosh workstations from performing proper name resolution in the local network if the Active Directory namespace ends with `.local`. Although there is a way to reconfigure the Macintosh to be able to correctly resolve network names in the `.local` namespace, covered in Chapter 17, "Integrating the Macintosh into a Small Business Server 2003 Environment," if you are installing SBS into a new network and you know there will be Macintosh workstations in the network at installation or in the near future, give your internal namespace an extension other than `.local`, such as `.lan` or `.office` or something similar. Do not use a `.mac` extension as that could cause conflicts with future Apple network services.

NOTE

The `.local` and `.lan` top-level domains (TLDs) are not reserved domains. That means those domains could be put into service at some point in the future and become routable domains. Four reserved domains are identified in RFC 2606 (`http://www.ietf.org/rfc/rfc2606.txt`) for testing: `.test`, `.example`, `.invalid`, and `.localhost`. Although it's unlikely that the domains `.local` and `.lan` would be used as live top-level domains in the near future, a systems administrator who wanted to be absolutely certain that his internal domain would never be publicly routed could use one of the four reserved domains. Doing so would present a special set of challenges, because the `.localhost` name has special functions for referring back to the local machine, and the other names do not imply permanence.

Wireless Network Access

One of the biggest challenges facing the small business consultant today is the increasing use of wireless devices on the network. Many SOHO router/firewall devices now include a wireless interface so that laptops and other devices with wireless network interfaces can connect to the local network. Connecting wireless devices to the SBS server presents two issues—securing the wireless connection and configuring access to server services.

The basic rule of thumb for the placement of the wireless access point is this: If the client that is connecting to the wireless access point needs to access the resources on the SBS server, the access point should be located on the internal network. If the wireless client only needs "guest" access for the purpose of getting to the Internet but not to resources on the server, the access point should be located on the external network. Figure 3.4 shows the two locations for wireless access points in the network.

Connecting a wireless client to an access point on the internal network gives that client an internal IP address and allows the client to interact with the rest of the internal network just as if it were connected to the wired internal network. Connecting to an access point on the external network is similar to connecting the workstation on the public Internet. In a properly configured dual-NIC SBS installation, this workstation will be unable to access file and print services on the server. The client could set up a VPN connection to the server to access as though the workstation were on the internal network, or the client could connect through Remote Web Workplace to a workstation on the internal network. In either case, if a workstation needs full access to the server, it just makes more sense to connect the workstation to an access point on the internal network.

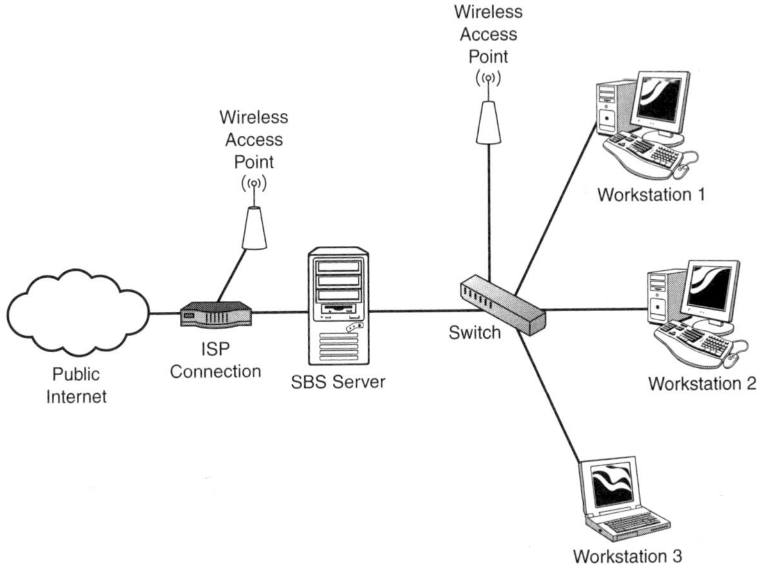

FIGURE 3.4 Network diagram featuring two possible locations for a wireless access point on the network.

Planning the Storage Layout

There are just about as many "best practices" for storage configuration on a server as there are people who configure storage on a server. Although there really is no "one size fits all" solution that works without issues for every SBS installation, this section addresses the main factors that should be considered when planning the storage layout for the new system.

The two main types of media that will be used to comprise the storage configuration on any server are disk media and backup media. Disk media storage has grown from single MFM/RLL drives to IDE to SCSI to SATA. Historically, backup media has almost exclusively been tape media of some type, whether DAT, DLT, LTO, and so on. These days, some shops are using external hard drives with either USB or FireWire connections as backup devices as well. But the function of each type of storage remains the same. Disk media is used for real-time access to data; backup media is generally accessed offline for archival or disaster recovery purposes.

The next section covers terminology as it relates to real-time and backup protection.

Fault Tolerance

Fault tolerance defines a system's capability to recover from a failure of hardware or software in such a way as to minimize the impact on the system. In most computer systems, hard disk drives are the first components to fail because they have the most moving parts and are accessed constantly while the system is powered on. Knowing this, most server systems are built with some form of fault tolerance for the disk system to minimize the impact when a disk drive fails.

Hardware Versus Software Fault Tolerance

SBS servers can achieve fault tolerance for the disk subsystems using either hardware or software solutions. Hardware solutions rely on specialized disk controllers to handle the management of the fault tolerance implementation selected, and these controllers are more expensive than standard disk controllers. Hardware fault tolerant solutions provide either a mirrored solution—where two disks of the same size act as one—or a *RAID (redundant array of inexpensive disks)* solution—where three or more disks function as a single drive. See the next section, "RAID Types," for a more detailed explanation of RAID arrays and their functions.

Microsoft servers can also implement mirrored and RAID solutions via software, avoiding the expense of a specialized disk controller card. Through the Disk Manager control panel, partitions of the same size can be mirrored by the operating system or combined into a RAID.

Although more expensive, hardware-based fault tolerance solutions are preferred over the software solutions for one reason—performance. Although the software implementations Microsoft provides for mirroring and RAID are less expensive from a hardware standpoint, the amount of overhead involved in managing the mirror or RAID has a significant impact on server performance.

Traditionally, SCSI RAID controllers are the devices of choice for fault tolerance solutions for the disk subsystem. But disk and controller manufacturers have been looking at less expensive options for the last few years because IDE/ATA drives are much less expensive than their SCSI counterparts and have similar performance specifications, which was not the case just a few years ago. Recently, a number of IDE-RAID and Serial ATA (SATA) RAID controllers have come on the market, and several major hardware manufacturers are beginning to incorporate these devices into their desktop and server lines. Over the next few years, new disk storage technologies will likely be introduced that will help drive down the cost of fault tolerant disk solutions for servers.

RAID Types

RAID, which stands for redundant array of inexpensive disks or redundant array of individual disks depending on whom you ask, is a specification for combining multiple disk units of the same size into a single logical unit for the purpose of improving read/write performance or providing fault tolerance or both. Although there are a number of RAID specifications, only a few are actually used in practice. Table 3.2 lists the most commonly used types of RAID and describes their functions, advantages, and disadvantages. The number of disks needed for each RAID type is listed as is the total available disk space for each type (the values are based on 40GB drives used as individual elements in the array).

TABLE 3.2 Commonly Used RAID Types

RAID Level	Format	# of Disks	Array Size	Description
0	Striping	2 or more	40GB * # of disks used	Technically not a RAID type because it provides no redundancy, RAID 0 arrays stripe the data written to the array equally across each disk in the array. This results in an increase in disk read/write performance, but if one of the devices in the array fails, the entire array fails.
1	Mirroring	2	40GB	RAID 1 arrays are disk mirrors. The data written to one disk is also written to the other. There is no read/write performance gain in a RAID 1 array, but if one of the devices fails, the other device kicks in, and no data is lost.
5	Striping with Parity	3 or more	80GB with 3 disks, 120GB with 4 disks, 160GB with 5; (n–1)*# of disks	RAID 5 arrays combine fault tolerance with improved read/write performance. When data is written to a RAID 5 array, a portion of the data is written to all but one member of the array. Parity information is written to the remaining member. If one member of the array fails, the remaining members have sufficient information to rebuild data on the array when read. RAID 5 is more efficient with disk space than RAID 1 but can cost more because more disks are needed than in a RAID 1 array.

TABLE 3.2 Continued

RAID Level	Format	# of Disks	Array Size	Description
10 (a.k.a. 0+1)	Striping with mirroring	4 or more (in multiples of 2)	80GB with 4 disks, 120GB with 6 disks, 160GB with 8	RAID 10 is really a RAID 0 (striped) array made up of RAID 1 (mirrored) elements. Two pairs of mirrored disks are connected, and data is striped across the pairs. Offers some read/write performance improvement over a RAID 1 array and adds fault tolerance to a RAID 0 array. There is a greater amount of overhead in processing this type of array and is costlier to implement because a minimum of four disks are needed. One element in each mirror can be lost with no data loss, but fault tolerance is effectively lost across the entire array with the loss of only one disk.
50 (a.k.a. 0+5)	Striping with parity sets	6 or more	160GB with 6 disks, 240GB with 8	RAID 50 is really a RAID 0 (striped) array made up of RAID 5 (parity) elements. Two or more sets of RAID 5 arrays are set up in a striped configuration. This configuration offers better read/write performance than RAID 10 but is much costlier in terms of disks needed at a minimum and the controller to manage the array. One element in each parity set can be lost with no loss of data, but fault tolerance is effectively lost across the entire array with the loss of only one disk.

One other advantage of a RAID configuration is that most RAID controllers can accommodate a *hot spare*—an extra disk drive on the controller that automatically becomes active if one of the other members of the array fails. Plus, when combined with a hot-swappable drive technology, the failed drive can be removed and replaced without bringing down the server. The upside is obvious because the system automatically rebuilds the necessary information on the newly activated disk if one fails and reduces the time the server spends without fault tolerance due to the failed drive. The downside is the overhead associated with rebuilding data onto the newly added drive, and that can be observed by end users during the rebuilding process. Use of a hot spare is more commonly found with RAID 5 implementations but can be used with a mirrored configuration as well.

Multiple Partitions Versus Multiple Spindles

Finding the ideal storage layout is a giant puzzle with a number of key pieces. In the end, the layout implemented is the result of a number of compromises with these pieces.

Ideally, some would suggest that an optimum SBS installation would have three *spindles*, or separate drive mechanisms. One spindle would contain the OS and key applications, one would contain the Exchange log files, and one would contain the Exchange mail databases. This layout would be optimized for performance because the type of disk access needed to read and process the Exchange log files (sequential) is different from the disk access needed to process the Exchange databases (random). User data could be stored on the spindle with the Exchange logs because most user data would be read and written sequentially, and any systemwide databases would be stored on the spindle with the Exchange databases because they would use a similar type of drive access.

But the cost of such a layout would keep a small business from implementing it. To achieve any level of fault tolerance, you would need to at least mirror each of the spindles, a total of six drives. If performance were truly the primary consideration, the two non-OS spindles would likely be a RAID 5 or RAID 50 array, jumping the number of disk drives up to at least eight. In the heady days of the .com spending of the late 1990s when startup capital seemed to come from the woodwork, allocating financial resources for this type of setup might have been possible. Not so today.

In the cost-aware economy of the mid-2000s, almost all organizations, especially small business owners, are looking for ways to reduce costs, and a requisition for a server as described previously might not even make it past the first approval signature needed. So the most cost-effective way to implement drive storage would be a single-spindle solution with some measure of fault tolerance. At a minimum, this would be a server with two hard drives mirrored—not an ideal scenario for performance but cost effective and has some degree of fault tolerance.

Many would argue that a server should really have two spindles—one for the operating system and one for data. The reasoning behind this is that if something were to happen to the drives containing the operating system, the data is still intact, and the server can be brought back to life fairly quickly by reinstalling and restoring the operating system configuration from backup. If the budget permits, each of the two spindles could be configured as separate RAID 5 arrays, or even a mirror for the OS spindle and RAID 5 for the data spindle.

But for some, the bottom line is everything, so the system must be built as inexpensively as possible. This usually means leaving the server operating on a single spindle, either a mirror or a RAID 5 array. Is this a bad configuration? No, but it does not present many opportunities for optimizing the storage space for speed. And the drive can still be logically divided into partitions to either segregate the data for organizational benefit or to help speed recovery times in case of a data disaster. Partitioning a single drive does not offer any performance benefits because the same drive mechanism is being used to read and write data to each of the partitions, so separating the Exchange log files onto a different partition from the Exchange databases will not have any positive performance impact on the server.

That being said, the SBS support community does have some general recommendations for basic data storage layout. The general rule of thumb is to have a C: partition of 12GB–16GB and a data partition as large as needed to handle the client's storage needs. Ideally, these would be on separate spindles for performance benefits, but at least partitioning a single spindle is recommended. The best solution for storage allocation cannot be boiled down to a single formula that works for every installation. The correct answer always depends on the needs of each individual installation, recognizing that cost will often be the mitigating factor.

Backup Technologies

Choosing the best backup system for the server also depends on a number of factors. Cost is certainly one of those, but so are reliability, speed, capacity, and ease of use, to name just a few. Although tape backup has been a mainstay for years and is probably still the default assumption of system builders, recent technology improvements have changed the backup landscape slightly, and that landscape is worth another look.

The biggest challenge facing any backup technology is capacity. Disk storage continues to increase in speed and capacity and drop in price. Tape backup systems have not enjoyed the same success. It is not uncommon to find small businesses needing servers with hundreds of gigabytes of disk storage. It is uncommon to find a tape technology that can back up that much data on a single cartridge that doesn't cost more than the server itself.

One limitation of the built-in backup solution provided through the SBS wizards is twofold. First, the wizard configures a backup process that attempts to back up all the data on the server in one job. Although certain areas of the server can be excluded from the backup job, that is the limit of the customization that can be achieved with the backup wizards. The SBS backup process is covered in greater detail in Chapter 13, "Exchange Disaster Recovery," and Chapter 18, "Backing Up SBS," and those chapters cover additional methods and built-in tools that can be used to streamline the backup process.

The second limitation of the SBS Backup Wizard is that it can only back up to a single tape device. If the data to be backed up is larger than the capacity of the tape device, the wizard fails. It has no mechanism to prompt to change a tape or interface with a tape loader. This is where the cost versus capacity challenge in tape devices really hits home for the SBS customer. If a client wants the simplicity of using the one-click backup offered by the SBS wizard but has 300GB–400GB of data stored on the server, he will need some sort of high-end LTO or other device that can handle the capacity. Given the cost of these devices, it probably makes more sense to look at a third-party backup solution and a midrange capacity tape auto-loader.

However, all hope is not lost. One option of the SBS Backup Wizard is to store the backup to a data file on disk. This can be a local disk on the server, a disk accessible across the network, or a removable USB or FireWire disk attached to the server. Many consultants have started looking seriously at the external USB and FireWire disk drives as an alternative to tape for a number of reasons. First is cost—several external hard drive units can be purchased for less than the cost of a midrange tape drive unit. Second is portability—with a removable drive, the backups can still be stored offsite, a requirement of some legislation affecting certain industries. Third is speed—accessing data on a disk is inherently faster than accessing the same data on a tape. In Chapter 18, the mechanics of implementing a backup rotation using a removable disk are covered in greater detail. For this chapter, if a removable disk backup solution is being considered for the server, make sure that the server has a USB 2.0 interface if a FireWire interface is not available. FireWire generally gives faster data transfer than USB 2.0, but if USB is the only option, the USB 2.0 interface is essential; USB 1.1 is just too slow to make that a practical option for backup.

Summary

Now that you've looked at all the options you need to consider for the design of the server and the network, you should be ready to prepare a proposal that outlines how the installation should look. Be sure to include the technical as well as the business justifications for the choices made in the proposal.

Best Practice Summary

- Client Access Licenses—Purchase a sufficient number of User CALs to cover all the employees in the organization. Only look at Device CALs in a shift-work environment where employees are sharing terminals.
- Terminal Services—If terminal service access is needed, install and configure a separate terminal server computer on the network. SBS 2003 cannot run Terminal Services in Application mode.
- Network configuration—Build the SBS server with two network cards and use a router/firewall device to connect the SBS server to the public Internet.
- DHCP configuration—Use the DHCP service from the SBS server and disable DHCP services on all other devices on the network (such as the router/firewall). Configure all workstations on the internal network to get a dynamic IP address from the DHCP service on the SBS server.

A highly generalized overview recommendation for the implementation of an SBS installation might look like this:

- Network layout—A hardware router/firewall connects to the ISP for Internet access. An SBS server with two network cards connects the router/firewall and an internal switch. All networked computers, including wireless computers needing normal access to the SBS server, are connected to the switch.

- Server storage—The SBS server has two spindles or partitions for data storage. The C: drive or partition is 12GB–16GB in size. The data drive or partition is as large as necessary to accommodate the organization's data storage needs.
- Backup storage—If using a tape drive for data backup and the capacity of the tape drive is less than the data size on the server, implement a third-party backup solution or customize a backup schedule using NTBackup (covered in detail in Chapter 18). If using removable disk drives, try to use a FireWire connection to an external disk enclosure with a drive large enough to store all the server data.

These are just guidelines. The actual implementation depends on the needs and restrictions of the installation site.

CHAPTER 4

Installing SBS 2003 SP1 on a New Server

IN THIS CHAPTER

- Installing Small Business Server
- SBS Configuration—To-Do List Part 1
- Configuring the Installation—To-Do List Part 2
- Troubleshooting Installation Issues

Those who have installed the initial release of SBS 2003 will find that installing SBS 2003 SP1 with the slipstreamed media to be a familiar process. This chapter is not for them. Instead, this chapter covers the SBS 2003 SP1 installation process for those who have not done any SBS installations or those who have minimal experience with the installation process.

This chapter covers only the installation of a server from the ground up. It does not contain any information about installing the service pack on an existing SBS installation. Information on the Microsoft SBS 2003 website (`http://www.microsoft.com/WindowsServer2003/sbs/downloads/sp1/default.mspx`) and the Small Biz Server site (`http://www.smallbizserver.net`) covers this topic in more than enough detail.

NOTE

Installation of the Premium Technologies is not covered in this chapter. See Chapter 23, "Internet Security and Acceleration Server 2004 Basics," for information on installing ISA 2004 and Chapter 14, "SharePoint and the Companyweb Site," for instructions on installing SQL 2000 and SP4.

Installing Small Business Server

As mentioned in previous chapters, one of the main benefits of SBS 2003 is the combination of all the Microsoft technologies on a single server. But the real magic comes during the installation process, when most of the components are installed at the same time instead of first installing the OS, then installing the web components, then installing Exchange, and so on. With the slipstreamed media, both Exchange 2003 and Exchange 2003 SP1 are installed at the same time, which is a significant time savings over doing both installs manually.

However, the installation process is more involved than a simple double-click-and-walk-away task. The installation process does take a few hours to finish, and it requires a significant amount of interaction on the part of the installer to complete successfully. This chapter breaks down the installation process of SBS 2003 SP1 Standard into its two main components: Base OS Installation and the Integrated Installation. The following section covers the configuration of the server after the basic installation has completed.

Installing the Core Windows 2003 Operating System

As expected, the first part of building the SBS server product is to get the Windows 2003 Server operating system on the box. Even though the OS on the SBS 2003 SP1 CD 1 has been tweaked slightly to include the product limitations, the installation process for the OS is virtually the same as installing Windows 2003 Server Standard Edition. Follow these steps to get the base OS on the box:

1. Boot the server from CD 1.
2. Press F6 and follow the instructions to load any additional disk drivers necessary.
3. Press Enter to set up Windows.
4. Press F8 to accept the license agreement.
5. Select the partition to use for the installation.
6. Format the partition with NTFS.
7. After Setup copies files to the disk, Setup restarts the computer and starts the graphical portion of the setup.
8. Make any necessary changes to the region and language options and click Next.
9. Enter the name and organization in the Personalize Your Software window.
10. Enter the product key and click Next.
11. Enter the name of the server and the administrator password and click Next.
12. Adjust the date and time as necessary and click Next.
13. Setup continues configuring the server and then restarts when complete.

BEST PRACTICE—ALWAYS INSTALL SBS MANUALLY

When computer hardware vendors preinstall the SBS 2003 software on a new server, the server configuration is set to make it easy for the vendor to build. The environment for each SBS installation is slightly different, however, so in many cases, and OEM installation simply isn't sufficient to meet the company's needs and may cause problems later.

Even if a new server is purchased with SBS 2003 preinstalled, it is best to wipe the drive and perform an installation manually. This way you can customize the installation to meet your needs from the onset and not have to worry about modifying any settings after the server has been put into production. You also usually get a cleaner Active Directory installation and are less likely to find traces of a previous server name left throughout the registry.

SBS Integrated Installation

Now that the core OS has been installed, setup continues with the SBS integrated portion of the installation. This is where basic information about the SBS environment is configured. Follow these steps to complete the integrated installation:

1. After the server reboots, log in with the administrator password created earlier.
2. The SBS integrated installation automatically starts. Click Next to continue.
3. The Setup Requirements window appears if there are any issues that setup has detected that keep it from completing successfully. One such item, having only one NIC in the server, is informational and can be bypassed by clicking Next, as shown in Figure 4.1. Other items need to be resolved as described in the window before installation can continue.

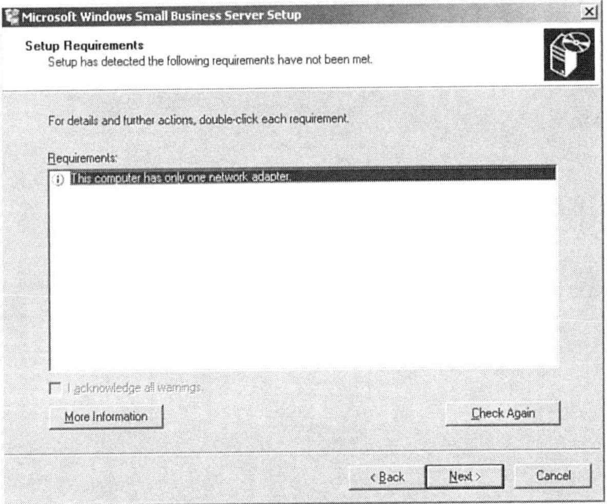

FIGURE 4.1 The Setup Requirements window displays any information, warnings, and errors related to the setup of SBS on the server before the installation process starts.

4. Enter the contact information for the server, as shown in Figure 4.2, and click Next.

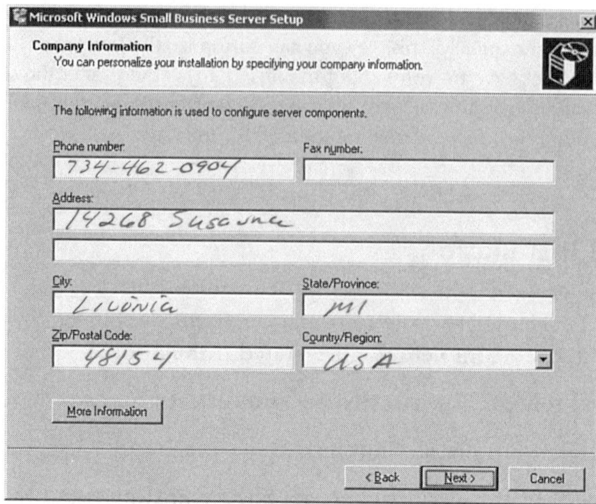

FIGURE 4.2 Completing the fields in the Company Information window populates that information in the appropriate places in the server configuration.

5. Enter the internal domain information, as shown in Figure 4.3, and click Next.

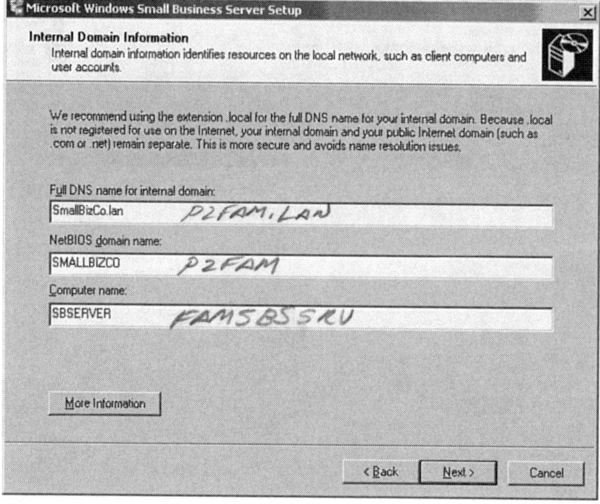

FIGURE 4.3 The Internal Domain Information window sets the fully qualified domain name as well as the NetBIOS domain name and the server name.

6. If you enter a top-level domain other than `.local`, setup presents a dialog warning you about using the domain name, as shown in Figure 4.4. If you specified a domain ending with `.lan`, click No and continue with setup.

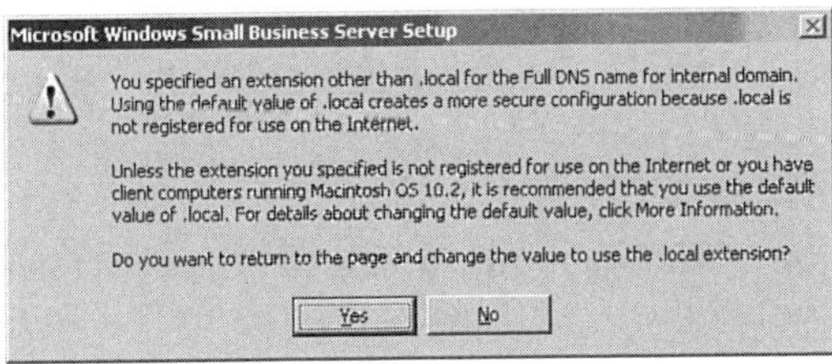

FIGURE 4.4 The SBS Setup Wizard assumes the use of a `.local` domain name and presents this dialog if anything other than `.local` is used.

7. If you have more than one NIC installed in the server, you are prompted to select which NIC to use as the local network adapter, as shown in Figure 4.5. Select the appropriate NIC and click Next.

NOTE

During the integrated install, and up until the point that the server is ready to connect to the Internet, the server NICs should be connected to a hub or switch that has no other connections. This allows setup to detect that the NIC has a network connection, but it still keeps the server isolated from potential malware attacks during the setup process.

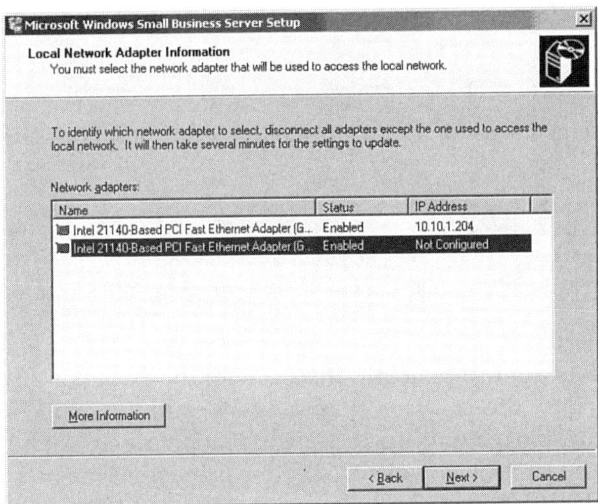

FIGURE 4.5 When two network cards are installed, one must be selected as the Local Network adapter, also known as the Internal NIC.

8. Enter the local network adapter information and click Next. The default IP address is 192.168.16.2, and the default subnet mask is 255.255.255.0.

9. Enter the administrator password so that the server automatically logs on after the next reboot to continue the installation process.

10. In the Windows Configuration screen, click Next.

The computer restarts after the domain configuration completes. When setup resumes, it finishes the Windows Server 2003 Configuration and the Microsoft Search installation.

SBS Component Installation

The Component Selection window appears, where you can select which SBS components to install and where to install them. As shown in Figure 4.6, on an initial installation, all components are selected to be installed and all default to install on `C:`.

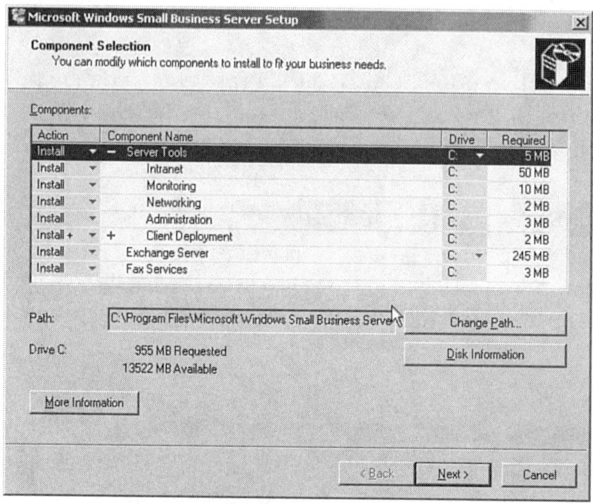

FIGURE 4.6 The components for the SBS integrated setup are set to install to `C:` by default.

> **NOTE**
>
> When the SBS integrated setup is launched from the Add/Remove Programs window after the initial installation and configuration, it opens to the Component Installation window.

The default action for each component is Install. With the exception of the Fax Services, the consensus among the SBS community is to install all the components listed, even if you think a component may not be used. The installation action can be changed by clicking on the action next to the component. Selecting None from the pop-up list prevents the installation of the component.

The most critical option at this point is deciding where to install each of the components. Although some of the components can be relocated to other places on the server after installation, it is best to identify the final location for each of the components at this stage of the install. Table 4.1 lists the default installation path for each of the SBS components.

TABLE 4.1 Default Installation Paths for SBS Components

SBS Component	Installation Path
Server Tools	`C:\Program Files\Microsoft Windows Small Business Server`
Exchange Server	`C:\Program Files\Exchsrvr`
Fax Services	`C:\WINDOWS`

To change the installation location for the components, select the component in the list and click the Change Path button. The individual components listed under Server Tools cannot have their locations changed separately. They all install under the same path selected for the Server Tools. Change the installation actions or path for the SBS components, if desired, and click Next.

The Data Folders page, shown in Figure 4.7, gives you the opportunity to further customize where some of the component data is installed. The default folder paths listed in the Data Folders page are based on the installation path selections in the Component Installation page.

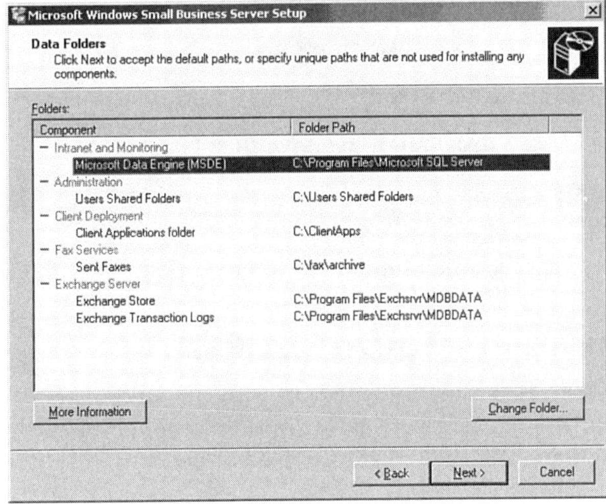

FIGURE 4.7 The installation location for each of the components can be further customized in the Data Folders page of the wizard.

If you have more than one partition or disk spindle available on the server (as discussed in Chapter 3, "Planning a New SBS Installation"), you may want to change the location of some of the data components listed off the `C:` drive.

BEST PRACTICE—LOCATION OF DATA FOLDERS

Many SBS consultants prefer to keep user data and operating system data separate. Ideally, the server operating system would reside on its own fault-tolerant disk, the Exchange logs and databases would each be on their own fault-tolerant disks, and the remaining data would reside on one of the Exchange disks. In the real world, you are likely to see a single fault-tolerant disk divided into multiple partitions. Even if this is the case, placing the non-OS data onto the second partition is still encouraged.

Follow these steps to complete the remaining portion of the integrated installation:

1. Change the folder path for each of the components, if desired, and click Next.
2. Verify the information in the Component Summary window and click Back to make any changes or click Next to continue with setup.
3. Setup starts the installation and configuration of the Exchange Server component.
4. Remove CD 1 and insert CD 2 when prompted.
5. Remove CD 2 and insert CD 3 when prompted.
6. Remove CD 3 and insert CD 4 when prompted.
7. Remove CD 4 and insert the Outlook CD when prompted.
8. In the Finishing Your Installation window, click Finish.
9. Click OK to restart the server.

At this point, the server reboots and moves to the next phase of installation.

SBS Configuration—To-Do List Part 1

After the server restarts, it automatically logs in with the Administrator's account (if you provided the Administrator's password earlier during setup) and launches the To-Do list. To finish the configuration of the server, you need to perform the appropriate tasks in the To-Do list.

The To-Do list, shown in Figure 4.8, is broken down into two sections: Network Tasks and Management Tasks. This section of the chapter covers the features of the Management Tasks.

Connect to the Internet

Before performing any other tasks on the server, you need to run the Connect to the Internet Wizard, otherwise known as the Configure E-mail and Internet Connection Wizard (CEICW). Click on the Start button on the Connect to the Internet line of the To-Do list to start the wizard.

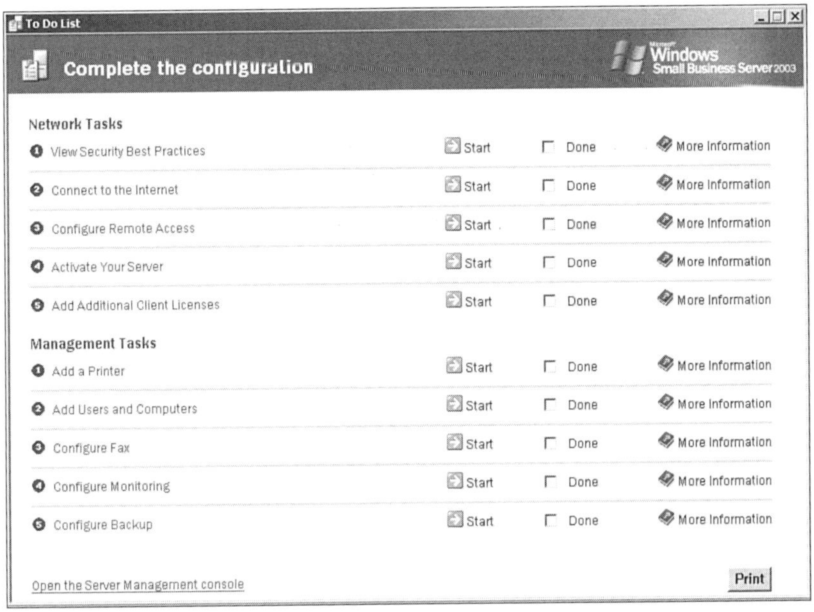

FIGURE 4.8 The To-Do List helps you track your configuration process.

NOTE

When SBS is installed on a server with two network cards, the NIC that connects to the Internet (referred to as the *external NIC* as opposed to the *internal NIC*) is disabled at the end of the setup process. The CEICW enables the external NIC as the wizard progresses.

When the CEICW launches, the first page of the wizard introduces the tasks that the wizard will perform. Clicking Next starts the wizard, which is divided into three main sections: Network Configuration, Firewall Configuration, and E-Mail configuration. Each section of the wizard is described in more detail in the following sections.

NOTE

In the list of tasks is a link that connects to the Required Information for Connecting to the Internet form. If you click on this link, you see a form that contains all the information you need to complete the wizard and configure the network correctly. However, the window is small, and even though it provides instructions on how to print the form, at this stage in the server setup no printers are defined or connected. The next few subsections of this chapter provide a table of the information needed to complete each section of the wizard.

Network Configuration

The first page of the wizard is the Connection Type page. Here is where you must select whether your Internet connection is dial-up or broadband. If you will be using a modem for the Internet connection, the modem must be connected to the server and installed as a device before launching the wizard. Select either Broadband or Dial-Up and click Next to move on to the next page in the wizard. Tables 4.2 and 4.3 list the information you need to complete both the dial-up and broadband connection settings.

TABLE 4.2 Dial-Up Connection Information

Dial-Up Connection Information	Description
Phone number	The number to dial in to the ISP
ISP username	The username needed to authenticate with the ISP
Password	The password needed to authenticate with the ISP
Static IP address (optional)	Needed only if the ISP has designated a static IP address for the connection
Preferred DNS server	The public DNS server provided by the ISP
Alternate DNS server (optional)	Another DNS server address provided by the ISP, if needed

TABLE 4.3 Broadband Connection Information

Broadband Connection Information	Description
Static IP address (optional)	Provided by the ISP if a static address has been designated for the connection
Subnet mask (optional)	Provided by the ISP if a static address has been designated for the connection
Default gateway (optional)	Provided by the ISP if a static address has been designated for the connection
Preferred DNS server	The public DNS server provided by the ISP
Alternate DNS server (optional)	Another DNS server address provided by the ISP, if needed
Service name (optional)	Needed only for a PPPoE connection
ISP username	Needed only for a PPPoE connection
Password	Needed only for a PPPoE connection

NOTE

Hopefully most server installs taking place these days use a high-speed broadband connection, so the remainder of steps in this chapter assumes a broadband configuration. Where applicable, information pertaining to dial-up configurations is included.

Follow these steps to complete the network configuration portion of the wizard:

1. In the Broadband Connection page of the wizard, select the appropriate connection type—local router with an IP address, connection that requires a username and password (PPPoE), or direct broadband connection—and click Next.

   If the connection that requires a username and password (PPPoE) option is selected, complete the page shown in Figure 4.9 and click Next.

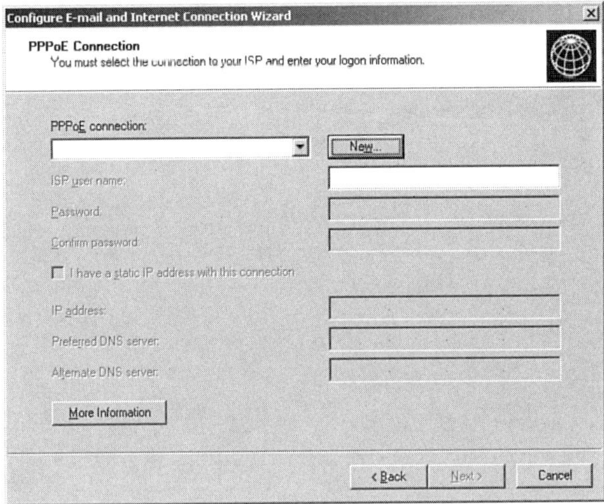

FIGURE 4.9 Information about a PPPoE connection can be entered in the PPPoE Connection page.

BEST PRACTICE—DEALING WITH PPPOE

In those installations where broadband network access is provided through a PPPoE configuration, the SBS server should not be set to handle the PPPoE login configuration. Instead, get a third-party hardware router/firewall to sit between the SBS server and the Internet and let that device maintain the PPPoE login configuration.

If the local router with an IP address option is selected, complete the page shown in Figure 4.10 and click Next.

2. In the Network Connection page, select the DHCP or Static IP option and click Next. If the Static IP option is selected, complete the information shown in Figure 4.11 before clicking Next. If the setup process detects a Universal Plug-n-Play (UPnP) router, it asks whether you want the wizard to configure the router. Click No if this dialog box appears.

3. Review the network configuration information and click Next.

NOTE

This chapter does not include information about ISA 2004 configuration on a new install. The installation and configuration of ISA 2004 is included in Chapter 23.

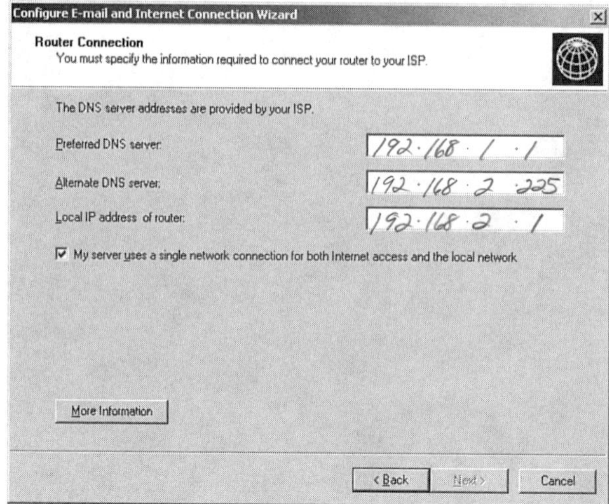

FIGURE 4.10 Enter the ISP's DNS servers and the router's local address in the Router Connection window.

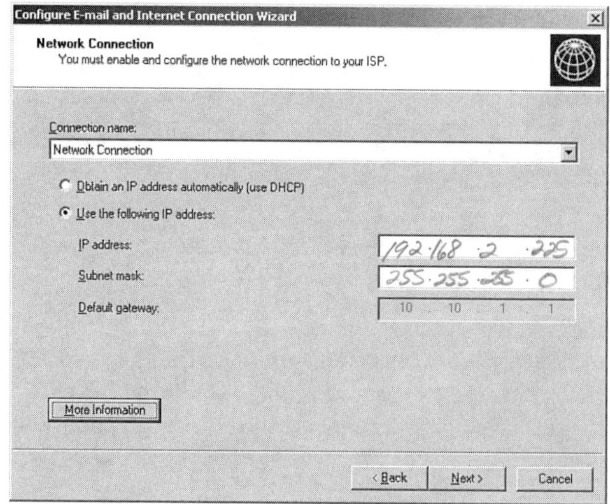

FIGURE 4.11 The address for the Network Connection, also known as the External NIC, is configured in the Network Connection page.

Firewall Configuration

The firewall section of the CEICW configures the Routing and Remote Access service as well as IIS to determine which resources can be accessed by computers coming in from the Internet. Follow these steps to complete this section of the wizard:

1. Select Enable Firewall and click Next.
2. Select the services that can be access from the Internet and click Next. If you select VPN from the list, you get a note that you must run the Remote Access Wizard after the CEICW completes to configure the server for inbound VPN connections.
3. Select the web services you want available to the Internet and click Next.
4. Select Create a new Web server certificate and then enter the public name for your server in the Web Server Name field. Then click Next.

Exchange Configuration

The last portion of the CEICW configures the Exchange server to act as either an SMTP server or as a POP3 collector. It also determines whether email is sent out directly to other servers (DNS) or to a server at your ISP (smarthost). Review the information listed in Table 4.4 and then follow the steps to complete the CEICW.

TABLE 4.4 Exchange Information

Email Options	Information Needed
Exchange uses DNS to deliver email	None
Exchange forwards all email to a smarthost	Name of the smarthost mail server
Exchange receives email directly from the Internet	None
Exchange connects to the ISP's mail server to retrieve messages (not the POP3 connector)	ISP's mail server name, type of connection (ETRN, TURN after authentication)
Internet Mail Domain	The address used for the mail server—that is, `smallbizco.net`.

1. Select Enable Internet email and click Next.
2. Select the appropriate email routing method and click Next.

   If you plan to route mail directly to other servers, select Use DNS to Route Email.

   If you plan to use a smarthost, select Forward All E-mail to E-mail Server at Your ISP and then enter the name of the mail server in the E-mail Server field.
3. Select Use Exchange in the E-mail Retrieval Method page and click Next. Even if you plan to use the POP3 connector to retrieve mail, do not select the Use the Microsoft Connector for POP3 Mailboxes check box at this time. Wait until all your users are defined and Internet access is working; then re-run the CEICW to configure the POP3 connector.
4. Enter your email domain name (do not include the "@") and click Next.
5. In the Remove E-mail Attachments page, leave the default settings to remove all attachments listed on the page. If you want to save attachments for later review, enable the Save Removed E-mail Attachments in a Folder check box and then browse to a folder on the server hard drive to store those attachments. Click Next.

CAUTION

If you save the removed attachments to a folder, make sure to exclude that folder from real-time scanning by your antivirus software. If the antivirus software tries to block the file from being saved by Exchange, the Exchange mail delivery process can break and cause other Exchange problems. The files in the folder can be scanned for viruses during a scheduled scan but must not be allowed to be scanned in real-time.

Finishing the Wizard

When the wizard has collected all the information necessary, you are presented with the summary page of the actions the wizard will take. After you have reviewed the summary and believe the information to be correct, click Finish to let the wizard make the necessary changes.

NOTE

Information about the settings used in the CEICW and the actions taken by the wizard are summarized in `C:\Program Files\Microsoft Windows Small Business Server\Networking\Icw\Icwdetails.htm`.

After the wizard completes the changes, you are prompted to enable password policies on the network. At this point, click No. You then see an alert advising you to check for the latest updates for the server now that it is connected to the Internet. When you click OK to close this alert, setup launches Internet Explorer and takes you to the Small Business Server 2003 downloads page. This behavior is different from the original release of SBS, which took you directly to the Windows Update site.

Additionally, you can check the Microsoft Update site (`http://update.microsoft.com/microsoftupdate`) to get the latest security updates installed before continuing with the server configuration.

Configure Remote Access

If you will be allowing incoming VPN connections to the network, you need to run the Configure Remote Access Wizard to establish the correct settings in Routing and Remote Access. Click on the Start button on line 3 of the To-Do list to start the wizard. Then follow these steps to complete the wizard:

BEST PRACTICE—BE CAUTIOUS WHEN SETTING UP VPN ACCESS INTO THE SBS NETWORK

THE SBS community is divided on the issue of VPN access. One camp takes the stand that VPN should never be opened because of the security risks. The other proclaims that with proper configuration, VPN can be more secure than other remote access methods. To make matters more interesting, both groups are correct.

Before opening up a VPN connection into your SBS network, you need to weigh the risks versus the benefits to determine whether VPN is really the best solution for you. A poorly planned VPN implementation can open your network to a number of virus, Trojan, and worm attacks. Using the Remote Web Workplace features of SBS can limit these risks, but even that solution has its own limitations and security holes. Review the information on VPN Quarantine in Chapter 24, "Internet Security and Acceleration Server 2004 Advanced Administration," for best practices on using ISA 2004 to help secure your VPN connections.

1. In the Welcome page, click Next.
2. In the Remote Access Method page, click Next.
3. In the VPN Server Name page, confirm that the value entered in the Server Name field is correct; then click Next.
4. Click Finish to close the wizard.

Activate the Server

Even though you have 30 days to activate the server, go ahead and run the Activate Your Server Wizard from the To-Do list at this point. After you have launched the wizard, follow these instructions to complete server activation:

1. Select the Yes, Let's Activate Windows over the Internet Now radio button and click Next.
2. If you want to register with Microsoft, click the Yes radio button. Otherwise, click No and then click Next.
3. After the activation process has completed, click OK to close the wizard.

Add Client Licenses

SBS 2003 comes with five Client Access Licenses (CALs) by default. To allow more users or devices to authenticate to the server, you need to add more CALs. If you have already purchased additional client license packs, you can launch the Add Additional Licenses Wizard from the To-Do list and follow these steps to add the licenses:

1. In the Welcome page, click Next.
2. In the License Agreement page, click the I Agree radio button; then click Next.
3. In the Contact Method page, click the Internet radio button; then click Next.
4. Enter the 25-character license code and click Add.
5. Verify that the license code has the correct number of licenses; then click Next.
6. After the licenses are activated, click Finish to close the wizard.

Configuring the Installation—To-Do List Part 2

Now that the network has been set up, you can continue with the necessary management tasks listed in the second part of the To-Do list. These tasks should be performed in the order listed because some of the steps need information from the previous tasks. The steps to complete the tasks are provided in the next sections.

Adding Printers

Using the Add a Printer Wizard is the same as launching the Add Printer Wizard from the Printers and Faxes window on a Windows 2003 server. The only difference here is where you launch the wizard.

By adding printers at this point in the setup process, the shared printers will be defined when you create users and set up client computers in the next section. Otherwise, this task can be performed at any time after setup is complete.

Adding Users and Computers

The Add Users and Computers task automates much of the work needed to connect a client workstation and create a user account to use it. Follow these steps to set up a user and an associated client workstation:

1. In the Welcome page, click Next.
2. Select the appropriate template for the user (User, Mobile User, Power User, or Administrator) and click Next.
3. In the User Information page, click Add to create new entries in the list.
4. Enter the information for the user and click OK.
5. Click Add again to create as many new entries in the list as desired. When finished adding users with this template, click Next.
6. Click the Set Up Computers Now radio button; then click Next.
7. In the Client Computer Names page, entries will already exist for the account names created earlier. You can add additional computers at this time, or just click Next to continue.
8. In the Client Applications page, click Next.
9. If desired, enable the Install Connection Manager or Install Activesync 3.8 check boxes to select those items for installation. Click Next to continue.
10. Review the information listed in the last page of the wizard and click Finish.

When the wizard completes, it presents a dialog giving instructions on how to set up the client computers. Click OK to close the dialog box.

Configuring FAX Services

If you have installed the FAX services, you can run the Configure Fax task now to set up FAX services. You need to have a FAX modem connected and installed prior to completing this task. Follow these steps to complete the wizard:

1. In the Welcome page, click Next.
2. Enter the company information as it will appear in the various FAX elements. Note that the company name can be no more than 20 characters. Click Next to continue.
3. Select the device that will be used to send Faxes from the list; then click Next.
4. Select the device that will be used to receive Faxes from the list. If you have more than one FAX device that will receive Faxes and want each one to have separate routing destinations, click the Set Specific Routing Destinations for Each Device radio button. Otherwise, click the Set Routing Destinations for All Devices radio button, and then click Next.
5. In the Inbound Fax Routing page, enable the check box next to each routing destination desired.
6. For each routing destination enabled, click Configure to set the appropriate destination information. Click Next to continue.
7. In the summary page, review the information for correctness; then click Finish.

Configuring Monitoring

The SBS Monitoring Configuration Wizard does not have to be run at initial setup. If you are not familiar with the Monitoring tools for SBS, you may want to review Chapter 19, “Monitoring and Reporting,” before running the wizard. Chapter 19 also covers the Monitoring Configuration Wizard in detail, so that topic will not be covered in this chapter.

Configuring Backup

The key step that must be performed before the Backup Wizard can be run is the proper installation of the backup device drivers. Whether you choose to back up to tape or disk, the server must be able to access the backup media before the Backup Wizard runs correctly.

Chapter 18, “Backing Up SBS,” covers SBS backups in depth, both using the SBS backup wizards and using other tools, including third-party solutions. For more information about configuring backup on the SBS server, review that chapter for full information.

Configuring Automatic Updates

Although Automatic Updates is not an item on the To-Do list, you should configure Automatic Updates as part of the installation/configuration process. The Automatic Updates icon appears in the Task Bar so long as it has not been configured. When you click on the icon, the Automatic Updates dialog appears, shown in Figure 4.12.

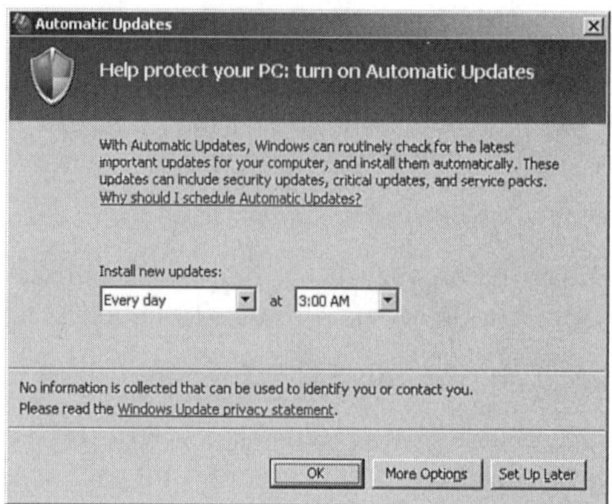

FIGURE 4.12 Automatic Updates wants to automatically install updates daily at 3:00 a.m.

If you just click OK in this dialog box, Automatic Updates will be configured with the default options, which is to download updates as they become available and install downloaded updates every day at 3:00 a.m. Instead of clicking OK in this dialog, click on More Options and select the Download Updates for Me, But Let Me Choose When to Install Them radio button in the next dialog box. Then click Apply to close the dialog. This allows you to schedule the installation of the updates after you have had a chance to test the updates on another system.

BEST PRACTICE—DO NOT CONFIGURE AUTOMATIC UPDATES TO AUTOMATICALLY INSTALL UPDATES AT A SCHEDULED TIME

As the SBS community learned from the release of Windows 2003 SP1, not all updates are designed for SBS and can cause problems when installed automatically. Several consultants who had updates set to install automatically encountered multiple problems when Windows 2003 SP1 was accidentally made available to servers running SBS 2003 through Automatic Updates. System administrators should install updates manually at a planned time to minimize downtime should any problems be encountered with the update.

Troubleshooting Installation Issues

The SBS setup process has a number of log files that document the steps taken during the installation of the server. Unfortunately, because different teams within Microsoft developed each of the component installation processes, not all the log files are stored in the same location. Table 4.5 lists the locations of the log files for the installation process.

TABLE 4.5 Locations of SBS Installation Log Files

`C:\Program Files\Microsoft Integration\Windows Small Business Server 2003\Logs`	Log files for the SBS installation process, including the `errorlog.txt` file
`C:\Documents and Settings\Administrator\Local Settings\Temp`	More logs from the setup process, including `addusr.log`, `errorlog.txt`, `ldif.log`, Microsoft Windows SharePoint Services 2.0 `Setup(0001).txt`, and `SearchSetup.log`
`C:\Exchange Server Setup Progress.log`	Log file for the Exchange installation
`C:\Program Files\Microsoft Windows Small Business Server\Support`	Log files for the configuration wizards, including the CEICW, Add User Wizard, Backup Wizard, and Monitoring Wizard

BEST PRACTICE—INSTALL SBS THREE TIMES

General wisdom in the SBS community is that to fully understand the installation process, you should go through three installs before attempting a production installation. The first time you do an install, you will get a feel for all the steps involved in the process. The second time, you will see more of the customization options available. By the third install, you will be comfortable with the potential hiccups in the process and be able to customize as needed.

Because an SBS server can take so many different configurations (one NIC, two NICs, Standard, Premium with SQL but no ISA, Premium with SQL and ISA, and so on.), you should try to go through a dry run of the installation process on a test box or in a virtual machine configured with similar settings to what you will be using in production. This helps the final installation go more smoothly.

In general, if an error is encountered during the setup process, the error dialog indicates which log file to review. This is not always the case, and becoming familiar with the log files and their locations is instrumental to successfully troubleshooting installation issues.

Two key install files are the `errorlog.txt` and `eventlog.txt` files located in the `C:\Program Files\Microsoft Integration\Windows Small Business Server 2003\Logs` directory. The `eventlog.txt` file tracks all the steps the installation process takes during the setup process. The following sample listing of this file documents the steps taken during the networking setup and domain configuration:

```
[mm/dd/yy,18:59:00] Setup.exe: ISetupManager::RunInstallFromList(IP
➥INSTALL) starting
[mm/dd/yy,18:59:00] WizardUI: entering CWizardUI::RunningComponent()
[mm/dd/yy,18:59:01] Networking Configuration: RAS configuration success
[mm/dd/yy,18:59:03] Networking Configuration: Networking->SetIpInformation()
[mm/dd/yy,18:59:03] Networking Configuration: About to BCreateProcess() :
➥netsh interface ip set address name={151A30CD-D1EE-4CB5-B22F-8A0E9CF391D9}
➥source=STATIC 192.168.16.2 255.255.255.0 NONE
[mm/dd/yy,18:59:21] Networking Configuration: Networking->SetIpDNS()
```

```
[mm/dd/yy,18:59:21] Networking Configuration: About to BCreateProcess() :
➥netsh interface ip delete dns name={151A30CD-D1EE-4CB5-B22F-8A0E9CF391D9}
➥169.254.142.195
[mm/dd/yy,18:59:27] Networking Configuration: Networking->SetIpWINS()
[mm/dd/yy,18:59:27] Networking Configuration: About to BCreateProcess() :
➥netsh interface ip delete wins name={151A30CD-D1EE-4CB5-B22F-8A0E9CF391D9}
➥169.254.142.195
[mm/dd/yy,18:59:30] Networking Configuration: About to BCreateProcess() : netsh
➥interface ip delete wins name={151A30CD-D1EE-4CB5-B22F-8A0E9CF391D9}
➥169.254.142.195
[mm/dd/yy,18:59:35] Networking Configuration: Renaming server
➥NIC:{151A30CD-D1EE-4CB5-B22F-8A0E9CF391D9}
[mm/dd/yy,18:59:36] Networking Configuration: Did not disable the selected
➥NIC:{151A30CD-D1EE-4CB5-B22F-8A0E9CF391D9}
[mm/dd/yy,18:59:36] Networking Configuration: Disabled all but selected NIC
[mm/dd/yy,18:59:36] Networking Configuration: Entering
➥DisableSharedAccessService()
[mm/dd/yy,18:59:36] Networking Configuration: SharedAccess service is
➥installed...
[mm/dd/yy,18:59:36] Networking Configuration: SharedAccess service is
➥RUNNING...  stopping the service.
[mm/dd/yy,18:59:37] Networking Configuration: Disabling the SharedAccess
➥service...
[mm/dd/yy,18:59:38] Networking Configuration: Exiting
➥DisableSharedAccessService()
[mm/dd/yy,18:59:42] Networking Configuration: TCP/IP binding order is changed
➥successfully
[mm/dd/yy,18:59:42] Networking Configuration: NetBiosOptions set for
➥Selected NIC
[mm/dd/yy,18:59:42] Networking Configuration: Networking->ConfigureSBSInstall():
    Checking to see if we want DHCP or WINS.
[mm/dd/yy,18:59:42] Setup.exe:
➥GetGlobalCustomProperty(238E7F41-8C49-4bb2-9723-9917A8811BE4)
[mm/dd/yy,18:59:42] Setup.exe:
➥GetGlobalCustomProperty(238E7F41-8C49-4bb2-9723-9917A8811BE4)
[mm/dd/yy,18:59:42] Setup.exe: AddGlobalCustomProperty
[mm/dd/yy,18:59:42] Setup.exe:
➥GetGlobalCustomProperty(238E7F41-8C49-4bb2-9723-9917A8811BE4)
[mm/dd/yy,18:59:51] Networking Configuration: Unbound all but the
➥selected NIC
[mm/dd/yy,18:59:51] Networking Configuration:
➥Networking->ConfigureSBSInstall():
    Just prompted for path, now checking for another DHCP
➥server present.
```

```
[mm/dd/yy,18:59:51] Networking Configuration: Networking install.
➥Attempting to detect DHCP server. Call to DHCP detection function
➥returned: IP: 34646208 return code: 10049
[mm/dd/yy,18:59:51] Networking Configuration: sysocmgr.exe
➥/u:C:\DOCUME~1\ADMINI~1\LOCALS~1\Temp\inf53.txt /q /r
➥/I:C:\WINDOWS\inf\sysoc.inf
[mm/dd/yy,19:02:13] Networking Configuration:
➥Networking->ConfigureSBSInstall():
    Looping for DHCP service.
[mm/dd/yy,19:02:23] Networking Configuration:
➥Networking->ConfigureSBSInstall():
    Checking again to see if it's still running!  :).
[mm/dd/yy,19:02:23] Networking Configuration:
➥Networking->ConfigureSBSInstall():
    We are set to install DHCP, so let's create the batch file.
[mm/dd/yy,19:02:24] Networking Configuration:
➥Networking->ConfigureSBSInstall(): finished configuration.
[mm/dd/yy,19:02:24] Networking Configuration:
➥Networking->SetIpWINS()
[mm/dd/yy,19:02:24] Networking Configuration: About to
➥BCreateProcess() : netsh interface ip delete wins
➥name={151A30CD-D1EE-4CB5-B22F-8A0E9CF391D9} 169.254.142.195
[mm/dd/yy,19:02:28] Networking Configuration: About to
➥BCreateProcess() : netsh interface ip delete wins
➥name={151A30CD-D1EE-4CB5-B22F-8A0E9CF391D9} 169.254.142.195
[mm/dd/yy,19:02:32] Networking Configuration:
➥Networking:DoInstall() - SBS
[mm/dd/yy,19:02:33] Networking Configuration: Networking Component -
➥SELECTED NIC - IP ADDRESS: 192.168.16.2
[mm/dd/yy,19:02:34] Networking Configuration: Networking Component -
➥NIC GUID: 151A30CD-D1EE-4CB5-B22F-8A0E9CF391D9
[mm/dd/yy,19:02:34] Networking Configuration: Networking Component -
➥SUBNET MASK: 255.255.255.0
[mm/dd/yy,19:02:34] Networking Configuration: Networking Component -
➥GATEWAY:
[mm/dd/yy,19:02:34] Networking Configuration:
[mm/dd/yy,19:02:34] WizardUI: entering CWizardUI::RunningComponent()
[mm/dd/yy,19:02:34] Licensing: Entering Install
[mm/dd/yy,19:02:34] Licensing: Action = IT_INSTALL
[mm/dd/yy,19:02:34] Licensing: Entering DoInstall
[mm/dd/yy,19:02:53] WizardUI: entering CWizardUI::RunningComponent()
[mm/dd/yy,19:02:53] Domain Configuration: CWinwKCfgDCPromo::DoInstall
[mm/dd/yy,19:02:53] Setup.exe:
➥GetGlobalCustomProperty(238E7F41-8C49-4bb2-9723-9917A8811BE4)
[mm/dd/yy,19:03:54] Domain Configuration: WriteNTNF
```

```
[mm/dd/yy,19:03:54] Domain Configuration: SetExtTimeSyncKey :
➥regkey successfully set to NoSync
[mm/dd/yy,19:03:55] Setup.exe:
➥GetGlobalCustomProperty(B51015E7-26A5-4c8f-B871-26ABA9BEFB65)
[mm/dd/yy,19:03:55] Setup.exe: ISetupManager::PersistTheData()
➥outputting information to [C:\Documents and
➥Settings\Administrator\Local Settings\Temp\SIT11904.tmp\REBOOT.INI]
[mm/dd/yy,19:03:56] Setup.exe: ISetupManager::PersistComponentData() starting
[mm/dd/yy,19:03:56] Setup.exe:
➥GetGlobalCustomProperty({8C212B25-D815-11D2-ACD9-00C04F8EEBA1})
[mm/dd/yy,19:04:00] Setup.exe: ISetupManager::PersistComponentData()
➥completing
[mm/dd/yy,19:04:01] Setup.exe: IsRunningUnattended
[mm/dd/yy,19:04:01] Setup.exe: AddGlobalCustomProperty
[mm/dd/yy,19:04:02] Setup.exe:
➥GetGlobalCustomProperty({9843461C-2F7A-4000-B91C-2DDD224C9E91})
[mm/dd/yy,19:04:02] Setup.exe: AddGlobalCustomProperty
[mm/dd/yy,19:04:07] WizardUI: entering CWizardUI::PromptForReboot()
[mm/dd/yy,19:04:07] Setup.exe:
➥GetGlobalCustomProperty({E0C022B6-2029-11D3-8DFC-00C04F797FB8})
[mm/dd/yy,19:04:07] Setup.exe:
➥GetGlobalCustomProperty(CEE76608-9790-4069-AAF6-ED6348C29032)
[mm/dd/yy,19:09:37] Domain Configuration: Force rebooting the machine
➥for dcpromo.
[mm/dd/yy,19:09:38] Domain Configuration: CWinwKCfgDCPromo::DoInstall:
➥exiting.
```

In this log sample, you can see the wizard change the Internal NIC from the APIPA address of 169.254.142.195 to the default of 192.168.16.2 and look at all the DHCP and WINS settings. Then it logs the `dcpromo` process and reboots the server so that the `dcpromo` process can complete.

When errors are encountered during setup, a note is logged in the `eventlog.txt` file. A sample of these notes follows:

```
[mm/dd/yy,18:30:37] setup.exe: ***ERRORLOG EVENT*** : ISetupComponent
➥had an InstallProblem while trying to set install action override:
➥Microsoft Exchange Messaging and Collaboration Services
[mm/dd/yy,18:30:38] setup.exe: ***ERRORLOG EVENT*** : ISetupComponent
➥had an InstallProblem while trying to set install action override:
➥Microsoft Exchange System Management Tools
[mm/dd/yy,18:30:38] setup.exe: ***ERRORLOG EVENT*** : ISetupComponent
➥had an InstallProblem while trying to set install action override:
➥Microsoft Exchange Domain Preparation
```

```
[mm/dd/yy,18:30:38] setup.exe: ***ERRORLOG EVENT*** : ISetupComponent
➥had an InstallProblem while trying to set install action override:
➥Microsoft Exchange Forest Preparation
[mm/dd/yy,18:30:38] setup.exe: ***ERRORLOG EVENT*** : Could not set

➥IR_MAINT on component: Updating Configuration
```

The ***ERRORLOG EVENT*** tag indicates that the item has been logged in the errorlog.txt file, and more information about the error can be found in that file. When you look in the errorlog.txt file, you will find information with the same date and time stamp as listed in eventlog.txt, and following those lines will be additional information about the errors encountered. The following lines are from the errorlog.txt file associated with the errors listed previously:

```
[mm/dd/yy,18:30:37] setup.exe: [2] ISetupComponent had an InstallProblem
➥ while trying to set install action override: Microsoft Exchange
➥Messaging and Collaboration Services
[mm/dd/yy,18:30:38] setup.exe: [2] ISetupComponent had an InstallProblem
➥while trying to set install action override: Microsoft Exchange
➥System Management Tools
[mm/dd/yy,18:30:38] setup.exe: [2] ISetupComponent had an InstallProblem
➥while trying to set install action override: Microsoft Exchange
➥Domain Preparation
[mm/dd/yy,18:30:38] setup.exe: [2] ISetupComponent had an InstallProblem
➥while trying to set install action override: Microsoft Exchange
➥Forest Preparation
[mm/dd/yy,18:30:38] setup.exe: [2] Could not set IR_MAINT on component:
➥Updating Configuration
[mm/dd/yy,18:58:02] WizardUI: [2] ISetupManager::GetGlobalCustomProperty()
➥failed in CPageBase::GetGlobalProperty(): GUID =
➥{F205AE18-9D39-4E3C-A4BA-12FBA060ED91}
[mm/dd/yy,20:40:28] Microsoft Integration: [2]
➥ISetupDataFile::GetPropertyValue() failed for account information in
➥ISetupManager::LoadPersistantComponentData(): filename = C:\Documents
➥and Settings\Administrator\Local Settings\Temp\SIT11904.tmp\REBOOT.INI,
➥component ID = {829300FF-C155-11D2-92EF-00C04F79F1A8}\
➥{DC3074B0-7DE8-43C5-B907-E9100CB5FFF2}, property name = (null)
[mm/dd/yy,20:40:29] Microsoft Integration: [2]
➥ISetupDataFile::GetPropertyValue() failed for account information in
➥ ISetupManager::LoadPersistantComponentData(): filename = C:\Documents
➥and Settings\Administrator\Local Settings\Temp\SIT11904.tmp\REBOOT.INI,
➥component ID = {829300FF-C155-11D2-92EF-00C04F79F1A8}\
➥{F333D98A-C152-11D2-92EF-00C04F79F1A8}, property name = (null)
[mm/dd/yy,20:40:36] Microsoft Integration: [2]
➥ISetupComponent::SetInstallActionByUniqueID() failed in
➥ISetupManager::LoadPersistantComponentData(): component name =
```

```
➥{685BC054-BB6F-46DB-8DB2-C2DB17DE3E8F}\{1F3267B2-721A-49E5-B688-3A10B81C0A8D},
➥action id = 2
[mm/dd/yy,20:40:37] setup.exe: [2] ISetupManager::AddGlobalCustomProperty
➥failed in ISetupManager::LoadPersistantData()
➥ ({df8ff64a-1967-4871-9e32-ca2f819bab81})
[mm/dd/yy,20:40:37] setup.exe: [2] ISetupManager::AddGlobalCustomProperty
➥failed in ISetupManager::LoadPersistantData()
➥ ({c248d3e3-632d-4435-888a-83035c144737})
[mm/dd/yy,20:52:25] WizardUI: [2] ISetupManager::GetGlobalCustomProperty()
➥failed in CPageBase::GetGlobalProperty(): GUID =
➥{FBCCE6F3-9E2D-464D-A4E7-12FBFD515395}
[mm/dd/yy,21:23:55] Server Configuration: [2] An error occurred while accessing
➥domain information. Open Active Directory Users and Computers, and
➥verify that objects appear. Rerun Setup.
[mm/dd/yy,21:23:56] Server Configuration: [2] CSuiteHelpComponentRoot::PreInstall:
➥RefreshAdmin failed with error [80004005]!
```

BEST PRACTICE—USE ERR.EXE TO LOOK UP MICROSOFT ERROR CODES

In the last line of the errorlog.txt sample listing, there is an error code [80004005]. Many Microsoft errors are listed as eight-digit hexadecimal values or possibly as a decimal value such as -2147467259. Microsoft provides a tool called err.exe that can help translate this value into a more meaningful description. err.exe is actually provided as a download from the Exchange download section at Microsoft, but the tool reveals information about errors for more than just Exchange.

To locate this tool, Google "Microsoft err.exe " and select the link from the Microsoft downloads section. Run the downloaded program to extract the program and its associated documentation to a PC's hard drive.

err.exe is a command-line tool that must be run from a command prompt to view its output successfully. To see what error 80004005 is, run err 80004005 from the command prompt. The following output from the command indicates that 8004005 is a generic error:

```
C:\>err 80004005
# for hex 0x80004005 / decimal -2147467259 :
  DDERR_GENERIC                                              ddraw.h
  DIERR_GENERIC                                              dinput.h
  DPERR_GENERIC                                              dplay.h
  DPNERR_GENERIC                                             dplay8.h
  DSERR_GENERIC                                              dsound.h
  DVERR_GENERIC                                              dvoice.h
  ecError                                                    ec.h
  MAPI_E_CALL_FAILED                                         mapicode.h
  STIERR_GENERIC                                             stierr.h
  E_FAIL                                                     winerror.h
# Unspecified error
# 10 matches found for "80004005"
```

The output of error also gives the specific header file where the error code is listed, which can help you identify specifically which error is relevant. For example, if you were troubleshooting an Exchange problem and got this error, you would look to the `MAPI_E_CALL_FAILED` error as the relevant message.

As with any troubleshooting tool, it can take some time to know exactly what to look for from the output of `err`. In most cases, this is time well spent.

In this particular case, the errors were caused by a low memory situation, and after the memory on the server was increased, the installation process completed successfully.

Summary

The installation of SBS 2003 from the SP1 integrated media is not significantly different from the original installation process. Outside inserting more CDs (if the DVD is not used), those who have done several SBS 2003 installations will not find many changes with this media. Those who have not done an SBS installation previously will find the process described in this chapter.

In addition, this chapter covers some basic guidelines for using the setup log files to troubleshoot installation problems. The log files are stored in three main log folders, and the Exchange installation log is stored in the root of `C:` just like every other Exchange installation. The two main setup log files, `eventlog.txt` and `errorlog.txt`, contain the bulk of the setup information needed to identify where problems occurred. The chapter also covered the use of the `err.exe` tool to translate Microsoft error codes from the log files.

The bottom line for server installation is that getting it right the first time is still critical for the long-term health of an SBS server. Even though the setup process is familiar to those who currently support SBS, going through a few test installs with the new slipstreamed media is still recommended prior to a production deployment.

Best Practice Summary

- Always install SBS manually—Even if SBS comes preinstalled on a new server, reinstall the system from scratch to ensure that the server is optimally configured for its environment.
- Location of data folders—Non-OS data, including Exchange and ISA logs and databases, should be placed on a drive other than `C:`. Ideally, multiple fault-tolerant disks would be used to store each type of data.
- Dealing with PPPoE—If the broadband network access is provided through a PPPoE account, use a third-party hardware router/firewall to maintain the PPPoE account connection instead of the external NIC of the SBS server.
- Be cautious when setting up VPN access into the SBS network—Look at all the security implementations and limitations before deciding to implement VPN into your SBS network. Review the VPN Quarantine features of ISA 2004 to plan the best VPN implementation if you do choose to go this route.

- Do not configure Automatic Updates to automatically install updates at a scheduled time—Updates can be configured to download automatically, but the system administrator should only install updates manually.
- Install SBS three times—Before you attempt your first production installation of SBS 2003 SP1, run through the installation process three times on a test box or in a virtual environment to become familiar with the installation process.
- Use `err.exe` to translate Microsoft hexadecimal error codes—`err.exe` can help you figure out what the error code means, which can help you track down the possible sources of the problem.

PART III

SBS 2003 Networking

IN THIS PART

CHAPTER 5

DNS, DHCP, and Active Directory Integration

IN THIS CHAPTER

- Review of Active Directory and DNS Integration
- Configuring DNS for the Internal Network
- Configuring DNS to Resolve Public Internet Addresses
- Configuring DHCP for the Internal Network
- Troubleshooting DNS, DHCP, and Active Directory Issues

The core of every SBS installation is a solid Active Directory infrastructure. Because Active Directory depends heavily on network technologies such as DNS, a successful and healthy SBS implementation must have a correctly configured network. This applies not only to the server but to the workstations as well. This chapter covers the default network configuration of an SBS installation in detail and looks at the problems that can arise when the configurations change.

Review of Active Directory and DNS Integration

With the release of the Windows 2000 server products, Microsoft introduced a new directory service to replace the flat domain directory structure of Windows NT. Active Directory is a much more complex directory structure and is dependent on knowing the structure of the network to function properly. To achieve this, Microsoft tied many functions of Active Directory into DNS and other networking technologies. But without a functioning and reliable DNS system, Active Directory is effectively useless. So even in a single-server network like most SBS installations, a basic understanding of DNS and how it integrates with Active Directory is important.

What Is DNS?

DNS stands for Domain Name System (or Domain Name Service or Domain Name Server, depending on your source) and is a mechanism for translating network computer names into IP addresses. DNS is like a large electronic phone book that computers the world over use to find each other.

Actually, DNS was devised more for humans than computers. Most humans have an easier time remembering words and phrases than numbers. Because all computer communication actually takes place using numeric values, this is essential for us. How much easier it is to remember `www.microsoft.com` or `www.google.com` than 207.46.156.156 or 64.233.187.99. Additionally, no one device knows all the names and addresses of all network devices connected to the Internet, but the structure of the DNS system takes care of that for us, too.

How DNS Works

When you open your web browser and type in `www.google.com`, the Google search home page appears magically on your screen. But actually many steps have to take place before that happens. First, your computer looks in its internal name cache to see whether an IP address for `www.google.com` has already been looked up. If it has, the computer uses the address from the cache and attempts to make the connection to the server sitting at that IP address. If there is no address in the local cache, DNS kicks in. The computer contacts the DNS server listed in the network properties for the connection and asks that server for the address for `www.google.com`. That DNS server then looks in its local cache to see whether it has looked up the address before. If it has, the DNS server sends the address back to the computer, and the computer commences contacting the web server. If the DNS server does not have the address either in its configuration or local cache, it turns to another server and asks for the address, and so the process goes until a DNS server that has the IP address for the name can be found.

How Active Directory Relies on DNS

When a Windows server runs the DNS service and participates in Active Directory, the DNS server stores more than just machine names and addresses. A large number of service (SRV) records can be stored in DNS to allow computers in an Active Directory environment to locate machines running specific services related to Active Directory. The DNS Management Console is the tool used to view and configure DNS settings on the server. To open the DNS Management Console, click on Start, Administrative Tools, DNS or type **`dnsmgmt.msc`** in a command prompt or after choosing Start, Run. Figure 5.1 shows the DNS Management Console display for the internal domain. In Figure 5.1, you can see the DNS host records (also known as A records) for the SBS server as well as several of the workstations that belong to the domain. In addition, there are other non-host records in this location that help the network do basic internal hostname lookups.

BEST PRACTICE—CREATING DNS ALIASES INSTEAD OF HOST RECORDS

As shown in Figure 5.1, the entry for the DNS name `companyweb` is not a host record (A record) but is an alias (CNAME) record. When a CNAME record is looked up in DNS, it returns another DNS name instead of an IP address. Then a lookup is done on this new DNS name, which, in the case of `companyweb`, returns the IP address of the SBS server's internal NIC.

If you need to create any new DNS records that point to existing servers or workstations, such as creating a DNS name for the server that is easier for users to remember, create the record as a CNAME instead of a host record. If you create the entry as an A record and you need to change the IP address of the server, you will have to remember to go back in DNS and change the address associated with the A record. If you create the record as a CNAME, when you change the IP address of the server, the CNAME record automatically picks up the new address of the server because it always points to the DNS name of the server and not the IP address.

To create a new CNAME record, follow these steps:

1. Right-click on the DNS forward lookup zone and select New Alias (CNAME).
2. Enter the name for the new host in the Alias Name field.
3. Enter the fully qualified domain name for the existing machine in the Fully Qualified Domain Name (FQDN) for Target Host field.
4. Click OK.

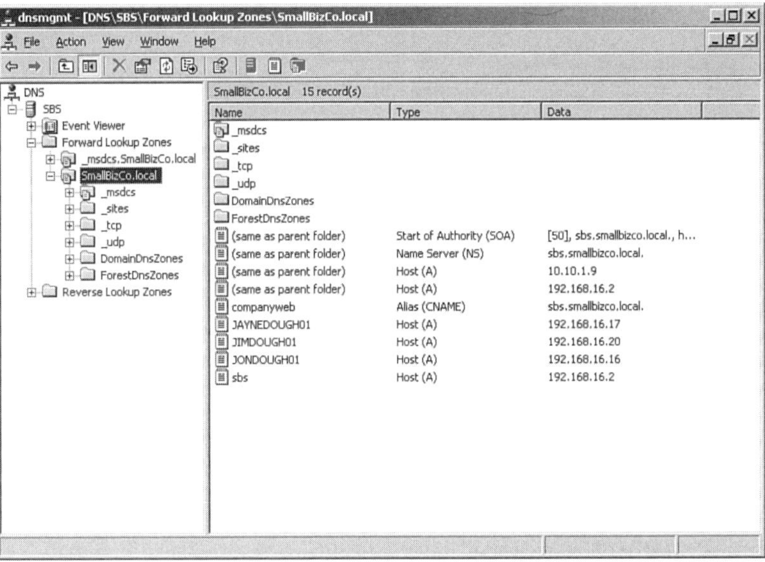

FIGURE 5.1 The DNS Management Console displays the hostname to IP address listings for computers on the internal network.

Figure 5.2 shows an expanded view of the `_msdcs` zone for the internal network. This is where the meat of network information for Active Directory is stored. The `_msdcs` zone is subdivided into four areas: `dc` for domain controller references; `domains` for core domain information; `gc` for global catalog references, and `pdc` for primary domain controller references. Although most humans would never need to know this information interactively, when a workstation attempts to authenticate against Active Directory or processes a user login on the domain, it uses DNS to look up these services to find where it needs to go to connect to, for instance, the appropriate Kerberos service.

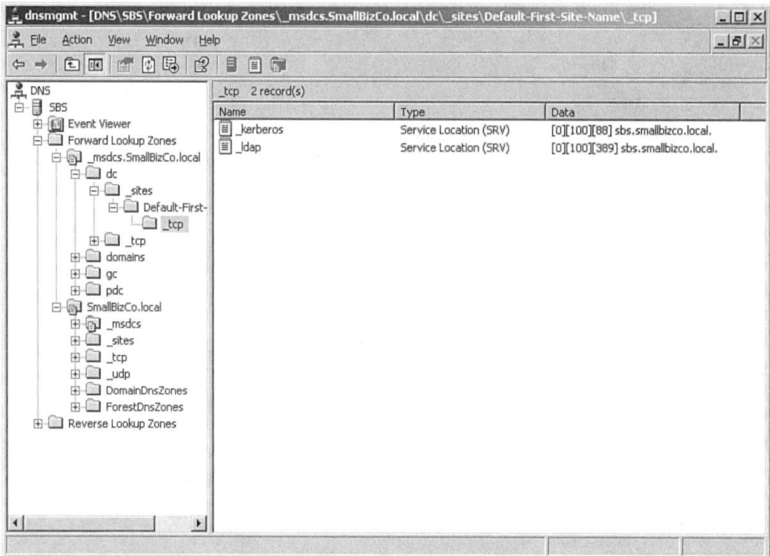

FIGURE 5.2 The `_msdcs lookup` zone contains lookup addresses for key Active Directory components.

A more detailed explanation of Active Directory, DNS, and the integration of the two is beyond the scope of this book. In fact, many books have already been published on Active Directory alone. For our purposes with this book, this basic understanding of the integration of DNS and Active Directory provides a foundation to be able to handle most issues that may arise in an SBS installation related to DNS and AD.

Configuring DNS for the Internal Network

When using the default configuration tools for setting up the server and workstations in an SBS environment, the network configuration should be set correctly for each computer to allow proper internal and external name resolution. Sometimes, however, knowing what should happen is not sufficient. Knowing what actually happens and comparing that to what should happen can shed light on problems you may encounter.

Standard DNS Server Configuration

The network portion of the Connect to the Internet Wizard, also known as the CEICW (Configure Email and Internet Connection Wizard) configures the network settings for both the internal and external network interfaces. As it relates to DNS, the NIC setup is straightforward—both interfaces reference the internal NIC's IP address as the DNS server. The following output of an `ipconfig /all` command in a command prompt shows a proper network configuration for a two-network card configuration after the CEICW has been run:

```
C:\Documents and Settings\Administrator>ipconfig /all

Windows IP Configuration

   Host Name . . . . . . . . . . . . : sbs
   Primary Dns Suffix  . . . . . . . : SmallBizCo.local
   Node Type . . . . . . . . . . . . : Unknown
   IP Routing Enabled. . . . . . . . : Yes
   WINS Proxy Enabled. . . . . . . . : Yes
   DNS Suffix Search List. . . . . . : SmallBizCo.local

Ethernet adapter Server Local Area Connection:

   Connection-specific DNS Suffix  . :
   Description . . . . . . . . . . . : 3Com 3C920 Integrated Fast Ethernet
➥Controller (3C905C-TX Compatible)
   Physical Address. . . . . . . . . : 00-08-74-40-5B-61
   DHCP Enabled. . . . . . . . . . . : No
   IP Address. . . . . . . . . . . . : 192.168.16.2
   Subnet Mask . . . . . . . . . . . : 255.255.255.0
   Default Gateway . . . . . . . . . :
   DNS Servers . . . . . . . . . . . : 192.168.16.2
   Primary WINS Server . . . . . . . : 192.168.16.2

Ethernet adapter Network Connection:

   Connection-specific DNS Suffix  . :
   Description . . . . . . . . . . . : Realtek RTL8029(AS) PCI Ethernet Adapter
   Physical Address. . . . . . . . . : 00-C0-F0-2B-7D-F9
   DHCP Enabled. . . . . . . . . . . : No
   IP Address. . . . . . . . . . . . : 10.10.1.9
   Subnet Mask . . . . . . . . . . . : 255.255.255.0
   Default Gateway . . . . . . . . . : 10.10.1.1
   DNS Servers . . . . . . . . . . . : 192.168.16.2
   Primary WINS Server . . . . . . . : 192.168.16.2
   NetBIOS over Tcpip. . . . . . . . : Disabled

C:\Documents and Settings\Administrator>
```

As you can see from the output, both the external and internal NICs point to the internal NIC for DNS. This forces all DNS lookups on the server to use the DNS Server service on the server to provide all name resolution.

Standard DNS Workstation Configuration

In general, workstations in an SBS environment should be configured to use DHCP to get their network configuration. In some cases, however, some workstations may be required to have a static IP configuration. The following listing shows the output from an `ipconfig /all` command for a standard workstation configuration:

```
C:\Documents and Settings\Administrator>ipconfig /all

Windows IP Configuration

        Host Name . . . . . . . . . . . . : JONDOUGH01
        Primary Dns Suffix  . . . . . . . : SmallBizCo.local
        Node Type . . . . . . . . . . . . : Hybrid
        IP Routing Enabled. . . . . . . . : No
        WINS Proxy Enabled. . . . . . . . : No
        DNS Suffix Search List. . . . . . : SmallBizCo.local
                                            SmallBizCo.local

Ethernet adapter Local Area Connection:

        Connection-specific DNS Suffix  . : SmallBizCo.local
        Description . . . . . . . . . . . : Intel 21140-Based PCI Fast
➥ Ethernet Adapter (Generic)
        Physical Address. . . . . . . . . : 00-03-FF-81-79-85
        Dhcp Enabled. . . . . . . . . . . : Yes
        Autoconfiguration Enabled . . . . : Yes
        IP Address. . . . . . . . . . . . : 192.168.16.16
        Subnet Mask . . . . . . . . . . . : 255.255.255.0
        Default Gateway . . . . . . . . . : 192.168.16.2
        DHCP Server . . . . . . . . . . . : 192.168.16.2
        DNS Servers . . . . . . . . . . . : 192.168.16.2
        Primary WINS Server . . . . . . . : 192.168.16.2
        Lease Obtained. . . . . . . . . . :
        Lease Expires . . . . . . . . . . :

C:\Documents and Settings\Administrator>
```

When setting the network configuration manually for a workstation, a few items must be configured correctly for the workstation to communicate correctly with the SBS network. First, the IP address and subnet mask must match the IP address range used for the internal network. Second, the default gateway must point to the SBS server's internal NIC (for a dual-NIC SBS configuration) or to the router/firewall (for a single-NIC SBS configuration). Third, the DNS server must be set to the SBS server's internal NIC. The `ipconfig /all` output from a workstation with a correctly configured network configuration looks like the following listing:

```
C:\Documents and Settings\Administrator>ipconfig /all

Windows IP Configuration

        Host Name . . . . . . . . . . . . : JONDOUGH01
        Primary Dns Suffix  . . . . . . . : SmallBizCo.local
        Node Type . . . . . . . . . . . . : Broadcast
        IP Routing Enabled. . . . . . . . : No
        WINS Proxy Enabled. . . . . . . . : No
        DNS Suffix Search List. . . . . . : SmallBizCo.local

Ethernet adapter Local Area Connection:

        Connection-specific DNS Suffix  . :
        Description . . . . . . . . . . . : Intel 21140-Based PCI Fast
➥ Ethernet Adapter (Generic)
        Physical Address. . . . . . . . . : 00-03-FF-81-79-85
        Dhcp Enabled. . . . . . . . . . . : No
        IP Address. . . . . . . . . . . . : 192.168.16.201
        Subnet Mask . . . . . . . . . . . : 255.255.255.0
        Default Gateway . . . . . . . . . : 192.168.16.2
        DNS Servers . . . . . . . . . . . : 192.168.16.2

C:\Documents and Settings\Administrator>
```

The workstation should not be configured to look to any other DNS servers besides the SBS server. If a secondary DNS server must be configured for a workstation, the SBS server's IP address must be listed first.

BEST PRACTICE—IPCONFIG /ALL

Anytime the server or workstation experiences communication difficulties, checking the network configuration of both with the `ipconfig /all` command is the first step to identifying where the problem lies. If you post in the SBS newsgroups or call Microsoft PSS for assistance, one of the first questions you are likely to be asked is to provide the output from this command for both the server and a workstation on the network.

To prepare the output from `ipconfig /all` for posting in a newsgroup or sending to a support professional in email, you'll need to save the output from the command to a file. The easiest way to do this is to enter the following command from a command prompt:

```
ipconfig /all > ipconfig.txt
```

This creates a text file named `ipconfig.txt` in the current working directory. The file can be opened in Notepad for review. One other quick way to create the file and review it immediately is to use the following command in the command window:

```
ipconfig /all > ipconfig.txt && ipconfig.txt
```

This command creates the `ipconfig.txt` file in the current working directory and immediately opens the file with Notepad.

Configuring DNS to Resolve Public Internet Addresses

So how does the DNS Server service provide name resolution for public Internet addresses if both network cards point to the SBS server for DNS resolution? For that, we need to look again at the DNS Management Console.

Using DNS Forwarders in the DNS Management Console

When the DNS Management Console comes up, right-click on the server name and select Properties; then click on the Forwarders tab. The dialog box shown in Figure 5.3 appears. The DNS Domain box should have one entry named All Other DNS Domains. The Selected Domain's Forwarder IP Address List box should have the IP addresses for your ISP's DNS servers listed. You should expect to see this configuration after the Connect to the Internet Wizard has been run on the server.

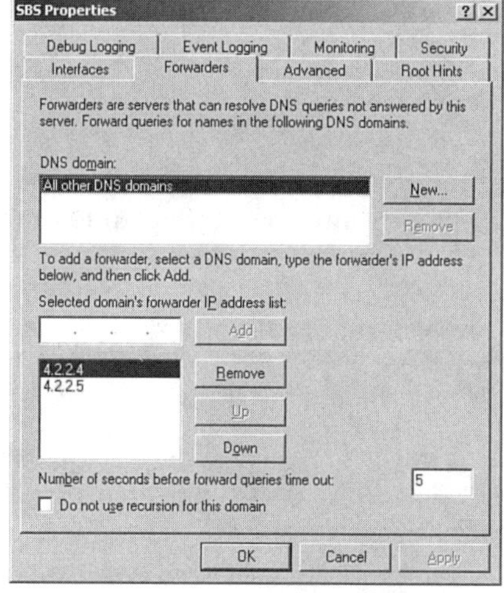

FIGURE 5.3 The DNS Management Console displays the DNS forwarder addresses.

As described earlier in this chapter, if the DNS service receives a request for an address that is not in its configuration, it first looks to its internal DNS cache for the address. If one is not found, the DNS Server service then contacts the first IP address listed in the Forwarders section and requests the address from that server. A second DNS server IP is strongly recommended in the case where the first server cannot be contacted for some reason.

Using Root Hints in the DNS Management Console

Being able to use DNS servers provided by the ISP helps reduce the DNS server load. When the DNS server cannot find an address in its local table or local cache, it makes one request to the ISP's DNS server and lets that server do all the lookup work necessary to find the address.

The DNS Server service does not have to use external DNS forwarders, however. The DNS Server service can make use or root hint servers and handle all the lookups itself instead of handing them off to the forwarder. If no IP addresses are listed in the Forwarders tab of the server properties in the DNS Management Console, the DNS server will automatically query the root hint servers listed in the Root Hints tab of the properties window. These root hint servers do not contain any DNS address information themselves, but they do contain addresses for other DNS servers that do provide the address information. When a DNS query comes in to the SBS DNS server for a server on the public Internet, the DNS service first queries the appropriate root hint server to find a DNS server to use to resolve the name; then will sends another query to that server to get the actual address to pass back to the client.

BEST PRACTICE—DNS FORWARDERS VERSUS ROOT HINTS

General wisdom in the SBS space is to use DNS forwarders for external DNS lookups. This reduces the load on the SBS DNS Server service for doing DNS lookups on the Internet. When the SBS server performs a DNS query for an Internet site by using the DNS forwarders, the SBS DNS Server service only makes one DNS query and relies on the DNS forwarder to do all the lookups necessary to get the IP address and return it to the SBS server.

Some small businesses have found that their ISPs may not provide the most reliable DNS forwarder servers. By configuring the SBS server to use the root hints servers, the SBS DNS Server service does all its own lookups, which may take multiple queries to get the actual IP address. But the root hint servers may be more reliable than the ISP's DNS servers.

The SBS server should be configured to use DNS forwarders as a general practice. But in cases where the ISP's DNS servers are not very reliable, configuring SBS to use the root hint servers is an acceptable alternative.

Recently, there have been security reports concerning *DNS poisoning* and the problem it can cause when using DNS forwarders. In short, DNS poisoning occurs when a DNS record is replaced with an IP address for a site not hosted by the DNS name owner. This effectively redirects web traffic to a different site for malicious purposes. Outside of ensuring that your ISP keeps its DNS servers patched and up-to-date, the only other workaround is to disable the use of forwarders and let the SBS server use the root hint servers for all DNS lookups. At this time, the SBS community still recommends the use of DNS forwarders but recognizes the threat of DNS poisoning and the use of the root hint servers as an acceptable alternative.

Configuring DHCP for the Internal Network

Anyone who has worked in a large network environment already knows and appreciates the value of DHCP (Dynamic Host Configuration Protocol) in providing dynamic IP address assignments and other network configuration settings. Although the benefits of using DHCP in a small network may not be immediately obvious to some, the technology is almost a requirement in the SBS world. This section provides an overview of DHCP and how it is used with SBS 2003.

What Is DHCP?

The DHCP protocol is defined in RFC 1541 (`www.ietf.org/rfc/rfc1541.txt`) and RFC 2131 (`www.ietf.org/rfc/rfc2131.txt`) as a way for network computers to acquire network configuration information from a remote server instead of a local configuration. In the early days of TCP/IP networking, every workstation and server was given a static IP address in the local configuration, and when the IP addressing scheme changed, each workstation had to be changed manually. In addition, a notebook computer that moved from one location to another had to have its network configuration changed each time it moved.

To automate the assigning of IP information to network clients, the BOOTP protocol was developed, which matched a machine's ethernet card MAC address to an IP address. When initializing the network interface, the workstation would send a broadcast on the network asking for a BOOTP server, and the broadcast included the MAC address of the workstation. The BOOTP server would receive the request, check against its internal database for the MAC address, and return configuration to the client so that the client could continue to connect to the network.

The BOOTP method still required a great deal of maintenance, however, in that any time a new workstation arrived, it had to be manually added to the BOOTP database. The same thing would happen if the network card in the computer was replaced.

DHCP was developed based on the BOOTP process but without many of the restrictions of BOOTP. The workstation's MAC address does not have to exist in a database on the DHCP server to get and IP address on the network, which cut down significantly on the management needed to get a network configuration working.

DHCP does more than just provide an IP address to a client workstation on the network. Many network settings can be configured on a workstation via DHCP. Table 5.1 shows a number of the settings that can be passed on to a workstation from a Microsoft DHCP server.

TABLE 5.1 Some Network Settings Configured Via the Microsoft DHCP Server

Setting	Description
Router	Sets the default gateway
Time server	Sets the address for a time server
DNS servers	Sets the addresses for DNS servers
Hostname	Sets the hostname for the client
DNS domain name	Sets the default DNS domain name for the client
NIS domain name	Sets the default Network Information Service domain name
NIS servers	Sets the addresses for NIS servers
NTP servers	Sets the addresses for Network Time Protocol servers
WINS/NBNS Servers	Sets the addresses for WINS and NBNS servers

TABLE 5.1 Continued

Setting	Description
SMTP servers	Sets the addresses for available Simple Mail Transport Protocol servers
POP3 servers	Sets the addresses for available Post Office Protocol servers
NNTP servers	Sets the addresses for available Network News Transport Protocols servers

DHCP can also be used to assign the same IP address to a workstation every time it makes a DHCP request. This is similar in function to the BOOTP process in that a reservation for the computer is made in the DHCP database based on the MAC address of the workstation's network card. This effectively gives the workstation a "static" IP address on the network. This is useful for network printer and other devices that need to have a fixed address on the network without having to configure the address manually on the device.

Default SBS DHCP Settings

The initial network setup for an SBS server creates a specific DHCP configuration for all installations. Table 5.2 shows the DHCP elements configured by the SBS setup and the default settings for each element.

TABLE 5.2 Default DHCP Settings as Configured by the SBS Setup

Content Area	Configuration	Default Settings
Scope Properties	Scope Name	SBS Scope
Scope Properties	Lease Duration	8 days
Address Pool	Address Range	192.168.x.1–192.168.x.254
Address Pool	Excluded Addresses	192.168.x.1–192.168.x.9
Scope Options	Router	Internal SBS IP address
Scope Options	DNS Servers	Internal SBS IP address
Scope Options	DNS Domain Name	Internal domain name
Scope Options	WINS/NBNS Servers	Internal SBS IP address
Scope Options	WINS/NBT Node Type	0x8

Keeping in line with the best practices for network configuration, the DHCP server gives a requesting client a valid IP address, points the workstation to the correct SBS IP address for DNS and WINS, and provides the correct internal domain name. The DHCP scope also excludes the first 10 addresses in the address range for machines that need a static IP address, such as the server's internal NIC.

In addition to using these settings during the initial install, these settings are updated back to these defaults when the Change IP Address Wizard is run. Running this wizard is the easiest way to rebuild a broken DHCP configuration on the server.

BEST PRACTICE—LET SBS PROVIDE DHCP SERVICES

When multiple devices on the network are capable of providing DHCP to the workstations on the network, the SBS server should be used to provide DHCP services. The SBS DHCP service is preconfigured with all the settings needed for workstations to connect successfully with the SBS network. Even if a third-party DHCP server can provide all the settings options (some do not support all the DHCP options), if any network configuration changes are made, the SBS server automatically updates the necessary settings in its DHCP configuration, where the third-party device would have to be manually configured.

Customizing DHCP Settings

For most environments, the default DHCP server settings preconfigured by the SBS wizards are sufficient to handle the workstation configuration needs. There may be times when specific network requirements necessitate an adjustment to these default settings. Only in those cases should the default settings for DHCP be modified at all.

DHCP settings are modified through the DHCP Management Console, which can be launched by choosing Start, Administrative Tools, DHCP or by entering **`dhcpmgmt.msc`** after choosing Start, Run or at a command prompt. In this console, you can also view the current DHCP address leases, as shown in Figure 5.4.

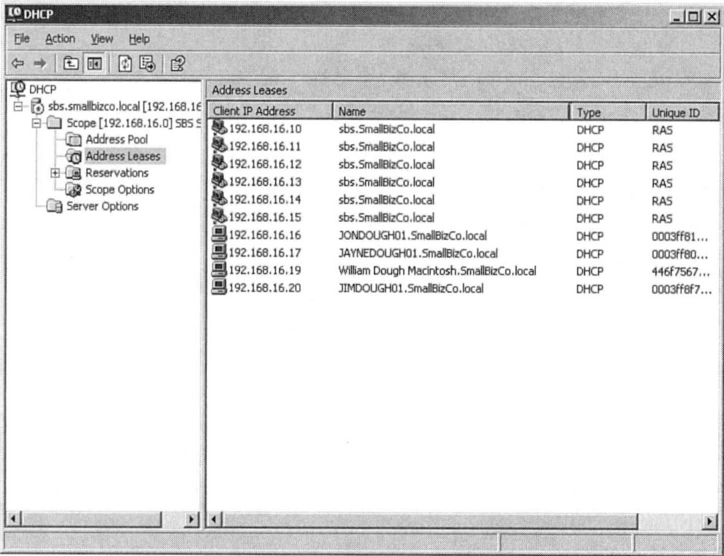

FIGURE 5.4 The DHCP Management Console shows the current DHCP address leases on the network.

Creating Additional Address Exclusions

One common modification to the default DHCP settings is to extend the range of excluded addresses. This would be done if more than 10 static IP addresses were needed in the local network. This can be achieved by either adding an additional exclusion range to the address pool or by deleting the existing exclusion range and creating a new one.

CAUTION

When modifying the DHCP address exclusion range, be sure to keep the IP address of the SBS internal NIC excluded.

Follow these steps to add an additional exclusion range to the DHCP address pool:

1. Open the DHCP Management Console.
2. Expand the server icon.
3. Expand the Scope folder.
4. Click on the Address Pool folder to view the existing address and exclusion ranges (see Figure 5.5).

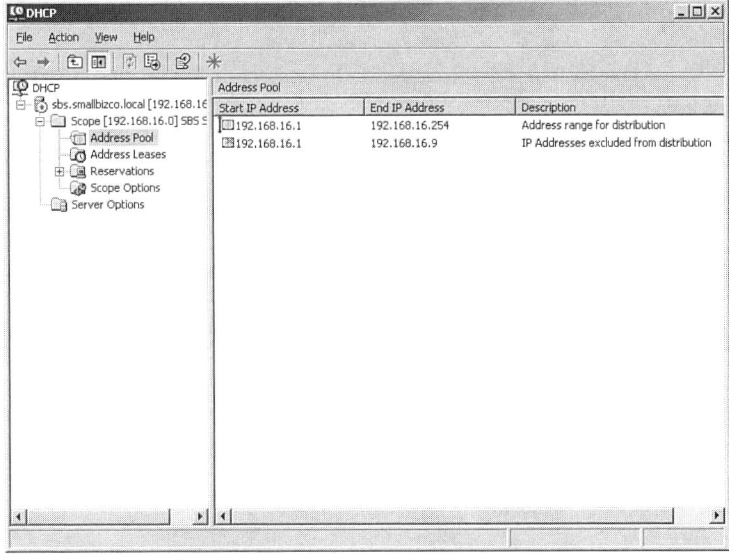

FIGURE 5.5 The existing address and exclusion ranges in the DHCP address pool.

5. Right-click on Address Pool and select New Exclusion Range.
6. Enter the starting and ending IP addresses to exclude (see Figure 5.6).
7. Click Add; then click Close.

Any new DHCP requests processed by the server will not receive an IP address in the exclusion range that was just added. Any existing DHCP address leases that may exist in the new exclusion range will not be affected until the workstation attempts to renew the lease for that address.

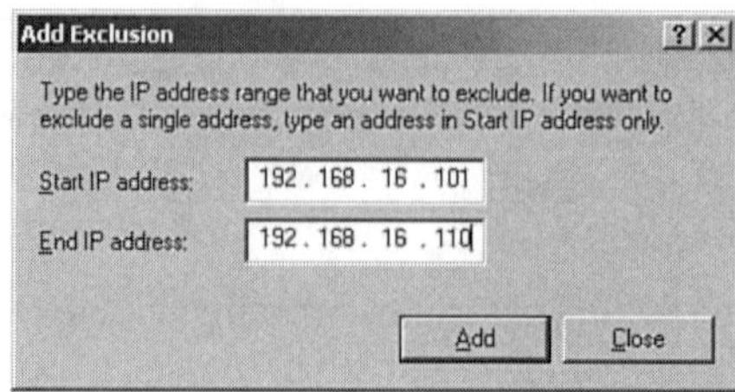

FIGURE 5.6 Specifying the starting and ending IP addresses to exclude from the DHCP scope.

Creating DHCP Address Reservations

Another common modification to the default DHCP settings is adding a DHCP address reservation for a specific device. This is done when a network device gets its configuration information from DHCP but needs to have the same IP address every time it comes on the network. To reserve an address for a specific device, you will need the MAC address from the ethernet card for the device. Follow these steps to add a new reservation to the DHCP configuration:

1. Open the DHCP Management Console.
2. Expand the server icon.
3. Expand the Scope folder.
4. Click on the Reservations folder to see any reservations that may already exist.
5. Right-click on Reservations and select New Reservation.
6. Provide the Reservation Name, IP Address, MAC Address, and Description in the New Reservation dialog box (see Figure 5.7).

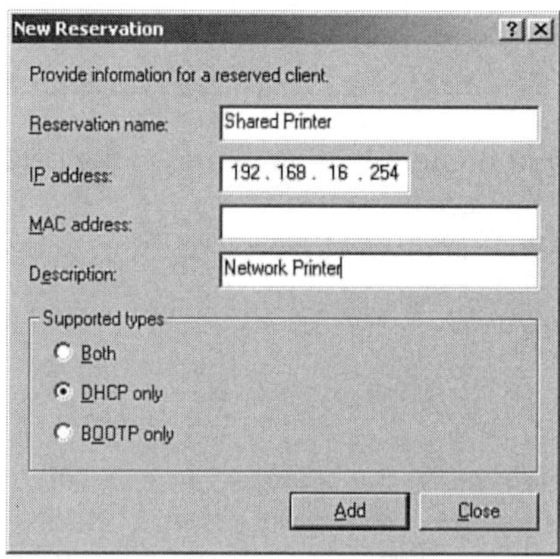

FIGURE 5.7 The settings for a new reservation entered in the DHCP Management Console.

7. Select the DHCP Only radio button. If BOOTP is used on the network, select either the Both or the BOOTP Only radio button instead.
8. Click Add; then click Close.

The next time the device requests a new DHCP address or attempts to renew its DHCP lease, it will be given the address specified in the reservation.

FINDING THE MAC ADDRESS

For a Windows workstation, you can get the MAC address for the network card by running `ipconfig /all` in a command window. If the device is on the network and you know the IP address it has received from DHCP, you can run `arp -a` from a command prompt on the server and get the MAC address for the device. The output from the command will be similar to the following:

```
C:\> arp -a
Interface: 192.168.16.2 --- 0x10003
  Internet Address      Physical Address      Type
  192.168.16.20           00-03-ff-8f-79-85     dynamic
```

Troubleshooting DNS, DHCP, and Active Directory Issues

Because of the interdependence of Active Directory and DNS, many DNS issues may actually seem to be Active Directory problems at first glance. The remainder of this chapter provides insight into some commonly experienced problems and troubleshooting tips to help resolve issues quickly.

Troubleshooting Internal DNS Lookup Issues

By far the most common internal network problems occur when the server or a workstation does not have DNS configured correctly. The next two examples identify the behavior seen and describe why the problem occurs.

Server Hangs at Applying Network Settings

With few exceptions, when an SBS server takes a long time to boot, and specifically appears to hang for 20 minutes or longer at the Preparing Network Connections portion of the boot process, the network cards on the server are pointing to an external server for DNS. The output of an `ipconfig /all` command on a server experiencing this problem might look like this:

```
C:\Documents and Settings\Administrator>ipconfig /all

Windows IP Configuration
```

```
   Host Name . . . . . . . . . . . . : sbs
   Primary Dns Suffix  . . . . . . . : SmallBizCo.local
   Node Type . . . . . . . . . . . . : Unknown
   IP Routing Enabled. . . . . . . . : Yes
   WINS Proxy Enabled. . . . . . . . : Yes
   DNS Suffix Search List. . . . . . : SmallBizCo.local

Ethernet adapter Server Local Area Connection:

   Connection-specific DNS Suffix  . :
   Description . . . . . . . . . . . : 3Com 3C920 Integrated Fast Ethernet
➥ Controller (3C905C-TX Compatible)
   Physical Address. . . . . . . . . : 00-08-74-40-5B-61
   DHCP Enabled. . . . . . . . . . . : No
   IP Address. . . . . . . . . . . . : 192.168.16.2
   Subnet Mask . . . . . . . . . . . : 255.255.255.0
   Default Gateway . . . . . . . . . :
   DNS Servers . . . . . . . . . . . : 192.168.16.2
   Primary WINS Server . . . . . . . : 192.168.16.2

Ethernet adapter Network Connection:

   Connection-specific DNS Suffix  . :
   Description . . . . . . . . . . . : Realtek RTL8029(AS) PCI Ethernet Adapter
   Physical Address. . . . . . . . . : 00-C0-F0-2B-7D-F9
   DHCP Enabled. . . . . . . . . . . : No
   IP Address. . . . . . . . . . . . : 10.10.1.9
   Subnet Mask . . . . . . . . . . . : 255.255.255.0
   Default Gateway . . . . . . . . . : 10.10.1.1
   DNS Servers . . . . . . . . . . . : 4.2.2.4
                                       4.2.2.3
   Primary WINS Server . . . . . . . : 192.168.16.2
   NetBIOS over Tcpip. . . . . . . . : Disabled
```

In this instance, when the server is in the Preparing Network Connections stage, it is attempting to register all its Active Directory information into the DNS server(s) listed on the NIC. Needless to say, the DNS servers hosted by the ISP are not going to accept any DNS registrations from just any server out on the Net, and it certainly does not recognize the nonroutable DNS suffix. When the attempt is made to register the DNS information with the remote server, the remote server will not respond, and the attempt will eventually time out. Unfortunately, the Active Directory startup routines are persistent and will keep making multiple attempts to register this information with the DNS server until it finally gives up. This process can take 20 minutes or longer, depending on how many external DNS servers are listed for each NIC.

This behavior also occurs when the internal NIC is listed as the DNS server for both NICs, but one of the NICs also has a secondary DNS server listed with an external address. The Active Directory DNS registration process is successful for the internal DNS server, but the server will attempt to register Active Directory information with each DNS server listed in the NIC configuration. The only way to avoid this situation is to have the internal IP address of the SBS server listed as the *only* DNS server for each network card in the server.

Connect Computer Wizard Fails to Find Users and Computers

Another common error occurs when a workstation is attempting to join the SBS domain using the Connect Computer Wizard. After starting the wizard from the web browser, an error is generated that says "The list of users and computers could not be found on the server. Make sure that the Small Business Server network adapters are configured correctly." The error occurs because the client workstation is not configured correctly, not because the server is misconfigured as the error applies. Microsoft has published KB article 837369 (`http://support.microsoft.com/?id=837369`) on this error. The KB article also indicates that the problem is the result of the client workstation having a DNS server entry that is not the SBS server's internal IP address. Again, this problem is resolved by modifying the network settings on the workstation so that it points to the SBS server as the only server for DNS.

NOTE

In SBS 2003 SP1, a different error is generated in this situation (see Figure 5.8). Instead of the cryptic error described previously, the error details the exact problem and gives steps to resolve the problem.

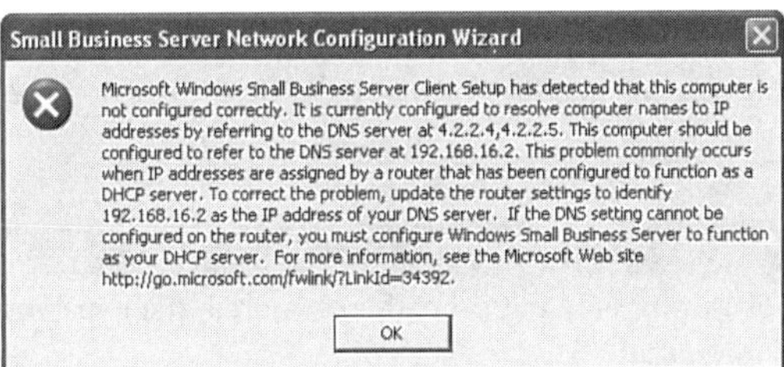

FIGURE 5.8 The Connect Computer Wizard describes the most common reason for not being able to complete.

Using `nslookup` to Search for Internal DNS Names

Sometimes you may run across a situation where internal DNS name resolution just doesn't work correctly but with no obvious cause. Perhaps users start reporting that when they open their web browser, the Companyweb page fails to load and generates a Page Cannot Be Displayed error. Or they are suddenly unable to open a share on another server or workstation in the local network. If the problem seems to be isolated to a single machine or a small group of computers, it is unlikely that a problem exists on the SBS server, so troubleshooting should start at the workstation.

The best tool to use to troubleshoot client DNS problems is the command-line tool `nslookup`. This tool is installed by default on every Windows 2000, Windows XP, and Windows 2003 system. For this type of troubleshooting, we will use `nslookup` in interactive mode, which is entered by typing **`nslookup`** at a command prompt or after choosing Start, Run. In interactive mode, you are presented with a > prompt where you can enter multiple lookup commands. Type **`exit`** at the > prompt to exit the interactive mode of `nslookup`.

To test the DNS lookup of a local system, enter the system name at the `nslookup` prompt and press Enter. If you enter the name of a local workstation (`jimdough01` in this example), you see a result similar to the following listing.

```
C:\>nslookup
Default Server:  sbs.smallbizco.local
Address:  192.168.16.2

> jimdough01
Server:  sbs.smallbizco.local
Address:  192.168.16.2

Name:    jimdough01.SmallBizCo.local
Address:  192.168.16.25
```

When `nslookup` first enters interactive mode, it displays the name and IP address of the default DNS server being used by the client. In the preceding example, the workstation is pointing to the local SBS server, which is the correct configuration. If you see a different server listed in the initial `nslookup` output, you know that the default DNS server for the workstation is not set correctly, which is the likely cause of the problem. In this example, the workstation can look up the name of the workstation `jimdough01` and get an IP address for the workstation.

NOTE

If the reverse DNS lookup zones are not properly configured, the initial response from `nslookup` generates the following output:

```
*** Can't find server name for address 192.168.16.2: Non-existent domain
Default Server:  UnKnown
Address:  192.168.16.2
```

If you see this response, you are not going to have problems doing DNS lookups through the server. You can resolve this issue by creating the reverse lookup zone for the internal network and adding a pointer (PTR) record for the SBS server in the zone.

When `nslookup` queries the name of a system that is not in the DNS table of the SBS server, it generates a response similar to the following listing. In this case, you would want to check the DNS entries in the forward lookup zone for the `smallbizco.local` domain and see whether there is an entry present for companyweb. In this example, there is not:

```
> companyweb
Server:  sbs.smallbizco.local
Address:  192.168.16.2

*** sbs.smallbizco.local can't find companyweb: Non-existent domain
```

In the following example, nslookup returns an address for companyweb from the server:

```
> companyweb
Server:  sbs.smallbizco.local
Address:  192.168.16.2

Name:    companyweb.SmallBizCo.local
Address:  192.168.16.8
```

However, the address returned is not the same as the address of the SBS server. In this case, we know that the failure to load companyweb in the workstation's Internet browser is because the DNS record is pointing to the wrong address.

As you can see from these few examples, nslookup can provide quite a bit of information on the local network with just a few commands. The next section takes a deeper look at how to use nslookup to troubleshoot DNS problems on the external network.

WHEN HTTP://COMPANYWEB RESOLVES TO WWW.COMPANYWEB.COM

Many web browsers have internal routines they use to try and find websites when a single-label name (such as companyweb is entered in the address bar. First the browser does a lookup on the name companyweb in the default domain. If no site is found, the browser starts guessing what the site might be by looking up the name as a domain name, starting with .com, then .net, then .org, and so on. So if the browser is set to go to http://companyweb when it starts and it cannot find a machine named companyweb in the local domain, it tries to load www.companyweb.com.

Recently this behavior was seen at a company with a heavy Macintosh population. After the SBS server was installed and all the PCs on the network were joined to the domain with the Connect Computer Wizard, the default web page was set to http://companyweb for the PCs. Wanting consistency across all platforms, the IT contact at the company set the default home page on the Macintosh workstations to be http://companyweb as well. Unfortunately, when the Mac web browsers were opened, they were redirected to http://www.companyweb.com instead.

The IT contact used nslookup on the Macintosh workstations to troubleshoot the DNS lookup problems, and even though the interface was slightly different than on the PC, he was able to determine that the Mac was not using the SBS server as the primary DNS server. He was later able to determine that the Macintosh was not set to get an IP address from the SBS DHCP server as he had originally assumed and after he made that change, the Companyweb web page opened as expected on the Macs in the organization. (For more information on Macintosh connectivity issues with SBS, see Chapter 17, "Integrating the Macintosh into a Small Business Server 2003 Environment.")

Some modern browsers no longer use this method for guessing what a user might have meant when a single-label name was given. Instead, if a single-label name cannot be found in the local domain, the web browser redirects the term to a search engine or to the page that comes up first in the search engine's query on that term. To see this behavior in action, use the Firefox browser to go to `http://companyweb` when the workstation DNS is pointed to a public DNS server. The page that appears is the Microsoft KB article on how to restore Companyweb after the Intranet component has been removed from SBS.

Troubleshooting External DNS Lookup Issues

System administrators learn quickly when there is a problem with the organization's Internet connection. Users tend to be quick to complain when they cannot get to a certain website, but often that call for help is phrased as "The Internet is down!" instead of "I am having trouble reaching this one site in particular even though other sites are working fine." So the first step in troubleshooting DNS problems on the Internet is asking a few pointed questions to determine the scope of the problem.

Certain Sites Have Intermittent Connection Problems

Intermittent problems are often the most difficult to diagnose because they do not always fail or do not fail in the same way every time they are encountered. When users complain that certain sites sometimes work and sometimes do not, but the problem is limited to a particular set of sites whereas others work with no difficulty, you will first want to take a look at EDNS as the source of the problem.

EDNS, often referred to as *Extended DNS,* is an enhanced DNS query process that has been implemented by default in Windows Server 2003. The EDNS specification allows for larger DNS query responses than standard DNS, and these larger responses can cause problems in some network configurations.

To turn off EDNS on the server and clear the DNS cache, enter the following two commands in a command prompt on the SBS server:

```
dnscmd /Config /EnableEdnsProbes 0
ipconfig /flushdns
```

The first command tells the server to send standard DNS queries instead of the extended DNS queries. The second command flushes the local DNS lookup cache on the SBS server and forces new lookups on all DNS requests. This modification should resolve the problem of intermittent connection problems to specific websites.

Connections to All External Sites Fail Periodically

The other side of the Internet connectivity coin comes when all access to external sites fails intermittently. If the actual Internet connection itself is good, meaning that you can access the SBS server from the Internet or you can access certain sites by IP address, the next step is to take a look at the DNS server on the SBS server. Again, you can use the `nslookup` tool to help with the troubleshooting.

The following is a sample nslookup session that attempts to determine whether there is a problem with the SBS DNS server:

```
C:\>nslookup
Default Server:  sbs.smallbizco.local
Address:  192.168.16.2

> www.google.com
Server:  sbs.smallbizco.local
Address:  192.168.16.2

DNS request timed out.
    timeout was 2 seconds.
*** Request to sbs.smallbizco.local timed-out
> www.sams.com
Server:  sbs.smallbizco.local
Address: 192.168.16.2

DNS request timed out.
    timeout was 2 seconds.
*** Request to sbs.smallbizco.local timed-out
> companyweb
Server:  sbs.smallbizco.local
Address: 192.168.16.2

Name:    sbs.Smallbizco.local
Address: 192.168.16.2
Aliases:  companyweb.Smallbizco.local
```

After starting nslookup, two queries to well-known websites fail. The error, `*** Request to sbs.smallbizco.local timed-out`, seems to indicate a problem with the DNS Server service on the SBS box. However, a third query for a local name, Companyweb, succeeds, which indicates that the server is working correctly. The next step would be to use nslookup to do a direct query against the DNS server or servers listed in the Forwarders section of the DNS Management Console. The following listing shows an example transcript:

```
> server 65.97.168.254
DNS request timed out.
    timeout was 2 seconds.
Default Server:  [65.97.168.254]
Address:  65.97.168.254

> www.google.com
Server:  [65.97.168.254]
Address:  65.97.168.254
```

```
DNS request timed out.
    timeout was 2 seconds.
DNS request timed out.
    timeout was 2 seconds.
*** Request to [65.97.168.254] timed-out
```

The first command listed in the example is used to change the DNS server that `nslookup` will use. In this case, we see a timeout when attempting to change the DNS server. Although this initial response is not unusual when changing DNS servers, it could be an indication that there is a problem with the remote DNS server. The second command is a lookup attempt against a well-known web address. In this case, we get two timeout responses from the request. This is a solid indication that there is a problem with the remote DNS server.

One method to confirm that the DNS servers listed as forwarders are having problems is to do a lookup against a different DNS server. When ISPs provide DNS server information for network connections, they usually provide the addresses for two servers so that in case the first server goes down, the second is available as a backup. Not all ISPs keep their DNS servers on different network segments, so if a network segment fails that prevents connections to one of the servers, it is likely that a connection to the second server will fail as well. To that end, many consultants and IT professionals keep a listing of alternate DNS servers available for use and testing. They may use DNS servers from other ISPs they have used in the past, or they may use well-known DNS servers.

The next step in this troubleshooting process is to test DNS resolution against the secondary server provided by the ISP. The same steps shown in the previous listing will verify whether the secondary server is working. If that test fails as well, try to use the DNS servers at 4.2.2.1 and 4.2.2.2, two well-known public DNS servers. Those servers generally respond to DNS lookup requests unless network routing problems prevent the client site from reaching the servers on the Net. Because these servers do respond to ping requests, a simple ping 4.2.2.1 or ping 4.2.2.2 will determine whether the servers are reachable. If these servers respond to DNS queries, the lookup problems exist with the servers specified as forwarders.

As mentioned earlier in the chapter, the DNS server on SBS does not have to have DNS forwarders specified. If no DNS servers are listed as forwarders, the DNS server uses the root hint servers for lookups. This would be one additional test that could be used to determine whether there is a problem with the forwarders. If the SBS DNS server begins processing lookups correctly when the forwarders are removed, the problem lies with the forwarders.

To resolve a problem with forwarders failing to respond to DNS queries, either remove the forwarders from the DNS Management Console and use the root hints, or configure alternate DNS forwarders in the console. The changes take effect immediately so there is no need to restart the DNS Server service, but it may be necessary to run an `ipconfig /flushdns` command after making the changes to clear out any bad DNS lookups from the local cache.

Troubleshooting DHCP Configuration Issues

In the SBS world, two main DHCP issues will crop up from time to time. The first is that the DHCP service on the SBS server will stop unexpectedly and generate errors in the event logs. This almost always occurs when a second DHCP server is activated on the internal SBS network. The SBS DHCP Server service detects the second DHCP server and shuts itself down to avoid conflicts. Unfortunately, in doing so the SBS box allows the rogue DHCP server to handle DHCP requests, usually passing on invalid configuration information. This problem often presents itself on the network as though the DHCP server is not configuring the workstations correctly. Only on further review will it become clear that the DHCP Server service on the SBS server is actually shut down and not handing out configuration information at all.

The SBS server generates two errors in the System event log at startup when it detects another DHCP server on the local network. The first error is a 1053 error from DhcpServer. The error description reads:

```
The DHCP/BINL service on this computer running Windows Server 2003 for
Small Business Server has encountered another server on this network with
IP Address, [IP address], belonging to the domain: .
```

The second error is a 1054 error, also from DhcpServer, reading:

```
The DHCP.BINL service on this computer is shutting down. See the previous
event log messages for reasons.
```

NOTE

In a dual-NIC configuration, the SBS server will not complain about an active DHCP server on the external network. In some cases, the server may be configured to get its external IP address from a DHCP server. The only time it will have problems is when it identifies another DHCP server on the internal network.

The second main issue occurs when the internal network IP address is changed on the server without using the Change IP Address Wizard. If the IP address on the internal NIC is changed in the network card configuration directly, the DHCP scope is not updated automatically. In this case, when a workstation boots up, it will not be able to get an address from the DHCP server and will end up with an Automatic Private IP Address (APIPA) in the 169.254.x.x range. This situation presents itself as a workstation no longer able to communicate with the network. Running an `ipconfig /all` command on the workstation and comparing that output to the output of an `ipconfig /all` command run on the server will reveal that the workstation and the server are on separate networks or that the workstation is looking to the wrong IP address for the SBS server. You may also see this situation if the server IP address is changed as described previously and the workstation has not had its DHCP lease renewed since the change. Again, the IP address range on the server and the workstation will be different.

To resolve this problem, the DHCP server settings can be modified manually, but the easier route is to run the Change Server IP Address Wizard, which will rebuild the DHCP scope automatically. When this wizard is run, however, the new DHCP scope will be set with the SBS defaults. Any customizations that had been made to the DHCP scope previously will be lost.

Troubleshooting DNS-Related Active Directory Issues

Problems with Active Directory can often be traced back to DNS configuration problems or service errors. Some of these issues have been mentioned earlier in the chapter (NIC settings pointing to an external server for DNS, for example), but a number of other errors that may seem like AD failures are really just problems with the DNS service itself. This last section of the chapter looks at a few ways to quickly recover from the DNS problems that may be causing Active Directory errors.

DNS 4004/4015 Errors

If you encounter a number of DNS 4004 or DNS 4015 errors in the event logs, the first place to check is the DNS configuration for Active Directory in the DNS Management Console. Compare the contents of the Forward Lookup Zone for the internal domain to those shown in Figure 5.1 earlier in the chapter. The main lookup zone must contain at least these four records:

(same as parent folder)	Start of Authority (SOA)
(same as parent folder)	Name Server (NS)
(same as parent folder)	Host (A)
server name	Host (A)

The first two records will have the internal FQDN of the server in the data field, and the last two will have the internal IP address in the data field, an example of which can be seen in Figure 5.1. If one of these records is missing or has incorrect data, the corrections can be made directly within the DNS Management Console by either adding the missing record or by editing a record and correcting any errors.

Netlogon

Figure 5.9 shows a portion of the Active Directory Forward Lookup Zone in the DNS Management Console. As with the Forward Lookup Zone for the internal domain discussed previously, some key elements must be present for Active Directory to function properly. In Figure 5.9, the `_msdcs` zone contains SOA (Start of Authority) and NS (Name Server) records just like the internal domain, and both of those records point to the internal FQDN of the SBS server. The `_msdcs` zone also contains an alias record, which points to the FQDN of the SBS server. Under the `domains` zone, there is a zone for the GUID for the domain as well.

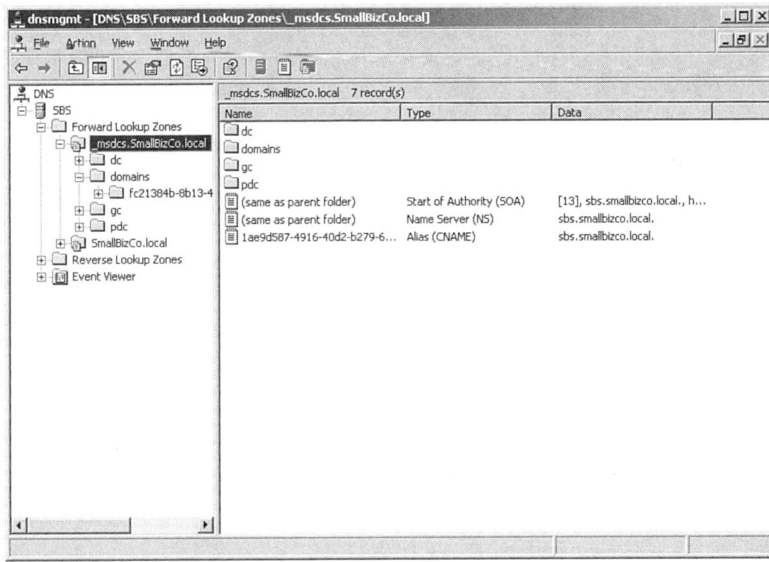

FIGURE 5.9 The `_msdcs` forward lookup zone contains records for the server and domain.

Because the DNS service relies on a database for storage of its information, it is subject to database corruption like other systems. One sign of database corruption is that the CNAME record for the server in the `_msdcs` lookup zone is missing. Fortunately, recovering from this database corruption is not difficult.

The Netlogon service is the component that ties the DNS service in with Active Directory. It maintains the DNS records for AD in two files located in the `config` directory under `system32`. The files are `netlogon.dns` and `netlogon.dnb`. If these files are missing when the Netlogon process starts, they will be created automatically with the proper DNS information for Active Directory. If the files are present but corrupt, the Netlogon service will start but may produce unexpected results.

The Netlogon databases can be repaired in a single command line. First, set the current directory in a command prompt to `C:\Windows\system32\config`. Then enter the following command:

```
net stop netlogon && del netlogon.* && net start netlogon
```

This stops the Netlogon service, deletes the `netlogon.dnb` and `netlogon.dns` files from the `config` folder, and restarts the Netlogon process. If you look in the `config` folder after running this command, you will find that both the `netlogon.dns` and `netlogon.dnb` files have been re-created. When you refresh the DNS Management Console display, you will find that the CNAME record for the server has been re-created if it was missing. This process also re-creates the `domains` zone under `_msdcs` if it was missing as well.

CAUTION

If you find that the `netlogon.dns` and `netlogon.dnb` files do not get re-created in the `config` folder and you see warnings in the Event log (Netlogon 5781), check and make sure that the DNS server listed in the TCP/IP settings for all NICs in the server are pointing to the internal IP address of the SBS server. If the NIC DNS settings point elsewhere, this process will not register the DNS records correctly.

`netdiag` and `dcdiag`

Another set of tools that are useful in diagnosing network and Active Directory issues are included in the Support Tools package. Because the Support Tools are not installed by default, the package must be installed before the `netdiag` and `dcdiag` tools can be used.

Because the output of both `netdiag` and `dcdiag` fills several screen pages, the output from the command should be redirected to a file for ease of searching. Use the following commands at the command prompt to run `netdiag` and `dcdiag` with verbose output, redirect the output to a file, and open the output file in Notepad after the command completes:

```
netdiag /v > netdiag.txt && netdiag.txt
dcdiag /v > dcdiag.txt && dcdiag.txt
```

When Notepad brings up the output file, search through the file for the terms "fail" and "fatal" to quickly identify problems that the tools have identified. If any problems are found, a Google search on the error messages from the output can help quickly track down the source of the problem, if the problem is not evident from the description in the file itself.

Running `netdiag /fix` also recovers any corruption within the Netlogon database files as well. This is effectively the same as stopping the Netlogon service, deleting the Netlogon database files, and restarting Netlogon as described previously.

BEST PRACTICE—INSTALL SUPPORT TOOLS

The Support Tools package contains a number of useful diagnostic tools besides `netdiag` and `dcdiag`. The Support Tools installer file `SUPTOOLS.MSI` is located on SBS installation CD #2 in the `\SUPPORT\TOOLS` folder. Double-click on the installer file and accept all the defaults through the installation process to install the package into the `C:\Program Files\Support Tools` folder on the SBS server.

Take some time to go through the output from the `netdiag` and `dcdiag` commands to see the type of information reported by the tools. After working with the tools for a while, you will develop an understanding of what you should and should not see in the command output that can help you quickly identify problems with the configuration of the server.

Summary

This chapter covered the interrelation of DNS, DHCP, and Active Directory in the SBS environment. Because DNS and Active Directory are so interdependent, the network settings of all systems in the SBS network must be configured correctly for workstations to participate in the local domain as well as access the Internet. The DHCP Server service will pass on the necessary information to client workstations when the SBS server is configured correctly. The `nslookup` command can be used to troubleshoot DNS lookup issues internally and on the Internet. The Netlogon service ties Active Directory together with DNS, and removing the databases while restarting the service can easily clear up corruption within the Netlogon databases. The `netdiag` and `dcdiag` commands are useful tools in diagnosing network and Active Directory issues.

Best Practice Summary

- DNS records—When creating additional DNS records for existing machines, create the records as CNAME records (DNS aliases) instead of A records (DNS hosts).
- `ipconfig /all`—Use this command as a starting point for troubleshooting connectivity problems from a workstation or the server.
- DNS forwarders—Configure SBS to use DNS forwarders where possible.
- DHCP servers—If you have a choice of the SBS server or another device acting as the DHCP server, let the SBS server provide DHCP to the network.
- Support Tools—Install the Support Tools package from installation CD #2 onto the SBS server as soon as possible after system installation.

CHAPTER 6

Internet Information Services

IN THIS CHAPTER

- IIS and Small Business Server
- Configuring the Default Websites
- Configuring Additional Websites
- Publishing Secure Sites on the Internet Using a Third-Party SSL Certificate
- Troubleshooting IIS Issues

When the World Wide Web was first introduced in the early 1990s, many people scoffed at the idea that others would want to look for information using such a graphics-heavy environment. Today, companies that do not have visually interesting websites often get overlooked by potential customers. The Web has changed significantly during its existence, and the servers that host the Web have as well.

When Microsoft first released its Internet Information Server (IIS), it lagged significantly behind other well-established server products. With each release of IIS, Microsoft has significantly improved the product, and it now ranks among the top web server products used by major web hosting facilities and direct providers alike.

IIS and Small Business Server

Many technologies included with SBS 2003 are web driven, so a good understanding of Internet Information Services (IIS) is important to successfully maintain an SBS server. This chapter provides a high-level overview of the makeup of IIS, identifies the key services that are dependent on IIS, provides instructions for how to modify IIS settings and create new websites, and offers troubleshooting techniques for resolving IIS problems quickly.

SBS Web Technologies

One of the first steps in the SBS deployment process is a web-driven process—the Connect Computer Wizard. This is just one of the many components of SBS that rely heavily on IIS. Table 6.1 lists some of the other commonly used features of SBS that are driven by IIS.

TABLE 6.1 SBS Tools That Run on IIS

Component	Location	Description
Connect Computer Wizard	`http://servername/connectcomputer`	Starts the wizard that connects a client workstation to the SBS network
Outlook Web Access (OWA)	`https://servername/exchange`	Allows remote users to access their email using a web browser
Outlook Mobile Access (OMA)	`http://servername/oma`	Allows users with web-enabled Smartphone devices to access their email remotely
Companyweb	`http://companyweb`	Provides a customizable front end to a SharePoint site for the organization
Remote Web Workplace	`http://servername/remote`	Provides access to many web-based remote utilities
Backup	`http://servername/backup`	Configures the built-in SBS backup component
Client Help	`http://servername/clienthelp`	Provides user guides for the various SBS technologies
Monitoring and Reporting	`http://servername/monitoring`	Configures the monitoring and reporting components
Terminal Services Web Client	`http://servername/tsweb`	Provides a web interface to the Remote Desktop Client

IIS by itself is a complex application and becomes even more complex when the SBS technologies are added into its configuration. The remainder of this section provides an overview of the different components that make up IIS and how those components are used to provide basic web services.

IIS Components

SBS 2003 uses IIS version 6, which was introduced with the released of the Windows 2003 server series. IIS 6 has some significant changes in its default install over IIS 5. Whereas IIS 5 was configured to be ready to serve any type of web information right out of the box, a focus on server and web security by the development team at Microsoft provided a default configuration that is very "locked down" in IIS 6. Another difference is that the configuration file for IIS 6, the metabase, is now a human-readable XML document instead of the corruption-prone binary file used by previous versions. The interface for managing IIS 6 is also different from its predecessors as will be evident when the IIS Management Console is opened by anyone familiar with earlier versions.

In SBS 2003, a shortcut to the IIS Management Console is located in the Administrative Tools folder of the Start menu. The management interface is broken down into three main parts, described in the following sections.

Application Pools

The first folder you see under the SBS server in the IIS Management Console is Application Pools. When you expand this folder, you see the application pool instances configured by default in IIS. Each pool is a process that runs in a separate program space, so that if a particular application pool runs into a problem and crashes or stops responding, only the web components tied to that pool are affected.

Figure 6.1 shows the standard application pools for SBS in the IIS Management Console. Under the DefaultAppPool entry, you can see the different websites or virtual directories managed by that pool process. In this configuration, if the ExchangeApplicationPool pool process were to crash, the Default Web Site (run by the Root application), Backup, Monitoring, and Remote virtual directories would continue to run without interruption.

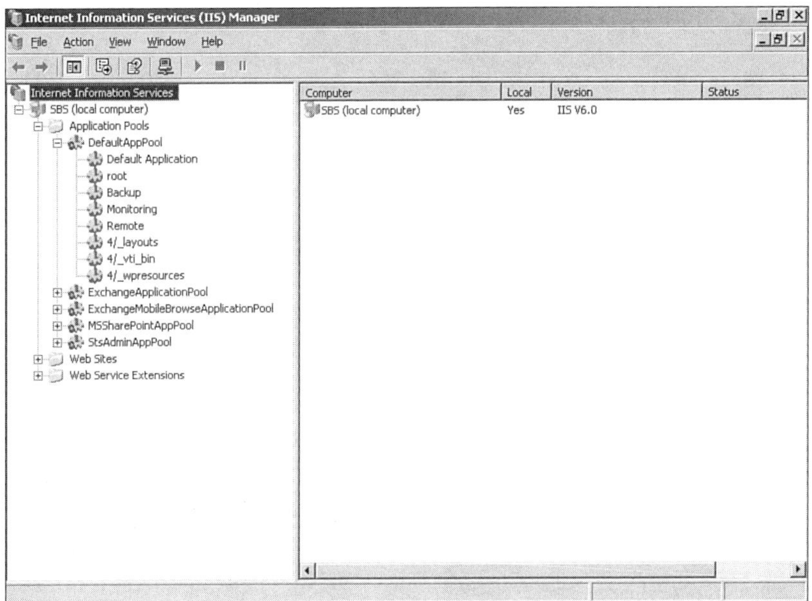

FIGURE 6.1 A standard SBS installation has five application pools defined, each with multiple nodes.

Each application pool process runs under a specific account on the server. This account is configured in the Properties page under the Identity tab as shown in Figure 6.2. Not all application pools run under the same account. The DefaultAppPool runs as the Network Service account, whereas the ExchangeApplicationPool runs as the Local System account.

In general maintenance, a system administrator will hardly ever review the status or configuration of the application pool instances. The settings of the application pool instances should not be modified without good reason because a misconfiguration of the application pool instance will render the web services that run in that application pool unusable.

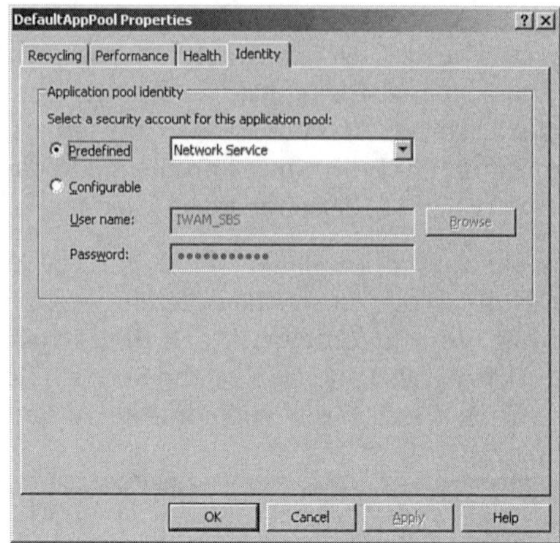

FIGURE 6.2 The Default Application Pool runs as the Network Service account.

Web Sites

The next folder under the server icon is the Web Sites folder. This is where the main website configuration information is viewed or modified. IIS 6 allows multiple websites to be run on a single server. Each site can contain multiple directories beneath it, and those directories can be file system directories based on the file location of the site, or they can be virtual directories, which appear as though they are part of the file system hierarchy but are actually in a different location on the file system. The settings configured in each website are applied to each directory or virtual directory underneath the site, unless specific settings are modified at that level. Figure 6.3 shows the standard layout for the Default Web Site configuration with an SBS installation.

Each website listed under the Web Sites section must be uniquely identifiable by the IIS server in some way. SBS uses a combination of IP address and host header to identify which website should process the incoming web request. Ideally, a separate IP address would be used for each site, but because SBS relies on a single IP address for each NIC, IIS must rely on host headers to differentiate between sites.

Web Service Extensions

The last folder under the server icon is the Web Service Extensions folder. This area lists all the web service extensions installed as well as their current status. As shown in Figure 6.4, some services are Allowed, and some are Prohibited. The biggest change from IIS 5 to IIS 6 is that the WebDAV service extension is Prohibited by default. This change is another in the long line of security improvements that Microsoft made with this version of the web server.

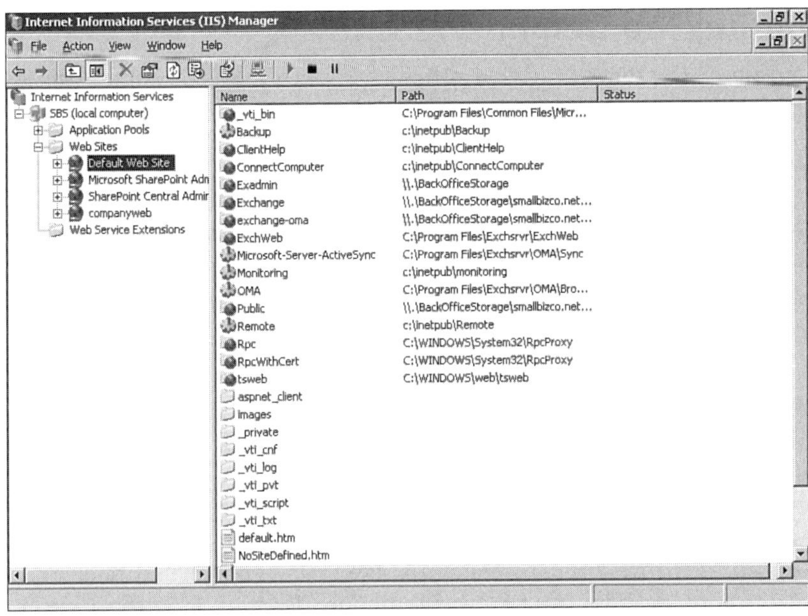

FIGURE 6.3 The Default Web Site contains a number of directories and virtual directories.

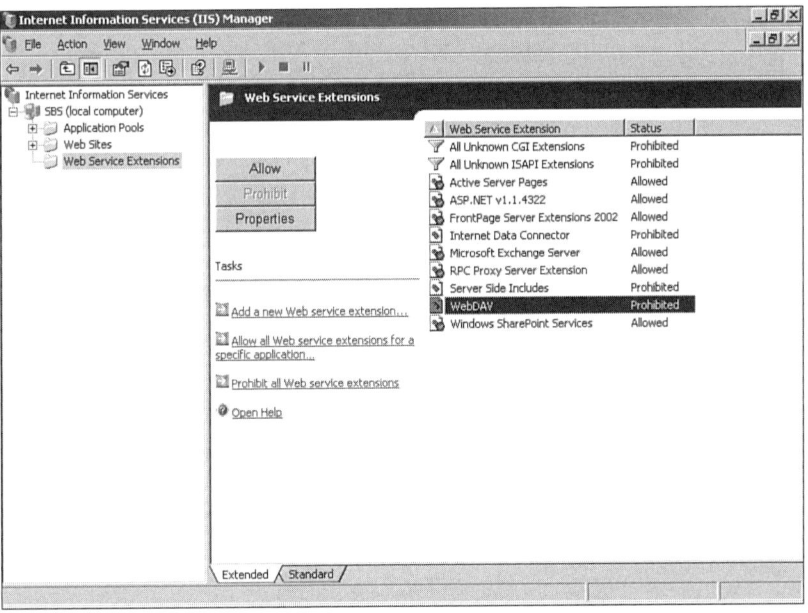

FIGURE 6.4 The WebDAV web service extension is prohibited by default, as are other web service components.

Configuring the Default Websites

With the possible exception of the Companyweb website, most SBS administrators who work in the IIS Management Console spend their time within the scope of the Default Web Site. Because this is where the configuration for the main SBS web page, the Outlook Web Access (OWA) web interface, the Remote Web Workplace interface, the ConnectComputer and ClientHelp pages, and the Backup and Monitoring interfaces are all configured, a thorough understanding of how this site is configured by default is essential to maintaining the operation of the web services for SBS. Any changes made to the Default Web Site, no matter how well intentioned, could end up crippling the web services for the entire organization.

Settings for the Default Web Site

When a typical SBS installation is performed "by the book," all the web services that rely on the Default Web Site configuration are configured so that they work well with each other. This chapter looks at the basic settings for the website and some of the virtual directories hosted in the Default Web Site. Some of the directories, such as the OWA directories (Exadmin, Exchange, Exchange-oma, ExchWeb, and Public) and the Remote Web Workplace directory (Remote) will be covered in more detail in their respective chapters.

The Properties page of the Default Web Site is broken down into nine main tabs, described in Table 6.2.

TABLE 6.2 Descriptions of the Settings Tabs for the IIS Web Site Properties Page

Tab Name	Description
Web Site	Stores the main identifier information for the site and the logging settings
Performance	Stores settings for limiting bandwidth and number of connections
ISAPI Filters	Lists the ISAPI filters that have been loaded and their status
Home Directory	Stores the main content location for the site, the access allowed to that content, and the application settings used, if any
Documents	Lists the default content page names and footer information for each page displayed, if used
Directory Security	Stores the authentication, IP/domain restrictions, and secure communication settings for the site
HTTP Headers	Stores settings for content expiration, custom HTTP headers, content ratings, and MIME types for the site
Custom Errors	Lists the locations for the files displayed for each of the HTTP error types
Server Extensions 2002	Provides access to SharePoint and/or FrontPage server extension settings, if installed

The most commonly accessed tabs in the Properties page are the Web Site, Directory Security, and Home Directory tabs. This is where the key settings are stored, and where the most damage can be done if not used correctly, so this chapter focuses on these areas. A more detailed discussion of the IIS settings is beyond the scope of this book.

Web Site

Figure 6.5 shows the default settings for the Default Web Site properties. The website is set to listen on all unassigned IP addresses, which means that if multiple IP addresses are on the server and another website is set to specifically listen on one of those addresses, this site will respond for all other IP addresses. In general, this setting should not be changed. The TCP port and SSL port are set to 80 and 443, respectively, which are the web defaults for normal and secure web traffic.

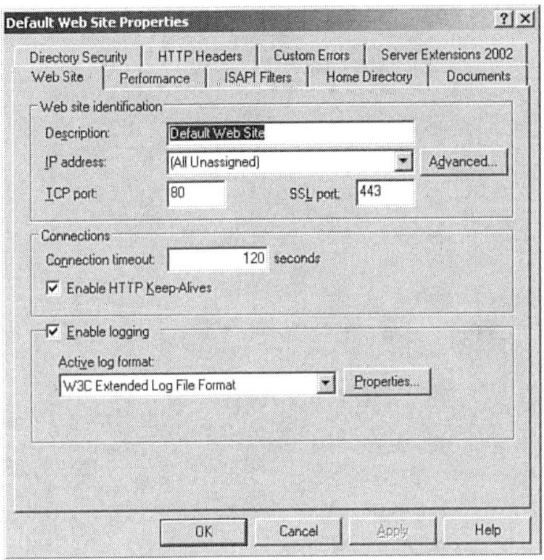

FIGURE 6.5 The Default Web Site Properties page Web Site tab shows the basic communications settings for the site.

Figure 6.5 also shows the connection timeout to be 120 seconds and HTTP Keep-Alives are enabled. By default, logging is enabled, and clicking the Properties button next to the Active Log Format drop-down menu allows access to specific settings related to logging. Logging is set to create a new log file daily in the `C:\WINDOWS\system32\LogFiles\W3SVC1` directory.

Directory Security

The Directory Security tab has three main sections: Authentication and Access Control, IP Address and Domain Name Restrictions, and Secure Communications. Figure 6.6 shows the settings for the Authentication Methods properties. The site is configured to allow anonymous access by default, and it does this by authenticating as the IUSR account for the server.

NOTE

The IUSR account, which is always named `IUSR_`*`servername`*, is one of several system-created accounts that allow access to certain areas of the server. These accounts have passwords assigned to them when they are created, but those passwords are not shared or accessible by normal methods. If the system is an OEM build, the IUSR account will be named based on the OEM image name and not the server name. This does not cause any performance issues, but might be confusing to the administrator on first glance.

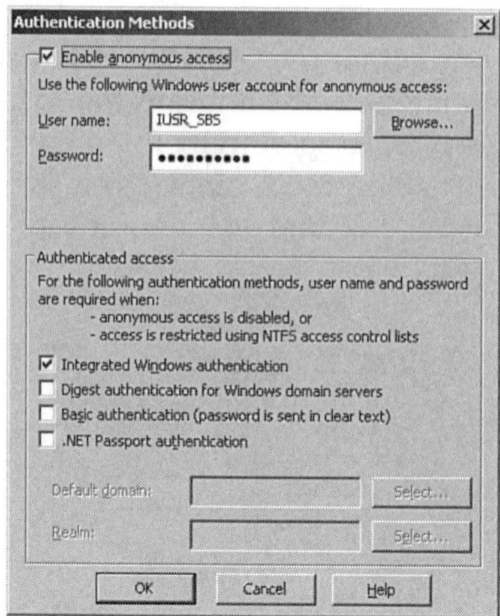

FIGURE 6.6 The default settings for Authentication Methods allow anonymous access to the site and use integrated Windows authentication in case authentication is needed or requested.

As shown in Figure 6.6, if and when authentication is needed for the Default Web Site, integrated Windows authentication will be used. Because anonymous access to the site is enabled by default on this page, the only time authentication would be needed is if one of the web directories required it or if NTFS permissions deny access to the IUSR account. Other settings that could be used for authentication are the Digest authentication for Windows domain servers, Basic authentication, and .NET Passport authentication. Digest authentication works only with Active Directory accounts and will not likely be used in an SBS configuration. Basic authentication sends a username and password to the server in clear text format and should be used only if the site requires an SSL (HTTPS) connection. The .NET Passport authentication uses the Passport service to authenticate users and again is not likely to be used in an SBS environment because there are additional fees associated with using Passport for authentication.

Figure 6.7 shows the settings for the default IP Address and Domain Name Restrictions settings. The default action in this window is to allow or deny access to the site and then specify exceptions to the default action.

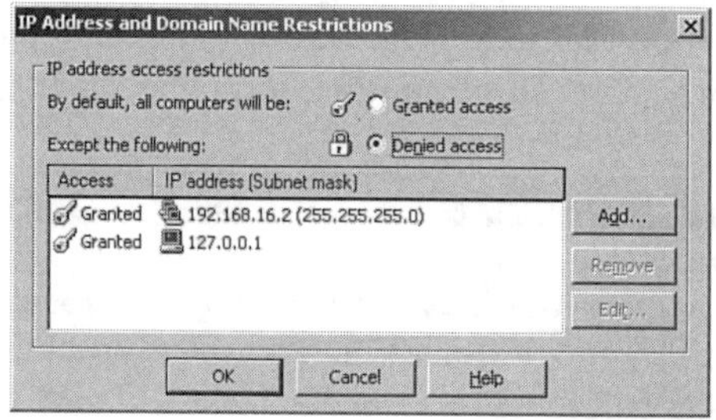

FIGURE 6.7 The IP Address and Domain Name Restrictions window shows only local addresses that can access the default website.

In this case, the only addresses allowed to connect to the Default Web Site are the localhost address, meaning that the server can connect to itself, and the local internal subnet. This is because when the Connect to the Internet Wizard (CEICW) was run, the Business website was set so that it was not published to the Internet. Had the Business website been selected to be available, the IP Address and Domain Name Restrictions window would have Granted Access selected, and the exceptions list would be empty.

In this configuration, if a computer from outside the local network attempted to access the main web page, IIS would return a 403.6 error, indicating that the IP address of the client had been rejected.

The real meat of the Directory Security tab lies in the Secure Communications section. This is where the SSL certificate created by the Connect to the Internet Wizard is stored and configured. Clicking on the View Certificate button in the Directory Security tab brings up a window showing the certificate created by the CEICW. Both the Issued To and Issued By fields have the public DNS name that was entered in the CEICW, meaning that this is a self-signed certificate.

Clicking the Edit button brings up the Secure Communications window, shown in Figure 6.8. Though there are several sections to this window, the only area that is of real interest to the SBS community is the Require Secure Channel (SSL) check box. If this check box is enabled, the website responds only to a page request over the SSL channel (port 443). If someone attempts to access the page with the standard web channel (port 80), IIS responds with a message that the page must be viewed over a secure channel and instructs the user to replace `http://` with `https://` instead.

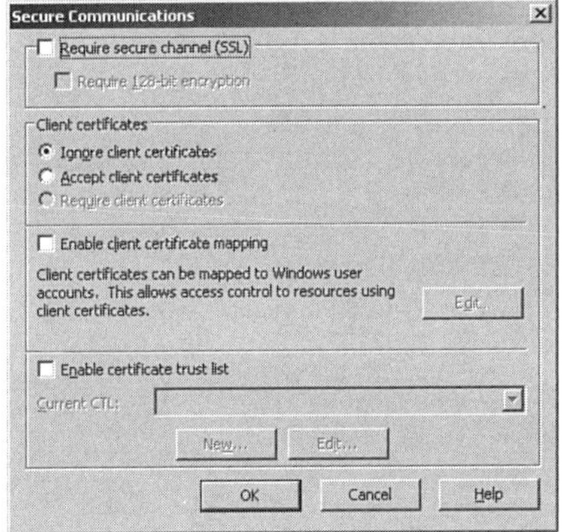

FIGURE 6.8 The Default Web Site settings do not require a secure connection to access pages on the site.

If the Require Secure Channel (SSL) check box is enabled here, the entire site would need to be viewed over SSL, which is not what is wanted by default. Each of the directories and virtual directories under the website can override this setting, but in general, SSL should be turned off at the site level and enabled where needed at the virtual directory level.

Best Practice—Leave Defaults as Defaults

With few exceptions, the settings for Default Web Site should not be modified. When a change is made at the top level of the website, the user is prompted to apply the change to all subwebs that would be affected by the change. If the user agrees to the changes to the subwebs, many of the services running under IIS on the SBS server can be taken out of action.

If you absolutely, positively, must make a change to the Default Web Site configuration, make sure that you do not apply the changes to any of the subwebs. When prompted for the inheritance overrides, make sure that none of the child nodes are selected and click OK in both prompts.

The Microsoft SharePoint Administration and SharePoint Central Administration sites are also configured automatically during the SBS installation and, to borrow a phrase, have no user-serviceable parts inside. Under normal server operation, there is never a time you will need to manage or maintain these site definitions, except to back them up. If you feel you really must modify any settings in these sites, which you shouldn't, make a backup of the site configuration before proceeding.

Home Directory

The Home Directory tab tells IIS where the main source of the content for the site is located. As seen in Figure 6.9, the source files can be located on the local system, a share from another system, or a URL redirection. In a default SBS install the Default Web Site files are stored in `c:\inetpub\wwwroot`. Table 6.3 lists the NTFS permissions for this folder.

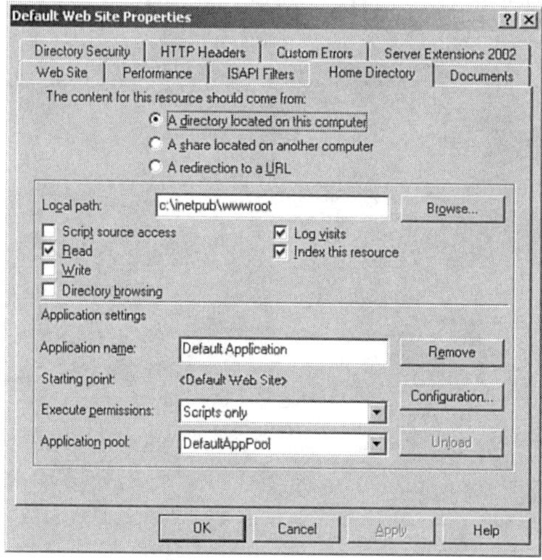

FIGURE 6.9 The Home Directory tab displays the path to the static files for the site as well as the application pool configuration.

TABLE 6.3 NTFS Permissions Assigned to Various Security Objects in the Website Root Folder

Security Object	NTFS Permissions
Administrators	Full Control
IIS_WPG	Read & Execute
	List Folder Contents
	Read
INTERACTIVE	List Folder Contents
Internet Guest Account	List Folder Contents
NETWORK	List Folder Contents
NETWORK SERVICE	List Folder Contents
SYSTEM	Full Control
Users	Read & Execute
	List Folder Contents
	Read

For security, only the Read permission should be applied at this level as per defaults. Enabling Script Source Access, Write, or Directory Browsing could open up your website to external users in unexpected ways. In addition, the Application Settings should not be modified. The Default Web Site should use the Default Application, the DefaultAppPool, and be set to execute Scripts Only, as shown in Figure 6.9.

Settings for the Companyweb Site

Although a more detailed outline of the settings for the Companyweb SharePoint site occurs Chapter 14, "SharePoint and the Companyweb Site," this section covers the basics of a default SBS installation for reference.

Web Site

The first of the key differences between the Default Web Site and the Companyweb website are in the Advanced Web Site Identification properties, shown in Figure 6.10. The Companyweb configuration uses host headers to differentiate traffic intended for this site from the other sites on the server. With this configuration, any web request destined for `http://companyweb` or `http://companyweb.SmallBizCo.local` is answered by this website on port 80.

The other key difference shown in Figure 6.10 is that Companyweb uses port 444 for SSL communications instead of 443. Because SSL web requests cannot use host headers to identify websites, the Companyweb website must listen on a different port number to allow incoming SSL access.

Directory Security

Unlike the Default Web Site, the Companyweb interface requires an authenticated connection. This is set in the Authentication and Access Control Settings of the Directory Security tab. As shown in Figure 6.11, the Enable Anonymous Access setting is disabled, and only Integrated Windows Authentication is enabled under Authenticated Access.

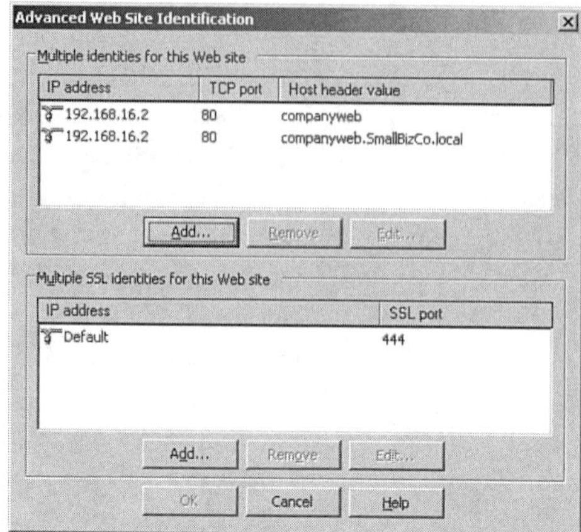

FIGURE 6.10 The Advanced Web Site Identification tab lists all the host header values to which the site will respond.

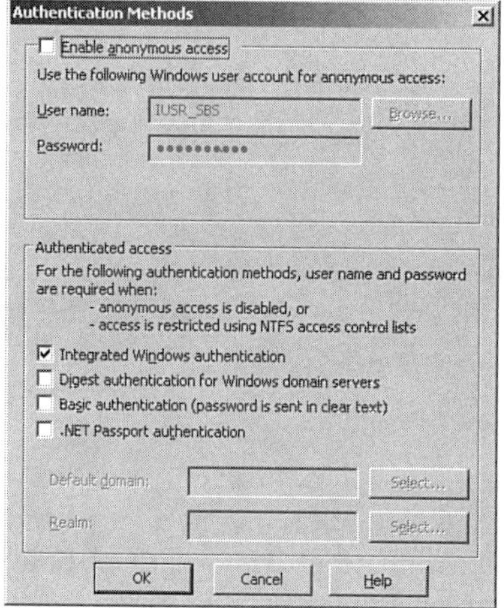

FIGURE 6.11 The Companyweb Directory Security Authentication Methods dialog shows that only authenticated users can access the site.

Under IP Address and Domain Name Restrictions, all computers are granted access. And although SSL connections to Companyweb are supported and recommended, they are not required under the Secure Communications properties of this tab.

Home Directory

Two settings differ in the Home Directory tab from the Default Web Site. First, the local path to the files for Companyweb is located in `C:\Inetpub\companyweb`. The NTFS security settings for that folder are listed inherited from `C:\Inetpub`. In addition, the application name used for Companyweb is *root*, even though it also uses the DefaultAppPool application pool.

Again, more detailed information about the configuration and use of the Companyweb interface can be found in Chapter 14.

Settings for the Microsoft SharePoint Administration Site

The Microsoft SharePoint Administration site is an admin site that manages the FrontPage Server Extensions installed with the default SBS installation. Table 6.4 lists the differences between the Microsoft SharePoint Administration site and other sites.

TABLE 6.4 Default Settings for the Microsoft SharePoint Administration Site

Setting	Location	Value
IP Address	Web Site	All Unassigned
TCP Port	Web Site	Random port above 6000
Local Path	Home Directory	`C:\Program Files\Common Files\Microsoft Shared\Web Server Extensions\50\isapi\_vti_adm`
Application Pool	Home Directory	None
Default Content Page(s)	Documents	`fpadmdll.dll`
Authenticated Access	Directory Security, Authentication and Access Control	Enable anonymous access Integrated Windows authentication No basic authentication

Settings for the SharePoint Central Administration Site

The SharePoint Central Administration site is the admin site for Windows SharePoint Services on the server, specifically for governing the Companyweb instance, but applying to other new SharePoint sites created on the server. Table 6.5 lists the differences between the SharePoint Central Administration site and other sites.

TABLE 6.5 Default Settings for the SharePoint Central Administration Site

Setting	Location	Value
IP Address	Web Site	All Unassigned
TCP Port	Web Site	8081
Local Path	Home Directory	`C:\Program Files\Common Files\Microsoft Shared\Web Server Extensions\60\template\admin\1033`
Application Pool	Home Directory	StsAdminAppPool
Application Name	Home Directory	Default App
Default Content Page(s)	Documents	`default.aspx`
Authenticated Access	Directory Security, Authentication and Access Control	No anonymous access Integrated Windows authentication No basic authentication

Configuring Additional Websites

As shown previously in the chapter, the default SBS installation configures four separate websites. In some cases, an SBS administrator may want to configure additional web services for internal use. These services can be set up as separate websites, or as directories under the existing main site. This section covers creating a new website, and the next section takes a closer look at adding virtual directories to existing sites.

Best Practice—Do Not Use SBS to Run a Public Website

The general consensus among the SBS community is not to use the SBS server as a public web server. Using SBS to host OWA and Remote Web Workplace as web apps is fine because both require SSL, encrypting all username and password information sent across the Internet. Historically, several significant attacks have targeted IIS servers hosting public websites. Because SBS hosts the core of the entire network, it should be protected as much as possible, including not allowing access to port 80 from the Internet.

Backing Up the IIS Configuration

As is the best practice in any situation, always make a backup of the IIS configuration before making any changes to it. Fortunately, this is a simple process, whether for backing up individual websites or the entire IIS configuration.

Backing Up Websites and Virtual Directories

The configuration for each individual website, and for each virtual directory within the site, can be saved to a file on disk. Backing up an individual site or virtual directory affords the administrator the opportunity to restore the single site or virtual directory if a problem develops with that site or directory without having to restore the entire IIS configuration. This is not so much a time-saving mechanism (the process to back up and restore the entire IIS configuration is quick) but a way to ensure that any changes made elsewhere in the IIS configuration are not overwritten in the process of restoring one element.

To back up a site or virtual directory to a file, right-click on the site or directory in the IIS Management Console, select All Tasks, and then select Save Configuration to a File. In the Save dialog box that comes up, enter the filename for the configuration and accept the default path or change the path to the location where you want the file saved. You can also encrypt the configuration file with a password. The file is saved in XML format and can be viewed with a text editor.

Alternatively, you can back up all the sites at the same time using this same method. Instead of running the Save Configuration to a File task from the individual site, you can right-click on the Web Sites folder and run the Save Configuration to a File task from there. This creates an XML file that contains the configuration information for all the sites configured in IIS. This does not save all the information stored in the metabase, only the website configurations.

Backing Up the Entire Metabase

There are two mechanisms for backing up the entire metabase within the IIS Management Console. With the server highlighted, you can select either Backup/Restore Configuration or Save Configuration to Disk from the Action, All Tasks menu in the console. The Backup/Restore Configuration item brings up the Configuration Backup/Restore dialog (see Figure 6.12), which lists all the backup points that can be used for restore. One backup is created when the IIS setup is run, and a number of automatic backups are done as part of normal maintenance. Only the most recent Automatic Backup configurations are kept. However, the automatic backups will not automatically overwrite manual backups created in this interface.

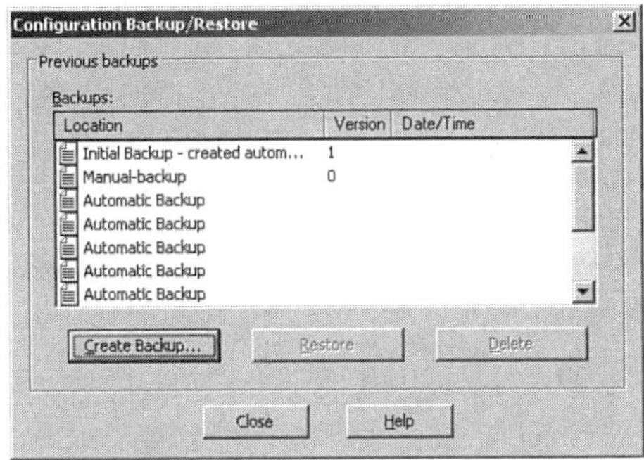

FIGURE 6.12 The Configuration Backup/Restore dialog lists the initial backup made during system installation, any manual backups made, and the most recent automatic backups.

To create a manual backup of IIS prior to making changes to the IIS configuration, follow these steps:

1. In the IIS Management Console, right-click on the local computer icon, select All Tasks, and then select Backup/Restore Configuration.
2. In the Configuration Backup/Restore dialog box, click Create Backup.
3. In the Configuration Backup dialog box, enter a name for the backup point. Optionally, you can enable the Encrypt Backup Using Password check box and enter and confirm a password for this backup point.
4. Click OK.
5. The backup point appears in the list. Click Close when finished.

Best Practice—Make Backups Before Making Any Configuration Changes to IIS

The importance of making backups to the IIS configuration cannot be stressed enough. Although the XML configuration of IIS 6 is less prone to corruption than the metabase format in earlier versions, even making seemingly simple changes to IIS can cripple the entire web operation of the server if a mistake is made. Because backups are so easy to make in IIS, there is no reason not to make a backup before looking at the IIS configuration, even if you are not planning on making changes.

Creating the New Site

Before you create a new site in IIS, you need a few pieces of information first. Table 6.6 highlights the key data points you need to create the site.

TABLE 6.6 Information Needed to Create a New Site in IIS

Setting	Description
IP address	The IP address the website will use to listen to incoming data. If the site will share an IP address with other sites, it will need a unique TCP port or host header to differentiate the site from other sites in the IIS configuration.
TCP port	Usually port 80, but may be different depending on the desired configuration.
SSL port	Usually 443, if configured. If you will not be using SSL for this site, you do not need to configure this setting. If this site will use SSL and other sites on the server will use SSL as well, this value must be something other than 443.
Host header	The unique hostname that web clients will use to connect to this site. This value must be set if this site is sharing an IP address with other sites in the IIS configuration.
Location of files	The path to the website files on the local server.

To create the new site, right-click on the Web Sites folder and select either Web Site or Web Site (from File) under the New submenu. When you select Web Site, the Web Site Creation Wizard starts and walks you through the process for configuring the new site. After you have completed the wizard using the information in Table 6.6, the new website appears in the IIS Management Console. If you need to configure SSL for the site, you have to manually edit the properties of the site because the wizard does not configure SSL on the site.

The other option for creating a new site is to create the site from an existing configuration file. This is a good method for restoring a corrupt site from a backup configuration. If you have created a backup file for a particular site or for all the websites using the method described earlier, you can use that backup file to create (or re-create) a website in IIS.

Use the following steps to test the backup/restore process for a single website. This example uses the Companyweb site as the test case. Make sure that you do a backup of the complete metabase before making any changes to your website configuration as a failsafe!

1. Right-click on Web Sites in the IIS Management Console, and select All Tasks, Save Configuration to a File.
2. Enter a name for the configuration in the File Name field and click OK.
3. Right-click on the Companyweb website in the IIS Management Console and select Delete. Remember, you are not uninstalling Companyweb, just removing the website configuration from IIS.
4. Click Yes when prompted to delete the site.
5. Verify that the Companyweb website is not listed in the IIS configuration.

6. Right-click on Web Sites and select New, Web Site (from File).
7. In the Import Configuration dialog box, click Browse and select the backup file you created in step 2. Click OK to close the file selection dialog box.
8. Click Read File. The list of sites in the backup file displays in the window.
9. Select the Companyweb configuration and click OK.

At this point, the Companyweb website configuration has been restored to IIS and is running again.

Managing Virtual Directories

In most cases, any additional web features you may want to add to the SBS server will not require a separate website in IIS. Instead, you may be able to simply add a virtual directory to the Default Web Site. This allows you to access the site securely from the Internet without having to set up an alternate SSL port. In addition, each virtual directory can have its own set of access permissions separate from the Default Web Site (compare OWA, Remote Web Workplace, and Monitoring and Reporting, all of which are virtual directories residing under the Default Web Site).

Virtual directories are managed differently from standard subdirectories in a website configuration. Even though both are accessed in the same way from a web browser (if the main website is `http://www.smallbizco.net`, a subdirectory or virtual directory named "webapp" would be accessed through `http://www.smallbizco.net/webapp`), a normal subdirectory would simply be created in the folder where the root of the web server is stored (`c:\inetpub\wwwroot for the Default Web Server`). A virtual directory, however, can exist anywhere on the server hard disk or even on another server on the intranet.

The process for backing up virtual directory configurations has already been discussed earlier in the chapter. In some cases, it makes sense to create additional backup configuration files for virtual directories in addition to backing up the website configuration entirely. This way an individual virtual directory can be removed and re-created without affecting the settings on the rest of the site. If you create a new virtual directory in a website, you should create a separate backup of the virtual directory configuration.

Creating a new virtual directory is similar to creating a new website. You can launch the Virtual Directory Creation Wizard by right-clicking on the website where you want the new directory and selecting New, Virtual Directory. The wizard requests three pieces of information from you: the name of the directory, the path to where the files for the directory are located, and the permissions that should be applied to the virtual directory.

After the virtual directory has been created, you can modify the settings for the directory to configure as needed. The properties for a virtual directory resemble the settings for a website configuration but have fewer options. Table 6.7 lists the five properties tabs available for virtual directories and the key items in each tab.

TABLE 6.7 Descriptions of the Settings Tabs for the IIS Virtual Directory Properties Page

Tab Name	Description
Virtual Directory	Stores the main content location for the directory, the access allowed to that content, and the application settings used, if any.
Documents	Lists the default content page names and footer information for each page displayed, if used.
Directory Security	Stores the authentication, IP/domain restrictions, and secure communication settings for the site.
HTTP Headers	Stores settings for content expiration, custom HTTP headers, content ratings, and MIME types for the directory.
Custom Errors	Lists the locations for the files displayed for each of the HTTP error types.

With a few exceptions, the settings in the virtual directory properties allow you to configure the virtual directory as if it were its own site. The key differences are that you cannot modify the IP address or port settings, nor can you enable FrontPage support if it is not already enabled on the parent site. Just about all other website settings, including application pool settings, can be modified in this area.

Installing Third-Party Web Services

SBS is not the only solution that builds much of its management interface on top of web services. Many other support solutions—antivirus software, antispam software, management and monitoring tools—have a web component to configure or monitor the software. Most of these software packages configure web services as part of the software installation package instead of relying on administrators to manually configure the web services.

Unfortunately, not all these tools have reached the level of web maturity that SBS has, and the installation process can trash the SBS IIS configuration. One notorious package is the Microsoft Customer Relationship Management suite, or MS CRM. By default, the CRM installation wants to install its web components into the Default Web Site, which is fine on a standalone server. However, many of the changes the CRM configuration makes to the Default Web Site breaks most of the SBS web tools. The CRM installation documentation does have a section detailing how to install CRM on an SBS server, but not all installers read the instructions to know that CRM can and should be installed into a separate site configuration on SBS and not the Default Web Site.

Other problems that can result from installing a third-party software web component on SBS are port conflicts. Some web management installations do install themselves into separate website configurations but fail to check and see whether any other websites are using a particular port to provide web services. Several software packages install themselves to listen on port 8080, which is unfortunately the same port that ISA uses for web proxy. Some also attempt to install on port 8081, which is where the SharePoint Central Administration site resides.

Best Practice—Installing Third-Party Web Services on SBS

Because of all the potential problems that can result with the installation of a third-party web solution on the SBS server, you should take several steps to make sure that the installation goes smoothly and that you have a way to get back to a running state if something does go wrong.

First, before installing the third-party software, make a backup of the IIS configuration using the methods described earlier in the chapter. This gives you a fallback position in case the software install has problems and uninstalling the software does not restore IIS to its previous configuration.

Second, if given the option, have the third-party software install into a separate website configuration. This keeps any changes it wants to make to the site configuration out of the Default Web Site and protects the existing web services on the SBS server.

Third, if the software wants to listen on a nonstandard web port—that is, a port other than 80—go through your IIS configuration and see whether any sites are already using that port. If so, be sure to select an alternate port number in the software installation. Do not allow a third-party software package to use port 8080 or 8081 for its web services, even if you are not currently running ISA on the server.

Publishing Secure Sites on the Internet Using a Third-Party SSL Certificate

One drawback to using the SSL certificate provided by the SBS setup wizards is that the certificate is not trusted by default for any web browser. In most cases, this results in a small annoyance when the web browser notifies the user that the certificate is not from a trusted authority each time the website is accessed. In other cases, it can prevent the user from accessing secure portions of the site altogether (see Chapter 17, "Integrating the Macintosh into a Small Business Server 2003 Environment," and the discussion of Internet Explorer 5 for the Macintosh). Most of the time, installing the SBS certificate into the workstation's certificate store as a trusted certificate can eliminate this behavior, but there are instances where this may not be practical or even possible.

It is possible to purchase and install a third-party SSL certificate in IIS to avoid all the issues related to the self-signed certificate SBS creates. There are a number of providers, and the cost can range from under $100 to several thousand dollars, depending on the type of certificate purchased. But before you can install a third-party certificate, you must generate a request file for the certificate. The following steps outline a process for generating a certificate request file and installing the certificate on the server:

1. Open the IIS Management Console.
2. Expand the server icon, expand Web Sites, right-click on the Default Web Site icon, and select Properties.
3. Click on the Directory Security tab; then click Server Certificate.
4. In the first page of the Web Server Certificate Wizard, click Next.
5. Select the Remove the Current Certificate radio button; then click Next.
6. In the Remove a Certificate page, you see the details for the self-signed certificate. Click Next.

7. Click Finish to close the wizard. You have now removed the existing self-signed certificate from the Default Web Site.
8. In the Directory Security tab, you will see that the View Certificate button is now grayed out. Click Server Certificate.
9. In the first page of the Web Server Certificate Wizard, click Next.
10. Select the Create a New Certificate radio button and click Next.
11. In the Delayed or Immediate Request page of the wizard, the Prepare the Request Now, But Send It Later radio button should be selected. Click Next.
12. In the Name and Security Settings page of the wizard, enter a name for the certificate, as shown in Figure 6.13, and click Next.

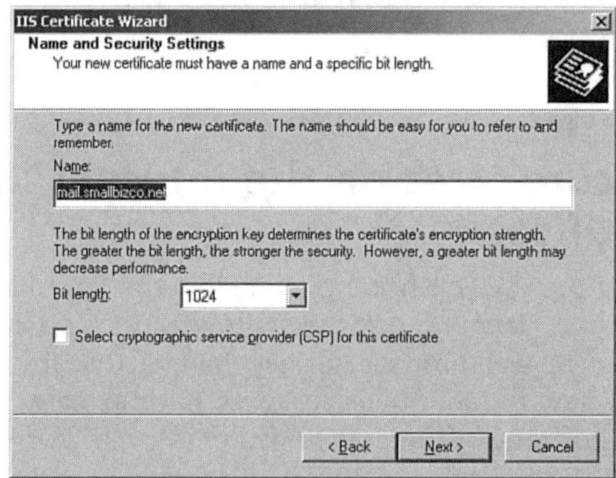

FIGURE 6.13 The Name and Security Settings page sets the name of the certificate and the size of the encryption key.

13. In the Organization Information page, as shown in Figure 6.14, enter or modify the Organization field, enter a name for the Organizational unit, and then click Next.

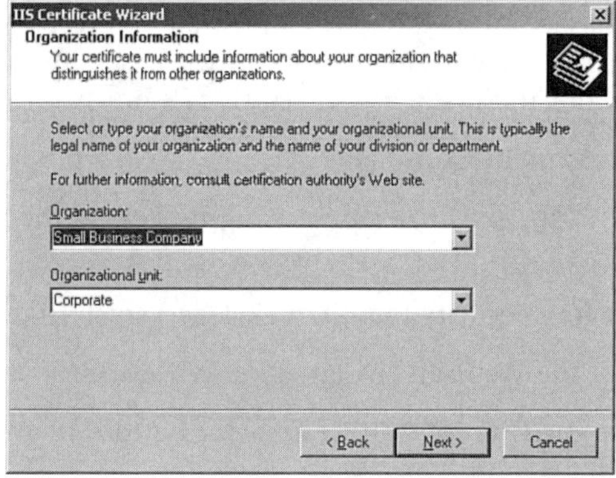

FIGURE 6.14 An organization and organizational unit name must be entered in the Organization Information page.

14. In the Your Site's Common Name page, enter the public Internet name of the server, as shown in Figure 6.15. This should be the same name that was used to create the self-signed certificate. Click Next.

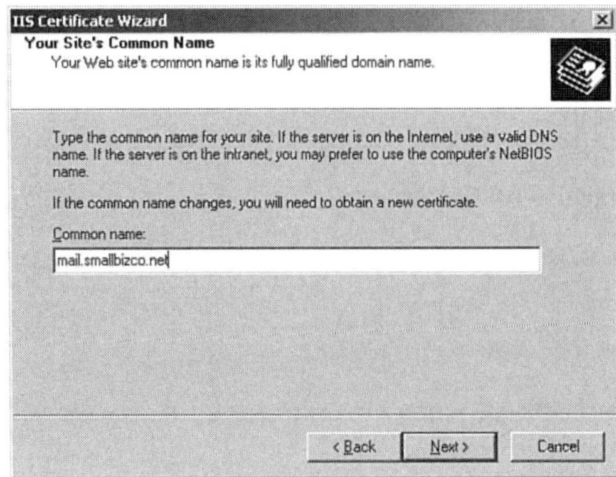

FIGURE 6.15 The public Internet name of the server must be entered into the Common Name field.

15. In the Geographical Information page, select the correct geographical information and click Next.

16. In the Certificate Request File Name page, enter the name of the file for the certificate request. The default filename is `c:\certreq.txt`. Click Next.

17. In the Request File Summary page, verify that the information listed is correct. If the information is incorrect, click Back to go back to the appropriate section of the wizard to correct the information. Otherwise, click Next.

18. Click Finish to close the wizard.

19. Submit the contents of the certificate request file to the vendor you have selected to generate the SSL certificate. This process differs depending on which vendor is selected.

20. After you receive the certificate file back from the vendor, save the certificate file to disk and run the Connect to the Internet Wizard on the SBS server.

21. In the Connection Type page, click the Do Not Change Connection Type radio button and click Next.

22. In the Firewall page, click the Do Not Change Firewall Configuration radio button and click Next.

23. In the Web Server Certificate page, click the Use a Web Server Certificate from a Trusted Authority radio button.

24. Click Browse to locate the certificate file on disk; then click Next.

25. In the Internet E-mail page, click the Do Not Change Internet E-mail Configuration radio button and click Next.

26. Click Finish to complete the wizard; then click Close when the configuration has completed.

The downside to this process is that while you are waiting for the certificate to get issued by the vendor, your Default Web Site will not have SSL protection, so it will not respond to any SSL requests. This means that services including OWA, Remote Web Workplace, and any other services that require SSL will not be available to the users on the server. If you are not sure how long your vendor will take to generate and deliver the certificate to you, you may want to consider this alternative method to generate and install a third-party certificate. This method involves creating a new site in the IIS configuration and using that site to create the certificate request and install the resulting certificate:

1. Open the IIS Management Console.
2. Expand the server icon; then right-click on the Web Sites icon and select New, Web Site.
3. In the first page of the Web Site Creation Wizard, click Next.
4. In the Web Site Description page, enter a name for the website, such as SSL Request, and click Next.
5. In the IP Address and Port Settings page, enter a unique host header for the site, such as sslrequest, and click Next.
6. In the Web Site Home Directory page, browse to the path for the default website, usually `c:\inetpub\wwwroot`; then click Next.
7. In the Web Site Access Permissions page, click Next.
8. Click Finish to close the wizard and create the site.
9. Right-click on the new site and select Properties.
10. Click on the Directory Security tab; then click Server Certificate.
11. In the first page of the Web Server Certificate Wizard, click Next.
12. In the Server Certificate page of the wizard, click the Create a New Certificate radio button; then click Next.
13. In the Delayed or Immediate Request page of the wizard, the Prepare the Request Now, But Send It Later radio button should be selected. Click Next.
14. In the Name and Security Settings page of the wizard, enter a name for the certificate and click Next.
15. In the Organization Information page, enter or modify the Organization field, enter a name for the Organizational Unit, and then click Next.
16. In the Your Site's Common Name page, enter the public Internet name of the server. This should be the same name that was used to create the self-signed certificate. Click Next.
17. In the Geographical Information page, select the correct geographical information and click Next.
18. In the Certificate Request File Name page, enter the name of the file for the certificate request. The default filename is `c:\certreq.txt`. Click Next.

19. In the Request File Summary page, verify that the information listed is correct. If the information is incorrect, click Back to go back to the appropriate section of the wizard to correct the information. Otherwise, click Next.
20. Click Finish to close the wizard.
21. Submit the contents of the certificate request file to the vendor you have selected to generate the SSL certificate.
22. After you receive the certificate file back from the vendor, save the certificate file to disk.
23. Open the properties page for the SSL Request website in the IIS Management Console, select the Directory Security tab, and then click the Server Certificate button.
24. In the first page of the Web Server Certificate Wizard, click Next.
25. The Pending Certificate Request page should appear, and the Process the Pending Request and Install the Certificate radio button should be selected. Click Next.
26. Browse to the location where the certificate file is located and click Next.
27. Click Finish to complete the wizard.
28. Right-click on the Default Web Site and select Properties.
29. Click on the Directory Security tab and click Server Certificate.
30. In the first page of the Web Server Certificate wizard, click Next.
31. Click the Replace the Current Certificate radio button and click Next.
32. In the Available Certificates page, shown in Figure 6.16, select the certificate that has been signed by the third-party vendor and click Next.

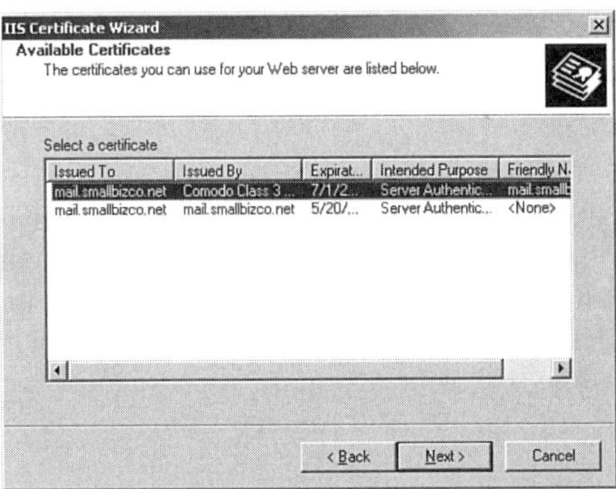

FIGURE 6.16 The Available Certificates page shows all available installed certificates, including previous versions of the self-signed certificate.

NOTE

If you have run the Connect to the Internet Wizard multiple times to re-create the self-signed SBS certificate, you may see more than one certificate listed. The self-signed certificates will have the same name in the Issued To column as in the Issued By column. The correct certificate to select is the one that has the vendor's name in the Issued By column.

33. In the Replace Certificate page, verify that the third-party vendor certificate has been selected; then click Next.
34. Click Finish to complete the wizard.

When completing the last steps to install the certificate on the Default Web Site, be aware that any active SSL sessions to the site may get interrupted as the change takes place. For that reason, this last task should be completed during a time when there is little or no SSL traffic on the server.

NOTE

These two methods for installing a third-party certificate work for systems not running ISA. For specific instructions on generating and installing third-party certificates with ISA installed on the server, see Chapter 24, "ISA 2004 Advanced."

Troubleshooting IIS Issues

Given that so many SBS services are tied to IIS, learning to quickly diagnose and resolve IIS problems will help keep you in the good graces of system users. This section covers several commonly encountered IIS problems and solutions, plus additional steps to help you get the information you need from your users to determine the real source of the problem. This chapter makes no attempt to be a definitive troubleshooting guide for all IIS issues that can arise, but it focuses on items that are either critical to SBS or are commonly found in an SBS environment.

Anatomy of an Error Page

Even though users may not realize it at first, the error page displayed by a web browser when problems are encountered accessing a website contains a wealth of information that can indicate to the system administrator where the source of the problem may be. Unfortunately, each of these error pages looks similar (lots of tiny black text on a white background), so after a while they generally gloss over the information presented and just try again later. When they do finally call in to report the problem, the call is generally phrased as "the Internet is down." Fortunately, you can ask them to read a couple of small lines to get you to the source of the error.

The typical IE error page is divided into three or more basic sections. The top section contains the basic error message—"The page cannot be found" or "Service unavailable" or "Bad request"—and may have a more detailed description of what the error means. The next section usually contains several options for the user to try and get around the error. The third section generally gives more technical information, or at least an attempt at it, to help better identify the problem.

Figure 6.17 shows a typical "page not found" error that a user may encounter. The middle section of the page lists an HTTP 404 error, which generally indicates that a URL has been incorrectly typed or that a section of the website has become unavailable.

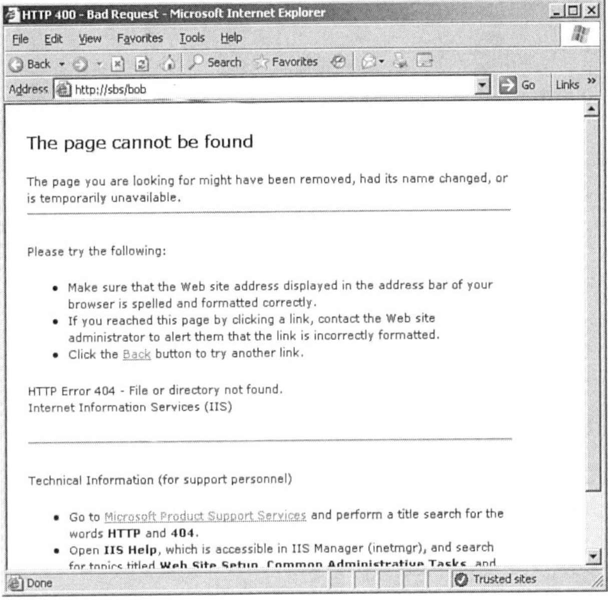

FIGURE 6.17 "Page cannot be found" error showing a 404 HTTP error.

Figure 6.18 shows a seemingly similar "page not found" error, but this time the page lists an HTTP 400 error instead of a 404 error. This generally indicates that the URL is correct, but there is a problem with the web service. In this example, this error results from the Default Web Site being stopped in IIS.

Service Unavailable

The Service Unavailable error in a web browser is pretty straightforward, both from the error page displayed and the troubleshooting steps to resolve it. When a user encounters a Service Unavailable error, that is literally the only information contained on the error page. There are no HTTP codes, no explanatory text, nothing. Only the words "Service Unavailable" in bold at the top of the window.

The key to resolving Service Unavailable errors is finding out what the user was attempting to access. If the user was accessing the Remote Web Workplace interface or one of the other SBS services, such as the Connect Computer Wizard or the ClientHelp directory, the first place to look is the application pools in IIS. If the DefaultAppPool is stopped, the Remote Web Workplace interface generates this error, as well the Backup and Monitoring modules in the Server Management Console. In many cases, the application pool can be started again, and services will be restored. You will still want to review the events listed in both the Application Log and the System Log to determine why the application pool stopped in the first place, if it was not stopped manually.

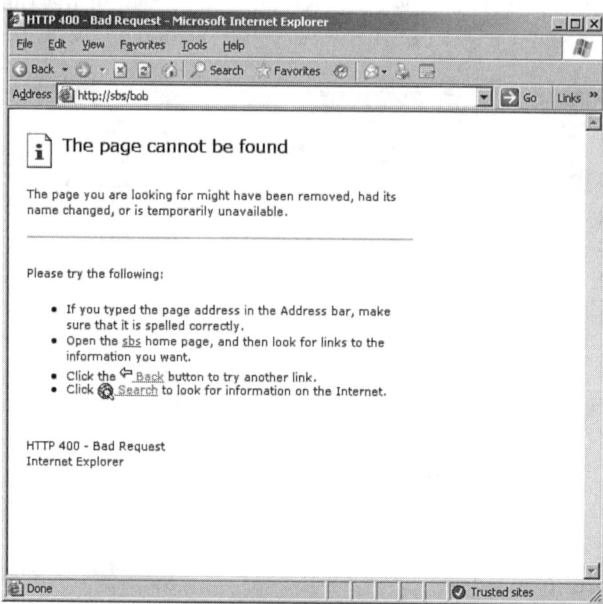

FIGURE 6.18 "Page cannot be found" error showing a HTTP 400 error.

Service Unavailable errors can also appear related to OWA. When a user gets a Service Unavailable error when trying to access his email or the Exchange Public Folders, there are two places to check. First, check in the Application Pools folder in IIS to see whether the ExchangeApplicationPool is started. If not, starting the application pool should restore access to the OWA interface. If it is started, next check the status of all the Exchange services. See Chapter 12, "Exchange Management," for additional Exchange troubleshooting information.

One common problem that can affect the OWA interface is when some or all of the Exchange virtual directories are removed from the Default Web Site configuration. Although those directories can be re-created manually if you have a known good server configuration to compare against, but this can be a tedious process because it involves more than just changes to IIS to get it back up and working again. Microsoft has a KB article (KB888033, `http://support.microsoft.com/?id=888033`) that details a way to have IIS rebuild all the Exchange virtual directories automatically.

When looking for the cause of Service Unavailable errors, you may open the IIS Management Console and find that all the application pools are stopped, and you may see a red X in the Web Sites icon. This indicates that the World Wide Web Publishing service is stopped and access should be restored after the service is started. Again, a look at the event logs is warranted when this core service is not running to help determine what might be the cause of the service failure .

Best Practice—Do Not Uninstall IIS from an SBS Server

Unfortunately, some assumptions related to supporting Microsoft products follow the "I can fix it by uninstalling and reinstalling it" mentality. This could not be further from the truth with SBS, and specifically with IIS. As detailed already in the chapter, many SBS components are dependent on a working IIS configuration. The process of uninstalling and reinstalling IIS completely eliminates all SBS configuration from the resulting metabase. To restore the configuration settings needed to get SBS back up and running as expected, every package that adds configuration changes to IIS must be reinstalled.

Many in the SBS community liken removing and reinstalling IIS to rebuilding the server from the ground up because just about as much effort is involved. If IIS is removed and reinstalled, the following tools must also be reinstalled: Exchange; SBS Administration Tools; Monitoring and Reporting; Intranet.

IP Address Restrictions

Occasionally you may encounter the "You are not authorized to view this page" error, as shown in Figure 6.19. Looking for the HTTP error code, Figure 6.19 shows a 403.6 error, indicating that the IP address of the workstation accessing the page has been rejected. This error is most often seen when attempting to access the Connect Computer Wizard from a nonlocal domain.

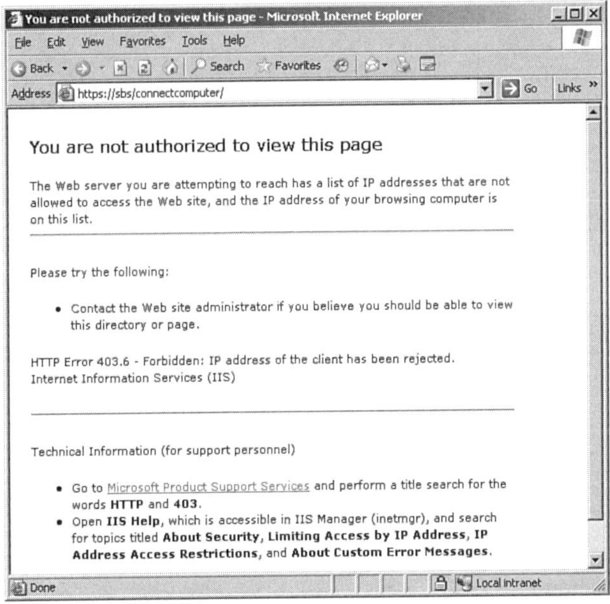

FIGURE 6.19 The 403.6 error indicates that the workstation IP is not in the allowed range for the site or page.

By default, the Connect to the Internet Wizard sets the IP address restrictions on the ConnectComputer virtual directory in IIS to be the local subnet for the internal NIC of the server. This prevents users from attempting to join workstations to the domain from across the Internet. It also prevents workstations on a different internal but routed network from accessing the page. But the most common cause of this error is if the IP address of the internal NIC on the server is changed without using the Change Server IP Address Wizard. That wizard not only changes the IP address on the NIC but also changes the IIS IP address restrictions for the Connect Computer Wizard, the DHCP scope, and a number of other places where the IP address is specified.

The issue is easy to troubleshoot. Open the properties of the website or virtual directory in the IIS Management Console and look at the IP address restrictions on the Directory Security tab. In the case of the connectComputer virtual directory, shown in Figure 6.20, you see the Denied Access radio button selected and the local subnet as well as 127.0.0.1 listed in the exceptions list. If the subnet does not match the internal NIC, you need to run the Change Server IP Address Wizard and then run the Connect to the Internet Wizard. Alternatively, if you want to restrict access to certain address ranges for other virtual directories, you can add those addresses or address ranges in this dialog box.

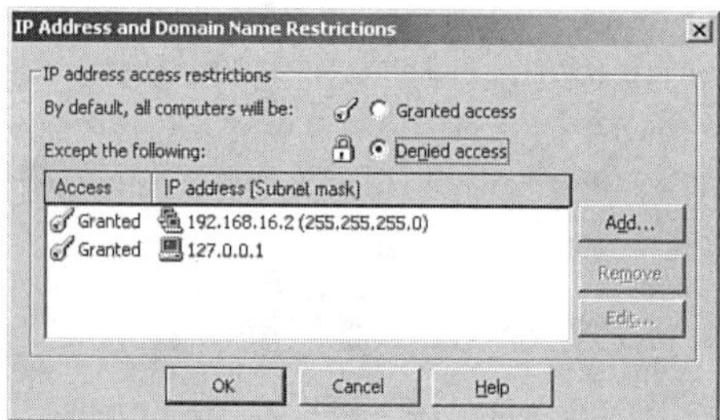

FIGURE 6.20 The ConnectComputer virtual directory restricts access to the localhost adapter and machines on the internal IP subnet.

Summary

IIS is an important component in an SBS installation because many of the SBS administration modules and user applications are web based. The Backup tools, Monitoring and Reporting components, and Connect Computer Wizard are all administration modules that run in the web space, as are the Outlook Web Access and Remote Web Workplace user tools. IIS is comprised of several modules that all work together to serve web applications—Application Pools, Web Sites, and Web Service Extensions. This structure affords a level of security and stability not found in earlier versions of IIS.

Although most SBS installations perform sufficiently with the default IIS configuration, it is possible to customize the configuration of IIS by adding additional websites or virtual directories to the Default Web Site. Because the IIS configuration is stored in a text file in XML format, it is not only less likely to get corrupted when changes are made, but backing up the configuration prior to making changes is much easier.

SBS 2003 includes the capability to generate a self-signed SSL certificate so that key tools can be accessed securely, including Outlook Web Access and Remote Web Workplace. In cases where the self-signed certificate is not sufficient to handle all security needs, a third-party SSL certificate can be purchased and installed on the server.

Troubleshooting IIS issues on an SBS server is fairly straightforward because the default configuration of IIS during server installation is stable and well documented. Common issues encountered in an SBS environment include services or components not running, misconfigured port numbers, and web-based applications that have modified the default configuration. In many cases, simply restoring the IIS configuration from a backup will recover from the problems. Alternatively, details in the error messages displayed in the web browser can help identify the source of the problems.

Best Practice Summary

- Default websites—The settings for the Default Web Site, Microsoft SharePoint Administration, SharePoint Central Administration, and Companyweb sites should not be modified. Because many services running on SBS are dependent on these default sites, any changes made could render core SBS services unusable. If any settings do need to be modified, try to make changes to the directories or virtual directories before modifying the site settings.
- Do not use SBS to run a public website—Even though IIS 6 is a much more secure product than its predecessors, there are still risks inherent with running a public website on the SBS server.
- Make backups before making any configuration changes to IIS—Because the stability of the metabase has increased with SBS 2003, there is no reason to avoid making backups of the IIS configuration prior to making any changes. The process of restoring the metabase configuration is simple and can get the web services back up and running quickly in case of trouble.
- Installing third-party web services on SBS—When a software product includes web management components, be sure to install the web parts into a separate website or at least a separate virtual directory on the server. Do not configure a third-party web component to use port 8080 or 8081 for their services.
- Do not uninstall IIS from an SBS server—Because so many services use IIS, uninstalling and reinstalling IIS requires the reinstallation of Exchange and all the SBS administration components as well. Use this method of recovery only as a last resort.

CHAPTER 7

Routing and Remote Access Service, VPN, and Firewalls

IN THIS CHAPTER

The Routing and Remote Access service (RRAS) is a vital component of Small Business Server 2003. The role of this service has been expanded from previous versions to provide new functionality that greatly improves security. Also, new wizards are available to automatically configure many aspects of remote access. These improvements are not limited only to the server portion but also to the client configuration as well.

In this chapter you learn the fundamentals of the RRAS along with examples on how to configure the most common options. Also, detailed information on accessing your server remotely is presented to give you some insight on the different methods available and when to use them.

Routing and Remote Access Service Basics

RRAS provides many essential services to your SBS network. However, many of its functions are determined by the way your server and network are configured.

The four major functions of RRAS are to provide the following services:

- Basic firewall
- Network address translation routing
- Remote access via dial-up
- Remote access via VPN

In SBS 2003 Standard Edition all these functions are handled by RRAS. If you have ISA Server 2004 installed (as part of SBS 2003 Premium Edition), the first two functions are taken over by ISA Server.

If you have ISA Server 2004 installed, you can skip the following sections up to the "Remote Access Basics" section because they do not apply to you. See Chapter 23, "Internet Security and Acceleration Server 2004 Basics," for information on configuring ISA Server as your firewall.

Using the RRAS Firewall

If you already ran the Configure Email and Internet Connection Wizard (CEICW) it is likely that you have configured the built-in firewall without much effort (or maybe without even knowing). Because the process is relatively simple, this chapter focuses on detailing the particulars of this service and providing in-depth information about certain common features.

Let's start by describing the main function of a firewall. The job of any firewall is to separate your internal (trusted) network from an external (not trusted) network, such as the Internet. This is an important function because it reduces the surface attack area of your network by exposing only those services that need to be accessed from outside.

For a firewall to be effective, both networks must be physically separated. Hence, one of the requirements to use RRAS as a firewall is that you must have two network cards. One card is connected to the local network, and the other card is connected to the Internet side, as shown in Figure 7.1.

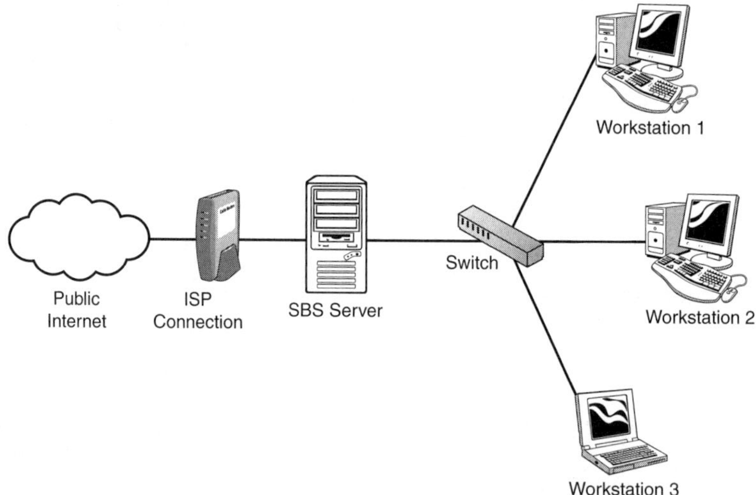

FIGURE 7.1 Network diagram of a typical installation using SBS as the firewall.

RRAS acts as a basic firewall because it can filter traffic only at the network layer (based the properties of the IP packet). Although it is not as fancy as ISA Server 2004, you still can protect your network effectively by restricting access not only by port number but also by source or destination address among other things.

Remember that although firewalls are important, they are not the be-all and end-all of network security. There are ways around firewalls (such as VPNs), and there is always the potential for having a vulnerable service behind an open port. Also, keep in mind that an improperly configured firewall can create a false sense of security.

Best Practice—Use ISA 2004 If You Have SBS 2003 Premium

If you already own the SBS 2003 Premium Edition, it is strongly suggested that you install ISA Server 2004. Not only does it provide a much more sophisticated firewall than RRAS, you also get more detailed reports and more control over what your users can access.

CEICW and the RRAS Firewall

Although CEICW takes care of most of the firewall configuration, you might be wondering exactly what it does. Understanding why and how ports are opened by the wizard is an important step toward improving your network security.

Table 7.1 lists the most common ports used in a typical SBS installation. By default, eight ports (marked with an asterisk) can be opened by the CEICW. Also, you can manually add other ports if you deem it necessary.

TABLE 7.1 TCP Ports Used in a Typical SBS 2003 Installation

TCP Port	Service	Description
21*	FTP	Enables the external file transfer
25*	SMTP	Enables incoming SMTP mail in Exchange
80*	IIS	Enables all nonsecure browser access, including: IIS websites and HTTPS redirectors
110	POP3	Enables external access to Exchange POP3 server
143	IMAP4	Enables external access to Exchange IMAP4 server
443*	IIS	Enables all secure browser access, including OWA, OMA, RWW, and RPC over HTTP
444*	Windows SharePoint Services	Enables external access to the SharePoint (Companyweb) website.
1723*	PPTP clients	Enables external PPTP VPN connections
3389*	Terminal Services	Enables access to Terminal Services using the Remote Desktop protocol
4125*	Remote Web Workplace	Enables Remote Desktop Connection via the Remote Web Workplace interface

**Denotes a port defined in the CEICW by default.*

7

Which ports are opened by the CEICW depends on the choices you make running it. For example, TCP port 444 will be opened only if you select Windows SharePoint Services Intranet Site on the Web Services Configuration screen.

Best Practice—Open Ports Only as Needed

Only open ports that are really necessary; opening ports that are not required can put your network at risk.

For example, if you use the POP3 Connector to retrieve email, allowing inbound SMTP access is not necessary. Unselect E-mail from the Services Configuration screen in CEICW to close it.

One nice feature of configuring your firewall using the CEICW is that if you have a hardware router/firewall installed on your network it can be automatically configured. If the device supports Universal Plug and Play (UPnP) the CEICW will not only open the ports on the RRAS firewall but also will open/forward the appropriate ports on the device. This eliminates much of the guesswork when manually configuring the hardware firewall.

Configuring the RRAS Firewall

As previously mentioned, the CEICW configures most basic functions of the RRAS firewall. However, there are a couple of things that you might want to do that are not directly configurable using the wizard. This section presents an overview of three common scenarios for configuring the firewall in an SBS network.

Creating a Packet Filter

At some point you might need to open an uncommon port to remotely access a service that resides on the server. For example, you might have a handheld device that needs IMAP4 or POP3 access to your mailbox in Exchange. Although opening another port in not really a best practice, sometimes you don't have a choice (although in this case you might want to consider buying a device that supports Exchange ActiveSync).

To create a packet filter to allow IMAP4 access (port TCP 143) through the RRAS firewall, follow these steps. These steps assume that the CEICW has been already run at least once.

1. Open the Server Management Console. On the left pane expand Standard Management and then select To Do List. Under Network Tasks and click on Connect to the Internet to open the Configure Email and Internet Connection Wizard.

2. On the welcome screen click Next. Assuming that you have already run CEICW previously, select Do Not Change Connection Type on the next screen and click Next.

3. Select Enable Firewall and click Next. On the Services Configuration Screen (see Figure 7.2) select all the services that you want to enable.

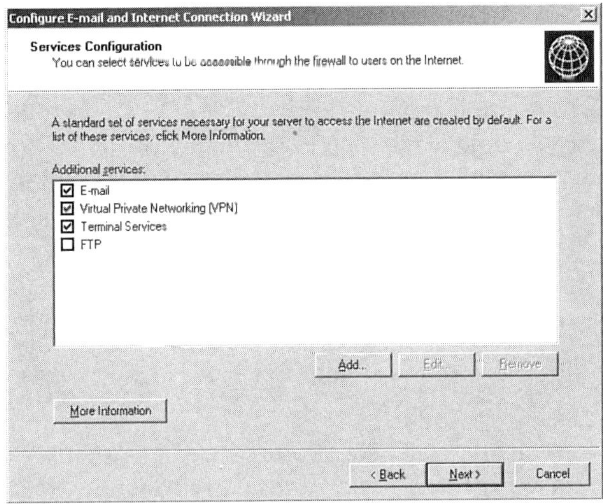

FIGURE 7.2 Services Configuration screen in the Configure Email and Internet Connection Wizard.

4. Click Add to create a new service. On the Add or Edit a Service screen (see Figure 7.3), enter **IMAP** as the service name, select TCP for the protocol, and enter **143** for the port number. Click OK to add the service and make sure that the check box next to the new service is selected. Click Next.

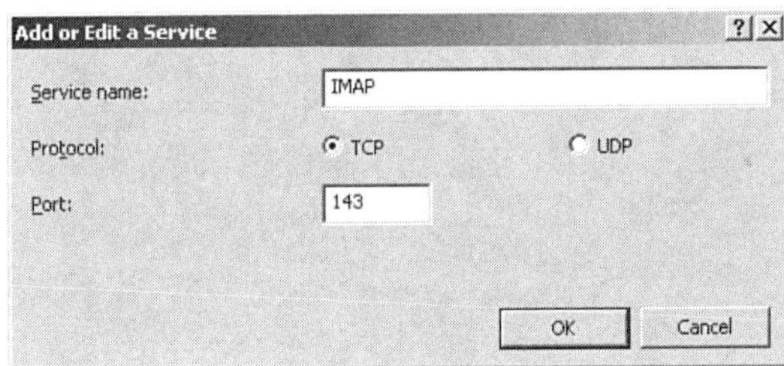

FIGURE 7.3 Add or Edit a Service screen in the Configure Email and Internet Connection Wizard.

5. Finish the wizard by clicking Next on the following screens and selecting Do Not Change Current Web Server Certificate and Do Not Change Internet E-Mail Configuration.

6. Optional: If you have a firewall in front of SBS that supports Universal Plug and Play (UPnP), the wizard attempts to configure it automatically. However, if your firewall does not support UPnP or it's disabled, you need to forward port 143 manually. Consult your router/firewall user guide for further instructions.

If the Microsoft Exchange IMAP4 service is running (which is disabled by default), you should be able to access the service externally.

Packet Forwarding to Another Device

There are cases where you need to allow access to an internal resource not allocated on the server. For example, you might have a web cam running on your network that you want to access remotely. For the purpose of this example, assume that the camera can be accessed via TCP port 8080.

The following steps outline how to forward a port from the external interface of your SBS box to a device located on the internal network:

1. Before configuring the port forwarding, make sure that the target device has a static IP assigned or a DHCP reservation.

2. Open the Routing and Remote Access console in Administrative Tools. Click on your server name to expand it and drill down to IP Routing, NAT/Basic Firewall. On the right pane right-click on Network Connection and select Properties.

3. On the Network Connection Properties screen click on the Services and Ports tab. Click on Add to bring up the Add Service Screen (see Figure 7.4). Type **`Webcam`** in the Description of Service box and select the TCP protocol. Enter **`8080`** as the Incoming and Outgoing Port and type the static IP of the device on the Private Address box. Click OK to save the changes and click OK again to close the Network Connection Properties.

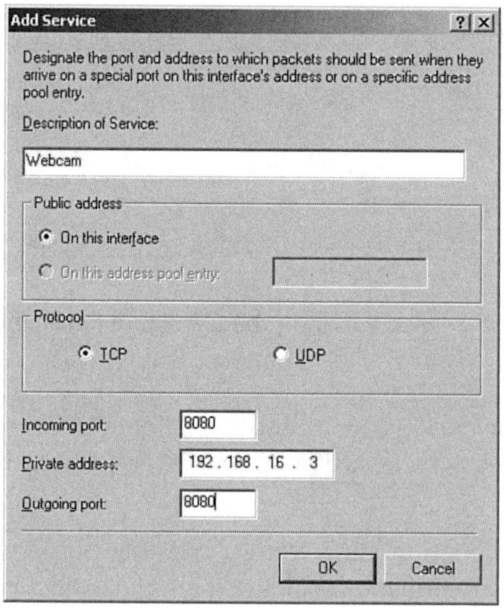

FIGURE 7.4 Add Service Screen on the Network Connection Properties of the RRAS Firewall

4. Optional: If you have a firewall in front of SBS you will need to forward port 8080 manually (even if your router is UPnP capable). Consult your router/firewall user guide for further instructions.

You should be able to access the webcam remotely by using the public IP of your server.

NOTE

One interesting feature that the RRAS firewall provides is port address translation. In other words, you can redirect traffic from one port on the external interface to another port on the target.

This is particularly useful for companies that have a single static IP. For example, assume that you have a Terminal Server alongside an SBS box, and you need to be able to access them both using RDP directly. You could change the listening port number on one of the servers, but that would prevent using Remote Web Workplace (RWW) to access it. A better alternative would be to leave both at 3389, but create forward port 3390 on the external interface and translate it to 3389 on the internal network. RWW keeps working, you have direct RDP access, and everybody is happy!

Filtering Connections

In some circumstances you might want to block certain IPs from reaching your server. For example, if you have seen numerous wrong password attempts from a specific IP, it might be wise to prevent it from even knocking at your door. Another use would be to block SMTP traffic (TCP port 25) from a specific IP address to curb spam.

With RRAS you can filter connections based on the source or destination IP address, port number, and protocol. The following steps outline the procedure to block a specific IP address from connecting to the server:

1. Open the Routing and Remote Access console in Administrative Tools. Click on your server name to expand it and drill down to IP Routing, NAT/Basic Firewall. On the right pane right-click on Network Connection and select Properties.
2. On the Network Connection Properties screen, click on Inbound Filters. Click on New to open the Add IP Filter screen (see Figure 7.5). Select the source network and on the IP address box type the address of the offending machine. For the subnet mask you can either specify a range of machines or, if you just want to block a single IP, type **`255.255.255.255`**. Click OK three times.

After completing the procedure the offending machine should be blocked at the firewall from attempting to contact your server. If you feel adventurous, you might want to play with those settings to restrict traffic based on the protocol and port number.

Best Practice—Regularly Test Your Firewall

Every once in a while get a port scanner and scan the external interface of your server. Make sure that every port you see open is supposed to be that way.

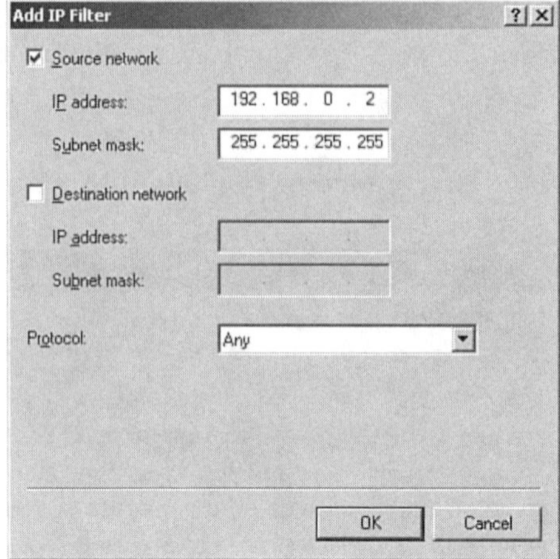

FIGURE 7.5 Add IP Filter screen on the Network Connection Properties of the RRAS firewall.

Remote Access Basics

There are many ways to access your server remotely. Although this section focuses on remote access using virtual private networks (VPNs) or dial-up, other remote access options are mentioned to compare them in terms of functionality and ease of use.

If you were to take a poll asking users what they like most about SBS, you would find that the ability to work remotely ranks high. Being able to read your mail and access files—or even your computer—from anywhere has become a necessity in today's business world, and it's one of the major reasons why people choose SBS.

Fortunately, remote access in SBS 2003 has improved significantly over previous versions. Not only it is easier to configure, but SBS also has a wide array of options to connect remotely in specific scenarios. Thanks to these improvements working remotely is more feasible than ever before, not to mention more secure.

Remote Access Options

Although working remotely can be a blessing, it can also become a nightmare (and I'm not talking about working at home at 2:00 a.m.!). SBS does a great job protecting your network, but enabling remote access is always a risk. On the other hand, this risk can be minimized by carefully considering all your remote access options and following the security best practices such as enforcing complex passwords and changing them frequently.

This discussion begins by addressing the following questions:

- What can you do with dial-up or VPN access?
- Is VPN or dial-up access necessary?
- When should you use VPN versus dial-up?

- How does VPN compare with other remote access alternatives?
- Which users need VPN or dial-up access?

Dial-up remote access is similar to accessing the Internet through a dial-up account. You connect to the server using a modem directly through a phone line. One of the main advantages of this is that you can access the network remotely even in the event of an Internet outage. The main disadvantage is speed; in most cases, the maximum speed attainable is 33.6 kbps, which is very slow. Another disadvantage is that you must have a line dedicated (at least partially) for this kind of access. Having said that, a dial-up connection will behave as part of your internal network (albeit much slower). In fact, you can even use it to connect to the Internet through your own server.

Virtual private networks on the other hand use a public network infrastructure (such as the Internet) to create a private link between two networks or computers. In other words, when you establish a VPN you are creating a secure tunnel between your computer and the remote network that goes through the Internet.

Not only can you access all the resources of the network as if your computer was physically connected to it, but traffic is encrypted in both directions while it travels the public network. When you connect to the VPN you can potentially do everything a local user would do (although it will be slower).

Best Practice—Enable Password Policies

Weak passwords and remote access do not mix. Enforcing a strong password policy is essential to keeping your data secure. Teach your users how to create pass phrases that are easier to remember and difficult to crack, and have your users change them regularly.

Risks of Using VPNs

VPNs are powerful, but they also present certain risks. Because VPN traffic is trusted, it effectively bypasses the firewall. This means that if you connect through VPN to a computer that has been infected with a virus or worm, you can potentially compromise the whole network because the virus/worm has unrestricted access to it. Also, if a hacker were to obtain access to the VPN, he would have access to the network, not just to a particular machine or service.

One of the main concepts in securing your network is to always give users the minimum access necessary to do their jobs. In that spirit the first thing you should evaluate is whether giving them VPN or dial-up access is required.

Best Practice—VPNs Are Not a Panacea

Although SBS makes VPNs easy, the truth is that they can be dangerous in the wrong hands. With so many options for remote access available in SBS, using VPNs is no longer a requirement. If a user only needs email access, it would be foolish to use VPN for that purpose.

Alternatives to VPNs

In the past VPNs were essential to work remotely. However, many new features in SBS 2003 make VPNs unnecessary in many cases. Table 7.2 shows several alternatives to VPNs for accomplishing certain tasks.

TABLE 7.2 Alternatives to Using VPN for Certain Activities

Activity	Alternative
Read email	Outlook Web Access—Access your email using a web browser.
	Outlook with RPC over HTTP—All the functionality of Outlook but remotely.
Connect to computers remotely	Remote Web Workplace—To connect to any workstation or server on your network.
Access files on the road	SharePoint—For files that need to be shared among several users either locally or remotely.
	Offline files—For files that are not being shared among users and that need to be available even when the network is not available.
	Remote Web Workplace—It can also be used to transfer files (if enabled).

In many cases using these alternatives can provide a better end-user experience. Also, from a practical standpoint using alternative methods can sometimes be the only way to access resources remotely because some providers may block VPN traffic while still allowing other (more common) protocols.

Guidelines for Using VPNs

From the previous discussion it becomes clear that VPNs are not for everyone. The question remains how to decide when the use of a VPN is really warranted. This section addresses these concerns by examining some common usage scenarios.

For administrative purposes VPNs can be really useful. The ability to see the whole network at once can be helpful for domain administrators to help diagnose and solve problems that involve several machines. Additionally, administrators are generally tech-savvy and take better care of their machines than regular users. Considering all this, granting administrators VPN access has many advantages and an acceptable risk level.

VPNs can also be helpful for users running an application locally that requires connecting to a resource in your network that is not available from the outside. For example, a user might need to connect to a database remotely. Setting VPN access for such users, where they can access the resource as required is a good idea.

Another example worth mentioning is printing to the SBS shared fax printer while you are on the road. You can potentially send faxes from anywhere in the world that has Internet access.

Best Practice—Practicing Safe VPN

Never establish a VPN from a computer not under your control (such as at an Internet Café). You will be giving that computer unrestricted access to your whole network and placing your network at risk.

Even allowing users to connect from their shared home PC is not a great idea because you don't have control of how well-kept those machines are. However, you can try to minimize that risk by implementing Network Quarantine Control. Use the following link to learn more about it: `http://www.microsoft.com/windowsserver2003/techinfo/overview/quarantine.mspx`

Configuring Remote Access

Configuring remote access using dial-up or VPN could not be easier with SBS 2003. As usual the built-in wizards take care of most of the heavy work, and they even take care of configuring the workstations.

Configuring the Server

The following steps outline how to run the Remote Access Wizard:

1. Open the Server Management Console. On the left pane expand Standard Management and then select To Do List. Under Network Tasks, click on Configure Remote Access.
2. On the welcome screen click Next. To enable remote access using VPN or dial-up, select Enable Remote Access and check the VPN Access and the Dial-in Access boxes (as shown in Figure 7.6). Click Next.

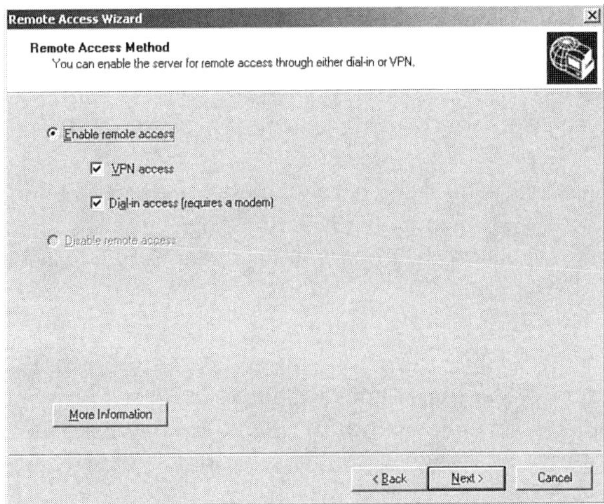

FIGURE 7.6 Remote Access Method screen in the Remote Access Wizard.

3. If the Client Addressing screen appears, you should either select the DHCP server to hand out the IP addresses to the remote clients (which is normally the SBS box) or set a static block of addresses for that purpose.
4. On the VPN Server Name screen type in the FQDN or public IP address of the server and click Next. This is the address that will be used to connect to the server

remotely, so a public DNS record should exist that points to the public IP of your server. You can create a new one—for example, vpn.smallbizco.net—or you could just use the same FQDN for which the SSL certificate was issued.

5. If you selected dial-up access in the Remote Access Method screen, the next screen asks you which modem(s) you want to use for incoming dial-up calls. Select the appropriate modem (as shown in Figure 7.7) and click Next. Remember that this modem should be used exclusively for remote access. If you have only one modem and you plan to use it as a fax, go back and disable dial-up remote access.

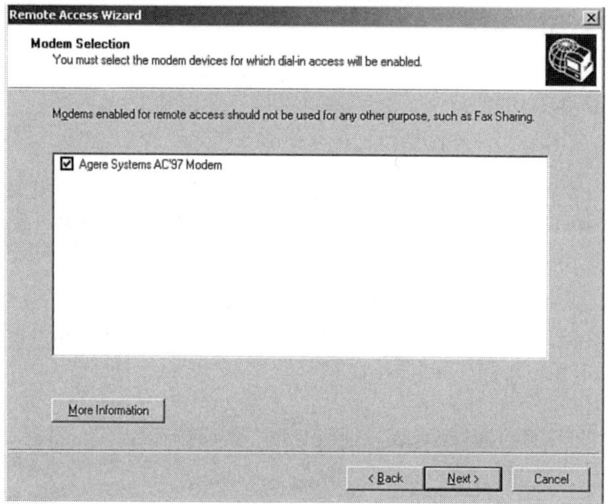

FIGURE 7.7 Modem Selection screen in the Remote Access Wizard.

6. The next screen asks you for the phone number to access the modem(s) selected in step 5. The primary phone number is required; only use the alternate if you have more than one line. Enter the phone number(s) and click two times to finish the wizard.

The server is now configured to accept incoming VPN connections. If you have a router/firewall in front of SBS that is not configured automatically, you need to forward port 1723 to the SBS box and allow protocol GRE 47 (sometimes called PPTP passthrough in some routers) for it work. Finally, if you haven't done so already, make sure that you enforce strong password policies in your network.

NOTE

This chapter focuses exclusively on using Point-to-Point Tunneling Protocol (PPTP) VPNs to connect individual devices to the network. However, other kinds of VPNs might adjust better to your situation. For example:

- Layer 2 Tunneling Protocol (L2TP) is commonly used as an alternative to PPTP. Although its functionality is similar, L2TP provides a higher level of security. This protocol uses certificates that are issued to the clients to mutually authenticate against the server, thus allowing you to restrict people from connecting using unapproved machines. Implementing L2TP requires a fair amount of manual configuration on both the client and the server.

- Gateway to Gateway VPNs are commonly used when a permanent connection between two offices is desired. Normally, this type of VPN requires a hardware router that supports that capability.

Configuring the Clients

Configuring the clients to connect remotely using VPN or dial-up is the easiest part of this process. If you already ran the Remote Access Wizard and the server is properly configured, the client configuration is almost automatic.

For computers that will be part of the domain but for which the Connect Computer Wizard has not been run yet, just select the Install Connection Manager when you are setting up the new computer on the Server Management Console. After that, run the Connect Computer Wizard (`http://sbs/ConnectComputer`) and wait for the applications to install.

For computers that already have been joined using the Connect Computer Wizard you need to redeploy the Connection Manager. Follow these steps:

1. Open the Server Management Console. On the left pane, expand Standard Management and then select Client Computers. On the right side, click Assign Applications to Client Computers.
2. On the Assign Applications Wizard, select the computers you want to deploy the Connection Manager and click Next.
3. Unselect any application you don't want to redeploy and click Next. On the next screen, select Install Connection Manager and click Next two times to finish the wizard.
4. The next time you log on to the client, the Connection Manager will be installed.

Finally, for any other computer you can download and install the Connection Manager from RWW. Follow these steps:

1. On the client open Internet Explorer and go to the RWW site (`http://mail.smallbizco.net/remote`). Unselect I'm Using a Public or Shared Computer and log in with your domain credentials.
2. On the welcome screen click on Download Connection Manager (as shown in Figure 7.8). Save the file to a location on your computer and run it. The program installs the Connection Manager to your machine.

After the Connection Manager has been installed, you should have an icon on your desktop named Connect to Small Business Server. You can also find it by opening the Connect To menu (or Network Connections folder).

7

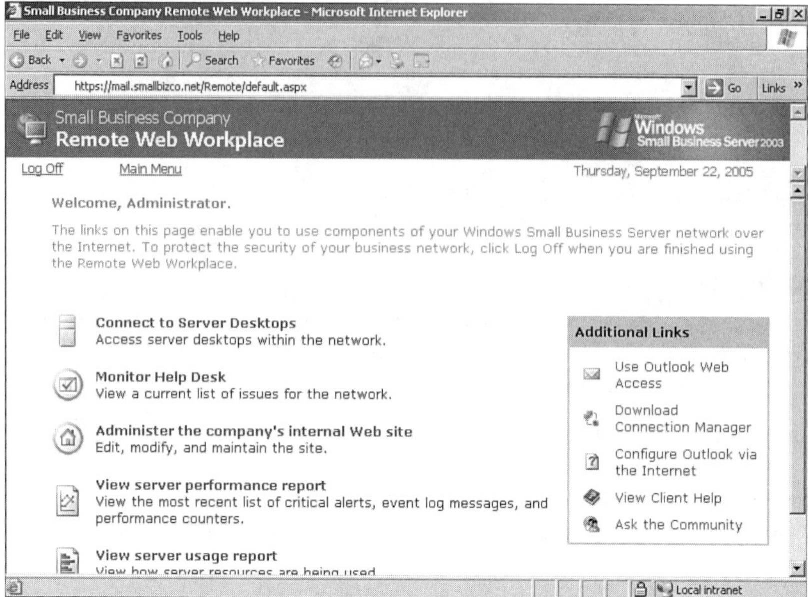

FIGURE 7.8 Connection Manager in RWW.

To connect via dial-up or VPN double-click on the desktop icon and type your domain credentials. If you want to connect using VPN, just click Connect. However, if you want to connect using dial-up, select Properties (see Figure 7.9) and select Dial a Phone Number to Connect. Click OK and then click Connect.

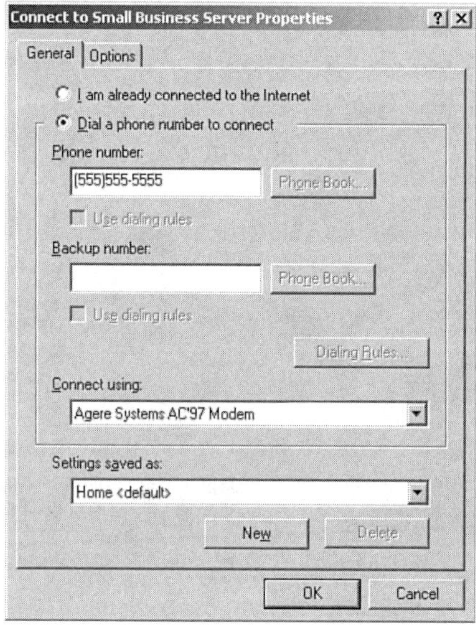

FIGURE 7.9 Connect to Small Business Server Properties screen.

Troubleshooting Routing and Remote Access Issues

Troubleshooting RRAS issues can sometimes be a painful process. So many elements are involved that pinpointing the cause of the problem is not as straightforward as you might hope. This section begins by addressing troubleshooting techniques for some of the most common problems.

A Service Cannot Be Accessed Remotely

You already configured the firewall, and you still cannot access a certain service from the Internet. There are many reasons why this problem can occur, but you can try to identify the problem in a systematic approach.

- Rerun the CEICW and make sure that the appropriate boxes are selected and that the required ports are opened.
- If you have a firewall in front of the server, make sure that the port is opened and forwarded to the SBS external network card.
- Verify that the service you want to access is running. Also, make sure that it's listening on the appropriate port. On the SBS box run `netstat -ano` in a command prompt to determine which processes are listening in which ports.
- Try connecting to the resource from the internal network first. For example, if you have trouble accessing SMTP, type **Telnet 192.168.16.2 25** from any machine on the network to see whether you get a response from Exchange SMTP server.
- Connect a computer on the external segment of the SBS server making sure that it's on the same subnet as the external network card. Try to connect from that location (using the external network card IP address). If you are successful, rule out that the problem is within the SBS box.
- Check whether your ISP is blocking that protocol. If this is the case, you might need to change ISPs or get a business class service that does not have such restrictions. Alternatively, you can use third-party services to redirect traffic to other ports (for example, DynDNS.org offers redirection for SMTP traffic).
- If you are using a DNS record (for example, `mail.smallbizco.net`) to access the resource, try using the public IP instead. Also, verify that the DNS record is resolving to the correct IP. Two great web resources for troubleshooting DNS issues are `www.dnsstuff.com` and `www.dnsreport.com`.
- Use a port scanner from different locations to determine where the fault occurs. FoundStone's SuperScan v4 is a great tool for this job (available for free at `http://www.foundstone.com/resources/proddesc/superscan4.htm`). Online scanners such as ShieldsUP (`www.grc.com`) are also useful.

You Want to Access Your Server Remotely, But Only a Dynamic IP Address Is Available

Ideally, everyone running SBS should have a static IP address. However, the reality is that sometimes you can't get a static IP in your area, or the cost is prohibitive.

You can use a dynamic DNS service to keep a DNS record that always resolves to your most current IP address. You can obtain this service from several third-party sites, such as:

- `www.DynDNS.org`
- `www.TZO.com`
- `www.ZoneEdit.com`

Using such services requires having either a router capable of running a dynamic DNS client or installing the client on your server. Also, some ISPs prevent certain services from being accessed remotely (most notably SMTP and HTTP access).

You Cannot Connect Remotely Using VPN—Error 721

If you cannot connect remotely using VPN, one possible cause is that port 1723 is not being forwarded to the SBS box. However, if you get error 721, this is usually caused if the GRE (Generic Routing Encapsulation) protocol is blocked.

If you are using a router, you must make sure that you enable protocol (not port!) GRE 47 through the router. This is sometimes called *PPTP* or *VPN passthrough.*

You Connect to the VPN Successfully, But You Can't Access Any Resources

This issue is likely caused by a routing problem. For a VPN to work, both machines must be on different subnets. In other words, if your server internal IP address is 192.168.16.2 with a subnet mask of 255.255.255.0, the machine originating the VPN connection can be on any range of IP addresses except 192.168.16.x.

This is a common problem for administrators who manage more than one SBS network. If you install and support SBS systems regularly and you plan to use VPN to access them, you should put your own network on a different subnet as your clients.

You Cannot Establish More Than Five Simultaneous VPN Connections

By default when you run the Remote Access Wizard, it creates only five VPN ports for PPTP and another five ports for L2TP. If this is insufficient, you need to increase the number of PPTP ports available. Follow these steps:

1. Open the Routing and Remote Access console in Administrative Tools. Click on your server name to expand it, right-click on Ports, and select Properties.
2. On the Port Properties screen, select WAN Miniport (PPTP) and click Configure to open the Configure Device dialog box (see Figure 7.10). On the Maximum Ports box select the appropriate number of ports that you want to have available.

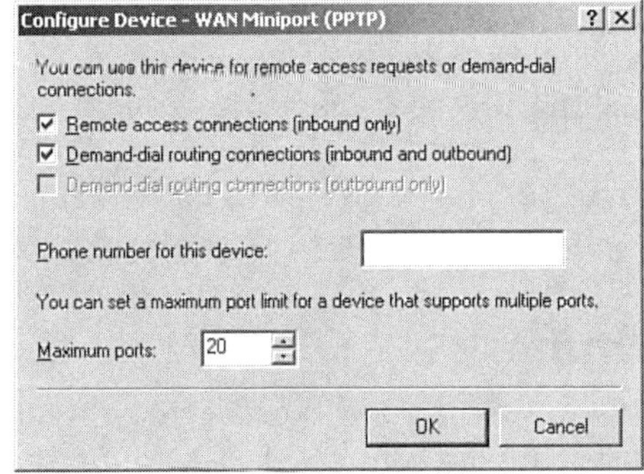

FIGURE 7.10 Configure WAN Miniport (PPTP) screen.

Internet Access Is Sluggish or Blocked While Connected to the VPN

Unfortunately, this is the expected behavior. When you activate the VPN connection, Internet traffic has to go through that connection, making it sluggish. If you are using ISA Server the client most likely will not be able to connect because it doesn't have the firewall client or the proxy settings enabled. In which case, the only workaround is to set the client to use ISA while connected to the VPN.

VPN Connection Keeps Disconnecting After a Period of Inactivity

By default the VPN connection will be dropped by the clients after 10 minutes of no activity. Although it is a good practice to disconnect the VPN as soon as you have finished using it, in some cases it might be necessary to increase this limit.

To modify that behavior, right-click on Connect to Small Business Server on the client and select Properties. Click on the Options tab, change the box that says Idle Time Before Disconnecting, and click OK.

More Troubleshooting Resources

You can find additional troubleshooting resources for the RRAS in Microsoft's TechNet:

- NAT/basic firewall troubleshooting—`http://www.microsoft.com/technet/prodtechnol/windowsserver2003/troubleshooting/routera.mspx`
- VPN troubleshooting—`http://www.microsoft.com/technet/prodtechnol/windowsserver2003/troubleshooting/vpn.mspx`

Summary

The RRAS in SBS 2003 provides important security features to your network. It also provides remote access capabilities via VPN and dial-up. Configuring these services can be achieved by running the built-in wizards and further modified to add more advanced features.

This chapter focused on detailing the features of the RRAS, configuring it as a NAT/basic firewall and to accept incoming VPN and dial-up connections. Also, the VPN capabilities of SBS were described in depth with special attention on enhancing the security of your network. However, firewalls and VPNs are a vast subject, and only so much can be covered in one chapter. The reader is encouraged to further familiarize himself with other firewall and VPN options not covered in this book.

Best Practice Summary

- Use ISA 2004 if you have SBS 2003 Premium—If you already own the SBS 2003 Premium Edition, install and use ISA 2004 instead of relying on RRAS for your firewall.
- Open ports only as needed—Only open ports that are really necessary; opening ports that are not required can put your network at risk.
- Regularly test your firewall—Every once in a while get a port scanner and scan the external interface of your server.
- Enable password policies—Weak or unchanging passwords are a security risk to your network, especially when remote access is enabled.
- VPNs are not a panacea—Think twice before enabling inbound VPN access to your SBS network and consider all the security risks of doing so.
- Practice safe VPN—Never establish a VPN from a computer that is not under your control.

CHAPTER 8

Terminal Services

IN THIS CHAPTER

- Understanding Terminal Services Operating Modes
- Installing and Configuring the Terminal Server
- Managing Terminal Servers
- Troubleshooting Terminal Service Issues

Of all the changes that Microsoft implemented in SBS 2003, the one that met with the largest uproar from the SBS community was the removal of Terminal Services support from the SBS server. Not all of the responses were negative, however. A large portion of the SBS community celebrated the loss of Terminal Services in Application mode because it removed one of the most significant security threats from the server.

Still, small companies that had been using Terminal Services on their SBS 2000 installations need to provide Terminal Services in the SBS 2003 environment. This chapter explains the basics of setting up Terminal Services in an SBS 2003 network and touches on some of the more common issues that network administrators may face.

Understanding Terminal Services Operating Modes

In the 2003 series of server products, Terminal Services features are provided in one of two modes: Remote Administration and Application. Remote Administration provides two remote desktop connections to a server for administration purposes. Application mode allows users to connect to run shared applications. But there are more differences than that, and they are detailed in the following two sections.

Remote Administration Mode

Almost all Windows 2003 servers support Remote Administration mode for remote access to the server console. A maximum of two simultaneous connections is allowed, and only members of the Domain Admins group can make a remote connection to the server when this mode is enabled.

When connecting to a server in Remote Administration mode, the administrator account has full access to the server as if she had logged on to the server console directly. The key thing to remember, however, is that you have *not* logged on to the server console directly unless you jump through a few hoops first.

Connecting to and Shadowing the Server Console

If you use the Remote Desktop Connection tool (mstsc.exe) or the Connect to Server Computers link from the Remote Web Workplace (RWW), you are connecting to one of the two remote administration sessions allowed in this mode. You can gain control of the actual console session in one of two ways, however.

First, if you are using the RDC tool, you would type **`mstsc /console`** to launch the remote connection and tell it to use the Console session instead of one of the two remote sessions.

Second, you could create a remote session and use the `shadow` command to control the existing console session. There are a few steps that you must take before you will be able to use the `shadow 0` command to control the existing console session. This information is documented in Microsoft KB article 278845 (`http://support.microsoft.com/kb/ 278845`).

By default, the SBS server is preconfigured with remote administration access enabled. You do not have to do any manual configuration to allow remote access to the server from inside the network. You need to enable Terminal Services access through the SBS firewall in the Connect to the Internet Wizard (CEICW) if you want to get access to the server desktop from outside the local network.

Application Mode

Terminal Services in Application mode is what most people think of when they think about a terminal server. When in this mode, a number of users can log in to the terminal server, run applications, and save data just as if they were logged in on a "normal" PC. There are a number of licensing restrictions regarding Terminal Services, more than can be appropriately addressed in this book. However, the section "Configuring Terminal Services Licensing Service" later in the chapter covers how to install appropriate Terminal Services licensing so that users can connect to the terminal server.

Before that can happen, however, a server has to become a terminal server first, and that involves installing Terminal Services in Application mode. Before you do this installation, consider a few items:

- Server Performance—Make sure that the server you plan to use as a terminal server has enough horsepower to handle the number of users and types of applications you plan to provide. Review the Microsoft whitepaper "Windows 2003 Terminal Server Capacity and Planning" (`http://www.microsoft.com/windowsserver2003/techinfo/overview/tsscaling.mspx`) for additional hardware guidelines.
- Domain controller—Do not plan on installing Terminal Services in Application mode on a domain controller. If you can demote the domain controller to a member server without impacting its other functions on the network, this might suffice; otherwise, look to a different server box that can maintain its role as a member server.

- Server licensing—Make sure that you understand your terminal server licensing needs. If you will be converting an existing Windows 2000 server (that's not a domain controller) into a terminal server, you will not need any additional TS CALs to connect Windows workstations. If your terminal server is based on Windows 2003 server, you will need to acquire TS CALs separate from the SBS CALs to provide licensed access to the server. Review Microsoft KB article 823313 (`http://support.microsoft.com/kb/823313`) and the Windows Server 2003 Terminal Server Licensing whitepaper (`http://www.microsoft.com/windowsserver2003/techinfo/overview/termservlic.mspx`) for more information.

Installing and Configuring the Terminal Server

Microsoft has provided a Quick Start guide for Terminal Services on its website (`http://www.microsoft.com/windowsserver2003/techinfo/overview/quickstart.mspx`), which outlines the basic steps to installing and configuring the terminal server service. The document does not specifically cover the installation and configuration of a terminal server on an SBS network, so a slightly more detailed how-to guide is included in this chapter.

Installing Terminal Services

After you have reviewed the requirements for terminal server in Application mode and have done the basic operating system load on the server computer, you can proceed to installing application services on the machine. Follow these steps to install Terminal Services on a Windows Server 2003 server:

1. Join the server to the SBS domain using the Connect Computer Wizard if it has not already been done. See Chapter 16, "Users and Computers," for more information.
2. Click Start, Control Panel, Add or Remove Programs.
3. Click Add/Remove Windows Components.
4. Click on the check box next to Terminal Server to turn it on.
5. Click Next. You get a warning about installing Terminal Services on the server and that already installed applications may fail to work after terminal server is installed. Click Next.
6. Make sure that the Full Security radio button is enabled and click Next.
7. Select the I Will Specify a License Server within 120 Days radio button and click Next.
8. Select Per User licensing mode and click Next.
9. Click Finish to close the wizard.

You need to restart the server before you can begin using the server as a terminal server. Click Yes in the restart prompt at the end of the wizard to restart the server immediately, or can click No and manually restart the server later.

Configuring Terminal Services Licensing Service

Before your terminal server becomes fully usable in its new role, you need to set up and configure the Terminal Services Licensing service. In the SBS environment, the Terminal Services Licensing service is usually installed on the SBS server. Follow these steps to install the licensing service on the SBS sever:

1. Click Start, Control Panel, Add or Remove Programs.
2. Click Add/Remove Windows Components.
3. Click on the Terminal Server Licensing check box to turn it on. Click Next.
4. Accept the default settings for making the license server available to the entire enterprise and the location for the license server database and click Next. Insert the CD and click OK if prompted.
5. Click Finish to close the wizard.
6. Click Start, Administrative Tools, Terminal Server Licensing.
7. Right-click on the SBS server listed in the right pane and select Activate Server.
8. Click Next in the first page of the Terminal Server License Server Activation Wizard.
9. Select the method to use to activate the TS CALs when they are installed (Automatic Connection is the default and recommended setting) and click Next.
10. Enter your company contact information and click Next.
11. Enter the optional company contact information if desired and click Next.
12. If you have TS CAL codes to enter, enable the Start Terminal Server Client Licensing Wizard check box and click Next; then follow the instructions in the Client Licensing Wizard to install your licenses. If you do not yet have TS CALs to enter, turn off this check box and click Finish.

Now you need to confirm that the terminal server can communicate with the licensing server. From the terminal server console, open the Terminal Server Licensing console from the Administrative Tools folder. If the terminal server can communicate with the licensing server, you will see the licensing server listed with a green check box in the server icon.

Best Practice—Running Terminal Server Licensing on the SBS Server

When you read the Terminal Server Quick Start guide from Microsoft, you will find that the Terminal Server Licensing service can be installed on the same server running Terminal Services in small environments. Even though SBS environments would fall under this recommendation, you should still install Terminal Server Licensing on the SBS box instead. Here are a few of the reasons:

- Backup—By default, the SBS backup process backs up the TS Licensing database as part of the nightly backup process. You do not need to run a separate backup job to ensure that the license database is protected.

- Disaster recovery—If something happens to the terminal server computer, the licensing database is still intact, and you can rebuild the terminal server and not have to worry about reregistering your TS CALs.
- Backward compatibility—Windows Server 2003 servers can host Terminal Server Licensing for terminal servers running Windows Server 2003 and Windows 2000 Server. If you ever had a mix of 2000 and 2003 servers acting as terminal servers, only the 2003 servers would be able to host the licensing database for all the terminal server licenses.

Managing Terminal Servers

Now that the terminal server is set up, the licensing server configured, and the users able to log in, you can start working on managing the terminal server. You need to set up applications for the users to use, and you may want to customize some of the access settings for the server. You will probably also be called on to help users who are having problems on the terminal server. The next three sections of the chapter cover these and other items related to terminal server management.

Installing Applications

Installing applications on a terminal server sometimes requires a different process than installing applications on a normal workstation. One of the first things you will notice about a correctly configured terminal server is that users are not accessing the server with administrator rights. As such, you will not be able to use the Assign Applications Wizard to install applications through the SBS logon script like you can for user workstations. (See Chapter 16 for more information about the SBS logon script and review Chapter 10, "Workstation Security," for a discussion about user rights on the workstation.)

This is not the only difference in the terminal server world, however. Because the terminal server is essentially a really souped-up shared workstation, applications must be able to have multiple instances open by different users at the same time. Not all applications have been written this way and would cause problems if they were accessed the same way they are run on a workstation. To that end, the terminal server recognizes when you are installing applications and takes some extra steps to help applications run in this multi-user environment.

8

The preferred method for installing applications on a terminal server is to use the Add or Remove Programs interface. In the Add or Remove Programs window, click the Add New Programs button in the left menu; then click the CD or Floppy button. If the program to be installed is on CD or floppy, the Install Program Wizard finds the installer and lets you select it, or you can click Browse and search for the installer in a different location. After you locate and launch the application installer, the Install Program Wizard remains open in the background. After the program installation is complete, click Next in the Install Program Wizard and then click Finish to close the wizard.

CAUTION

Do not close the Install Program Wizard until the application installation has finished. The wizard warns you about this twice before you can close it so that you cannot accidentally close the wizard before the application installation has completed. The application may fail to work correctly if the Install Program Wizard finishes first.

Alternatively, you can simply run the application installer on the terminal server without going through the Add or Remove Programs interface. In some cases, the terminal server service recognizes that an application installer has been started and the service automatically launches the Install Program Wizard, but not all applications install in the same way, so the service cannot detect every installer and launch accordingly.

BEST PRACTICE—INSTALLING MICROSOFT OFFICE ON A TERMINAL SERVER

The process for installing Office 2003 on a terminal server is much simpler than with earlier versions of Office. Microsoft has developed a web page (`http://office.microsoft.com/en-us/assistance/HA011402071033.aspx`) with information on preparing for a deployment of Office 2003 on a terminal server. Before you install Office on the terminal server, review this document and make sure that your licensing for Office is appropriate for use in a terminal server environment. Standard OEM or off-the-shelf installs of Office do not include the rights to run Office on a terminal server. Contact your Microsoft licensing specialist to ensure that you have the proper licenses necessary to run Office from the terminal server.

Running Terminal Services Configuration

The Terminal Services Configuration console provides an interface to view and modify settings related to the connection between the client and the terminal server. These options are divided into two areas in the console, which can be found in the Administrative Tools folder.

In the Connections folder of the console is the default RDP-tcp connection. The properties pane of the connection, shown in Figure 8.1, has eight tabs. Table 8.1 provides a summary of the settings available in each of these tabs.

TABLE 8.1 Settings Tabs in the RDP-tcp Connection Properties

Tab Name	Settings
General	Security layer and encryption options; determines what level of security and encryption the connection will use
Logon Settings	User logon credential selection options; determines whether to accept the credentials provided by the client or to log on to a specific account
Sessions	Timeout and reconnection options; determines which timeout settings will be used
Environment	Initial program launch options; determines whether users get full desktop or just an application upon logon
Remote Control	Remote observation and control options, determines if and how use sessions can be remotely controlled or observed

TABLE 8.1 Continued

Tab Name	Settings
Client Settings	Remote device connection options; determines what remote resources are made available in the terminal session
Network Adapter	NIC options; determines which NIC to use for the connection and how many simultaneous connections can be used
Permissions	Security options; determines which users or groups can access the connection

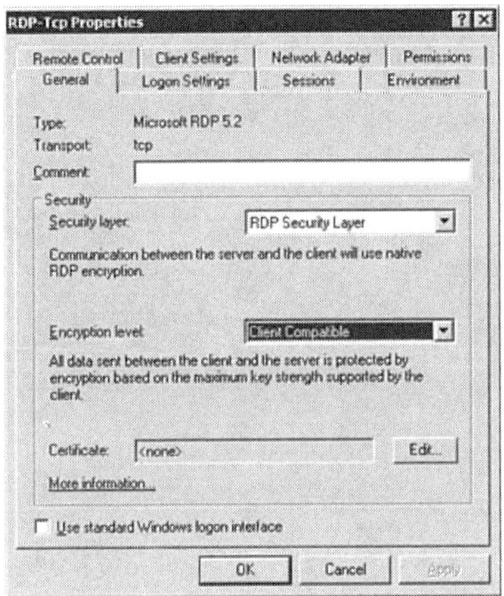

FIGURE 8.1 Properties of the RDP-tcp connection in the Terminal Services Configuration console.

In most SBS installs, these settings do not need to be modified. For those concerned with the security of the remote connection, you could look at modifying the encryption settings available in the General tab. The FIPS Compliant setting allows for the strongest encryption on the connection, but some remote clients, including the Remote Desktop Client for Macintosh, do not support that level of encryption and would not be able to connect.

The other folder available in the Terminal Services Configuration console is the Server Settings folder, shown in Figure 8.2. The seven options available here are self-explanatory and govern all connections to the terminal server.

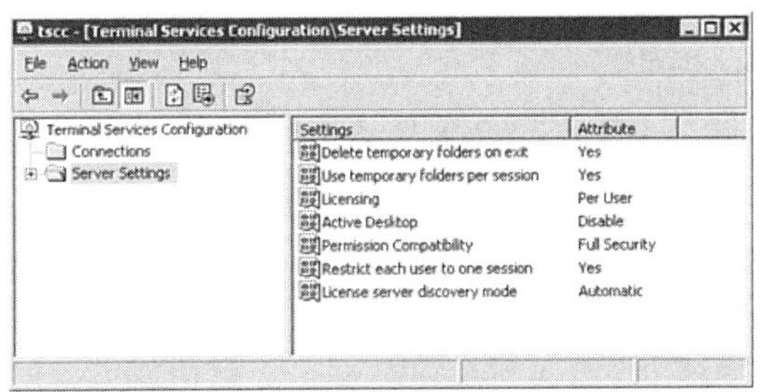

FIGURE 8.2 Terminal Server Configuration Settings include the licensing mode of the server.

Make note of the Licensing option in this area because this is where you can change the licensing mode of the server from Per User to Per Device. In most cases, you will want to use Per User. However, if you need to change the licensing mode of the server for troubleshooting purposes, this is where you would make that change.

Running Terminal Services Manager

The Terminal Services Manager console provides information about the active sessions on the terminal server. As shown in Figure 8.3, when the Terminal Services Manager console is first opened, it lists all the existing sessions on all the terminal servers in the environment. In most SBS installations, this mostly likely will be only one server. Note that this window does not show any information about the SBS server itself because it supports only remote administration.

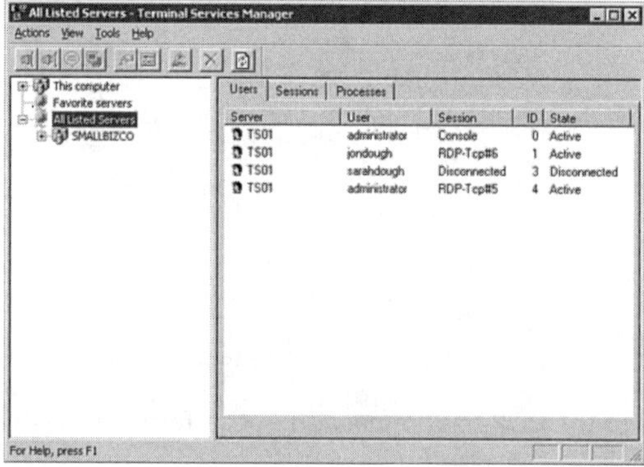

FIGURE 8.3 Terminal Services Manager lists all sessions on the server.

For each session, several pieces of information are listed. Table 8.2 lists and describes the information available for the connection. In addition, the green head icon (shaded in Figure 8.3, the last connection in the list) indicates the currently active connection. When you have multiple connections to the terminal server, such as a console connection and an RDP connection as shown in Figure 8.3, this helps you identify which session you are in so that you do not accidentally log yourself out.

TABLE 8.2 Session-Specific Information in the Terminal Services Management Console

Column	Description
Server	Identifies the server hosting the session
User	Identifies the user who initiated the session
Session	Identifies the location of the session. This will be the Console, the RDP-tcp connection number, or Disconnected if the user has dropped the session
ID	Identifies each session with a unique number
State	Indicates whether the session is active or disconnected
Idle Time	Indicates how long the session has been idle
Logon Time	Indicates the time that the session was first established

The real power in the Terminal Services Manager console is in interacting with the different sessions. Although you can take some action on the sessions when logged in on the terminal server console, you will not get the full ability to manage the sessions until you connect to the server remotely. The following list describes the interaction options and how or when you might want to use them:

- Connect—Allows you to take over the session. When you select this option, you are prompted to enter the password of the user who owns the session. After you enter the correct password, the user is disconnected from the session, and the session becomes active on your screen.
- Disconnect—Drops the user from the session. The session stays active on the server, but the user is no longer in control of the session, and the session state changes to Disconnected.
- Send Message—Allows you to send a message to the user session through a pop-up box on the session screen. Useful for letting a user know if the server needs to be restarted or for other administrative communication.
- Remote Control—Allows you to share control of the remote session with the user. Depending on the configuration set in the Terminal Services Configuration console, the user may need to grant you access to the remote control session, but by default this authorization is not needed. You can remotely control only an active session, not a disconnected one.
- Reset—Kills the remote session immediately. All resources used by the session are immediately released, and any unsaved work in open applications is lost. Think of this as the remote equivalent of powering the session off.
- Status—Displays a window of TCP/IP statistics for the session.
- Log Off—Disconnects the user session, but by sending a logoff command to the session. This can be done on active and disconnected sessions and is safer than doing a Reset on the connection.

Your time spent in the Terminal Services Manager console will likely be for one of two reasons: remote controlling user sessions to assist with problems or clearing out disconnected sessions. One of the hardest lessons to teach new terminal server users is to use the Log Off button instead of the big X to close the terminal server session. In some cases, this can lead to multiple disconnected sessions for a single user, tying up system resources on the terminal server. Periodically, you need to run the Terminal Services Manager console to see whether there are scores of disconnected sessions, especially sessions that have been idle for long periods of time. If and when you find them, right-click on the session and select Log Off.

Troubleshooting Terminal Service Issues

After you set up the terminal server environment, you should have relatively few problems related to daily operation. However, some issues and resolutions are worth mentioning in this chapter.

Internet Explorer Enhanced Security Configuration

For terminal servers based on Windows Server 2003, you have to modify the Internet Explorer Enhanced Security Configuration on the server before terminal server users will be able to browse the Web from the terminal server. To change the configuration, open Add or Remove Programs from Control Panels; then click Add/Remove Windows Components. Select the Internet Explorer Enhanced Security Configuration item in the components list, click Details, and turn off the For All Other User Groups check box. Click OK; then click Next and click Finish to complete the changes.

Best Practice—Internet Explorer Enhanced Security Configuration and Administrators

Even though you will want to disable the Internet Explorer Enhanced Security Configuration for your users, you will still want to leave it enabled for administrators. Even though the terminal server is being used as a workstation, you will still want to protect it from as much malware as possible. Leaving the Internet Explorer Enhanced Security Configuration enabled for administrators is one step to helping keep the server and the rest of the network safer.

Terminal Server Missing from Remote Web Workplace

Occasionally when a terminal server is installed into an existing SBS network, the new terminal server will not show up on the RWW page. For a more in-depth look at how RWW interacts with remote desktops, including terminal servers, see Chapter 15, "Remote Web Workplace." This issue, however, is generally resolved by correcting one value in the Registry on the SBS server. Look in the `HKEY_LOCAL_MACHINE\SOFTWARE\Microsoft\SmallBusinessServer\RemoteUserPortal\KWLinks` key for the `AppTS` value and make sure that it has been set to 1. The standard warning about making changes to the Registry applies, so get a backup of the Registry before you make any changes, if you need to make changes.

Users Unable to Log In to Terminal Server

If users are unable to log in to the terminal server and receive the message shown in Figure 8.4, the local Remote Desktop Users group may not have been set up correctly on the server during its configuration. To see what groups have been added to the Remote Desktop Users group on the Terminal Server, right-click on My Computer and select Manage. Then expand System Tools, Local Users and Groups, Groups; then right-click on Remote Desktop Users and select Properties. If the correct groups are not listed in the Members pane, click Add and add them to the list.

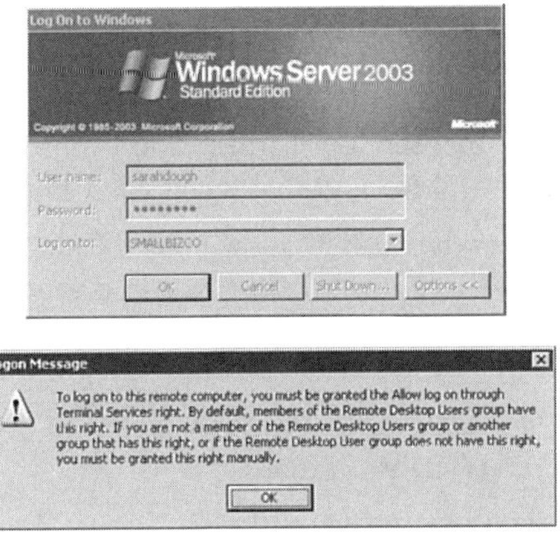

FIGURE 8.4 Access Denied error when logging in to the terminal server remotely.

Another reason users may not be able to access the terminal server relates to Terminal Server Licensing. If a user or workstation accessed the terminal server before the licensing service was configured and the TS CALs were installed, the user was granted a temporary token. This temporary token allows the user to access the terminal server for up to 90 days if a permanent license is not installed in the meantime. In some cases, the permanent license does not get installed correctly, and the user will start getting warnings that indicate that the Terminal Services temporary token will expire in a certain number of days. After the token expires, the workstation should request a permanent license and receive it from the TS Licensing server, provided a license is available. You may need to remove the temporary token from the workstation following the instructions in Microsoft KB article 187614 (`http://support.microsoft.com/?kbid=187614`), which also includes information on how to clear temporary tokens from Macintosh clients.

Summary

Deploying and managing Terminal Services in a Windows network environment can be complicated, and this chapter did not address all possible scenarios that you might encounter if you choose to implement Terminal Services in your SBS network. However, getting a terminal server up and running is not rocket science, and the basic steps to set one up are fairly straightforward. First, you have to install a separate server to run Terminal Services in Application mode. The SBS server supports only Remote Administration mode starting with SBS 2003. After you have the basic server OS installed, you will install Terminal Services on the new server, install Terminal Server Licensing on the SBS server, and then install your TS CALs.

Managing the terminal server is also not difficult and will mostly be done through the Terminal Services Management console. Through this console, you can remotely control other users' sessions, view the status of existing sessions, and clear out disconnected sessions as needed. The Terminal Services Configuration console provides an interface for you to configure other aspects of the terminal server environment for your users.

With the advent of RWW and the push to allow users to work remotely, you may find yourself in a position to need Terminal Services even in a very small business environment. Knowing the basics of configuring and managing a terminal server may be more of a necessity than an option as the use of SBS continues to grow around the world.

Best Practice Summary

- Running Terminal Server Licensing on the SBS Server—For performance and fault-tolerance reasons, install the Terminal Server Licensing services on the SBS server and not on the terminal server.
- Installing Microsoft Office on a terminal server—If you need to install Office on a terminal server, read the Office Deployment whitepaper and make sure that you have appropriate Office licensing.
- Internet Explorer Enhanced Security Configuration and administrators—To help protect the terminal server as much as possible, do not remove the IE enhanced security configuration for administrators on the terminal server. Only users should have this configuration removed.

PART IV

Security

IN THIS PART

CHAPTER 9

Server Security

IN THIS CHAPTER

- Physical Security
- File-Level Security
- Share-Level Security
- Password Security
- Troubleshooting Security Issues

Given that the intent with SBS is to have all the main business operations residing on a single server, securing that server against accidental and deliberate damage becomes even more important than in a more traditional multiserver Windows environment. In some small business environments, physical security of the server may be lacking or even nonexistent. Many companies encounter problems with employees who steal or sabotage company data. With the added risk of all the network-based attacks the server will be subjected to simply by connecting it to the Internet, keeping a server secured is more of a challenge than just a few years ago.

This chapter covers four main aspects of security as it relates to the SBS server: physical security, file security, share security, and password security. It also documents some commonly encountered security problems and offers ways to troubleshoot and resolve those problems quickly.

Physical Security

Even with the best password, file, and network policies in place to secure access to the server, there is no substitute for solid physical security of the server. If anyone, thief or employee, has physical access to the server, company data can be deleted, compromised, or stolen. If the server box itself can be removed from the company site, any number of methods can be employed to access data stored on the server disks, even removing the disks and placing them in another machine in some cases.

Ideally, any server, including an SBS server, should be physically located in a locked area and access to the location should be limited to just a few key company employees. This reduces the risks of theft, accidental damage, and the temptation for employees to use the server as a desktop workstation, which could lead to the inadvertent loading of viruses or other malware on the server.

Securing the server computer is more than just protecting it and the data it contains from theft. Environmental issues can cause just as much damage. When Tropical Storm Allison struck the Texas coast and dumped rain on the area for five days in 2001, the resulting flood caught many IT operations off guard. Several data centers were destroyed outright because they were housed in otherwise secure locations underground that were not immune to the flooding. Those centers have now been rebuilt in secure areas above ground to eliminate flooding risks.

Water damage comes from more than just flooding. Broken water and sewer lines running above a server room can destroy a server computer with a much smaller volume of water. Not to mention fire, electrical spikes, or even spilled coffee.

Of course, physical security can be taken to the extreme, but many small businesses simply cannot afford these extreme measures. But just because an extreme security solution cannot be implemented does not mean that no attempt to secure the server physically should be made.

The location of the server should be selected in such a way as to minimize the risks of the physical world as much as possible. How many times have you heard the story of the server that was shutting down unexpectedly every night, only to find out that the janitorial staff was unplugging the server from the wall to plug in the floor sweeper? Although this story may be urban legend, it demonstrates the point that even when you think you have complete control over your environment, you may not.

One physical security aspect often overlooked is the ambient temperature of the area where the server is located. If the server is stored with other heat-generating equipment in a confined space, the air temperature in that space will be higher than in other areas. Prolonged exposure to higher temperatures reduces the server's capability to vent heat out of the computer enclosure, which results in a shorter life span for the computer components most sensitive to heat.

Small businesses may not have the physical or financial resources to protect their network resources in an enterprise-class server room, but you should still make every effort to ensure that the server is as physically protected as possible.

Best Practice—Power Protection

Without fail, one of the most compromised aspects of server security is power protection. An uninterruptible power supply (UPS) is an absolute necessity to help protect an SBS installation, yet there are many times when no UPS is used, or if one is put into place, it does not have sufficient capacity.

As the price of small office sized UPS systems continues to drop, it becomes easier for the small business consultant to justify obtaining a larger UPS unit than the client might otherwise agree to. The general guideline for what size UPS to purchase is not really measured in amp-hours or system uptime in case of failure. The general rule is "buy as much as you can afford."

Most UPS systems now include monitoring software that can be installed on the server so that the server is alerted when the UPS goes on battery power. Many consumer-grade units include a USB connection from the UPS to the server, but a unit that has a serial (RS-232) connection should be used to connect to a server. Although the SBS community at large is still split over the stability of using USB devices on a server, an RS-232 serial connection does and will work reliably and should be selected if there is any doubt whether a USB interface will be reliable enough to protect the server.

Ideally, a UPS for a server should have only the server and possibly the server monitor connected to it. A UPS with more than one computer connected is going to have a shorter uptime during a power failure than if the server alone is connected. The amount of uptime is important, especially when the server is monitoring the UPS device, so that the server has plenty of time to perform a normal shutdown when the UPS goes on battery power.

File-Level Security

One of the biggest challenges for new system administrators, whether running SBS or another of the Windows Server products, is understanding how permissions on files and folders works. Even those who have worked with Windows server products for years can get confused from time to time. The next two sections of the chapter cover the basics of both NTFS file permissions and share permissions and the interaction between the two. It also covers the default NTFS and share permissions on several key directories unique to an SBS installation.

NTFS File Permissions

Prior to Windows NT, the Microsoft Windows file system had no security. Anyone who could physically access the PC could access all files on the volume. With Windows NT, Microsoft introduced the NT File System (NTFS) and the concept of file-level security to workstations and servers. The implementation of NTFS has matured with each release of the server product line, but the essential principles remain the same.

NTFS permissions can be applied at the file or folder level. These permissions can be viewed or modified in the Security tab of the object properties window. Figure 9.1 shows the default NTFS permissions on the root of drive `C:` on an SBS 2003 installation. Figure 9.2 shows the permissions for the file `boot.ini` in the root of drive `C:`. As you can see in the two figures, different permissions are available for volume/folder permissions than for file permissions. Tables 9.1 and 9.2 outline the permission settings for both the volume/folder permissions and file permissions.

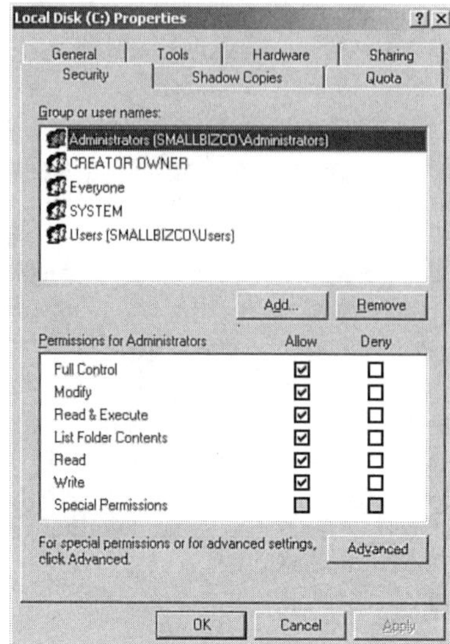

FIGURE 9.1 NTFS permissions for the `C:` volume in a default SBS installation.

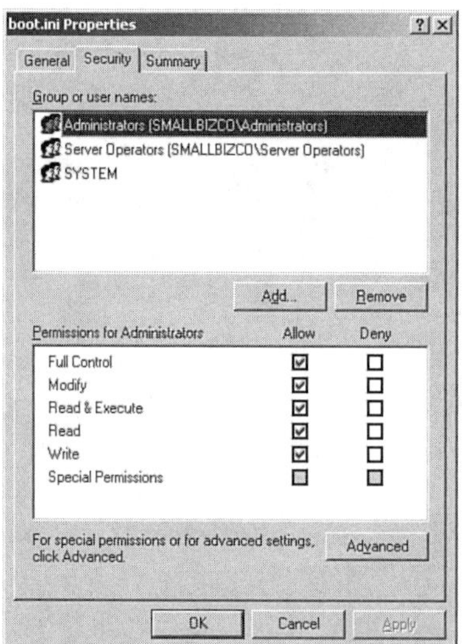

FIGURE 9.2 NTFS permissions for the `boot.ini` file.

TABLE 9.1 NTFS Volume/Folder Permissions

Permission	Action
Read	Allows objects to read the contents of a volume/folder, including file attributes and permissions
Write	Allows objects to create new files and folders within a volume/folder, write attributes on files and folders, and can read permissions and attributes on files and folders

TABLE 9.1 Continued

Permission	Action
List Folder Contents	Grants objects the same rights as the Read permission but also enables the object to traverse the full folder path
Read & Execute	Gives objects the same rights as the List Folder Contents permission and allows objects to execute programs stored in the volume/folder
Modify	Gives objects the same rights as the Read, Write, List Folder Contents, and Read & Execute permissions and allows objects to delete files and folders within the volume/folder
Full Control	Gives objects full access to the contents of the volume/folder as well as the capability to change permissions and take ownership

TABLE 9.2 NTFS File Permissions

Permission	Action
Read	Allows objects to read the contents of the file, including attributes and permissions
Write	Allows objects to change the contents of a file and read but not change the attributes and permissions
Read & Execute	Grants objects the same access as the Read permission and allows objects to execute a program file
Modify	Grants objects the same access as the Read, Write, and Read & Execute permissions, as well as allowing objects to delete the file
Full Control	Grants objects full access to the file, as well as the capability to change permissions and take ownership

Applying NTFS Permissions

Viewing and modifying the NTFS permissions on a file or folder is done through the Security tab of the Properties page on the file or folder, as shown previously in Figures 9.1 and 9.2. Different permissions can be applied to different security groups or individual user objects as necessary.

Some special security groups exist in this realm that are not used elsewhere in a Windows network. One in particular is the Creator/Owner group. The membership of this group cannot be modified directly. Instead, when a user creates a file in a folder, that user becomes the creator/owner of that file, and permissions assigned to that group apply to that user for the files she owns in the folder.

Permission assignments are cumulative. For example, suppose that the account `jondough` is a member of both the Domain Users group and a custom group called Accounting. In a directory on the server where accounting files are stored, the Domain Users group is given Read permissions but nothing else. The Accounting group is given Write permissions but nothing else. The effective permissions for `jondough`, because he is a member of both groups, are Read and Write for the files in the folder.

Allow and Deny Permissions

When assigning permissions to a user or group, you can choose to Allow or Deny the permission in the assignment. Selecting Allow in the permissions list grants the permission to the user or group. Selecting Deny in the permissions list revokes that permission from the user or group. The Deny permission almost always overrides an Allow permission when an object has both permissions assigned through multiple groups.

Taking another look at the example in the previous section, suppose that the system administrator wanted to make sure that Domain Users could not write to any files in the Accounting folder and only members of the Accounting group could. If the system administrator assigns the Deny Write permission to Domain Users, the user `jondough` would not be able to write to any files in the folder. His effective permissions would be Allow Write from the Accounting group and Deny Write from the Domain Users group, and because Deny takes higher priority over Allow, he would not be able to write to any files in this folder.

CAUTION

Using the Deny permission without careful forethought can lead to significant problems with file permissions. If Deny permissions are assigned to the Domain Users group, every account in the domain will be locked out of that permission for that folder. For that reason, it is best not to apply the Deny permission to Domain Users for anything other than Read and Write permissions. If the Deny permission is applied to Modify or Full Control for the Domain Users, the folder effectively becomes locked out for all users because no account would then have permission to go back in and make changes to the permissions on the objects.

Permission Inheritance

When permissions are set on a folder, those same permissions also apply to all the files and subfolders within that folder as well. By default, all objects in a folder inherit the permissions of the parent folder unless a separate set of permissions has been applied to the object. When viewing the permissions of an object, inherited permissions appear grayed out in the Security tab, indicating that those permissions were applied to one of the parent folders of the object.

Inherited permissions for an object can be turned off in the Advanced Security Settings window. Click on the Advanced button in the Security tab to open this dialog. Figure 9.3 details the Advanced Security Settings dialog for the `C:\Windows\config` folder.

In the Permissions tab, you can see all the security groups that have been granted permission to the folder and the location from which the permissions were inherited. The Allow Inheritable Permissions from the Parent to Propagate to This Object and All Child Objects check box is enabled, indicating that this folder should inherit all permissions from the parent folder, which is `C:\Windows` in this case. If any additional permissions had been assigned at this level, this check box would also propagate those permissions to child objects in addition to the inherited permissions.

If you wanted to remove permission inheritance and create a completely new set of permissions on the folder, click this check box to turn it off. On doing so, you are presented with a Security dialog box asking what you want to do with the permissions. You can Copy the permissions, which creates a new set of permissions matching the settings that had been inherited, or Remove the permissions, which clears all settings. If you choose to Remove the settings, be sure to grant sufficient settings that you can later go back and modify the permissions before you apply the changes and close the Properties dialog. Doing this without granting additional permissions first can yield the folder inaccessible.

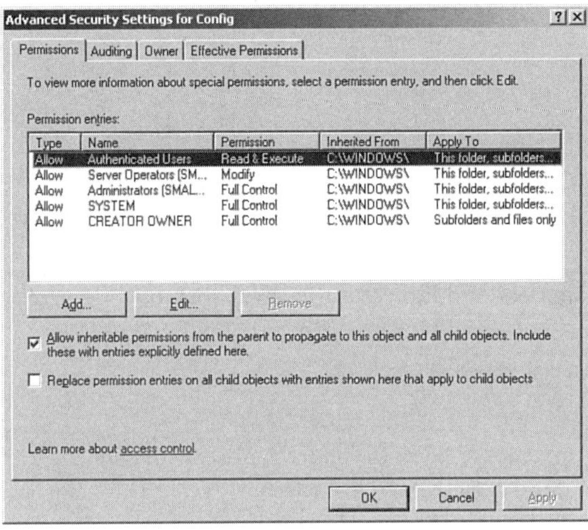

FIGURE 9.3 The Advanced Security Settings window.

With Windows 2003, the permission inheritance rules for the Deny permission were modified slightly. In previous NTFS implementations, a Deny permission applied to all subfolders and files through inheritance and could not be overridden. In the 2003 implementation, however, an explicit Allow permission can override an inherited Deny permission. Going back to the example used earlier in the chapter, if the Domain Users group is given the Deny Write permission on the Accounting folder, no users in the domain will be able to write to any files within that folder. Suppose that a subfolder of Accounting, called 2005 for example, has the Allow Write permissions assigned to the Accounting group. Even though the Deny permission is inherited from the parent folder, the explicit Allow Write permission overrides the Deny, and members of the Accounting group will be able to write to files in the 2005 folder.

Special Permissions

In addition to the standard permissions listed previously in Tables 9.1 and 9.2, Special Permissions can be applied to a file or folder. These Special Permissions are essentially subsets of the regular permissions that allow you to fine-tune the access you may want to grant to a particular set of users. These special permissions are accessed by either adding a new permission entry in the Advanced Security Settings dialog or by editing an existing security entry. Figure 9.4 shows the Permission Entry page for an object, and Table 9.3 details the Special Permissions and their capabilities.

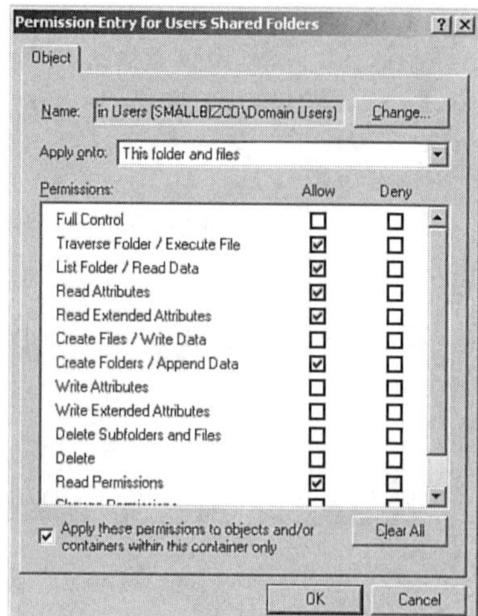

FIGURE 9.4 NTFS Special Permissions for the Users Shared Folders folder.

TABLE 9.3 NTFS Special Permissions

Permission	Action
Traverse Folder/ Execute File	For folders, allows the object to navigate through the subfolder structure on disk. For files, allows the object to execute a program file store in the folder.
List Folder/ Read Data	For folders, allows an object to see the names of files and subfolders. For files, allows an object to view the contents of the file.
Read Attributes	Allows an object to view the attributes of a file or folder.
Read Extended Attributes	Allows an object to view the extended attributes of a file or folder. Extended attributes are generally defined by an application and vary from program to program.
Create Files/ Write Data	For folders, allows an object to create new files within the folder. For files, allows an object to change or replace the contents, but not the attributes, of a file.
Create Folders/ Append Data	For folders, allows an object to create new subfolders within the folder. For files, allows an object to append data to the end of an existing file but not to alter the remaining contents of the file.
Write Attributes	Allows an object to modify the attributes on an existing file or folder within the folder.
Write Extended Attributes	Allows an object to modify the extended attributes on an existing file or folder within the folder.
Delete Subfolders and Files	Allows an object to delete a file or subfolder, even if the standard Delete permission has not been granted.
Delete	Allows an object to delete a file from the current folder.
Read Permissions	Allows an object to view the security permissions on a file or folder.
Change Permissions	Allows an object to modify the security permissions on a file or folder.
Take Ownership	Allows an object to change the owner information on a file or folder to the object.
Full Control	Allows an object to perform all Special Permissions.

Ownership

One other item available in the Advanced permissions window is the Owner tab, shown in Figure 9.5. In this window, you can see who owns a particular file or folder, and you can change the object that owns the file or folder. File ownership affects two aspects of the object. First, file ownership is used to calculate space used against disk quotas, if quotas are enabled. Second, the owner of a file has the permissions assigned to the Creator/Owner group for the folder assigned to the owner for that file.

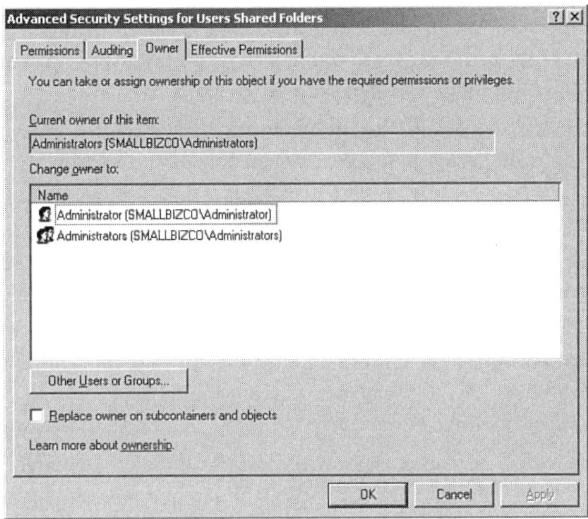

FIGURE 9.5 The Owner tab for the Users Shared Folders folder.

With Windows Server 2003, Microsoft has provided a new command-line tool to work with file ownership—`takeown`. This tool can be used by an administrator to either take ownership of the object or assign ownership of the object to another user on the network. Table 9.4 lists the command-line parameters for the tool.

TABLE 9.4 Command-Line Parameters for `takeown.exe`

Parameter	Action
`/F filename`	Changes the owner of the file or files specified by *`filename`*. *`filename`* can be the name of a single file or a wildcard pattern to change multiple files.
`/A`	Changes the owner of the file or files to the Administrators group instead of the user who runs the tool.
`/R`	Changes all files in the directory specified with the `/F` parameter and its subfolders.
`/S` *`system`*	Forces the `takeown` action to occur on the remote computer *`system`*.
`/U [`*`domain`*`\]`*`user`*	Changes the file owner to the user specified by *`user`* and the optional domain specified by *`domain`*.
`/P [`*`password`*`]`	Uses the password specified by *`password`* to authenticate as the user specified with the `/U` flag. Prompts for a password if none is specified.

To change the owner of a file in the current directory to the currently logged-on user, enter **`takeown /f filename`** at the command prompt. In addition to wildcards, environment variables can also be used with the tool. For example, `takeown /f %windir%\*.txt /r /a` would change ownership of all the `.txt` files in the Windows system directory and all its subdirectories to the Administrators group. You must have Modify permissions or the Take Ownership special permission to change ownership on a file or folder.

Best Practice—Setting NTFS Permissions

Setting permissions on files and folders can lead to great confusion when trying to sort out what access an object has to a particular file or folder if some thought is not given in advance. Follow these guidelines when setting permissions on a file or folder.

Set as few permissions as necessary. The more permissions are set, the more potential for conflicting permissions that result in incorrect access to files and folders.

Set permissions based on security groups, not individual user objects. If special access is needed for an area of a folder tree, create a special security group for that access and assign permissions to that group. Then add or remove users to the group as necessary. It is easier to modify the group memberships on a user object to change the access needed on the file system than try to remember every place that user object was given permissions in the file system.

Use the Deny permission sparingly. It is often better to remove permission settings for a file/folder than to attempt to Deny access to the object. Misapplying the Deny setting can cause many unintended permissions conflicts. Never apply the Deny permission to the Everyone group.

Set permissions on folders instead of files where possible. If radically different permissions are needed on a single file in a folder with many other files, a better solution may be to move the file in question to a different location with different permissions.

Leave the default permissions as defaults. Unless you have a good reason, there is generally no need to modify the permissions on any objects within the `c:\Windows` folder, the `c:\inetpub` folder, the `Program Files` folder (especially the `Exchsrvr` folder), or any of the other default folders. Permissions within the Users Shared Folder can be modified as needed to allow access to files between users, but those changes should be made at the user folder level, not at the parent folder.

Encrypted File System

Another security feature included with NTFS is the Encrypted File System. When applied, files marked as encrypted are unreadable by other users. This additional level of protection can keep sensitive data secure even if NTFS permissions are modified to grant access to the folders where the encrypted files are stored.

File encryption uses the user's domain certificate to encrypt the file. By default, only two accounts can access the contents of a file after it has been encrypted—the user who encrypted the file and the domain Administrator account. The domain Administrator account is the default Recovery Agent that can access the contents of the file in case the user is no longer able to access the file, either because of a certificate problem or because the user is no longer with the company.

File encryption can be enabled on a file or a folder. When encryption is set on a folder, all the existing contents of the folder and any new items put into that folder will be encrypted. Likewise, individual files within a folder that has been marked for encryption can have the encryption removed.

File encryption can be enabled on server shares as well as local file paths. Follow these steps to set up encryption for a folder on a domain share:

1. Right-click on the desired folder and select Properties.
2. In the General tab, click Advanced.
3. In the Advanced Attributes dialog box, enable the Encrypt Contents to Secure Data check box as shown in Figure 9.6.

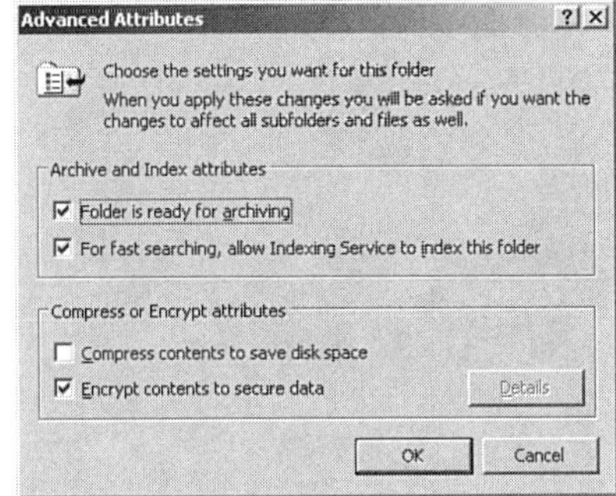

FIGURE 9.6 Folder encryption settings in the Advanced Attributes dialog.

4. Click OK to close the Advanced Attributes dialog.
5. Click Apply to encrypt the files within the folder, and then click OK to close the folder Properties dialog.

Share-Level Security

Shares give domain users access to areas of the server disk across the network. SBS system administrators are familiar with a number of these shares, including the Users Shared Folders share. These network shares have their own security permissions that determine whether and how a user account will access the share. Table 9.5 describes the different share permissions available.

9

TABLE 9.5 Share Permissions

Permission	Description
Read	Allows objects to see file and folder names, open files and programs, and see file and folder attributes for objects stored within the share
Change	Allows objects to create new files and folders, modify contents, delete files and folders, and modify file attributes in addition to the actions allowed by the Read permission
Full Control	In addition to the actions allowed by the Read and Change permissions, allows objects to change permissions on files and take ownership of files

These share permissions work in conjunction with the NTFS permissions that have been assigned to the file path on the server. This is possibly the single most confusing aspect of Windows system administration for new and experienced admins alike. When dealing with share and NTFS permissions in combination, the more restrictive permission is the one that wins out. Table 9.6 shows the effective permissions for various combinations of share and NTFS permissions.

TABLE 9.6 Share and NTFS Permissions in Combination

Share Permission	NTFS Permission	Effective Permission
Read	Modify	Read
Change	Full Control	Modify
Read	Full Control	Read
Full Control	Read	Read
Full Control	Full Control	Full Control

Share permissions are accessed in the Sharing tab of a folder's Properties dialog box by clicking on the Permissions button. This brings up the Share Permissions dialog, shown in Figure 9.7, which shows the default share permissions for the Users Shared Folders folder.

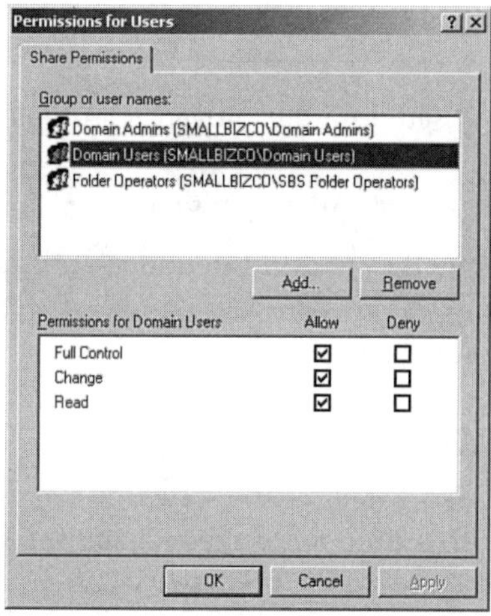

FIGURE 9.7 Share Permissions for the Users share.

Of the three groups listed in the dialog box, two should be familiar to most Windows administrators—Domain Admins and Domain Users. By default, the Domain Users group is given Full Control permission for the share because the user needs Full Control access to her folder inside the Users share. The Domain Admins group is also given Full Control over the share so that the administrators can manage access to resources through the share and not just from the server console.

The third group may not be as familiar—the Folder Operators group, which is also given Full Control permissions by default. This group is created by the SBS installation, and members of the group are able to manage shared folders on the server and in Active Directory. This group contains the Domain Power Users group by default, so any account created as a Power User will be able to manage shared folders on the SBS network.

Like the NTFS permissions dialog, the individual permissions can be set to Allow or Deny. Just like with NTFS permissions, the Deny permission overrides the Allow permission, so care must be taken when setting the Deny permission on a shared folder.

Best Practice—Setting Shared Folder Permissions

In general, the Domain Users group should be given Full Control permissions on a share where user data is stored. This allows you to restrict access to areas within the share with NTFS permissions, if needed.

When you create a new share using the Share a Folder Wizard, you are given several options for setting share permissions. You can choose from the following options:

- All users have read-only access.
- Administrators and Folder Operators have full access; other users have read-only access.
- Administrators and Folder Operators have full access; other users have read and write access.
- Use custom share and folder permissions.

To give the Domain Users group Full Control, you must select the last option and enter the permissions manually.

Remember that setting share permissions affects how users access data through the share. If the Domain Admins group is given only Read permission on the share, a member of the group will be unable to modify any settings on files and folders when accessed through the share. When a member of the Domain Admins group accesses the files from the server console, only the NTFS permissions will apply.

Password Security

Password security is a topic that can generate a lot of heated discussions among users and system administrators alike. The lines are generally divided between having passwords that are difficult to guess or crack by a malicious outsider and having passwords that are easy for users to remember without having to write them down (which would make it easier for a malicious outsider to access). Even when these parties agree that more secure passwords should be used, the argument can then turn to enforcement and implementation.

SBS 2003 contains several tools to help make managing secure passwords easier for the system administrator. The primary element is the Small Business Server Domain Password Policy group policy object that is applied to the SBS domain. The settings in this policy object can be managed through several SBS wizards. At the end of the Connect to the Internet and the Repair Internet and E-mail Settings Wizards, if the password policies have not been enabled, the user running those wizards is asked whether he wants to enable the password policies. The policies are primarily managed through the Configure Password Policies Wizard found in the Users section of the Server Management Console.

Configure Password Policies

Figure 9.8 shows the Configure Password Policies dialog box. The password policy is broken down into three requirements: password length, password complexity, and password age.

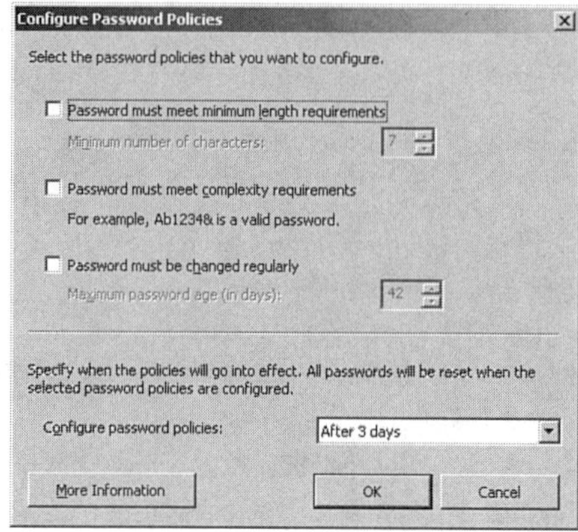

FIGURE 9.8 The Configure Password Policies dialog box allows the administrator to make password restrictions as tough or as lax as desired.

Password Length

When the Password Must Meet Minimum Length Requirements check box is enabled, all users are forced to have a password with at least as many characters as identified in the setting. The general rule is that the longer the password is, the tougher it is to break, even when password-cracking tools are used. When this setting is enabled, a number from 0–14 can be used as the minimum length. When the value is set to 0, or if this option is not selected, a user account can have a blank password, which is generally not desired.

Just because a password is long does not necessarily mean that it is secure. The password "smallbusinesscompany" would meet a minimum length requirement of 14 characters, but is still not a very secure password. Setting a minimum password length alone is not enough to ensure a secure password.

Password Complexity

When the Password Must Meet Complexity Requirements check box is enabled, all users must have a password that meets Windows password complexity rules. The Windows rules are made up of two sections. The first part of the rules prevents a user from using all or part of his username or logon ID as part of the password. The second part of the rule is that the password must contain characters from three of the following four character groups:

- Uppercase characters
- Lowercase characters
- Numeric characters (0–9)
- Non-alphanumeric characters (!, @, #, $, and so on)

The Configure Password Policies dialog box gives the password "Ab1234&" as a password that would meet complexity requirements. It contains characters from all four of the character groups, and so long as the account name does not start with "ab" or have "1234" in the ID, it should work for most user accounts.

Making a password complex also makes it more difficult to remember. One currently used method to help make complex passwords easy to remember is to use pass phrases or acronyms based on longer passages. For example, you might take a phrase from a Dr. Seuss book, such as "Oh, the places you will go!" and convert that into a pass phrase. With a few tweaks, that phrase might turn into the password "0tpUwg!" which uses characters from all four character groups (the number 0 for the word "oh", upper- and lowercase letters, and a special character "!").

NOTE

Some non-alphanumeric characters can be used in passwords but could cause problems when being accessed from some systems. For example, the "!" and "@" characters have special meanings in most UNIX systems and might not be passed along as part of the password.

Again, only setting complexity requirements may not be enough to create a secure password. For example, the password "B0b!" would meet complexity requirements, but because of its length, it might not take long to crack.

Password Age

Even the best passwords are of no use of they have been compromised. If a malicious outsider somehow learns a user's password, even if the password is long and complex, the outsider will be able to access that user's account until that password is changed. Thus the notion of changing passwords on a regular basis comes into play. When the Password Must Be Changed Regularly check box is enabled, all users will not be able to keep their passwords longer than the value listed. The Windows default for this setting is 42 days, but the value can be set anywhere from 0 to 999.

Many enterprise environments set password expiration between 30 and 90 days depending on their environment and level of risk. Generally, if the risk of password compromise is low, a longer password age can be set. If the risk is high, a shorter password age should be set.

Policy Enforcement

When a change is made to the password policies you can specify when the updated policies will go into effect by selecting a value from the Configure Password Policies drop-down list. The selections range from Immediately, which puts the new policy into effect as soon as you click OK, to 7 days, which gives you a week to alert your users to the new password requirements and give them time to make changes. After the policy goes into effect, a user with a password that does not match the policy will be unable to access the network until the password is changed to one that meets the new requirements. For that reason, it is best to set the policy enforcement out several days to give you and your client time to address any questions or concerns that may arise before the policy goes into effect.

Small Business Server Domain Password Policy Group Policy Object

The Configure Password Policies Wizard is a friendly front end that modifies the settings in the Small Business Server Domain Password Policy group policy object. Although the best way to modify settings in this object is to use the wizard, an understanding of how the policy looks can help if problems arise related to password issues.

The Small Business Server Domain Password Policy object can be found in the Server Management Console, under Advanced Management, Group Policy Management, Forest:, Domains, [*internal domain name*]. To bring up the policy in the Group Policy Object Editor, right-click on the policy object and select Edit. The settings related to password policy are found under Computer Configuration, Windows Settings, Security Settings, Account Policies, Password Policy, as shown in Figure 9.9.

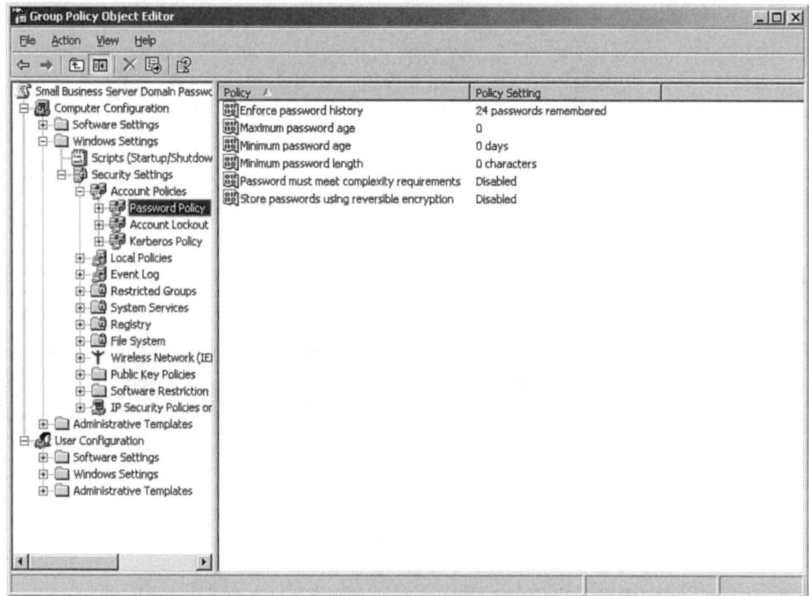

FIGURE 9.9 The policy elements for the Small Business Server Domain Password Policy object.

> **NOTE**
> For more information about managing group policy objects, see Chapter 20, "Group Policy."

You can see in Figure 9.9 that there are more options for password policy in the group policy object than can be set in the Configure Password Policies Wizard. The Enforce Password History, Minimum Password Age, and Store Passwords Using Reversible Encryption elements can be modified only in this environment. The first two of these elements can be used to keep users from changing their password when required and then changing back to a previously used value. Windows systems default to remembering the last 24 passwords that have been used, which is the maximum value. With this setting enabled, a user would have to change his password 24 times before being able to use a previous password again. The Minimum Password Age element specifies how often a user can change his password. With the default value of 0, a user can change a password as many times as desired during the same day. Increasing this value prevents a user from changing a password more than one time on any given day. The intent, of course, is to discourage users from changing their passwords rapidly to get through the stored password history and get back to the password they had been using.

The Store Passwords Using Reversible Encryption policy should never be changed from the default value of Disabled. With this setting, passwords are stored in Active Directory using one-way encryption, meaning that if someone were to get a copy of the encrypted password, she could not determine the original password. If this setting is changed to Enabled, the password is stored using two-way encryption, meaning that the original password can be calculated if the encrypted password is captured.

Any changes made to the policy object in this interface take effect the next time group policy is updated for the server and workstations, or the update can be forced using the **`gpupdate /force`** command on the server and workstations. Any changes made to the password history, minimum password age, and reversible encryption elements will not be changed by subsequent runs of the Configure Password Policies Wizard.

Best Practice—Setting Password Requirements

First, enable password policies on the SBS server. The degree of security applied to the password policy may vary from location to location, but the organization should be held to a common password policy.

Second, encourage users not to use their SBS password for any other password-enabled services. Many users use the same password for several network services to help them remember those passwords more easily. If the user uses her SBS password for a POP3 mail account, that password is transmitted across the Internet in clear text where a malicious outsider can capture it.

Third, set a maximum password age. Although this may not make you the most popular system administrator, it is a good mechanism to help counter any password compromises.

Finally, make sure that you have the buy-in from the company's management before implementing any password policies. Discuss the issues with the decision-makers and make sure that they understand the risks and benefits. But absolutely get their approval, or you may find that you or a different support organization is coming back in to reset the password policies.

Troubleshooting Security Issues

The most common problems encountered related to the security issues covered in this chapter are permissions problems, usually because someone made a change to the permissions on a file or folder without checking to see what the possible impact would be. Fortunately, there are tools and straightforward processes to check to see what and where security permissions have been set.

Common Access Problems

The following are commonly encountered problems related to file/folder access:

- Lack of permissions—A user is expecting to be able to access a file or folder but cannot because permissions have not been set on the file or folder. The user may not belong to a group that does have the desired permissions, or the permissions may not have been applied.
- Too many permissions—A common reaction of an inexperienced system administrator is to simply grant Full Control to more and more groups until access issues are resolved. Often having the system wide open is more problematic than being too restrictive.
- Permission conflicts—In most cases, conflicts occur when a Deny permission is set and yields unexpected results. In many cases, restricting access to resources can be better handled by removing permissions than by denying them.
- Files or folders moved or copied—When files and folders are moved or copied to different volumes using Explorer, the permission settings may not transfer as expected. After copying a set of files or folders, double-check the resulting permissions to see that they match those of the original location.
- NTFS and share permissions in conflict—When NTFS and share permissions are not in sync, users generally report that they have limited access to the files they are trying to use.

Although there is no guaranteed, one-size-fits-all rulebook for troubleshooting access problems, some general steps can be followed to help identify where the problem lies:

1. Listen, listen, and then listen some more. When an access problem is described, try to get an understanding of exactly what is happening. The best technician is going to be less effective if the problem is not understood fully. Take the time up front to get as much detail as possible before heading down the wrong troubleshooting path.
2. Examine group memberships for the user in question. In most SBS environments, group memberships will not change much from the defaults applied when the user account is created. However, if a user belongs to two groups that have conflicting permissions on a file or folder, looking first at the group membership may help quickly find the source of the conflict.
3. Examine the files or folders that are being accessed. Sometimes it's best to look for the obvious before hunting down the obscure. Check to make sure that the files or folders exist in the expected location. Check for read-only flags on files. Look to see whether explicit NTFS permissions have been assigned to files instead of the containing folders, and then ask why. Check for the presence of the CREATOR OWNER group and that it has appropriate permissions. Look up the folder path to see whether any Deny permissions have been set along the way.
4. Check the permissions on the share being used to access the files and folders. Look to see whether multiple shares have been created to access the same folder on the

server volume. Different shares can be assigned different permissions, which can lead to confusion. Make sure that the share has the same desired maximum permissions that are assigned in the NTFS permissions.

Effective Permissions

One quick way to see whether a user has the permissions expected in a folder is to look at the user's effective permissions for that folder. When a user belongs to multiple groups, or multiple permission assignments have been inherited down a folder tree, it may not be readily apparent what permissions the user actually has in a given location. Fortunately, the Effective Permissions tool can display that information without much time or effort.

The Effective Permissions tab is located in the Advanced Settings dialog box of a file or folder's Security settings, as shown in Figure 9.10. To verify user or group NTFS permissions settings, open the Effective Permissions tab, click Select, identify the appropriate object, and click OK. When the dialog updates, you see the permissions that the user or group has on the particular file or folder. In this example, if the user Jayne Dough was reporting problems saving files into a directory, you could see from the Effective Permissions window that the account only had Read access to the folder.

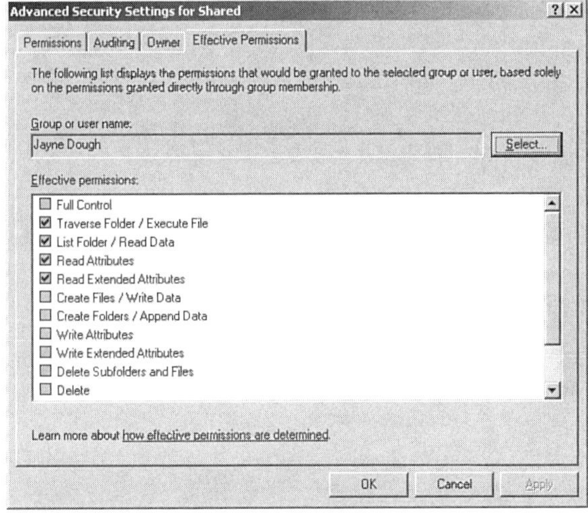

FIGURE 9.10 Viewing effective permissions for a user on a folder.

Summary

This chapter examined several aspects of security for an SBS installation. The physical security of the server computer should not be overlooked. Keeping the server away from common areas reduces the chance of accidental disconnection or damage. Providing adequate power and temperature protection helps maintain the integrity of data on the server.

Server data is protected with a combination of NTFS and share permissions. NTFS permissions are applied to files and folders and allow users to read, write, modify, and delete files. Individual permissions can be either allowed or denied, with the Deny permission having higher precedence than the Allow permission. All files and folders lower in the directory tree inherit permissions applied to a folder, unless explicitly removed and replaced with other permissions. NTFS special permissions allow for finer control of access to file resources. File ownership is used to calculate disk space used when disk quotas are enabled. The CREATOR OWNER group permissions apply only to the owner of a file. Files and folders on the server volumes can also be encrypted so that only the user and the Administrator can view the contents.

Share permissions determine the maximum level of access that a user can have to a shared directory on the server. Users and groups can be granted the ability to read files and folders, change files and folders, or have full control over the contents of the share. When share and NTFS permissions are applied in combination, the more restrictive of the permissions is applied.

Strong passwords provide another level of security for data on the server. Password policies can be put in place to ensure the continued security of passwords on the network. The password policy can control the minimum length, complexity, and age of passwords. The policy can be modified in two ways—by using the Change Password Policies Wizard or by modifying the Small Business Server Domain Password Policy group policy object directly. Unless the number of remembered passwords or the minimum password age values need to be modified, the wizard should be used to set password policy.

Best Practice Summary

- Power protection—With the continuing drop in the price of Uninterruptible Power Supplies (UPS), there are fewer reasons not to get a large unit. Use a UPS that has a serial connection to the server and monitoring software so that the server can shut down normally in case of an extended power outage.
- Setting NTFS permissions—Set as few permissions as possible to avoid unnecessary confusion. Apply permissions to security groups, not to individual user objects. Avoid using the Deny permission, and never apply the Deny permission to the Everyone group. Apply permissions to folders instead of files. Leave default permissions as defaults and do not modify permissions on the root of `C:` or the Windows directory.
- Setting shared folder permissions—Give Domain Users Full Control permissions on shares and use NTFS permissions to restrict access. When accessing data through a share, the more restrictive of the share and NTFS permissions apply.
- Setting password requirements—Enable password policies on the server. Encourage users not to use their SBS password for any other accounts. Set a maximum password age, but be reasonable. Get support from business management prior to implementing password policies.

CHAPTER 10

Workstation Security

IN THIS CHAPTER

- Windows XP Service Pack 2
- Local Administrator Access for Users
- Antivirus Tools
- Antispyware Tools
- The Managed Network
- Let's Not Forget About Office
- The Educated End User and Security Review Process
- Protecting Data from the Inside
- Troubleshooting Workstation Security

Once upon a time, the network consultant worried most about the threat from the floppy drive. At one time all viruses and all attacks on the network barring physical attacks came from a worker at the office placing a disk in a drive and launching a file. At that time most viruses attached themselves to a Word file or perhaps even a boot sector. As long as the antivirus software was kept up-to-date on the workstation, you were relatively assured that you could stay one step ahead of the virus. Viruses spread through *sneakernets*, the slang description for a bunch of computers whose means of transporting files was having a floppy disk moved from one computer to another. Thus, like in a virus infection in humans, physical contact was key to transmitting the computer virus in most small networks.

But as technology connects us every moment of our lives, so too has the capability for viruses to be transmitted increased. When the networks that most of us rely on were first designed, there was no need to put protections for workstations inside the office. All we needed to protect networks was a well-designed, well-defended perimeter. But then two inventions changed the way we do computing forever—and changed the boundaries of our network.

The laptop and the Internet moved the boundaries of computer networks away from the ISA Server and Cisco Pix and into the homes of small businesses. It moved the threat window from the time it took to move infected files around via floppy disks to now where within 24 hours, proof of concept of exploit code is posted on the Web. You must think of workstation security as protecting someone from an epidemic. What is the best protection for an infectious disease? Ensuring that you are not exposed in the first place and obtaining inoculations when you realize you cannot remove all the risk of exposure. The computer world is no different. There are three tenets to risk management in a network:

- Accept the risk.
- Mitigate the risk.
- Transfer the risk.

This chapter assumes that you have completed the process of identifying those assets in the firm you need to protect. You have identified those databases and devices that contain the data you need to most protect due to regulation or other requirements. Typically, for most firms, this is a category of data called *personal identity information (PII)*. In the healthcare industry, this data is *electronic patient healthcare information (ePHI)*. Both PII and ePHI have as their risk factors, a risk of business impact due to the required disclosure laws now on the books in many locations. Furthermore one could argue that sitting down and making a reasonable determination of the risk factors in your network is both a good business practice to ensure that your security dollars are well spent and just good business period. If your firm and your clientele depend on a source of data for your revenue above all other pieces of data on your network, this process will help you and your clients streamline that data and assign the proper protection.

Traditionally in risk management there is an equation that allows you to put a dollar value, a budget in place:

$$ARO \times SLE = ALE$$

You first look at the *annualized rate of occurrence (ARO)* for these events. What historically has been the impact of viruses? Then you determine the *single loss expectancy (SLE)* for the risk, which is based on the costs to clean up from the risk. Multiply the two to determine the *annual loss expectancy (ALE)* to determine whether it's less expensive to "clean up from the mess" or to "prevent the mess" in the first place. That amount you calculate—the dollar amount to clean up the machines—should be less than the cost of the item needed to prevent the event from occurring in the first place. If it is not, there is no question that prevention is cheaper than cleaning up.

Best Practice—Security Budget Calculation

Sit down early on with your client and determine the client's environment and level of tolerance for security issues. Setting this budget early in a proactive way will help you set forth the design goals of the network.

Although this chapter focuses on some key processes to ensure more protection of the workstations, should always keep in mind this equation and the overall part that workstations play in the security of your network. Your best protective device may not be technology at all; it may in fact be an educated end user. Make sure that in your budget of security actions you also remember that education will go a long way to the overall security of your network.

Network threat modeling is a relatively new concept but is key for any size firm. Understanding where your data if stored and flowing and the appropriate amount of resources to apply to protecting that key data is more an art than a science.

Windows XP Service Pack 2

When Windows XP was shipped, it was built for the threats and risks on the Internet at that time. But then the world changed, and so did the operating system. Although XP Service Pack 2 is merely called a "service pack," there are many changes, enough to arguably call it nearly a new operating system. The reason that administrators have taken time to deploy it is indeed due to these changes and the interaction with line-of-business applications.

The major changes for XP SP2 include the Windows Firewall, Internet Explorer, Outlook Express, Data Execution Prevention, Automatic Updates, and the Security Center. These changes are detailed in the following sections.

Windows Firewall

First and foremost, in Windows XP SP2, the firewall is enabled by default for standalone workstations and when joined to the SBS domain, has minimal ports exposed for optimum network connectivity. The administrator then has two options: Allow the end user to manually add applications exceptions to work through the firewall, or allow the exception via group policy at the server level. Regardless of the choice taken, keep in mind that it is safer to build a firewall exception for the application instead of building a port exception. The reason for this is that if you build a port exception, the port will remain open at all times. If you, instead, build an exception based on the application, when the application is not in use, the opening to the Internet will be closed.

For SBS 2003 SP1, the settings can be found in the Group Policy Management Console under Computer Configuration, Administrative Templates, Network, Network Connections, Windows Firewall.

There are two profiles: one is a Domain profile, and the other is a Standard profile for those times the machine is "off" the domain. The system understands when you are on and off the domain. Everything that is needed to ensure a near fully functioning workstation is prebuilt into the SBS 2003 SP1 platform.

Chapter 20, "Group Policy," covers the key elements of this group policy, but one area needs to be identified here as a potential issue with workstations, and that is antivirus settings. The policy in particular that allows an end user's machine to build its own exceptions is the following settings:

```
Windows Firewall:  Define Program Exceptions:  ENABLED
Windows Firewall:  Define Port Exceptions:  ENABLED
Windows Firewall:  Allow local port exceptions:  ENABLED
```

10

These settings are detailed in the following three sections.

`Windows Firewall:  Define Program Exceptions:  ENABLED`

From the Explanation inside the group policy screen, it states that Define Program Exceptions allow you to view and change the program exceptions list defined by group policy. Windows Firewall uses two program exception lists: One is defined by group policy settings, and the other is defined by the Windows Firewall component in Control Panel.

If you enable this policy setting, you can view and change the program exceptions list defined by group policy. If you add a program to this list and set its status to Enabled, that program can receive unsolicited incoming messages on any port that it asks Windows Firewall to open, even if that port is blocked by another policy setting, such as the Windows Firewall: Define Port Exceptions policy setting. To view the program list, enable the policy setting, and then click the Show button. To add a program, enable the policy setting, note the syntax, click the Show button, click the Add button, and then type a definition string that uses the syntax format. To remove a program, click its definition and then click the Remove button. To edit a definition, remove the current definition from the list and add a new one with different parameters. To allow administrators to add programs to the local program exceptions list that is defined by the Windows Firewall component in Control Panel, also enable the Windows Firewall: Allow Local Program Exceptions policy setting.

If you disable this policy setting, the program exceptions list defined by group policy is deleted. If a local program exceptions list exists, it is ignored unless you enable the Windows Firewall: Allow Local Program Exceptions policy setting.

The selections in this screen that are placed by the SBS preselections are

```
%WINDIR%\PCHealth\HelpCrt\Binaries\Helpctr.exe:*Enabled.Remote
➥Assistance - Windows Messenger and Voice
%WINDIR%\PCHealth\HelpCrt\Binaries\Helpsvc.exe:*Enabled.Offer
➥Remote Assistance
%WINDIR%\SYSTEM32\Sessmgr.exe: *Enabled:RemoteAssistance
```

`Windows Firewall:  Define Port Exceptions:  ENABLED`

The syntax here is Port, Transport, Scope, Status, and Name. Port is defined as a decimal port number, Transport is either TCP or UDP, Scope can be a "*" for all networks or specifically listing a range of IP addresses, Status is Enabled or Disabled, and Name is a text string.

In the case of SBS 2003 SP1, it's

```
135:TCP:*:Enabled:Offer Remote Assistance-Port
```

Remember though that it's better to build the exception based on the application name and not the port address.

`Windows Firewall:  Allow Local Port Exceptions:  ENABLED`

From the Explanation in the group policy console:

This setting allows administrators to use the Windows Firewall component in the Control Panel to define a local port exceptions list. Windows Firewall uses two port exceptions lists; the other is defined by the Windows Firewall: Define Port Exceptions policy setting.

If you enable this policy setting, the Windows Firewall component in the Control Panel allows administrators to define a local port exceptions list.

If you disable this policy setting, the Windows Firewall component in the Control Panel does not allow administrators to define a local port exceptions list.

If you do not configure this policy setting, the ability of administrators to define a local port exceptions list depends on the configuration of the Windows Firewall: Define Port Exceptions policy setting. If that setting is not configured, administrators can define a local port exceptions list. If it is enabled or disabled, administrators cannot define a local port exceptions list.

All these domain settings allow for full functioning of the network. In your environment you may need to add exceptions for antivirus or other programs. One of the easiest ways to determine what software is being blocked by the XP SP2 firewall is to review the blocked settings in the firewall log file located at `C:\WINDOWS\pfirewall.log` (ensuring that you have enabled the dropped packets logging).

Internet Explorer

The next major change is tighter security for Internet Explorer and additional options for control of ActiveX controls. ActiveX is the proprietary set of rules for how web browsers and programs should share information. ActiveX controls have full access to the operating system. As such, it can and historically has caused security issues. Therefore, as part of your overall security strategy, you can present those allowed ActiveX components using group policy as well.

The default for Windows XP SP2 is to disable the execution of ActiveX controls and Active Scripting in the Local Machine zone. Specifically the new settings are

- `URLACTION_ACTIVEX_ RUN`—Resolves to Disallow.
- `URLACTION_ACTIVEX_OVERRIDE_OBJECT_SAFETY`—Resolves to Disallow.
- `URLACTION_SCRIPT_ RUN`—Resolves to Prompt.
- `URLACTION_CROSS_DOMAIN_ DATA`—Resolves to Prompt.
- `URLACTION_BINARY_BEHAVIORS_BLOCK`—Resolves to Disallow.
- `URLACTION_JAVA_PERMISSIONS`—Resolves to Disallow.

Additional ActiveX Restrictions

In addition to the built-in protection, you can add additional restrictions via group policy as described in Microsoft KB article 883256 (`http://support.microsoft.com/?id=883256`).

For the SBS server, the XP SP2 template is already installed on the server. Click on Start, Run; then type **`gpedit.msc`**, and press Enter.

Expand Computer Configuration or User Configuration, Administrative Templates, Windows Components, Internet Explorer, and Security Features, and then click on Add-on Management.

Under there are two settings. The first, Deny All Add-ons Unless Specifically Allowed in the Add-on List, enables the Deny setting.

From the Explanation:

This policy setting allows you to ensure that any Internet Explorer add-ons not listed in the Add-on List policy setting are denied.

By default, the Add-on List policy setting defines a list of add-ons to be allowed or denied through group policy. However, users can still use the Add-on Manager within Internet Explorer to manage add-ons not listed within the Add-on List policy setting. This policy setting effectively removes this option from users; all add-ons are assumed to be denied unless they are specifically allowed through the Add-on List policy setting.

If you enable this policy setting, Internet Explorer allows only add-ons specifically listed (and allowed) through the Add-on List policy setting.

If you disable or do not configure this policy setting, users may use Add-on Manager to allow or deny any add-ons not included in the Add-on List policy setting.

NOTE

If an add-on is listed in the Add-on List policy setting, the user cannot change its state through Add-on Manager (unless its value has been set to allow user management—see the Add-on List policy for more details).

Now select the next policy entitled Add-on List and define the allowed ActiveX components to look similarly to Figure 10.1.

TABLE 10.1 ActiveX Components to Allow in Group Policy

Component	GUID	Description
Remote Web Workplace	{F414C260-6AC0-11CF-B6D1-00AA00BBBB58}	Javascript
	{B54F3741-5B07-11cf-A4B0-00AA004A55E8}	VBScript
	{7584C670-2274-4EFB-B00B-D6AABA6D3850}	Microsoft RDP Client Control (redist)
Outlook Web Access	{8D91090E-B955-11D1-ADC5-006008A5848C}	`DEGetBlockFmtNamesParam` Class
	{2D360201-FFF5-11D1-8D03-00A0C959BC0A}	DHTML Edit Control Safe for Scripting
	{2933BF90-7B36-11D2-B20E-00C04F983E60}	XML DOM document
	{F6D90F11-9C73-11D3-B32E-00C04F990BB4}	XML DOM document
	{F6D90F16-9C73-11D3-B32E-00C04F990BB4}	XML HTTP
	{ED8C108E-4349-11D2-91A4-00C04F7969E8}	XML HTTP request
	{3050f4f8-98b5-11cf-bb82-00aa00bdce0b}	Microsoft HTML component
	{B45FF030-4447-11D2-85DE-00C04FA35C89}	SearchAssistantOC
	{8856f961-340a-11d0-a96b-00c04fd705a2}	Microsoft web browser
WSS	{3050F819-98B5-11CF-BB82-00AA00BDCE0B}	`HtmlDlgSafeHelper` class
	{47B0DFC7-B7A3-11D1-ADC5-006008A5848C}	`DEInsertTableParam` class
	{E18FEC31-2EA1-49A2-A7A6-902DC0D1FF05}	Office 11 `name.dll`
	{9F9C4924-C3F3-4459-A396-9E9E0D8B83D1}	SharePoint OpenDocuments class

TABLE 10.1 Continued

Component	GUID	Description
	{BDEADE9E-C265-11D0-BCED-00A0C90AB50F}	SharePoint Spreadsheet Launcher
	{65BCBEE4-7728-41A0-97BE-14E1CAE36AAE}	Microsoft Office List 11.0
	{E543A17A-F212-49C0-B63D-BF09B460250E}	`OISClientLauncher` class
	{07B06095-5687-4D13-9E32-12B4259C9813}	STSUpld `UploadCtl` class
	{3FD37ABB-F90A-4DE5-AA38-179629E64C2F}	SharePoint Spreadsheet Launcher
	{BDEADEF4-C265-11D0-BCED-00A0C90AB50F}	SharePoint Stssync handler
	{003FAFEF-54E3-4D94-9765-44C55997A91C}	`MsSvAbw.AddrBookWrapper`
ConnectComputer (client setup)	{485D813E-EE26-4DF8-9FAF-DEDF2885306E}	`NSHelp` class
Microsoft Office	{E18FEC31-2EA1-49A2-A7A6-902DC0D1FF05}	Office 11 `Name.dll`

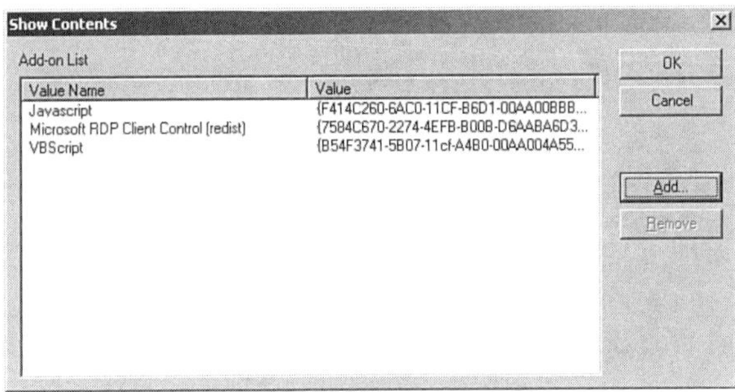

FIGURE 10.1 Sample of allowed ActiveX add-ons.

You can use a workstation to determine the baseline settings. Inside Internet Explorer on XP SP2, click on Tools, Manage Add-ins; then right-click on the top of the menu bar and enable ClassID so that you can view the code. Although this is a valuable add-on, you may need to do the legwork and manually type in these ActiveX codes. An additional resource for these CLSID codes can also be found at `http://castlecops.com/ActiveX.html`.

Additional Internet Explorer Security Changes

Additional changes include a built-in pop-up blocker and changes in MIME type handling that better defend social engineering and phishing attacks.

Outlook Express

Although typically not a major impact to a small firm using Outlook 2003, the email changes in Outlook Express add the capability to block external HTML content such as those in *web bugs*. Web bugs are little bits of code that can track that email through the Internet. Web bugs tell the system how far that email has traveled.

Data Execution Prevention (DEP)

Included both in XP SP2 and Windows 2003 SP1 is a new feature that adds memory protection to help prevent malicious code from executing on your machines. Although more available in hardware, software DEP does give a layer of protection, nonetheless. If it sees a pattern of malicious software, it prevents the execution of the code, thus blocking any potential for damage.

Automatic Updates

Windows XP SP2 has the necessary updates to be easily attached to a Windows Software Update Service patch management system as well as automatically updating itself.

> **Best Practice—Use Windows XP SP2**
>
> There is no doubt that XP SP2 goes a long way toward better protecting your network. The built-in defense in depth layers that it has available are still severely underused by the entire tech industry. Install it and take advantage of the power it has built in.

Security Center

Finally, one of the most important features is the Security Center that monitors antivirus, automatic updates, and firewall settings. If any of the three are set in an unsafe manner, a red icon shows up in the system tray alerting the end user to an insecure system. Make sure that employees in the firm are trained on this icon and, if they see it, that they alert you to the problem if you are unaware of the noncompliance.

An excellent resource for the specific Windows XP SP2 group policy settings as well as all the other group policy settings can be found at `http://www.microsoft.com/downloads/details.aspx?familyid=7821C32F-DA15-438D-8E48-45915CD2BC14&displaylang=en`.

If you find that applications are being blocked by the XP SP2 firewall, you may want to review the log file at `C:\WINDOWS\pfirewall.log` (the default location) and make sure that dropped packets are tracked. Remember that if you are still running Windows with full rights for the end user, that workstation should be able to make any outbound connection. If you need a static entry for a "listening" port, the easiest way to determine this is to enter **`netstat -ano`** at the desktop and review the ports shown as Listening. On a workstation, click Start, Run, cmd. Type in at the DOS prompt **`netstat -ano`**. Now click on Task Manager, then on the Processes tab, and click View to add "select columns," and add the PID. Look for the image name of the antivirus software and write down the PID number. In the `netstat` window, look to see what port that PID application is using that is marked as Listening. This will still be the port the antivirus uses and must be open to function properly. You should see programs such as antivirus software running and using a specific port. Add this port to your group policy deployment to push this out to all workstations.

Local Administrator Access for Users

As showcased in Microsoft KB article 320065 (`http://support.microsoft.com/?id=320065`) under the category of Computer Configuration\Windows Settings\Security Settings\Restricted Groups, add a group under the local computer that will be restricted users and add your organizational unit members there.

Unfortunately, if it was as easy as this, we would all be operating our workstations in this manner. Chapter 21, "Managing Workstations Through Group Policy," lists some of the specific items you can consider locking down; however, it's recommended by Microsoft to use the Groups feature instead of adjusting every item, line by line. The reality is much different. Many line-of-business applications run in offices require either local administrator rights or power user rights. Now power user rights many not sound that unreasonable until you read Microsoft Knowledge Base Bulletin 825069 (`http://support.microsoft.com/default.aspx?scid=kb;en-us;825069`), which clearly states that a member of the Power Users group may obtain administrator rights; therefore, the use of Power User is not recommended.

Although running as a restricted user is not the answer to all virus and worm issues, it does go a long way toward blocking one particular threat in a firm—that of the end user who is tricked into downloading a piece of unwanted software. That unwanted software could easily include Trojans, backdoors, keystroke loggers, or other malicious software. Protecting your users by preventing them from being tricked into downloading software goes a long way toward helping the overall defense in depth. Discuss this process with your clients.

The first step is to change one user's machine to restricted user and identify all the software that will not properly operate in this mode. Typically, the application will not launch from the normal process. An easier way may be to simply determine that an application has the Designed for Windows XP logo because those applications are required to support running in restricted user mode. You may want to investigate software vendors that have obtained this logo for their software.

If the software is not certified, you must determine what Registry permissions need to be adjusted. Two software tools, FileMon and RegMon (both of which are available at `http://www.sysinternals.com` free of charge), can be used to identify these Registry and folder permission changes.

You may first begin this process by using Google to see whether anyone else has gone through this process with the application you are attempting to do this on. You may find that someone has already identified the Registry and file permissions.

Change the workstation to restricted user, launch RegMon with RunAs rights, and now launch the application. Right click and click on RunAs; enter administrator credentials to review those Registry keys that the software applications are requiring full rights on and note these.

As a general rule, the file location needs to be opened up as well as the Registry keys for the application. In some cases you may find that the application dynamically adds so many Registry keys to certain hives to make it nearly impossible to specifically identify those Registry settings. Thus you may need to balance the time you spend to perform this process with the benefit from protection. You may end up merely opening an entire hive such as ClassesRoot. Note that in this example, it is not the author's preferred recommendation, but rather the accepted balance between time spent attempting to identify the needed hives, versus the benefit of at least ensuring that some protection is offered to the end user. Exposing the entire ClassesRoot hive is not preferred, but rather a compromise.

Those items on which you need to adjust the permissions are as follows:

- Assign full permission to `C:\Program Files\Intuit`.
- Assign full permission to `C:\Program Files\Common Files\Intuit`.
- Assign full permission to `HKEY_LOCAL_MACHINE\SOFTWARE\INTUIT`.
- Assign full permission to `HKEY_CLASSES_ROOT`.

Although you could walk around to each workstation and manually add these Registry and file permission changes, in a network setting, you can use the power of group policy to perform these steps to the needed workstations. Identify those users who need these settings.

Setting Up a Security Group

The first step is to set up a security group that includes only those users who need these rights. There is no need to deploy these settings to all authenticated users, but only to the needed user.

Click on Server Management and then on Active Directory Users and Computers. On the right-hand side of the screen is the Add a New Security Group option. Go through the wizard to add a new security group, making sure that it has a descriptive name, unique enough so that you know what the group is used for. Add only those users to whom you want the policy applied.

Now you need to build a policy to set the permissions. In SBS 2003, open up the Group Policy Management Console. Under the domain, right-click and select Create and Link a GPO Here. Name the group policy, again using a descriptive name so that you can know that you have added the policy. Do not adjust an existing policy, but rather ensure that you are setting up a new one. Right-click on the newly named policy and click Edit to begin the process of building the policy. Scroll down to Computer Configuration, Windows Settings, Security Settings, and then to File System, as shown in Figure 10.2.

Click on Add File, and a window that looks like a standard computer browser window appears. In the Folder location box, type in `C:\Program Files\Intuit` and click OK (see Figure 10.3).

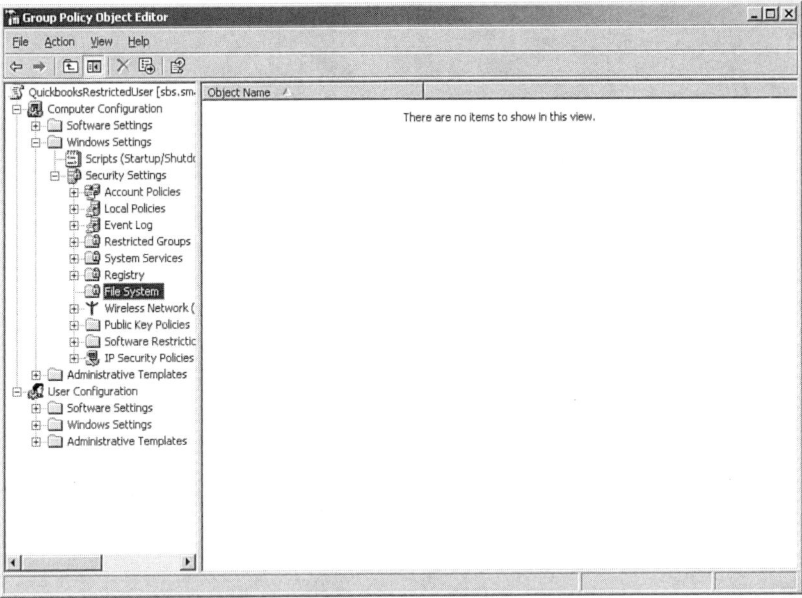

FIGURE 10.2 Drilling down to the File System settings.

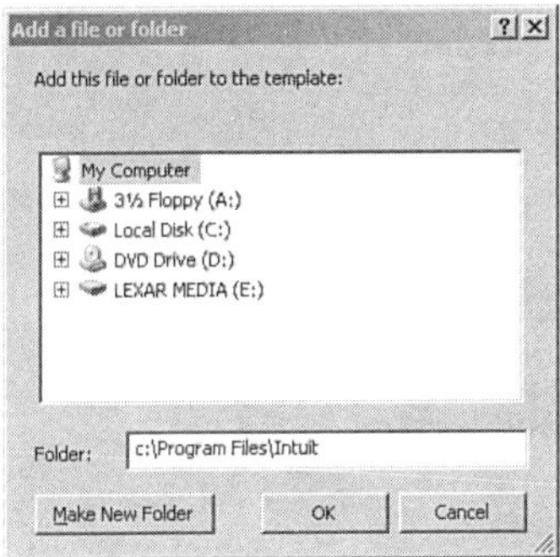

FIGURE 10.3 Adding the name of the folder on which to adjust permissions.

Click on Advanced and then click on Find Now. Scroll down and click to add the specific security group you built earlier, and specifically add Full Control (see Figure 10.4).

In the Add Object dialog box, select Configure This File or Folder Then and Propagate Inheritable Permissions to All Subfolders and Files (see Figure 10.5).

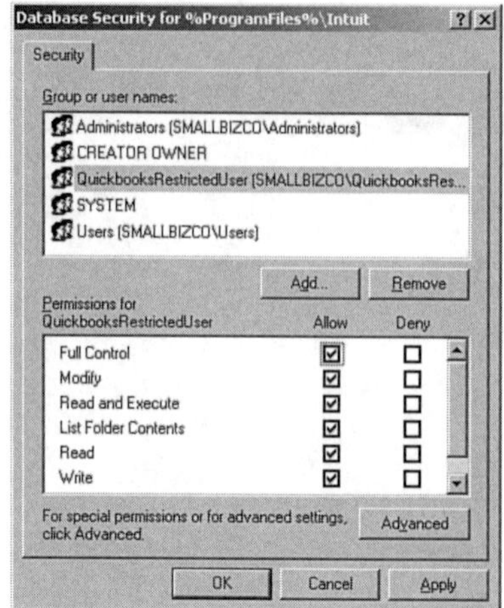

FIGURE 10.4 Browsing to find the security group and adding full rights.

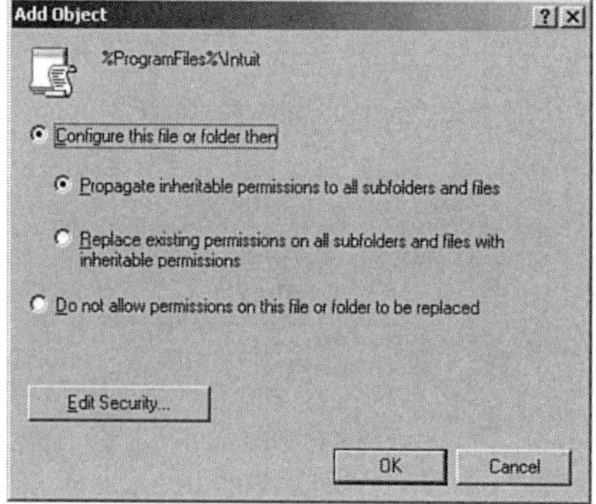

FIGURE 10.5 Adding propagation rights.

Now do this again for `C:\Program Files\Common Files\Intuit` following the same instructions. The resulting screens for files should look like Figure 10.6.

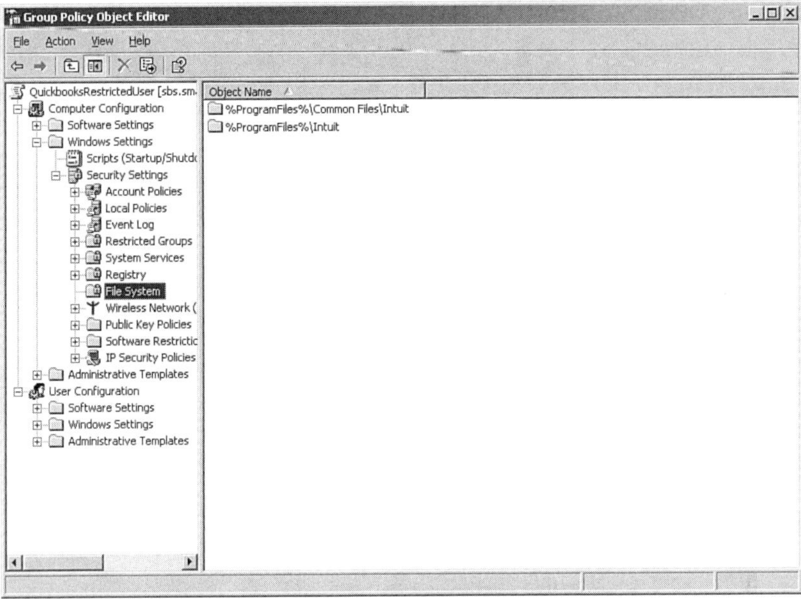

FIGURE 10.6 Resulting screen showing results of adding file permissions

Now perform the same process for the Registry keys. In the same window, select the hive of Registry and right-click on Add Key. Remember, you don't need to use the HKEY part of the hive. You want to add permissions to HKEY_LOCAL_MACHINE\SOFTWARE\INTUIT. We remove the HKEY_LOCAL MACHINE and when building our rule, only need MACHINE and then the SOFTWARE key and then add a slash "\" and the word "Intuit," as shown in Figure 10.7.

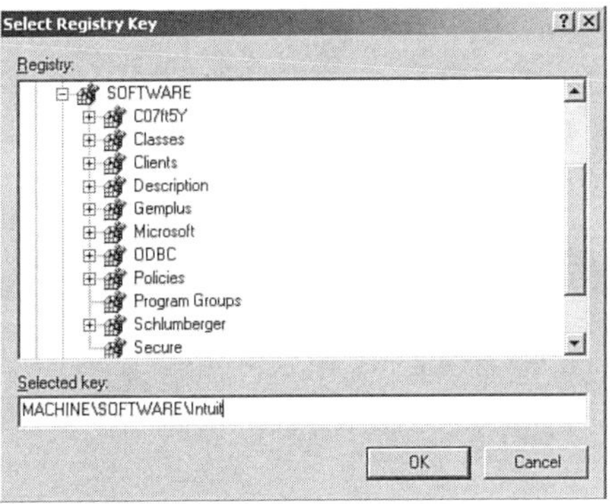

FIGURE 10.7 Adding the Registry key of Intuit.

10

As before, adjust the permissions of this entry you made, scrolling down and finding the security group you added earlier. Add full permissions and allow propagation. Finally, once again, choose Registry, Add key; browse to the entire key of CLASSES_ROOT (see Figure 10.8) and change the permissions to your security group to Full Control.

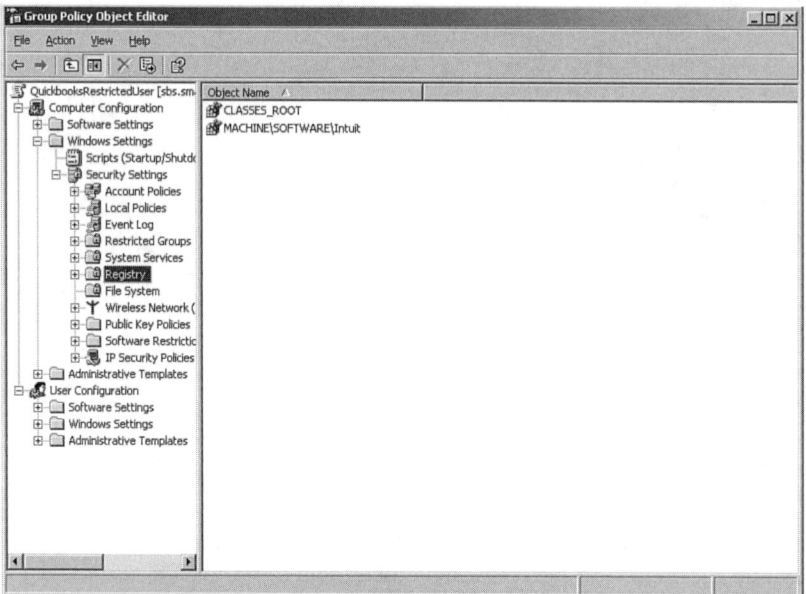

FIGURE 10.8 Resulting view of Registry keys.

After those four steps are complete, type `gpupdate /force` in a command prompt or in Start, Run to force the policy's effect. You should now be able to use this software in restricted user mode on your workstations.

The key to this process is finding the hives that need to be adjusted for permissions. It is preferable to have software that supports restricted user mode from the beginning, so keep this in mind when identifying line-of-business software for your clients' use.

Note

For an alternate method (and quite probably more secure method) of adjusting the permissions of the registry hives, review the instructions at http://www.quickbooksgroup.com/webx?14@@.eeb323b/9. This method also allows the user to update the program for payroll updates.

Microsoft Vista will utilize more of this restricted user mode concept. Therefore, if you purchase this software that supports this now, you will be better able to protect your desktops in the future.

Antivirus Tools

In your firm, you can have antivirus software in many places and on many machines. The key element in choosing antivirus software is to ensure that it is in a position to block and scan before the viruses enter your desktops. The optimal goal for the consultant is to ensure that the end user never sees the antivirus warning sign that the virus has gotten to the desktop. It is therefore recommended that the solution be centrally managed, ensuring that the viruses and even potential for viruses do not enter your system.

Therefore whether you choose to block attachments using the SBS email attachment blocking, or that of your antivirus program, choose one to remove those attachments that have no immediate business need. Furthermore on a regular and annual basis review the security events in the network and reevaluate as needed.

This chapter does not recommend one antivirus over another, with one exception: Ensure that the antivirus solution you choose includes coverage of the server, the workstations and the Exchange server.

In the SBS community, the solutions most often installed include the following:

- Symantec Corporate Edition
- Sophos
- Trend CSM
- Panda Antivirus
- McAfee
- Nod32
- AVG

On all these platforms, it is recommended to adjust the automatic download of virus identification signature files as often as you can, or as often as the vendor supports the updating. In the antivirus industry, the vendors call the same virus by different names, thus one of the annoyances of dealing with different vendors in the servers you work with is this lack of naming consistency. The next best practice that is recommended is to choose one antivirus platform and truly understand all the options and settings included in that product. Typically there are tweaks and adjustments in each software. Take the time to learn a platform to best support that.

An excellent resource for keeping aware of viruses and other incidents is the FSecure web log at `http://www.f-secure.com/weblog/` where the company tracks late-breaking issues.

Be aware though that antivirus is *reactive* and not *proactive*; thus, the software always needs a computer to get infected first. Blocking your historical methods of infection to ensure that you are protected proactively is the proper solution. Review your vendors' response times and compare them with other vendors that have solutions designed for the small business. One such historical comparison can be found at http://www.f-secure.com/news/response/f-secure_speed_of_response.pdf, but this information is easily found on the Web.

When you install any one of these antivirus consoles on the server, you typically need to adjust it to handle a proxy server, and you probably need to add any web interface site to the trusted site zones using the Enhanced IE to get it to function properly. If you need to do any standalone scanning of workstations off the network due to infections (see the "Troubleshooting Workstation Security" section later in this chapter for more information), you may need to have a functioning Internet Explorer to use these web-based tools. You may need to remove the workstation drive to a *sandbox*, by making it a slave drive on another testing system to scan and clean the drive.

When setting up the antivirus, consider your risk zones just like in patch management. Workstations need full scanning with few exceptions. For servers, many database designers recommend that you do not scan their databases. Furthermore it's always recommended that you exclude the file location of Exchange; therefore, the exclusions and settings you need for the server have no bearing on the scan settings you need in place for the workstations. Adjust these based on your data and needs. An example of setting up these zones can be found in Wayne Small's whitepaper on installing Trend Micro CSM on SBS, which can be downloaded at http://www.sbsfaq.com/Visual%20Guides/Trend%20CSM%20on%20SBS2003.pdf.

Viruses are nothing more than code whose goal it is to do bad things to your system. Whether the maliciousness is an annoyance or completely destructiveness, it's still code. As such, antivirus scanners will gather examples of this code, determine an identifier of the binary or code, and update the antivirus signature files to block and scan for that malicious code. Most antivirus software performs background monitoring. Every time a file is opened or accessed, the binaries in that file are compared to these signatures. Antivirus software includes the capability for its signatures to scan for other similar style of attacks. This process is called *heuristics*, whereby the antivirus engine looks for similar patterns of attack and flags that as a potential for viruses as well. The disadvantage to this model is the potential for false-positives. There have been times when software code that is not virus laden is flagged as a virus. When setting up your selections for dealing with non-email–based viruses, you may not want to set the action to delete but rather to quarantine. On the off chance that a key file is flagged, you can recover from this misidentification easier. More information about antivirus software can be found at http://www.symantec.com/region/reg_eu/resources/antivirus.html and in the book *The Art of Computer Virus Research and Defense* by Peter Szor, Addison Wesley Professional, ISBN: 0321304543.

In an office where the goal is to ensure that you never have a virus show up on the desktop, you may need to use something like the Eicar test virus to showcase how the desktop antivirus interface looks so that the end user understands what to look for. Go to http://www.eicar.org/anti_virus_test_file.htm to find several methods to test entry methods for viruses. Consider preparing a short awareness document to tell the end user how to handle a virus infection. Have a prepared list of procedures for the on-site owner or end user to perform so that the attack can be minimized.

Best Practice—Educating the Business Owner on Handling Viruses

Because most of you are not on your client's premises full-time, it is key that you educate staff on the best way to handle an outbreak. Prepare a demonstration of what the antivirus software should look like when activated and discuss processes for quarantining systems.

Resources such as the Virus Bulletin that test to ensure that antivirus vendors protect for the top 100 viruses in the wild (`http://www.virusbtn.com/vb100/archives/products.xml?table`, sign up and register for access) may help you identify vendors. Some, if not many, of these online platforms require ActiveX and a working Internet Explorer so online scanners may not be viable in a severely infected box.

Some of the free online virus scanners include

- `http://www.pandasoftware.com/activescan/` (ActiveX)
- `http://housecall.trendmicro.com/housecall/start_corp.asp` (ActiveX)
- `http://www.ravantivirus.com/scan/indexie.php` (ActiveX and Java)

Antispyware Tools

Recently viruses have been making less of an impact in networks and spyware more so. Both types of malicious software, viruses and spyware, could honestly be treated as one category. The industry, however, treats them as two separate types of unwanted software. The reality is that any unwanted software is just that, unwanted software. The antispyware industry is moving from the standalone desktop model to the managed solution model. Currently, of the top-rated antispyware software as ranked by *Consumer Reports*, only a few have a corporate version.

Best Practice—Choosing the Right Vendor

The typical argument in the community is to choose a vendor who specializes in a particular type of malware, either antivirus or antispyware. However, many products are beginning to overlap, and the two types of malware are beginning to be difficult to distinguish. Bad code is bad code no matter what you call it. The general consensus is still to pick a solution for each "genre" or type of malware.

Some of the high-rated antispyware tools are

- Microsoft AntiSpyware (beta), free to individual users, but a fee for the corporate version
- Webroot by Spy Sweeper
- Computer Associates eTrust Pest Patrol
- Spybot Search and Destroy
- Ad-Aware SE Plus

- McAfee Antispyware
- Trend Micro PC-Cillin Internet Security
- Counterspy

Spyware is similar to viruses and has similar symptoms. The Microsoft AntiSpyware website at `http://www.microsoft.com/athome/security/spyware/spywaresigns.mspx` describes the following symptoms of spyware; also see Table 10.2.

TABLE 10.2 Symptoms of Spyware on Your System

Symptom	Explanation
I see pop-up advertisements all the time.	Some unwanted software bombards you with pop-up ads that aren't related to a particular website you're visiting. These ads are often for adult or other websites you may find objectionable. If you see pop-up ads as soon as you turn on your computer or when you're not even browsing the Web, you may have spyware or other unwanted software on your computer.
My settings have changed, and I can't change them back to the way they were.	Some unwanted software has the capability to change your home page or search page settings. This means that the page that opens first when you start your Internet browser or the page that appears when you select Search may be pages that you do not recognize. Even if you know how to adjust these settings, you may find that they revert back every time you restart your computer.
My web browser contains additional components that I don't remember downloading.	Spyware and other unwanted software can add addi tional toolbars to your web browser that you don't wantor need. Even if you know how to remove these toolbars, they may return each time you restart your computer.
My computer seems sluggish.	Spyware and other unwanted software are not necessarily designed to be efficient. The resources these programs use to track your activities and deliver advertisements can slow down your computer, and errors in the software can make your computer crash. If you notice a sudden increase in the number of times a certain program crashes, or if your computer is slower than normal at performing routine tasks, you may have spyware or other unwanted software on your machine.

The difference between spyware and viruses is merely the attack vector. Spyware typically attacks via the web browser. As such, antispyware software's main goal is to freeze the browser settings and look for changes in Registry settings and startups. There is overlap between spyware and viruses, and this blurring of the edges between the two will probably only become more significant in the future. A discussion of the approach of analysis of the Microsoft AntiSpyware product can be found at `http://www.microsoft.com/athome/security/spyware/software/isv/analysis.mspx`. In that article the categories for spyware are identified as listed in Table 10.3.

TABLE 10.3 Spyware Criteria

Category	Explanation
Deceptive behaviors	Includes problems with notice and consent about what is running on the user's machine, control over the actions taken by the program while it is running on the machine, and installation and removal of the program from the machine at the user's discretion.
Privacy	Issues in collecting, using, and communicating the user's personal information and behaviors without explicit consent.
Security	Negative impact on the security of the user's computer or attempts to circumvent or disable security, including but not limited to evidence of malicious behaviors.
Performance impact	General impact on performance, reliability, and quality of the user's computing experience (for example, slow computer performance, reduced productivity, corruption of the operating system, or other issues).
Industry and consumer opinion	The software industry and individual users play a key role in helping to identify new behaviors and programs that could present risks to the user's computing experience.

As you can see the characteristics are similar to viruses. Both are unwanted code on your system.

The Managed Network

Right now the industry of desktop protection is somewhat fragmented. Antivirus over there; antispyware over here. Although some corporate desktop products have included antispyware in their antivirus software, or antispyware in their patching tools, the industry is still working toward a cohesive control of desktops in the small business space. At least in the SBS network with Active Directory, you can leverage the ability to take advantage and lock down desktops and control. However, the typical small business consultant doesn't just maintain networked machines, she also maintains the home machines of employees of the firm. Unfortunately, not many tools are available to centrally manage machines that are not joined to the domain. The best tool you have for such services is just utilizing several remote control programs available in the marketplace. Some of the options include

- Logmein Pro, Logmein Reach—Remote control software that includes audit reports that can be used for billing purposes; only requires port 80 and 443 access (`http://www.logmein.com`).
- Gotomypc—Remote control software that only requires port 80 and port 443 access (`http://www.gotomypc.com`).
- PCAnywhere—Symantec's non-web–based remote control software. The disadvantage is that if the router is reset, you may lose the remote access due to the blockage of the ports (`http://www.symantec.com`).
- Webex—Offers several packages for remote connectivity that include a request/confirmation process where the client approves the access (`http://www.webex.com`).

- Office Live meeting—Microsoft's higher end packages can be utilized for remote access as well (`https://main.placeware.com/ordering/lmbuy_it/buy_it.cfm?promocode=2730`).
- Radmin—Remote access package (`http://www.radmin.com/`).
- VNC and Tight VNC—Free remote control software (`http://www.tightvnc.com/`.
- Remote Desktop Protocol—Built into Windows XP is the native desktop version of Terminal Services that allow you to remotely connect.

In each of these products, there is a concern that such remote control tools can be easily introduced into a network where there is no policy blocking them. Make sure that your end users know when they can and cannot be installed, and review the logging mechanism of each platform. Some of the newer ones such as Logmein have built-in logging capability.

Best Practice—Ensuring Remote Access

Even on your non-networked clients, it is key to have remote access for remote cleanup. Have a plan to be able to remotely manage these home machines as well by using such tools as Remote Desktop and Logmein.

The important thing to keep in mind with all these solutions is to ensure that you can control any desktop that may attach to your network. Remember that any desktop attaching remotely back to your network may affect the health of your own network.

Let's Not Forget About Office

Although this chapter doesn't go into great depth about the settings you can adjust and change in Office 2003, you may want to review the detail group policy settings that can be controlled. To control Office applications, you first need to make sure that the `.adm` file for Office is loaded in the Group Policy Management Console on the server. You can obtain this file from this location along with the files that should be where you start first to review what you might want to control: `http://www.microsoft.com/downloads/details.aspx?FamilyID=BA8BC720-EDC2-479B-B115-5ABB70B3F490&displaylang=en`

The key settings that a consultant should consider reviewing on an as-needed basis are the ones surrounding macros (see Table 10.4).

TABLE 10.4 Office 2003 Group Policy Settings Surrounding Security

Examples of Security Settings in Office:
Disable VBA for Office applications
Automation Security
Word: Macro Security Level
Word: Trust all installed add-ins and templates
Word: Trust access to Visual Basic Project

TABLE 10.4 Continued

Examples of Security Settings in Office:
Excel: Macro Security Level
Excel: Trust all installed add-ins and templates
Excel: Trust access to Visual Basic Project
Access: Macro Security Level
Access: Trust all installed add-ins and templates
PowerPoint: Macro Security Level
PowerPoint: Trust all installed add-ins and templates
PowerPoint: Trust access to Visual Basic Project
Publisher: Macro Security Level
Publisher: Trust all installed add-ins and templates
Outlook: Macro Security Level

For Outlook 2003, the security settings surround email and attachments, as described in Table 10.5.

TABLE 10.5 Outlook 2003 Group Policy Settings Surrounding Security

Examples of Security Settings in Outlook:
Prevent users from customizing attachment security settings
Allow access to email attachments
List of file extensions to allow:
Disallow access to email attachments
List of file extensions to disallow:
Outlook virus security settings
Apply individual settings for Outlook virus security
Configure Add-In Trust Level
Select Add-In Trust Level:
Security Zone for loaded Messages
Item Scripting
Scripting
Allow Active X One Off Forms
Disable Remember Password check box for Internet E-mail settings dialog
Prompt user to choose security settings if default settings fail
Check to prompt the user; uncheck to automatically select
Do not automatically sign replies
Disable automatic signing of signed messages on replies

10

As part of your security review process, make sure that the appropriate amount of balance between control by the administrator and control by the end user is chosen. Some individuals in the firm can be trusted to properly control their systems, and some need to be better protected from the myriad of choices and tricks used to entice the end user into clicking and downloading.

The Educated End User and Security Review Process

Your best defense for your workstation perimeter is truly an educated end user. Recent years have seen the increase of *blended threats* where viruses drop Trojans, or a machine is made into a *bot* to be used in a larger attack on another system or systems, or even *rootkits* where programs that were once only in the UNIX system are now are being introduced to the Windows administrator. Rootkits are designed to be undetected programs that silently gather data or other malicious tasks. Although the Windows administrator can control the workstations and can ensure that antivirus is kept up-to-date along with antispyware, the reality is that your best defense is a well-trained end user. Understanding social engineering attacks, choosing strong passwords, monitoring physical safety—all these are key elements that need help from the end users in your network.

So, what's the first step toward an educated end user? First and foremost is an acceptable use policy. Before you can set the security goals of your firm and put in place the technology tools to assist you in meeting these targets, you need to identify with the business owner what is deemed acceptable.

Is the firm you are consulting for bound by regulations to protect certain kinds of data? Is the data required to be handled and transmitted in a certain manner? Where is data stored throughout the network? All these questions need to be answered before you can set an acceptable use policy.

Sample policies can be found at the SANS.org website but need to be tailored to your needs and possibly reviewed by a human resource attorney. What does your firm consider acceptable in the office? Is unlimited instant messaging part of the acceptable business use of computer equipment at your firm? For some firms, IM is part of the business structure and is not considered a time waster. However, there should be guidelines and notification that conversations done on business equipment can be logged, reviewed, and tracked. For most firms, illegal downloading of digital assets is considered inappropriate at best, illegal at worst.

Best Practice—Educating the User

No other single device or technology can secure a network as well as an educated end user. As Steve Riley, Senior Security Product Manager for Microsoft recommends, place security posters in bathroom stalls. You will have a captive audience because there won't be anything else for them to read (`http://nativeintelligence.com/posters/security-posters.asp`).

Consider awarding employees for selecting strong passwords or conforming to best practices. Award those who handle desktop data security appropriately.

Make sure that the staff is informed that only approved software is allowed and that only those parties who have the rights to download should be downloading. Stress to everyone in the office how they too are a part of the security fabric of your network. Consider as part of your managed services, information about common security hoaxes and scams on the Internet. Some of the best resources for being aware of such scams include the web resources such as Snopes.com and the Oops newsletter from Sans.org. You may want to consider sending monthly reminders to your clients of these social engineering issues.

Tables 10.6 and 10.7 present two sample checklists that can serve as memory joggers for you to think about this as an ongoing process that needs to be reviewed regularly.

TABLE 10.6 Monthly Security Checklist

Issue	Done	Comment
Review Help desk requests.		
Discuss any security issues with client.		
Malware/Spyware		
Viruses		
Backup running and tested.		
Disk space growth reasonable.		
Daily monitoring email reviewed and all questionable items cleared.		
Review ports open on firewall.		
Review services running, memory use growth.		
Review security bulletins for patch issues (at the top of each bulletin).		
Operating system patches deployed.		
Application patches deployed.		
Hardware updates deployed.		
Patch issue follow up.		
Review Microsoft Security Advisories.		
Take action as appropriate.		
Run MBSA or other tool report checking that passwords have been updated per schedule.		
Review hoaxes with clients.		
Review junk mail levels and set IMF filter accordingly.		
Perform test restore routine.		
Perform Image (if part of backup plan).		

TABLE 10.7 Annual Security Checklist

Issue	Done	Comment
Review Security policy for changes/revisions.		
Review changes/additions to group policy settings based on security policy changes.		
Discuss any security issues with client for yearly technology review.		
Review updating/retirement of assets.		
Review updating/retirement of applications.		
Review maintenance agreements.		
Review annual disk growth.		
Perform full restore to alternative hardware as test.		
Perform annual risk analysis.		
Determine annual security budget.		
ARO×SLE = ALE—Annualized Rate of Occurrence×Single Loss Expectancy = Annual Loss Expectancy.		
Review password change policy.		
Run MBSA tool to review status of network.		
Review insurance policies.		
Perform a "what if the worst occurs" analysis and what's the risk of it occurring?		

10

Use this monthly and annual review process to ensure that your desktop security goals are being met.

Protecting Data from the Inside

There are two emphases in protecting data inside your network. The first is protecting data from outside intruders; the second is protecting data from inside intruders. Protection of data from outside intruders includes all that has been previously discussed in the chapter, as well as one more key element: ensuring that the data you need to protect is not kept on the desktop. Built into SBS 2003 is a My Documents redirection that places the data on shared folders on the server.

But what about protecting data from unauthorized access inside the network? The best protection for this risk is to follow the best practice of allowing access to the data only to those persons who need access. Thus only allow that user/workstation the bare minimum permissions it needs to access the data on the network.

The next concern that invariably comes up is the risk of external drive or device access. USB thumb drives have recently come under attack as a security issue, yet the risk from unauthorized retrieval of data is no different from floppy disks, MP3 players, cell phones with memory chips, emailing documents, faxing documents, or, in the case of Fawn Hall, stuffing documents down pieces of clothing and walking out of the office with them. For all these threats, the countereffort must be weighed with the loss of business agility. Block CD-ROMs and USB thumbdrives in a small office, and you may restrict a key business process that the company uses to obtain external data.

Although there are solutions such as Windows Right Management Services that will allow you to restrict emails or documents to be only opened by certain parties, the reality is that you cannot prevent an "analog attack" on your digital documents. Your best prevention for that attack is written security policies and educated end users.

Troubleshooting Workstation Security

If all your clients see the value in spending the money in the proactive security manner rather than the reactive manner, this chapter could end here. The reality is much different. Even if your clients do have a managed and controlled network, they will probably not have a well-working, well-functioning machine at home unless they are taking the same sort of steps of ensuring that antivirus, patching, and antispyware are in place, and restricting uneducated end users from running as administrator. The reality is that, probably more often than not, you will get asked about an ill-running machine or one inundated with pop-ups.

A workstation or standalone computer that is virus- and spyware-infected is typically an ill-running machine that just doesn't act as "peppy" as it once did. It could also be evidenced by the router showing a log of traffic patterns and activity. After you identify a machine, or a server for that matter, that has been infected and is possibly no longer your machine anymore, your first plan of attack should be to remove that computer from the location and isolate it to ensure that you limit the risk of exposure. Again, remember the illness analogy. If you have an extremely sick, infectious patient, you remove him and quarantine the patient during treatment. For a workstation, merely unplug the network connection from the back of the workstation. If you suspect the server, merely unplug the RJ45 network connection from the wall.

The typical security consultant keeps a *jump bag* or toolkit of security tools to help him deal with desktop issues. Recently, a post to the incidents.org website listed one consultant's recommended jump bag. Consider building one of your own for those tools that you regularly use to clean or deploy workstations. Many, if not all, of the tools on this list are freely available on the Web, and the links for each can be found in Appendix A, "SBS Resources." Build your own CD-ROM or USB thumbdrive toolkit and always keep a copy of the latest `.dat` file signatures on that thumbdrive to ensure that you can easily scan an infected machine. Table 10.8 lists some possible items for your security toolkit.

TABLE 10.8 Security Toolkit

Antivirus Tools
McAfee Stinger (updated routinely)
Symantec AV Corporate Edition (your antivirus solution)
Microsoft Malware Removal Tool (released monthly)
Current Symantec AV Intelligent Updater
Response Kit
NetCat (available now at SecurityFocus)
SysInternals AccessEnum
SysInternals AutoRuns
SysInternals Contig
SysInternals DiskView
SysInternals FileMon
SysInternals ListDLLs
SysInternals Page Defrag
SysInternals ProcessExplorer
SysInternals PS Tools
SysInternals RegMon
SysInternals Rootkit Revealer
SysInternals Sdelete
SysInternals ShareEnum
SysInternals Sync
SysInternals TCPView
SysInternals Miscellaneous tools
Heysoft LADS
myNetWatchman SecCheck
Inetcat.org NBTScan
FoundStone BinText
FoundStone Forensic Toolkit
FoundStone Fport
FoundStone Galleta
FoundStone Pasco
FoundStone Rifuti

TABLE 10.8 Continued

Response Kit
FoundStone Vision
FoundStone ShoWin
FoundStone SuperScan
WinDump
Nmap
Tigerteam.se SBD (encrypted netcat)
GNU-based unxutils (from `unixutils.sourceforge.net`)
Good copies of Windows binaries (`netstat`, `cmd`, `ipconfig`, `nbtstat`)
Spyware Tools
AdAware (updated defs in same directory)
CWShredder
Hijack This
MS AntiSpyWare Beta
Spybot Search and Destroy (updated defs in same directory)
BHO Demon
Security Tools (this is my usual place to dump the `.zip` or `.exe` installers)
Heysoft LADS (list alternative data streams)
Inetcat.org NBTScan
MS Baseline Security Analyzer
MS IIS Lockdown Tool
Sam Spade
SSH Client (SSH.com or Putty)
SysInternals Tools
Foundstone Tools
BlackIce PC Protection
Kerio Personal Firewall
Zone Alarm Personal Firewall
WinPcap
WinDump
Ethereal Installer
Nmap for Windows (client version)
Utilities
Adobe Acrobat Reader Installer
CPU-Z
FireFox Installer
Macromedia Flash and ShockWave Installers
QuickTime Standalone Installer
VNC Installer
WinZip ISCAlert Installer
Service Packs (on a 2nd CD)
Windows XP SP2
Windows 2000 SP4 (+rpc/lsass critical patches or SRP when released)
Windows 2003 Server SP1

To this list you could add the Administrator's NT password reset disk information located at `http://home.eunet.no/~pnordahl/ntpasswd/` and WinPE or Bart's PE `http://www.nu2.nu/pebuilder/`. PEs are preinstallation or maintenance operating systems that allow the technician to boot from a safe operating system but still have tools to clean and disinfect the system safely. You can even have a bootable USB thumbdrive that can reset the local administrator's password, but don't forget, in a network, for devices still on the network, all you need to do is go to the user menu on the console and reset the password.

If you have a severely impacted machine, the only way you may be able to clean and clear severe malware is one of three methods:

- Boot from safe mode and use antispyware tools to remove the unwanted software.
- Boot with WinPE or Bart's PE. Keep in mind that for many small business consultants who are not system builders, you will not have access to Microsoft's WinPE and will have to rely on Bart's PE.
- Remove the hard drive from the machine, attach it as a slave drive on another segregated test machine, and use antivirus/spyware to scan the drive.

Even after these three methods have been used, you may have situations where you cannot trust the system anymore. Especially in an office situation, you have to ask yourself, can you trust this system?

Best Practice—Flattening the Machine

There comes a point that you must ask yourself and the business owner, "How much time am I taking in cleaning this up?" versus "How much time will it take to rebuild this?" If the reason you are taking so much time to clean the workstation is that there is key data on that machine, you should have proactively fixed that problem first. There's no reason that a workstation should have key data with no backup. You should have no hesitation rebuilding a workstation. If you do, you have a bigger problem.

In most cases, security intrusions occur when the system is not properly maintained. The typical way that rootkits and other extreme forms of malware enter a system is through a weakness. Weak passwords, not patching, misconfiguration—all these are chinks in your armor that could allow something to occur. If you suspect that a real intrusion has occurred, and you are not in an industry that requires regulatory investigation, your best method to determine whether something truly has occurred is to contact Microsoft Product Support Services (PSS) and request a security investigation. This investigation may use tools from PSS that perform an online analysis of your system. The goal of the analysis is to give you recommendations and guidance for preventing the issues in the future. Keep in mind that the recommended way to recover from an intrusion is to be formatted and reinstalled from known CD-ROM media, have all security patches installed, and then and only then be reattached to the network. More of this is discussed at `http://www.cert.org/nav/recovering.html`.

Summary

Entire books have been written on recommendations for securing the Windows desktop. This chapter briefly touched on some of the realistic implementations that a small business consultant can realistically and effectively do to help her clients better protect their desktops and, in turn, better protect the network.

The basic protections of the network must be in place for the workstations as well:

- Patching
- Antivirus and antispyware
- Firewall

And last but not least—control. Control that includes input from the Human Resources Department for security policies first before the technological processes are put in place to enforce that control.

Security of the desktops is a process that needs to be carefully discussed with the business owner and the best balance between business needs and business data protection found to fit the environment.

Best Practice Summary

- Security budget calculation—Work with clients in advance to determine their acceptable risk and budget levels.
- Use Windows XP SP2—Update all workstations to Windows XP SP2 to give you more control and tools.
- Removing local administrator—Consider deploying workstations without full rights to the desktop. The use of local administrator is usually not needed by all in the firm.
- Educating the business owner on handling viruses—Always install a server-based antivirus that covers the server, workstation, and email.
- Choosing the right vendor—Antispyware is currently mostly a standalone desktop product, but you may consider corporate centrally managed versions.
- Educating the user—Keeping your end users up to date in security awareness may require unusual methods for implementation but will be your most effective security tool.
- Flattening the machine—Don't hesitate to reformat and reload a workstation if you find you cannot trust that system anymore.

PART V

Exchange

IN THIS PART

CHAPTER 11

Client Connectivity

IN THIS CHAPTER:

- Using Outlook
- Using Outlook Web Access
- Using Outlook Mobile Access (OMA)
- Using ActiveSync
- Troubleshooting Client Connectivity

In a Small Business Server network environment, the Microsoft Exchange Server is the central repository for all company email, contacts, and calendar information. But the employees needing access to that information don't interact directly with the Exchange server itself. Rather, they use various clients that communicate with the Exchange server on their behalf, similar to the way a web browser interacts with data stored on a web server.

This chapter discusses the four Exchange clients available inside and outside the SBS network, namely: Outlook, Outlook Web Access (OWA), Outlook Mobile Access (OMA), and ActiveSync. This chapter also covers available methods for connecting these clients to the Exchange server, and finally, troubleshoots connectivity issues. For information on the Mac Exchange client, Entourage, see Chapter 17, "Integrating the Macintosh into a Small Business Server 2003 Environment."

Using Outlook

As part of the Microsoft Office suite, Microsoft Office Outlook (see Figure 11.1) is the most widely used Exchange client in SBS networks today. It provides personal and shared access to email, calendars, contacts, tasks, notes, journals, and public folders. With the addition of third-party plug-ins, Outlook can be extended to include support for blogs, RSS feeds, and newsgroup readers. Microsoft even offers a *mini-CRM* plug-in for Outlook called *Business Contact Manager Update* as a free download at `http://www.microsoft.com/office/outlook/contactmanager/prodinfo/default.mspx`. Because a great many books—too many to mention here—dedicated to the features and functionality of Outlook are available today, this chapter focuses on a few key features, setup, and connectivity.

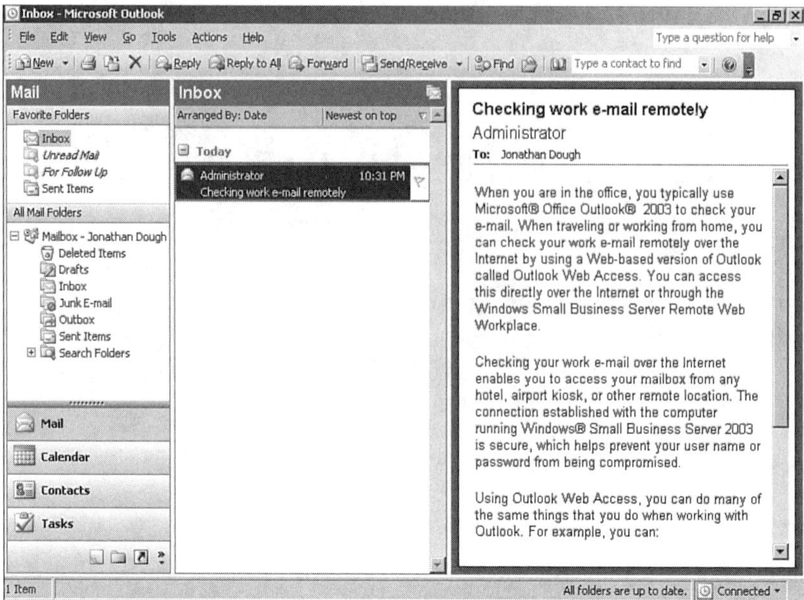

FIGURE 11.1 Outlook 2003 sports a new look over previous versions and offers vast technological improvements such as Cached Exchange Mode.

Installing Outlook

Outlook is included in all versions of Microsoft Office 2003, and it also comes bundled in both SBS 2003 Standard and Premium Editions. During the initial installation of SBS, the Outlook files are copied into a folder on the server for later distribution to client computers. By default, those files are located in the `C:\ClientApps\outlook2003` directory.

> **CAUTION**
>
> It is important to note that even though the Outlook files reside on the server for distribution to client machines, the Outlook application itself should never be installed on the SBS server. Microsoft doesn't support installing Outlook and Exchange on the same machine, due to conflicts with the Messaging Application Programming Interface (MAPI). See Microsoft KB article 266418 for more details (`http://support.microsoft.com/?id=266418`).

After the Outlook install files have been successfully copied onto the SBS server during installation, you can put away the original Outlook disc and yellow 25-digit product key sticker for safekeeping. The only time you will need the 25-digit code is when manually installing Outlook 2003 on a client workstation from the CD. All further Outlook 2003 installs can be initiated from the server using the built-in wizards. If the workstation needing Outlook installed is new to the network, run the Set Up Client Computers Wizard. Or if the workstation is already a member of the SBS domain, run the Assign Applications to Client Computers Wizard. To run either of these wizards from the Server

Management MMC console, open Server Management, click Standard Management, click Client Computers, and select the wizard from the task pane on the right.

Alternatively, if you need to install or reinstall Outlook 2003 from a client workstation, installation can be initiated manually by browsing to `\\servername\ClientApps\outlook2003` and double-clicking the `Setup.exe` program.

Cached Exchange Mode

Cached Exchange Mode in Outlook provides access to employee mailbox information normally stored in Exchange, even in the event of a network outage or if the Exchange server is unavailable. This is accomplished by storing a copy of the user's data from the Exchange mailbox on the local user's machine in an Offline Folder (OST) file. A copy of the address book is also stored locally as an Offline Address Book (OAB) file. The client's mailbox still resides on the Exchange server, but most of the traffic takes place between Outlook and the OST file, even when network conditions are normal.

Best Practice—Download and Review the Microsoft White Paper, "Enabling a Superior Client Experience with Microsoft Office Outlook 2003"

This 36-page whitepaper is a must-read for any SBS administrator seeking a better understanding of the new connectivity features in Outlook 2003, how Cached Exchange Mode works, Exchange/Outlook synchronization, and automatic conflict resolution. It also discusses the optimal settings for each possible bandwidth scenario for mobile users who need to connect to Exchange. The whitepaper can be downloaded for free from Microsoft's website: `http://www.microsoft.com/office/outlook/prodinfo/enabling.mspx`.

Outlook automatically synchronizes the local OST file with the Exchange server. If you watch the lower right corner of the Outlook status bar carefully, you can see it flash a message when synchronization occurs, followed by a message that says "All folders are up to date." The OAB file synchronization also happens automatically, but only once per day.

NOTE

If necessary, users can manually initiate synchronization of the OST file by clicking the Send/Receive button in Outlook. Likewise, the automatic once-per-day synchronization of the OAB file can be initiated manually by clicking on Tools, Send/Receive, and Download Address Book. However, manual synchronization of the OST and OAB files is rarely necessary when Cached Exchange Mode is enabled. In fact, as the network administrator you may want to disable manual and scheduled synchronization to minimize unnecessary traffic on the Exchange server, unless the user is also using POP3, IMAP, or HTML-based webmail accounts such as Hotmail or Gmail.

Obviously, storing all this information in the OST and OAB files increases Outlook's footprint on the local machine. But there are several trade-off benefits such as a reduction in network traffic and reduced load on the Exchange server. It also gives users the ability to continue to access their data if the Exchange server goes offline. This data is available even if they disconnect from the network intentionally, which is especially beneficial for laptop users who often move between various wireless access points. While disconnected from the network they can compose email, look up contacts, and make schedule changes with no Internet or LAN access whatsoever. When they eventually reconnect to the network, the folders and contents can be synchronized with the Exchange server. Newly composed email and calendar updates on the laptop are sent up to the Exchange server, and new messages, schedule changes, and other mailbox updates are brought down to the OST file on the local machine.

CAUTION

Desktop search engines installed on client machines such as MSN Desktop Search can negatively affect performance of the Exchange Server. When these desktop search engine applications interact with Outlook and MAPI clients they can increase CPU usage, cause I/O spikes on the Exchange Server, and create bottlenecks for Remote Procedure Calls (RPC). For more detailed information on locating these client applications installed on workstations on the network and minimizing their negative effects, see Microsoft KB article 905184 (`http://support.microsoft.com/?id=905184`).

NOTE

Some features such as new email notification, uncached public folder access, free/busy lookup, and delegate support work with Outlook in Cached Exchange Mode, but only when Outlook has a live network connection to the Exchange server. If the network connection drops, these features cease to function until network connectivity is reestablished. A detailed explanation of the various synchronization modes and folder states available in Outlook is located in the "Troubleshooting Cached Exchange Mode" section found later in this chapter. .

When Outlook 2003 is initially installed on a client machine, Cached Exchange Mode in enabled by default. But when upgrading a client machine from a previous version of Outlook to Outlook 2003, Cached Exchange Mode is not enabled automatically. You may need to enable it yourself manually.

To enable Exchange cached mode in Outlook 2003, follow these steps:

1. Open Outlook, click Tools, E-mail Accounts.
2. In the E-mail Accounts dialog box, click View or Change Existing E-mail Accounts, and click Next.
3. In the Outlook Processes E-mail for These Accounts in the Following Order box, select the name of your Exchange server, and click Change.
4. Check the Use Cached Exchange Mode check box.
5. Click Next and click Finish.
6. Close and restart Outlook.

To disable Cached Exchange Mode in Outlook, simply uncheck the Use Cached Exchange Mode in step 4 in the preceding list. Also, Cached Exchange Mode can be disabled on the Exchange server by the network administrator.

NOTE

For an in-depth explanation of how Cached Exchange Mode works, including Registry keys that control synchronization timing, the order in which folders are synchronized, issues that affect performance degradation, and best practices, see Microsoft KB article 870926 (`http://support.microsoft.com/?id=870926`).

Disabling Cached Exchange Mode negatively affects network performance because of the increase in traffic between Outlook and Exchange. But it is more secure in the event of a computer theft because sensitive company information is safe back on the Exchange server and not stored in an OST file on the stolen machine.

Best Practice—Computers Using Cached Exchange Mode Should Protect Their OST Files Using NTFS Partitions

Computers running Outlook in Cached Exchange Mode should use the NTFS file system on the hard drive containing the OST and OAB files due to the potential for theft or misuse of sensitive information, particularly laptops and computers in public areas. You may also evaluate the possible need for encryption on those drives to comply with federal regulations if company email includes Protected Health Information (PHI) or financial information such as credit card numbers. A security solution is only as strong as its weakest link. It doesn't do any good to have firewalls protecting your Exchange server if that same data is in an OST file on a FAT32 partition in your salesman's laptop—especially if that laptop gets left at the local coffee house or stolen in an airport terminal.

Configuring Outlook Via the Internet, or RPC over HTTP

If you take a poll of SBS administrators and consultants and ask them what their favorite features of SBS are, Outlook via the Internet (also called RPC over HTTP) will definitely be in the top five of that list. It allows users outside the network firewall to use Outlook remotely to access their mailbox and public folders, and remote workers can access that information without the need for a *Virtual Private Network (VPN)* or dial-up remote access into the server. This is a huge cost savings from hardware and administrative standpoints. It also improves security because you no longer need to open up your entire network via VPN or dial-up just to give a remote worker access to his inbox. If you enable Cached Exchange Mode in Outlook, this minimizes the required bandwidth and offers an improved end-user experience, especially over slow Internet connections such as dial-up or busy Wi-Fi spots.

What Is RPC over HTTP?

First, to disassemble the acronyms, RPC over HTTP stands for *Remote Procedure Call over HyperText Transport Protocol*. To break that down even further, a *Remote Procedure Call (RPC)* is a command issued to a remote computer. In this instance, those RPC commands are related to processing email. The "over HTTP" in basic terms means that Outlook is communicating with the Exchange server over the Internet the same way a web browser views web pages. This makes it easier to establish a connection to the Exchange server, even if you are behind a firewall.

How RPC over HTTP Works

Because you don't want anyone on the Web executing commands on your server or reading your email as it passes by, all RPC traffic is wrapped in HTTP packets and encrypted in Secure Sockets Layer (SSL). Although it is technically *possible* to send RPC over HTTP without encryption, it poses a major security risk. So the default implementation of RPC over HTTP in an SBS environment includes SSL encryption. Stick to the default SBS settings, and you'll be fine.

The mention of SSL should clue you in that you'll need a certificate. You can go out and buy a certificate from a third-party vendor, but SBS has the capability to generate its own certificates, and those are free. So Outlook takes the certificate from the SBS server and uses it to encrypt the RPC packets with the public key before sending them across the Web. The SBS server then receives the encrypted packets and uses its private key to decrypt the packets and processes the RPC information inside. If an unauthorized computer on the Web intercepts the packets, they're useless because they're encrypted and can't be opened without the private key.

Preparing the Server for Outlook Via the Internet

Before configuring the client to use Outlook via the Internet, some configurations and items need to be put in place to prepare the SBS server:

1. If you haven't done so already, purchase a domain name such as `www.smallbizco.net`.
2. Contact your Internet Service Provider (ISP) and have the ISP set up an *A record* for you. This is not the same thing as an *MX record* (those are for email). The A record should be formatted *`servername.domain.com`* or *`servername.domain.net`* and point to the public IP address of your router. So, for example, if your server name is *SBS*, your domain is `smallbizco.net`, and your router's IP address is 217.142.22.7, you would ask your ISP to create your A record for `sbs.smallbizco.net` and point it to 217.142.22.7. Important: in this example, `sbs.smallbizco.net` is your *Fully Qualified Domain Name (FQDN)* for your SBS server. You'll need this information in step 6.
3. Launch the Configure Email and Internet Connection Wizard (CEICW) in SBS. To do this, open the System Management console, expand Standard Management, click on Internet and email, and then click on the green Connect to the Internet button.
4. If you ran CEICW during your initial installation of SBS, your Internet connection should already be set up. Click Do Not Change Connection Type and click Next.
5. On the following screen, make sure that the Allow Access Only to the Following Web Site Services from the Internet radio button is checked and check the box next to Outlook Via the Internet.

6. On the Web Server Certificate page, click the Create New Web server Certificate radio button, and enter your FQDN from step 2. In our example we'll use `sbs.smallbizco.net`, as shown in Figure 11.2.

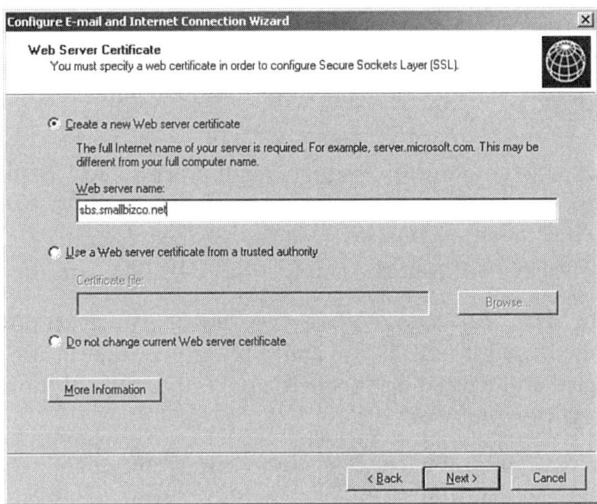

FIGURE 11.2 The information in the Web Server Name box must match exactly the A record on file with your ISP.

Best Practice—Create Your SSL Certificate Using Your Fully Qualified Domain Name, Not Your Public IP Address

Although it is possible to create an SSL certificate for SBS using the public IP address of the router, this is generally not recommended, for several reasons.

First, it's easier for users to remember names instead of numbers—for example, `sbs.smallbizco.net` instead of `217.142.22.7`. When they're typing in the address for Remote Web Workplace (RWW), OWA, OMA, or Outlook via the Internet, they'll appreciate the easy-to-remember name instead of the IP address. And if you use an FQDN instead of an IP address, users won't need to know or even care if you ever change ISPs.

Second, most small businesses typically do not own their public IP address—their ISP owns it. So if your SSL certificate is hard-coded to that IP address and you switch ISPs down the road, your new public IP address will not match the address on your old SSL certificate. You'll have to create a new certificate and install it on the server and on the client machines. But if you create your SSL certificate using your FQDN and then change ISPs, all you need to do is have your new ISP create a new A record for you. You'll still need to rerun CEICW to update your DNS server information. But after your new ISP creates that A record for you on its servers, as far as your certificates are concerned, you won't have to lift a finger, and neither will your users.

7. Click Next, click Do Not Change Internet E-mail Configuration, click Next again, and click Finish.

Configure Outlook Via the Internet on the Client

Because installing Outlook via the Internet is not especially intuitive in nature, Microsoft has included a dynamic page on the RWW that walks users through the install process. Not only does it outline the process step-by-step, but because the page is created dynamically, it inserts the correct answers to all the questions you'll come across, such as the name of your proxy server. To review this document, open Internet Explorer and go to `https://server/remote`; then click on Configure Your Computer to Use Outlook over the Internet.

As you'll notice, before delving into the actual install process itself, the instructions on that page walk the user through a self-conducted "pre-flight" check of sorts. The user needs to have three things: either Windows XP Service Pack 1 with KB #331320 patch or Windows XP Service Pack 2 (without the patch), Outlook 2003, and the SSL certificate.

When you browse to `https://server.domain.com/remote`, you are prompted to install the server's certificate; install it now. If you aren't prompted, that means that the certificate is already installed and trusted on this machine. Important: Without this certificate installed, RPC over HTTP won't work.

After those conditions are met, the user is ready to install Outlook via the Internet. Here is a succinct, but complete, version of the two-page ASP setup document found on RWW:

1. To open the Mail Setup dialog box, open Control Panel, double-click Mail, and click on Show Profiles.
2. If you already do have an existing profile, locate the profile and click Properties, click E-mail Accounts, click View or Change Existing E-mail Accounts, and click Next. Click Change and skip to step 4.
3. If you don't have a profile, click Add, type a profile name, click OK, click View or Change Existing E-mail Accounts, and click Next. In the E-mail Accounts dialog box, click Add, click Microsoft Exchange Server, and click Next.
4. In the Microsoft Exchange Server box, type the name of the local Exchange server—for example, **`sbs.smallbizco.local`**. It is also recommended that you also check the Use Cached Exchange Mode check box for improved performance.
5. In the User Name box, type your username, but do not click the Check Name button. Click More Settings.
6. On the Connection tab, click the Connect to my Exchange Mailbox Using HTTP check box, and click the Exchange Proxy Settings button.
7. On the Exchange Proxy Settings dialog box, in the Use This URL to Connect to My Proxy Server for Exchange, enter ***`server.domain`*`.com`**—for example, **`sbs.smallbizco.net`**.
8. Check the three boxes for Connect Using SSL Only, Mutually Authenticate the Session, and On Slow Networks, Connect Using selections.
9. In the Principle Name for Proxy Server enter **`msstd:`*`server.local`*`.com`**—for example, **`msstd:sbs.smallbizco.net`** (see Figure 11.3).

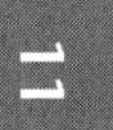

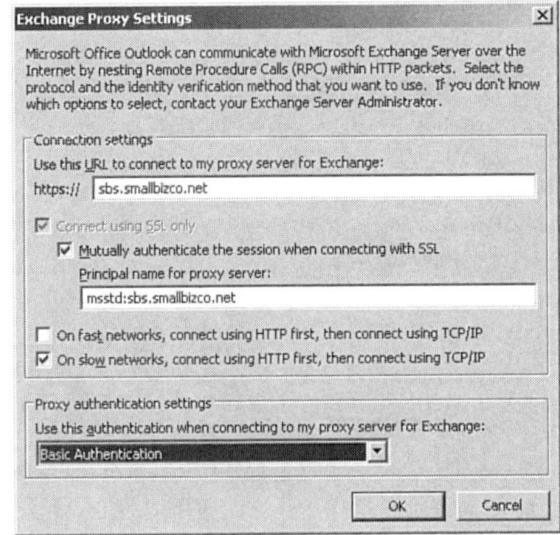

FIGURE 11.3 The URL in the Connection Settings box must match the A record on file with your ISP and your SSL certificate.

10. For Proxy Authentication Settings, choose Basic Authentication. Click OK twice, and then click Next, Finish, and Close.

You can now test your configuration by starting Outlook and entering your username and password. Outlook via the Internet is picky about the username format, and more detailed information about this can be found in the "Troubleshooting Outlook Via the Internet" section later in this chapter.

Using Outlook Web Access

Outlook Web Access, or OWA, allows remote users to access email, contacts, calendar items, tasks, and public folders remotely using only a web browser. OWA is often described by clients as "Outlook in a web browser," because it looks so similar to Outlook. In fact, the average passerby may not be able to tell the difference between the two. This similarity is by design to help minimize the learning curve for network users. If the users can operate Outlook at the office, they should be able to access the same data stored on the Exchange server using OWA with minimal training and the proper URL.

Enormous similarities aside, there are key differences between Outlook and OWA. For example, although Outlook can cache information locally and function offline, OWA requires a live network or Internet connection to the Exchange server. And although Outlook requires a disc or network install point and credentials to install the application on a client machine, OWA is just a website accessible via a URL through a web browser and doesn't need to be installed on the client.

The key thought to keep in mind is that there are benefits and drawbacks to both technologies. There is no perfect solution, and clients may require a combination of Outlook and OWA to fit their business needs. OWA is an excellent choice for high- or low-bandwidth environments and allows multiple users access to their Exchange data without storing multiple profiles on the local machine. But it's not as robust as Outlook and is unavailable when there is no network connectivity. So the rule of thumb is to use Outlook 2003 for the *knowledge worker* who spends all day accessing Exchange data, and use OWA for the occasional user and shared computer user at the office, or for the knowledge worker who wants to check her email and schedule from home.

OWA has actually been around for a while and was available in previous versions of SBS. Enhancements in bandwidth reduction, compression, and forms-based authentication, and an improved user interface built into Exchange Server 2003 make the new version of OWA 60% to 70% faster for low-bandwidth users. The faster logon time and page load times improve the end user experience. Better compression cuts OWA traffic across the wire by 40% to 60%, resulting in a cost savings for pay-by-the-byte bandwidth customers.

From an administrative standpoint, OWA is installed and enabled by default on the SBS server. Users inside and outside the firewall type in an abbreviated http:// URL in a standard web browser and are then automatically redirected to the https:// SSL secured 128-bit login page, so their credentials and all other traffic are encrypted.

Network users inside the firewall can access OWA in two ways; by opening the URL `http://servername/exchange` in their web browser, or by clicking on the Remote E-mail Access hyperlink on the default SBS intranet located at `http://companyweb`.

Users outside the corporate firewall can access OWA via the Internet. But external OWA access is disabled by default, so the administrator must enable access. To enable OWA for external users, follow these steps:

1. Click Start, and click Server Management.
2. Expand the Standard Management tree and click Internet and E-mail.
3. Click Connect to the Internet to launch the CEICW Wizard, and click Next.
4. On the Connection Type page click Do Not Change Connection Type radio button, and click Next.
5. On the Web Services Configuration page, check the Allow Access Only to the Following Web Site Services from the Internet radio button, make sure that the Outlook Web Access box is checked, and click Next.
6. If you have already set up RPC over HTTP earlier in this chapter, you should now see an existing SSL certificate (for example, `sbs.smallbizco.net`) on the Web Server Certificate page. If so, click Do Not Change Current Web Server Certificate, and click Next.
7. On the Internet E-mail page, click Do Not Change Internet Email Configuration, and click Next.
8. Review your changes on the final screen, and click Finish.
9. The CIECW Wizard now automatically opens the proper ports for you in the RRAS (SBS Standard) or ISA Server (SBS Premium) firewall. In the case of OWA, the external ports needing to be open are port 80 (http) and port 443 (https). When the wizard has completed successfully, you should see four green check marks next to Network Configuration, Firewall Configuration, Secure Web Site Configuration, and E-mail Configuration. Click Close.

Best Practice—Make Sure That the Proper Ports Are Open on Both the Firewall and the Router

It may seem like a platitude, but never assume anything, especially in a network environment. Even though the SBS wizards open the necessary ports in the firewall, that doesn't mean your job is done. Always double-check to make sure that corresponding ports are also open on the router connecting the SBS server to the Internet. Some ISPs block all inbound port traffic on routers they control, and you have to contact them with the specific port numbers you need opened. More than a few SBS administrators have run the wizards, tested OWA or RWW from the Internet, failed, and immediately assumed that the wizards didn't "take" and the problem was inside SBS. Learn from their pain, and before you bang your head in frustration, call the ISP and make sure that those router ports are open.

10. If you have not already done so, the CEICW Wizard now prompts you to enable password policies. Click Yes.

CAUTION

Having strong passwords on a network is always a good idea. But after you enable OWA, RWW, or any of the other SBS technologies that allow access to your network from the Internet, it is critical that strong passwords be enabled. After you open ports in your firewall, the only things keeping company information safe from prying eyes on the Internet are a username and a password. Because most companies use an employee's username in her email address, a hacker already has one of the two puzzle pieces, and even strong passwords need to be changed routinely.

11. Check the Password Must Meet Complexity Requirements check box and select a password length, an expiration frequency, and an effective date that meet your company's individual needs (see Figure 11.4). Click OK.

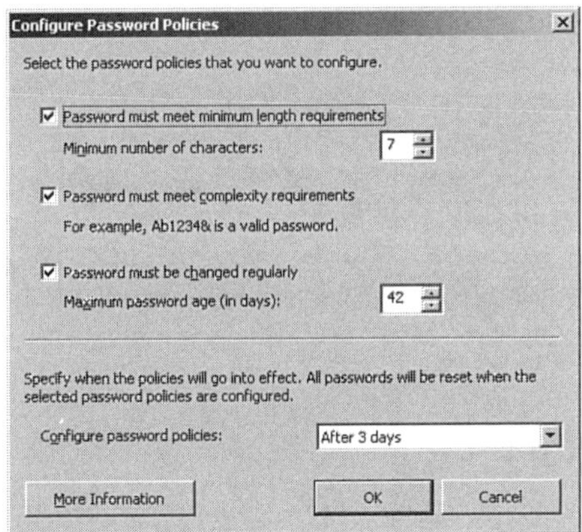

FIGURE 11.4 It's especially important to enable strong password policies when using OWA and other remote features in SBS.

> **NOTE**
>
> If you're unsure about which password settings to use, you can always rerun the Configure Password Policies Wizard again at a later time. It's located in Server Manager, Standard Management, Users, Configure Password Policies. You can click the More Information button to learn about all the options in Figure 11.4.

Whether connecting to OWA inside the firewall or across the Internet, three different varieties of OWA are available in SBS 2003: OWA Basic, OWA Premium, and OWA Premium with ActiveX. When initially logging in to OWA, the user is given a choice of OWA Basic or Premium; OWA Premium with Active X is not shown on the login menu (see Figure 11.5). The user must also choose one of two OWA security settings; either Public or Shared Computer or Private Computer. The advantages and drawbacks of each OWA version and security settings are discussed in detail.

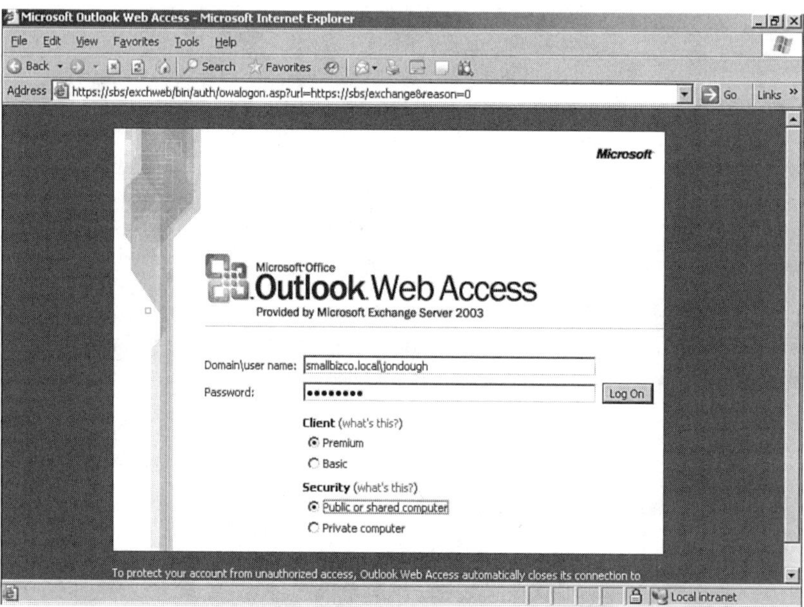

FIGURE 11.5 OWA allows users to choose client and security settings that match their environment.

Outlook Web Access Basic

OWA Basic is just like the name sounds—the most basic version of email access via a web browser (see Figure 11.6). As nice as having many features can be, sometimes less is more, especially in low-bandwidth or high-security scenarios. Because OWA Basic runs in a single web browser window, it loads faster than OWA Premium. It's also useful in Mac and UNIX environments.

However, OWA Basic can't pop up additional windows or dialog boxes, so it lacks key features, including spell checking, search capabilities, the capability to mark messages as read or unread, and new mail notification. To check for new mail the user must manually refresh the browser window, typically by pressing F5 in Internet Explorer, Firefox, or Opera.

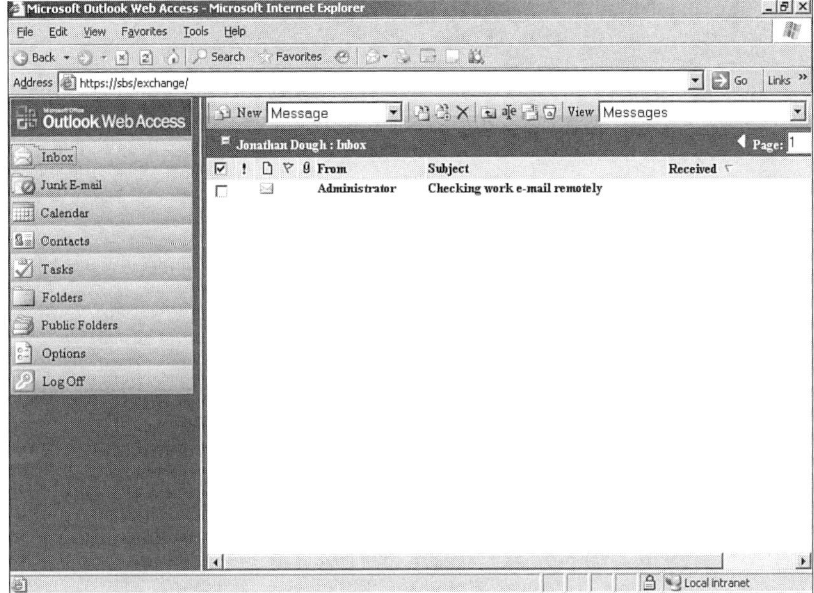

FIGURE 11.6 OWA Basic offers a simple and straightforward interface.

Outlook Web Access Premium

If given a choice, most users opt for OWA Premium (see Figure 11.7). The feature set in Premium is much closer to what users are accustomed to in Outlook 2003, and the layout is nearly identical. Feature improvements over Basic include spell checking, message flags, reminder windows, message sensitivity, and search capabilities. Premium also includes the aesthetic features such as the Reading Pane and five different OWA color schemes available in the Options menu.

Spell Checking

The spell checking available in OWA is great feature, but this is not the full version of spell checking found in Outlook 2003. OWA Premium spell checking checks only the first 96K of the email, and it checks only the reply portion of the email. Also, because the spell checking is performed by the server and not on the client or web browser, you cannot add new words to the dictionary. Keep in mind that spell checking is not available in OWA Basic.

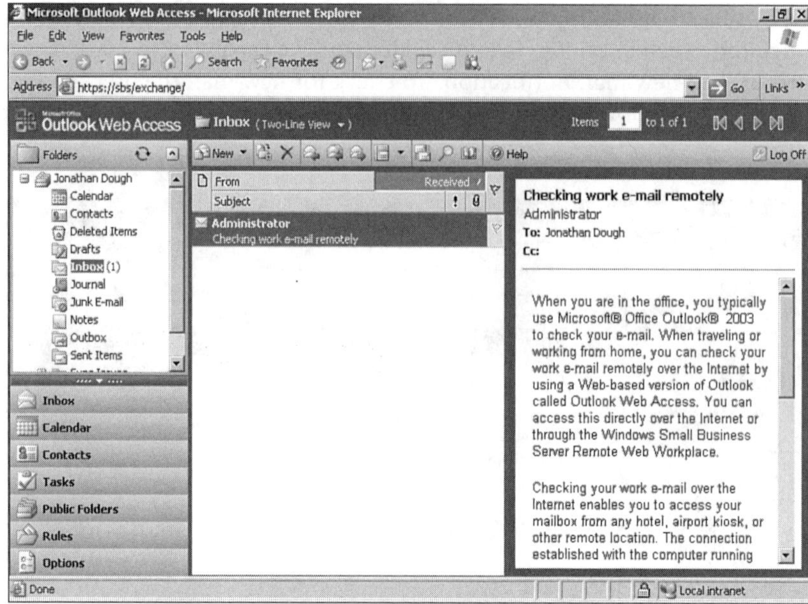

FIGURE 11.7 OWA Premium mimics the features and layout of Outlook 2003 (refer to Figure 11.1).

Outlook Web Access Premium with ActiveX

The third, and most overlooked, version of Outlook Web Access is OWA Premium with ActiveX. This is OWA Premium with an ActiveX control installed on the client machine. The necessary ActiveX control, called the S/MIME control, can be downloaded and installed from the Options page in OWA Premium (see Figure 11.8).

Once installed, the ActiveX control can be viewed or removed from the Add/Remove Programs Wizard in the Control Panel of Windows. The system requirements are a client OS of Windows 2000 or greater, the web browser must be IE6 or higher, and the user must have sufficient privileges to install the ActiveX control locally.

The ActiveX version of OWA supports S/MIME, which is the standard for sending signed and encrypted email. This makes sure that your email content is always encrypted when going over the network. It also allows better drag-and-drop attachment handling.

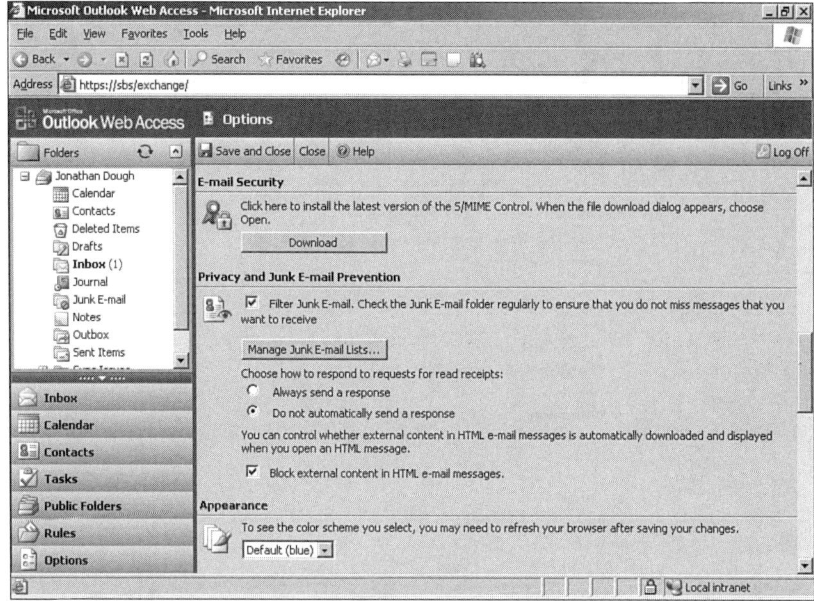

FIGURE 11.8 Downloading and installing the S/MIME ActiveX control turns OWA Premium into OWA Premium with ActiveX.

Best Practice—Download the Outlook Web Access Administration Kit

As powerful and useful as OWA is, more features are hidden under the surface that can be unlocked by downloading and installing the Outlook Web Access Administration Kit from the following URL: `http://www.microsoft.com/exchange/downloads`.

In a nutshell, the OWA Admin Kit allows a network administrator to configure the registry keys that control OWA, and it gives you a single location to see all the OWA settings available. You also get an in-depth explanation of what each setting does. The OWA Administration tool requires IE6 or higher, and for security reasons, it should be installed on a separate workstation on the domain, not on the SBS server.

After installation of the `OWAAdmin.MSI` file, an icon will be added to the Microsoft Exchange program group in the Start menu called Outlook Web Access Administration. Alternatively, you can access the OWA Admin tool from the URL `https://servername/OWAAdmin` in Internet Explorer (see Figure 11.9).

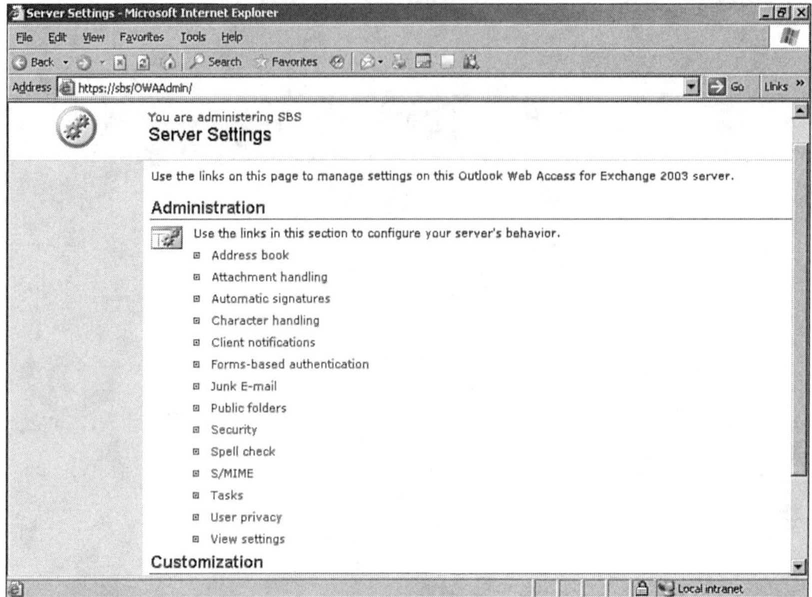

FIGURE 11.9 The Outlook Web Access Administration Kit exposes the hidden settings in OWA.

Perhaps the single biggest reason to download and use the OWA Administration Kit is to enable remote workers or users without a dedicated workstation to change their domain password through OWA. Without this feature, all OWA users must periodically log in to a workstation on the domain or VPN in to the network to change their password when it expires. True, OWA does notify users that their domain password is about to expire, and that's helpful, but a standard installation of SBS doesn't allow password changes through OWA. If the user's password expires and he keeps entering the password repeatedly, the user account will become locked, and that's a sure-fire recipe for a help desk call.

To enable the ability to change passwords in OWA, open the OWAAdmin toolkit as described previously, click on Security, scroll down to the Enable Change Password section, click the Yes radio button, and click OK (see Figure 11.10). Before enabling this feature, you should also read Microsoft KB article 297121 (`http://support.microsoft.com/?id=297121`).

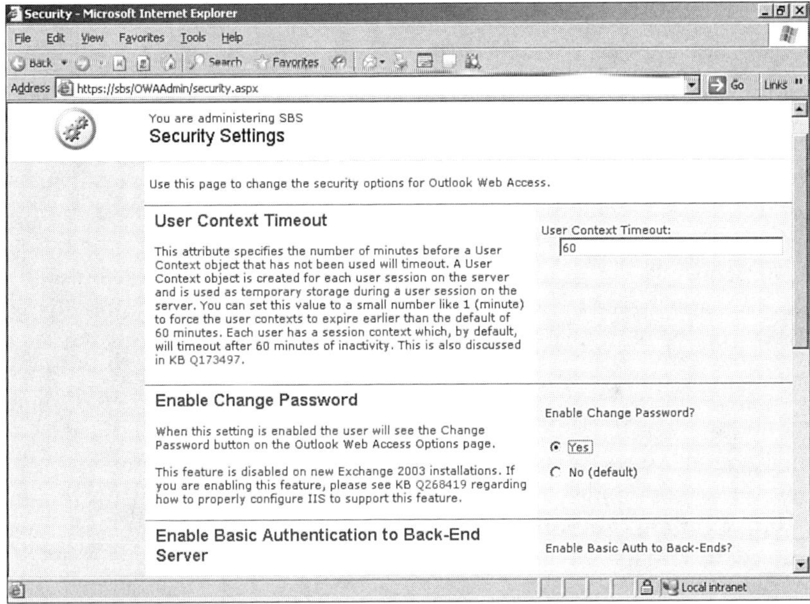

FIGURE 11.10 The Security tab contains several options, including the ability to change passwords in OWA.

If you successfully installed the change password configuration, OWA users should see a new button on their Options tab in OWA (see Figure 11.11).

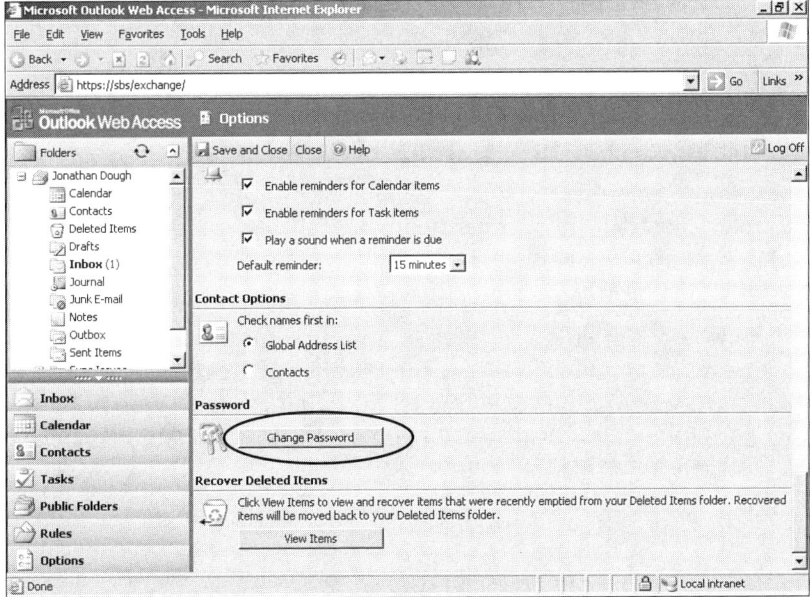

FIGURE 11.11 Notice the new Change Password button between the Contact Options and Recover Deleted Items sections.

Outlook Web Access Security Settings

The OWA login screen provides two security options: Public or Shared Computer and Private Computer.

Public or Shared Computer Security Setting

The Public or Shared Computer security configuration for OWA is selected by default and is the most secure configuration. Users are automatically logged off after a short period of inactivity (default 15 minutes). This setting is beneficial for web kiosks, computer labs, or computers in public places. Because this configuration "times out" more quickly, users may be inadvertently logged off when typing long emails or when temporarily distracted by a phone call or visitor, so instruct users to periodically save their work when using public mode.

Private Computer Security Setting

The Private Computer security configuration for OWA is often used at remote offices, warehouses, employees' homes, and other locations where the computer is in a more secure physical location. Users of this setting are automatically logged off after a longer period of inactivity (default 24 hours).

> **NOTE**
>
> Most SBS administrators consider the 15–20 minute window too long for a session timeout on a public machine. Fortunately, the session timeout duration, or *cookie authentication timeout*, can be adjusted manually by the network administrator. To adjust this OWA setting and others such as custom logon pages, attachment blocking, and forms-based authentication, see the Microsoft knowledge base article 830827, "How to manage Outlook Web Access features in Exchange Server 2003" (`http://support.microsoft.com/?id=830827`).

Using Outlook Mobile Access (OMA)

When users are away from their personal computer or handheld organizer, they can still access their email, contacts, and calendar stored in Exchange using a web-enabled cell phone and OMA (see Figure 11.12). OMA is lightweight on the features, but it more than makes up for that with speed.

The abbreviation OMA is often confused with OWA, but the two technologies are vastly different in appearance and function. To mentally differentiate the two, remember that Outlook *Web* Access (OWA) is for web browsers in computers, and Outlook *Mobile* Access (OMA) is designed for mobile phones or cell phones. By default, OMA is enabled for all mailbox-enabled SBS domain user accounts.

The LCD displays on cell phones are notoriously tiny, and the buttons on phones are equally small. So OMA is designed with a minimalistic interface that can be controlled using just a couple of buttons on the cell phone. If you don't have a web-enabled cell phone, you can still test drive OMA via a standard web browser on a desktop or notebook computer.

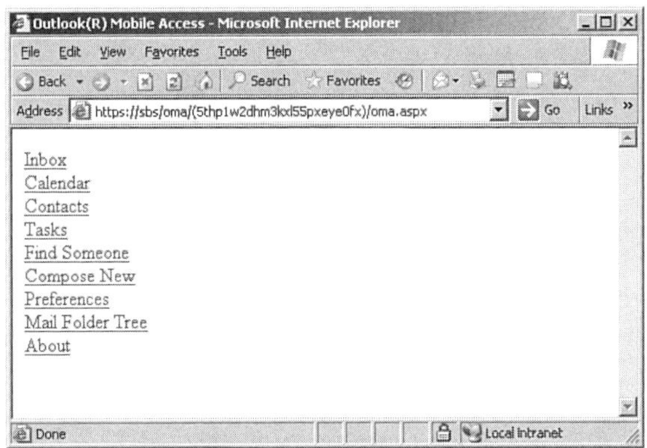

FIGURE 11.12 OMA may be used from a cell phone's web browser to access information stored in Exchange.

To access OMA inside the SBS firewall, go to the URL `http://servername/oma`, where *`servername`* is the name of your SBS server—for example, `http://sbs/oma`.

To access OMA *outside* the corporate firewall from the Internet, go to the URL `http://servername.domainname.com/oma`—for example, `http://sbs.smallbizco.net/oma`.

It is important to note that SBS installs OMA with Exchange by default, and it is automatically enabled inside the firewall. But, just like OWA, it uses ports 80 (http) and 443 (https), and you must run the Configure Email and Internet Connection Wizard (CEICW) to enable OMA access to the Internet.

To use OMA from a web-enabled cell phone, follow these steps:

1. Open the web browser on your mobile phone and verify that it is connected to the Internet. Enter the URL of your SBS server into the web browser in the format *`servername.domainname`*`.com/oma`—for example `http://sbs.smallbizco.net/oma`.
2. When OMA responds, enter your username and password and click OK.
3. Typically, OMA authenticates your username and password and replies "The device type you are using is not supported. Press Ok to continue." This is normal. Click OK.

That's all there is to it. The OMA main menu includes Inbox, Calendar, Contacts, Tasks, Find Someone, Compose New, Preferences, and About.

The data updated via OMA is relayed back to the Exchange Server in real-time, and navigation is simple because a Home link is at the bottom of each screen.

NOTE

One handy feature OMA includes is the capability to change the domain user's password. Unfortunately, OWA doesn't include this functionality by default. So if the OWA users on your network report that OWA keeps counting down the days until their password expires, you have two choices: Install the Outlook Web Access Administration Kit mentioned earlier in this chapter, or have the users log in to OMA and change their password from there.

Because of the lack of keyboard, email attachments, or graphics, OMA is better suited for reading email, calendar items, tasks, and contacts than it is at creating them. OMA is nice for quick information lookups, provided that it can cache your username and password on the phone.

If users' credentials and URL can't be cached because of the limitations of the phone, users probably won't adopt OMA. Entering a username, password, and URL each time, quickly becomes tedious. For example, for Jonathan Dough to enter his username and password, he would need to press the following keystrokes on the cell phone keypad (example—for the letter "S" press the #7 key four times, and so on):

Username:

`j o n d o u g h` 5> 666> 66> 3> 666> 88> 4> 44>

Password:

`p a 5 5 w 0 r d` 7> 2> 5> 5> 9> 0> 777> 3>

This demonstration shows 23 keypresses for the username, and 18 button presses for the password. And that doesn't even include entering the URL first of `http://sbs.smallbizco.net/oma`.

For many users, the make-or-break for OMA depends on ease of use, and that judgment hinges on the actual phone itself, not on OMA. Most new cell phones offer a feature called *T9 Predictive Text Input* where the phone guesses what word you're trying to type to ultimately save you keystrokes. T9 is helpful for composing brief emails or SMS messages, but it doesn't work for usernames, strong passwords, or URLs.

The bottom line is that OMA is a breeze for the administrator, but the cellular equipment ultimately determines whether users will adopt this Exchange client.

Using ActiveSync

Described simply, the job of ActiveSync is to synchronize the content of mobile devices with the Exchange server. Likewise, ActiveSync can synchronize content between the mobile device and a host desktop PC to back up the mobile device in case of power failure or service replacement.

ActiveSync Versions

The original Windows SBS 2003 release came with ActiveSync 3.7 installed. SBS Service Pack 1 upgraded ActiveSync to version 3.8 with minor improvements and is the current version. ActiveSync 4.0 is the successor to 3.8, with support for the Windows Mobile 5.0 operating system for handheld devices.

Mobile Devices

PocketPCs for use with SBS 2003 are handheld devices that run either Windows Mobile 2002, 2003, or 2003 Second Edition, which is the current version. The next operating system release for PocketPCs, also slated for release in late 2005, is called Windows Mobile 5. These mobile devices fall into three categories, discussed in the following sections.

PocketPC

Of the three Windows Mobile device types available, PocketPCs are in the middle of the pack, regarding size; they are larger than the SmartPhones but smaller than the Phone Editions. PocketPC devices can be basic no-frills or high-end with Bluetooth, 802.1x WiFi, and can even include a digital camera. What differentiates the PocketPC from the other two categories of devices is that PocketPCs don't include a phone. The screen size is large (unlike the SmartPhone), and, depending on the model, you can enter text via a stylus or possibly a built-in or snap-on mini keyboard. Who is it for? Your typical user who needs to take her data on the road and doesn't need always-on Internet access.

PocketPC Phone Edition

Take everything that the PocketPC has, add built-in phone capability, make the case a bit larger to hold those extra electronics, and you have a PocketPC Phone Edition. The built-in phone is useful for making calls or data transmission. These devices are top of the line in features and capabilities. If you don't mind the larger form factor, PocketPC Phone Edition devices are as close as you can come to having your cake and eating it too. Who is it for? Road warriors, techs, and consultants who don't have time to hunt down a public WiFi hotspot, and who don't want to hassle with plugging their PocketPC into a regular cell phone.

SmartPhones

Take a cell phone with a normal small screen, give it the brains of a Windows Mobile device, and you've got a SmartPhone. SmartPhones come in flip-phone or conventional "eyeglass case size" form factors. They don't have a stylus for input, so they're more geared toward reading email and making calls. Who is it for? Sales reps and executives who need to keep in touch and like the smaller form factor but who don't need to send a lot of emails from the road.

Synchronization

ActiveSync is typically installed on the client workstation by checking the Install ActiveSync 3.8 check box when running the Set Up Client Computers Wizard in the Server Management Console. If a client machine is already a member of the domain, you can add ActiveSync by performing the following steps:

1. Click Start, Server Management, Standard Management, Client Computers, and click Assign Applications to Client Computers.
2. In the Assign Applications Wizard window, click Next, highlight the computers that need ActiveSync installed, click Add, and click Next.
3. On the Client Applications screen, ignore the check boxes and just click Next.
4. On the Mobile Client and Offline Use screen, check the box next to Install ActiveSync 3.8, click Next, and click Finish.

After adding ActiveSync 3.8 to the workstation, follow the instructions from the hand-held device manufacturer for installing the cradle and initializing the PocketPC or

SmartPhone. When you plug the cradle into the USB port and insert the PocketPC into the cradle, Windows XP automatically detects the device and ActiveSync launches. To properly configure ActiveSync, follow these steps:

1. On the New Partnership screen, choose Standard Partnership, and click Next.
2. When asked Specify How to Synchronize Data, choose Synchronize with Microsoft Exchange Server and/or This Desktop Computer, and click Next.
3. Enter the server name—for example, `sbs.smallbizco.net`. The URL should match your SSL certificate and should omit the "http://" prefix.
4. Check the This Server Uses an SSL Connection check box.
5. Enter your domain username (for example, **`jondough`**), your domain password, your domain (for example, **`smallbizco`**), check the Save Password box, and click Next (see Figure 11.13).

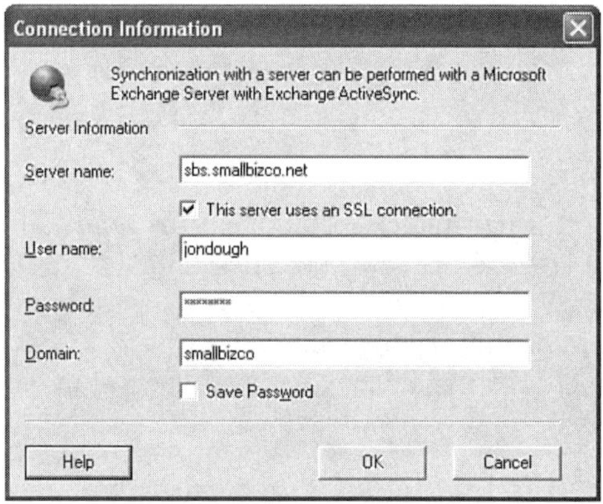

FIGURE 11.13 ActiveSync can use your credentials to connect to Exchange through the cradle, via infrared, or across a wireless connection.

6. In the Mobile Device window, check the boxes next to Calendar, Contacts, and Inbox. By highlighting Calendar or Inbox and then clicking the Settings button, you can specify additional options such as downloading email attachments. Contacts has no additional settings. When you are finished specifying any additional options, click Next.
7. On the next window, ActiveSync gives you the two options on how to handle items that may already exist on your PocketPC. The first option, Delete Any Items, is more destructive but avoids possible duplicates. The second option, Keep the Items on My Device, is a safer option but may result in duplicate items. Choose the appropriate selection for your handheld device, or if this is a new PocketPC, click OK.
8. Enter a unique device name to identify this handheld. The default ID is Pocket_PC, but that ID may have already been used before. Enter an appropriate name to your liking, and click Next.

9. The Select Synchronization Settings screen contains six more synchronization items: AvantGo Channels, Internet Explorer Favorites, Synchronized Files, Microsoft Outlook Notes, Microsoft Pocket Outlook Databases, and Microsoft Outlook Tasks. Important: If you select any of these items, they will only synchronize when the PocketPC is docked in the cradle. ActiveSync only synchronizes your Calendar, Contacts, and Inbox over the air remotely.

10. Click Next, and click Finish. ActiveSync automatically begins synchronization. When synchronization has finished, check the status window. All items should show a status of Synchronized. If so, you're done!

If any items say "Sync status is on the device", you need to check the device for an error report. Most likely the device is missing the SSL certificate from the SBS server. To remedy this, follow these steps:

1. On the PocketPC, click Start, Programs, and ActiveSync. Look for a blue hyperlink that says "Errors" and click it. If you receive an error code `INTERNET_45`, the PocketPC is missing the Root Certificate from the SBS server.

2. To locate the Root Certificate on your desktop PC, click Start, Run, type **`MMC`** and click OK. In the MMC console, click File, Add/Remove Snap-In, and click Add. In the Add Standalone Snap-Ins window, click Certificates, Add, My User Account, and then click Finish, Close, and OK.

3. To select the Root Certificate, expand Certificates - Current User, expand Trusted Root Certificate Authorities, click Certificates, and select the SBS certificate—for example, `sbs.smallbizco.net` (see Figure 11.14).

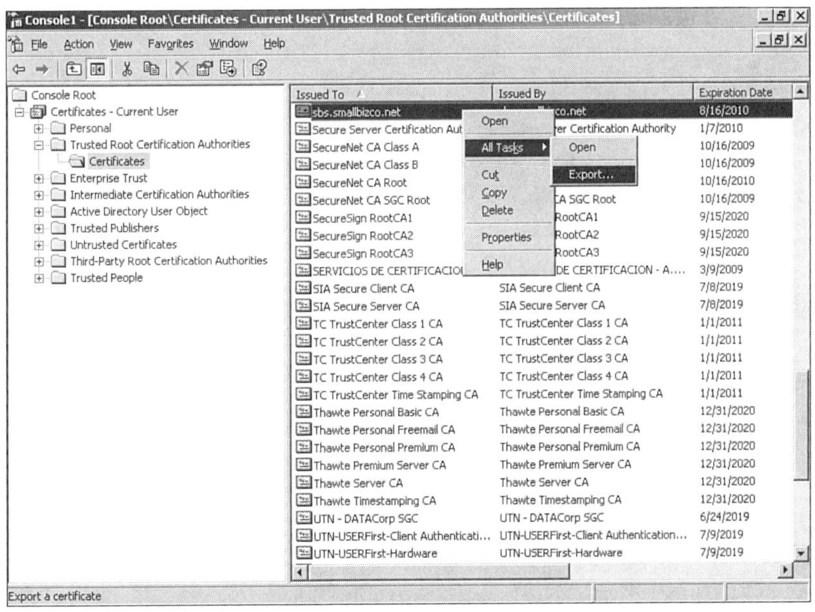

FIGURE 11.14 The Root Certificate can be found in the Console Root Directory.

4. To export the Root Certificate, right-click the certificate, click All Tasks, and click Export. The Certificate Export Wizard launches on the workstation. Click Next, select DER Encoded Binary X.509 (.CER), click Next again, and save the file on your hard drive as `wirelesscert.cer`. Click Next and then click Finish.

5. Locate where you saved the `wirelesscert.cer` certificate, and, with the PocketPC still in the cradle, copy and paste the certificate to the PocketPC.

6. On the PocketPC click Start, Programs, File Explorer, and locate the `wirelesscert.cer` on the device. Click the certificate one time, and then click Yes to install it.

7. Finally, synchronize the PocketPC again. There should be no errors.

NOTE

A valuable reference detailing the function of mobile devices and synchronization in a small business network is the Microsoft "Small IT Solution for Mobility," available here: `http://www.microsoft.com/technet/itsolutions/smbiz/sitmob/default.mspx`.

To aid in troubleshooting, detailed step-by-step instructions with screen shots on how to synchronize a PocketPC with Exchange 2003 are available on Daniel Petri's, MVP's MCSEworld website: `http://www.petri.co.il/how_to_sync_ppc_with_exchange_2003.htm`.

Troubleshooting Client Connectivity

Microsoft offers extensive information online for troubleshooting Exchange clients on the TechNet website (`http://technet.microsoft.com/default.aspx`). The following section details some of the most common support issues with Exchange clients you may encounter in the SBS environment.

Troubleshooting Cached Exchange Mode

The following modes and notes visible in the lower right corner of the Outlook status bar indicate in which mode Outlook is functioning and the status of the offline folders:

- Disconnected—This folder was last updated at (time). Status: There is no network connectivity with the Exchange server.
- Trying to connect—This folder is trying to update. Status: Establishing connection with the Exchange server.
- Connected—All folders are up-to-date. Status: Cached Exchange Mode is enabled, and local OST and OAB folders are up to date.
- Online—Status: Cached Exchanged Mode is disabled and Outlook is communicating directly with the Exchange server.
- Offline—This folder was last updated at (time). Status: Cached Exchange Mode and Outlook will not try to automatically synchronize with the Exchange server.

TIP

While working in Offline mode, clicking the Send/Receive button on the Standard Outlook toolbar temporarily puts Outlook in Connected mode, manually synchronizes the folders, and then automatically returns Outlook to Offline mode. This also brings up an Outlook Send/Receive Progress dialog box with helpful synchronization and error information. Unfortunately, the box closes automatically after attempting synchronization, leaving you no time to view the window contents. But if you click on the pushpin icon located in the lower-right corner of the window, this pins the window open even after synchronization is complete. You can also click on the Send/Receive drop-down list, Send/Receive Settings, and Show Progress to bring up the last synchronization box if it has already closed.

A common tech support call comes from users who state that Outlook is running, but they haven't gotten any new email in quite some time. Ask the user if the mode indicator on the Outlook status bar says Disconnected or Offline. If it does, have the user click the word Disconnected or Offline and uncheck the Work Offline selection. Outlook should then attempt to connect to the Exchange server to synchronize the folders.

If Work Offline is already unchecked, make sure that the user has network connectivity. If network connectivity is already established, verify that the user has valid credentials on the Exchange server. This can be done by having the user attempt to access OWA with Internet Explorer using his username and password. This simple test also ensures that the Exchange server is running and available.

Another area with valuable troubleshooting information is the SyncIssues folder located in the Folder List view in the Navigation Pane in Outlook. If Outlook is disconnected from the Exchange server, you should see two subfolders named Conflicts and Local Failures. If Outlook is connected to the Exchange server, you should also see a third folder called Server Failures. Look in these folders for possible synchronization errors.

Offline Folder Is Running Out of Space

During the initial installation of Cached Exchange Mode, the offline data file created is in ANSI format, which has a 2GB size limit. For most users, 2GB is plenty of space for their Outlook content. But for users who need more space, a multilingual format called Unicode offers a 20GB folder size limit. If a user has a large number of items in his mailbox and is experiencing slower performance in Outlook, he may be using an ANSI data file that is running out of space. To determine which mode the offline file is in (ANSI or Unicode), follow these steps:

1. Open Outlook; click on Tools, E-mail Accounts, View or Change Existing E-mail Accounts, and click Next.
2. Select your email account, and click Change, More Settings.
3. On the Advanced tab is a Mailbox Mode box. If you are already running in Unicode mode, it will say, "Outlook is running in Unicode mode against the Microsoft Exchange Server."

If you are running in ANSI mode, unfortunately, there is no built-in provision for converting an existing ANSI folder to Unicode. Instead, you need to create a new Outlook data file in Unicode format and then import the existing data into the new file. For step-by-step instructions on this process, open Outlook, click Help, and search on "Unicode". The article "Convert a Non-Unicode Data File (`.pst`) to a Unicode Data File (`.pst`)" contains the necessary instructions.

Troubleshooting Outlook Via the Internet

A common error experienced by clients using Outlook over the Internet is supplying the username in an incorrect format. This error doesn't sound like a big deal, but it's very frequent because most domain users are accustomed to typing only *`username`* in the username field when they log on to their workstations. But to use Outlook via the Internet, a slight modification is required by the user. Clients need to add the prefix *`domain\`* or `domain.local\` to their username, so the correct result should be in the format `domain\username` or `domain.local\username`. Tables 11.1 and 11.2 give examples of correct and incorrect name formats.

TABLE 11.1 The Correct Username Formats for Outlook Via the Internet

Correct Formats	Correct Username Examples
`domain\username`	`smallbizco\billdough`
`domain.local\username`	`smallbizco.local\billdough`

TABLE 11.2 Common Incorrect Examples of Username Formats for Outlook Via the Internet

Incorrect Formats	Incorrect Username Examples
`username`	`billdough`
`servername\username`	`sbs\billdough`
`domain.com\username`	`smallbizco.net\billdough`
`servername.domain\username`	`sbs.smallbizco\billdough`
`servername.domain.com\username`	`sbs.smallbizco.net\billdough`
`servername.domain.local\username`	`sbs.smallbizco.local\billdough`

As you can see, there are numerous ways for the client to get this wrong, and only two ways to get it right. Out of habit, most will usually try the first incorrect example, `username`. When that doesn't work they may be pretty confused because `username` works fine with both the domain login and the RWW login. Users may try several other incorrect combinations before finally either giving up or picking up the phone to call you.

When you get that call, have the user look at the title bar of the username and password dialog box. At the top, the window will say "Connect to 'server.domain.local'". Instruct the user to use the domain name in the middle, a backslash, followed by the username. He can also use `domain.local\username`, but not `domain.net\username`, as mentioned previously.

Troubleshooting Outlook Web Access

The most common OWA issue is clients using an incorrect URL depending on whether they are inside the firewall. On the LAN the correct URL is `http://servername/exchange`. Outside the LAN, the URL should be `http://servername.domainname.com/exchange`.

Troubleshooting Outlook Mobile Access (OMA)

Because the interface and features of OMA are minimal, troubleshooting is also minimal. Typically OMA just works without any unnecessary care or feeding, but there are a couple of issues to be aware of with OMA.

Invalid Password Characters in OMA

This is a rather minor issue, but some mobile phones don't allow mixed-case characters when entering passwords, specifically some Motorola/Nextel phones. The problem lies with the cell phone itself, not with OMA. So if you're enforcing strong passwords on your network, make sure that the cell phone can enter upper-and lowercase alphabetical characters and other "special" characters. If the phone has input limitations, be sure and educate the network users to avoid using those characters in their network password.

"Item no longer exists" Error

When browsing to `http://servername/oma` internally or `http://servername.domain.com/oma` externally, the web browser returns the error, "Item no longer exists. The item you are attempting to access may have been deleted or moved."

Usually this error pops up after an administrator has added an additional SMTP address (such as `info@smallbizco.net`) to an existing domain user account, and deleting the offending SMTP address does not resolve the error.

The fix is simply changing an IIS virtual directory setting from the `.local` suffix to the proper `.com` or `.net` suffix to match your SSL certificate on the SBS server.

To find and repair the offending entry, follow these steps:

1. Click Start, Server Management; expand Advanced Management, Internet Information Services, Local Computer, Web Sites, Default Web Site (see Figure 11.15).

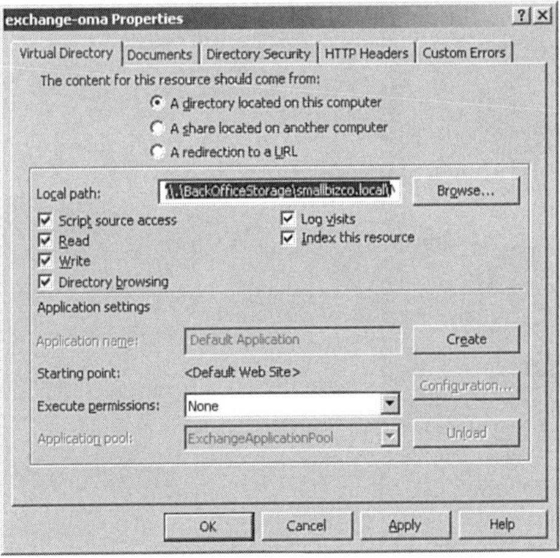

FIGURE 11.15 An incorrect local path in the Exchange-OMA virtual directory is usually the culprit of "Item no longer exists" OWA errors.

2. Right-click the exchange-oma virtual directory and click Properties. On the Virtual Directory tab in the Local Path box, look at the entry. It may read `\\.\BackOfficeStorage\smallbizco.local\MBX`. If so, change it to match the domain suffix on your SBS certificate—for example, `\\.\BackOfficeStorage\small-bizco.net\MBX`.

Troubleshooting ActiveSync

By far, the single most common problem with ActiveSync is due to Windows Integrated Authentication not being set on the `/Exchange` virtual directory in IIS. To verify or enable this, follow these steps:

1. Open the Server Management Console.
2. Expand Advanced Management.
3. Expand Internet Information Services.
4. Expand Servername (local computer).
5. Expand Web Sites.
6. Expand Default Web Site.
7. Right-click the Exchange virtual directory (see Figure 11.16).
8. Select Properties from the pop-up menu.

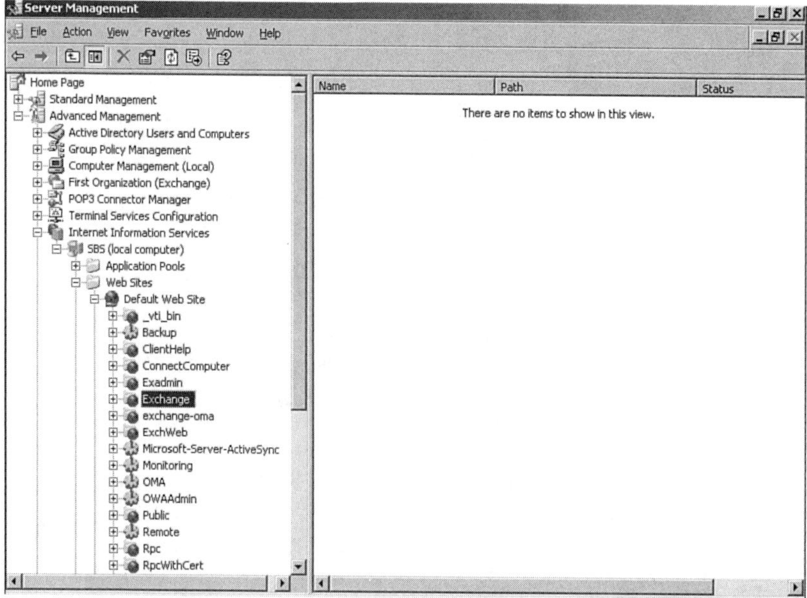

FIGURE 11.16 Drill down to the Exchange virtual directory in IIS to locate the Exchange Properties dialog box.

9. In the Exchange Properties dialog box, click on the Directory Security tab.
10. In the Authentication and Access control box, click the Edit button (see Figure 11.17).
11. In the Authenticated Access box on the Authentication Methods dialog box, the Integrated Windows Authentication check box should be checked.

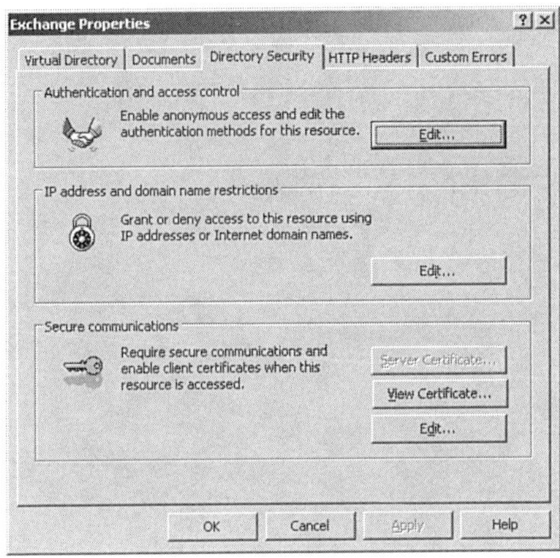

FIGURE 11.17 Click Edit to modify the authentication and access control settings.

12. Click OK to close the Authentication Methods window.
13. Click OK once more to close the Exchange Properties window.

Summary

This chapter looked at the available Exchange clients: Outlook, Outlook Web Access, Outlook Mobile Access, and ActiveSync. All four clients access the same information stored in Exchange, but the level of detail and functionality varies for each client. It is common for knowledge workers to utilize multiple Exchange clients, depending on their physical location and available bandwidth. This chapter also outlined key design and performance features and common troubleshooting issues.

Best Practice Summary

- Download and review the Microsoft whitepaper, "Enabling a Superior Client Experience with Microsoft Office Outlook 2003"—This whitepaper is a network administrator's best friend when you need an in-depth look at how Outlook connects with the Exchange Server, and how to leverage the new features to improve end user access to the Exchange data.

- Computers using Cached Exchange Mode should protect their OST files using NTFS partitions—Sensitive company information is stored in the offline files, and if a laptop is lost or stolen, information can be easily compromised if it isn't stored on a protected folder on the hard disk.
- Create your SSL certificate using your Fully Qualified Domain Name, not your public IP address—Many factors can lead to a change in IP address, which would require generating a new certificate and deploying it to every workstation that had the old one stored.
- Make sure that the proper ports are open on both the firewall and the router—Having the correct ports open in the SBS firewall doesn't matter if those same ports are not opened at the external firewall.

CHAPTER 12

Exchange Management

IN THIS CHAPTER

- Default Mailbox Management Configuration
- Junk Mail and Viruses
- Microsoft Connector for POP3 Mailboxes
- Receiving Mail with Multiple Domains
- Troubleshooting Exchange Management Issues

SBS 2003 installs with Exchange Server 2003 standard and offers several additions not found with previous versions of Exchange. SBS 2003 takes advantage of Outlook Web Access, Outlook Mobile Access, and Exchange Server ActiveSync. SBS also provides a tool to download POP3 (Post Office Protocol) email into the Exchange server that is not available with other server solutions. SBS administrators can also use the Intelligent Message Filter (IMF) Exchange add-on to help control spam on the network. To keep those features running smoothly, the Exchange part of SBS 2003 must be managed and maintained.

Default Mailbox Management Configuration

During setup Exchange features are easily configured through the use of the Configure Email and Internet Connection Wizard. The wizard configures the following settings by default.

- Deleted Items Retention—Set to 30 days. Changes can be made as well by running the Backup Configuration Wizard. Here you can change the value or turn the value on or off.
- Circular Logging—Enabled to save drive space. It is recommended that you use this configuration only if a backup solution has not been selected. Circular logging is disabled after the Backup Configuration Wizard has been run.
- Idle User Sessions—The timeout interval is set to 10 minutes.
- SMTP Connector—The connector is created and configured with any send/receive options you select for Internet email.

- Default Recipient Policy—The default policy is created and set to your domain name. It also applies the policy to all for SMTP email addresses.
- The Microsoft Connector for POP3 Mailboxes—The connector is installed. Through the CEICW or the POP3 Connector manager you can define POP3 mailboxes that are to be downloaded to Exchange mailboxes.
- Maximum Number of Concurrent Connections—For Message Delivery the maximum number of concurrent connections is set to 500.
- Outbound Connections—Limited to 10.
- Email Attachment Types—Attachment filtering can be utilized.
- Mail Clients—Clients assigned an address within the specified local IP range are allowed to relay mail through the SMTP virtual server.

In addition to these settings, you should also be aware of the mailbox management process in Exchange and what it does for your mail server. By default, the mailbox management process is set to Never Run. However, the mailbox management process can perform some important tasks and should be enabled on the SBS server.

One of the most important tasks handled by the mailbox management process is the online defrag of the mail databases. Through the course of normal operation, mail data is added and removed from the mail database, and over time a large amount of unused space becomes scattered across the database. The online defrag process rearranges the storage within the database so that all the empty database records are moved to the end of the database file. You can also start the mailbox management process manually by right-clicking on the server object in Exchange System Manager and selecting Start Mailbox Management Process. This can be helpful when troubleshooting Exchange-related issues as discussed in Chapter 13, "Exchange Disaster Recovery."

Junk Mail and Viruses

Email has quickly become one of the most popular ways that people communicate with each other. With it we can instantly send pictures, send attachments, or give someone information that just a few years ago would have required a phone call or fax, or would have taken days to receive.

Junk mail is typically defined as unsolicited email or pop-ups sent to you without your prior knowledge or approval. Also described as *spam*, these emails usually contain an advertisement for a product or service. This type of email not only wastes large amounts of network bandwidth and server resources but also costs companies millions with loss of labor by employees viewing or deleting them. Junk email is considered spam; however, not all spam is considered junk email.

A *virus* is a computer program loaded onto your computer without your knowledge. These programs are made by man, but have the capability to replicate themselves to other computers without others knowing it is happening. After the virus program is executed, it steals available memory and resources from the system making the unit unusable.

Both have become a significant problem for mail system administrators. Some problems stem from receiving spam and virus-infected attachments, some from the measures other companies have taken to curtail the flow of spam into their systems. The next two sections discuss each of these scenarios in more detail.

Recipient Filtering and Tar Pitting

A number of third-party solutions have come and gone over the years to help combat spam and viruses. Unfortunately, most of those work only on messages after they have been received by Exchange and processed into the message store. As the volume of received messages increases, this approach becomes less efficient. Exchange 2003 implements two features to help combat this problem.

Recipient Filtering in SBS 2003

Recipient filtering is a new feature in Exchange 2003 that allows the SMTP server to drop or reject email not addressed to a mail-enabled account in Active Directory. This is beneficial in two ways. First, it cuts down on the number of messages that have to be processed into the message store in Exchange, which reduces the load on the database. In an SBS environment, this might not seem like a significant issue, but considering that some sites have been hit with several thousand messages a minute in a reverse NDR attack (see the following sidebar), it can become a problem quickly.

Best Practice—Preventing the Reverse NDR Attack

A reverse NDR attack occurs when a spammer or other malicious individual sends a flood of email messages to a server with bad recipient addresses and bad return addresses. In normal Exchange operations, these messages are received by the SMTP server and passed on to Exchange for processing. Only when Exchange attempts to put the message in the message store does the process recognize that the address is invalid. At that point, Exchange generates a Non-Delivery Report (NDR) an sends it back to the sender.

This is where the invalid return address comes into play. When Exchange attempts to deliver the NDR back to the sender, it gets hung in the outgoing mail queue while Exchange goes through its normal process of attempting to send the message. By default, Exchange attempts delivery for 48 hours before deleting the message. When thousands upon thousands of these undeliverable NDRs begin filling up the queue, however, not only does the Exchange/SMTP process slow down, but it can slow down the entire server. In addition, server disk space is used up quickly for storage of these messages that will simply never get delivered.

The best way to prevent a reverse NDR attack is to simply refuse delivery of messages with invalid mail addresses at the SMTP server level so that no NDR is generated within Exchange. If Exchange is not configured this way, the pain inflicted by a reverse NDR attack can be sudden and severe.

Follow these steps to enable recipient filtering on the SBS server:

1. In the Server Management Console, expand Advanced Management, First Administrative Group (Exchange), Global Settings.
2. Right-click on Message Delivery and select Properties.

3. Click the Recipient Filtering tab.

4. Enable the Filter Recipients Who Are Not in the Directory check box, as shown in Figure 12.1, and click OK.

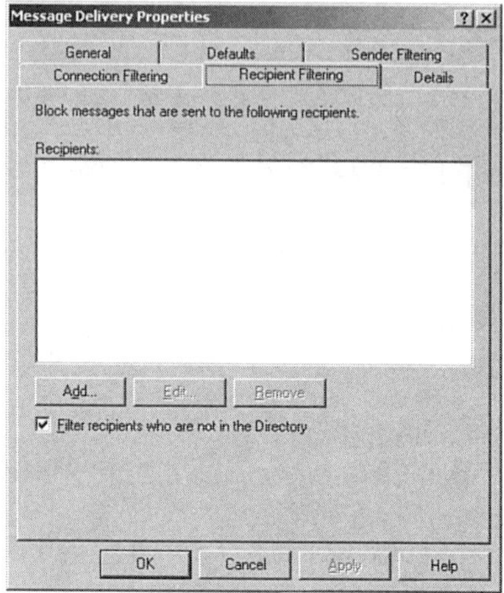

FIGURE 12.1 Recipient filtering is first enabled in the Message Delivery properties.

5. A dialog box appears indicating that you must manually enable recipient filtering on the SMTP virtual server. Click OK.

6. Under the Exchange node, expand Servers, *your server name*, Protocols, SMTP.

7. Right-click the Default SMTP virtual server and select Properties.

8. On the General tab, click the Advanced button.

9. In the Advanced dialog box, click Edit.

10. In the Identification dialog box, enable the Apply Recipient Filter check box, shown in Figure 12.2, and click OK.

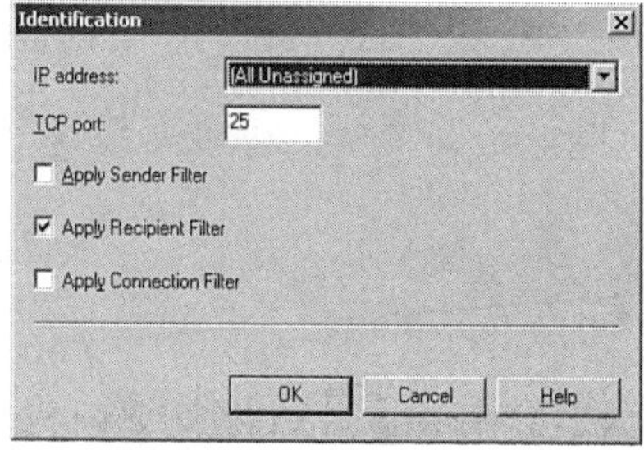

FIGURE 12.2 Enable the recipient filter in the Default SMTP Virtual Server properties.

11. Click OK twice more to close out the Default SMTP Virtual Server properties.

There is one significant downside to enabling recipient filtering on an Exchange server. When recipient filtering is enabled, a spammer can run scripts against your server's SMTP service looking for valid email addresses. If the script gets an immediate rejection for an email address, the spammer knows to mark that address as invalid and not to use it again. If the script does not get an immediate rejection, the address can be marked as valid and sold to bulk mailers or used directly by the spammer. Fortunately, there is a way around this issue by using tar pitting.

SMTP Tar Pitting

The tar pit feature was first introduced in Microsoft KB article 899492 (`http://support.microsoft.com/kb/899492/`) as a hotfix for Windows Server 2003. The feature is also included in Windows Server 2003 SP1 and is described in Microsoft KB article 842851 (`http://support.microsoft.com/kb/842851`).

In normal operations when recipient filtering is enabled, an SMTP request for an invalid email address gets an immediate `5.1.1 User unknown` response. Enabling the tar pit feature delays the error message, which generally causes problems for spammers running scripts against the mail server.

By default, the tar pit feature is enabled when SBS SP1 is installed in a slipstreamed media version. If you are adding SP1, you can enable tar pitting by following the instructions in Microsoft KB article 842851. The necessary code is on the service pack installed version but not yet enabled. Only SBS installations performed with the SP1 slipstreamed media have the value enabled out of the box.

Exchange Intelligent Message Filter (IMF)

Another tool that Microsoft provides to help counter spam on Exchange servers is the Intelligent Message Filter (IMF). This free download from Microsoft's website can be installed on any Exchange 2003 server. The IMF works with both the SMTP and Exchange services to help mail administrators filter or block unwanted email from the server.

The IMF scans each piece of incoming email at the SMTP service and assigns a Spam Confidence Level (SCL) value, ranging from 1–9, to the message based on a number of factors. Then, depending on the configuration, the message is blocked or delivered based on two different filters. The first filter is the blocking filter. When the IMF installs, it sets a value of 8 for this filter. This means that any message with an SCL value of 8 or 9 will have one of four actions taken on it. Those actions are

- Archive—The message is moved into an archive folder on the system for later review by the mail administrator.
- Delete—The message is deleted from the system with no other action taken.
- No Action—The message is passed through to the next phase of filtering.
- Reject—The message is not delivered, and a rejection email is sent to the message sender.

Any message with an SCL value of 7 or less at the first filter gets passed on to the second filter automatically.

The second filter determines whether the message is delivered to the user's Inbox or the Junk Mail folder. Again, the default value on this at installation is 8, meaning that a message with an SCL value of 8 or higher gets put into the user's junk mail folder. Again, messages with an SCL value of 7 or less get stored directly in the user's Inbox.

Follow these steps to install the Exchange IMF on SBS:

1. Download both the Exchange Intelligent Message Filter and the Filter Update for Exchange Intelligent Message Filter from Microsoft.
2. Start the IMF install by double-clicking on the `ExchangeIMF.MSI` file.
3. Click Next on the opening page of the wizard.
4. Select the I Agree radio button on the End User License Agreement page and click Next.
5. When the components finish installing, click Finish to close the wizard.
6. Launch the Filter Update by double-clicking on the `Exchange 2003-KB883106-v2-x86-ENU.exe` file.
7. In the first page of the Installer Wizard, click Next.
8. Select the I Agree radio button on the Licensing Agreement page and click Next.
9. When the update completes, click Finish to close the installer.

After the IMF has been installed, you need to configure it for your environment. If you accept the default installation values, mail with an SCL value of 8 or higher will get filtered into the user's Junk Mail folder, and all other messages will be delivered into the Inbox. You can change the values of the filter at any time, but you may want to start with a more aggressive filter configuration. Follow these steps to configure the IMF:

1. Open Exchange System Manager.
2. Expand Global Settings and open the Properties for Message Delivery.
3. Click on the Intelligent Message Filtering tab.
4. Select the desired values for the Gateway Blocking Configuration and the Store Junk E-mail Configuration. Figure 12.3 shows the settings for a moderately aggressive junk mail filter. Click OK when complete.
5. In the Exchange System Manger, expand Servers, *your server name*, Protocols, SMTP.
6. Right-click on the Intelligent Message Filter and select Properties.
7. Enable the check box for the Default SMTP Virtual Server and click OK.

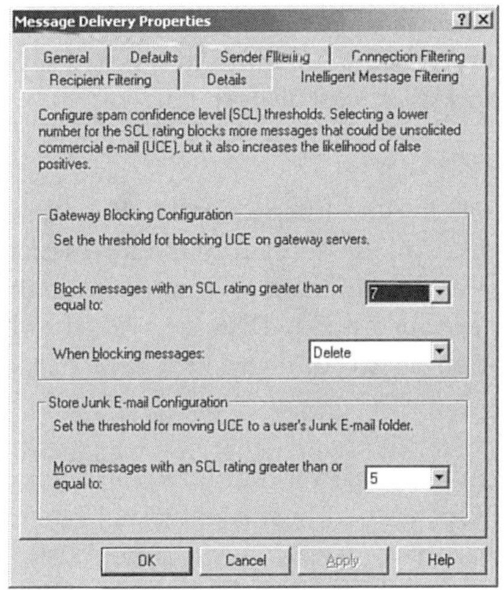

FIGURE 12.3 Settings for the Intelligent Message Filter.

Best Practice—Install the Intelligent Message Filter on All SBS Installations

Any server not running any third-party antispam solutions should definitely install and use IMF on SBS because there is no cost, and the immediate benefit of reduced spam is invaluable. Even if other third-party programs are being used, the IMF can still be used to provide additional protection. In the same way that no single antivirus or antispyware program catches every threat across the board, no single antispam product can either. When possible, always use two comparable tools to protect against unwanted items, and when one of those tools (IMF) is free, there is no financial reason to avoid it.

Getting Mail Delivered Despite Antispam Measures

Many organizations have begun taking drastic measures to combat the flood of spam their accounts are receiving. They have started using a number of new technologies that have made it more difficult for smaller businesses to get mail through to their clients. The following are a few examples of the technologies used to fight spam:

- Blacklists—The ISP obtains updated lists from organizations such as `www.ordb.org` for suspected spam servers. These lists contain servers/domains that have been listed as having *open Relay* servers and could be used for spamming.
- Dynamic IP lists—Most ISPs designate these for residential use. ISPs such as AOL view that residential users would be using their ISP's SMTP servers for sending mail (smart host), so there should not be a need for receiving mail directly from a dynamic IP that appears in the list. In turn, the direct connection would be denied.
- Reverse DNS lookups—Before a connection is accepted, the remote email server performs a DNS lookup on the originating server ensuring that the IP being presented matches the domain name.

How Mail Gets Delivered

Exchange can use two methods to send email to other mail servers. These are commonly referred to as *DNS delivery* and *smart host delivery*.

DNS

By default Exchange uses DNS to send Internet email. It is through the use of DNS records and MX records registered for a public domain that addresses are discovered and email is routed. When Exchange needs to send mail, it attempts to look up the MX record for the remote domain's mail server using a public DNS server. It then takes the IP address listed for the remote server and attempts to connect to the remote mail server directly.

Smart Host

A smart host is a "middleman" email server that forwards/sends email for your domain's email server on its behalf. When a smart host is in place, Exchange takes outgoing mail and sends it to another mail server that you specify (the smart host). The smart host then sends your email to the destination mail server. This feature makes it appear that email from your domain is originating from the smart host server. A good example of this would be if you or someone else uses Outlook Express to send email through your ISP's SMTP servers.

Routing All Mail Through DNS

If your have a static IP address for your network, this is usually the best option for delivering mail. Here are some reasons why:

- No "middleman" is needed.
- You don't have to rely on third-party email servers to ensure delivery of email.
- You have more control over email delivery.
- The server continues to attempt to resend email if needed.

When you run the CEICW, you can choose to have mail delivered through DNS by selecting the Use DNS To Route E-mail button in the E-mail Delivery page of the wizard. The wizard then creates the Default SMTP Virtual Server and the SmallBusiness SMTP Connector and configures both to route mail directly using DNS.

> **NOTE**
>
> If you think you have a static IP, check with your ISP to make sure that it really is a static address. Some ISPs use DHCP reservations to reserve a specific IP address for a client, but the address still shows up in the dynamic address pool.

Routing All Mail Through a Smart Host

If you do not have a static IP address, or if you cannot get a reverse DNS pointer record for your static IP address, you may have difficulty delivering mail directly from your site. There are other reasons that you may choose to router your email through a smart host, including the following:

- You avoid antispam measures to larger ISPs.
- It may be the only way to send email when using a dynamic IP.
- The server continues to attempt to resend email if needed.
- Some ISPs view access to their email servers as a Premium Service. In this case, you may need to subscribe to an additional third-party email service.

The smart host configuration can also be set in the CEICW. In the E-mail Delivery page of the wizard, select the Forward All E-mail To E-mail Server At Your ISP radio button and then enter the address for your ISP's SMTP mail server.

> **NOTE**
>
> Smart hosts can be created or identified by either IP or FQDN (fully qualified domain name). FQDN is preferred to avoid any possible issues with unexpected IP changes. If you use an IP address to specify a smart host, the address must be enclosed in square brackets.

If your ISP requires you to authenticate to its smart host to send mail (not all do), you need to manually enter the authentication settings in Exchange System Manager. Follow these steps to add outbound authentication for the SMTP server:

1. Open Exchange System Manager.
2. Expand Servers, *your server name*, Protocols, SMTP.
3. Right-click on the Default SMTP Virtual Server and select Properties.
4. Click on the Delivery tab and then click Outbound Security.
5. Select the Basic Authentication radio button, enter the username and password for the mail server, as shown in Figure 12.4, and then click OK when finished.

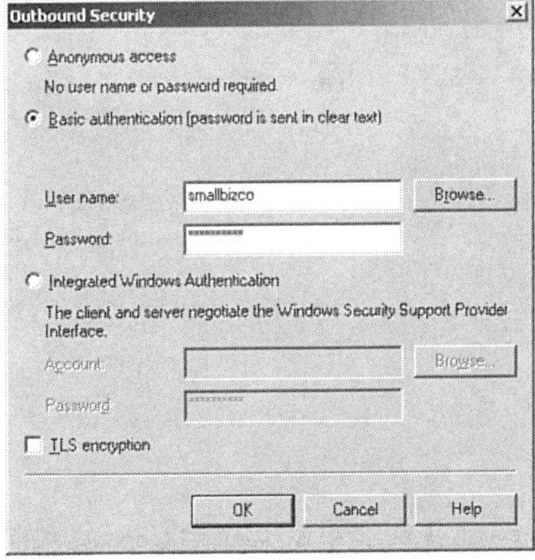

FIGURE 12.4 Setting the outbound authentication information in the SMTP Virtual Server.

6. Click OK to close the Properties of the Default SMTP Virtual Server.
7. Expand the Connectors node in Exchange System Manager.
8. Right-click on the SmallBusiness SMTP Connector and select Properties.
9. Click the Advanced tab; then click the Outbound Security button.
10. Select the Basic Authentication radio button; then click the Modify button.
11. Enter the username and password for the ISP mail server connection and click OK. When the authentication has been set, as shown in Figure 12.5, click OK to close the window.

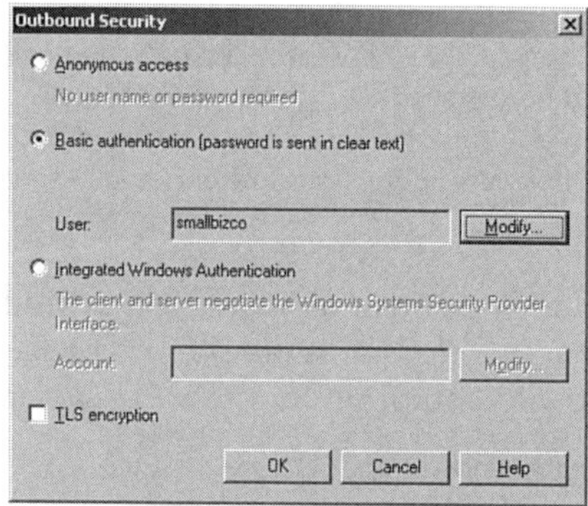

FIGURE 12.5 Setting the outbound authentication information in the SMTP Connector.

NOTE

Outbound SMTP authentication information must be entered in both the Default SMTP Virtual Server and the SmallBusiness SMTP Connector objects before Exchange can successfully route email through the smart host.

12. Click OK twice to close the SmallBusiness SMTP Connector Properties window.

Routing Some Mail Through DNS, Some Through Smart Host

In some rare circumstances, you may find a need to route some mail through a smart host and some mail through DNS. One large ISP in the United States has reconfigured its SMTP servers so that attempts to authenticate to a smart host from an Exchange server fail, even though connection attempts from other mail systems work successfully, forcing some businesses to use third-party smart host systems to route mail. The following steps walk you through the process of setting up a new SMTP mail connector and configuring Exchange to route mail appropriately:

1. Open Exchange System Manager.
2. Right-click on Connectors and select New, SMTP Connector.

3. In the General tab, enter a name for the connector.
4. Select the Forward All Mail Through This Connector to the Following Smart Hosts radio button and enter the SMTP address for the smart host.
5. In the Local Bridgehead section, click Add, select your Exchange server from the list, and click OK.
6. Click the Address Space Tab.
7. Click Add, select SMTP, and then click OK.
8. Enter the name of the domain you want to route through the smart host, as shown in Figure 12.6. Click OK when finished.

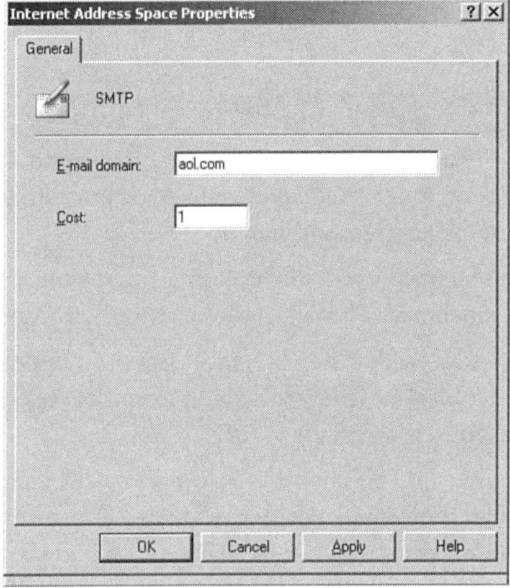

FIGURE 12.6 Enter the mail domain in the SMTP connector Address Space Properties page.

NOTE

Address space defines the domains or mail addresses to route through the connector. Routing through a connector is done through the closest match to an address space. Wildcards can be used in address spaces, as follows:

- `*`—Includes all external domains
- `*.net`—Includes all external domains with the `.net` extension
- `aol.com`—Specifies the domain only.

Exchange selects which connector to use based on the address spaces listed for the connector. If more than one connector has the same name space, the cost is the deciding factor. For a typical SBS server, you will not have multiple connectors with the same name space, so dealing with cost values is not as critical as with larger Exchange installations.

9. Repeat steps 7 and 8 to add additional domains for delivery through this connector.

CAUTION

Do not list your inbound domains on an SMTP address space for a connector. Internal domains are handled through recipient policy.

10. Close the SMTP Connector properties when finished.
11. Open the properties for the SmallBusiness SMTP Connector.
12. Click on the Address Space tab, select the * SMTP space from the list, and click Modify.
13. Change the cost on the * space to 2 or higher.
14. Click OK twice to close the SmallBusiness SMTP Connector properties.

Best Practice—Route Outbound Email Through a Smart Host

Even if you can get a static IP address and have no issues delivering email directly to recipients through DNS, your best option for reliable email delivery is to route your mail through a smart host. Some of the more compelling reasons include

- Performance—When all mail is routed through a smart host, the SBS server does not have to queue up and attempt redelivery of email to sites that do not respond on first request.
- Blacklist protection—Even with a static IP address, you still run a risk of a site misidentifying you and adding you to a blacklist, preventing you from delivering mail to that site. Routing your mail through a smart host minimizes that risk.
- Reverse NDR protection—If you choose not to implement recipient filtering as described previously, you can still avoid performance issues related to a reverse NDR attack. Even if your server gets hit and generates a large number of NDRs, routing outbound mail through your smart host puts the burden of filtering through the bogus NDR messages on the smart host and not on the SBS server. This also reduces the number of messages that would end up in the badmail folder, which reduces the risk of running out of disk space on the server in case of such an attack.

Microsoft Connector for POP3 Mailboxes

Many small businesses still use and rely on their ISPs to handle the maintenance and flow of their email everyday. This job could be as small as managing a single email box to handling many individual email accounts for all the company's employees. The Microsoft Connector for POP3 Mailboxes, also referred to as the POP3 Connector, gives small businesses the capability to download and distribute POP3 email into individual mailboxes automatically.

The POP3 Connector included with SBS 2003 has been completely redesigned compared to previous versions. In prior versions there were issues with the capability to move large amounts of email. This has been addressed along with a user-friendly interface that allows increased usability.

The POP3 Connector supports

- Individual user mailboxes for POP3 accounts—The capability to download mail for a single user from a remote POP3 server and then deliver this mail to a valid user account on the Exchange server.
- Global POP3 mailboxes—The capability to download mail, for multiple recipients stored in a single remote mailbox and then deliver this mail to all valid user accounts on the Exchange server.

NOTE

For global POP3 mailboxes to be used, there must be a defined Exchange user account that matches the username specified by this account.

- Mailing lists—You can include POP3 accounts in lists such as Internet mailing lists.
- Diagnostic logging—Multiple levels of logging are available to help troubleshoot problems if encountered.
- Scheduling—You can schedule mail retrieval in 15 minute increments. The user interface also includes a "retrieve now" button to allow for immediate retrieval of email for testing purposes.

How Does the POP3 Connector Work?

The POP3 Connector performs a complex set of tasks to pull mail from the POP3 server and store messages into the correct location in Exchange. This process is described in the following steps:

1. The POP3 Connector service initiates a connection to the remote POP3 server.
2. The service then connects and logs on to the remote POP3 server.
3. Email is retrieved and then placed into the `Program Files\Microsoft Small Business Server\Networking\POP3\Incoming Mail` folder.
4. After all email has been retrieved from the remote server—CDO (collaborative data objects) then picks up the mail in the Incoming Mail folder.
5. Email headers are modified with the local Exchange mailbox user information.
6. The mail is then placed into the `inetpub\mailroot\Pickup` folder.
7. All nonroutable email is placed in the `Program Files\Microsoft Small Business Server\Networking\POP3\Failed Mail` folder by the CDO service.
8. All email placed in the `Pickup` folder is then processed by the local SMTP service and forwarded on to the addressed user.

Limitations of the POP3 Connector

One of the main complaints about the POP3 Connector is that it does not offer as many features as other third-party POP3 solutions. Some of the restrictions of the POP3 Connector include

- POP3 allows you to schedule email downloads in 15 minute increments, but unfortunately the minimum is 15 minutes.
- Messages downloaded to a local hard disk are placed on that hard disk and not stored on the server. In turn this type of email is available from one computer only, unless accessing the machine from a remote source.
- BCCs are not recognized when using a global mailbox configuration. Email headers are stripped after email is delivered to the ISP's POP3 mailbox. The connector does not have the necessary delivery information to determine who the intended recipient is. The email is then dropped.
- Messages delivered through the POP3 Connector do not get processed by the IMF. This is because the POP3 Connector bypasses the SMTP process to deliver messages into the Exchange message store.

NOTE

For more information on POP3 and BCCs, see `http://support.microsoft.com/default.aspx?scid=KB;EN-US;265739`.

Configuring the POP3 Connector

The POP3 Connector is enabled after POP3 mailboxes have been created manually, or it can also be done through the Configure Email and Internet Connection Wizard. POP3 mailbox maintenance is handled through the POP3 Connector Manager. Here you can add, remove, change, or edit existing POP3 mailboxes on-the-fly using the POP3 Connector Manager. For bigger jobs, the CEICW allows you to configure both POP3 and Exchange mailboxes at the same time.

To configure the POP3 Connector settings manually, follow these steps:

1. In the Server Management Console, expand Advanced Management.
2. Select the POP3 Connector Manager in the console tree; then click the Open POP3 Connector Manager link in the right pane.
3. In the Mailboxes tab, click Add.
4. Enter the name of the external POP3 server, the port number (if the server uses a nonstandard POP3 port), and the username to access the POP3 account, and then enter the password for the account twice.

Now you need to configure the account as a user mailbox or a global mailbox. The next two sections describe the difference between the two and the necessary information needed to complete the account information.

Routing Mail from a Global Account

Some ISPs collect all incoming email for a mail domain and store the information in one POP3 account. In other words, any email destined for any account at `smallbizco.net` would be stored in a single account on the ISP's mail server instead of in individual mailboxes for each account. If you connected to this account with Outlook or Outlook Express, you would see that the messages downloaded would have different "to:" addresses, but they would all be in the same mail domain.

When the POP3 Connector processes mail from a global account, it downloads all the messages from the POP3 server, looks at the addressee, and delivers that message to the addressee in Exchange. For this to work correctly, each addressee must have a mail account in the Exchange server.

Delivery of mail with a global account can fail in at least two ways. First, if a message is delivered with the recipient in the BCC field and not the TO field, the message will not get delivered. The POP3 Connector can process messages only for recipients in the TO or CC fields of the message body. This is why mailing lists are also a problem. When a message is delivered to a mailing list address, the user's address does not appear in the TO header or the CC header, and the delivery of the message fails.

To complete the setup of a global account in the POP3 Connector Manager, follow these steps:

1. In the Mailbox Information section, select Global Mailbox from the Mailbox Type drop-down menu, as shown in Figure 12.7.

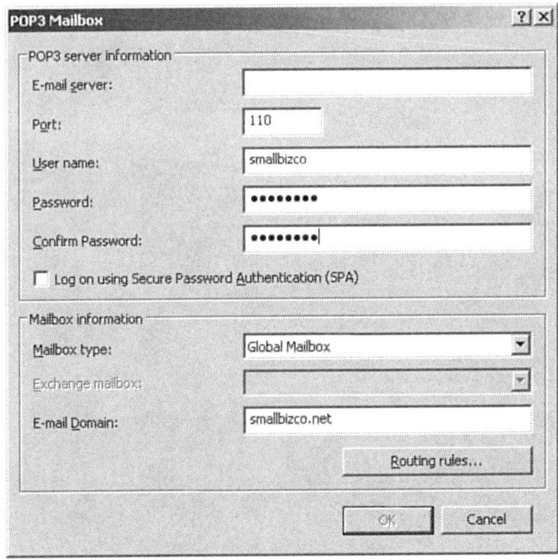

FIGURE 12.7 Entering the settings for the global mailbox in the POP3 account setup dialog.

2. Enter the email domain for the server in the Email Domain field.
3. If you have POP3 mail addresses that do not have a matching account on the server, click the Routing Rules button; then click Add.
4. Add the address information in the Text In To: Or CC: Line field; then select the Exchange mailbox to receive those messages, as shown in Figure 12.8. Click OK when finished.

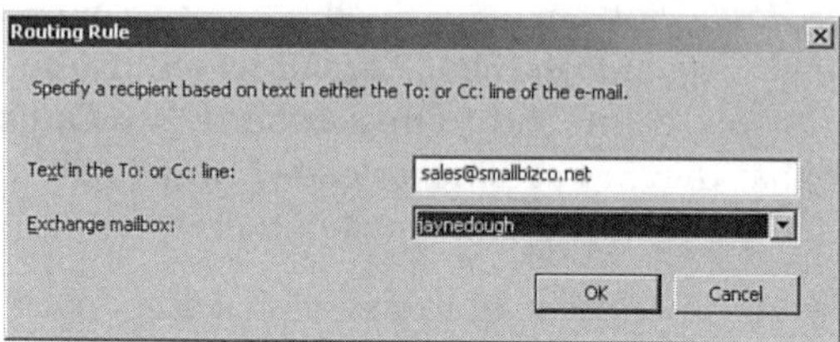

FIGURE 12.8 Entering routing rules for global mailbox settings.

5. Click OK to close the POP3 Account window. Click Add to add other POP3 mailbox mappings, or click OK to close the POP3 Connector Manager.

Routing Mail with Individual Accounts

Most ISPs allow you to have an individual mailbox on their mail server for each user on your mail server. The configuration of the POP3 Connector for this setup is much simpler than for the global mailbox setup. To configure the POP3 user to forward messages to a specific user, follow these steps:

1. Under Mailbox Information, leave the Mailbox Type as User Mailbox.
2. Select the desired user mailbox in the Exchange Mailbox drop-down menu, as shown in Figure 12.9.

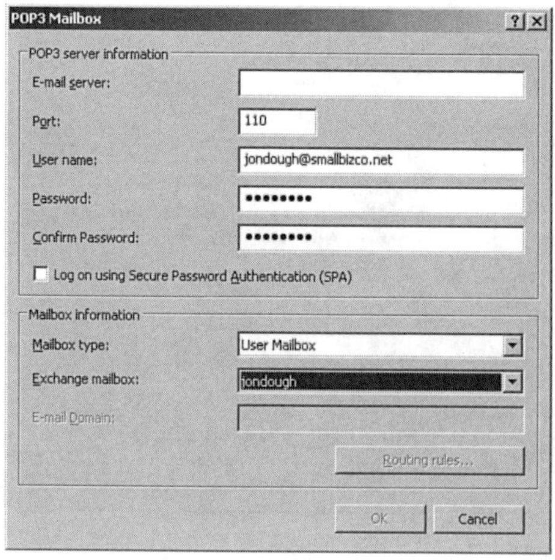

FIGURE 12.9 Entering the settings for an individual mailbox in the POP3 account setup dialog.

3. Click OK to close the POP3 account window. Click Add to add other POP3 mailbox mappings, or click OK to close the POP3 Connector Manager.

Best Practice—Use the POP3 Connector as a Transitional Tool, Not as a Mail Solution

Even though the POP3 Connector made its first appearance with SBS 4.5, it has always been intended as a transitional tool. Microsoft developed and provided the POP3 Connector as a way for companies to migrate away from POP3 mail delivery and use SMTP mail instead. Because of the issues related to the POP3 Connector, the SBS community recommends using the connector only as an interim workaround until full SMTP mail delivery can be established on he SBS server.

Receiving Mail with Multiple Domains

One question that appears regularly in the SBS community is how to set up Exchange to accept email from more than one domain. In the Connect to the Internet Wizard (CEICW), the Exchange Configuration field only allows for one email domain name, so the assumption has been that SBS can only receive email for one domain name.

Because SBS 2003 uses Exchange 2003 Standard Edition for email, the same features available for Exchange 2003 are also available for SBS 2003, including the capability to work with multiple mail domains. To take advantage of these features, you have to work outside the wizards.

Adding Additional Email Addresses

Associating additional email addresses with a single-user account is fairly straightforward. Each user object in Active Directory can have more than one email address associated with it. In fact, with a default SBS installation, three email addresses already are associated with each user object. These addresses can be seen in the E-mail Addresses tab of the user properties page in Active Directory Users and Computers, shown in Figure 12.10. Two of the addresses are SMTP addresses—one has the external mail address for the user and is marked as the primary address; the other is an address for the internal domain. There is also an X.400 address that is used internally by Exchange and will never be seen by the average user.

To add another address for the user, follow these steps when the E-mail Addresses tab is open:

1. Click New.
2. In the E-mail Addresses Type list select SMTP Address and click OK.
3. Enter the full email address and click OK.

The new address appears in the list, and when you close the user properties dialog, Exchange will now accept incoming mail for that address and deliver it to the user.

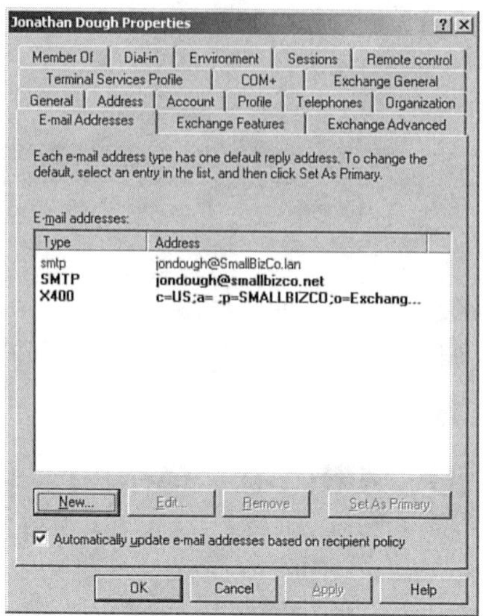

FIGURE 12.10 Each user starts with three email addresses defined.

NOTE

One reason to add an additional address for a user is to give the user an alias address. In the examples, the user Jonathan Dough has a logon ID of jondough. By default, his email address is `jondough@smallbizco.net`. If he wanted to use a different address, such as `jonathan.dough@smallbizco.net`, instead, you can add this to the list of addresses for his user object, and he will be able to receive messages at that address. If he wants `jonathan.dough@smallbizco.net` to appear as the return address on all his outgoing mail, you need to select that address in the E-mail Addresses tab and click the Set As Primary button.

Recipient Policies

If you need to add an additional mail domain name for all users on the network, adding the address to each user object individually is not the best approach. Instead, use recipient policies to make changes across the entire organization.

When Exchange is initially configured through the CEICW, the wizard creates a recipient policy in Exchange. Any new accounts created on the server get their email addresses assigned based on the settings in this policy. When the Default Recipient Policy object is created, it contains the three email domain names described previously, as shown in Figure 12.11.

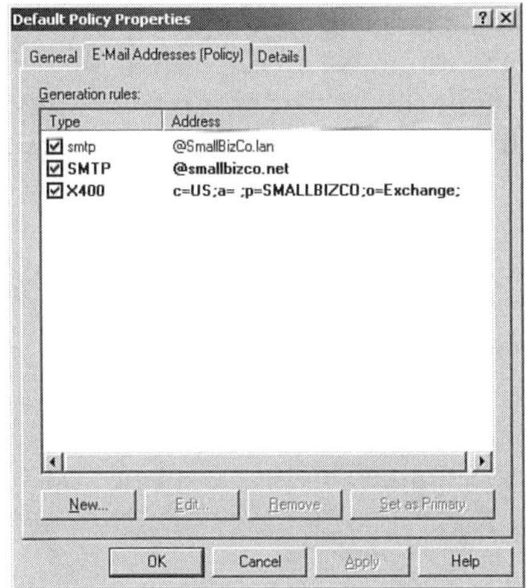

FIGURE 12.11 The default recipient policy contains the three basic address settings configured by the CEICW.

To add another mail domain to the Exchange server, follow these steps:

1. Open Exchange System Manager and expand Recipients.
2. Click on Recipient Policies and double-click on Default Recipient Policy.
3. Select the E-Mail Addresses (Policy) tab and click New.
4. Select the SMTP Address item from the E-mail Addresses Type list and click OK.
5. In the Address field, enter the email domain name, as shown in Figure 12.12.

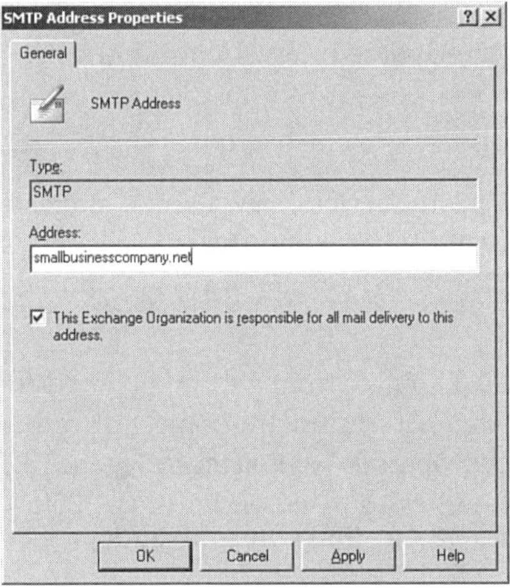

FIGURE 12.12 Entering a mail domain into the default recipient policy.

6. If mail to this new domain gets delivered to severs other than the SBS server, clear the This Exchange Organization Is Responsible for All Mail Delivery to This Address check box. For more information about split mail delivery issues, see the "Routing Mail for a Nonauthoritative Zone" section later in the chapter.
7. Turn on the check box next to the new domain name in the Generation Rules list.
8. Click OK when finished. You get a pop-up window asking whether you want the new SMTP address to be added to all existing recipients. Click Yes or No to add this mail domain to each user object in the domain or not.

If you respond Yes to the dialog box, a new email address is created for each user object in Active Directory. That task is performed by the Recipient Update Service.

Recipient Update Service

Not much guesswork is needed to figure out what the Recipient Update Service is and does. When active, it applies any changes to any of the recipient policies to all user objects across the network. In an SBS standard installation, this service is configured to run at all times, so that any time a change is made to the default recipient policy (or ay other recipient policies), those changes are immediately applied.

This behavior can be modified in one of two ways. First, the Recipient Update Service can be disabled. This is done by opening the Recipient Update Service objects and setting the Update Interval to Never Run instead of Always Run. To make these changes, follow these steps:

1. In Exchange System Manager, expand Recipients.
2. Select Recipient Update Services and double-click on the update service object to open its properties.
3. Select Never Run from the Update Interval drop-down list.
4. Click OK to save the changes and close the dialog.

If you disable the Recipient Update Services, new users you create will still get all the addresses defined in the recipient policy when they are created, but no objects on the network will have any changes applied automatically if you make additional changes to the default recipient policy.

The second way to prevent a user object from getting updated with changes to the recipient policies is to restrict that behavior in the user object directly. This is done in the E-mail Addresses tab of the user properties page, refer to Figure 12.10, by disabling the Automatically Update E-mail Addresses Based on Recipient Policy check box. This exempts this user object from having global updates applied.

NOTE

Why would you want to exclude a user from having recipient policy changes applied? If the user is configured to use a different email domain than the server default as his default address, every time a change is made to the default recipient policy, his return email address will change to match the system default. If you disable the automatic update through the Recipient Update Service for that user account, his customized email settings will not be affected by any changes to the recipient policies. On the other hand, if you need to make changes for his account because of changes to the recipient policy, you have to make those changes by hand.

Routing Mail for a Nonauthoritative Zone

Dealing with split delivery mail domains is not as uncommon in the small business environment as you might think. Many small businesses rely on split delivery mail solutions, especially when the POP3 Connector is being used.

Simply put, a split delivery mail system is a mail setup where not all the accounts for an email domain exist on a single mail server, in this case, the SBS server. And the CECIW cannot handle a split delivery mail domain during Exchange configuration, so if this scenario applies to you, you need to configure the setup manually.

The problem arises when Exchange is told that it is the authoritative server for the split delivery mail domain. When a user on the SBS network attempts to send email to an account that does not reside on the SBS server, Exchange immediately returns the message as undeliverable because it cannot find that mail address in Active Directory.

The best solution for this situation is to configure Exchange so that it is not the authoritative server for the domain. To change this configuration, follow these steps:

1. In Exchange System Manager, expand Recipients, and select Recipient Policies.
2. Double-click on Default Policy.
3. Click the E-mail Addresses (Policy) tab.
4. If the mail domain to reconfigure is set as the Primary mail domain (it appears in bold in the list), select the internal SMTP address and click Set As Primary.
5. Select the external mail domain and click Edit.
6. Turn off the This Exchange Organization Is Responsible for All Mail Delivery to This Domain check box, shown previously in Figure 12.12, and click OK.
7. Select the external mail domain and click Set As Primary.
8. Click OK to close the policies.

Troubleshooting Exchange Management Issues

Exchange is a complex product, and the SBS implementation of Exchange makes it more so. One chapter in a book cannot begin to cover all the troubleshooting possibilities for Exchange. The remainder of this chapter instead covers some of the commonly encountered issues with Exchange related to topics covered in the chapter.

Troubleshooting Outbound Mail Delivery

Many outbound mail delivery issues can be identified with just a couple of basic tools—Exchange System Manager and `telnet`. When you suspect outbound mail delivery problems, open the Exchange System Manager and look at the outbound SMTP queues (which can be found under Servers, *your server name*, Queues). When you have Exchange set to deliver mail through DNS, you see a queue for each mail domain where Exchange has recently attempted delivery. The status of the queue is listed in the State column, shown in Figure 12.13. If the status is anything other than Ready, you must identify and resolve the problem before Exchange can deliver mail.

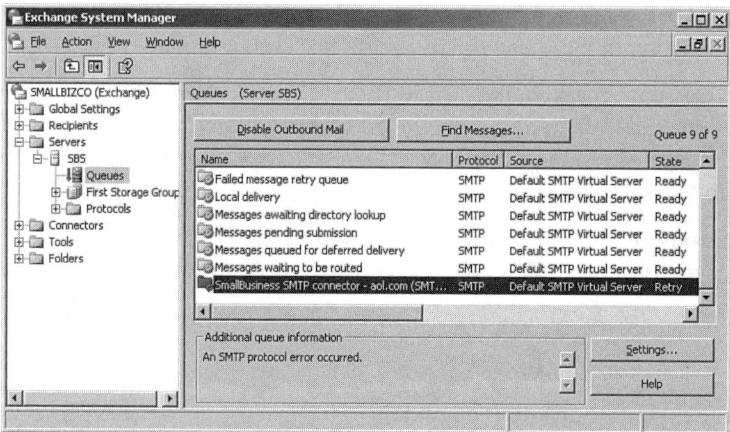

FIGURE 12.13 Exchange System Manager displays the status of each outbound mail queue.

When you highlight the problem mail queue, the Additional Queue Information field gives you an indication of the problem. In Figure 12.13, the queue for delivery to `aol.com` is in a Retry state, meaning that Exchange will make another attempt to deliver mail to `aol.com`. The Additional Queue Information area indicates that the last connection attempt failed because of an SMTP protocol error. In most cases, this is likely not a protocol error, but a delivery refusal.

You can narrow down the cause in one of two ways from here. First, you can enable SMTP logging and review the information collected in the log file. Follow these instructions to enable SMTP logging:

1. In Exchange System Manager, expand Servers, *your server name*, Protocols, SMTP.

2. Right-click on the Default SMTP Virtual Server and click Properties.
3. Turn on the Enable Logging check box; then click Properties.
4. In the Logging Properties General tab, select the Daily radio button under New Log Schedule and note the location of the SMTP log files (`C:\Windows\System32\LogFiles` by default).
5. Click the Advanced tab; then enable all the check boxes under Extended Logging Options. You can choose to omit the last three fields, as shown in Figure 12.14, because they do not apply to SMTP traffic.

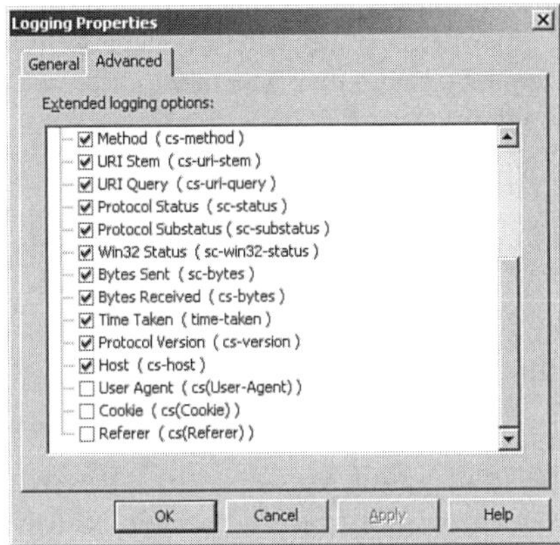

FIGURE 12.14 Enable most of the Extended Logging Options to collect useful information in the SMTP logs.

6. Click OK twice to save changes and close the Default SMTP Virtual Server properties.
7. Right-click on the Default SMTP Virtual Server and select Stop.
8. When the SMTP virtual server stops (a red sign appears on the icon), right-click on the virtual server again and select Start.

Now that you have SMTP logging enabled, you can force Exchange to make another connection attempt and record the transaction in the logs. You can do this by right-clicking the connector in the Queues listing and selecting Force Connection.

Next, you can review the information in the SMTP log file. Browse to the folder where the log files are stored (`C:\Windows\System32\LogFiles` by default), open the `SMTPSVC1` folder, and open the most recent log file. The following listing displays a typical response you might get from a refused connection:

```
year-mo-da 15:22:20 hostserverIP OutboundConnectionResponse SMTPSVC1 SBS - 25 -
➥ - 554-+(RTR:BB)++http://postmaster.info.aol.com/errors/554rtrbb.html
year-mo-da 15:22:20 hostserverIP OutboundConnectionResponse SMTPSVC1 SBS - 25 -
➥ - 554-+AOL+does+not+accept+e-mail+transactions+from+dynamic+or+residential
```

In this example, you can see that AOL responds to the connection attempt and does not accept connections from IPs that are registered as residential or dynamic by ISPs. AOL even provides a URL in the error that gives you more information about why it refused the connection.

NOTE

Some mail hosts handle refusing mail in different ways. AOL refuses to accept the connection, but in such a way that no NDR is generated. The Exchange SMTP queue continues to attempt delivery to AOL until the delivery timeout is received, at which point, it generates its own NDR indicating that the message could not be delivered within the time configured on the server. Other ISPs refuse the connection in such a way that an NDR is generated immediately and tells the sender exactly why the mail has been rejected. It is easier to troubleshoot delivery failures when these NDRs are generated because they generally indicate which black list or other spam-blocking tool they used to refuse your request.

Another way to investigate mail delivery problems is to make a manual SMTP connection to see what is happening. This can be useful for those occasions when no information about the connection problem is listed in the SMTP logs. You use the `telnet` tool to connect to the mail server and attempt mail delivery to see how the remote system responds.

Before you can `telnet` to the mail server, you need to know where the mail server is. Use `nslookup` to find the address or name of the mail server. Follow these steps to find a remote mail server using `nslookup`:

1. In a command prompt window, type **`nslookup`** and press Enter.
2. At the `nslookup` prompt, type **`set type=mx`** and press Enter.
3. Type the mail domain and press Enter.

`nslookup` returns the mail exchanger record(s) for the mail domain. After you have noted the name or address of the remote mail server, type `exit` and press Enter to quit `nslookup`. Now you can use `telnet` to attempt a manual message delivery by following these steps:

1. At the command prompt, type `telnet [name of mail server] 25` and press Enter.
2. If you receive a 220 response from the mail server, type `ehlo [your mail domain]` and press Enter.
3. If you receive a number of 250 responses, type `mail from: [your return e-mail address]` and press Enter.
4. If you receive a 250 response, type `rcpt to: [address of recipient]` and press Enter.
5. If you receive a 250 response here, you will be able to send a message to that user successfully, so you can type `quit` and then press Enter to close the `telnet` session.

If you get anything other than a 220 response on the initial connection or a 250 response after any of the other steps, review the SMTP server responses and continue troubleshooting from there. Some responses make it obvious what the problem is. For example, if you don't have the correct server address for a mail domain, you may get a `550 5.7.1 Unable to relay` error. Other errors may not be as obvious, but you can at least look up the errors on the Internet and see what may be causing the problems.

Troubleshooting IMF

One indicator that there may be a problem with the configuration of the IMF is users reporting that they are not getting the messages they are expecting. The first place to look for trouble is the SMTP log file. The following two samples from the SMTP log file show two different mail delivery sessions:

```
year-mo-da 16:05:10 [remoteIP] - SMTPSVC1 SBS [externalIP] 0 EHLO - - 250 0
year-mo-da 16:05:14 [remoteIP] - SMTPSVC1 SBS [externalIP] 0 MAIL -
[ic:ccc}+from:+user@remotedomain.net 250
year-mo-da 16:05:18 [remoteIP] - SMTPSVC1 SBS [externalIP] 0 RCPT -
➥+to:+jondough@smallbizco.net 250 0 0 17 0 SMTP -
year-mo-da 16:05:36 [remoteIP] - SMTPSVC1 SBS [externalIP] 0 DATA -
➥<SBS8FCc6OiA86YmJueD00000002@smallbizco.net> 250
year-mo-da 16:05:41 [remoteIP] - SMTPSVC1 SBS [externalIP] 0 QUIT - - 240
year-mo-da 16:06:11 [remoteIP] - SMTPSVC1 SBS [externalIP] 0 EHLO - - 250
year-mo-da 16:06:21 [remoteIP] - SMTPSVC1 SBS [externalIP] 0 MAIL -
➥+from:+spam@spam.net 250
year-mo-da 16:06:31 [remoteIP] - SMTPSVC1 SBS [externalIP] 0 RCPT -
➥+to:+jondough@smallbizco.net 250
year-mo-da 16:07:32 [remoteIP] - SMTPSVC1 SBS [externalIP] 0 QUIT - - 240
```

The difference between these two sessions in the log is the `DATA` response line in the first listing. This line indicates that the message was accepted for delivery and queued into the Exchange process. The second listing has no `DATA` line, which means that no message was queued for delivery in Exchange. In this example, the IMF was configured to delete messages with an SCL of 8 or higher.

If a user complains that she is not receiving messages from a particular person, you can search through the SMTP logs for that email address and see whether a connection attempt has even been made. If it has and you see the email address listed in one of the `MAIL` lines in the log, you will see a corresponding `DATA` line after the message has been queued for delivery.

One option to identify whether IMF is blocking messages that it should not be is to set the Gateway Blocking Configuration to take No Action on messages at that level. This allows those messages to pass through to the next filter, where they get dumped into the Junk Mail folder for the client.

Alternatively, you can set the Gateway Blocking Configuration to Archive. This places blocked messages into a folder (`C:\Program Files\Exchsrvr\Mailroot\vsi 1\UceArchive` by default) as individual `.eml` files. In the SMTP log, you will not see the `DATA` entry for messages that get moved to the Archive folder, and if you do not monitor this folder, you could run out of disk space quickly during a spam attack on your server. You can open the messages stored in this folder with Outlook Express, but it is highly recommended that you use Notepad or some other text viewer instead to prevent any malicious content that may be in the message from being executed in Outlook Express from the server.

Best Practice—Setting Appropriate SCL Values Using Outlook

Unfortunately, Microsoft did not provide many easy-to-use management tools to keep a handle on IMF after you have it installed. Though a few third-party IMF management tools are available now, they are still considered "works in progress" and should be used with care. One useful management tool for IMF settings comes included with every SBS installation in the world—Outlook.

By following the instructions posted in the "You Had Me At EHLO" blog (`http://blogs.technet.com/exchange/archive/2004/05/26/142607.aspx`), you can get Outlook to display the SCL value for each message in the mail display listing. Then you can review the messages that are getting dumped into the Junk Mail folder to determine whether adjustments to the IMF values are needed.

This method is recommended when first setting up IMF on a server to determine what the best value for the Gateway Blocking Configuration should be. By setting the Gateway Blocking Configuration action to No Action and setting the Store Junk E-mail Configuration value to a lower number than the Gateway Blocking Configuration, all mail that would get blocked at the gateway will be delivered into the Junk Mail folder. Over a period of time, you can review the messages that get delivered to the Junk Mail folder and their respective SCL values and determine a baseline value to use for gateway blocking. After you have developed a feel for how IMF assigns SCL values to different types of messages, you can make the adjustment to the Gateway Blocking Configuration and set it to Delete when ready. The same approach can be used to determine whether the value for Store Junk E-mail Configuration is correct.

Just remember that IMF does not have any configuration options other than setting these two values. If you want more granularity in your spam filtering, you need to investigate third-party products. Many have advanced configuration settings such as blacklists and white lists (mail domains that always get blocked or always get delivered, respectively), quarantines, and user-level configurations.

Troubleshooting POP3 Connector

Troubleshooting issues with the POP3 Connector is similar to troubleshooting outbound mail delivery. Setting up and reviewing the extended logging with the POP3 Connector and using `telnet` to test connectivity are your primary tools.

The logging level for the POP3 Connector is set in the Troubleshooting tab of the POP3 Connector Manager. The four levels are

- None—No information is placed in the event logs by the POP3 Connector service.
- Minimum—Only security audit information (successful and failed logins) and critical errors are stored in the event logs.
- Medium—Logs messages from the Minimum setting plus other informational messages.
- Maximum—Logs every step of the POP3 Connector process in the event logs.

When you encounter problems with the POP3 connector, set the logging level up to Maximum and restart the POP3 Connector service. Then force connection attempts by clicking the Retrieve Now button in the Scheduling tab of the POP3 Connector Manager. After the connection attempt has had time to complete, you can open the Event Viewer and go through the messages related to the POP3 Connector. Fortunately, when logging is set to Maximum for the POP3 Connector, you can view each step of the entire process to see where problems are actually occurring. Unfortunately, so much information is stored in the logs, it may take a long time to sort through the data to find the information you need.

CAUTION

Do not forget to set logging back to Minimum (or none) and restart the POP3 Connector service when you have finished your troubleshooting session. Otherwise, your event logs will fill up quickly and could cause other problems on the server. The logging settings will not actually change until the service has been restarted.

Alternatively, you can use `telnet` to verify access credentials and message availability on the remote POP3 server. Follow these steps to connect to the server and see how many messages are waiting:

1. At a command prompt, type `telnet [remote mail server] 110` and press Enter.
2. At the `+OK` prompt, type `user [pop3username]` and press Enter.
3. At the `+OK` prompt, type `pass [pop3password]` and press Enter.
4. At the `+OK` prompt, type `list` and press Enter. This shows the number of messages waiting for download and the size of each message.

This process verifies several pieces of the POP3 puzzle. First, if the username and password are not correct, you get a `-ERR` response after the password entry line. Second, you can see whether messages are waiting to be downloaded. This can be helpful if you suspect mail delivery problems at the other side. You can simply keep repeating the list command to get the current count and size of the messages and watch for changes to indicate when new messages have arrived.

CAUTION

You can also use Outlook Express or another POP mail client to verify the username and password on the remote server. Be sure that when you build a profile in a mail client for testing purposes that you configure the profile to leave the messages on the POP3 server when checking mail. Otherwise, those messages will be deleted from the server, and the POP3 Connector will not be able to download and deliver them.

One scenario in particular that can cause much grief for an SBS administrator is when a user has her POP3 mail account configured for use in Outlook or Outlook Express. If more than one POP3 client is pulling mail from the POP3 server, irregular mail delivery is practically guaranteed. When a new SBS server is installed in an environment where users had been relying solely on POP3 for mail delivery, you should make sure that all users remove the POP3 account configuration from their mail clients for the POP3 Connector to work correctly.

One last step to verify that a message on the POP3 server will get delivered correctly is to issue the `retr` command in the POP3 `telnet` session to view the contents of the message without deleting it from the server. Simply type `retr [message#]` after authenticating to the POP3 server, and the server will send the entire contents of the message. At that point, you can look through the headers for the TO: and CC: fields for a valid address for your server. If an address within your domain space is not listed in the TO: or CC: fields, the message downloads to the server but does not get delivered, unless you specify a mailbox to receive delivery of all undeliverable messages.

Summary

This chapter covered some of the main management aspects of the Exchange and POP3 Connector services included with SBS 2003. Most of the main settings for Exchange are configured through the Connect to the Internet Wizard, but some features, such as mail delivery to multiple domains and the Intelligent Message Filter require manual setup by the system administrator. The chapter also addressed other issues related to the prevention of spam and virus attacks on the server and gave troubleshooting steps for several processes related to mail delivery and processing. With this information, an SBS system administrator should be better prepared to handle the day-to-day management of Exchange and its related components.

Best Practice Summary

- Preventing the reverse NDR attack—You can use a combination of recipient filtering and tar pitting to protect your server against the reverse NDR attack.
- Install the Intelligent Message Filter on all SBS installations—Because the IMF is a free tool and does not conflict with other antispam tools, it should be installed on all SBS servers.
- Route outbound email through a smart host—To protect against current and future problems that could impact your server's capability to deliver mail to other servers reliably, you should configure your server to send all outbound email through your ISP's SMTP server.
- Use the POP3 Connector as a transitional tool, not as a mail solution—If you must use the POP3 Connector at all, use it only to transition mail services away from POP3 toward full SMTP.
- Setting appropriate SCL values using Outlook—Enable the display of SCL values in the Outlook client and monitor the operation of the IMF to determine the ideal values to set for Gateway Blocking and Junk E-mail Delivery configurations.

CHAPTER 13

Exchange Disaster Recovery

IN THIS CHAPTER

- Understanding the Exchange Database Structure
- Understanding Exchange Backup Methods and Requirements
- Recovering Exchange Databases from Backup
- Repairing a Damaged Exchange Database
- Recovering a 16GB Mail Database
- Troubleshooting Exchange Disaster Recovery Issues

There are no prizes for realizing that email has become ubiquitous. Email addresses can be found on everything from candy wrappers to billboards. Not only is email replacing the Fax machine, but its attachments are replacing mailed and couriered documents from orders and contracts to graphics and multimedia. Email is also replacing telephone communications in areas such as inquiries, complaints, and help desk.

It is no surprise then that Microsoft Exchange is part of the base platform of Small Business Server. Exchange provides huge benefits in terms of collaborative communication between staff, customers, and suppliers, locally via the network and remotely via the Internet, Outlook Web Access, and Outlook over HTTP. There is also huge growth in Mail-enabled mobile devices such as Smartphones and PDAs directly synced to Microsoft Exchange.

One missed order or complaint can be disastrous for a small or medium-sized business. The messaging system is therefore both time sensitive and business critical.

All systems fail, and there is always a risk that at sometime Microsoft Exchange will be unable to service email. However, this need not be a showstopper. Both the Microsoft Exchange and the SBS developer teams have provided many enhancements in SBS 2003 and in Exchange Server 2003 to minimize the downtime and its impact on the business's users, suppliers, and customers.

With a full SBS wizard-generated backup, the server, users, mailboxes, and data can all be brought back online quickly. Using Microsoft Exchange Server's Deleted Mail and Deleted Mailbox retention, users and administrators can recover items within minutes. Should the Exchange database be infected, corrupted, or lost for any reason, a database can be brought back online to continue servicing mail while still running user mailboxes restored via the Recovery Storage Group.

These features dramatically increase uptime while simultaneously reducing recovery time. Still, this does not cure all ills, and, depending on the nature, severity, and criticality of the disaster and the urgency of reconnection, you may need to call on a number of techniques and tools to recover mailbox and/or other data such as public folders.

Bear in mind that Murphy's Law holds true. If it can happen, it will happen; it's just a question of when. Provided that you are prepared, when disaster strikes, it need not be the total disaster it first appears to be, so plan, implement, and practice—above all, practice. Keep in mind that a backup is only as good as the last time you actually restored it.

This chapter discusses Microsoft Exchange databases, the types of disasters that can occur, the tools used for backup and recovery, and how and when to use them.

It can't be emphasized strongly enough that you should not just read and follow these steps and methods after disaster has struck but use them to plan, implement, and practice.

Understanding the Exchange Database Structure

An increasing number of wizards both in Microsoft and other vendor products is available for use in backing up and restoring Microsoft Exchange. These wizards are mini applications with easy-to-use graphical user interfaces (GUIs) that collect data and options and then automatically configure all required settings.

Although these tools take the tedium and risk out of complex, multifaceted operations, it is important to understand what should be backed up, why it should be done, and the process by which it occurs. Without understanding these fundamentals it is almost impossible to plan and implement an efficient disaster recovery program and resolve or work around the issues. Moreover, such knowledge lends a framework and context to the various processes, techniques, and tools used for data recovery.

This chapter concerns itself with the backup and restoration of Microsoft Exchange data, not the SBS server, Exchange Server, or its messaging components. Restoration of the server can be achieved through restoring a full system backup, a disk image, or a recovery reinstall of the Exchange Server using the `/DisasterRecovery` switch.

The choice of backup media undoubtedly will be determined by the business's cost/benefit analysis together with the needs and the risk analysis. The media to be used, whether it be tape, hard disk, tape via hard disk, network addressed storage (NAS), or other, may affect the speed of backup and recovery, but it does not affect the basic method.

The following are the main elements of Microsoft Exchange relating to data backup:

- Exchange storage groups
- The Mailbox Store
- The Public Folder Store

- Extensible Storage Engine (ESE) databases
- The log files
- Circular logging
- The checkpoint file
- Transactions

Exchange Storage Groups

Because SBS 2003 contains Exchange Server 2003 Standard Edition, it can have only one storage group accessible by MAPI (Messaging Application Programming Interface) clients such as Microsoft Outlook. Table 13.1 lists the two stores created by default in an SBS 2003 installation.

TABLE 13.1 SBS 2003 Exchange Message Stores

Store	Description
Mailbox Store	Also known as the private store, this store contains folders and data that are private to a user.
Public Folder Store	This store is the repository for collaborative information shared by all Exchange users on the network.

On installation, these two stores are created as First Storage Group, as shown in Figure 13.1.

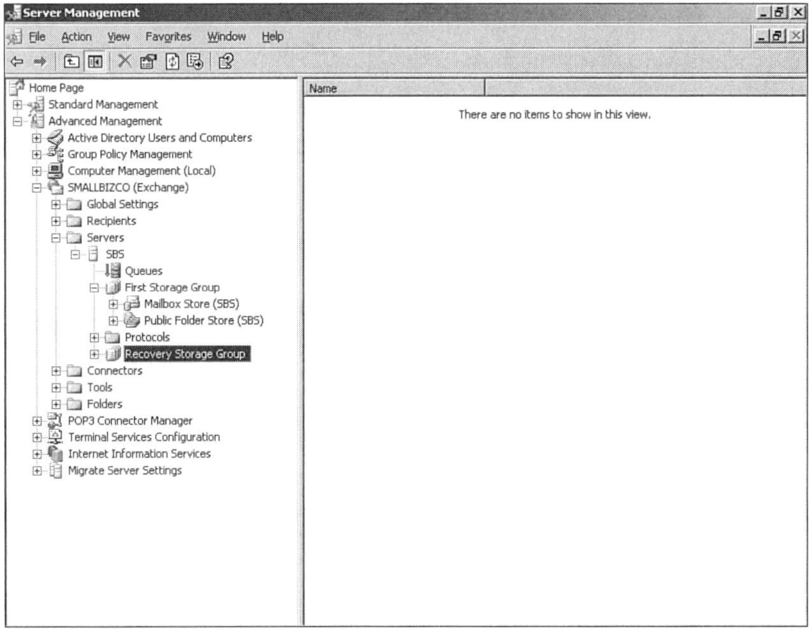

FIGURE 13.1 SBS storage groups.

In addition, you can create a Recovery Storage Group not accessible by MAPI clients but responsive to the Exchange API for the recovery of a Mailbox Store or its contents.

In Microsoft Exchange 2003 Standard each storage group store consists of two databases that work together. These are Microsoft Extensible Storage Engine databases denoted by extensions `.edb` and `.stm`. It is important to keep these two files together at all times whether copying, moving, or backing up because they form parts of a whole. The internal schema for the `.stm` database is stored in the `.edb` database.

A database signature, which is a 32-bit random number combined with the time that the database was created, is stored as a header in both files. If these files get out of synch, (as would be the case if one file were backed up one day and the other the next), the database will be unrecoverable.

Extensible Storage Engine (ESE) Databases

Exchange Server 2003 uses ESE98, an Extensible Storage Engine (ESE), as its database engine. This was previously known as Joint Engine Technology (JET) Blue. The ESE is optimized for fast retrieval of data because this is the database's main function. Properties of ESE databases include

- Transaction-based
- Relational
- Multiuser
- ISAM (Indexed Sequential Access Method) table management
- Fully Data Manipulation Language (DML) capable
- Fully Data Definition Language (DDL) capable
- Low-level Application Programming Interface (API) exposed

The ESE allows applications to store records, create indexes, and access those records in a variety of ways. You can find the location of the files that underlie the databases in the Mailbox Store Properties window, shown in Figure 13.2, and the Public Folder Store Properties window, shown in Figure 13.3.

The `.edb` File

The `.edb` database file contains folders, tables, messaging data, attachments, indexes, and metadata for MAPI messages and other items in the Exchange store such as the internal schema for the `.stm` file.

By default, SBS creates the files as `Priv1.edb` and `Pub1.edb` for the respective Mailbox and Public Folder Stores.

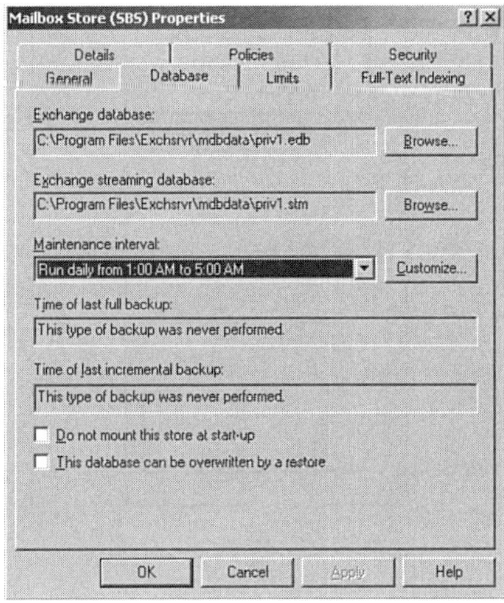

FIGURE 13.2 Property sheet showing the location of Mailbox Store database files.

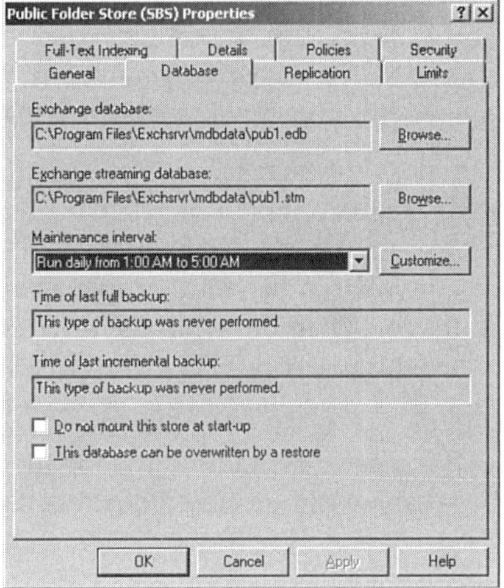

FIGURE 13.3 Property sheet showing the location of Public Folder database files.

The `.stm` File

The `.stm` database file (also known as the streaming file) contains Internet messages in their native format, such as MIME, which are written directly (streamed) to the file as a temporary storage point until the email is accessed by a client such as Outlook.

By default SBS creates the files as `Priv1.stm` and `Pub1.stm` for the respective Mailbox and Public Folder Stores.

Figure 13.4 illustrates how the `.edb` and `.stm` files together with the uncommitted transaction log files constitute the total Exchange data.

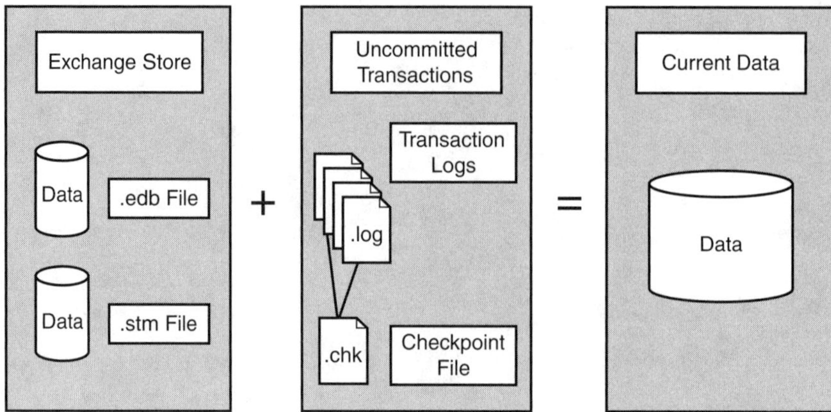

FIGURE 13.4 Exchange current data.

Log Files

As Microsoft Exchange receives data, it simultaneously writes the information to a transaction log and to memory, until the load on the server allows for the data to be written to the database. If a database shuts down unexpectedly, uncommitted transactions can be restored by replaying the sequentially numbered transaction log files into the database.

There are a series of transaction logs for each store. The sequential filenames prefixed with an `E`, have a `.log` extension, and contain a seven-character hexadecimal number: the letter and first two characters identifying the database. By default, each log file (except the temporary log currently being written to—for example, `E00tmp.log`) is exactly 5 megabytes (5,242,880 bytes) in size. When the temp file reaches 5 megabytes, it is saved as the next sequentially numbered transaction log.

Each storage group also maintains two reserve log files, `Res1.log` and `Res2.log`. These are created to reserve disk space. If the drive containing the log files runs out of disk space, these will be used so that the database can be closed down in a consistent state without data loss.

Figure 13.5 shows the transaction log location in the property sheet.

Best Practice—Data Storage

Take into account the mail usage and retention practices of the business and plan to store your Exchange data and log files on disks or partitions with ample free space for additional copies of the databases and logs in a recovery or repair situation. The additional space required can be considerable, and free space of at least 120% of your projected maximum Exchange database size (`.edb plus .stm` files plus `.log` files if hosted on the same partition) is recommended.

Figure 13.6 shows the default log file directory `MDBData` and examples of the log files themselves.

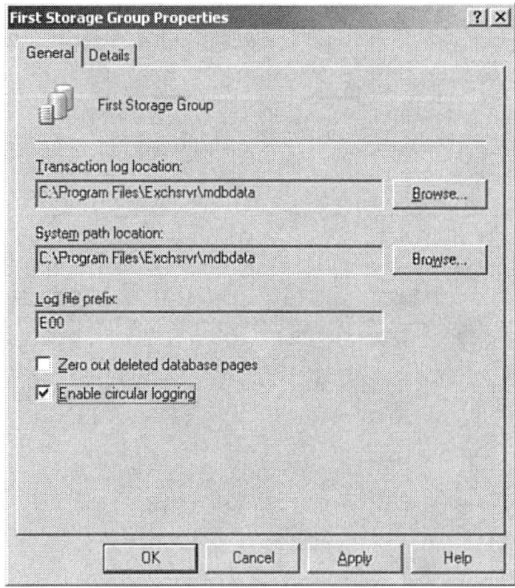

FIGURE 13.5 Transaction log location.

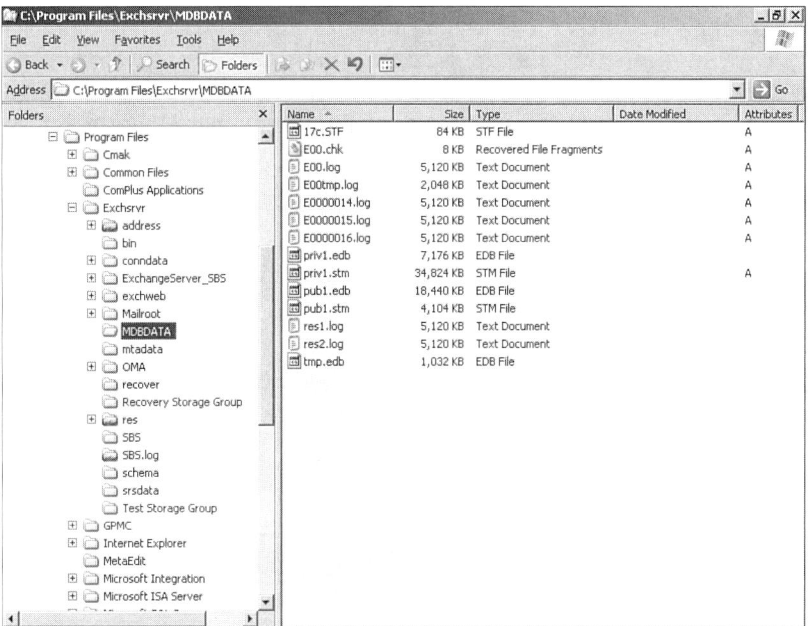

FIGURE 13.6 Default log file directory.

Circular Logging

Circular logging is turned on by default in SBS 2003 installations to protect systems that have not configured an Exchange-aware backup, which deletes committed log files, from filling the hard drive partition. The SBS Backup Wizard disables circular logging on completion.

Best Practice—Disable Circular Logging

Configure an Exchange-aware backup as soon as practical after setup to ensure that circular logging is disabled and a full System State backup run and verified. Immediately after disabling circular logging, a full backup of Exchange should be run to provide the base point for future backups.

Because you cannot recover Exchange 2003 data that is more recent than the last Normal backup without a complete set of transaction logs, you should not have circular logging enabled in production environments. Circular logging is usually used for Public Folder Stores that contain Network News Transfer Protocol (NNTP) feeds (newsgroup posts) where roll-forward capabilities are not required.

Checkpoint File

Each storage group has a checkpoint file. This file has a `.chk` extension with a prefix containing the letter and the two numbers that identify the storage group it and the logs refer to. This prefix is also the prefix of the related log files with the database identifier.

The purpose of the checkpoint file is to track the progress of transaction logging and which logs have been committed to the database. Transaction log files accumulate over time, and this tracking can dramatically reduce the amount of time taken during a recovery because the logs need only to be rolled forward from the point indicated in the checkpoint file.

Although the checkpoint file is not essential to a backup, ideally it should be backed up together with the ESE databases and the Exchange logs.

Transactions

Microsoft Exchange is transaction based. A *transaction* is defined as an inseparable set of database operations such as inserts, deletes, and updates that must be executed either in their entirety or not at all.

A transaction should adhere to the following ACID properties:

- Atomic—The operation occurs in its entirety or not at all.
- Consistent—The database is left in a consistent state at all times.
- Isolated—Changes are not available while in an intermittent state.
- Durable—Once committed, transactions are preserved in the database even in the event of a system failure.

The database engine commits data only when it can verify that it has successfully committed that data from memory to the transaction log file on disk. Figure 13.7 illustrates the transaction process.

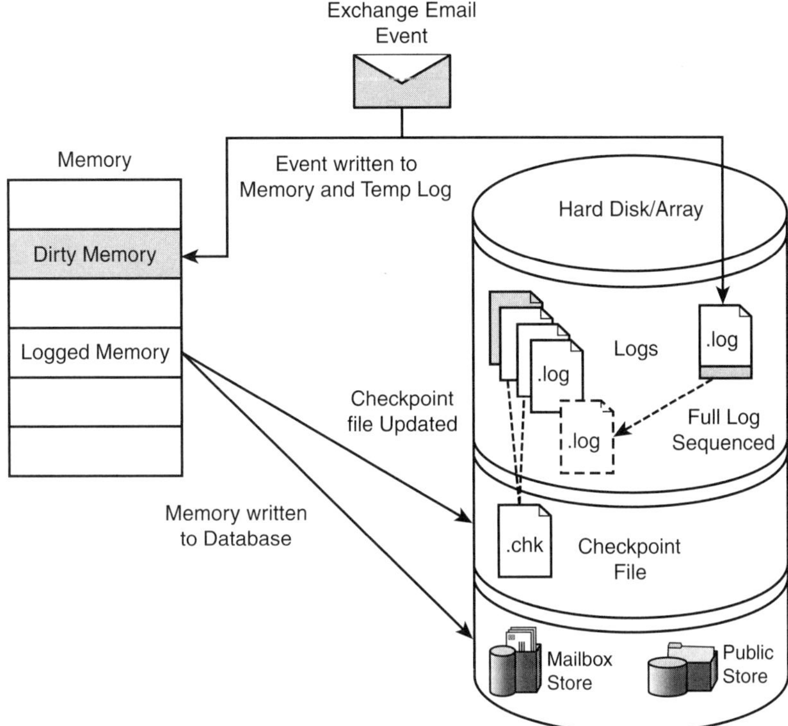

FIGURE 13.7 The transaction process.

Typical Transaction Logging Process

The following list outlines the steps that take place in the Exchange message transaction process:

1. The user sends a message.
2. MAPI calls the Information Store to tell it that the user is sending the message.
3. The Information Store starts a transaction in the database engine and makes the corresponding changes to the data.
4. The database engine records the transaction in memory by dirtying a new page in memory.
5. Simultaneously, the database engine secures the transaction in the transaction log file and creates a log record. When the database engine reaches the end of a transaction log file, it rolls the file over creating a new log file in sequence.
6. The database engine writes the dirty page to the database file on disk.
7. The checkpoint file gets updated.

Understanding Exchange Backup Methods and Requirements

Now that you have a better idea how the Exchange databases are structured and data flows through the Exchange processes, you will be better able to understand the different backup methods used with Exchange and the requirements to back up the databases successfully. There are basically two types of Exchange backup: online and offline.

Online Backup

Online backups are made while the Exchange 2003 services are running and use the Exchange streaming backup API. The Exchange 2003 online backup API automatically synchronizes and gathers the Exchange 2003 database and transaction log data that will be required for successful restoration using the same channel as normal database access. Although this can take longer than offline backups, it has the advantage of not interrupting users' use of email services, and as each 4K page is passed through the database engine to be written to backup media, its checksum is verified. Any error found is reported as a `-1018` error, and the backup is terminated.

Figure 13.8 shows a representation of the Exchange backup process.

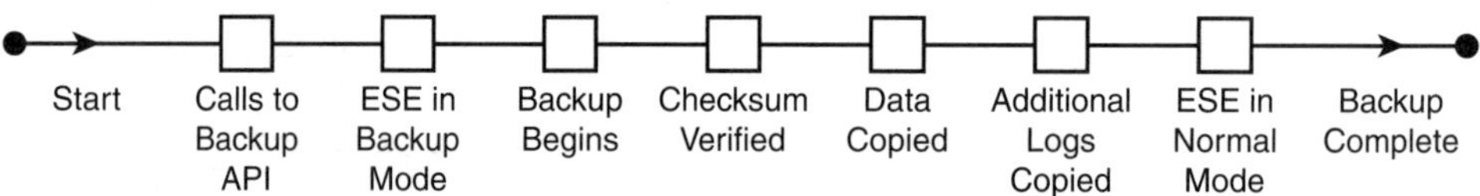

FIGURE 13.8 The Exchange backup process.

There are four types of online backups of an Exchange database: normal, copy, incremental, and differential. In Exchange 2003 these processes are as described in the following sections.

Normal (Full) Backup

The Backup application backs up the ESE database files (`.edb` and `.stm`) and at least one of the log files. On completion, the backup application deletes all committed log files indicated by the pointer in the checkpoint file. A patch page is then added to the database containing details of messaging transactions that occurred in Exchange while the backup process was running.

Note that without circular logging, or an Exchange-aware backup process such as this, the log files would accumulate until all disk space was consumed. This is a common problem with badly configured and/or administered Exchange Servers.

The steps in detail are as follows:

1. The backup agent establishes a connection to and communication with the Microsoft Exchange Information Store service (MSExchangeIS).

2. The checkpoint is frozen. New data continues to be written to the databases, but the Checkpoint pointer is not updated until the backup ends.
3. The first log file that must be copied to the backup media is recorded in the database header in the Current Full Backup section.
4. The copying of the databases begins. Changes during the backup that cannot be reconstructed fully from the log files are not flushed to disk. Instead, an extra file page is created and attached to the end of the `.edb` file as a mini header containing information relating to the transaction log files required to recover the database. This information can be seen in the Patch Current Full Backup section in a restored but not yet rolled forward database using `ESEutil /MH` from a command line. The information stored there overrides the Log Required field in the Database header.
5. Because log files cannot be backed up while open, the current temp log file is closed and sequenced regardless of its size immediately after copying the database files.
6. The transaction log files required to reliably restore the databases are now copied to the media. This includes all transaction log files such as those flagged in the checkpoint file and including the file just closed.
7. Based on the Last Backup Date/Time information stored in the database headers together with the logs that were required and the information in the Checkpoint file, those transaction logs not required for a successful restore of the database are deleted from disk.
8. The Previous Full Backup section of the database header is updated with the Date/Time and Log Range of the backup just completed.

Copy Backup

A copy backup is similar to the Normal backup with the exceptions that it does not delete the old log files and does not update the database headers to indicate that the backup has occurred. This can be useful for creating a rollback copy of the Exchange data prior to a restore or repair of the databases in the event that the restore or repair was unsuccessful.

Daily Backup

In Exchange Server 2003 a daily backup is the same as a copy backup.

Incremental Backup

Unlike normal and copy backups where the current transaction log file is closed and sequenced after the databases have been copied, with incremental backups, it is rolled over at the beginning. All the sequentially numbered log files are then copied to the media, and those not required for successful database recovery are deleted for disk. The Current Incremental Backup section of the database header is then updated with the Date/Time and log range of the backup just completed.

For an incremental backup to be useful in a disaster recovery you must have a normal or copy backup containing the ESE databases and an unbroken sequence of transaction log files.

Differential Backup

A differential backup is similar to an incremental backup with the exception that the old transaction log files are not deleted, and the Current Incremental Backup section of the database header is not updated.

Offline Backup

Offline backups are file-level backups made while the Exchange 2003 services are shut down or the data stores dismounted.

It is highly recommended that you do not use offline backups except in special cases immediately prior to recovering databases. Their one advantage is that because they do not check data integrity during the backup process they can be performed in cases where an online backup may fail due to data corruption.

To ensure the integrity of the data and transactions, including those in memory and as yet uncommitted to disk, you should use online backups.

Security Permissions

The user account that you are logged in to must have the requisite permissions or rights assigned when trying to back up or restore Microsoft Exchange data. Only those accounts with Domain Level Backup Operator rights can back up Exchange 2003 databases. To restore Exchange 2003 backups, the account must have full Exchange administrator rights for the domain.

Table 13.2 lists the minimum account levels needed for backup and restore.

TABLE 13.2 Minimum Account Levels for Backup and Restore

Operation	Minimum Account Level
Exchange backups	Domain backup operator
Exchange restore operations	Full Exchange administrator
Windows backups	Local backup operator
Windows restore operations	Local administrator rights

Note that you can assign users Domain Backup Operator permission without granting them full administrator rights. You can also use Run As to perform operations such as scheduled jobs in a security context other than that of the logged-on user.

Table 13.3 lists the group memberships and backup and restore privileges assigned to various security groups.

TABLE 13.3 Group Memberships and Backup and Restore Privileges

Group Membership	Backup Privileges
Local Administrators group	Members can back up most files and folders on the computer where the account is a member of the Local Administrators group. If the computer is an Exchange 2003 member server, you cannot back up Exchange database files unless you are also a member of the Backup Operator or Domain Administrator group.

TABLE 13.3 Continued

Group Membership	Backup Privileges
Domain Administrators group	Members can back up all files and folders on all computers in the domain.
Local Backup Operators group	Members can back up all files and folders on the computer where the account is a member of the Local Backup Operators group.
Domain Backup Operators group	Members can back up all files and folders on all computers in the domain.
Any other domain or local group	Members can back up all files and folders that the account owns. Members can back up files or folders for which the account has Read, Read and Execute, Modify, or Full Control permissions.

Backing Up Exchange Using the SBS Backup Wizard

By default, the SBS Backup Wizard automatically configures and schedules Microsoft NTBackup to perform a full, online, Exchange-aware backup of the server, which includes the Exchange stores and logs together with Windows System State and user data.

There is no need (and in fact no option) to select the Exchange stores and logs when configuring the Backup Wizard. If you open the wizard-generated backup file in NTBackup, as shown in Figure 13.9, you will see that it included the Exchange Information Store First Storage Group. This is saved as `C:\Program Files\Microsoft Small Business Server\Backup` as `Small Business Server Backup Script.bks` in a default SBS install.

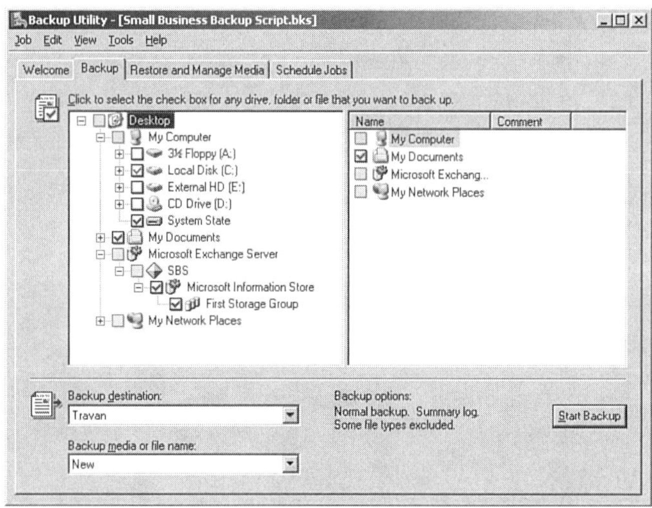

FIGURE 13.9 SBS wizard-generated backup.

By default SBS 2003 hides the Exchange Installable File System (IFS) drive, previously seen as the M virtual drive. If this is visible for any reason, you should add the entire drive to the list of file exclusions in the Backup Wizard.

At the Storage Allocation for Deleted Files and Email screen, shown in Figure 13.10, you can configure the period of time Exchange retains deleted emails and mailboxes before flushing them from the system. Users and administrators can then recover these items during the retention period directly from disk without recourse to the backup media.

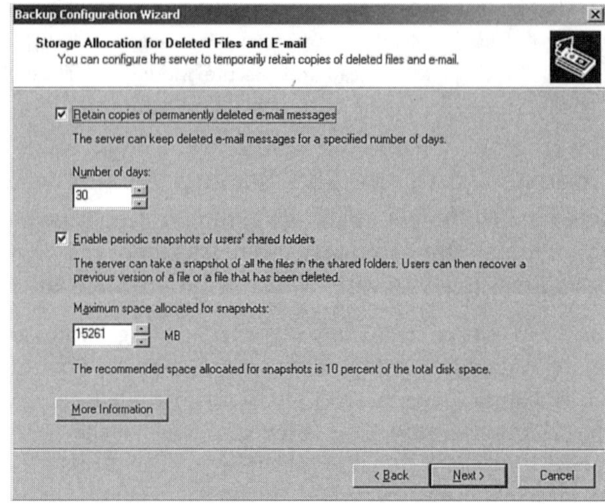

FIGURE 13.10 Storage allocation for deleted files and email.

Before setting the retention period, consider the following issues:

- The volume of email
- The size of the email
- The size of the database and logs on disk
- The effect this will have on performance
- The effect on the size and duration of the backup
- The effect on the free space available on disk for a recovery or repair
- The effect that this will have on the duration of a restore

One thing to be aware of is that although the wizard-created backup uses the Volume Shadow Copy service in part, the Microsoft Exchange Server 2003 Writer for the Volume Shadow Copy service can conflict with NTBackup. If the Exchange Writer is enabled, it precludes the capability to simultaneously back up Exchange stores and System State. Microsoft has therefore disabled the Exchange Writer as part of the SBS setup.

Using NTBackup

The SBS Backup Wizard configures a restorable backup set that includes System State as well as your Microsoft Exchange data stores and is the easiest and recommended way to back up SBS. The wizard is a wrapper around NTBackup and a number of other services, but you can configure these manually if you want.

You can configure and run NTBackup independently depending on your plan and needs using either the GUI in the wizard or manual mode, or scripted via the command line.

Windows Server 2003 Backup uses Volume Shadow Copy services (VSS) to back up System State, but backs up the Exchange Server stores directly. The System State Backup Shadow Copy Provider changes the state to Backup in Progress, and other processes cannot then access the Information Store.

Exchange 2003 SP1 supports Volume Shadow Copy when used with backup tools that include an Exchange Server 2003 aware Volume Shadow Copy Service Requestor. Due to the lack of such a requestor in NTBackup you need to configure the backup independently of a System State backup. Some third-party software does include the requestor, however, and can back up System State and Exchange stores simultaneously using the Volume Shadow Copy service.

Not all Exchange data that may be required for a successful restore is backed up with the System State. Exchange relies on IIS for its SMTP component and for Web Services for Outlook Web Access (OWA). Exchange stores the configuration data in Metabase Stores in IIS. By default, the data is stored in two files in the `C:\WINDOWS\system32\inetsrv\MetaBack folder`.

The `.MDn` file, where *n* is a version number, holds the metadata, whereas the `.SCn` file holds the schema. You can create a one-time backup of these files using the GUI from the IIS Manager by selecting *computer name*, Action, All Tasks, Backup/Restore Configuration (as shown in Figure 13.11); then select Create Backup. You can then include these files in your Exchange backup, as shown in Figure 13.12.

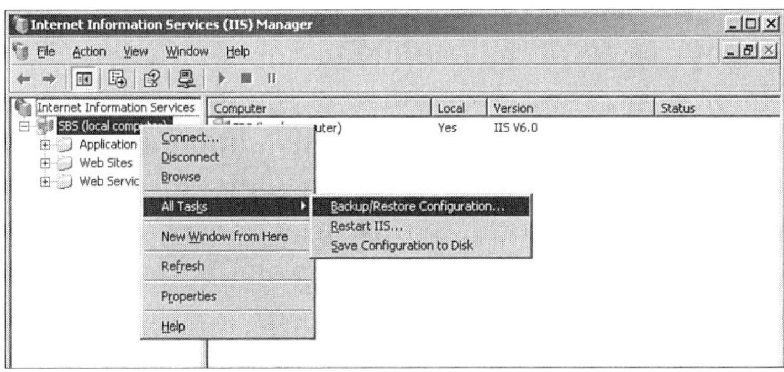

FIGURE 13.11 Back up IIS metadata.

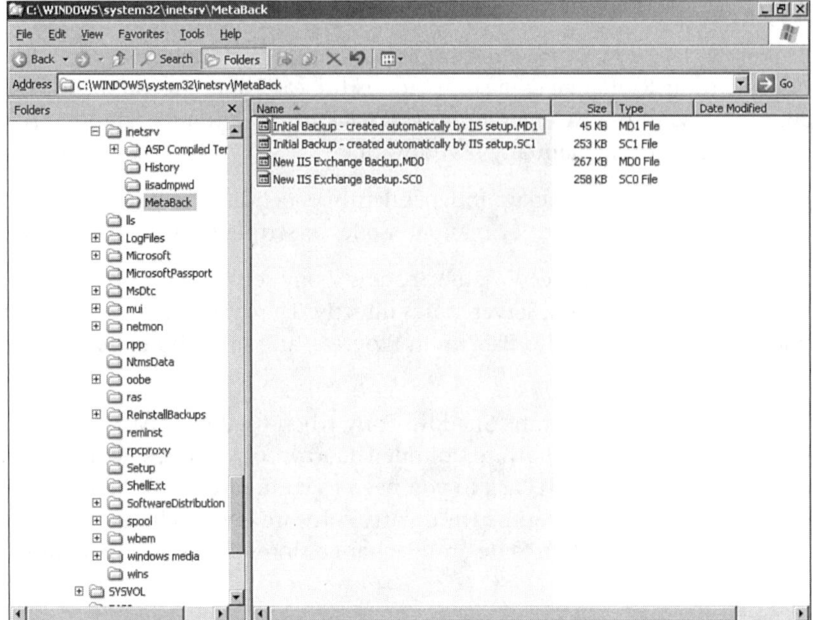

FIGURE 13.12 IIS metadata backup files.

As stated previously, you should not back up the Exchange Installable File System (IFS, `M`) drive if it is visible. Neither should you back up the database or log files unless the databases are dismounted and offline. Although it is strongly recommended that you use only online Exchange-aware backups, you may have reason to do an offline backup. In that event, dismount both the Private and Public Folder Stores before backing them up. You should also exclude the directories containing the databases and the log files (by default, `C:\Program Files\exchsvr\mdbdata\`) from selection.

It will be necessary to configure properties in the public and private folders that the SBS Backup Wizard would normally configure automatically. These include

- Circular logging
- Deleted item retention
- Deleted mailbox retention
- Do not permanently delete items and mailboxes until the store has been backed up

Using ExMerge

The Exchange Server Mailbox Merge Wizard (ExMerge) is a powerful tool used to extract and import information from and to Exchange private mailboxes using Outlook `.pst` files.

Since its creation in 1997 as a tool to remove Melissa virus-infected messages, it has grown into a sophisticated multithreaded application with considerable search and filtering capabilities on single or multiple mailboxes in a store.

ExMerge can extract and copy, move, or delete messages by selecting or excluding folders by specific subject, by attachment name, or by date/time range.

It can be used in a one- or two-step process from a GUI interface or command line and supports logging and scripted calls to a configuration (`.ini`) file.

Best Practice—ExMerge

Download the latest version of ExMerge appropriate to the version of Exchange and install it to the `%Program Files%\Exchsrvr\bin` directory. Add the `%Program Files%\Exchsrvr\bin` directory to the Systems Path variable so that ExMerge can locate required Exchange DLLs, and you can easily execute both it and other utilities such as ESEutil and ISinteg from the command line. Prepare yourself by reading the comprehensive manual. Add ExMerge to your toolkit and practice using it.

The latest version of ExMerge supports Outlook Calendar, Contacts, Journal, Notes, Tasks, Views, and Folder rules.

Although ExMerge works with both the First Storage Group and the Recovery Storage Group, it cannot extract data from Public Folders nor can it handle all data and metadata. Its search and filtering cannot find a string in a substring or an attachment to a message nested within another message.

ExMerge requires Receive As and Send As permission for the mailboxes to be able to import and export information. The logged-on user Account must have Service Account Administrator permissions at the organization, site, and configuration levels of the Administrator program and have both permissions on the mailboxes.

ExMerge is ideally suited to creating *brick level* (individual mailbox) backups and archives. Although it cannot write data directly to backup tape, it can to other media such as internal or external HDD or NAS that can be programmatically moved to tape. It can also create incremental backups by either of the following:

- Merge—Copy only new messages and folders skipping all messages and folders previously copied.
- Replace—Replace data only if the copy in the source store is more recent.

ExMerge uses a sophisticated process that helps recover all uncorrupted data even if individual mailbox folders contain corrupted messages. All messages in a mailbox folder are extracted collectively to minimize remote procedure call (RPC) traffic and time. On encountering an error, ExMerge automatically skips the message and then begins copying the messages that remain in the folder individually. After reaching the end of the folder, the tool then resumes copying messages collectively again until another error is encountered. This makes it an ideal recovery tool.

Another feature of ExMerge is that it is highly scriptable. You can create sophisticated `.ini` files (either manually or by saving your setting to files as seen in Figure 13.13). You can then script calls to the appropriate file for a variety of backup and disaster recovery operations.

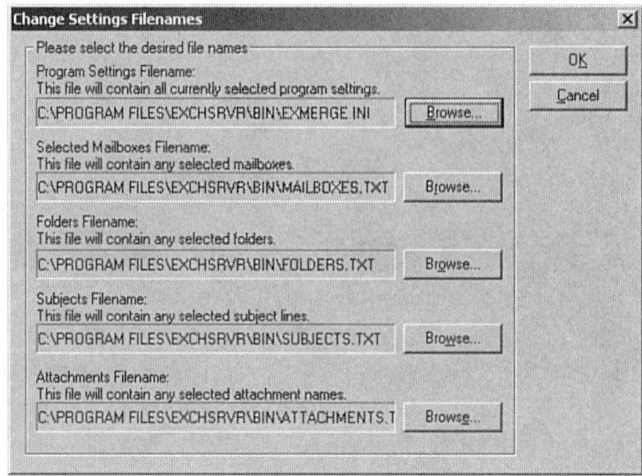

FIGURE 13.13 ExMerge Change Settings Filenames window.

Using Third-Party Solutions

Although not specifically necessary, it's possible and common to use third-party backup solutions with SBS and Microsoft Exchange. These vary in price, feature set, and usability from those that are simple wrappers around the NTBackup software to those that fully support the backup APIs and VSS.

Third-party backup solutions can provide support for features that the SBS NTBackup does not, such as disk imaging, optical media, brick level backup and restore, and Microsoft Exchange backup via Volume Shadow Copy Services.

Additionally, there are vendor and service provider solutions that include offsite backup to remote storage backup via broadband and snapshot or streaming backup to NAS or *hot spare* servers.

In evaluating backup software for SBS and Microsoft Exchange 2003, consider the following:

- Price (cost/value benefit).
- Use of and support for MS Backup APIs (Exchange aware).
- Use of and support for Volume Shadow Copy services (VSS aware).
- Proprietaries and support for the backup hardware/medium.
- Whether it allows for online or offline only backup and restore.
- The duration of the backup and restore scenarios and methods.
- Reliability and appropriateness of the solution.
- The degree of difficulty.
- Documentation.
- Vendor support and longevity in the market—archived backups may be many years old.

If you are going to use VSS aware backup software to back up your SBS Exchange databases, you need to turn on the Exchange Writer. You can do this by editing the Registry value located in

```
HKLM\SYSTEM\CurrentControlSet\Services\MSExchangeIS\ParametersSystem
```

and setting the Disable Exchange Writer value to a Value Data of 0. Either toggle the value to 1 or delete the Registry entry when no longer required.

NOTE

Be aware that enabling the Exchange Writer inappropriately can cause system errors and data loss. Make sure that the backup solution you are using supports it.

CAUTION

The usual warning about editing the Registry applies. Great care needs to be taken. You should have a known good backup of the Registry and know how to restore it in the event of disaster or lockout.

Recovering Exchange Databases from Backup

The sole point of an Exchange backup is for the data to be restored to disk at some point in time and the data to be accessed via client applications. Do this often to validate the integrity of your backup, practice your techniques, and fine-tune and reevaluate the process for timing to suitability.

A large percentage of backups fail to restore successfully. This can be for a variety of reasons from devices that are no longer compatible with the archived backup to operator error that may be due to lack of training or practice.

Having a backup on media and a backup log that states that the backup process verified the data transfer is not enough. A backup operator should restore data from the media to the hard disk and verify it at least once a month and do a full disaster recovery restore and verify (possibly to a test server or the Recovery Storage Group and a dummy RestoreVerify user) at least once a quarter. This is the only way to verify the disaster recovery plan and will highlight any issues with the media, the hardware, the operator, or the efficiency of the plan itself.

The aim here is to successfully restore the most current or archived data in the least time, with a minimum of disruption to the business and its ongoing services.

As part of your disaster recovery implementation plan, you should create a recovery checklist, similar to the following, that is appropriate to your own environment and plan:

- Have the last full backup media available.
- Have the incremental/differential backup media available.

- Issue users and concerned parties an outage advice.
- Dismount the Mailbox and Public Folder Stores that you are restoring.
- Set This Database Can Be Overwritten (may be optional).
- Determine the database and log file locations of the files to be restored (optional).
- Ensure that there is sufficient free space on the volume or volumes to be used.
- Offline copy the current database and log files to another location (optional).
- Make sure that the Mailbox and Public Folder Store names in Exchange System Manager match your backup media (may be optional).
- Make sure that the Microsoft Exchange Information Store service (MSExchangeIS) is running.
- Select the backup files that you want to restore from your backup media.
- Restore the selected files.
- Make sure that the restore process was successful.
- Replay the transaction log files (`ESEutil /cc`) (optional).
- Mount the databases (stores).
- Advise users and concerned parties that messaging services have been resumed.
- Complete and sign off on the issue and process update in the server log book. (You do have a server log book and keep it current don't you?)

This list is by no means definitive and needs to be tailored to your own processes. In restoring Exchange, patience under pressure is a virtue, and time is the key.

Events Requiring Exchange Recovery

Many scenarios may require the recovery of Exchange data:

- Catastrophic loss of the SBS server (hardware/HDDs)
- Migration of the SBS server to new hardware
- Loss of the Exchange 2003 server (Exchange database and transaction log files also lost)
- Loss of the Exchange 2003 server (Exchange databases and transaction log files intact)
- Lost database/storage group
- Lost Exchange databases
- Lost mailbox
- Lost mail item (deleted mail)
- Corruption in the data stores

Some events, such as lost email or lost mailboxes, may be recovered almost instantly if deleted item retention is turned on in Exchange and the recovery is attempted within the retention period. Otherwise, recovery will require restoration from backup media via one or more methods.

Your backup plan should take into account the possible types of disaster and the type of backup and schedule that is both cost effective and timely for the business. Your disaster recovery plan needs to incorporate a suitable range of recovery methods based on the recovery time best suited to each disaster and the business needs.

Recovery Process

As mentioned previously, Microsoft Exchange 2003 has features that reduce the time required to recover from disasters. In that context two terms apply here, *soft recovery* and *hard recovery*.

Soft Recovery

An uncontrolled shutdown of the Exchange 2003 Server databases can leave them in a `State: Dirty Shutdown`, as indicated by an entry in the headers. On remounting the databases, if Exchange finds them in this state, it attempts a soft recovery by automatically playing back the relevant log files as indicated by the pointer in the checkpoint file. This ensures that the Exchange databases operate in a consistent state.

Hard Recovery

A hard recovery occurs after you restore a database from backup, either automatically as for example when you select the Last Backup Set option in NTBackup's Restore Wizard, or use the `ESEutil /cc` option from the command line. A hard recovery replays the available logs into the database to bring it up to date, after which, on remounting, an additional soft recovery is also triggered.

Using the SBS Backup Wizard to Restore

The backup created by the SBS Backup Wizard is a full System State backup, including an Exchange aware, online backup of Microsoft Exchange data stores and logs.

The backup can be restored either as part of the complete system restore from Directory Services Restore mode or from the Windows 2003 Server install prior to the SBS server and component server setup. In this event, the system will be brought back online with Exchange operational and the data stores as they were at the time of the backup.

There is no separate SBS Wizard for restoring Exchange data only. However, you can restore Exchange data using NTBackup and other techniques outlined in the following sections by selecting to restore only the Microsoft Information Store\First Storage Group from the SBS backup.

Using NTBackup to Restore

NTBackup uses application programming interface (API) calls to the Exchange Extensible Storage Engine (ESE) to restore Exchange database files and their associated log files.

Figure 13.14 shows a typical flowchart of a restore operation.

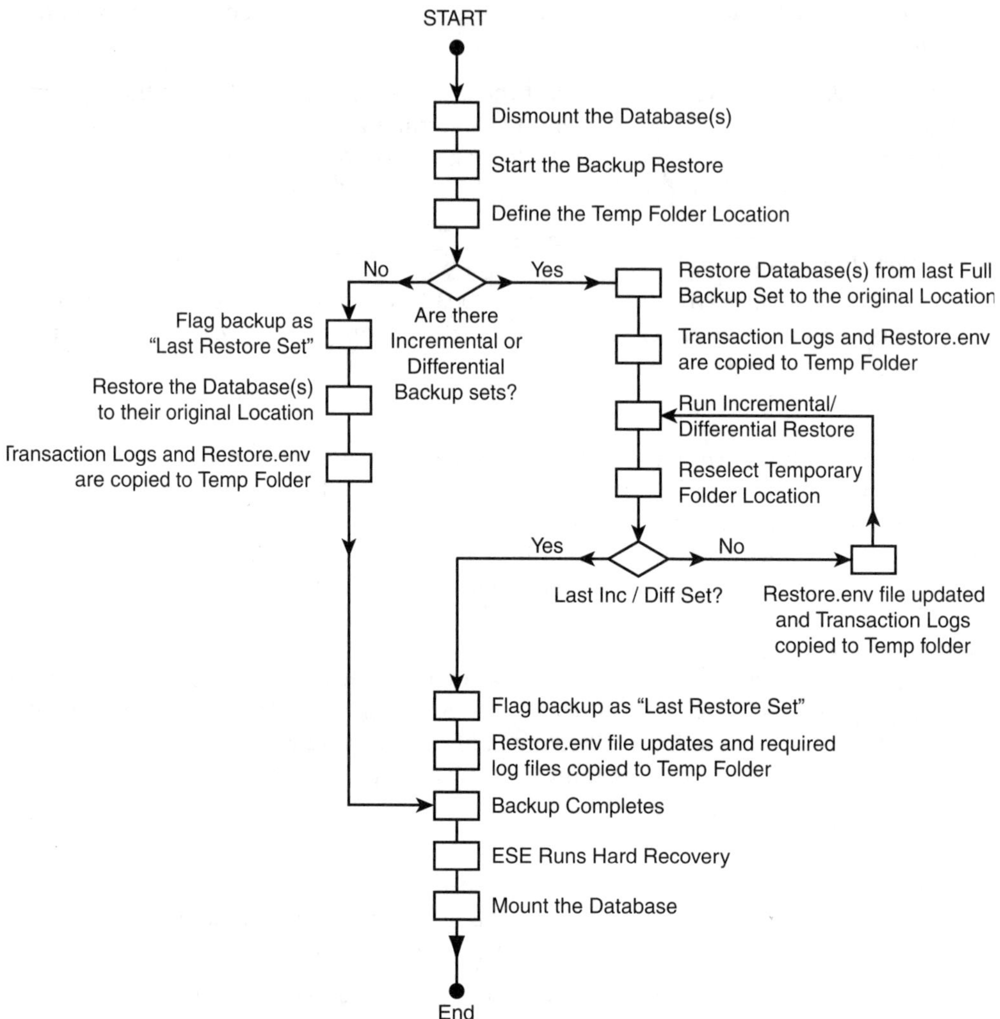

FIGURE 13.14 Flowchart of a restore operation.

A direct overwrite restore operation requires that the data stores be dismounted until the restore process has been successfully completed. With large databases, and slow backup media, this can take some time considering that transfer and repair rates can be in the order of 3 to 6GB per hour. There are also latency issues associated with making changes in Exchange.

Do not stop the Exchange Information Store service (MSExchangeIS), and if it is stopped, restart it from System Services.

To dismount the store, right-click on the store in Exchange System Manager and select Dismount Store. A red down-arrow icon indicates that the store is dismounted as can be seen in Figure 13.15.

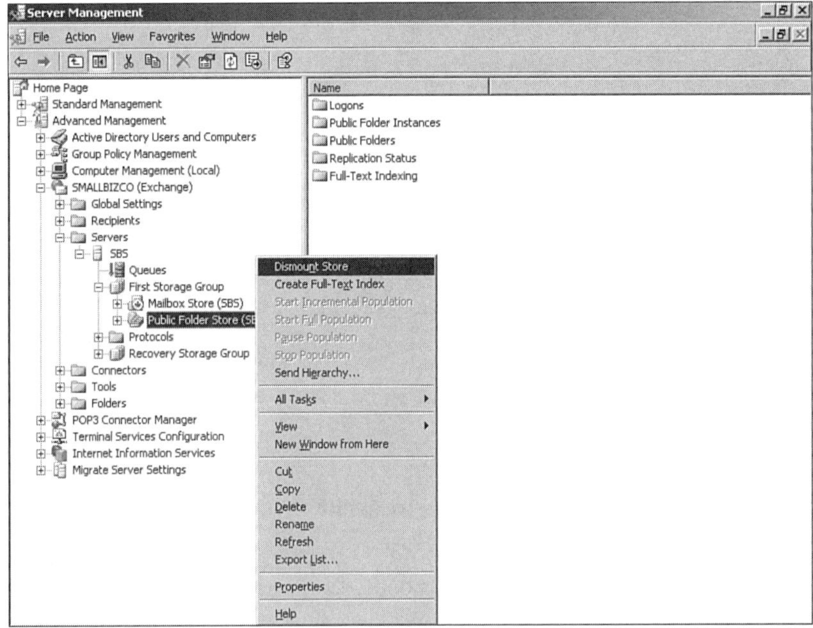

FIGURE 13.15 Dismounting Exchange stores.

Best Practice—Copy/Move Data

Copying and moving data on the same partition is much faster than doing so between partitions, across the LAN, or to/from backup tape or external storage. Having ample room on the Exchange partition can dramatically reduce the time involved in recovery/restore operations of large Exchange databases.

If you are restoring the databases to their original location and you have not re-created the databases in the interim, you do not need to set the This Database Can Be Overwritten By a Restore property on the database as shown in Figure 13.16. This is required only if the GUID (Unique Identifier) of the source and destination databases are different, as would be the case in a move of data in a migration, or if for some reason you have to create new databases before you restore. However, not selecting the overwrite option can increase the time required for the system to mount the store.

Note that the storage group and database display names also need to match. If they do not, you can rename the storage group and database names from the submenu of these items in the Exchange System Manager and Folder Explorer.

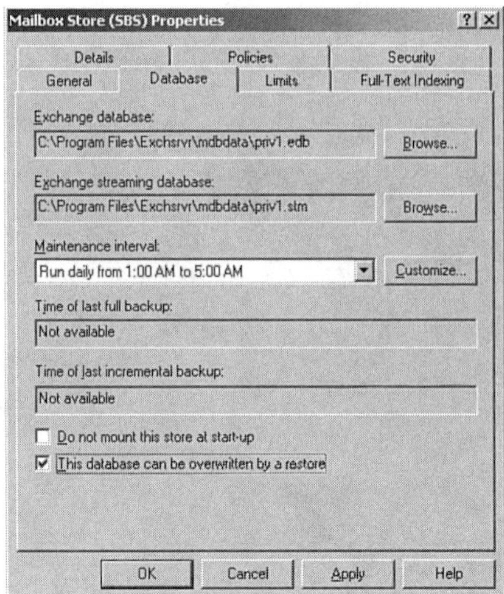

FIGURE 13.16 This database can be overwritten by a restore.

In essence, the process is as follows:

1. Backup informs the ESE that a restore process has begun, and ESE enters restore mode.
2. The database (`.edb` file and `.stm` file) is copied from the backup media to the database folder.
3. The backup log files are copied to the defined temporary folder.
4. Information about the restore process is written to the `restore.env` file. This replaces the "restore-in-progress key" of earlier versions. This file keeps track of the storage group that the database belongs to, the paths of the database files when they were backed up, the path to the database when they were restored, the range of log files that were restored, and other data.
5. A new instance of ESE is started, and the log files are replayed into the database.
6. If you did not select the Last Restore Set option in the backup restore, you need to run a hard recovery manually using the `ESEutil /cc` command at the temporary folder containing the restored log files.
7. The stores are remounted.
8. Once remounted successfully, the system is back online, and Exchange actively services messaging.

You must restore a full backup set before you can restore a differential or incremental backup set. The `restore.env` file is created by the restore of a full online or copy database. Restoring differential or incremental backups is reliant on its existence. Because of this reliance the incremental and differential backups need to be restored to the full backup's temporary folder.

Because the old databases are overwritten, it may be useful to take an offline copy of the database and log in the event that they are needed if the restore fails. The backup may be unrecoverable, and the database may need to be repaired and/or additional data extracted from it.

Using the Recovery Storage Group

The Recovery Storage Group was designed to aid in speedy recovery of Exchange data with a minimum of downtime for the business/users by allowing the recovery of mailboxes while the Exchange server continues to service messaging requests. This also saves the need for a separate recovery server.

Individual or multiple mailboxes restored to the Recovery Storage Group from a backup can be combined or merged with live mailboxes directly from the Exchange System Manager with a few clicks using the Exchange Task Wizard. Using ExMerge and its advanced features, more selective mailbox data including previously purged messages can be merged or copied to live mailboxes.

There are, however, limitations as follows:

- You cannot use the Recovery Storage Group to recover public folders.
- You can only recover data from an Exchange database that is between Microsoft Exchange 2000 Service Pack (SP) 3 and the version of Exchange running on the Recovery Storage Group server. The database will be upgraded to the version currently running on the Recovery Storage Group server in the process.
- Because the Recovery Storage Group uses a unique identifier created in Active Directory, if the Exchange configuration in Active Directory has changed, databases re-created, or mailboxes deleted from the Active Directory, the association between the objects will not be able to be established for the recovery of data. The `msExchMailboxGUID` and `msExchOrigMDB` are the identifiers set in Active Directory on the user object that owns the mailboxes and the database object in the Recovery Storage Group, respectively.
- When you recover a database to the Recovery Storage Group, its unique identifier (being its distinguished name, the value for `msExchOrigMDB` in the Active Directory) must match that of the distinguished name of the database you will be restoring.
- If the `msExchMailboxGUID` for each mailbox in the two stores match, the association can be made, and the data recovered.
- The only functionality allowed for the Recovery Storage Group, is recovery. To this extent the following functional differences are in place.
- Mail cannot be sent to or from a database in a Recovery Storage Group. The only protocol available to it is MAPI.
- Active Directory accounts cannot be connected to user mailboxes in a Recovery Storage Group, and new mailboxes cannot be created there.

- System and mailbox management policies including online maintenance and defragmentation are not applied to the Recovery Storage Group.
- The databases cannot be set to mount automatically at startup of the Information Store service.
- To move the path to the database in the Recovery Storage Group, you need to delete and re-create the group with the new name and path details.

Best Practice—Recovery Storage Group

Do not leave a Recovery Storage Group longer than necessary for the recovery operation. It takes up needless space and can conflict with other operations.

The Recovery Storage Group is easily created from the Exchange System Manager with the default settings as shown in Figure 13.17.

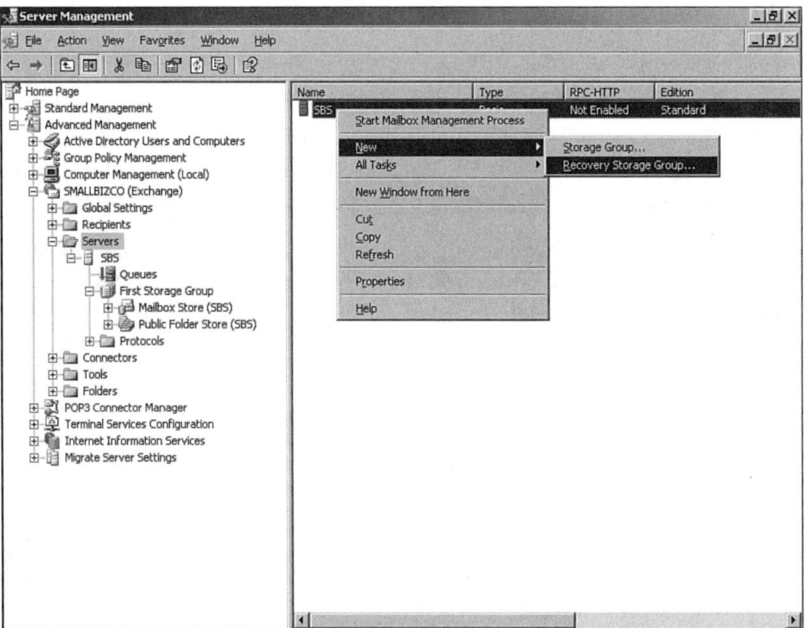

FIGURE 13.17 Creating the Recovery Storage Group.

The Mailbox Store for the Recovery Storage Group is also easily created by selecting Add Database to Recover from the Action menu for the Recovery Storage Group and selecting the database to recover as shown in Figure 13.18.

Once the Recovery Storage Group and its Mailbox Store exist, any restore from backup of the Exchange databases to the original location will automatically be directed to the Recovery Storage Group.

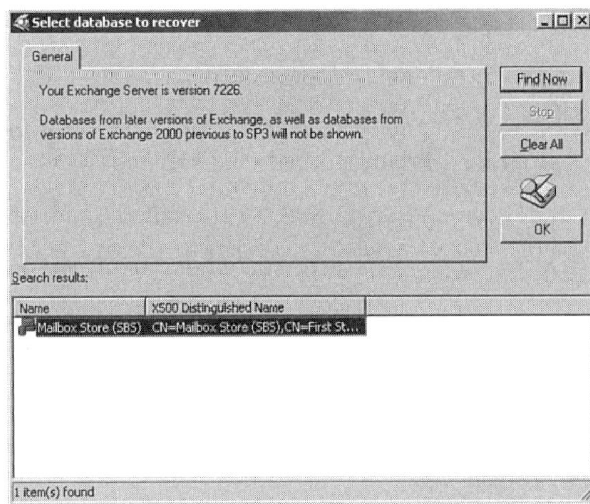

FIGURE 13.18 Creating the Recovery Storage Group Mailbox Store.

If you want to allow a normal restore to the storage group itself while the Recovery Storage Group exists, you can set a Registry key to override the behavior as follows:

```
HKLM\System\CurrentControlSet\Services\MSExchangeIS\ParametersSystem
```

Create a DWORD value called `Recovery SG Override`, and set its Value Data to 1. Remember to flip this value or delete the key when finished to avoid future accidents.

The ability to copy or merge from the Recovery Storage Group to the default (First Storage) group can provide a means of dramatically reducing the recovery downtime. The technique uses a *messaging dial tone database*.

A new (clean) database is created and users are brought online immediately to provide Dial Tone Service. Although there is no access to historic data, the business is online, and messaging can move forward.

Data can be restored to the Recovery Storage Group from backup and/or repaired or recovered database and logs. The most important online mailboxes can then be progressively populated with the historic data in the Recovery Storage Group. Although expeditious, the process can still take considerable time, particularly if the mailboxes are large.

In a variation that inserts a brief downtime, but can dramatically reduce the rebuild time, the databases are switched.

When the data has been satisfactorily restored to the Recovery Storage Group, both the Mailbox Store and the Recovery Storage Group are dismounted. The databases are then swapped, placing the high-volume database back as the users' live mailboxes and the low-volume database, which can be merged in minimal time, as the RSG database.

Having the two databases in the same partition helps decrease transfer times during the swap process. Minimizing the amount of data being merged into the mailboxes also lessens the impact on other running server processes.

The steps for creating and using the dial tone messaging are as follows:

1. Stop the databases in the default storage group.
2. Copy all transaction logs for the storage group to a safe location. These may be required if the original log files are purged when the databases are mounted.
3. Move or rename the (`.edb` and `.stm`) files for the failed database (if it exists).
4. In Exchange System Manager, mount the failed database. The following warning appears:

```
"At least one of this store's database files is missing. Mounting this
➥store will force the creation of an empty database. Do not take this
➥action if you intend to restore an earlier backup. Are you sure you want
➥to continue?"
```

5. Select Yes, and Exchange generates a new database. When you mount the DataStore from which the files have been removed, Exchange Server 2003 creates blank database files. As users attempt to access their mailboxes, Exchange creates new mailboxes in the database, and the users are able to send and receive mail. The user objects retain their original Exchange attributes (including `msExchMailboxGUID`). Because the new mailboxes have the same GUID values as the old mailboxes, Task Wizard or ExMerge can successfully transfer data between the Recovery Storage Group database and the dial tone database.
6. Set up the Recovery Storage Group and the Recovery Storage Group database.
7. Restore the original database or backup to the Recovery Storage Group. You may need to repair and/or hard recover the database before you are ready for the swap and remount.
8. Disconnect from both databases and swap the database files between the original storage group and the Recovery Storage Group.
9. After swapping the dial tone database into the Recovery Storage Group and the original database back to its original storage group, users can access their previous data (including rules, forms, and offline or cached mode `.ost` data files); however, until the merge from the RSG is done, they cannot access items in the dial tone database.
10. Using Exchange Task Manager or ExMerge, merge data from the dial tone database back into the original database to bring the user mailboxes up to date.
11. The Recovery Storage Group can then be dismounted, archived, and deleted along with the database.

For the process to be efficient, you should definitely practice the technique on a spare server or virtual machine.

Using ExMerge to Restore

ExMerge is a powerful tool, not only for backing up Exchange data to `.pst` files, but also for merging `.pst` data into existing mailboxes. It can, however, be used only with mailboxes, and not public folders. In moving data to and from `.pst` files, some metadata can be lost, and the process breaks Exchange's single storage, so the sum of the resultant data may be significantly greater than the original.

As shown in Figure 13.19, ExMerge allows for both single step restore, in which the backup to `.pst` files, merge, and cleanup occur as a single transaction, and dual step restore, where you can either export (back up) to `.pst` files or import/merge `.pst` files to mailboxes.

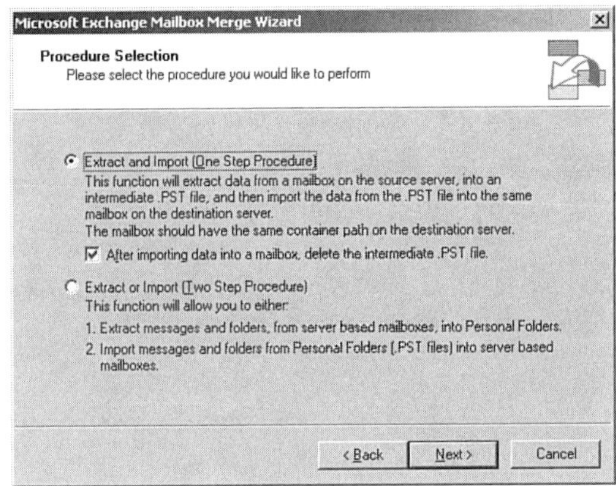

FIGURE 13.19 ExMerge step selection.

Although some of the functionality has been incorporated into the Exchange Tasks Wizard of the Recovery Storage Group, ExMerge provides far greater control over data to be recovered.

With scripting, and the use of the `.ini` file, which can be created by saving the options from the GUI, even greater functionality, such as the ability to map disparately named mailboxes and `.pst` files, can be achieved . ExMerge cannot, however, create destination mailboxes on the server if they do not exist.

The data selection criteria provide the following options:

- Data:
    - User messages and folders.
    - All user data, including messages, folders, calendars, contacts, tasks, journal items, and notes.
    - Associated folder messages.
    - Some hidden data such as folder rules and views.

    - Folder permissions.
    - Will overwrite the permissions on the target folder with those on the source.
    - Items from Dumpster.
    - Will copy all deleted items still available for recovery.

- Import Procedure:
    - Copy data into the target store.
    - Will copy to target store regardless and may result in duplicate messages.
    - Merge Data into the target store.
    - Will only copy messages that do not exist on the target.
    - Replace existing data on the target.
    - Will overwrite messages on the target.
    - Archive data to target store.
    - Copy from source to target, deleting the message on the source when the source is an Exchange mailbox.

- Folders:
    - Select to process or ignore selected folders and subfolders.

- Dates:
    - Select a message date range for the operation based on the delivery or last modified time.

- Message Details:
    - Filter on Message Subject and Attachment name at the top level only.
    - The filter includes options for Substring and Full string match ignoring case or for an Exact string match. The filter uses the following operation: (Date Criteria) AND (subj.1 OR subj.2 OR subj.n...) AND (att.1 OR att.2 OR att.n...).

Using Third-Party Solutions to Restore

Third-party software solutions may provide for restoration of either the entire Exchange database or individual mailboxes either directly or via the Recovery Storage Group and the backup APIs. Functionality varies based on vendor and price. Carefully consider your requirements set before selecting a package and verify that not only the backup but also the restore functionality is suitable and timely.

Repairing a Damaged Exchange Database

Exchange 2003 post SP1 is far more "self healing" than previous versions; however, at times when corruption will occur and you will need to manually repair the databases offline. Two prime command-line tools are available for use with errors that can occur at the page, database, or application store level: ESEutil and ISinteg. ESEutil checks and fixes individual database tables, whereas ISinteg checks and fixes links between tables.

It is always best to restore from a backup whenever possible. A repair may delete an unknown number of corrupted data pages and/or links to bring the database back to an operational state, and these may not be immediately obvious. Consider a repair a last option.

If you restore from a backup, you ensure that you have a good, clean, stable database that will start and run on your server. In almost every circumstance, it is faster and more reliable to restore from a backup than to perform a hard repair on the database.

Repair requires both considerable disk space (for the original, copy, temp, and restored database) and time.

Depending on the source and destination (for example, from tape to HDD, between disks, or within the same partition), transfer rates can be as slow as 3–6GB per hour. The repair process itself can run at approximately 4–6GB per hour, and the ISinteg check at a similar 3–6GB per hour. If this is not run on separate hardware, the process can impact the server's capability to service "normal" operations.

It is worth warning here that ESEutil commands can be dangerous to the uninitiated.

ESEutil can be looked at from several aspects: The harmless `/m` options, such as `/mh`, that provide an extensive read-out of information about the database; those manually run actions that occur as part of Exchange's own processes, such as the `/cc` command that ensures consistency; the more risky operations that affect the data, such as the `/d` defragment option, which performs a special operation to compact the databases; and the high-risk operations such as `/p`, which does a page level repair.

The tools should not be used indiscriminately, and you should make sure that you have an offline copy of your databases and logs before running these commands. For example, consider an offline defragmentation only if you are moving an Exchange Server database or after a database repair. Performing offline defragmentation when it is not required could affect performance.

Additionally, because offline defragmentation actually creates the new database, database files, and log file signatures, a new defragmented database file will have a different database signature. Because the databases and transaction logs point to each other based on signatures, all previous backups of this database are invalidated by the offline defragmentation. You should create new backups of Exchange Server 2003 databases immediately after offline defragmentation.

Overall, ESEutil is a rich tool that any operator involved in Exchange recovery processes needs to be familiar with. Table 13.4 explains some of the command-line options, their functions, and descriptions.

TABLE 13.4 ESEutil Command-Line Options

Command	Function	Description
`ESEutil /c`	Restore	Performs a hard recovery after a database restore
`ESEutil /cc`	Hard recovery	Performs a hard recovery after a database restore
`ESEutil /d`	Defragment	Defragments the `.edb` database and overwrite
`ESEutil /d /p`	Defragment	Defragments and leaves new database in the Temp folder
`ESEutil /g`	Integrity	Verifies the integrity of a database
`ESEutil /i`	Bypass	Bypasses database and streaming file mismatch error
`ESEutil /k`	Checksum	Verifies the checksums of a database
`ESEutil /m`	File dump	Generates formatted output of various database file types
`ESEutil /mh`	Verify	Verifies the state of an Exchange database
`ESEutil /mk`	Checksum	Provides information about the checkpoint file
`ESEutil /ml`	Integrity	Performs integrity check on log files
`ESEutil /mm`	Metadata dump	Database metadata dump
`ESEutil /p`	Repair	Hard repair a corrupted store database; discards corrupt pages
`ESEutil /r`	Recovery	Recovery repair Exchange 2003 log files
`ESEutil /y`	Copy	Copies a database, streaming file, or log file

After ESEutil has been run in a mode that affects the data, ISinteg should be run until it reports that there are zero errors.

NOTE

If ISinteg is run multiple times and does not correct the database corruption, you must use the ExMerge utility, which can skip individual corrupt messages, to extract data from the database to `.pst` files or another database.

ESEUTIL /r

`ESEutil /r` performs soft recovery to bring a single database into a consistent or Clean Shutdown state. This is a nontrivial operation to repair the database after a restore.

ESEutil takes the parameters `/r` [Base log file number. Usually `E00`] `/i`.

ESEUTIL /p

The `/p` option used on its own discards corrupt pages while overwriting the database. There is no guarantee that the database will be usable if critical or sufficient pages are discarded, so there is serious potential to lose the database altogether. If the operation was not run on a copy, it would be catastrophic.

The use of `ESEutil /p` should be considered an absolute last resort measure only.

`ESEutil /d /p` on the other hand has a different result. The `/d` tells ESEutil to defragment the designated database. The `/p` option used after the `/d` instructs ESEutil to leave the newly created defragmented database in the temporary work area and not to overwrite the original database.

Note that the order of the command-line options is important.

ISINTEG

ISinteg is the tool that sees and treats the Exchange database as a relational database.

ISinteg scans the tables and B-trees that organize the ESE pages into their logical structures. It looks at the mailboxes, public folders, and other parts of the information store, checking for orphans, incorrect values, and broken references.

ISinteg builds an Exchange database, `Refer.mdb`, of reference counts. It then browses the tables, compares the counts found to the counts in the reference database, and, if running with the `-fix` switch, updates these counts to the values it considers correct.

What appears valid to ESEutil from a physical data point of view might not be valid from a logical database view. Because ISinteg focuses on the logical level, it can repair and recover data that ESEutil can't. Valid data that was unavailable because of a broken reference in the database may be made available again after ISinteg repairs the link.

ISinteg has two modes. The default Test mode, which runs the specified tests and reports the results, and the Fix mode, where ISinteg runs the specified tests and attempts to fix any errors. Table 13.5 shows some of the operator options.

TABLE 13.5 ISinteg Command-Line Switches

Command	Function	Description
`ISinteg -test`	Test(s)	Use with a variety of command lines
`ISinteg -test Alltests`	All tests	Run all tests
`ISinteg -fix`	Fix	Fix any inconsistencies in your database
`ISinteg -s`	Server	Specify server name
`ISinteg -l`	Log	Log filename
`ISinteg -dump`	Dump	Create a verbose dump file of store data
`ISinteg -verbose`	Verbose mode	Display a detailed report of issues discovered

It is important to run ISinteg until it no longer reports any errors. Running the command once will not guarantee that the Information Store is functioning properly. The process can take some time depending on the size of the Information Store and the power and resources of the computer on which it is run.

Recovering a 16GB Mail Database

SBS 2003 currently contains Exchange Server 2003, which has a total database size limit of 16GB for each of the Public and Private stores.

That is not a great deal of storage these days, particularly given the quantity and size of attachments sent and stored with messages. To some extent, pressure is alleviated by Exchange's single instance storage, but it is becoming more common to find databases that have inadvertently hit the 16GB limit triggering the messaging database to shut down and making the store unmountable.

Although Exchange 2003 SP2 increases the data store size to 75GB and the simplest solution is to upgrade the Exchange Server, you may come across instances where this is not possible or practicable.

If you cannot upgrade to Exchange 2003 SP2, you can temporarily increase the size of the data store to 17GB by creating a new Registry value by following these steps:

1. Open the registry at:
   `HKEY_LOCAL_MACHINE\SYSTEM\CurrentControlSet\Services\MSExchangeIS\<Exchange Server Name>\Private-<hexadecimal GUID>.`
2. Create a new DWORD: Temporary DB Size Limit Extension.
3. Set the value data to 1.

CAUTION

The usual warning about editing the Registry applies. Great care needs to be taken. You should have a known good backup of the Registry and know how to restore it in the event of disaster or lockout.

This is only a temporary solution, however, while you are repairing the database. It is strongly recommended that you stop the Simple Mail Transfer Protocol (SMTP) service and the Microsoft Exchange MTA Stacks service (if it is running) before you mount the Mailbox Store to ensure that additional data does not flow into the database. The next time that the Exchange services are started, the size limit reverts to 16GB.

Use one or more of the following to reduce the size of your database before the size limit reverts to 16GB:

- Have users clean up their mailboxes.
- Remove database content using ExMerge.
- Purge deleted, unused, and nonessential mailboxes.
- Reduce the Deleted Items Retention period. (Setting it to 0 deletes all deleted items.)

Follow these steps to physically reduce the size of the store database. The Mailbox Store is listed in this set of steps, but the same process will work for the Public Folder Store:

1. Open Exchange System Manager.
2. Expand Servers, *<SBS Server Name>*, First Storage Group.
3. Right-click on the Mailbox Store and select Properties.
4. Select the Database tab; then click Customize next to Maintenance Interval.
5. Enable the time area starting with the next 15 minute interval and select several hours past that time in the Schedule window; then click OK.

6. Wait for the online maintenance task to run. It will start at the next quarter hour and may run for several hours, depending on how much data was deleted prior to running the maintenance.
7. Monitor the application event log to see when the online maintenance task completes.
8. After the online maintenance task completes, dismount the Mailbox Store.
9. Open a command prompt and change into the MDBDATA directory.
10. Make a copy of the priv1.edb and priv1.stm files to a different location on the sever or another workstation.
11. Make sure that you have at least 36GB of free disk space on the drive.
12. Run **eseutil /d priv1.edb** and wait for it to complete. This could take several hours.
13. Run **isinteg -s <servername> -fix -test alltests** at the command line.
14. Type **1** and press Enter to select the Mailbox Store (note that it must be offline for isinteg to work).
15. Type **Y** and press Enter to start the process.
16. Review the output of the command. If you see any errors or fixes listed for any of the tests, repeat the isinteg command. Continue running the isinteg command until the number of errors and fixes drops to zero, or until the number stays the same on multiple test runs.
17. Look at the size of the combined database files. If the size of both files is less than 16GB, remount the databases.
18. Get a backup of the Mailbox Store and then allow users back into Exchange.

NOTE

The 16GB size limit for the Exchange Private Mailbox Store database and the 16GB size limit for the Exchange Public Mailbox Store database is the sum of the size of both the respective .edb and the .stm files. Exchange System Manager displays only the space used by the .edb file as the mailbox size. It does not include the space that the .stm file uses. Also, when you put a limit on a mailbox, you limit the storage only in the Priv.edb file but not in the Priv.stm file.

Troubleshooting Exchange Disaster Recovery Issues

During an Exchange 2003 restore, a restore.env file is created in the selected temporary folder. This file holds path information about the Exchange data, aiding the restore process in matching files with corresponding email stores. If the restore fails and the cleanup process does not delete the file, you can examine it in Notepad, or with ESEutil from the command line using the /cm extension.

Well-written applications display meaningful error messages when issues are encountered. Most applications create log files of the running processes, including any issues encountered by the process. The location of these logs can sometimes be obscure, so you may need to look in the application properties, the application folder, or the system folder, or even perform a search of the system.

In some instances, the application itself allows you to specify the location of the log file or requires you to specifically initiate one with a subcommand such as `-dump`. It is good practice to know how to require the creation of these logs and where these files are located for the tools you will be using well before you need to do a disaster recovery under pressure.

Errors are usually also written to the System and Application event logs by the application, and the system writes events that it encountered as a result of the operation, and you can view these in the Event Viewer. Bear in mind that system and hardware events may be equally relevant. Take note of the exact error message and any references and/or error numbers.

If the resolution is not obvious, you can use the resources listed in Appendix A, "SBS Resources," to help track down the cause of and resolution to the problem.

Summary

Exchange disaster recovery is not trivial. The impact of the disaster, the time taken to recover, and the degree of success of that recovery depend on how well the recovery has been planned for, how well the plan has been implemented, and how well the plan has been practiced prior to any actual disaster taking place.

Exchange disaster recovery is not "set and forget." Things change over time. The volume and reliance on messaging, the tolerance to outage, the tools available, the hardware available, and the operators available are all variables within the overall plan, which should be reassessed regularly.

SBS 2003 with Microsoft Exchange contains sufficient and powerful tools for successful backup and restore of Exchange messaging data. Third-party tools are also available that may enhance or simplify some of the processes; however, at the very least the recovery operator should be comfortably familiar with the included tools because situations may occur where the third-party tools are not available.

With proper planning, implementation, and practice, the most catastrophic disaster can be recovered from.

Best Practice Summary

- Data storage—Take into account the mail usage and retention practices of the business and plan to store your Exchange data and log files on disks or partitions with ample free space for additional copies of the databases and logs in a recovery or repair situation. The additional space required can be considerable, and free space of at least 120% of your projected maximum Exchange database size (`.edb` plus `.stm` files plus `.logs` if hosted on the same partition) is recommended.
- Disable circular logging—Configure an Exchange-aware backup as soon as practical after setup, ensuring that circular logging is disabled and a full System State backup run and verified. Immediately after disabling circular logging, a full backup of Exchange should be run to provide the base point for future backups.
- ExMerge—Download the latest version of ExMerge appropriate to version of Exchange and install it to the `%Program Files%\Exchsrvr\bin` directory. Add the `%Program Files%\Exchsrvr\bin` directory to the Systems Path variable so that ExMerge can locate required Exchange DLLs, and you can easily execute both it and other utilities such as ESEutil and ISinteg from the command line. Prepare yourself by reading the comprehensive manual. Add ExMerge to your toolkit and practice using it.
- Copy/move data—Copying and moving data on the same partition is much faster than doing so between partitions, across the LAN, or to/from backup tape or external storage. Having ample room on the Exchange partition can dramatically reduce the time involved in recovery/restore operations of large Exchange databases.
- Recovery Storage Group—Do not leave a Recovery Storage Group longer than necessary for the recovery operation. It takes up needless space and can conflict with other operations.

PART VI

Web Technologies

IN THIS PART

CHAPTER 14

SharePoint and the Companyweb Site

IN THIS CHAPTER

One of the most exciting features with Small Business Server 2003 is the presence of the Companyweb intranet site, which is based on Windows SharePoint Services. The Companyweb intranet provides SBS 2003 users with a wide array of tools for sharing contacts, calendars, links, announcements, documents, and photos all within a familiar, easy-to-use, and easy-to-customize web-based interface. In this chapter we look at the default Companyweb implementation but focus primarily on customizing the Companyweb site for various needs.

Overview of Windows SharePoint Services

Windows SharePoint Services (WSS) is a web-based collaboration solution that allows users to better store, share, and collaborate on documents and projects. To appreciate how WSS can benefit a typical SBS customer, it is necessary to have an understanding of the various objects available within a WSS site.

Essentially, almost everything within a SharePoint site is part of a list of some form, often simply displayed in an appropriate manner. For example, look at some of default objects available for you to create:

- Document libraries
- Picture libraries
- Contact lists
- Event lists
- Task lists

- Custom lists
- Discussion boards
- Surveys
- Web pages

Although these templates represent many common use scenarios, the beauty of WSS is your ability to not only customize these templates but also to create new lists suited exactly to meet your needs.

Overview of the Companyweb Implementation for SBS

SBS 2003 includes a preconfigured WSS intranet site at `http://companyweb`, shown in Figure 14.1. The Companyweb implementation of WSS provides a default set of objects ready to be used or customized. These objects include five separate document libraries, a picture library, lists for announcements, links, vacation schedules, help desk items, and general discussions. Although these objects are preconfigured for you in the default Companyweb implementation, almost all these can be reproduced on any WSS site. The exception to that statement is the Incoming Faxes library. The Companyweb implementation of WSS includes Fax Library objects in addition to Document Library and Forms Library objects. The Fax Library object is unique to SBS and allows faxes received via SBS Shared Fax to be automatically routed and stored in a SharePoint library.

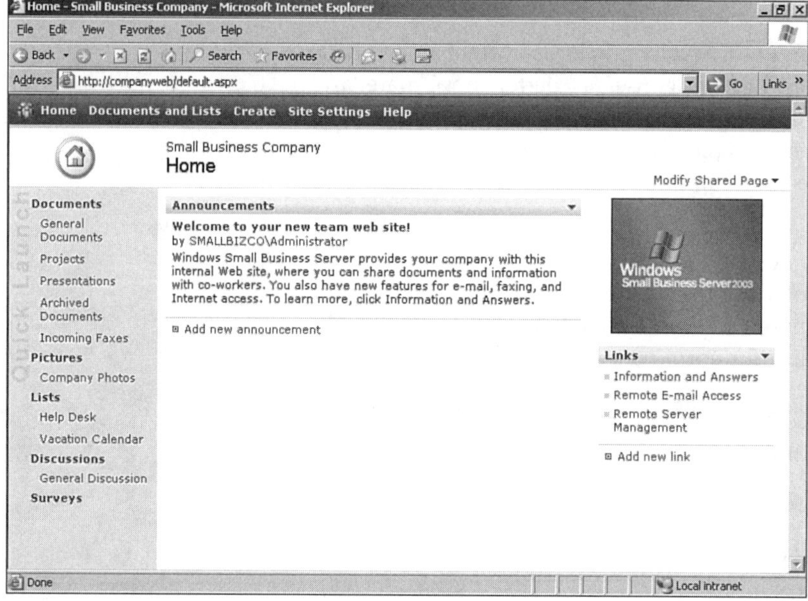

FIGURE 14.1 The default Companyweb home page.

Default File Locations for Companyweb

From an installation standpoint, the Companyweb has two main file groups. First, there are the support files that are available for all SharePoint sites to use. These files include items such as icons, graphics, and site templates. By default, these are installed in the `C:\Program Files\Common Files\Microsoft Shared\Web Server Extensions\60\` directory. The other half of the Companyweb installation is the SharePoint databases. WSS uses one database to store configuration information for the WSS server, as well as a separate content database for each WSS site that stores all site content. Therefore, the number of WSS databases on a given WSS server will always be equal to the number of WSS sites on the server plus one.

By default, WSS uses the Microsoft SQL Data Engine (MSDE) as its database engine. MSDE supports separate instances, where each instance appears and behaves as a separate MSDE installation. SBS creates a separate MSDE instance for Companyweb, which by default is installed to `C:\Program Files\Microsoft SQL Server\MSSQL$SHAREPOINT\`, with the actual database files in the data subdirectory.

14

Best Practice—Move SharePoint Databases from Default Location

WSS uses a Microsoft SQL database as its data store. As a result, all content within a WSS site (including Companyweb) lives in the database. This is true not only for list items such as contacts and announcements but also for pictures in photo libraries and documents in document libraries. Therefore, if you create a new document and save it to a document library within Companyweb, you will not be able to find the document by searching the server's hard drives.

Storing the Companyweb contents within the database presents several advantages, most of which are related to indexing and searching of items. However, this results in the single database file on the server growing as new items are added to the Companyweb site. This poses a potentially serious problem as the SharePoint databases are installed by default to the `C:` drive on the server. It is therefore possible for the Companyweb database to consume all free space on the `C:` drive. Because the `C:` drive is also the system partition, consuming all the available free space on the system partition will crash the server. As a result, the best practice is to move your Companyweb databases off the system partition.

Moving Companyweb Databases

The best method to move SharePoint databases is to not have to move them to begin with. When running the SBS integrated setup, you have the option to specify where you want to install the Companyweb databases, which allows you to redirect the installation target location to a data partition.

If you have already completed your SBS installation and the Companyweb databases are in the default location on the `C:` drive, you can successfully move the Companyweb databases to another partition. By default, the Companyweb installation has two databases: `STS_Config` and `STS_<servername>_1`. Each of these databases needs to be moved using the following steps:

1. Log on to your SBS server and open a command prompt.

2. Stop the web server using the following command:

   ```
   iisreset /stop
   ```

3. Stop the SharePoint Timer Service:

   ```
   net stop sptimer
   ```

4. Launch the OSQL utility:

   ```
   osql -E -S %computername%\SharePoint
   ```

5. To detach the default configuration database, enter the following command (press Enter after each line; the prompt will increment accordingly):

   ```
   EXEC sp_detach_db 'STS_Config', 'true'
   GO
   ```

6. To detach the default content database, enter the following command:

   ```
   EXEC sp_detach_db 'STS_<servername>_1', 'true'
   GO
   ```

   where *<servername>* equals the name of your SBS server.

7. Using My Computer, move the configuration and content databases to their new location. Be sure to copy both the database (.mdf) and transaction log (.ldf) files for each database.

8. Return to the command window running the OSQL utility.

9. To attach the Configuration database, enter the following command:

   ```
   EXEC sp_attach_db 'STS_Config', '<new_path>\STS_Config.mdf',
   '<new_path>\STS_Config_Log.ldf'
   GO
   ```

   where *<new_path>* equals the directory to which you moved the database files.

10. To attach the content database, enter the following command:

    ```
    EXEC sp_attach_db 'STS_<servername>_1',
    '<new_path>\STS_<servername>_1.mdf',
    '<new_path>\STS_<servername>_1_log.ldf'
    GO
    ```

11. Exit the OSQL utility by pressing Ctrl+C.

12. Restart the SharePoint Timer Service:

    ```
    net start sptimer
    ```

13. Restart the web server:

```
iisreset /start
```

Default Permissions for Companyweb

WSS uses its own role-based permissions structure for controlling permissions to each of the various elements within the Companyweb site. By default, the Companyweb defines four different permission roles (also known as site groups within WSS) as shown in Table 14.1.

TABLE 14.1 Default Permission Roles Within Companyweb

Role	Description
Reader	Read-only access to the site and list contents
Contributor	Able to add/edit/delete contents of document libraries and lists
Web Designer	Able to create lists and document libraries, as well as customize site pages
Administrator	Full control of site

These roles (or site groups) within WSS are similar in function to security groups within Active Directory. Because users can belong to any number of site groups, you can grant permissions to individual elements (lists) within the Companyweb site to site groups instead of individual users. By adding users to site groups, each user inherits the same permissions as the site groups the user belongs to. One feature currently not present within the WSS security model is the capability to nest site groups, or have one site group be a member of another site group. Although this capability would prove beneficial in a larger, rather complex WSS deployment, it is most often not needed in a typical SBS Companyweb deployment.

As you know, when creating user accounts within SBS by using the provided Add User Wizard, you may select from one of four predefined templates: User, Mobile User, Power User, and Administrator. From a Companyweb standpoint, both the User and Mobile User templates grant the user Web Designer permissions to the Companyweb, whereas the Power User and Administrator templates grant the user Administrator permissions to the Comanyweb. If you do not want all your users to have a minimum of Web Designer rights within the Companyweb, you have several options to customize permissions within the Companyweb.

Customizing Permissions for Companyweb Site

WSS allows you to define your own security roles for site access, so you are not bound to the four default roles mentioned previously. For example, suppose that you have several users who you want to be able to add and edit list items, but you do not want them to be able to delete list items. However, the default Reader role allows users only to view items, not to add new items or edit existing items. Likewise, the default Contributor role allows users to add new items, edit existing items, and delete items. As a result, you need to create a new role to meet your needs, selecting from the available list rights as shown in Figure 14.2.

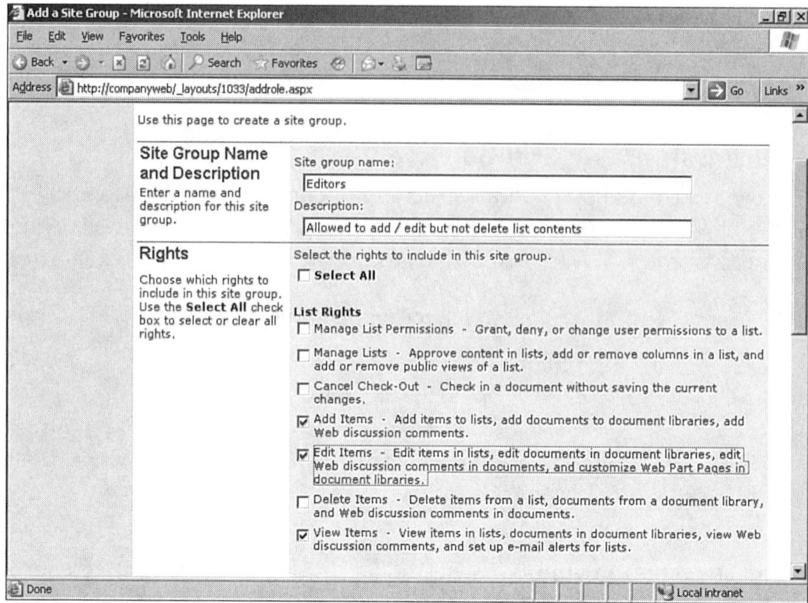

FIGURE 14.2 The list rights available when creating a new site group.

Virtually all configuration tasks for Companyweb take place within the Companyweb site, under Site Settings. To maintain site groups, from the Site Settings page, follow the link to Go To Site Administration; then follow the link for Manage Site Groups. On this page, you can create a new site group to meet your needs. Figure 14.2 shows a new site group called Editors being created that grants View, Add, and Edit permissions to list contents but does not include Delete permissions.

Now that we have created the Editors site group, we need to add users to this group. Again, access Manage Users via the Companyweb site by opening Site Settings. In the Manage Users page as shown in Figure 14.3, select the users you want to assign to the Editors group and click to Edit Site Groups of Selected Users. Here you can choose the site groups you want the selected users to belong to and update their membership.

You'll notice that the Companyweb Manage Users page includes four users that you may not recognize: Administrator Tmpl, Mobile User Tmpl, Power User Tmpl, and User Tmpl. These are the disabled user accounts that SBS uses for templates when creating new user accounts. As a result, you can edit the Companyweb permissions granted to new users created with user templates by editing the site group membership of the template accounts themselves. For example, if you wanted any user created with the User template to have only Contributor level access within Companyweb, you could simply open the User Tmpl and change its site group from Web Designer to Contributor. As a result, all future user accounts created with the User template will have Contributor level access to the Companyweb instead of the default Web Designer access.

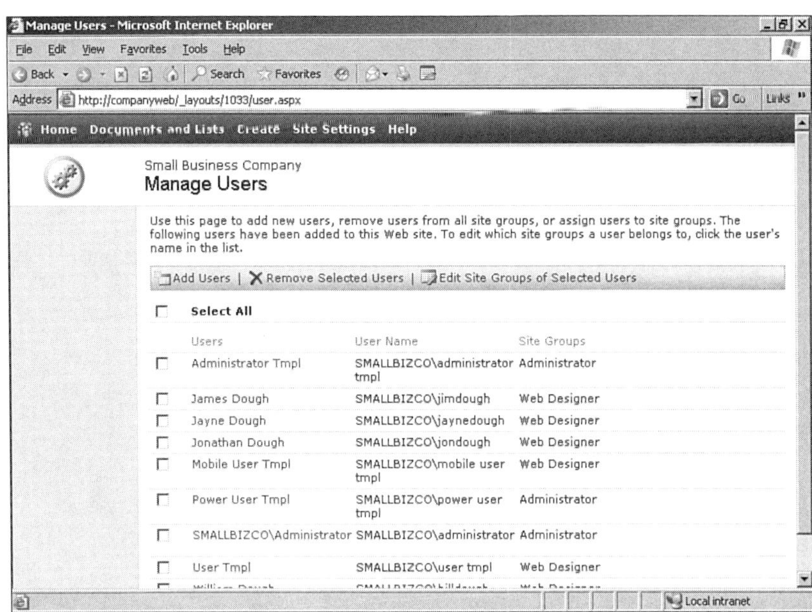

FIGURE 14.3 The Companyweb Manage Users page.

As mentioned previously, virtually all the configuration tasks for Companyweb are executed within the Companyweb Site Settings. However, there is one key exception to this rule when it pertains to Companyweb permissions. Within Active Directory Users and Computers, there exists a Security Group under the My Business, Security Groups Organizational Unit called SharePoint Administrators. Members of this Security Group automatically have Administrator level access to the Companyweb site, regardless of the permission levels explicitly granted within Companyweb itself. By default, SBS adds the Domain Power Users security group as a member of the SharePoint Administrators security group. As a result, any user who is a member of the Domain Power Users security group will have Administrator level access to Companyweb. Therefore, if you want to restrict the permissions of any users who are members of the Domain Power Users security group, you need to either remove the user from the Domain Power Users security group, or remove the Domain Power Users security group from the SharePoint Administrators security group.

Customizing Permissions for Companyweb Lists

By default, site groups within Companyweb apply to all elements in the Companyweb site. So a user who belongs to the Contributor site group has permission to view, add, edit, and delete items in each individual document library and list. On occasion, you will have a need for custom permissions for a given object, as shown in Figure 14.4. For example, suppose that all your users have Contributor level access to the entire Companyweb site. However, you want to restrict a certain document library so that only a few specific users have access.

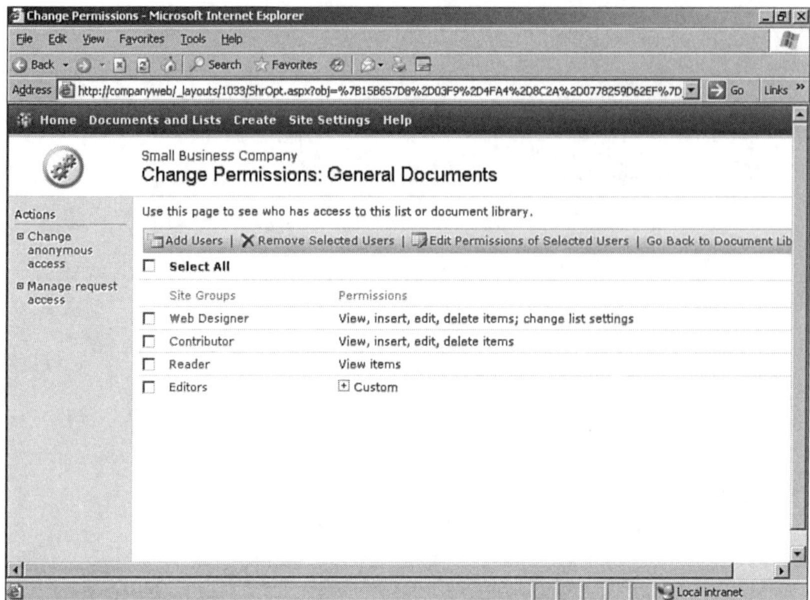

FIGURE 14.4 The Change Permissions page for the default General Documents document library.

When you access any object (document library, list, and so on) within Companyweb, you will notice a group of Action links in the left pane. So, to customize access permissions for the General Documents library, simply open the library and then follow the Modify Settings and Columns link. In the General Settings section, select the link to Change Permissions for This Document Library, which opens the page as shown in Figure 14.4. From here, you can add the specific users you want to have access and what permissions you want each user to have within this document library. Additionally, you will want to remove the site groups that you do not want to have access to the document library.

In this scenario where you are configuring specific permissions for a given object in the Companyweb site, you are somewhat limited by what permissions you can grant to individual users. For example, the object permissions do not provide an option to have a user be able to add and edit items but not delete items. If you need this level of advanced permissions, you can create a new site group as mentioned previously. With the new site group you can specify View, Add, and Edit permissions, and then add the users you want to have these permissions for the document library. Finally, add the new site group to the document library permissions list instead of the individual users to obtain the desired result.

Best Practice—Modify Default Permissions for Companyweb

As with virtually any technology, you want to grant users just enough rights to perform their job. By default, SBS grants all users a minimum of web designer rights within the Companyweb. The interesting aspect of WSS is that it is a relatively new technology to the small business customer. As a result, it is difficult to predict which users will simply use the Companyweb, and which users will fully utilize and stretch the limits of your Companyweb. As a result, there is a definite benefit to providing your users with web designer access to the site, so that your users can experience and experiment with the site. When you start to get an idea of who your SharePoint power users are going to be, you can edit permissions for your other users and let your SharePoint administrators go to town. Besides editing the permissions of your other users, you also want to be sure to edit the permissions of the template accounts so that new users created from these templates will get the appropriate permissions.

Customizing the Companyweb Interface

One of the greatest benefits of WSS to SBS end users is the ability to customize their WSS site(s) on-the-fly to meet their needs. Users can customize a wide range of items, from adding new lists, adding/removing fields from existing lists, creating custom views of list data, and creating personalized pages.

Applying a Theme to the Companyweb Interface

A simple way of customizing the Companyweb interface is to apply a different theme to the site. By default, WSS ships with 21 different themes including the default blue theme. To apply a different theme to the Companyweb site, access Site Settings. Within the Site Settings page, under the Customization heading, you see a Apply Theme to Site link. Follow this link to see a list of installed themes you can choose from, as well as a preview of each theme. Figure 14.5 shows the default Companyweb page after applying the Compass theme.

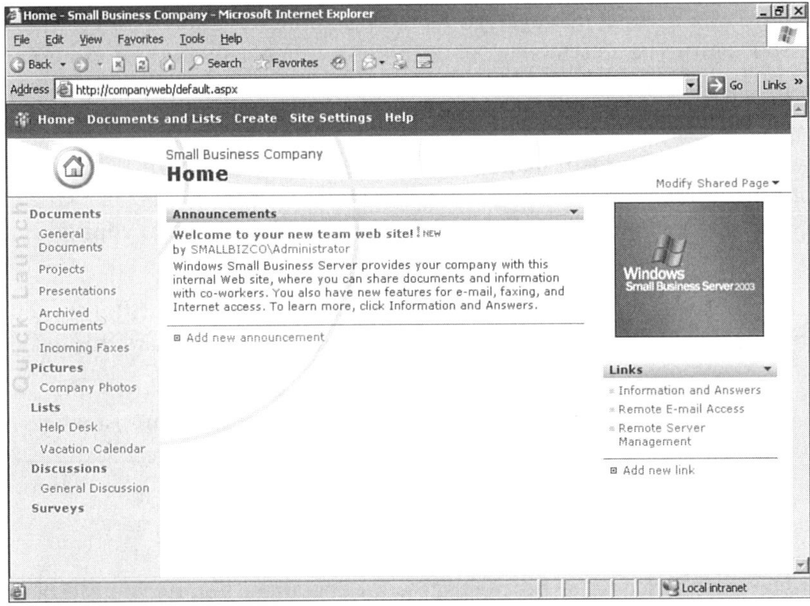

FIGURE 14.5 Companyweb home page after applying the Compass theme.

Creating and Managing Objects and Lists

As mentioned earlier in this chapter, the default Companyweb implementation on SBS includes several predefined objects. One of the truly great aspects of WSS is the capability to customize almost everything about the site, including these predefined objects. Not only can you customize the predefined objects, but you also can create your own objects to meet your unique needs.

WSS includes several object templates for you to choose from when creating new objects, including document libraries, picture libraries, links, contacts, events, tasks, and custom lists. Although each of these objects includes predefined fields, you can easily customize any object by adding and removing fields to meet your needs. To customize the field list for an object, open the object (either from the QuickLinks pane on the main page or from the Documents and Lists page); then click on Modify Settings and Columns in the left-hand pane to open the Customize page. On the Customize page, under the Columns section, you will notice links for adding a column and changing the order of columns. You can also edit or delete a column by clicking on the column name.

When adding a new column, you have several options to choose from as far as formatting and contents are concerned. For example, your new field can be a single line of text, a date/time value, a number, currency, or a yes/no value. In addition, you can also have a choice field, a lookup field, or a calculated value. Although it may not be obvious at first, these last three choices provide amazing flexibility when it comes to building SharePoint solutions for your organization. For example, assume that you have decided to use a SharePoint document library to store documents relating to company projects. However, you have specific requirements for viewing and finding documents. Your project documents fall into one of three main categories: correspondence, quotes, and technical specifications. You want to be able to view all documents of a given type (for example, quotes) for all projects; likewise, you want to be able to view all documents for a specific project in chronological order.

To meet your project document management goals, you decide to create additional fields in your document library to store specific data about your documents (also known as *metadata*, or data about your data). You create two additional fields in your document library:

- Document Type—A choice field formatted as a drop-down list with three options: Correspondence, Quote, Technical Spec. Additionally, you require this field to have a value.

- Project—Let's assume that you have already created a SharePoint list for your projects—Project Number, Customer, Start/End Dates, and Project Manager. For the project field in your document library, you create a lookup field that looks up the Project Number field from your Projects list.

Now that you have added these two fields to your document library, you can begin to upload documents and fill in the metadata fields. As you populate your document library with project documents, you can use the Filter button to filter your view, to only show documents for a specific project, for example.

Best Practice—Use Metadata Instead of Subfolders in Document Libraries

Most users are familiar with using multiple folders within a file system to sort and organize documents into similar types or subjects. As a result, users new to WSS and the Companyweb document libraries will feel the need to create subfolders to organize their documents. The problem with subfolders is that they limit what qualities can be used to sort and view documents.

Although many users are familiar with using folders, they often would benefit from being able to sort and view their documents in ways not possible when using a traditional directory structure to organize their files. For example, an organization may have a directory structure where each customer has a folder, then in each customer folder is a folder for each project for that customer, and each project folder has separate folders for document types—for example, quotes, correspondence, and so on. Although this structure makes it easy to find a specific document when you know the customer, project, and document type, this structure does not allow you to easily view all correspondence to a specific customer for all projects. This is where using metadata instead of subfolders becomes beneficial.

By using metadata to identify your documents, you still can easily find a specific document, only instead of drilling down through subfolders, you filter the document library view to show only the project and document type you're looking for. Additionally, if you want to view your documents in less traditional ways—for example, all correspondence for a specific customer, or all quotes created on a specific day—you have that ability at your fingertips as well, simply by filtering your view on the metadata fields.

Creating New Views for Objects and Lists

We've mentioned how you can filter object views to get exactly the data you want. However, if you have certain filters you or your users are always entering, you will start to lose productivity as you are constantly filtering your views. The good news for you is that not only does WSS allow you to define custom views, but you also have more flexibility in how you sort, filter, and display your data with custom views than you do with regular filters.

Let's use the project document library example again. You access this document library multiple times per day, and you find that 95% of the time you are filtering the view to show only documents you created. To create a new view, open your document library and click on Modify Columns and Settings in the left pane. At the bottom of the page that opens, you see a list of current views, as well as a link to Create a New View. When you click to create a new view, you see you have several options to customize your view. First, you need to name your view, which should be something meaningful because this name will appear in the list of available views. You can also select whether you want this view to be a public view or a personal view. A personal view appears only in the list of available views for the user who created it, whereas a public view is available to all users. Next you can select what columns you want to see in your view, as well as the order you want the columns displayed. After selecting the columns to view, you can specify how you want the view sorted (for example, ascending on created date), filtered (for example, `Created By equals <your display name>`), and grouped (for example, ascending on project number). Note that for many of these options, you can select multiple fields. For example, you can have your view show multiple grouping levels, grouping first on project and next on document type as shown in Figure 14.6.

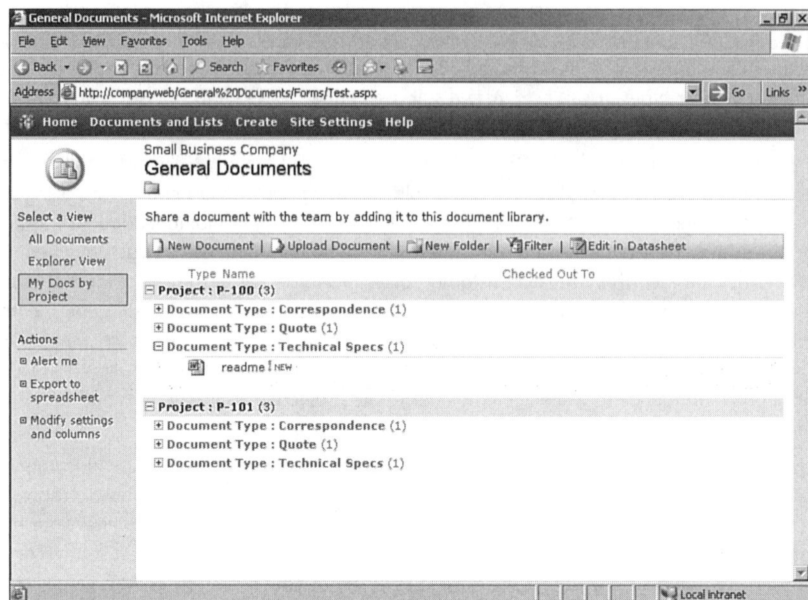

FIGURE 14.6 A custom document library view with multiple grouping levels.

It is important to note that when creating custom views, WSS includes two global variables when defining filters: [Today] and [Me]. [Today] obviously returns the current date, and [Me] returns the current user. In the custom view example used previously, if you wanted this custom view to be available to each of your users (allowing them to see the documents they created, grouped by project and document type), you could either help each of them to create a personalized view with a filter value of `Created By equals` *`<user display name>`*, or you could create one public view with a filter value of `Created By equals [Me]`, which provides the same results.

Best Practice—Premium Customers: Upgrade Your SharePoint Database Engine to Full SQL Server

Microsoft Small Business Server 2003 Premium Edition includes Microsoft SQL Server 2000. By default, Companyweb on SBS uses the Microsoft SQL Data Engine (MSDE), which is the little brother to full-fledged Microsoft SQL Server 2000.

The primary benefit of upgrading your SharePoint data engine to full SQL is the ability to enable full-text search on your Companyweb site. Enabling full-text search not only allows you to search list contents within your Companyweb site but also allows you to perform full-text searches against indexed contents of any document stored in a SharePoint document library.

To upgrade your SharePoint data engine to full SQL and enable full-text search for SharePoint, follow the instructions in the `premiuminstallsteps.htm` file on the Small Business Server Premium Technologies CD.

By default, SharePoint is capable of indexing Microsoft Office documents to support full-text search. If you want to have SharePoint index other document types (for example, `.pdf` files), you need to install an iFilter for that document type. Note that most vendors (including Adobe) provide iFilters free for download.

Creating Personalized Pages

In addition to creating personalized views for SharePoint libraries and lists, users can also personalize most web part pages on a SharePoint site, including the companyweb main page. For example, on the Companyweb main page, you have a link for Modify Shared Page. If you choose to add web parts or design this page, the changes made are visible for everyone. However, if you click on Modify Shared Page and choose Personal View, you will notice that the Modify Shared Page link changes to Modify My Page. As a result, any web parts you add or any other design changes you make affect your personal page only.

Understanding and Working with Web Parts

So you've heard the term before, but what exactly is a *web part*? Simply stated, a SharePoint web part is a container for displaying information on a web part page, which is nothing more than a SharePoint web page that holds web parts. By default, any list or library you create in a SharePoint site can be displayed as a web part. The Companyweb main page is itself a web part page, with the SBS image, Links list, and Announcements list each being a web part.

Customizing a web part page is simple. As mentioned earlier, you can customize the Companyweb main page by clicking on Modify Shared Page and selecting either Add Web Parts to add a new web part to the page, or Design This Page to rearrange existing web parts on the page. Whether adding new web parts to the page or simply rearranging existing web parts, the process is literally drag-and-drop.

As mentioned previously, any list or library you create in a SharePoint site can be viewed as a web part. In addition, you can customize a web part view just like you can customize a list or library view. First select Modify My Page and then browse for a web part. In your company web part directory, find the document library or list that you want to display, and drag that web part to your Companyweb page. After the web part is on the page, you can access the web part menu by clicking on the down arrow icon at the right side of the web part header bar and selecting Modify Web Part. The right-hand pane of the page that was displaying your available web parts changes to show options for this one particular web part. By default, the selected view field displays Current View; however, you can select any of the views you may have already created for this particular list or document library. Alternatively, you can click on Edit the Current View to customize the view to meet your needs.

Besides being able to display SharePoint lists and libraries as web parts, there are also many third-party custom web parts that provide a variety of functionality, from displaying data from foreign systems (for example, accounting applications or even Outlook/Exchange) to displaying current information such as weather and news to simply giving you more options on how you display your native SharePoint items. For example, many free SharePoint web parts are available online, from Office integration web parts from Microsoft to the MSNBC web parts available by default in the SharePoint Online Gallery to Tim Heuer's RSS FeedReader web part available at `www.smilinggoat.com`. In addition to free web parts, a growing number of companies sell high-quality web parts, which range from the effective and affordable, such as Programs Unlimited's (`www.programsunlimited.com`) calendar web part, which lets you have a web part calendar view of any library or list with a date column, complete with color coding, to CorasWorks' (`www.corasworks.net`) lineup of impressive workflow and integration web parts, which includes its Outlook Integration web part.

Best Practice—Create a Separate Document Library to Store Your Web Part Pages

Web part pages created within the SharePoint interface must be stored in a document library. To keep your SharePoint site as organized as possible, a best practice is to create a separate document library solely for web part pages instead of using one of your existing document libraries.

In addition to keeping your site better organized, creating a separate document library for web part pages also gives you better control over those pages. By using a separate document library, you can customize the permissions on that document library (as discussed earlier in this chapter) to prevent users from deleting web part pages from the library. Note that users you want to be able to create web part pages will need to have Web Designer permissions for your SharePoint site.

Besides the Companyweb main page, you can create additional web part pages. To do so, begin by clicking on the Create link at the top of the main page to open the Create page. Scroll to the bottom of the page and click to create a new Web Part Page. The New Web Part Page page allows you to enter a name for your new web part page, select a layout, and choose which document library you want to save the page in. Click Create to create your new web part page. When the page opens, you can place web parts where you want them to build your own custom web part page. One example use for a web part page would be to place multiple copies of Tim Heuer's RSS FeedReader all over the page, with each individual web part subscribing to different RSS feeds, thus creating your own RSS feed page for you and your users.

Creating New Sites in SharePoint

Although SBS provides the predefined Companyweb, you can actually create additional SharePoint sites, either as new top-level sites or as subsites below Companyweb.

Creating New Subsites Under Companyweb

There are many benefits to having subsites under your Companyweb site. A prime example is to have a separate subsite devoted to each of several different projects. SharePoint provides native functionality for easily creating subsites, as shown in Figure 14.7.

Creating a new subsite is simple. From your Companyweb page, follow the Create link. At the bottom of the list of available objects, follow the link for Sites and Workspaces, which takes you to the page shown in Figure 14.7. Here you can specify the title and description as well as the URL and permissions for the subsite. The title and description appear on the main page of the subsite and can be changed at any time from within the subsite's Site Settings. The URL is obviously how you and your users will access the subsite. Finally, you have the option to use the same permissions as the parent site, or use unique permissions. The default option is to use the same permissions from the parent site. This option results in the subsite inheriting permissions from the parent site. As a result, the subsite will not have its own user list or site group list. If you want to restrict access to the subsite, you'll want to choose to use unique permissions. In that case, you then need to explicitly grant users permissions to the subsite and create any site groups you may want.

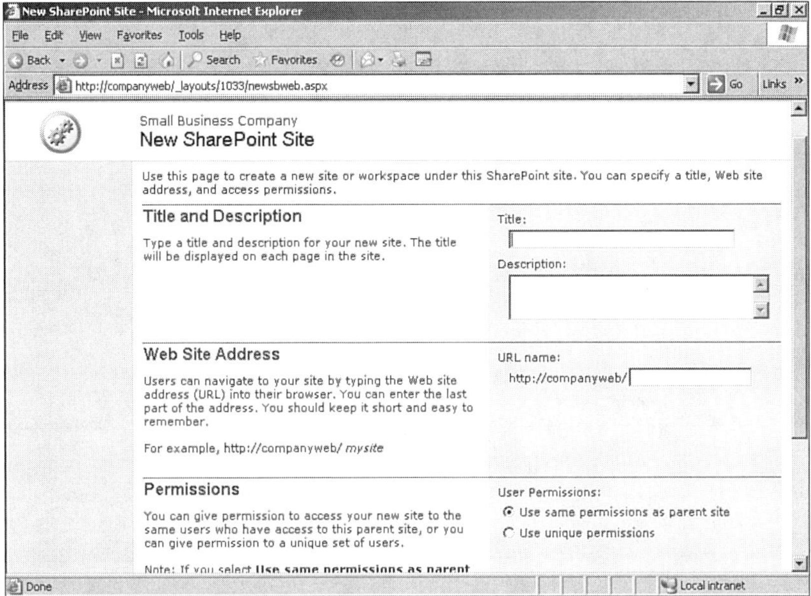

FIGURE 14.7 The New SharePoint Site creation page.

To access subsites you have created, you have several options. First, you can directly access a given subsite by entering its URL (for example, `http://companyweb/mysubsite`). Alternatively, you can access a listing of all your subsites from your Companyweb. To do this, follow the link for Documents and Lists. In the left-hand pane under See Also, follow the Sites link. Depending on how many subsites you create, and how long you keep them, you may want to consider creating a new Links list for your subsites. In the long run, this is going to be the easiest way to maintain your site listing if you are creating many subsites and keeping them for archival purposes. For example, you may want to create a new subsite for each major project and keep those subsites alive even after the project has completed. However, on a daily basis you only need to access active projects. By creating a new Links list for your subsites, you could add a custom column that would indicate whether the subsite is inactive. As a result, you could customize list and web part views to show only active subsites by default.

Best Practice—Use Site Templates to Streamline Creation of Companyweb Subsites

An added benefit of WSS is the ability to save a WSS site as a template. Continuing with the example of creating a subsite for each project, you will most likely have a certain set of objects that you want each subsite to have, such as a document library, contact list, events calendar, task list, and links list. Instead of creating each of these objects every time you create a new project subsite, you can use an existing subsite that already contains these objects to create a new site template.

To create a site template, open the site you want to use as a template. Follow the Site Settings link and then the Go to Site Administration link, as shown in Figure 14.8.

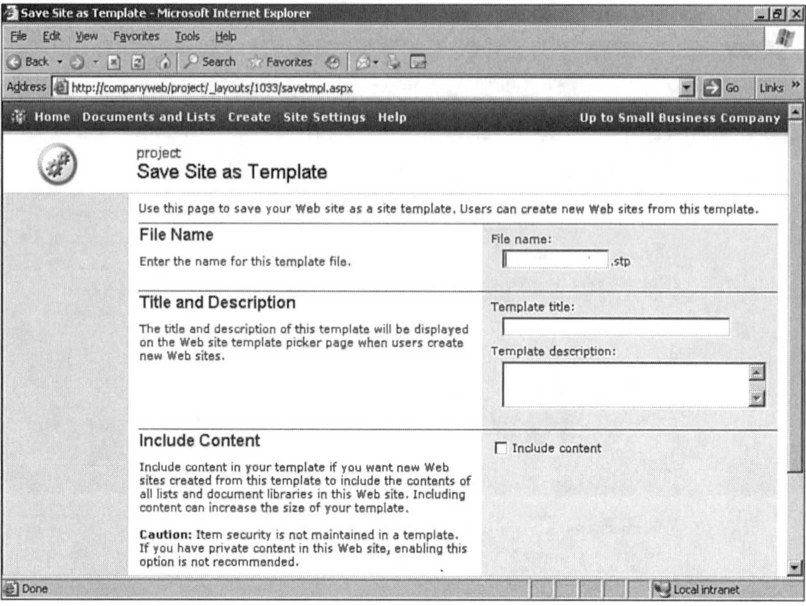

FIGURE 14.8 The Save Site As Template page.

When saving a site as a template, you need to specify a filename for the template. This must be unique but can be any arbitrary name. The template title should be meaningful, and an accurate description should be entered. When you are creating a new subsite and get to the Template Selection page, the template title you enter here appears in the template list. Likewise, the description you enter is the description displayed when the template title is selected.

Finally, you will notice that, when creating a site template from an existing site, you have the option to include content. This is particularly useful if you have many documents that each project needs. For example, if you are using a checklist to track when certain tasks common to each project are completed, you could upload the blank checklist document to the document library before creating the site template. As a result, that document will be present in the document library for each new site you create using this site template.

Creating New Top-Level SharePoint Sites

In addition to creating subsites below your Companyweb site, you can also create additional top-level SharePoint sites. To create a new top-level site, the first thing you need to do is to create a new blank website:

1. Log in to your SBS server and open the Internet Information Services MMC (select Start, All Programs, Administrative Tools, Internet Information Services [IIS] Manager).

2. In the IIS MMC, expand <*your_servername*> and click on Web Sites.

3. From the Action menu, select New, Web Site
4. Click Next to start the New Website Creation Wizard. Enter a description for the new site and click Next to continue.
5. As shown in Figure 14.9, change the IP Address from (All Unassigned) to the internal IP of your SBS server (192.168.16.2 by default).

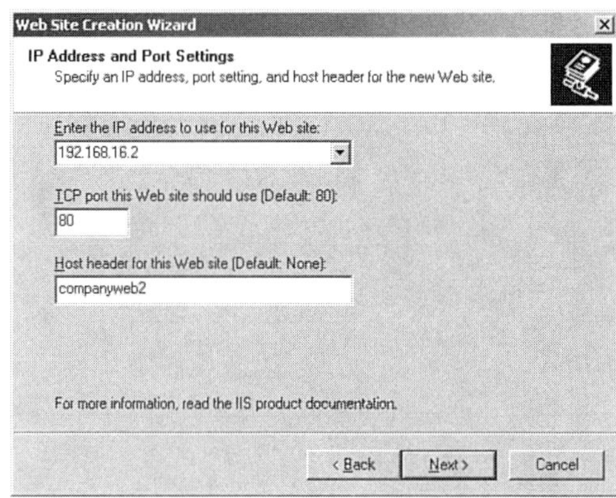

FIGURE 14.9 The Web Site Creation Wizard IP Address and Port Settings page.

6. Enter the host header value for your new website and click Next. The host header value should match the URL you want to use to access the new site. Figure 14.9 shows `companyweb2` as a host header value. As a result, you would enter **`http://companyweb2`** into your browser to access this site.
7. Click the Browse button to select an installation path for your website. Expand `C:\Inetpub` and click on Make New Folder to create a new folder under `C:\Inetpub`. For simplicity, use your host header value from step 6 as your folder name.
8. Uncheck Allow Anonymous Access to This Web Site and click Next.
9. Click Next to accept the default permissions; then click Finish to complete the Web Site Creation Wizard and close the IIS MMC.

Now that you have created a new blank website, you need to extend WSS so that the new website will be a SharePoint site:

1. On your SBS server, open SharePoint Central Administration (select Start, All Programs, Administrative Tools, SharePoint Central Administration).
2. When SharePoint Central Administration opens, follow the link to Extend or Upgrade Virtual Server.
3. Click on the website you just created.
4. Click on the Extend or Create a Content Database link.

5. The Extend or Create Content Database page appears, with several option groups for the new SharePoint site. Under the Application Pool group, select to Create a New Application Pool. Enter a name for the new application pool and select the Predefined Network Service for the security account (see Figure 14.10).

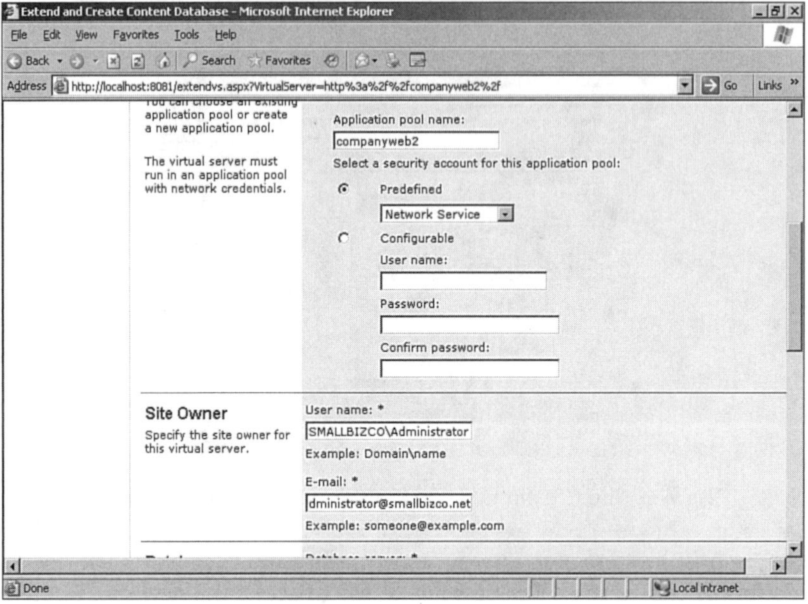

FIGURE 14.10 The Extend or Create Content Database page with recommended values.

6. In the Site Owner section, enter the required user account and email address for the site owner.

7. In the Database Information section, verify that Use Default Content Database Server is selected. This uses the default `<`*`servername`*`>\SHAREPOINT MSDE` database instance but still creates new configuration and content databases for the new site.

8. Accept the default values for the Custom URL and Quota Template sections. In the Language section, select the language you want the new site to use. Note that by default, the only language available is the language represented by the version of SBS. As a result, if you have an English version of SBS, by default English is going to be the only language available. However, you can add language packs, which is discussed later in this chapter.

9. Click OK to extend WSS to the new website. Click OK to acknowledge the message that WSS was successfully extended.

Now that you have created the new website and successfully extended WSS, you need to create a new DNS alias mapping the host header value (for example, `companyweb2`) to the internal IP address of the SBS. For specific steps on how to create a new DNS alias, see

Chapter 5, "DNS, DHCP, and Active Directory Integration." After you have created the necessary DNS alias, you can access your new top-level site and begin customizing to meet your needs.

It is also important to note that creating a new site (whether a subsite or another top-level site) results in the creation of a new content database. By default, this database is created in the data directory of the `SHAREPOINT` instance's installed location, which by default is on the `C:` drive. As a result, consider moving this content database to prevent site content from consuming valuable free space on your system partition.

Backing Up and Restoring SharePoint Data

To adequately administer WSS, it is important to be familiar with the unique aspects of backing up and restoring SharePoint sites. As mentioned earlier in this chapter, each WSS site depends on two separate SQL databases. One database stores the site configuration, and the other stores the site contents including list items as well as documents within site document libraries. To restore the Companyweb in a disaster-recovery scenario, you need to have a System State backup of your SBS server, as well as backups of your system partition, the MSDE installation directory, and all SharePoint databases.

The good news is that SBS includes built-in support to successfully back up and restore Companyweb in a disaster recovery scenario. SBS ships with NTBackup, as well as a backup snap-in and wizard within the Server Management Console. SBS's built-in backup wizard backs up all the components necessary to restore your Companyweb site in a disaster recovery scenario.

However, it is not only conceivable but probable that at some point in time you will need to perform an item-level restore within your Companyweb site. As mentioned earlier, all content within the Companyweb site lives in the content database for that site. As a result, what happens if one day at 4:30 p.m. one of your users accidentally deletes a file out of one of the Companyweb document libraries and needs to get it back? Traditional restore methods would require you to restore the entire content database. Sure, that would allow you to get this document back, but it would also result in losing all other work saved to the entire Companyweb site since the last backup, which is not acceptable.

Best Practice—Schedule At Least One Native SharePoint Backup Each Business Day

WSS includes the capability to back up SharePoint sites. Although NTBackup provides a means for disaster recovery of a SharePoint site, it does not provide many options for item-level recovery of individual documents, photos, or list items. To be able to perform item-level restores, you must have a WSS backup of your site.

In a typical Companyweb deployment, users may be using the Companyweb site constantly throughout the workday, adding, editing, and deleting documents, photos, and list items. As a result, having to roll back to a backup even 24 hours old could significantly impact your business. However, each business is different, and each will therefore have a different time period it is comfortable with potentially losing, whether it be 2 hours, 4 hours, or even a day. Determine what works best for your scenario and schedule your SharePoint backups accordingly. At a minimum you should schedule one SharePoint backup per day.

In this scenario, you can use a native WSS back up to perform a parallel restore to a temporary site. At that point, you have the production Companyweb site running without the deleted document, and a parallel Companyweb site running as it existed at the point it was backed up, complete with the document you need to recover. From here, you can go to the parallel site, open the document you want to recover, save it to the desktop, and then upload it to the production companyweb site. However, before you can perform this type of recovery, you must first schedule SharePoint backups:

1. Log in to your SBS server, open My Computer, and create a new folder on a data partition on which to save your Companyweb backups.
2. Open Control Panel, Scheduled Tasks, Add Scheduled Task. When the Scheduled Task Wizard starts, click Next.
3. Click Browse. Browse to `C:\Program Files\Common Files\Microsoft Shared\Web Server Extensions\60\bin\`. Click on stsadm.exe and click Open.
4. Change the task name to something meaningful—for example, Companyweb Backup - 11am.
5. Select to perform this task weekly and click Next.
6. Select the time you want the backup to start, and the days of the week you want it to run. Click Next.
7. Enter Administrator credentials and click Next.
8. Select Open Advanced Properties for This Task When I Click Finish and click Finish.
9. On the Task tab, remove the command from the Run field and replace it with the following:

   ```
   "%SystemDrive%\Program Files\Common Files\Microsoft Shared
   ➥\Web Server Extensions\60\Bin\Stsadm.exe " -o backup -url http://Companyweb
   ➥ -filename target -overwrite
   ```

   Where `target` equals the full path of the backup location you created in step 1 plus a filename (for example, `D:\Companyweb Backup\11am`). Note that this filename does not require an extension but should be unique from any other filenames you are using for other Companyweb backups. For example, if you are scheduling Companyweb backups for 11 a.m., 2 p.m., and 5 p.m., each scheduled task must use a different filename.
10. Click OK. Enter Administrator credentials if prompted and click OK.
11. Repeat steps 2 through 10 for each additional scheduled backup you want to perform.

After you have created your Companyweb backup schedules, you should manually run each scheduled task to verify that the backup files are created where you expect them. When your scheduled tasks are successfully creating backup files for your Companyweb site, you have the means necessary to perform item-level restores of documents, photos, and list items within your Companyweb site.

As mentioned earlier, to restore individual items to your Companyweb, you need to create a new subsite and restore your Companyweb backup to this site. The procedure for restoring individual documents and photos is as follows:

1. Log in to your SBS server and open a command prompt.
2. At the command prompt, enter the following command to create the new subsite:

```
"%SystemDrive%\Program Files\Common Files\Microsoft Shared\Web Server
➥ Extensions\60\Bin\Stsadm.exe " -o createsiteinnewdb -url
➥http://companyweb/sites/RestoredSite -ownerlogin
➥DOMAIN\administrator -owneremail administrator@DOMAIN.local
➥-databasename STS_RESTORE
```

3. At the command prompt, enter the following command to restore your Companyweb backup to the newly created subsite:

```
"%SystemDrive%\Program Files\Common Files\Microsoft Shared\Web Server
➥ Extensions\60\Bin\Stsadm.exe " -o restore -url
➥http://Companyweb/Sites/Restoredsite -filename target -overwrite
```

   Where `target` equals the full path and filename of the Companyweb backup file you want to restore (for example, "`D:\Companyweb Backup\11am`").

4. Open your web browser and browse to `http://companyweb/sites/restoredsite` to view your newly restored parallel site. To restore library items (documents, photos, faxes), for each item you want to restore, find the item in the restored site, right-click on it, and select Save Target As to save the document to the local hard drive. After you have saved each item you want to restore to your local hard drive, you can browse to `http://companyweb` and upload each item to the correct library.

   When it comes to individual list items (contacts, announcements, and so on), there isn't a way to actually restore these items. Instead, you find the items in the restored site and use that to re-create the item in your production Companyweb site.

After you have restored your individual library and list items, you will want to remove the `restoredsite` subsite from Companyweb, as well as corresponding databases. This is necessary not only to allow for future restores but also for proper disk space management. When you create the `restoredsite` subsite, you also create a new database for the restored site content, and this database is populated during the restore process. As a result, you end up with twice the disk cost because you have two separate databases with virtually all your Companyweb content. Additionally, by default the `restoredsite` database is created in the data folder under the MSDE installation directory. Therefore, it is important to realize that if your `SHAREPOINT MSDE` instance is installed on your `C:` drive, the restore process creates a new database on your system drive. So, to remove the `restoredsite` subsite and content database, follow these steps:

1. On your SBS server, open SharePoint Central Administration (select Start, All Programs, Administrative Tools, SharePoint Central Administration).
2. Under the Virtual Server Configuration section, click Configure Virtual Server Settings; then click on Companyweb.
3. Under the Virtual Server Management section, click Delete Site Collection.
4. Type the subsite URL (**`http://companyweb/sites/restoredsite`**); then click OK and click Delete.
5. To remove the content database, under the Virtual Server Management section, click Manage Content Databases.
6. Click STS_RESTORE; then click Remove Content Database and click OK. Close SharePoint Central Administration.
7. To delete the database from the `SHAREPOINT MSDE` instance, open a command prompt and enter the following command:

```
osql -E -S <SERVERNAME>\SharePoint -Q "drop database sts_restore"
```

Where *<SERVERNAME>* equals the netbios name of your server.

Extending Companyweb with FrontPage

One of SharePoint's true strengths is the capability to extensively customize virtually all aspects of a SharePoint site from within SharePoint's web interface. However, you have even more options for customizing your SharePoint sites using Microsoft FrontPage 2003. Although the possibilities of SharePoint combined with FrontPage 2003 are virtually limitless, we will focus on how to use FrontPage to extend the SharePoint interface and overcome a few speed bumps you may encounter from following some of the customizations included in the chapter.

For example, you may have noticed that after you have created a custom web part page, there isn't any way to place a shortcut to that web part page on the Companyweb main page. The best you can do is place a shortcut to the document library that that web part page lives in, or add it to a Links web part on the main page as well, which isn't exactly an ideal solution. But you can put a direct link to that web part page on the Companyweb main page using FrontPage 2003.

Open FrontPage 2003 and select File, Open Site. In the Site Name field, enter **`http://companyweb`** and click Open. The site opens, and you can see all the individual pages and directories that make up your Companyweb site. Double-click on `default.aspx` to open the Companyweb main page. From here, you can easily add additional links to either the QuickLaunch bar on the right side of the page, or even the SharePoint header bar at the top of the page. After you've added your new link, simply save the page, and your changes will be visible on the Companyweb home page.

Besides adding links to the main page, you can further customize your web part pages. Depending on the layout you chose when you created your custom web part page, you may have noticed that different web part zones on the page had different orientations—for example, some zones organized web parts vertically, whereas others organized web parts horizontally. If you have a web part page where you don't like the orientation of the zones, you can easily change that within FrontPage. With your Companyweb site open in FrontPage, open your web part page (in the folder list, expand the document library where your web part page lives, and double-click on the web part page). Find a web part in the zone whose orientation you want to change and right-click on the web part. In the context menu that appears, select Web Part Zone Properties. On the dialog box that opens, you can specify that the layout for that zone be either horizontal or vertical. Click OK to close the dialog box; then save your web part page.

When it comes to creating web part pages, many people would prefer not to just create a top-level web part page without having to store it in a document library. Although creating a web part page in the SharePoint web interface requires that the page be stored in a document library, you can easily create a top-level web part page in FrontPage without having to store it in a document library. To do so, in FrontPage simply select File, New, which opens the Activity pane on the right side of the FrontPage window. From the Activity pane, click More Page Templates, go to the Web Part Pages tab, and select the layout you want for your new page. After you've created the new web part page, you can add web parts and further customize your page within FrontPage. Note that because this is a top-level web part page, you need to place a link to this page somewhere on your Companyweb, or you will only be able to access this page by entering its direct URL.

One of the most exciting things you can do with FrontPage 2003 and SharePoint is to convert your normal web parts to Data View web parts and establish data connections between web parts. What exactly does that mean? Take the project documents you've been using throughout this chapter, where you have a document library that stores all your project documents and a SharePoint list that stores your project information. Let's say that you also have a SharePoint list that stores your customer information and a contact list that stores customer contacts. You're using lookup fields in the projects and contacts lists to look up customers from the customers list, and a lookup field in the document library to look up projects. This allows you to select the customer that each contact and project is related to, and to select the project that each document is related to. How can you filter and view all this data in a coherent and efficient manner? Wouldn't it be great if you could select a customer from a list and automatically see all the contacts and projects that relate to that customer? Well with SharePoint and FrontPage 2003, you can! The following steps allow you to create this functionality with a custom web part page:

1. Start by creating a new web part page and adding the necessary web parts (Customers, Contacts, Projects, and Project Documents), placing them where you want them on the page.
2. Edit the view of each web part to include the columns, filters, and groupings that you want.

3. Open your web part page in FrontPage 2003.
4. For each web part on the page, right-click on the web part and select Convert to XSLT Data View to convert the web part to a Data View web part. This effectively alters the web part so that it is aware of the data it is displaying, so it can provide that value to other web parts.
5. After you have converted each web part to a Data View web part, right-click on the Customers web part and select Web Part Connections. This starts the Web Part Connections Wizard that allows you to filter other web parts (Projects and Customers) based on the value selected in this web part (Customers).
6. The Web Part Connections Wizard starts. In the Action field, select Provide Data Values To and click Next.
7. Select Connect to a Web Part on This Page and click Next.
8. In the Target Web Part field, select the target web part (Contacts).
9. In the Target Action field, select Filter View Using Data Values From and click Next.
10. Choose the columns from each web part that have matching values. This usually is the lookup field in the target web part and the field in the source web part that the lookup field points to. For example, when you set up your Contacts list in SharePoint, let's say that you created a lookup field called Customer. The Customer lookup field pulled its values from the Name field of the Customer list. As a result, in this stage of the wizard, you would select the Name field from the Customer web part, and the Customer field from the Contact web part. Click Next.
11. In the Create Hyperlink On field, select the same field from the source web part (Customers) as you did in the prior screen. Verify that Indicate Current Selection Using is checked, and that the field value matches that of the Create Hyperlink On field. Click Next; then click Finish.
12. Repeat steps 5 to 11 to connect the Customers web part to the Projects web part, and repeat again to connect the Projects web part to the Documents web part.
13. Save your web part page.

After you've finished the preceding steps, you can open your web part page in SharePoint. When you do, you will notice that the first customer in your customer web part is selected. As a result, the Contacts web part shows only contacts for that customer, and the Projects web part shows only projects for that customer. Additionally, the first project in the web part is selected by default, so the Documents web part only shows documents for that project. You can select a different project to view related documents, or select a different customer, which updates the Contacts, Projects, and Documents web parts accordingly. In little time, you were able to create a custom dashboard for your specific needs, which represents the great value that SharePoint offers.

Working with Multiple Languages in SharePoint

Depending on your specific location, you may need to have a SharePoint site that uses a different language from that used by your specific version of SBS, or you may have a multinational company with unique language requirements, with employees speaking English, Hebrew, and Japanese, for example. By default, WSS uses the same language as the host operating system, so if you have an English version of SBS, your SharePoint site will also be in English. However, Microsoft provides multiple language packs that you can download for free to create additional SharePoint sites using alternate languages. The one catch, however, is that you must specify the language you want to use for your SharePoint site when you create the site. However, because the Companyweb installation is scripted as part of the SBS integrated setup, the Companyweb will always be installed with the same language as the SBS server; there is no way to change the default Companyweb to a different language after the fact.

To obtain additional language packs for WSS, browse to `http://www.microsoft.com/downloads/details.aspx?displaylang=en&familyid =E7EEC77D-4365-4B66-8E8D-9D079C509679`, select the language you want, and download to your server. When complete, run the `STSTPK.exe` package on your server to install the language pack you selected. After the installation is finished, you will be able to select the additional language when creating a new site.

As mentioned earlier, it is not possible to reconfigure the default Companyweb site to use a different language than the SBS operating system. However, you do have a few different options. First, if you have multiple language requirements such as the English, Hebrew, and Japanese example mentioned previously, you could create subsites for additional languages. For example, if you had an English version of SBS, you could use your English default Companyweb site, download the Hebrew and Japanese language packs, and create one subsite using the Hebrew language pack and another subsite using the Japanese language pack, so that each group of users has a SharePoint site in its native language.

Troubleshooting SharePoint Issues

SharePoint is arguably one of the more challenging SBS components to troubleshoot when problems arise. Fortunately, however, you rarely see issues with SharePoint—it usually just works. But what do you do when it doesn't?

The first step in troubleshooting SharePoint issues is to determine whether you truly have a SharePoint issue or some other issue that only shows itself when you're accessing your SharePoint site. Examples of other issues that could appear when trying to access your SharePoint site include network connectivity issues, firewall issues, and permissions issues.

Verify that you can reach your server and that DNS is resolving properly. This is accomplished simply by opening a command prompt and pinging Companyweb. You should receive a response from the IP address of your server. If you don't, you know you have either a network connectivity or DNS issue to troubleshoot.

Firewall issues can be tricky, although they rarely prevent you from completely accessing the Companyweb site. One common issue you may see when Internet Security and Acceleration (ISA) Server is installed is a dialog box prompting for user credentials. This most often occurs because your http request is being routed through ISA's proxy service because it is not recognized as an internal website. In this case, you can open Internet Explorer properties, go to the Security tab, and add `http://companyweb` to your Local Intranet zone. Additionally, you can go to the Connections tab, LAN Settings and add Companyweb to the list of addresses excluded by the proxy service.

Permissions issues can often appear similarly to firewall issues—with prompts for user credentials. However, unlike firewall issues, entering proper credentials never lets you access the Companyweb site. In this instance, you want to make sure that you are not experiencing an issue with the specific client PC, by having the same user log on to another PC and try to access the Companyweb site. If the user can access the site from another PC, you know you do not have a permissions issue within the Companyweb; otherwise, the user would not be able to access the site from any location.

If the user cannot access the site from another PC, a Companyweb site administrator needs to verify that the problem user has the proper permissions to access the Companyweb site. If site permissions appear okay, you will want to log on to the server to check the user's AD account and verify that it is not locked out or disabled.

Although network connectivity and firewall issues are the most common, it is possible that you may encounter an issue with WSS itself. If you have eliminated client-side issues, such as network connectivity and firewalls, and have verified that you do not have a permissions problem, you want to begin looking at your server. Check the obvious items first by verifying that your necessary services are started. These include the MSSQL$SHAREPOINT service and the SPTimer service. If both of these services are started, verify that the Companyweb web site is started within IIS. If your services and website are started, check the logs. WSS is relatively new technology and as a result is very good about logging errors to the Windows Event logs. Open your Event Viewer and access the Application log. Check for any errors relating to WSS. If you find a related error, open the error and note the Event ID and description. Open a web browser and navigate to `http://www.eventid.net`. Enter the Event ID from your error and review the results. Additionally, don't be afraid to consult the many resources that the SBS community has to offer, which are outlined in Appendix A, "SBS Resources."

The Definitive Remove and Reinstall Companyweb How-To Guide

Under most deployment scenarios, you should not need to remove or reinstall your Companyweb site. However, if you find yourself in this position it is important to know how to perform this level of maintenance.

With any reinstallation process, there is a chance for data loss. As a result, if you have any documents or content from your current Companyweb site that you want to save, be sure to either extract these items from your Companyweb site and save them to disk or make sure that you have a valid SharePoint backup as discussed earlier in this chapter so that you can perform item-level restores into the new site if necessary.

A true benefit of SBS is the work that Microsoft has done for you in terms of providing comprehensive wizards to streamline installation and maintenance tasks. As with most aspects of SBS maintenance, Companyweb removal and reinstallation are best handled via the SBS wizards, specifically the SBS integrated installation wizard. Reinstalling Companyweb via the SBS integrated installation wizard does not reinstall the Companyweb content database if it already exists.

To access the SBS Integrated Installation Wizard, follow these steps:

1. On your SBS server, open Control Panel, Add/Remove Programs.
2. In the Currently Installed Programs list, locate Windows Small Business Server 2003 and click Change/Remove.
3. Click Next to start the Windows Small Business Server 2003 Installation Wizard. Click Next again.
4. As shown in Figure 14.11, select Maintenance next to Server Tools. You then can select your desired action (Remove or Reinstall) for the Intranet component (Companyweb). Click Next.

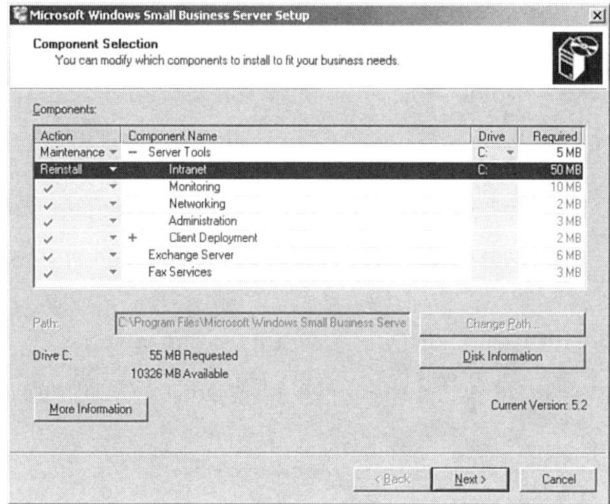

FIGURE 14.11 The SBS Installation Wizard Component Selection screen.

5. Select to manually enter password and click Next.
6. Click Next to begin maintenance actions. Insert SBS CD3 when prompted and click OK.
7. Click Finish to complete the installation wizard.

If the integrated reinstallation process does not solve your problem, or if you want to start over with a blank, default Companyweb site, a complete manual removal and installation of Companyweb will be required, which can be accomplished by using the following steps. More information is also available via Microsoft knowledge base article 829114: How to Remove and How to Install the Windows Small Business Server 2003 SharePoint Services Companyweb Web Site.

1. Follow the preceding steps to remove the intranet component from SBS.
2. Open Control Panel, Add/Remove Programs and remove Microsoft SQL Server Desktop Engine (SHAREPOINT).
3. Delete the following registry keys:

   ```
   HKEY_LOCAL_MACHINE\SOFTWARE\Microsoft\SmallBusinessServer\Intranet

   HKEY_LOCAL_MACHINE\SOFTWARE\Microsoft\Microsoft SQL Server\SHAREPOINT

   HKEY_LOCAL_MACHINE\SOFTWARE\Microsoft\Shared Tools\Web Server Extenstions
   ➥\Ports\Port /LM/W3SVC/4:
   ```

   (Do not delete `/LM/W3SVC/1:` If any other `/LM/W3SVC/x:` keys are present, back them up and then delete them.)
4. Open Internet Information Services Administration console.
5. Expand Web Sites and delete both the Companyweb site and the SharePoint Central Administration site. Do not delete the Microsoft SharePoint Administration site.
6. Expand Application Pools. You want to keep the following four application pools: DefaultAppPool, ExchangeApplicationPool, ExchangeMobileBrowseApplicationPool, and MSSharePointAppPool. Delete all other application pools.
7. Rename `C:\Program Files\Microsoft SQL Server\MSSQL$SHAREPOINT` directory (if present).
8. Rename the `C:\Intepub\Companyweb` directory (if present).
9. Follow preceding set of steps to complete integrated installation of intranet component.
10. When reinstalling the intranet component via SBS Integrated Setup, the setup process prompts for SBS CD3. If your SBS media does not include SBS SP1, when you insert SBS CD3 you receive the error "The drive contains a disk for Windows Small Business Server 2003 with no Service Packs. When the prompt appears, insert a disk for Windows Small Business Server 2003 with Service Pack 1." To complete the installation, you need to point SBS setup to the updated intranet installation files. If you receive this error, follow steps 11-14 to provide setup with the updated files. If you do not receive this error, skip to step 15.
11. Start a command prompt and change the working directory to the folder where you downloaded SBS SP1, or your CD drive if you have SBS SP1 on CD. (Note that you will want SBS SP1 CD2 inserted.)

12. Type the following command and press Enter:

```
SBS2003-KB885918-SP1-X86-ENU.exe /x
```

13. When you are prompted for a location to place the extracted files, create a temporary folder such as `C:\SBSSP1`.
14. Run the SBS Integrated Setup to reinstall the intranet component. When setup prompts for SBS CD3, point setup to the `temp` folder where you extracted the updated setup files in the previous step.
15. After the integrated installation completes, reapply WSS SP1 from SBS SP1 CD 1 or from your download location.
16. After installing WSS SP1, reapply SBS SP1 from SBS SP1 CD 2 or your download location.
17. If your previous Companyweb installation was using full SQL server, you will need to upgrade the recently reinstalled SharePoint WMSDE instance to full SQL server by following the instructions found on the SBS Premium Technologies CD. Note that after upgrading the SharePoint database to full SQL, you must install SQL SP 4 from the SBS SP1 CD 3.

Summary

The Companyweb implementation of WSS in SBS provides small business customers with a collection of tools and functionality that can be used by any small business. Additionally, WSS represents an impressive toolset for anyone, and especially the small business customer. The ability to quickly and extensively customize a SharePoint site, combined with the opportunity to create practical business applications, better communicate and collaborate, and better organize company resources presents amazing value and potential to the SBS customer.

Best Practice Summary

- Move SharePoint databases—Protect free space on your system partition by moving SharePoint databases to alternate location.
- Modify Companyweb default permissions—Change default permissions to grant users only the permissions they need.
- Use metadata—Use metadata fields in document libraries to better organize, filter, search, and sort your documents.
- Upgrade from MSDE to SQL Server—Premium customers upgrade to full SQL to take advantage of full-text search capabilities.

- Create web part pages document library—Keep your existing document libraries clean and organized by creating a separate document library solely for web part pages.
- Use site templates—Streamline site creation by creating templates of preconfigured sites.
- Schedule daily SharePoint backups—Daily SharePoint backups (in addition to full nightly server backups) provide the greatest flexibility in allowing for item-level restores.

CHAPTER 15

Remote Web Workplace

IN THIS CHAPTER

- Overview of the Remote Web Workplace Interface
- Using Remote Web Workplace
- RWW Behind the Scenes
- Customizing Remote Web Workplace
- Troubleshooting Remote Web Workplace

Even though SBS 2003 has many uniquely implemented technologies, the most exciting technology that is unique to SBS 2003 is Remote Web Workplace (RWW). Many consultants have reported that this feature alone has accounted for the sale of SBS to potential clients who were otherwise lukewarm about the SBS product. Many other consultants have asked Microsoft when RWW will be made available for other platforms. For now, RWW belongs only to SBS and will probably remain that way for the foreseeable future.

One component of RWW, the capability to remotely control servers and desktops through a web interface, is often alluded to as RWW itself. This chapter covers all the aspects of the RWW interface, including the remote control capabilities.

Overview of the Remote Web Workplace Interface

On the surface, RWW is simply a web menu—a web page with links to a number of other resources. In its presentation, it provides an interface to tools that a remote user would need to access regularly. The interface is sparse because it is intended to be used across the Internet with a lower-speed connection.

The RWW interface is accessed across an SSL connection to keep the traffic going across the Internet encrypted. The website is published using the public Internet name for the server. If the public name is `mail.smallbizco.net`, RWW would be accessed at `https://mail.smallbizco.net/remote`. This interface requires that port 443 (the HTTP SSL port) be open through the firewall to the SBS server.

NOTE

The RWW interface can also be accessed at `http://mail.smallbizco.net/remote` and will redirect to `https://mail.smallbizco.net/remote` thanks to an ISAPI filter configured in IIS. However, for this redirection to work, you would have to have port 80 open to the SBS server, a practice not recommended by the SBS community at large due to the security issues it poses. Although most users may have trouble remembering to type `https` in the web address for RWW, they can (and should) bookmark the URL for easier access after they get to the main login page.

When you make the initial connection to RWW, you are prompted to enter your username and password to access the site. This is the same as your domain logon credentials. You do not need to enter the username in the form of *domain\username*.

Two other items are available on the logon page. The Connection Speed drop-down menu allows you to select the speed of your connection to the Internet. Selecting the appropriate speed here helps determine the way some information is provided to you through the RWW interface, primarily when remotely controlling machines on the internal network. The other item is the I'm Using a Public or Shared Computer check box. When this check box is enabled, the RWW interface logs you off after 20 minutes of inactivity. When the box is not checked, the inactivity timeout increases to two hours. After you enter your credentials successfully, you get to the main view for your account.

There are two main views for RWW: the administrator view and the client view. When a user logs in to RWW, the user's security level determines which of the two views is presented. The differences between the two views are detailed in the next two sections.

Administrator's View

Figure 15.1 shows the default Administrator view, which is divided into two main sections. The items believed to be most commonly accessed in this view are listed on the left, and the remaining items are in the box on the right.

Table 15.1 briefly describes the four primary icons in the interface.

TABLE 15.1 Description of the Administrator Menu Items

Item	Description
Connect to Server Desktops	Opens connections for remote desktop access to any servers in the network, including terminal servers. Discussed in detail in the "Connecting to Server Desktops" section later in the chapter.
Connect to Client Desktops	Opens connections for remote desktop access to any Windows XP workstations in the network. Discussed in detail in the "Connecting to Client Desktops" section later in the chapter.
Monitor Help Desk	Opens a connection to the Help Desk tool in the Companyweb SharePoint interface. This item is present only if Companyweb has been published to the Internet through the Connect to the Internet Wizard.
Administer the Company's Internal Web Site	Opens a connection to the Site Settings section for the Companyweb SharePoint interface. This item is present only if Companyweb has been published to the Internet through the Connect to the Internet Wizard.

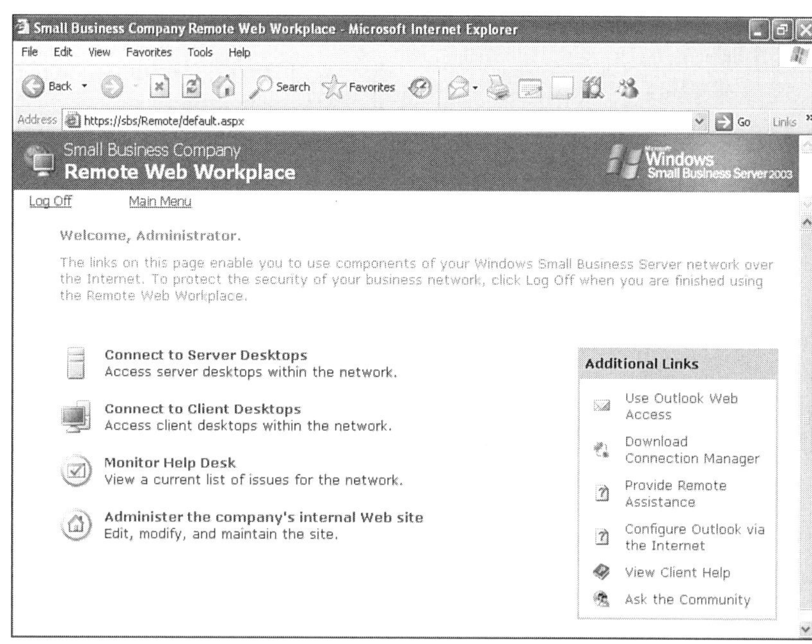

FIGURE 15.1 Administrator's initial view.

The remainder of the RWW items for administrator accounts are contained in the Additional Links box. Table 15.2 briefly describes these items.

TABLE 15.2 Description of the Additional Links Items

Item	Description
Use Outlook Web Access	Connects to the Outlook Web Access interface using the current credentials. Discussed in detail in the "Connecting to OWA" section later in the chapter.
Download Connection Manager	Downloads the Connection Manager tool to help connect the remote workstation to the SBS network. See Chapter 7, "Routing and Remote Access Service, VPN, and Firewalls," for more information about the Connection Manager tool.
Provide Remote Assistance	Opens a page of instructions for how to start a Remote Assistance session with a user on the internal network.
Configure Outlook via the Internet	Opens a page of step-by-step instructions for configuring a remote workstation to use RPC over HTTP to connect Outlook 2003 to the Exchange server across the Internet. See Chapter 11, "Client Connectivity," for more information about Outlook over the Internet.
View Client Help	Opens the Client Help web page interface.
Ask the Community	Opens a new web browser instance to the Small Business Server Community page where you can access the SBS newsgroups, find a user's group, or view the blogs of several SBS MVPs.

Client View

Figure 15.2 shows the Client RWW view. This view has fewer options and only one basic menu structure.

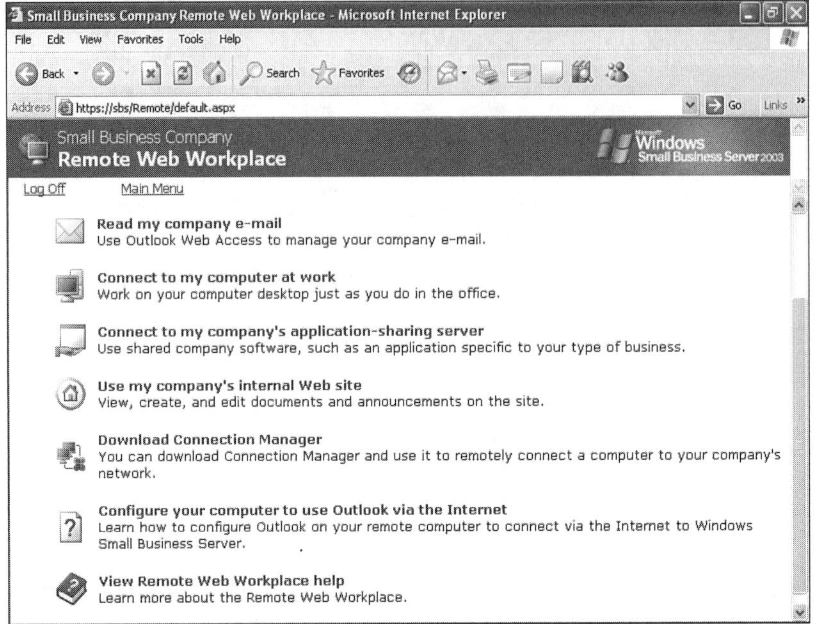

FIGURE 15.2 Client initial view.

Table 15.3 briefly describes the function of each item shown in Figure 15.2.

TABLE 15.3 Menu Items in the Client View

Item	Description
Read My Company E-mail	Connects to the Outlook Web Access interface using the current credentials. Discussed in detail in the "Connecting to OWA" section later in the chapter.
Connect to My Computer at Work	Opens connections for remote desktop access to any Windows XP workstations in the network. Discussed in detail in the "Connecting to Client Desktops" section later in the chapter.
Connect to My Company's Application-Sharing Server	Opens connections for remote desktop access to any terminal servers in the network. This item appears only if terminal servers are set up in the network.
Use My Company's Internal Web Site	Opens a connection to the Companyweb SharePoint site. This item is present only if Companyweb has been published to the Internet through the Connect to the Internet Wizard.
Download Connection Manager	Downloads the Connection Manager tool to help connect the remote workstation to the SBS network. See Chapter 7 for more information about the Connection Manager tool.

TABLE 15.3 Continued

Item	Description
Configure Your Computer to Use Outlook Via the Internet	Opens a page of step-by-step instructions for configuring a remote workstation to use RPC over HTTP to connect Outlook 2003 to the Exchange server across the Internet. See Chapter 11, "Client Connectivity," for more information about Outlook over the Internet.
View Remote Web Workplace Help	Opens the Client Help web page interface.

Using Remote Web Workplace

Each of the tools linked from RWW is fairly self-explanatory. You can access Outlook Web Access (OWA) and the Companyweb site without using the RWW interface, but accessing those sites through RWW may be easier for your users. In fact, because users can get to OWA, Companyweb, and many other features through RWW, some companies only share the RWW web address with their users who need remote access. Remembering or bookmarking a single entry point is simpler for some users than having to remember one bookmark for OWA, one for RWW, and a separate one for Companyweb.

One of the biggest myths related to RWW is that you cannot access the RWW interface from a Macintosh or a web browser that does not support ActiveX controls, such as Firefox. This is simply not the case. The Firefox browser and almost all Macintosh web browsers can access most of the functions of RWW with minimal differences. Only the connections to server and workstation desktops will not work because those connections are handled with an ActiveX control.

NOTE

The only browser that simply will not work at all with RWW is Internet Explorer for the Macintosh, and even then only under one condition. Internet Explorer for the Macintosh has no mechanism for interacting with SSL certificates that have not been generated by "trusted" third-party providers. When IE for the Mac encounters the self-signed certificate generated by SBS, it will not continue the connection. For more information about Macintosh web browsers and the self-signed SSL certificate with SBS, see Chapter 17, "Integrating the Macintosh into a Small Business Server 2003 Environment."

This section of the chapter covers the most commonly used features of RWW, how they work, and how they differ from standard access methods.

Connecting to RWW

The first step to accessing any of the features of RWW is to log in to the interface. From inside the network, open `https://servername/remote` in your browser. From outside the network, use `https://publicdnsname/remote` instead. If you configured your SBS server with the self-signed certificate, you will get a prompt alerting you that the certificate is from an untrusted source. You can click OK to bypass the warning or, if you are using a computer that you will use to access RWW regularly, you can install the certificate in the local certificate store to bypass this warning every time you access the logon page. The SSL certificate is automatically stored in the proper certificate store on workstations that have been joined to the domain using Connect Computer, so you should not see this warning on workstations on the internal network.

When you get the logon page, enter your network username and password and press Enter to log in. You can also adjust your connection speed in the drop-down menu. After you are logged in, you get either the Administrator menu or the Client menu, depending on your account permissions.

Connecting to OWA

In traditional Exchange installations, OWA Access is accessed through its own web page, usually `https://publicdnsname/exchange`. This interface is also available with SBS and is covered in more detail in Chapter 11. The significant difference between accessing OWA directly through its web interface and the RWW interface is in the way authentication is handled.

When you access OWA through its own page, you have to enter your username and password to access the site. When you access OWA through the RWW interface, you do not need to give a username and password a second time. RWW passes the credentials you used to log in to RWW to OWA so that the OWA interface is brought up directly for your user account.

One particular item to note here is that you can only access *your* Exchange account through OWA from RWW. Because no authentication prompt appears when you click on Use Outlook Web Access from the Administrator view or Read My Company E-mail from the Mobile User's view, you cannot provide different credentials and access a different mailbox.

By default, RWW attempts to access OWA using the Premium interface, which gives the most Outlook-like look and feel. When you access OWA through RWW from a browser other than Internet Explorer on Windows, you get the Basic OWA interface instead.

One other difference between Internet Explorer for Windows and other browsers is in the way the Log Off function is handled within OWA. If you click the Log Off button in the OWA premium interface, you get the OWA logon screen inside the RWW shell. If you then click on the RWW Main Menu link, you are taken back to the RWW logon page. Clicking Log Off from the OWA Premium interface logs you out of the RWW session as well. If you select Log Off from the OWA Basic interface, however, you still get the OWA logon screen, but when you click the RWW Main Menu link, you are taken back to the RWW menu. The Log Off from the Basic OWA interface does not impact the logon credentials for OWA.

Connecting to Companyweb

The entry point into Companyweb is different depending on whether you logged in to RWW as an administrator or as a normal user, and is present only if access to the Windows SharePoint Services intranet site has been enabled in the Connect to the Internet Wizard (CEICW). For more information on this configuration setting, see Chapter 14, "SharePoint and the Companyweb Site." From the Administrator's menu, you can jump into the Help Desk section of Companyweb, or you can access the Site Settings. The user menu takes you straight to the root of the Companyweb site. In either case, you are prompted for your username and password to access Companyweb. The single sign-on support for OWA does not apply to Companyweb.

When using Internet Explorer for Windows, if you log out of RWW and log back in without closing the IE window, you are prompted for authentication credentials again when you try to access any of the Companyweb links in the RWW menu. This is not the case with other browsers. The credentials used to access Companyweb continue to be stored in the browser until the browser window is closed and reopened. This could present issues if you are verifying user access to Companyweb through RWW.

For example, if you connect to RWW from a non-IE Windows browser, log in as Administrator, and access Companyweb, you are prompted to enter your username and password, which is the same Administrator logon information you provided when logging in to RWW. After you have made changes to the Companyweb interface and want to test it as a regular user, you might log out of RWW and log in again without closing the window. No matter how you log in to RWW, when you click on one of the links that takes you in to the Companyweb interface, you will not be prompted to log in again. Companyweb uses the same credentials that had been entered earlier. The only way to ensure that you get completely disconnected from Companyweb when you log out of RWW is to close the browser window and open a new one before trying to access Companyweb through RWW again.

Connecting to Server Desktops

Connecting to servers using the remote desktop protocol is one of the main administrative uses of RWW in the SBS community. When administrators log in to RWW, the first link listed in the Administrator menu is Connect to Server Desktops. This link opens the remote desktop ActiveX control and lists all servers in the network. This list includes the SBS server, any member servers, any domain controllers, and any terminal servers in the domain. This list is the only way to access the SBS server, member servers, and domain controllers through RWW.

> **NOTE**
>
> Only Windows 2003 servers and Windows 2000 servers running Terminal Services appear in the server list. Regular Windows 2000 servers do not support remote desktop and cannot be accessed using this interface.

Terminal severs are a bit different. Because users need access to the terminal server desktop, a special menu item is made available in the uses RWW menu—Connect to My Company's Application-Sharing Server. When a user selects this item, a list of available terminal servers appears for the user to select from. No other servers are listed in any RWW interface for non-administrator users.

Figure 15.3 shows the Connect to Server Desktops interface with the Optional Settings menu expanded. From this screen, you can select the server computer to connect to, specify any particular settings you want for the connection, and select the screen size for the connection.

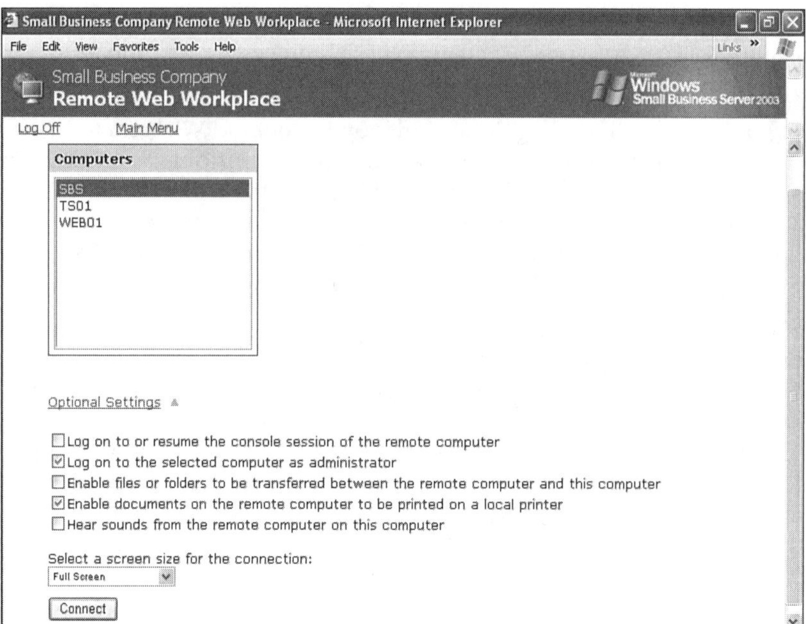

FIGURE 15.3 Options for connecting to server desktops.

Table 15.4 briefly describes the connection options available for server connections.

TABLE 15.4 Options for Connecting to Server Computers

Item	Description
Log On to or Resume the Console Session of the Remote Computer	Allows you to connect to the console session of the server, not just a standard remote session. See Chapter 8, "Terminal Services," for an explanation of connecting to console sessions versus remote sessions.
Log On to the Selected Computer as Administrator	By default, the connection to the remote computer uses the same username provided for the RWW session. Removing this check box allows you to provide a different username for the connection.
Enable Files or Folders to Be Transferred Between the Remote Computer and This Computer	When enabled, this option creates a network drive mapping for each drive on the local computer at the remote computer.
Enable Documents on the Remote Computer to Be Printed on a Local Printer	When enabled, this option creates a printer object on the remote computer for each printer defined on the local computer.
Hear Sounds from the Remote Computer on This Computer	When enabled, audio from the remote computer, if any, will be mapped to and played on the local computer. This includes system alert sounds as well as other audio, if audio is supported on the remote computer.

By default, only the Log On to the Selected Computer as Administrator and Enable Documents on the Remote Computer to Be Printed on a Local Printer options are enabled.

CAUTION

Not all printers connected to the local machine can support remote desktop printing. Most USB printers and some printers connected via the parallel port will not work in this configuration.

You can also select the screen size you want to use for the remote connection from the drop-down menu. The default setting is Full Screen, but other standard screen sizes (640x480, 800x600, 1024x768, 1280x1024, and 1600x1200) can be selected as well.

When you click Connect, the ActiveX client makes a connection to the remote machine through the Terminal Services Proxy port (4125). The Terminal Services Proxy services on the SBS server get the incoming connection on port 4125, get the name of the machine from the connection, and then open a connection to port 3389 (the remote desktop port) on the destination machine and tunnel data between the remote machine to the internal machine. This data connection is configured automatically in the CEICW, but if you have a standalone router/firewall between the SBS server and the Internet, you will have to configure the firewall to allow port 4125 inbound to the SBS server before remote machine connections will work.

Connecting to Client Desktops

Connecting to client desktops (called Connect to Client Desktops in the admin menu and Connect to My Computer at Work in the user menu) is similar to the server desktop connections, with a few key differences. First, only Windows XP workstations with Remote Desktop enabled are listed in the selection screen. Windows XP workstations that have been joined to the domain using the Connect Computer Wizard have this configuration enabled by default. Second, the option to connect to the console session is not available in this interface because console connections are the only connections supported in Windows XP. This also means that only one person can be logged in to the Windows XP workstation at a time. If someone is using the workstation locally and a remote user attempts to connect to it, the local user could be logged off or have his session taken over and be locked out of the connection while the remote connection is in place. Otherwise, the steps to connect to a client desktop are the same as connecting to a server desktop.

One issue that users may complain about is performance when connecting to their desktops remotely. The user interface in Windows XP is more graphical than the interface in Windows Server 2003. Even though the remote connection transmits only screen information and keyboard/mouse data across the network, an XP workstation with a high-resolution background image or special cursor images can significantly slow down the session to a point that the user may feel it's unusable. Many of these graphics can be reduced and overall performance improved by selecting a slower connection speed at the initial RWW logon screen. This is one complaint about the RWW interface—you can adjust the connection speed setting only at the initial logon.

Best Practice—Set the RWW Connection Speed to Modem (28.8Kbps)

When showing users how to log in to the RWW interface, have them select the Modem (28.8 Kbps) option in the Connection Speed drop-down menu. This setting configures the remote desktop connections to use minimal graphics on the remotely connected desktop to improve performance across the network. When choosing this setting, the user's desktop background image will not be displayed, and the Start menu and other interfaces will revert to classic mode, reducing the amount of visual data that must be sent across the wire.

Even when connecting across a high-speed connection in both directions, this setting significantly improves remote desktop performance. If users complain about the lack of graphics, you can have them step up the options one at a time until they reach a balance of the visual environment they are used to and a connection speed they can live with. In most cases, though, users get used to the quicker speed they get by using the lowest connection speed setting.

RWW Behind the Scenes

Now that you know more about how RWW works on the user side, you may well want to learn about the inner workings of RWW. This section of the chapter explores the files and settings that make RWW tick.

RWW File Locations and Registry Settings

The SBS installation places all the files related to RWW in the `C:\inetpub\Remote` directory. This directory contains the ASPX files and the `Web.Config` file that drives the web application as well as a folder for image files. There is no special security for the files in this folder—the security settings are inherited from the `C:\inetpub` folder.

The Registry settings related to RWW are located in `HKLM\Software\Microsoft\SMallBusinessServer\RemoteUserPortal`. In addition to the Registry values at that level, two subkeys, AdminLinks and KWLinks, help determine which menu options are visible in the Administrator and Client views. These values are set as part of the CEICW process and have their values determined by the options set in the firewall configuration section.

RWW IIS Configuration

RWW is created in IIS as a virtual directory off the Default Web Site. This Remote virtual directory runs as an application off the DefaultAppPool object. Table 15.5 lists the default settings for the Remote virtual directory for each of the tabs in the virtual directory properties.

TABLE 15.5 Default Settings for the Remote Virtual Directory

Tab	Setting	Value
Virtual Directory	Local Path	C:\inetpub\Remote
	Script Source Access	Disabled
	Read	Enabled
	Write	Disabled
	Directory Browsing	Disabled

TABLE 15.5 Continued

Tab	Setting	Value
	Log Visits	Enabled
	Index This Resource	Enabled
	Application Name	Remote
	Execute Permission	Scripts Only
	Application Pool	DefaultAppPool
Directory Security	Enabled Anonymous Access	Enabled
	Integrated Windows Authentication	Enabled
	Digest Authentication for Windows Domain Servers	Disabled
	Basic Authentication	Disabled
	.NET Passport Authentication	Disabled
	Require Secure Channel (SSL)	Enabled
	Require 128-bit Encryption	Enabled
	Ignore Client Certificates	Selected
	Enable Client Certificate Mapping	Disabled

Customizing Remote Web Workplace

Because RWW is a web interface, there are several ways to customize it to meet your particular wants or needs. This section provides information on several customizations you may want to look at for your RWW installation.

CAUTION

Be warned that some of the customizations listed here involve changes to the Registry on the SBS server. Be sure to make a good backup of the Registry before making any changes detailed here.

Changing the Look and Feel of RWW

The RWW logon page and web page headers are built from images in the Remote directory. The two key images involved in the logon page are `login.gif` and `RwwOEMlogo.gif`. The `RwwOEMlogo.gif` file is a white image that displays in the lower right-hand corner of the white login box. This image file is 135x20 pixels in size and does not appear to display because the rest of the window it displays in is also white. `Login.gif` is the image that displays as the top banner of the logon page, and is 448x175 pixels. You can change the contents of these two files to alter the appearance of the RWW logon page; just keep in mind that the image dimensions should remain the same to keep in line with the code. The files should be backed up before making any changes. Those who are more adventurous can look at the `logon.aspx` file and adjust the table settings to alter the appearance even further. Just be aware that code errors in this file could break the logon process and keep users from accessing RWW.

The other image files stored in the Remote\images directory can also be modified as desired to change the appearance of the RWW menu. The top banner of each RWW page is essentially a table with a gray background to match the background of the SBS logo image that appears on the right of the banner.

Increasing the Default Timeout Values in RWW

As noted earlier in the chapter, the default timeout values for RWW are 20 minutes when the Public Computer check box is enabled during RWW logon and two hours otherwise. These values are stored in the Registry as `PublicTimeOut` and `TrustedTimeOut` under `HKLM\SOFTWARE\Microsoft\SmallBusinessServer\RemoteUserPortal`. These values are stored in minutes, so by default `PublicTimeOut` is 20 (0x14), and `TrustedTimeOut` is 120 (0x78). If you increase these values in the Registry, they take effect the next time a user logs in to RWW.

Excluding Systems from Remote Control List

By default, all Windows XP workstations on the network show up in the Connect to Client Computers and Connect to My Computer at Work lists. You may find that there are some systems that you do not want to make available to your users for remote control. You can add a Registry value to exclude certain systems from the list. Follow these steps to add the value:

1. Open `regedit` and browse to `HKLM\SOFTWARE\Microsoft\SmallBusinessServer\RemoteUserPortal`.
2. Right-click on RemoteUserPortal and select New, String Value.
3. Name the new value `ExcludeList`.
4. Add the workstation names you want to exclude, separated by commas—for example, `jondough01,sarahdough01,jimdough01`.
5. Close `regedit`.

The next time users log in to RWW and pull up the list of desktops, the computers listed in the Registry value will not display. Again, there is no way to selectively allow systems to appear based on user or group information. This is an all or nothing change.

Prevent Users from Connecting Local Drives to the Remote Computer

The option to allow users to connect the disk drives from their local computer to the remote computer when remotely controlling a workstation through RWW is a useful feature in some environments and a security nightmare in others. One of the advantages of using RWW over VPN is that you never allow a computer from outside the SBS network direct network access to any of the other systems. The Enable Files or Folders to Be Transferred Between the Remote Computer and This Computer option in RWW unfortunately does exactly that.

If you have a corporate policy that prohibits remote, unprotected computers from having direct file access to other systems on the network, you do not want to have this option enabled for your users. Use the following steps to modify RWW to prevent that option from showing for your users. Unfortunately, there is no way to make this option selective based on user account or other criteria. This modification is an all or nothing prospect, and because this modification is not officially supported by Microsoft, you may not be able to get support if you encounter problems after making these changes.

1. Browse to the `C:\inetpub\Remote` directory on the server.
2. Make a copy of the `selectpc.aspx` file and name the backup `selectpc_original.aspx` or something similar.
3. Open `selectpc.aspx` in Notepad or another text editor.
4. Find the following lines in the file:

```
<asp:CheckBox TabIndex="7" id="checkDrives" runat="server"
➥CssClass="optionText"></asp:CheckBox><BR>
<asp:CheckBox TabIndex="8" id="checkPrinters" runat="server"
➥CssClass="optionText" Checked="True"></asp:CheckBox><BR>
<asp:CheckBox TabIndex="9" id="checkAudio" runat="server"
➥CssClass="optionText"></asp:CheckBox><BR><BR>
```

5. Change those three lines (each line should start with `<asp:CheckBox`) as follows:

```
<asp:CheckBox TabIndex="7" id="checkPrinters" runat="server"
➥CssClass="optionText" Checked="True"></asp:CheckBox><BR>
<asp:CheckBox TabIndex="8" id="checkAudio" runat="server"
➥CssClass="optionText"></asp:CheckBox><BR><BR>
<asp:CheckBox TabIndex="9" id="checkDrives" runat="server" visible="false"
➥CssClass="optionText"></asp:CheckBox><BR>
```

6. Save the changes to the file, and the option will not be visible the next time a user views all the options.

Be sure that each of those lines does not wrap—there should only be three lines, and each one should start with `<asp:CheckBox`.

Troubleshooting Remote Web Workplace

Most troubleshooting issues related to RWW involve network troubleshooting. Generally, if you can access any part of RWW, you can access all of the functions. There are times when this is not the case, but the design of RWW was intentionally kept simple, and as a result, most issues can be quickly identified and resolved.

The first step to troubleshooting any problem related to RWW is to see whether the problem exists when RWW is accessed internally as well as externally. In other words, you need to see whether the problem lies at the Internet boundary or on the SBS server itself.

If you can access the RWW feature from the internal network but not from across the Internet, you need to check the firewall configuration to see what network access is being allowed. If you suspect that the problem may be on the SBS server itself, your best bet is to rerun the CEICW and let it reset the default settings for RWW and the network configuration. If you suspect that an external firewall might be at fault, check to make sure that ports 443, 444, and 4125 are open and directed to the SBS server.

Best Practice—Troubleshooting External Network Connectivity from Inside the Network

When you have SBS running in a two NIC configuration behind an external firewall, it can be difficult to determine whether a network configuration problem with the firewall or the external NIC on the server is the cause of the problem. One way to narrow down the source of the problem is by using a laptop and a small network hub. Figure 15.4 shows the network layout for this configuration.

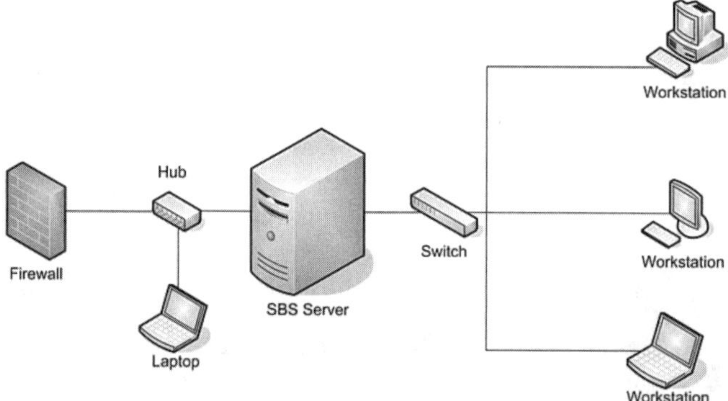

FIGURE 15.4 Connecting a hub and laptop to the external network.

Connect the hub between the SBS server and the external firewall. This will not impact your Internet connection but will allow you to connect the laptop to the network between the server and the firewall. Connect the laptop to the hub as well, and configure the laptop with an IP address on the same subnet as the external NIC on the server. Now you can access the server as if you were coming from the Internet and eliminate any problems that the firewall might be causing.

If you can access the server resources fine from the laptop connected to the external interface but not from a machine across the Internet, you need to look at the configuration of the firewall first. If you cannot access the resources on the server from the laptop, you need to look at the server configuration first.

The remainder of this chapter provides some insights for troubleshooting problems where RWW cannot be accessed externally but can be accessed internally.

Cannot Connect to RWW

The trick to identifying the root cause of the problem that keeps you from accessing RWW from the Internet is to look closely at the error that you get in Internet Explorer. Not the generic error that appears at the top of the error page (although that can help narrow down the issue with some errors), but the HTTP error code that appears toward the bottom of the page, usually a 400-series error. In many cases, a quick Google search on the HTTP error can point you in the right direction.

For example, if you get this error when accessing RWW, "HTTP Error 403.6 - Forbidden: IP address of the client has been rejected," the Remote Web Workplace check box was not enabled during the firewall configuration portion of the CEICW. When RWW is not enabled in the CEICW, the IIS virtual directory for RWW has a restriction on which IP addresses can access the virtual directory, and those addresses fall in the internal IP address range.

On the other hand, you might get this error: "Cannot find server or DNS Error." This usually indicates that access to the site is not enabled. If you cannot access any of the secure sites on the server such as OWA, check to make sure that port 443 is open on your firewall.

Cannot Access Companyweb Through RWW

If you get a "The page cannot be displayed" error when attempting to access any of the Companyweb links, more than likely port 444 is not correctly forwarded to your SBS server. You can verify this by attempting to telnet to port 444 on your public network interface. If you get a "Could not open connection to the host" response from telnet, the port is not correctly forwarding to the server. If you get a blank screen after issuing the telnet command, the port did respond, and the problem lies elsewhere. You can only confirm this for certain by connecting from outside the network, or using the hub connected to the external NIC described in the preceding "Best Practice—Troubleshooting External Network Connectivity from Inside the Network," sidebar.

If you cannot access Companyweb through RWW because the menu items are not present, you need to rerun the CEICW and make sure that the Windows SharePoint Services intranet site is enabled in the firewall portion of the CEICW. If that option is not enabled, the RWW menu will not display the Companyweb items.

Cannot Remotely Control Workstations Through RWW

This can be one of the trickiest access problems to troubleshoot with RWW because so many pieces are involved. The first item to test is to make sure that you can make a remote desktop connection to the Windows XP workstation directly from another machine on the local network. You can do this with the Remote Desktop Client or by trying to telnet to port 3389 on the workstation. If you get no response from the workstation, you may need to check the firewall settings on the workstation to make sure that remote desktop is enabled.

If you can connect to the workstation directly, the next step is to test the RWW remote connection from a machine inside the network. If you can access the workstation directly but cannot get to it through RWW on the internal network, you need to check and see whether a process is listening on port 4125 on the server. By default, port 4125 does not have an active listener and will not show up in the output of a `netstat -aon` command. When a remote control session is active, you will see a process active on port 4125 in the output of `netstat -aon`, and that process will be the IIS worker process (`w3wp.exe`). If you find any other process listening on port 4125, you've got a misconfiguration or other problem on the server.

Finally, if you can connect to the workstation through RWW from an internal machine, test the connectivity from the external NIC using the laptop and hub test described in the previous "Best Practice" sidebar. If you can connect from the laptop but not from a machine across the Internet, your firewall is most likely misconfigured and not forwarding port 4125 to the SBS server.

One other error you might encounter when trying to remotely connect to workstations or servers through RWW is a Javascript error similar to the following:

```
Line: 272
Char: 4
Error: Invalid procedure call or argument
Code: 0
```

This error occurs when the client workstation attempting to make the connection has a screen resolution of 1600×1200 or greater, and you attempt to make a Full Screen connection to the remote workstation. Setting the screen size in the remote connection to 1280×1024 or less prevents this error, as does lowering the resolution on the client workstation to something lower than 1600×1200.

Summary

Upholding the adage that good things come in small packages, RWW provides a huge value to SBS, despite its relatively simple implementation. The relatively straightforward selection of remote features grouped together into a simple and easy-to-navigate web interface helps make RWW attractive to administrators and users alike. Through the RWW web interface, you can access your email, access the Companyweb SharePoint site, and remotely control servers and workstations.

This chapter covered the features and limitations of RWW as well as explaining how the underlying structure works. The chapter also provided information about customizing the RWW interface from the look and feel of the login page to restricting access to certain features of remote workstation connectivity, including steps for how to keep a workstation from being included in the list of available resources.

Best Practice Summary

- Set the RWW connection speed to Modem (28.8Kbps)—Choosing the lowest connection speed option when logging in to RWW gives you the best performance when connecting to remote desktops.
- Troubleshooting external network connectivity from inside the network—Connecting a hub and a laptop to the external NIC on the SBS server allows you to test network access from outside the network without going through the firewall, allowing you to determine whether the firewall configuration is causing problems.

PART VII

Client Connectivity

IN THIS PART

CHAPTER 16

Users and Computers

IN THIS CHAPTER

- Managing Users in SBS 2003
- Managing Computers in SBS 2003
- Troubleshooting User and Computer Issues

Chances are that, outside of new installations, system upgrades, growth, or massive turnover in an organization, you will not spend much time managing users and computers in a small business network.

Managing Users in SBS 2003

As with almost every other aspect of managing technologies on the SBS server, there are two ways to create and manage user objects: with the wizards or without the wizards. Although it may seem obvious to the reader who has come this far through the book that the expected response here is to use the wizards to create and manage users, there are still some administrators who come from an enterprise background who still want to create and manage users by hand. Even if they have adopted the wizard mantra for other aspects of managing an SBS server, something as simple as managing users can be just as easily done by hand, right? Not exactly.

Even though SBS has wizards to deal with most aspects of managing user objects after they have been created, some tasks still can only be performed using the traditional server management tools. However, just because some tasks must be performed outside the wizards does not mean that the whole process of user management should be done without the wizards. As is the general rule for everything else in the SBS world, start with the wizards and then move on.

All the user-related tasks can be found in the Users node of the Server Management Console. This includes the wizards as well as shortcuts to the non-wizard tools.

Administrator and Power User Access

SBS administrators are not the only accounts that can manage users and computers on the SBS network. Users created with the Power User template can also manage aspects of the server environment, including a subset of user management functions. For power users to access the Server Management Console, however, they have to log on to the server directly. The default security settings for SBS 2003 do not permit power users to log on directly at the console, so the user would have to make a remote connection to the server to access the management tools. The Remote Web Workplace (RWW) interface will not allow a power user to remotely connect to the server, so the power user wanting to manage the server will have to use Remote Desktop to get to the server console.

Because power users are not full administrators, they do not have access to the entire suite of management wizards that administrators do. Table 16.1 lists the differences in user management tools between administrators and power users.

TABLE 16.1 Access to User Management Tools By Administrators and Power Users

Tool	Administrator	Power User
Add a User	Yes	Yes
Add Multiple Users	Yes	No
Add User to a Group	Yes	Yes
Rename User	Yes	Yes
Change User Properties	Yes	Yes
Change User Permissions	Yes	No
Configure Password Policies	Yes	No
Configure My Documents Redirection	Yes	No
Change Mailbox and Disk Quota Limits	Yes	Yes
Offer Remote Assistance	Yes	No
Disable Account	Yes	Yes
Remove User	Yes	No

Additionally, the Server Management Console interface has a different look to it for power users than full administrators. Figure 16.1 shows the default layout for the Power User Server Management Console.

Adding Users

If you are new to SBS but have read through the other chapters in this book, you should have a good understanding of all the technologies that have custom configurations applied to work correctly in the SBS environment. On the surface, it may seem that a task as simple as adding a user might not really benefit from being done through a wizard. However, the rest of this chapter looks into all the different options that are set for user objects when the wizards are run. There are times, however, when a user object is needed on the server that falls outside the scope of what the wizards can do, so the chapter provides some insight into that situation as well.

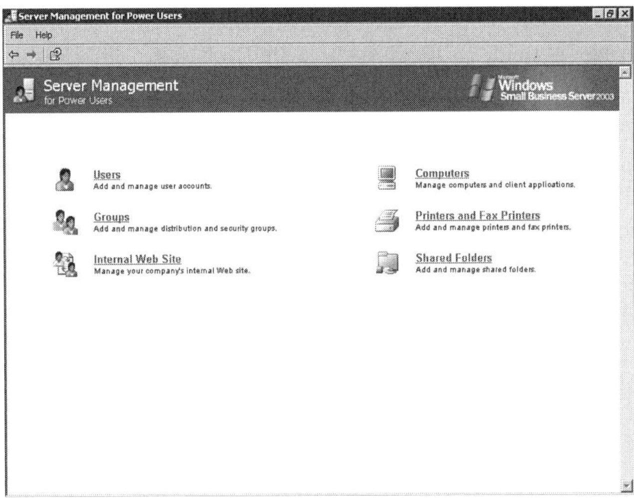

FIGURE 16.1 The Power User Server Management Console has fewer options available than the full Server Management Console.

Using the Add User Wizard

The interface for the Add User Wizard is the same for administrators and power users. There are a couple of minor differences in some of the wizard pages, however, based on the limitations of what the power user can do.

Here are the steps to completing the Add User Wizard:

1. Open the wizard and click Next on the first page.
2. Enter the first and last names for the user account. The logon name is filled in with the first and last names together. Change the logon name and email aliases if desired in this page and click Next when finished.
3. Enter a password for the user and click Next.
4. Select the appropriate template for the user being created and click Next.

CAUTION

When a power user gets to the Template selection page, the only template options available are the User template and the Mobile User template. A power user cannot create a user with administrative privileges on the network, so the Power User template and the Administrator template are not available in this page. See the "Understanding User Templates" section later in the chapter for a more detailed explanation of each of the template options.

Think carefully before creating a user with the Power User template. Accounts created as power users have enhanced privileges on the network. Be sure not to grant those permissions to a user object unless you are absolutely sure that you want that person to be able to use those enhanced permissions.

5. If you want to set up a computer for this user, enter a name for the workstation in the Computer Name field. Otherwise, click the Do Not Set Up a Computer button. Click Next when finished.
6. If you selected to add a computer, the wizard presents two additional pages relating to the installation of client software on the workstation. This interface is covered in greater detail in the "Assigning Applications to Computers" section later in the chapter. Click Next on each page after the desired settings have been selected.
7. Review the summary of actions to be taken by the Add User Wizard and click Finish to create the user object.

The summary page gives you a glimpse into the many tasks that the Add User Wizard performs. It creates the user object, creates a home directory for the user, creates a mailbox in Exchange for the user, adds the user to the appropriate security groups (based on the template selected during the wizard), adds the user to the default distribution group for Exchange, adds the user to the Companyweb setup with the permissions determined by the template, and assigns a disk quota for the user. If a new computer object was requested during the wizard, the wizard creates the computer object, assigns several applications to the computer, and configures settings for multiple applications on the workstation.

NOTE

To really understand what goes on with the Add User Wizard, you can use the FileMon and RegMon tools from SysInternals (`http://www.sysinternals.com`) and monitor the server while the wizard does its magic. Be warned, however, that you will need to export the data into a spreadsheet and have ample time to sort through just the entries that the `addusr.exe` tool adds to the logs from both programs.

When the Add User Wizard completes, the newly created user appears in the users list in the Server Management Console. Many administrators who are new to SBS will not find these users immediately when looking for them in Active Directory Users and Computers. This is because the Add User Wizard places the user objects into the MyBusiness, Users, SBSUsers Organizational Unit (OU) instead of the Users container that most non-SBS administrators are familiar with. This is done primarily to be able to make use of Group Policy, and even though SBS does not have group policy objects predefined at that level, the structure is created to allow for customization through group policy later, if needed.

Using Active Directory Users and Computers

UserDirectory Users and Computers (ADUC) Management Console, but any users created in this manner should not be typical network users. Instead, if you choose to create users in the ADUC Console, you should only create specialized users, such as backup administrator accounts and so on.

Best Practice—Add Users with the Add User Wizard

This may seem obvious given the focus of the book as a whole, but the SBS global community continually runs across queries for help from those who have not followed this mantra. When you add regular domain users to the network, use the Add User Wizards to ensure that the proper permissions and access are granted to the user object. The only users that could be created manually are specialized accounts that serve specific functions on the network and are not regular user objects.

Changing User Permissions

The Change User Permissions Wizard restores default settings to a user object by reapplying one of the SBS user templates to the object. The wizard can be used to create a user mailbox in Exchange, create a home folder, restore security and distribution group memberships, reset SharePoint access, and reset disk quotas.

Only network administrators can run the Change User Permissions Wizard because the wizard allows the operator to add Power User and Administrator templates to an existing user, and that could give an existing Power User object the ability to elevate his own permissions on the network. Rather than build a separate wizard that allows only a power user to reapply the User or Mobile User template to an existing user object, Microsoft chose to simply not make this wizard available to Power User accounts.

NOTE

When a power user selects a user object in the Server Management Console, a link named Change User Permissions does appear. However, when the link is clicked, the user object's properties page is displayed, not the Change User Permissions Wizard.

The second page of the Change User Permissions Wizard, shown in Figure 16.2, allows the operator to select which template to apply. Another significant selection must be made here, also.

Two radio buttons appear beneath the list of templates. You can select whether to replace the existing permissions granted to the user, or you can add the permissions defined by the template to the user, keeping any permissions that do not otherwise conflict with the template attached to the user object. The default setting in the wizard is to replace all the permissions for the user with the permissions from the template. This selection makes sense if a user received elevated permissions or the user permissions became corrupt and needed to be reset to defaults.

Alternatively, you can choose to have the settings in the template added to the existing settings for the user object. You might select this option if you had added a user, based on the User template, to some custom security groups, and then decided to apply the Mobile User settings to the user object. If you chose to replace the user settings with the template settings, the user would be removed from the custom security groups. If, however, you had several users that needed some custom settings configured, you could look at creating your own user template that contains all the settings you need for a group of users on the network.

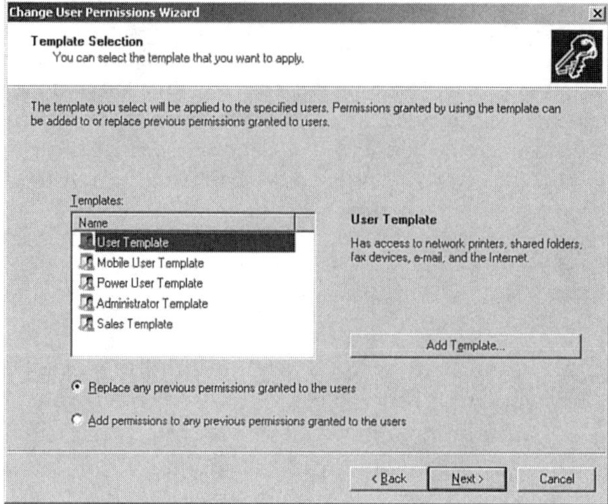

FIGURE 16.2 Any user template can be applied to an existing user object.

Understanding User Templates

A user template is simply a collection of permissions and other settings that can be applied to a user or group of users quickly, instead of having to apply each permission or setting change manually to each user. Each user template is actually stored as a disabled user object in Active Directory in the same OU as the regular user accounts. To see most of the settings stored in the template, you can open the template object in ADUC, as shown in Figure 16.3.

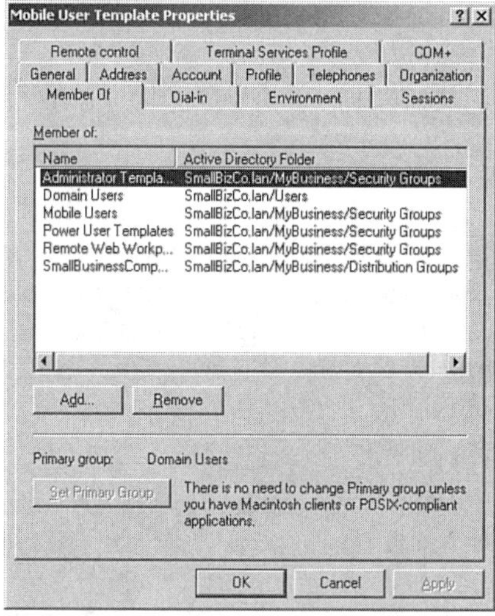

FIGURE 16.3 The security groups for a template can be viewed in the template object properties.

Creating and Modifying User Templates

Your best bet to understanding how user templates work is to go through the Add Template Wizard. This wizard is accessed from inside the Change User Permissions Wizard by clicking the Add Template button, shown previously in Figure 16.2. Or, you can run the `addtmpl.exe` program file from `C:\Program Files\Microsoft Windows Small Business Server\Administration` folder.

In the second page of the wizard, you specify a name and description for the template. You can also configure the template to be the default template used by the Add User Wizard, and you can select whether the template is visible to power users running the Add User Wizard.

In the next page of the wizard, you can select which of the existing domain security groups will apply to the template. Only existing groups are displayed in the wizard window. If you need to add security groups, you will need to do so in the ADUC Management Console. See the section "Working with Security and Distribution Groups" later in the chapter for more information on adding new security groups.

CAUTION

Be warned that you can add administrator-level security groups to the template, even if you allow power users to use the template. It might seem that if you add the Domain Admins group to the template, for example, and allow power users to create users with this template, a power user could create a new user with Domain Admin rights, log in to the domain with those rights, and have full control over the network. However, when a power user attempts to create a user with administrator-equivalent groups in the template, the Add User Wizard halts when trying to apply those permissions, and the power user is warned that she cannot fully configure the account and is given the option to keep or remove the user account.

The next page of the wizard allows you to select which Exchange distribution groups will apply to the template. You should include the default domain distribution group to the template to make sure that any user accounts created with the template receive email sent to the company distribution list. For more information on working with distribution groups, see "Working with Security and Distribution Groups" later in the chapter.

The SharePoint Access page of the wizard allows you to select the default access the template will have to the SharePoint sites on the server. You can select from Reader, Contributor, Web Designer, or Administrator, or you can prevent access to SharePoint sites by selecting none of the options.

The Address Information page allows you to include address information for the template. If you have a site with multiple users in multiple locations, you might choose to create a template based on the site address so that when users are added with the site-specific template, the correct address information is populated automatically to the user accounts. Alternatively, you can leave this information blank.

The Disk Quotas page, shown in Figure 16.4, is where you specify what the disk quota limits will be for the template, if any disk quotas are applied at all. The SBS default limits are populated in the wizard page but can be modified as necessary.

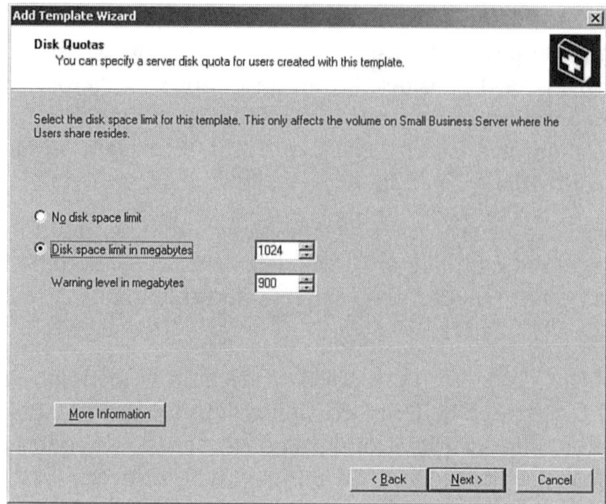

FIGURE 16.4 Templates can have disk quotas set by default.

Although customizing user templates can reduce user administration time, the level of complexity of a small business environment may not justify the time and effort needed to plan and develop custom templates. In a five-user network, for example, developing more than one custom template may be overkill. In a five-user network that is growing to 25 users, however, it may be justified.

Setting and Modifying User Limits

One of the objectives of the default SBS installation settings is to help protect a novice network administrator from misconfigurations that could end up crashing the server. Many of these are related to putting limits on disk space used so that the server system drive does not fill to capacity and bring down the system.

User configuration in SBS is no different. The SBS wizards place space limits on user accounts for mailbox size and disk space storage. These limits help keep the size of the Exchange database in check, and the disk capacity on the server is protected as well.

You may find, however, that the default limits provided by SBS simply do not match your environment. This section covers how to review and modify those settings.

Mailbox Usage

User mailboxes in the SBS implementation of Exchange 2003 are limited to 200MB. A warning is mailed to the user when the capacity of his mailbox reaches 175MB, but when the limit of 200MB is reached, all mail activity—sending and receiving included—is blocked. These limits are set at the Mailbox Store and can be modified there if you want to change (or remove) the limits across the entire network.

You can get to the Mailbox Store Properties window, shown in Figure 16.5, from Server Management, Advanced Management, First Administrative Group (Exchange), Servers, *servername*, First Storage Group, Mailbox Store (*servername*), Properties. The Limits tab displays the current settings.

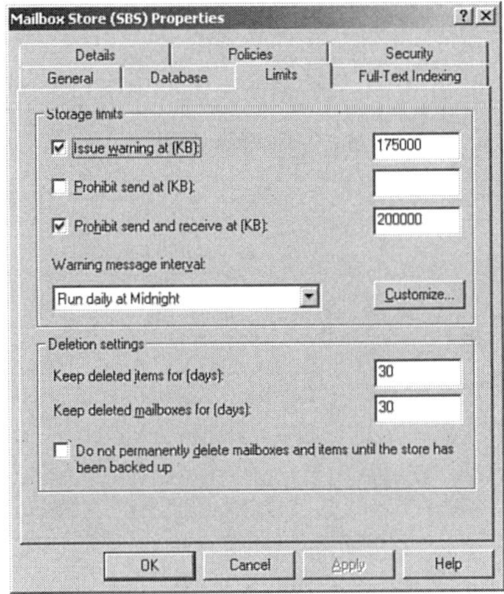

FIGURE 16.5 The default SBS mailbox limits are 175MB for the warning and 200MB to prevent sending and receiving.

Also listed in the Limits page is the deleted items retention period, which is 30 days by default. Any of the settings on this page can be changed as needed for your particular environment. If the network has only five or six users and the volume of email sent and received by the user base is low, you may be able to remove the limits on the Mailbox Store and allow the users to store more email on the server than the limits would otherwise allow. On the other hand, you will need to keep a closer eye on the total size of the Mailbox Store if you remove the limits, because a Mailbox Store without limits can unexpectedly grow to the maximum 16GB size quickly and without warning. If that happens, follow the instructions in Chapter 13, "Exchange Disaster Recovery," to restore access to the database.

Actually, though, the settings for the mailbox limits are not enforced at the Mailbox Store level. The final arbiter for mailbox size limits is actually Active Directory. Each user object has settings that determine how much mail can be stored in the Mailbox Store. When you open the Storage Limits dialog from the Exchange General tab of the user's properties, shown in Figure 16.6, you see that the default setting is to use the Mailbox Store defaults for both the storage limits and deleted item retention. Modifying the values in this area of the user properties sets the actual values that will be used for that particular user.

At this point, you may be wondering why this discussion began with settings in the Mailbox Store and user properties instead of with the explanation of a wizard. Simply put, there is no wizard for modifying these settings. When you click on the Change Mailbox and Disk Quota Limits link in the Server Management Console, the Small Business Server Help and Information window opens with links explaining how to make changes to mailbox and disk quota settings for individual users and for all users. If you need to make changes to any of these settings, you make the changes in the Exchange configuration and in Active Directory, just like you would in a non-SBS network.

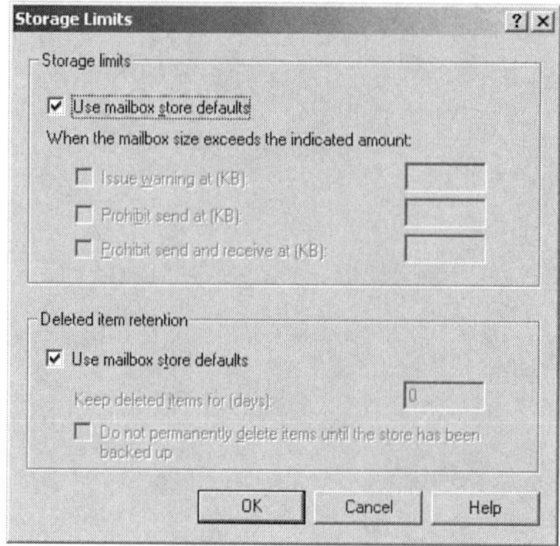

FIGURE 16.6 Storage limits and deleted item retention settings are actually stored in each user object's properties.

Disk Usage

As mentioned in the preceding paragraph, disk usage limits on the server are not configured with a wizard but directly in the properties of the volume where you want to set or modify limits. Settings for both individual users and all users are modified in the same location, the properties window of the volume, shown in Figure 16.7.

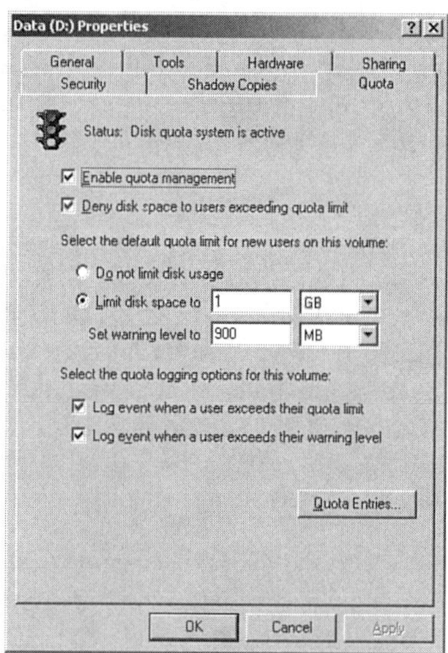

FIGURE 16.7 Disk quota limits are set for an entire volume.

By default, SBS enables quotas on the volume where the User Shared Folders are stored. If all of SBS is installed on a single volume (not a good idea), the quota applies to the entire disk. If the User Shared Folders are stored on a different partition, such as `D:` in Figure 16.7, only that partition has quotas enabled. The default limits are 900MB for the warning and 1GB for the hard block.

Individual user quota entries can be set or modified by clicking the Quota Entries button on the Quota tab. The resulting Quota Entries window, shown in Figure 16.8, lists all the user objects, including user templates, their quota limits, and the amount of space used in size and percentage of quota.

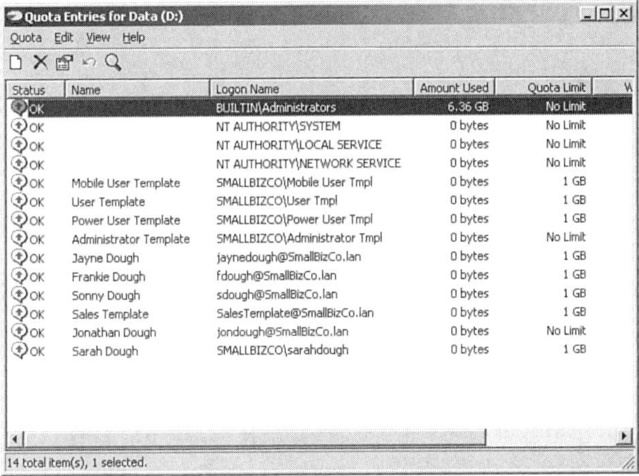

FIGURE 16.8 The Quota Entries window details the quota settings for all user objects on the network.

From this window, you can edit the quota settings for the individual objects by double-clicking on the object. You can also add or delete quota entries using the icons in the toolbar. The Add User Wizard and the Remove User Wizard take care of the necessary quota entry management automatically. If you do remove a quota entry from the list, the next time that the user attempts to store data on the volume, the quota entry will be re-created with the default settings from the volume.

> **NOTE**
>
> If you delete a user object from the network without using the wizards, the quota entry for the user may not get removed. You can easily spot these entries because the Name field shows `[Account Information Unknown]`, and the Logon Name displays a user SID. You can safely remove any entries like this from the Quota Entry screen.

Working with Security and Distribution Groups

Security groups and distributions groups have their own nodes in the Server Management Console tree. The level of management needed for these groups is not as complex as for user objects, but because user templates can use custom security and distribution groups, they are worth at least a brief mention.

Security groups and distribution groups are the two types of groups that can be defined in Active Directory. A security group is used to allocate or restrict access permissions to areas on the network for the members of the group. A distribution group creates a mail alias in Exchange that delivers messages addressed to the group to the mailboxes of each of the members of the group.

Managing Security Groups

When you select the Security Groups node in the Server Management Console, the list of all the security groups defined on the network appears, along with links for security group tasks. Table 16.2 describes the three tasks that can be performed on security groups from the Server Management Console.

TABLE 16.2 Server Management Tasks Related to Security Groups

Task	Description
Add a Security Group	Opens the Add Security Group Wizard, which walks you through the process of naming and adding users to a new group
Change Group Properties	Opens the ADUC Properties page for the selected security group
Remove Security Group	Deletes the selected security group from the network

Each security group has four tabs in the Properties page: General, which includes the name and description of the group; Members, which lists the user and other objects that belong to the group; Members Of, which lists the groups to which this group belongs; and Managed By, which identifies the user object responsible for managing the group, if any. These settings can be viewed by double-clicking on the group in the list, or by clicking the Change Group Properties task when the group object is selected.

Managing Distribution Groups

The same basic tasks present for security groups are also available for distribution groups in the Server Management Console, but one other task, Manage POP3 E-mail, appears as well. Whereas the properties page for a security group has only four tabs, the properties page for a distribution group has seven. The first four are the same as the security group, and the additional three are related to Exchange. Table 16.3 lists the settings organized into each of the tabs.

TABLE 16.3 Exchange Settings for Distribution Group Objects

Tab Name	Settings Available
Exchange General	Alias name, display name, message size limits, and message restrictions
E-mail Addresses	Lists all the addresses that will be delivered to the distribution group
Exchange Advanced	Advanced settings, including simple display name, hiding the group from Exchange address lists, and delivery report settings

Managing Computers in SBS 2003

For users to get the full experience of SBS, their computers must be joined to the domain. But adding the workstation to the domain through the Network Identification Wizard or just joining the domain through the System control panel is not sufficient to receive all the benefits of SBS domain membership. To get the full effect, you must rely on the wizards.

Just like with the user management wizards discussed at the beginning of the chapter, not all computer management wizards are available to domain power users in the Server Management Console. Table 16.4 lists the tasks related to computer management and their availability to administrators and power users.

TABLE 16.4 Access to Computer Management Tools by Administrators and Power Users

Tool	Administrator	Power User
Set Up Client Computers	Yes	Yes
Create Remote Connection Disk	Yes	Yes
Assign Applications to Client Computers	Yes	Yes
View Computer Settings	Yes	Yes
Set Up Client Applications	Yes	No
Manage Computer	Yes	No
View Event Logs	Yes	No
Offer Remote Assistance	Yes	No
Connect to Computer via Terminal Services	Yes	No
Remove Computer from Network	Yes	No
Set Up Server Computers	Yes	No
View Services	Yes	No

In addition, the power user version of the Server Management Console has only one grouping of tasks for computer management. The administrator version has nodes for Client Computers and Server Computers. The only item from Table 16.4 that is present in the Server Computers node is the View Services task, which brings up the Services console for the selected server computer.

Getting computers joined to the SBS network is a two-step process. The first step is to create the computer object in Active Directory and configure the settings on the network for the computer object. The second step is to join the computer to the domain and complete the configuration processes on the computer. These two steps are broken down in the next two sections.

Adding Computers to the Network

Three different methods can be used to create a computer account on the domain. Two of them are wizards; the third is a manual process.

Using the Add User Wizard

At the end of the Add User Wizard is a page where you can configure a computer for the user being added. In the Set Up Client Computer page of the Add User Wizard, you can specify the name of the computer to add for the user. If you choose to add the computer, whose default name will be the user's logon name with "01" added to the end, the next page in the wizard is the Client Applications page. In this page, you select which of the predefined applications are pushed out to the workstation when it logs in to the network. For more information about managing client applications, see the "Assigning Applications to Computers" section later in the chapter.

Table 16.5 lists the default applications on this page. Some of these applications are mandatory, and, although the check box next to them can be disabled, you will get an error that the installation cannot be removed or modified.

TABLE 16.5 Default Client Applications

Application	Description	Mandatory
Client Operating System Service Packs	Windows 2000 SP4, Windows XP SP1 (pre-SBS SP1) or Windows XP SP2 (post-SBS SP1)	Yes
Internet Explorer 6.0	IE 6.0 installs if the client workstation has an earlier version installed	No
Microsoft Office Outlook 2003	Outlook 2003 SP1 is installed postSBS-SP1	No
Shared Fax Client	Only installed if shared FAX services are installed on the server	No

The next page in the Add User Wizard is the Mobile Client and Offline User page. In this page, you can select to install the Connection Manager or ActiveSync 3.8 on the workstation. The Connection Manager allows the workstation to connect to the SBS network from an external network. The ActiveSync 3.8 install not only installs the ActiveSync 3.8 client on the workstation, but it also copies the self-signed SSL certificate, created by the CEICW, to the workstation so that the user can access the server using a secure connection from a PDA synched with the workstation.

Using the Set Up Client Computers Wizard

The Set Up Client Computers Wizard allows you to create a new computer account not specifically associated with a user account. You would use this wizard if you are adding a new workstation to the network but not adding a new user at the same time. You might also need to run this wizard if an existing computer account had to be removed from the domain for some reason.

In the second page of the wizard, shown in Figure 16.9, you can add one or more computer names to the network. Simply enter the name of the computer in the Client Computer Name field and click Add for as many computer objects as you want to add.

The next two pages of the wizard are exactly the same as the Client Applications and Mobile Client and Offline User pages in the Add User Wizard. Table 16.5 discussed the default applications available in this page, and the "Assigning Applications to Computers" section later in the chapter covers how to customize the list of applications available. One other group of settings can be modified in this page by clicking on the Advanced button. This brings up the Advanced Client Computer Settings dialog where you can enable or disable application settings for the client computer. The settings are listed and described in Table 16.6.

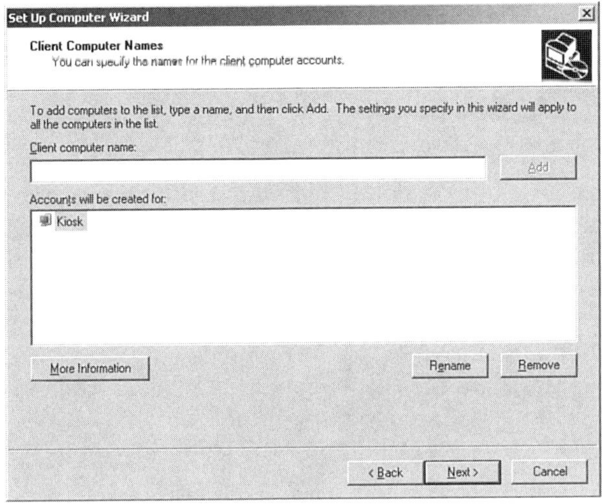

FIGURE 16.9 Multiple computer objects can be added at one time in the Set Up Client Computers Wizard.

TABLE 16.6 Advanced Client Computer Settings

Option	Description
Internet Explorer Settings	Modifies the connection settings and populates the Favorites menu
Outlook Profile Settings	Configures the Outlook Profile for the user account to connect to the SBS server
Desktop Settings	Creates desktop shortcuts and places links in the My Network Places folder
Fax Printer	Sets up a printer object for the shared Fax printer on the server (if FAX services have been installed on the server)
Printers	Adds printer objects for all shared printers on the server
Fax Configuration Information	Configures fax settings on the workstation and synchronizes those settings with the server
Remote Desktop	Enables Remote Desktop connectivity for workstations running Windows XP Pro

Using Active Directory Users and Computers

Client computers can be set up manually in Active Directory Users and Computers, but there are a few catches to this method. First, you need to add the computer to the Active Directory tree in the My Business, Computers, SBSComputers organizational unit. If you add the computer object to the Computers container immediately below the root of the domain, the computer object will not be able to be fully managed by SBS.

Second, you have to manually configure applications for the computer using the Assign Applications to Client Computers Wizard, discussed in more detail in the next section, "Assigning Applications to Computers." This step is handled automatically by the Add User and Set Up Client Computer Wizards.

Third, if the computer account is set up manually, you may encounter problems running the Connect Computer Wizard, described in the "Using the Connect Computer Wizard" section later in the chapter. If you manually create the computer object and do not run the Connect Computer Wizard with a domain admin-level account, you will not be able to join the workstation to the domain.

The bottom line here is that unless you have a workstation that you do not want to be managed by SBS and you want to take care of every aspect of managing that computer account manually, use one of the wizards to set up the client workstation. You will save yourself time up front and avoid headaches down the road.

Assigning Applications to Computers

This chapter already introduced the client application setup process used during the client computer setup wizards. But beyond the steps in the wizards, what exactly does the assign application process do?

When the assign applications process runs, it creates a set of files and folders on the SBS server that will be accessed by the workstations when the user logs on. Table 16.7 lists the key components, their locations, and a brief description of their functions.

TABLE 16.7 Components of the Assign Applications Process

Component	Location	Description
`SBS_LOGIN_SCRIPT.bat`	*domainname*\sysvol*domainname*\scripts	Runs at each user login and calls the client application setup program
Client Application Setup Wizard	*servername*\clients\setup\setup.exe	The program file that runs the setup for the selected client application installs
Workstation Install File	*servername*\clients\response*workstationname*\apps.dat	The response file used by the Client Application Setup Wizard, unique to each workstation
Application Install Location	*servername*\ClientApps\	Stores a folder for each application listed in the Client Applications page of the computer setup wizards

When the Set Up Client Computer Wizard is run, the wizard creates a folder for each workstation under *servername*\clients\response. Then the `apps.dat` file is built for the workstation, indicating which of the applications stored in *servername*\ClientApps should be installed on the workstation. The content of a sample `apps.dat` file is as follows:

```
<?xml version="1.0"?>
<root><apps><app id="{F28193FE-08F8-4eae-B714-D425838F46FE}" canChangePath="0"
➥diskSpace="943718400" needsReboot="1" time="45" order="1" refCount="1">
<name><![CDATA[Client Operating System Service Packs]]></name>
```

```
<cmdLine><![CDATA[]]></cmdLine><defaultPath><![CDATA[%systemdrive%]]>
</defaultPath></app>
<app id="{A792B130-2B57-44e8-87FB-0B5C3BC2EDE7}" canChangePath="0"
➥diskSpace="73400320" needsReboot="1" time="15" order="2" refCount="1">
<name><![CDATA[Internet Explorer 6.0]]></name>
<cmdLine><![CDATA["\\SBS\ClientApps\IE6\ie6setup.exe " /C:"ie6wzd /s:""#e""
➥/V:I /Q:A /R:N"]]></cmdLine>
<defaultPath><![CDATA[%programfiles%\Internet Explorer]]></defaultPath></app>
</apps>
<miscdata autoLogoff="0" userCanChange="0" isUpgrade="0" mobile="0" activeSync="0"
➥optionsMask="511"/></root>
```

Although the file data may seem a little difficult to read at first, after you have analyzed a few of the files, it becomes easier to process. In this sample, two applications are defined for the workstation. The first is identified as application ID `{F28193FE-08F8-4eae-B714-D425838F46FE}`. It needs approximately 950MB of free disk space to install, and it needs a reboot when complete. The name of this piece is the Client Operating System Service Pack, and it executes the installation from a command-line provided by the script. The second application needs only 75MB of disk space to install and also requires a reboot. This application is Internet Explorer 6.0, and the setup program at `\\SBS\ClientApps\IE6\ie6setup.exe` uses the command-line parameters identified in the `<cmdline>` tag. The `<miscdata>` tag tells the setup application not to automatically log the user off at the end of the install, not to allow the user to change any of the settings for the installation, and that the workstation does not need the connection manager or ActiveSync installed.

Adding Other Client Applications for Installation

If you have additional applications that need to be added to all workstations in the domain, you can add entries for those applications to show up in the Set Up Client Computers Wizard. Doing this is a two-step process.

Preparing the Applications for Installation

The first step to adding applications for client installation is to prepare the application installer on the network. The application installer ideally resides in the ClientApps share along with the other application installers, but you can locate the installer elsewhere on the network. If you choose to put the installer in a different location, you need to create a new share that points to the path where the installer is located, and you need to set Full Control permissions on the share for domain users and add Read and Execute permissions for appropriate users and groups on the folder, and those permissions must be applied to all subfolders as well.

When you have the installation path ready, you need to copy the installer information into that path. For some applications, this may be as simple as copying the contents of the installation CD to the share. For other applications, such as Office-related installs, you may need to do an administrative install to build the installer directory on the server for the application. After the install data has been put on the server, you are ready to move to the second step.

CAUTION

Before adding new client applications for the entire network, make sure that you understand and are compliant with the licensing restrictions for the software.

Running the Set Up Client Applications Wizard

The last step to adding the application to the Client Applications list is to run the Set Up Client Applications Wizard. This wizard is found in the Client Computers node of the Server Management Console. Follow these steps to complete the wizard:

1. Launch the Set Up Client Applications Wizard and click Next.
2. In the Available Applications page, click Add.
3. In the Application Information dialog box, shown in Figure 16.10, enter the name of the application and click Browse to locate the installer program on the server. Click OK when finished.

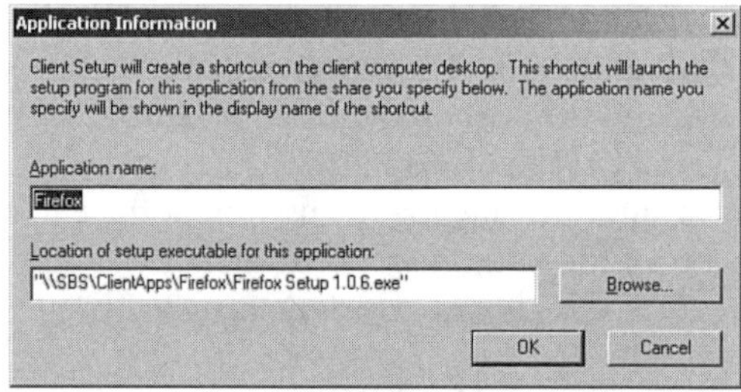

FIGURE 16.10 The Application Information dialog box collects information that will be used to create the installation shortcut on the user's desktop.

4. If there are spaces in the path to the installer, you get a warning dialog box. Click Yes to continue; then click Edit and add double quotation marks around the path to the installer program and click OK.
5. Click Next; then click Finish to close the wizard.
6. If you have added new applications, you get a dialog asking whether you want to assign the applications to client computers now. If you click Yes, the Assign Applications Wizard launches. If you click No, the Set Up Client Applications Wizard closes with no further action.

As you can see in Figure 16.10, the new application appears as a shortcut on the user's desktop. The shortcut points to the application installer listed in the Application Information dialog box. The user still has to double-click on the shortcut to install the application.

Using the Connect Computer Wizard

The real magic of adding the client computer to the network is done in the Connect Computer Wizard. Each time you add a workstation to the domain using the Add User or Set Up Client Computers Wizard, the wizard displays a dialog box telling you to run the Connect Computer Wizard to complete the computer setup process. This particular wizard is a web tool, not a program that is run locally. In addition, not all of the wizard runs in the web interface—some of the last steps of the wizard are included in the SBS logon script. This section of the chapter breaks down the parts and pieces of the Connect Computer Wizard.

The Web Component

The Connect Computer Wizard is accessed from the SBS server at `http://`*`servername`*`/connectcomputer`, which launches the first part of the wizard. The first page of the wizard provides a single link, Connect to the Network Now, which can be selected. When the link is clicked, the workstation downloads an ActiveX control from the server, and an installation prompt appears. After the ActiveX component is downloaded and run, the Small Business Server Network Configuration Wizard starts.

In the first page of the wizard, you enter the username and password of a user on the network, usually the name of the user who will be using the workstation. In the next page of the wizard, shown in Figure 16.11, you can select which users on the network will be assigned to the workstation and whether a local profile needs to be copied into that user's new profile on the workstation.

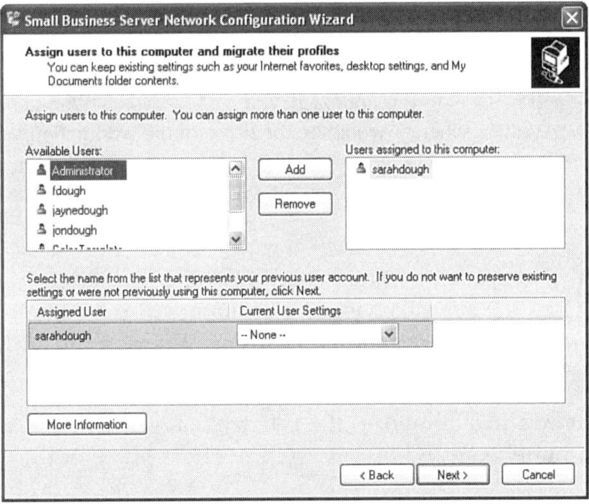

FIGURE 16.11 The Connect Computer Wizard allows you to select which network users will be assigned to the workstation.

Best Practice—Administrator Access and the Connect Computer Wizard

Part of the process of the Connect Computer Wizard is to give the assigned users selected in the Assign Users page of the wizard administrator access to the workstation. The domain user objects are placed in the local Administrators group on the workstation after the workstation is joined to the domain. Doing this allows the remainder of the workstation management tools to run correctly because the additional tools require that the user running them have local administrator access on the box.

This scenario flies in the face of what many IT consultants are trying to accomplish, which is limited user access to the local machine to help combat virus and Spyware problems. When a user accesses the workstation with User or Power User permissions, the chance of unintended software installation (such as Spyware or Trojans) is reduced. However, reducing a user to User or Power User permissions on a workstation in an SBS network will keep some of the computer maintenance tools from working correctly.

One suggestion that frequently comes up in discussions within the SBS community is to go back and remove the user object from the local Administrators group after the workstation has completed the Connect Computer Wizard process. However, if additional application installs need to be pushed to the workstation, those installs will fail using the regular SBS management tools unless the user is added back to the Administrators group.

One option to consider is to create a security group in the domain (perhaps called "Workstation Admins") and add the security group to the local Administrators group on each of the workstations. Then, when an update is needed that requires local admin access on the workstation, you could go back and add the Domain Users group to the Workstation Admins group on the network, and the next time the user logs in, she will have local administrator access to the workstation and not necessarily be any the wiser about it. After the software push has been completed across the network, you could go back and remove the Domain Users group from the Workstation Admins group, and the next time the user logs in, she will no longer have administrator access to the workstation.

To have even more granularity to this approach, you could create a "Workstation *X* Admins" group for each workstation, where *X* would be the name of the workstation, and then add and remove the Domain Users group or individual user objects to the group to fine-tune your control over who has admin access to the workstation.

The next page of the Connect Computer Wizard is where you select the name for the computer. The page lists the available workstation names in the domain. If you logged in with the username that had a workstation assigned to it during the Add User Wizard, that workstation name will be selected automatically.

The final page of the wizard summarizes the activity that will take place. After you click Finish, the workstation reboots and moves on to the next phase of the process.

The Reboot Cycle

When the web portion of the wizard completes, the workstation reboots. When the workstation comes back up, it automatically logs in with the user object created in the web section of the wizard and makes changes to the network settings of the workstation. This is where the workstation name is changed and the join to the domain is complete.

This is also the point in the process where the new domain user profile is created and the settings from the old profile are copied, if a source profile was selected in the web section of the wizard. After these steps have been completed, the wizard reboots the computer one last time.

The Logon Script

After the last reboot completes, the user is presented with a standard logon window. At this point, the user can log in with his domain username and password, and the domain logon script completes the wizard process. The user sees a dialog box prompting the user to run the Client Setup Wizard. When the user clicks the button to start the installation, the `\\servername\clients\setup\setup.exe` wizard program is launched. This wizard collects the name of the workstation and opens the appropriate `apps.dat` file in the `\\servername\clients\response` folder. After this information is collected, the wizard begins.

The second page of the wizard allows the user to enter his password so that when the workstation reboots after the completion of the wizard, the user will be automatically logged back in. The wizard then begins the installation of the server packages. The latest operating system service pack is installed first, followed by Internet Explorer 6.0 (if it is not already installed), followed by any other applications selected during the Set Up the Client Workstation Wizard. After the wizard has completed the installation, the workstation reboots. The next time the user logs in, the workstation is ready for use.

16

NOTE

The logon script runs every time the user logs in, but the user generally only sees the Client Setup Wizard screen once. On subsequent launches, the Client Setup Wizard compares the contents of the `apps.dat` file to the applications already installed on the workstation, and if there are no differences, the Client Setup Wizard completes silently, and the user is none the wiser.

When additional applications have been added using the Set Up Client Applications Wizard, the Client Setup Wizard creates a shortcut on the user's desktop that points to the installer for the new application(s).

Adding Servers

The process of adding servers to the SBS network is similar to the process for adding client computers but does not have as many options. There are two main methods for adding servers, discussed in the following sections.

Using the Set Up Server Computers Wizard

The best way to set up a new server and connect it to the network is to run the Set Up Server Computers Wizard in the Server Computers node of the Server Management Console. The first page of the wizard asks for the name of the computer. The second page of the wizard determines whether the server will get a dynamic IP address through DHCP or whether it will have a static IP address and what that address will be. The last page of the wizard summarizes the setup for the server computer and instructs you to run the Connect Computer Wizard to complete the process.

CAUTION

There is a known issue with the IP address information not getting set correctly if the server name has capital letters in the Set Up Server Computers Wizard. See KB 889029 (`http://support.microsoft.com/?id=889029`) for more information.

On the SBS server side, the wizard creates the computer object in the MyBusiness, Computers, SBSServers OU. If you give the server a static IP address, the wizard also modifies the DHCP settings to exclude the IP address assigned to the new server from the DHCP scope, if the address is not already within an excluded range of addresses.

When the new server runs the Connect Computer Wizard, it goes through a similar process to a client computer. The wizard comes up, asks for a username and password (which should be a domain admin account), and then asks the user to select which computer name to use for the server. Then the wizard finishes and restarts the server. The server logs in with the SBS account created in the wizard, changes the name and domain affiliation of the server, and makes changes to the network configuration, if needed. The server then reboots again, and the server is now ready to participate as a member of the SBS domain.

Manually Joining the Server to the Domain

Because much less configuration is done to a server during the Connect Computer Wizard than for a client workstation, you may opt to join the server to the domain manually. You still need to perform a couple of manual configuration items if you choose to go with this option.

First, when you join the domain from the member server console, the computer object is placed in the Computer container in Active Directory. You need to move the computer object into the appropriate OU after the computer has been joined. Member servers go into the MyBusiness, Computers, SBSServers OU. Domain controllers should already be in the Domain Controllers OU as a result of the `dcpromo` process, but you should confirm this.

Second, if the server is using a static IP address, you need to make sure that the IP address has been excluded from the DHCP scope on the SBS server so that a conflicting address is not handed out to a workstation by the DHCP server process.

Best Practice—Adding a Domain Controller to the SBS Network

If you want to add an additional domain controller to the SBS network, use the `dcpromo` tool to configure the new server correctly. The `dcpromo` tool takes care of all the configuration necessary on the server to get it to participate correctly in Active Directory, so no other steps are needed. Because not every server that could be added to the SBS network, such as a dedicated web server or a terminal server, needs to be a domain controller, be absolutely certain that you need another domain controller on the network before you run `dcpromo`.

Troubleshooting User and Computer Issues

The single most commonly asked question in the SBS community relates to the Connect Computer Wizard. A quick scan of Google Groups for Connect Computer yields thousands of threads reporting the same problem. With SBS 2003 prior to SP1, the error read "The list of users and computers could not be found on the server. Make sure that the Small Business Server network adapters are configured correctly." After SPS 2003 SP1 has been installed, a more reasonable error message is presented, which reads "Microsoft Windows Small Business Server Client Setup has detected that this computer is not configured correctly." The error message goes on to describe how to resolve the problem, but the simple answer is this: The IP configuration for the workstation needs to have its DNS server settings changed to point to the IP address of the SBS server. If the client workstation points to any other IP address for DNS, the Connect Computer Wizard will fail.

When trying to troubleshoot other errors related to the Connect Computer Wizard and its related components and other wizards, several log files can help lead you to the source of the problem. Table 16.8 lists and describes many of these log files.

One last troubleshooting tip for resolving user and computer problems in the SBS environment is to make sure that the wizards have been run. In many cases, running the Change User Permissions Wizard to reset the settings for a user object can resolve access and other problems being encountered. This is especially the case if you suspect that a user or computer object was created without using the wizards. A quick search in the Active Directory Users and Computers console for the user or computer object can tell you whether the object was created with a wizard. If the object can be found in the default Computers or Users containers just beneath the root of the domain, the object was not created by the wizard.

TABLE 16.8 Log File Locations and Descriptions for User and Computer SBS Wizards

Filename	Location	Path	Description
SBSClientApps.log	Workstation	C:\Program Files\Microsoft Windows Small Business Server\Clients	Logs activities of the Client Setup Wizard (applnch.exe) at user logon
SBSNetSetup.log	Workstation	C:\Program Files\Microsoft Windows Small Business Server\Clients	Logs network configuration activities of the Connect Computer Wizard
Sbsmig.log	Workstation	C:\Program Files\Microsoft Windows Small Business Server\Clients	Logs changes to the workstation name and group memberships as part of the Connect Computer Wizard
add_security_group_wizard.log	Server	C:\Program Files\Microsoft Windows Small Business Server\Support	Logs activities of the Add Security Group Wizard
add_template_wizard.log	Server	C:\Program Files\Microsoft Windows Small Business Server\Support	Logs activities of the Add Template Wizard
add_user_wizard.log	Server	C:\Program Files\Microsoft Windows Small Business Server\Support	Logs output from the Add User Wizard
change_user_permissions_wizard.log	Server	C:\Program Files\Microsoft Windows Small Business Server\Support	Logs activities of the Change User Permissions Wizard
delgroup.log	Server	C:\Program Files\Microsoft Windows Small Business Server\Support	Notes any groups deleted using the Server Management Console tasks
delusr.log	Server	C:\Program Files\Microsoft Windows Small Business Server\Support	Notes any users deleted using the Server Management Console tasks
ExtWiz.log	Server	C:\Program Files\Microsoft Windows Small Business Server\Support	Logs activities from the Set Up Client Applications Wizard
PassPol.log	Server	C:\Program Files\Microsoft Windows Small Business Server\Support	Logs activities from the Configure Password Policies Wizard
scw.log	Server	C:\Program Files\Microsoft Windows Small Business Server\Support	Logs activities from the Set Up Client Computers and Set Up Server Computers Wizards

Summary

This chapter has broken down many of the wizards used to manage users and computers to show you some of the work that gets done "behind the scenes" in the SBS environment. If nothing else, the reader should come away from this chapter with a better appreciation for the work done by the wizards as well as a reference for tools to use to troubleshoot problems that do arise.

Best Practice Summary

- Add users using the Add User Wizard—Although it may seem obvious to some, using the Add User Wizard in SBS is more than just a strong recommendation. A number of customizations are applied to a user object with the wizard that would take too long to perform by hand.
- Administrator access and the Connect Computer Wizard—The Connect Computer Wizard adds the user to the Local Administrators group on the workstation as part of the setup process. If you choose to remove the user from the Local Administrators group after the initial configuration of the workstation, be aware that some of the SBS user and computer management processes will fail, such as adding new applications through the SBS logon script.
- Adding a domain controller to the SBS network—Use `dcpromo` instead of the Set Up Server Computers Wizard to join a new domain controller to the SBS network.

CHAPTER 17

Integrating the Macintosh into a Small Business Server 2003 Environment

IN THIS CHAPTER

- Sharing Files with a Macintosh from an SBS Server
- Secure Website Access
- Accessing Exchange from the Macintosh
- Remote Connectivity Tools for the Macintosh

For the last few years, Apple Computer has been producing products that have become increasingly popular among the home user market—the iMac, the eMac, and now the Mac Mini. These devices have started making their way into the business arena as well. In certain industries—graphic design, audio production, advertising, publishing, and so on—the Macintosh platform has always been present, but some Windows administrators have been reluctant to figure out how to incorporate the Macintosh platform into their Windows networks.

The SMB market seems to have a greater presence of Macintosh devices interacting with Windows-based PCs than the enterprise space. To that end, the SMB consultant has been struggling to discover how to connect the Macs to the network in such as way that he doesn't impact the way users on either platform expect to work.

This chapter outlines the steps necessary to configure both the Macintosh devices and the SBS server to allow the Macintosh platform equal opportunity access to the services provided by the SBS server.

Best Practice—Keep Mac OS Up to Date

Just like Microsoft, Apple periodically releases updates and security fixes to Mac OS. With Mac OS 9 and earlier, users had to run the Software Update control panel to check for updates from the Apple servers. Later versions of OS 9 included the option to schedule update checks weekly, but the process is still manual.

Mac OS X has an automatic update feature that checks weekly for updates by default. As with Automatic Updates on Windows XP, Software Update can be configured to automatically download the files for important updates in the background, so when the user is notified that updates are available, the files are ready for installation.

Mac users should be given permission and encouraged to install these updates when they become available.

Sharing Files with a Macintosh from an SBS Server

Sharing files between Macintosh and PC workstations has always been a challenge. The process has always been a little easier on the Macintosh side of the fence because Macintosh workstations have long been able to read and write PC-formatted floppy disks and CDs. Storing files on a common server is the easiest way to share files between platforms, but even that approach is not without its difficulties. This section covers the configurations necessary to allow Macintosh clients to connect to the SBS server and store files on the server.

Connecting Using Services for Macintosh (Mac OS 9 and/or Mac OS X)

Microsoft began providing file-sharing support for the Macintosh platform back with Windows NT with a product called Services for Macintosh. When Services for Macintosh was installed on a Windows NT server, the server would appear to a Macintosh client as though it were an AppleShare server, the standard server technology from Apple. To do this, Services for Macintosh had to do two tasks. First, it had to install and configure the AppleTalk protocol on the network interface so that the Macintosh workstations could see the NT server on the network. Second, it had to add another file format layer on top of NTFS to mimic the Apple Files System (AFS). Given these two modifications, Macintosh workstations could connect to a Windows NT server and share files on the server with other Macintosh clients and with PC workstations.

With the release of Windows 2000 came an update to Services for Macintosh. These updates included some significant changes in the way that Services for Macintosh was installed and configured on the server. No real changes were made to the AppleTalk network protocol; it has remained fairly constant since Apple first introduced it. But significant changes were made to the way the file system was handled because the newer Macintosh operating systems used an updated file system to handle larger sized drives.

The Services for Macintosh product did not change significantly from Windows 2000 to Windows 2003, and there is no difference between the version that comes with SBS and the version included with other Windows 2003 server versions. Unfortunately, some of the limitations introduced with the Services for Macintosh product with Windows 2000 have remained.

Still, Services for Macintosh remains the only way to connect Macintosh computers running Mac OS 9 or earlier to a Windows server without a third-party product. And for an environment that has Macintoshes running both OS 9 and OS X, Services for Macintosh is the only way to connect both platforms to the server so that files can be shared effortlessly between the platforms.

Services for Macintosh uses the AppleTalk network protocol to allow Mac OS 9 and Mac OS X workstations to connect to the SBS server as though it were an AppleShare server. There are several key differences between the way a Macintosh sees files and folders on an AppleShare server and the way Windows PCs see files and folders on a Windows share. When using this method to allow Macs to access files on the server, you will have to create a new share on the server for the Macs to use, even if the share already exists for Windows PCs.

Best Practice—Installing File Services for Macintosh

If the network environment has Macintosh workstations running both Mac OS 9 and Mac OS X, you should configure the server with File Services for Macintosh and run AppleShare connections on both Mac OS versions. This is the only way to guarantee file compatibility between the OS 9 and OS X workstations without going to a third-party product.

Installing File Services for Macintosh

Services for Macintosh is not installed on an SBS server by default. Use the following steps to install Services for Macintosh on the SBS server:

1. Open Add or Remove Programs in the Control Panel.
2. Click Add/Remove Windows Components.
3. Select Other Network File and Print Services and click Details.
4. Enable File Services for Macintosh.
5. Click OK.
6. Click Next.
7. Wait for the components to install, and click Finish.
8. Close the Windows installer and the Add or Remove Programs Control Panel.

Configuring File Server for Macintosh

After the service is installed, the server must be configured so that the Macintosh clients can see the server and access shares. By default, Services for Macintosh is configured only to allow connections from Macintosh clients that have the Microsoft User Authentication Module (UAM) installed. Because most systems will not have that component installed yet, the server needs to be reconfigured to accept connections from clients with the UAM installed or those still using the clear-text authentication method provided by Apple. Ultimately, you will want to install the UAM on all Macintosh workstations and change this setting back to Microsoft because the Microsoft UAM encrypts the username and password for authentication across the network.

Follow these steps to configure Services for Macintosh to allow the Apple clear-text authentication method and identify the name of the server as it will appear on the Macintosh network:

1. Right-click on My Computer (server) and select Manage.
2. Right-click on Shared Folders and select Configure File Server for Macintosh.
3. Change Enable Authentication to Apple Clear Text or Microsoft.
4. Click Apply and then click OK.
5. Make note of the server name listed in the Server Name for AppleTalk Workstations field. You will need this name later.

Creating Shares on the Server

Unfortunately, Services for Macintosh cannot use existing Windows shares, so if you want to have Macintosh clients access data on existing Windows shares, you will have to re-create those shares specifically for the Macintoshes. Any future shares can be created as both Windows and Macintosh shares at the same time, but any existing shares that need to be accessed by both platforms will need to have separate entries in the share listings. Follow these steps to create Macintosh shares for existing Windows shares:

1. Right-click on My Computer and select Manage.
2. Expand the Shared Folders icon.
3. Right-click on Shares and select New Share.
4. Click Next.
5. Enter the path to the folder on the hard drive or click Browse to select the folder.
6. Click Next.
7. If the folder selected is already shared to your Windows clients, uncheck the Microsoft Windows Users check box.
8. Enable the Apple Macintosh Users check box and enter a name for the share in the Share Name field.
9. Click Next.
10. Click Finish.
11. Click Close.
12. Right-click on the new share and select Properties.
13. Uncheck the This Volume Is Read-Only check box and click OK.
14. Close the Properties window.

Installing the Microsoft UAM

To take advantage of the additional security provided by the Microsoft UAM, you need to install it on each Macintosh that will connect to the server using Services for Macintosh. Follow these steps to download and install the correct UAM for the Macintosh:

1. Go to: `http://www.microsoft.com/mac/otherproducts/otherproducts.aspx?pid=windows2000sfm`.
2. Install the appropriate UAM for your operating system:
   - OS X:
     1. Download the `UAM for OS X 10.1 or later` installer.
     2. Open the `MSUAM_for_X` folder and run `Install MSUAM for X.pkg`.
   - OS 9 and earlier:
     1. Download the `UAM for OS 8.5 to 9.2 installer`.
     2. Open the `MSUAM_for_Classic` folder and copy the `MS UAM 5.0` file into the `AppleShare Folder` in the `System Folder`.

Enabling AppleTalk on the Macintosh (OS X Only)

Macintosh computers running Mac OS 9 or earlier have the AppleTalk network protocol enabled by default. With Mac OS X version 10.2 and later, the AppleTalk protocol is disabled by default. For Macintosh computers running OS X 10.2 or later, AppleTalk must be enabled on the workstation. Follow these steps to enable the AppleTalk protocol on the Mac OS X workstations:

17

1. Open System Preferences by selecting the Apple menu, System Preferences, as shown in Figure 17.1.

FIGURE 17.1 The Apple menu contains links to several operating system functions, including a shortcut to the System Preferences application.

2. Click the Network icon.
3. Select Built-in Ethernet and click Configure.
4. Click the AppleTalk tab and enable the Make AppleTalk Active check box.
5. Click Apply Now and close System Preferences.

Configuring Directory Access on the Macintosh (OS 10.2 and Later)

In addition to enabling AppleTalk in the Network preferences, the AppleTalk protocol must also be enabled in the Directory Access application. Follow these steps to enable AppleTalk and disable the Active Directory and SMB components within Directory Access. These instructions and figures specifically cover the user interface in Mac OS 10.3. The steps still apply to Mac OS 10.2, but the interface will appear slightly differently. These steps cannot be completed on Mac OS 10.1 and earlier.

1. Open the Directory Access application by selecting Macintosh HD, Applications, Utilities, Directory Access.
2. Click the lock to make changes (see Figure 17.2).

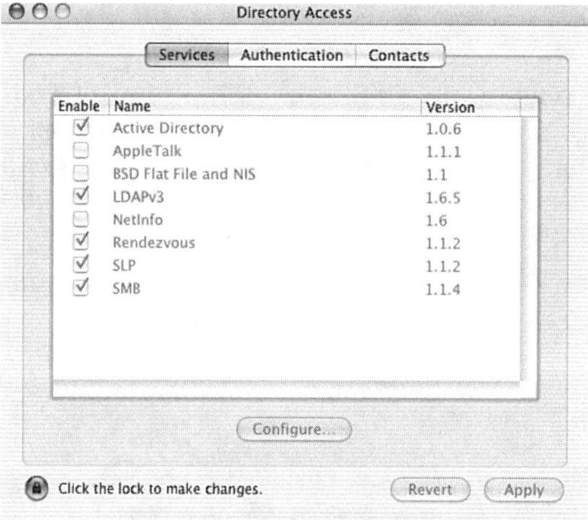

FIGURE 17.2 Directory Access settings can be locked and unlocked to prevent accidental configuration changes.

3. Enter the appropriate username and password for the Macintosh.
4. Disable Active Directory, SMB, and LDAPv3.
5. Enable AppleTalk (see Figure 17.3).
6. Click Apply and quit Directory Access.

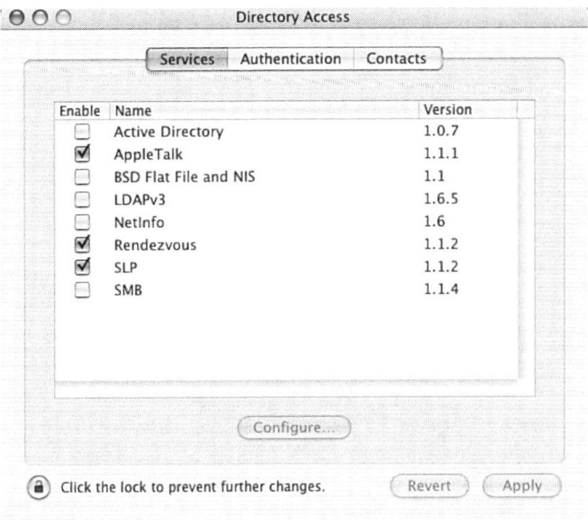

FIGURE 17.3 In an AppleTalk-only environment, only AppleTalk, Rendezvous, and SLP are needed in Directory Access.

Connecting to the Server—Connect to Share Method (OS X Only)

Now that the server and the workstation are both configured, you can connect to the server share from the Macintosh. In Macintosh-speak, this is known as *mounting a volume* because a new disk volume icon appears on the desktop when the share connection is made. There are two methods for doing this from a Mac OS X workstation. Follow these steps to use the Connect to Share method:

1. From the Finder, press Command-K (Apple key plus the "k" key).
2. In the Server Address field, enter `afp://servername`, where `servername` is the AppleTalk name of the server listed in the File Server for Macintosh properties.

> **NOTE**
>
> If you know the share you want to connect to, you can enter the share name at the end of the URL, as in `afp://`*`servername`*`/Users Shared Folders`. This will mount the share directly instead of presenting you with a dialog showing all the available shares.

3. Click Connect.
4. Enter the username and password to connect to the server.
5. Select the volume or volumes you want to mount (see Figure 17.4) and click OK. The volume(s) will mount on the desktop.

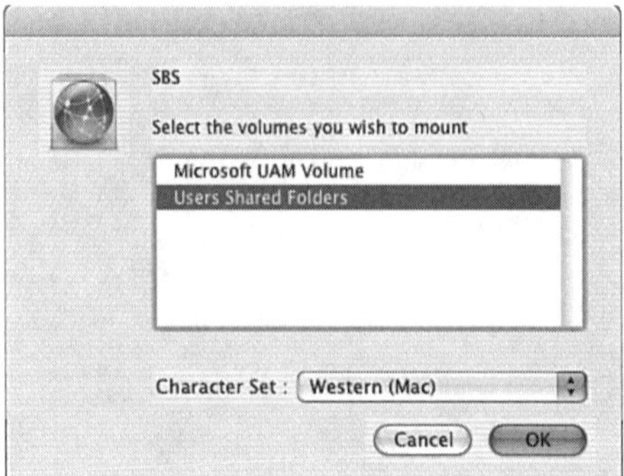

FIGURE 17.4 The Connect to Server dialog displays all the available volumes on the server.

CAUTION

One problem that has been reported across the Macintosh SBS community is a timeout problem when connecting shares using the AppleTalk method under OS X. Periodically, shares on the server will get disconnected from the Macintosh for no apparent reason, forcing the user to reconnect to the share to access the resources on it. Most of the time, this problem can be resolved by adjusting the Power Save settings. Another fix is detailed in Microsoft KB article 297684 (`http://support.microsoft.com/?id=297684`). Yet another workaround is to force the Mac OS X AppleTalk connection to use pure AppleTalk instead of AppleTalk over IP, which is the default (and faster) connection method.

To force a volume mapping to use AppleTalk instead of AppleTalk over IP, enter **`afp:/at/`*`servername`*** in the Server Address field instead of `afp://`*`servername`*. By using the AppleTalk protocol instead of AppleTalk over IP, the connection to the server is regularly updated, avoiding the timeout issues. However, using true AppleTalk adds additional traffic to the network and significantly slows down the file access to the server. Use this method only as a last resort to address this problem.

Connecting to the Server—Browse Method (OS 10.3 and Later Only)

Another way to access the volumes on the server is to browse to them through the Finder interface directly. With OS X 10.3 and later versions, the Finder window contains a Network icon in addition to the regular file shortcuts. Follow these steps to use the browse method to access resources on the SBS server:

1. Open Macintosh HD.
2. Click the Network icon in the left panel.
3. Look for the server name in the right pane (see Figure 17.5). It may take up to a minute for the server name to appear. You may also need to look for the server in the Local folder if one is displayed.
4. Double-click on the server name.
5. Enter the username and password and click Connect.

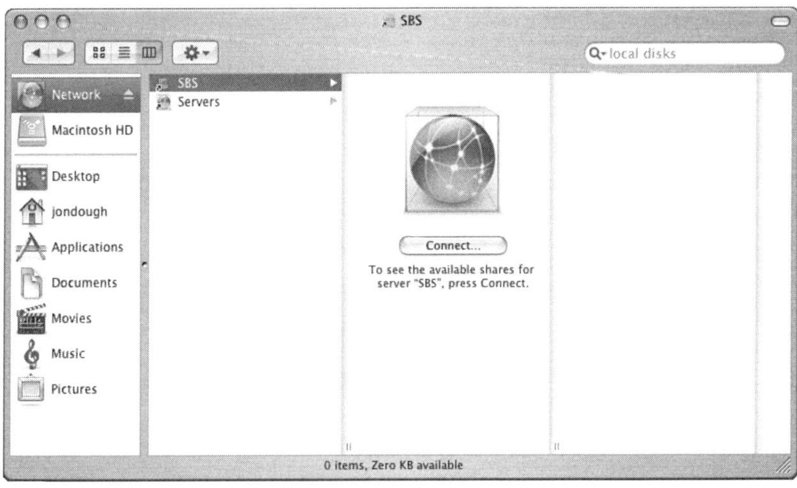

FIGURE 17.5 Mac OS X displays available servers in the file browser interface.

6. Select the share from the list presented.
7. The share now appears on the desktop and in the volume list in the left pane (see Figure 17.6).

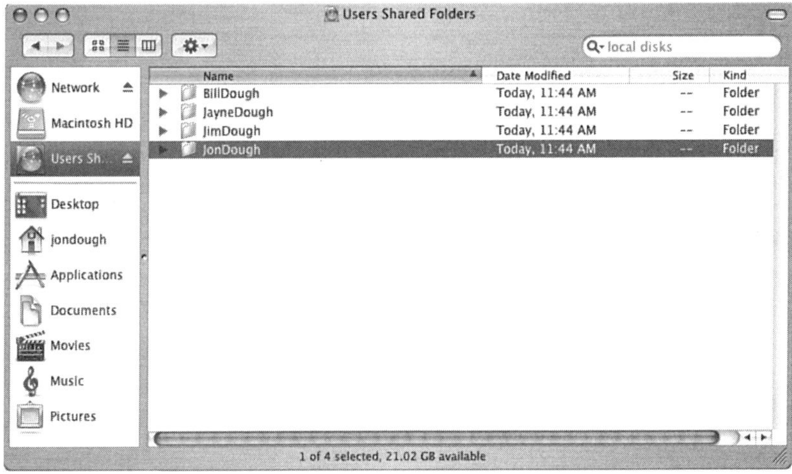

FIGURE 17.6 Network volumes are listed in the top left of the file browser interface.

Connect to the Server—Chooser Method

This method for connecting to a share on the SBS server is the only method that can be used by Macintosh workstations running OS 9 or earlier. Although it is possible to use this method on a Macintosh running OS X, it can only be done when Classic mode has been started. Unless the Macintosh user is running applications in Classic mode that need to access data on the server, it is not recommended that you use this method with Mac OS X. Follow these steps:

1. Open Macintosh HD.
2. Open System Folder, then Apple Menu Items, and double-click Chooser. Alternatively, you can select the Chooser icon from the Apple menu (Mac OS 9 and earlier only, see Figure 17.7).

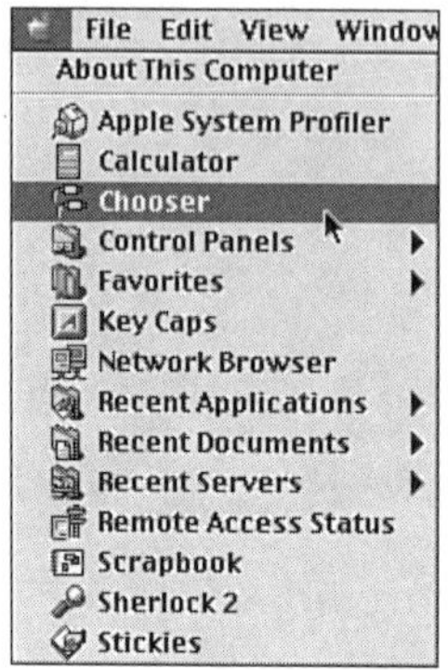

FIGURE 17.7 The Chooser application can be easily found in the Apple menu under Mac OS 9.

3. Classic mode starts up if not already running (Mac OS X only).
4. Click the AppleShare icon, select the server in the right-hand pane, and click OK.
5. Enter the username and password and click Connect.
6. Select the volume or volumes to mount and click OK. The volume(s) will mount on the desktop.
7. Close the Chooser.

Connecting Using SMB (Mac OS X 10.3 Only)

With Mac OS 10.2, Apple added the capability for the Mac OS to connect to shares on a Windows server using native Windows methods. This can be done thanks to a service called Samba that is used to connect to SMB shares. The Samba implementation in Mac OS 10.3 was improved significantly over the implementation in Mac OS 10.2, so if a Macintosh workstation is going to regularly access a Windows server using SMB, it should be upgraded to at least Mac OS 10.3, if not 10.4. This section of the chapter covers the issues related to accessing SMB shares and the steps to follow to correctly configure the server and the workstation.

Best Practice—Connecting Macintosh Workstations Using SMB

If the only Macintosh workstations in the network are running Mac OS X 10.3 and later, use the SMB method for connecting the Macintoshes to the server. Although using the AppleTalk method described earlier in the chapter will work, the SMB connection method is easier to manage from the server, and the Macintosh workstations will benefit from faster network connections than when connecting over AppleTalk.

The `.local` Issue

There are several prerequisites that you need to confirm before you can connect a Macintosh to an SBS server using SMB (Windows) shares. First, you need to know the internal domain name of the network. If the internal domain name ends in `.local` (for example, `domainname.local`), you need to change the network configuration on the Macintosh before you can continue. This is because the Rendezvous service introduced into Mac OS X in version 10.2 uses multicast DNS with a `.local` name to function. The Macintosh will not be able to successfully use the SBS DNS server to resolve addresses in the `.local` domain if multicast DNS is enabled on the Mac. This has changed with Mac OS 10.4, which can look up names in the `.local` namespace by default.

Best Practice—Setting Up a New Active Directory Namespace

As discussed in Chapter 3, "Planning a New SBS Installation," if you are planning a new SBS installation, select an internal domain name that does not end with `.local`. If you discover that there will be a mixture of PCs and Macintosh computers on the network prior to an SBS installation and there is not an existing Active Directory network, use `.lan` or `.office` or some other top-level domain name that is not a public domain and not `.local`. Also, avoid the temptation to use `.mac` in the domain namespace because this unregistered top-level domain may very well be used by Apple Computer in the future in support of their .Mac network services.

Even if there are not any Macintosh systems on the local network, the SBS community is beginning to move away from the use of `.local` in the Active Directory namespace as a best practice.

If your network does not have a `.local` internal domain name, or if you are running Mac OS 10.4, you can skip to the "SMB Signing" section later in the chapter. Otherwise, follow these steps to configure the Macintosh to be able to successfully resolve names in the `.local` namespace.

First configure DNS on the Macintosh by following these steps:

1. Open System Preferences by selecting the Apple menu, System Preferences.
2. Click the Network icon.
3. Select Built-in Ethernet and click Configure.

4. Enter the IP address of the Windows server in the DNS Servers field.
5. Enter the internal domain name in the Search Domains field.
6. Click Apply Now.
7. If an address appears next to the IPv6 Address field, click Configure IPv6 and select Off from the Configure IPv6 drop-down menu.
8. Click OK.
9. Quit System Preferences.

Next enable unicast `.local` resolution by performing these steps (Not needed for OS 10.4 or later.):

1. Open the Terminal application (select Macintosh HD, Applications, Utilities, Terminal).
2. At the command prompt, type **`sudo su`** and press Return.
3. Enter the password for the current user account and press Return.
4. Type **`cd /usr/sbin`** and press Return.
5. Type **`cat > EnableUnicastDotLocal`** and press Return. You will not see a command prompt at this point.
6. Enter the following four lines exactly as shown, pressing Return at the end of each line (the filename is `local.ONE` not `local.L`):

```
#!/bin/tcsh
echo domain.local > /etc/resolver/local.1
grep -v domain /etc/resolv.conf >> /etc/resolver/local.1
echo search_order 2 >> /etc/resolver/local.1
```

7. After you press Return at the end of the last line, press Control-D. The command prompt appears again.
8. Type **`chmod +x EnableUnicastDotLocal`** and press Return.
9. Type **`/usr/sbin/EnableUnicastDotLocal`** and press Return.
10. Type **`cat /etc/resolver/local.1`** and press Return. You should see `domain.local` and the IP address of the server listed in the output, which will look similar to the following:

```
domain.local
search domainname.local
nameserver 192.168.16.2
search_order 2
```

11. Press Control-D and quit the Terminal application.

SMB Signing

All Windows 2003 domain controllers enable SMB encryption by default. The Mac OS uses a package called Samba to enable the Mac to connect to SMB shares on a Windows server, but the implementation of Samba in Mac OS 10.3 and earlier cannot make encrypted connections to SMB shares. Connecting a Mac to an SMB share on an SBS server requires disabling the SMB signing policies for the SBS server. If your company security policy prohibits you from modifying these security policies, you need to enable AppleTalk connectivity to your server instead using the steps listed in the "Connecting Using SMB (Mac OS X 10.3 Only)" section of the chapter.

> **Connecting Down-Level Clients to SBS Server Shares**
>
> The Macintosh is not the only SMB client that cannot interact with SMB encryption. Windows 98 PCs, UNIX/Linux systems, and many network-aware multifunction printer devices (those that include scanning features particularly) also cannot connect to SBS shares by default. Following the steps in this section to disable SMB signing by creating a new group policy object allows these other devices to connect to the server shares as well. See Chapter 20, "Group Policy," for more detailed information on group policy and its use with SBS.

Instead of making changes to the Default Domain Policy to disable SMB signing, create a new group policy object with the appropriate policy settings. This is in line with the additional group policy objects created by the SBS setup. Follow these steps:

1. On the SBS server, open the Server Management console.
2. Expand Advanced Management.
3. Expand Group Policy Management.
4. Expand the forest.
5. Expand Domains.
6. Select the local domain. The SBS policy objects display in the right-hand pane along with the Default Domain Policy as shown in Figure 17.8.
7. Right-click the domain icon (*domainname*.local) in the console tree and select Create and Link a GPO Here.
8. Enter **`SMB Signing Disabled`** for the GPO Name and click OK.
9. Right-click on the new GPO in the right-hand pane and select Edit to open the Group Policy Object Editor.
10. Under Computer Configuration, expand Windows Settings.
11. Expand Security Settings.
12. Expand Local Policies.
13. Select Security Options.
14. In the right-hand pane, scroll down to Microsoft Network Server: Digitally Sign Communications (Always) and double-click on the policy object.

17

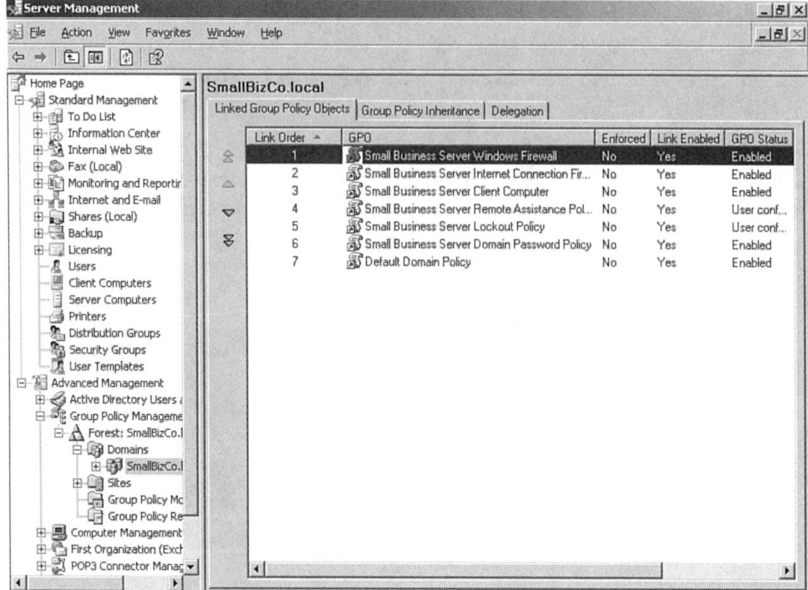

FIGURE 17.8 All the Group Policy Objects for the domain are listed under the domain object in the console.

15. Select the Disabled radio button and make sure that the Define This Policy Setting check box is enabled as shown in Figure 17.9.

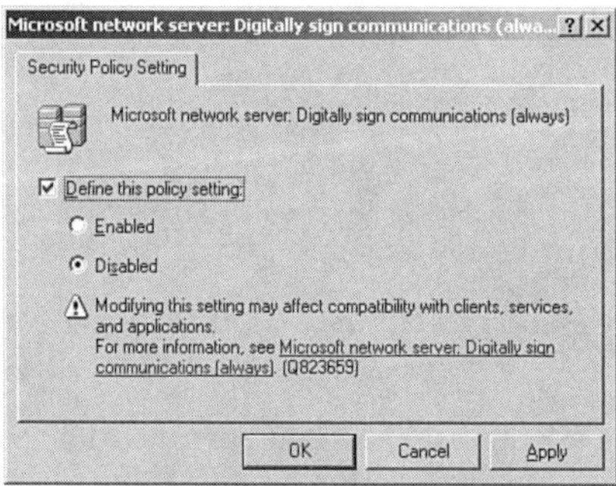

FIGURE 17.9 The security policy setting needs to be disabled to allow SMB access from the Macintosh.

16. Click OK.

CAUTION

Other published documents that discuss disabling SMB signing advise disabling the Microsoft Network Server: Digitally Sign Communications (If Client Agrees) setting as well. This is *not* recommended because it could cause problems with other PCs configured to require SMB signing by default. If a Windows XP workstation has the Microsoft Network Client: Digitally Sign Communications (Always) setting enabled and the server has this second setting disabled, the Windows XP workstation will not be able to access any shares on the server. The only item that needs to be disabled in the SBS server group policy is the Microsoft Network Server: Digitally Sign Communications (Always) item for Macintosh and other down-level clients to connect to SMB shares successfully.

---

17. Close the Group Policy Object Editor.
18. Using the arrows in the pane, move the SMB Signing Disabled policy just above the Default Domain Policy in the window.
19. Right-click on the SMB Signing Disabled policy object and select Enforced. In the Linked Group Policy Objects window, the SMB Signing Disabled object should show Yes under both Enforced and Link Enabled. Figure 17.10 shows the correct placement of the SMB Signing Disabled policy object as well as the correct Enforced and Link Enabled settings.

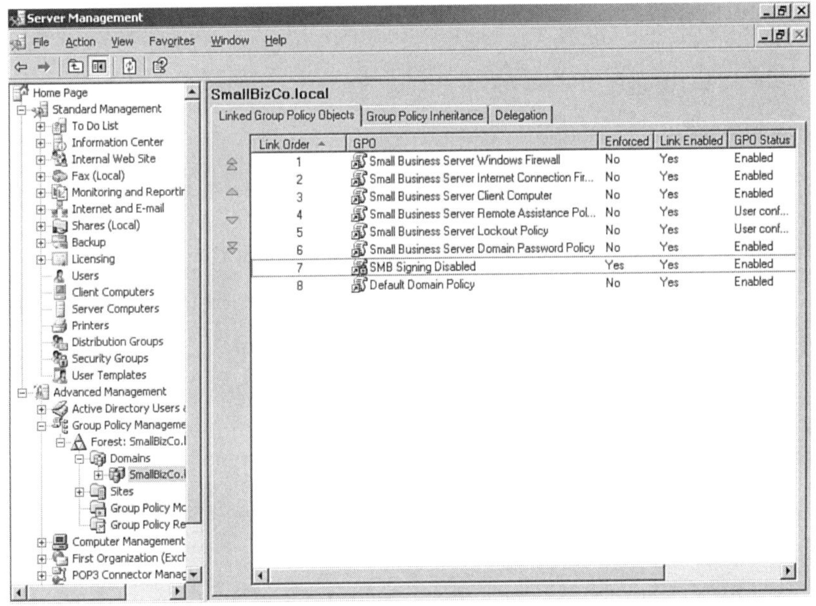

FIGURE 17.10 The new SMB Signing Disabled policy is Enforced and Enabled.

20. Open a command prompt on the server.
21. Type **`gpupdate /force`** and press Enter.
22. When the policy update completes, close the command prompt.

Configure the Mac for Active Directory Access

Despite rumors to the contrary, Mac OS X systems running 10.2 or later can participate in Windows Active Directory networks. This is not required for the Macintosh to access shares on the server, nor does it give system administrators the same level of control over the Macs as PCs through group policy or logon scripts because the Macs will not process either. But with a Mac correctly configured in an Active Directory environment, Windows domain credentials can be used to log on to the Mac, and individual user profiles for those domain users can be stored on the Mac hard drive.

To join the Macintosh to Active Directory, begin by configuring Directory Access by following these steps:

1. Open Directory Access (select Macintosh HD, Applications, Utilities, Directory Access).
2. Click the lock to make changes.
3. Enter the password for the local Macintosh account.
4. Enable SMB and click Configure.
5. Enter the NetBIOS name of the domain in the Workgroup field. If the full domain name is `SmallBizCo.local`, the NetBIOS domain name would be `SmallBizCo`.
6. Enter the IP address of the server in the WINS Server field.
7. Click OK twice.
8. Click Apply.

Next join the Macintosh to the Active Directory Domain by following these steps:

1. In the Directory Access application, select Active Directory and click Configure.
2. In the Active Directory Forest field, enter the fully qualified domain name of your SBS domain (for example, `domain.local` or `domain.lan`).
3. In the Active Directory Domain field, enter the fully qualified domain name of your SBS domain (for example, `domain.local` or `domain.lan`).
4. In the Computer ID field, enter a unique network name for the Macintosh.
5. Click the arrow next to Show Advanced Options.
6. Clear the Authenticate in Multiple Domains check box.
7. Enable the Prefer This Domain Server check box and enter the fully qualified domain name of your SBS server (for example, `server.domain.local` or `server.domain.lan`).
8. Click Bind.
9. Enter the username and password for a domain account that has permissions to add a workstation to the domain. If you want the Macintosh to belong to an OU (Organizational Unit) or container other than `Computers.domain.local`, make the appropriate changes in the Computer OU field.

10. Click OK. The Macintosh goes through a five-step process to join the domain. When it is successful, the Bind button changes to Unbind as shown in Figure 17.11.

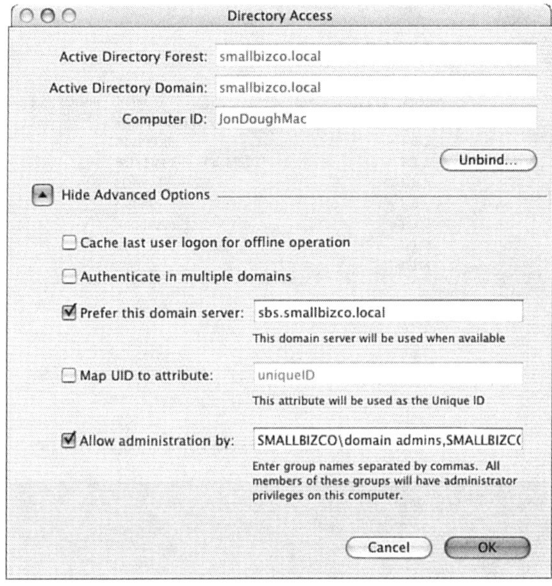

FIGURE 17.11 Joining a Mac to Active Directory is configured in the Directory Access application.

11. Click OK.
12. Click the Authentication tab.
13. Select Custom Path from the Search drop-down menu.
14. Click Add.
15. Select `/Active Directory/domain.local` and click Add.
16. Click the Services tab.
17. Enable the Active Directory check box.
18. Click Apply.
19. Quit Directory Access.

17

Logging In with Active Directory Credentials

Most Macintosh systems are configured to automatically log on with the default username and password at boot time. To log on to the Macintosh with the Active Directory account, you would need to first log off the currently authenticated account. To do this, click on the Apple menu and select Log Out *[current user]*, where *[current user]* is the full name of the currently logged in account. Then click Log Out to complete the logoff process. At this point, you are presented with a logon screen that includes an icon for Other. When you click on Other, you can enter the username and password for a domain user in *domainname\username* form and authenticate against Active Directory. Note that doing this creates a new profile on the Macintosh for the domain user account that will have none of the settings or documents from the local user profile.

If you want to have the option of logging in with the Active Directory account when the Macintosh is turned on, you need to disable the automatic logon feature of the OS. To do this, select System Preferences from the Apple menu and click on the Security icon. Activate the Disable Automatic Logon check box and quit System Preferences. The next time the Macintosh is restarted, the logon window will be presented.

Follow these steps to connect to a share on the SBS server from the Macintosh:

1. From the Finder, press Command-K (Apple key + k).
2. In the Server Address field, enter **`smb://netbiosservername/sharename`** and click Connect.
3. Enter the domain username and password for access and click OK.
4. A new window with the contents of the share opens.

NOTE

You can also enter **`smb://netbiosservername/`** without the sharename, and after you authenticate you will be prompted to select which share to connect.

You can also use these alternative steps to connect to a share on the SBS server from the Macintosh:

1. Open Macintosh HD.
2. Click the Network icon in the left panel.
3. Shortly, you should see several items: Servers and one or more folders with the NetBIOS and fully qualified names of the domain.
4. Double-click on the folder with the NetBIOS name of the domain.
5. After a moment, icons for the server and other workstations in the domain appear in the folder as shown in Figure 17.12. Double-click on the server icon.
6. Enter network authentication information—the domain should be filled in, and you will probably need to change the username—and click OK.
7. Select a share from the pop-up list and click OK. The share now appears as an icon on the desktop and in the left panel of the Macintosh HD window.

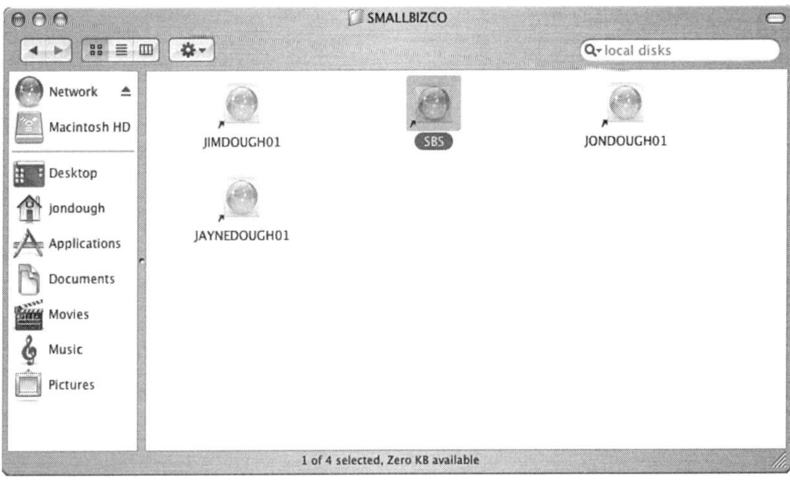

FIGURE 17.12 When correctly configured, the Macintosh can see all NetBIOS machines in the local domain.

Secure Website Access

The release of SBS 2003 provided a much-needed feature—SSL Security Certificates at no additional cost. Well, no monetary cost, anyway. These certificates are self-signed. So although the certificate enables SSL communications on the SBS server (for Outlook Web Access [OWA], Remote Web Workplace, and other services), it is not specifically a trusted certificate. In the Windows world, this is not much of a problem. When you connect to a site using a self-signed certificate, you are presented with a warning indicating that the certificate is not valid, specifically pointing out that it is signed by a nontrusted authority. To get past this, you click Yes and go on.

Not surprisingly, the behavior is a little different in the Macintosh world. Using Microsoft Internet Explorer on the Mac to connect to these same sites results in a hard block. IE generates an error, not a warning, and refuses to continue access to the site. However, Microsoft has discontinued production on IE for the Mac.

Fortunately, there are workarounds. Unfortunately, none of them involve IE for the Mac.

People using Netscape 4.x or 7.x for the Mac are prompted with a similar warning when accessing these sites. Netscape gives you the option to add the security certificate to its own certificate store. This is the only way to work around this problem for Macs running OS 9.

There are also times when access to one of these sites takes place outside the context of the web browser. Mac OS X has its own internal certificate store. The Safari web browser and other services in Mac OS X use this store. It is also used by Entourage 2004 to connect to an Exchange server. You can import these self-signed certificates into the OS store as a trusted certificate, and that allows Safari and other tools that look to the OS store for certificates to communicate securely with the server without generating warnings or errors.

Exporting the SSL Certificate from SBS

The self-signed certificate on SBS is stored in the certificate store, not as a file on the disk. To get the certificate into a format that the Mac can use to add to its own store, the certificate must be exported from the certificate store on the server into a file. Follow these steps to export the self-signed SSL certificate from the server:

1. Open Internet Information Services (IIS) Manager.
2. Expand the server and then expand Web Sites.
3. Right-click Default Web Site, and then click Properties.
4. Select the Directory Security tab, and then click View Certificate.
5. Select the Details tab, and then click Copy to File.
6. In the Certificate Export Wizard, click Next.
7. On the Export Private Key window, select No, Do Not Export the Private Key, and then click Next.
8. On the Export File Format window, select DER Encoded Binary X.509 (.CER), and then click Next.
9. On the File to Export window, browse to a location that you can access from the Macintosh, enter a filename, and then click Next.
10. Click Finish to complete the wizard.

Importing the SSL Certificate into the Macintosh Certificate Store

After you export the OWA certificate and copy the certificate file to the Mac OS X computer, you can add the certificate as a trusted certificate using either the UNIX interface on the Macintosh or a third-party utility, such as the freeware program CerttoolGUI 0.1. This utility is available at either of the following websites:

```
http://macupdate.com/info.php/id/10947

http://www.versiontracker.com/dyn/moreinfo/mac/18496
```

Follow these steps to add the certificate using CerttoolGUI 0.1:

1. Rename the certificate file to have a .DER extension instead of .CER, and then copy the file to the root of the Macintosh hard disk drive.
2. Start CerttoolGUI.
3. Click Add Certificate. The certificate appears in the CerttoolGUI certificate list.
4. Select the certificate, and then click Import Certificates. The certificate state appears as added.
5. Close CerttoolGUI. Safari will no longer warn about the certificate.

Follow these steps to add the certificate using the UNIX interface on Mac OS X:

1. Copy the certificate file to the root of the Macintosh hard disk drive. Do not rename the file.
2. Open the Terminal application (select Macintosh HD, Applications, Utilities, Terminal).
3. Type **`cd /`** and then press Enter.
4. Type **`sudo certtool i certname.cer d k=/System/Library/Keychains/X509Anchors`** and then press Enter, where `certname.cer` is the name of the certificate file.
5. When prompted, enter the password for the local Macintosh account.
6. To verify that the certificate was added correctly, type **`sudo certtool y k=/System/Library/Keychains/X509Anchors | grep yourdomain`** and then press Enter, where `yourdomain` is the SBS 2003 domain. If the certificate was added correctly, you will see two or more lines starting with Common Name that displays the name of the server.

Accessing Exchange from the Macintosh

As in the Windows world, people use many different email clients with the Macintosh platform. Two clients interface with Exchange directly (Outlook 2001 and Entourage 2004), whereas the rest must rely on POP3 or IMAP services to connect with the Exchange server. For example, all versions of Entourage prior to Entourage 2004 and Outlook Express for the Mac connect to an Exchange server using IMAP according to best practices. Other third-party mail clients generally use POP3 to connect to a mail server, but a few support both POP3 and IMAP.

This section covers configuring both the Macintosh mail clients and the Exchange services on SBS to allow a variety of Mac-based mail clients to interact with the Exchange server in SBS 2003.

Best Practice—IMAP Instead of POP3

Because so many mail clients now support the IMAP protocol in addition to POP3, there is rarely a need to enable POP3 services on SBS to allow external clients to get to their email. Additionally, the performance benefits of IMAP far outweigh those of POP3.

The main difference between IMAP and POP3 is the way each protocol handles mail on the server by default. POP3 by default attempts to download all messages from the server and then deletes the messages from the server when the connection is done. In an Exchange environment, this is not desired. Although every POP3 mail client has settings to instruct the client to leave the messages on the server instead of deleting them from the mailbox on the server, this is usually not the default setting, and it only takes one time to forget to enable that feature and remove all mail from the server on the first connection.

IMAP, on the other hand, leaves all messages on the server by default, and when it makes its initial connection, it collects only the mail header information for each message instead of downloading the entire message. The full message contents are downloaded only when the user opens the message in the IMAP client. This significantly reduces the amount of time necessary to make the initial mail connection and allows the user to select which messages to download completely. The performance increase is especially significant when there are multiple mail messages with large attachments. POP3 downloads all the messages and attachments by default, whereas IMAP downloads only the header information.

POP3 has been a reliable and familiar mail protocol for a long time, but IMAP is now the preferred protocol to use when interfacing with an Exchange server.

Both POP3 and IMAP have a security risk in that the user's username and password are sent across the network to the server in plain text. Anyone monitoring port 110 or 143 going into your network could get the authentication information for accounts accessing POP3 or IMAP services and thus gain access to other services on the network.

Enable IMAP on SBS

Exchange 2003 does not enable POP3 and IMAP by default as Exchange 2000 did. To allow Macintosh email clients to make an IMAP connection to the Exchange server, the IMAP service must be started and set to automatically start when the server boots. To do this, open the Services control panel, double-click on the Microsoft Exchange IMAP4 service, change the Startup Type to Automatic, click Apply, click Start, and then click OK.

CAUTION

When enabling IMAP services on the SBS 2003 server, you need to enable port 143 inbound on all firewalls if you want external clients to collect email using IMAP. Internal clients can connect as soon as the IMAP services are enabled, but you need to follow the instructions in Chapter 7, "Routing and Remote Access Service, VPN, and Firewalls," to enable inbound IMAP connections through the RRAS firewall, or review Chapter 24, "Internet Security and Acceleration Server 2004 Advanced Administration," to manually create a server publishing rule in ISA 2004 for IMAP.

Outlook Express

Outlook Express 5 is the latest release of Outlook Express for the Mac. Although it is an OS 9 product, it can be run under Mac OS X in Classic mode. Because Outlook Express 5 is an older product (it has not been updated since October 2002), it should really be used only as a stopgap measure to interact with the Exchange server for email until another, more robust mail client can be installed and used. If Outlook Web Access can be accessed from the Mac, it would be a better choice than Outlook Express in most cases.

Mac OS 9 and `.local`

Interestingly enough, Macs running Mac OS 9.2 also have the same `.local` name lookup problem, even though the Rendezvous service is not supported on Mac OS 9.2. Using Outlook or Outlook Express on Macs running OS 9.2 can also cause problems if the internal domain name ends in `.local`. When an OS 9.2 machine does a lookup for a name in the `.local` namespace, the OS does a multicast DNS lookup instead of a direct DNS query against the DNS server to try and resolve the name to an IP address.

There is no "one size fits all" workaround in Mac OS 9.2 to get past the `.local` lookup problems as there is for Mac OS 10.3. With OS 9.2, you have to resort to using Hosts files on the Macintoshes to map the names with the internal IP addresses. Fortunately, creating the Hosts file on the Mac is not difficult. Unfortunately, the Hosts file must be updated every time there is a change on the network, and the Hosts file will never work when looking up names for machines that are getting their addresses from DHCP.

Follow these steps to create a Hosts file on a Mac OS 9 machine:

1. Use SimpleText to create a new file on the desktop.
2. Enter **`[machinename].[domainname].local A 192.168.x.x`** in the file, where **`machinename`** is the name of the server or workstation, **`domainname`** is the name of the domain, and `192.168.x.x` is the IP address of the machine. Press the Tab key between each section. Repeat this step for as many entries as are needed with each entry on a separate line.
3. Save the file to the Mac desktop.
4. Open the TCP/IP control panel by selecting the Apple menu, Control Panels.
5. Click Select Hosts File.
6. Locate the file you just saved on the desktop, select it, and click Open.
7. If a Hosts file already exists, you are prompted to replace the contents of the existing Hosts file with the selected file. Click OK.
8. Close the TCP/IP control panel and click Save to activate the new configuration.

You now will be able to connect to internal machines by name.

Follow these steps to add an IMAP profile to Outlook Express:

1. Open Outlook Express.
2. Select Tools, Accounts from the menu.
3. In the Accounts window, click New.
4. Enter the display name and click the right arrow (see Figure 17.13 for the window layout).

FIGURE 17.13 The setup assistants in Mac OS 9 often use "forward" and "back" arrows to navigate through the wizard.

17

5. In the Internet E-mail Address window, enter the public email address for the user. Click the right arrow to continue.
6. In the Email Server Names window, select IMAP from the drop-down menu, and enter the name or IP address of the SBS server in both the Incoming Mail and Outgoing Mail fields. Click the right arrow to continue.
7. In the Internet Mail Logon window, enter the user's logon name in the Account ID field and enter the password in the Password field. Click the right arrow to continue.
8. Enter a name for the account in the Account Name field. This name is displayed in the main folder list to identify this account from others that may be configured in the application.
9. Click Finish when done.
10. Close the Accounts window.

After the account has been configured, it displays in the folder list in the left pane of the Outlook Express interface. To start the initial connection with the Exchange server, click the Send & Receive button in the button bar. When the transaction completes, an expansion arrow appears next to the account folder. When this folder is expanded, Outlook Express displays the Inbox and a listing of all the unread messages.

Figure 17.14 shows the default status of all the folders on the Exchange server in the Outlook Express configuration. By default, Outlook Express IMAP connections only connect to and download messages in the Inbox. Outlook Express downloads all the names of the folders for the mail account, but it does not download the headers of any messages in any of those folders until the folder is subscribed. To subscribe to a folder, select that folder in the right pane and click the Subscribe button in the button bar. At that point, Outlook Express adds the folder to the list in the left pane and downloads the mail headers for any items in that folder.

Mac OS X Mail

Mac OS X includes an email application, called Mail, with the OS. During the initial Macintosh setup, the user is prompted to configure Mail to connect to the .Mac mail service, but additional accounts can be added to Mail, including IMAP connections to Exchange on SBS.

Follow these steps to add an IMAP configuration to the Mail application in Mac OS X:

1. Open the Mail application.
2. Open the Mail application preferences (type **`Command-`**, or select Mail, Preferences from the menu).
3. Click the Accounts tab.
4. Click the + in the lower-left corner of the Accounts window.

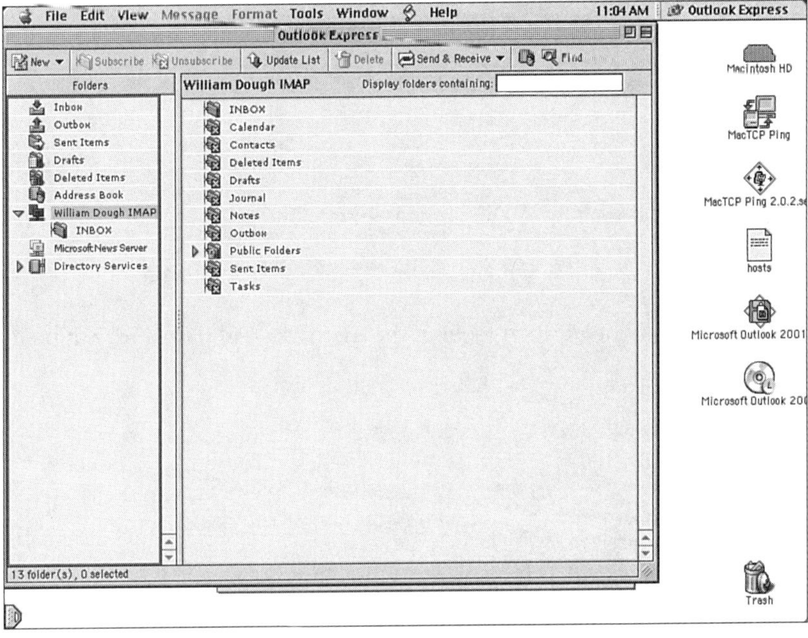

FIGURE 17.14 Outlook Express for Macintosh can make an IMAP connection to the Exchange server.

5. Select IMAP from the Account Type drop-down menu.
6. Enter a descriptive name for the account in the Description field.
7. Enter the public email address in the Email Address field.
8. Enter the username in the Full Name field.
9. Enter the name or IP address for the SBS server in the Incoming Mail Server field.
10. Enter the user's logon name in the Username field (no domain name is necessary).
11. Select Add Server from the Outgoing Mail Server (SMTP) drop-down menu.
12. Enter the name or IP address for the SBS server in the Outgoing Mail Server field.
13. Select Password from the Authentication drop-down menu.
14. Enter the user's logon name and password in the User Name and Password fields. The window should now look like Figure 17.15.
15. Click OK. The Accounts window should now look like Figure 17.16.
16. Close the Preferences window.

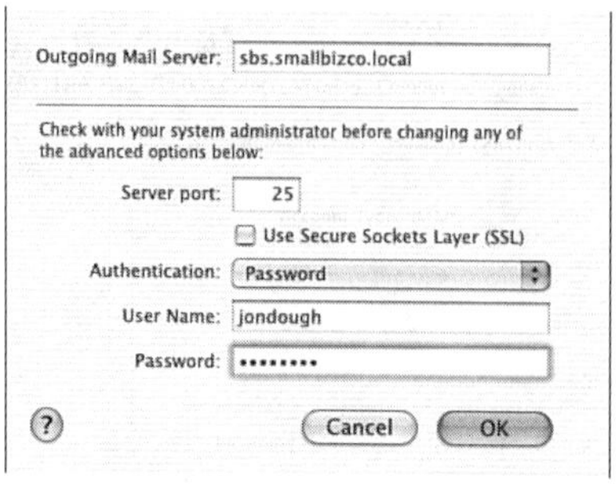

FIGURE 17.15 SMTP authentication requires the username and password, but no domain name is needed.

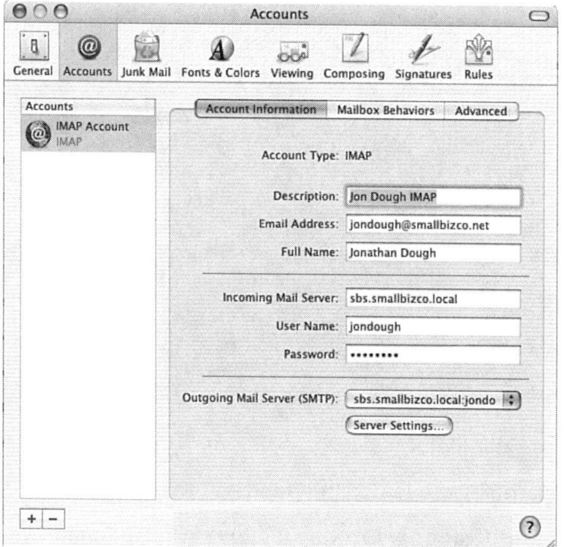

FIGURE 17.16 The Mail application can also use IMAP to communicate with the SBS Exchange server.

When Mail finishes making the IMAP connection and has transferred all the information from the mail server, the main application window should appear as shown in Figure 17.17. Messages in the Exchange Inbox appear in the Inbox tray in the left pane. Sent messages appear in the Sent Items tray.

When you expand the mail service tray (usually listed at the bottom of the left pane), you see all the folders from the Exchange server account. However, because IMAP only handles mail items, you do not see the Outlook calendar when you select the Calendar folder. Instead, you see a mail item that contains an ICS file attachment. Double-clicking on the ICS attachment launches iCal and attempts to add the calendar item into the iCal schedule.

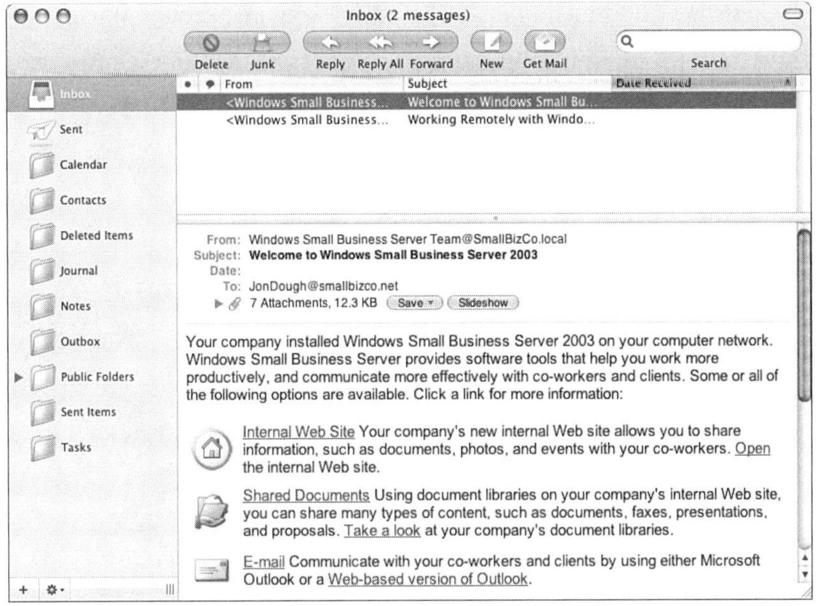

FIGURE 17.17 The IMAP connection in Mail pulls the mail folder information from the Exchange server.

Entourage X

When Microsoft introduced Office X for Mac OS X, it dropped the Outlook product in favor of a new mail and calendaring tool called Entourage. Although Entourage had the look and feel of the other Office applications under OS X, it lacked one significant function—Exchange support through MAPI. In fact, until Microsoft released Office Update 10.1.4, Entourage could not connect to an Exchange server other than as a POP3 client. The Exchange compatibility promised in Office Update 10.1.4 only delivered IMAP and LDAP functionality to connect to the Exchange server, not true MAPI connectivity as with other Exchange clients. A full discussion of the pros and cons of the Entourage X mail client has been documented in the Entourage Special Report at MacWindows, `http://www.macwindows.com/entourage.html`.

> **NOTE**
>
> If you are using Entourage X in your environment, make sure that Entourage has been updated to Office Update 10.1.6. Updates can be downloaded from `http://www.microsoft.com/mac/downloads.aspx`.

Follow these steps to set up Entourage X to communicate with your SBS Exchange server:

1. Open the Accounts window (select Tools, Accounts) in Entourage.
2. Select the Exchange tab and click New.

3. In the Basic User Information field, click the Configure Account Manually button.
4. In the Account Settings tab, fill in the Account Name, Account ID, Password, Domain, Exchange Server, Name, and Email Address fields with the appropriate information (see Figure 17.18).

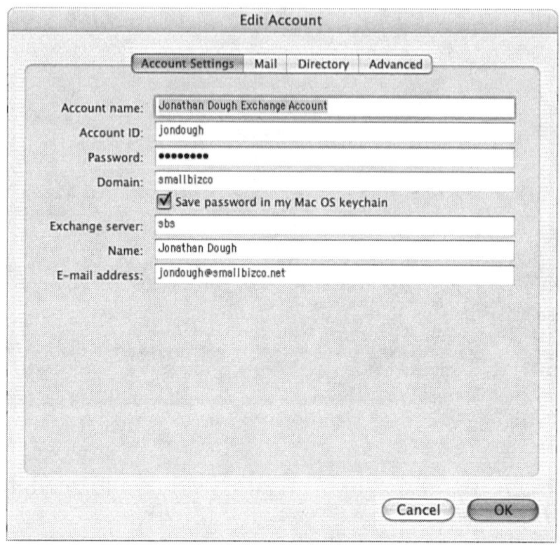

FIGURE 17.18 The Entourage X Account Settings tab contains the necessary information to connect to the Exchange server.

5. Click on the Mail tab and enter the name of the SBS server in the SMTP Server field.
6. Click on the Directory tab and enter the name of the SBS server in the LDAP server field.
7. Click on the Advanced tab and enter **`[servername]/public/`** in the Free/Busy Server field, where `[servername]` is the name of the SBS server.

NOTE

Use of the Free/Busy server in Entourage X is sketchy at best. Because it uses OWA to update the calendar information, directory security settings in IIS for the Public folder URL have a significant impact on how well this feature functions. When Entourage X was released, OWA for Exchange 2000 did not require SSL for connections, so Entourage X expects no SSL for this connection. If SSL is used (which it is by default in SBS 2003, you will need to modify the Security settings in the Advanced tab by enabling the DAV Service Requires Secure Connections (SSL) check box, unless you are still using the self-signed certificate provided by SBS. Otherwise, you could turn off the SSL requirements on the Public folder in IIS (not recommended) or upgrade to Entourage 2004 and follow the configuration information listed later in this chapter (highly recommended).

8. Click OK and close the Accounts window.

After the account is set up, Entourage connects to the Exchange server, downloads all the folder and mail information, and displays the contents of the Exchange mailbox as shown in Figure 17.19.

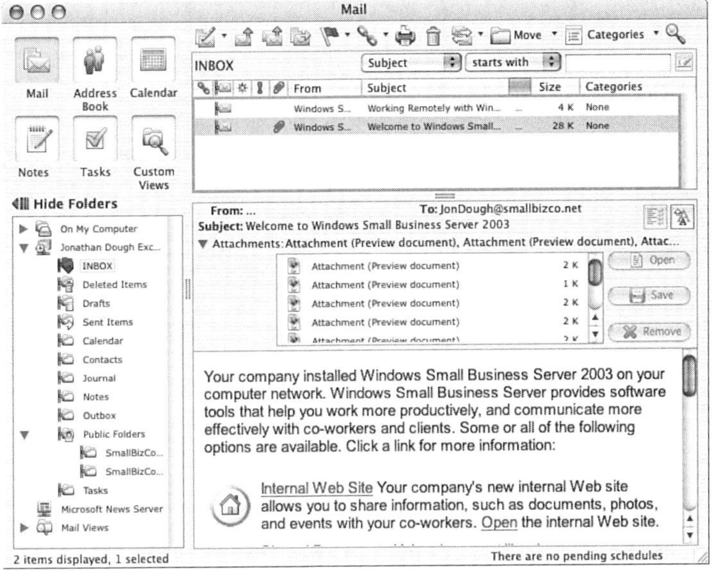

FIGURE 17.19 The Entourage Mail window displays the folders and mail items for the user's mailbox on the Exchange server.

Exchange

Making an Exchange-aware connection to the mail server is advantageous because the Exchange connection allows you to access more than just mail items and calendar items represented as mail objects. With a full Exchange connection, a mail client can access the Contacts and Public folders on the server and have a better interaction with calendar items. This section looks at three ways to have the full Exchange mail experience from the Macintosh.

Best Practice—Outlook 2001 and Entourage 2004

To get the best possible integration with the Exchange mail server from the Macintosh, use the Outlook 2001 client on Macs running Mac OS 9 or earlier and Entourage 2004 on Macs running Mac OS X. Outlook 2001 has better integration with the Exchange server, but because it has not been updated in several years, it may not be fully compatible with future updates to Exchange 2003.

Entourage 2004 comes the closest to full Exchange integration of any Entourage client released to date. It uses Outlook Web Access as its engine to connect, so in some ways, it is nothing more than a well-written front end to OWA. However, it does have a similar look and feel to Outlook 2003 on the PC and can be used with ease on PowerBooks that move between connecting locally and connecting remotely.

More information on configuring Outlook 2001 and Entourage 2004 is contained within this section of the chapter.

Outlook Web Access (OWA)

The only real difference between Outlook Web Access (OWA) on a Macintosh and a PC is that the Macintosh can only access the Basic version of OWA. When the OWA interface is loaded from a Macintosh, the user is presented with the familiar logon screen, except the only options available are selecting from a Public or Private computer. The option to select from Premium and Basic is not even displayed.

The Basic version of OWA lacks several features of the Premium version. Most notably visible when the OWA interface is fully loaded is the lack of a preview pane. To read a message, the user must click on the message header, and the message contents are displayed in the main web frame instead of opening in a separate web browser window. Other features missing from the Basic version are the interface to add and edit mail routing rules, spell checking tools, and the ability to modify the appearance of the OWA interface.

The biggest challenge to running OWA from a Mac was explained earlier in the chapter. If the SBS installation is using the default self-signed SSL certificate, Internet Explorer for the Mac cannot be used to access OWA. Safari, Netscape, and Firefox are browsers that can interact with OWA from a Mac when the self-signed certificate is used. Each of these programs has its own way of handling the self-signed certificate and will generate a warning when the self-signed certificate is encountered. With Netscape and Firefox, the certificate can be installed into the program's certificate store to avoid the warning each time OWA is accessed. Safari uses the Mac OS X certificate store to check, so the steps earlier in the chapter on installing self-signed certificates into the Mac OS X certificate store will avoid the warning in Safari each time OWA is accessed.

Outlook 2001

Outlook 2001 was the last Macintosh mail client released by Microsoft that fully integrates with Exchange. Fortunately, Outlook 2001 is still available as a free download from the Microsoft website (`http://www.microsoft.com/mac/downloads.aspx#Outlook`) and will run under both Mac OS 9 and earlier and all versions of Mac OS X that have Classic installed and enabled. Like its PC-based counterpart, Outlook 2001 makes a MAPI connection to Exchange for full functionality. As such, the configuration to connect Outlook 2001 to the Exchange server is very similar. Remember that if the Mac is running Mac OS 9.2 and the internal domain includes `.local`, you will need to add the SBS server to a Hosts file on the Mac for proper name resolution. See the steps to do this in the "The `.local` Issue" section earlier in the chapter.

Follow these steps to configure Outlook 2001 to communicate with the SBS server. These steps assume that this is the first time Outlook 2001 has been run on the Macintosh:

1. Launch Outlook 2001.
2. Enter the username and organization information into the appropriate fields and click OK.
3. Select the appropriate time zone and click OK.
4. Enter a name for the Outlook profile.
5. Enter the internal name of the SBS server in the Microsoft Exchange Server field.

6. Enter the user's logon name in the Mailbox Name field.
7. Click Test Settings (see Figure 17.20).

FIGURE 17.20 Outlook 2001 needs the name of the server and a user account to test the connection to the Exchange server.

8. When the test completes successfully, click Create Profile.
9. Enter the login information and click OK.
10. Outlook connects to the server and displays the full Exchange mailbox, as shown in Figure 17.21.

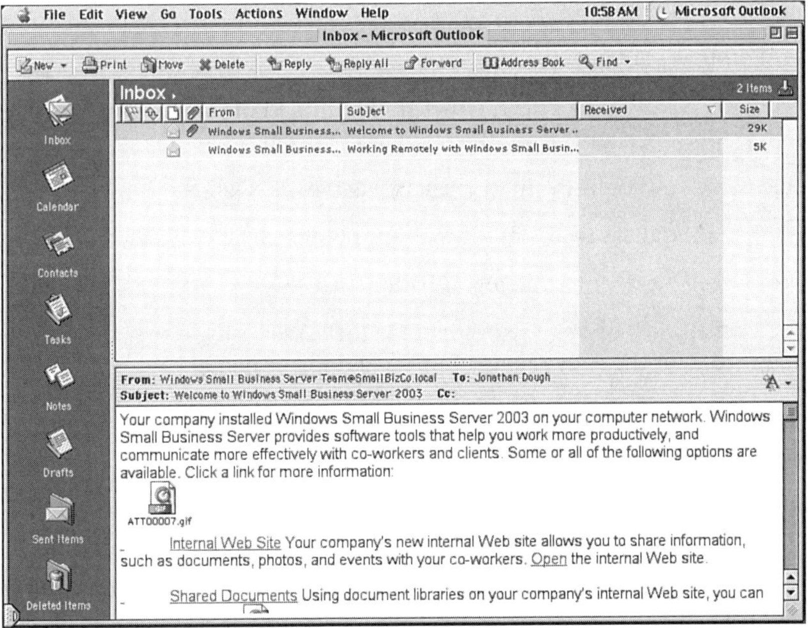

FIGURE 17.21 Outlook 2001 interfaces with all the features of Exchange mail server.

Entourage 2004

With the release of Microsoft Office 2004, people who want to use Entourage to connect to an Exchange server are going to be pleased with the enhancements made to Entourage and the ease with which it can interact with Exchange 2003. This section specifically covers connecting Entourage 2004 to an SBS 2003 server, but the steps can be extrapolated to any Exchange 2003 server that publishes OWA.

> **NOTE**
>
> SBS owners can get a copy of Entourage on CD by calling 1-800-360-7561 (in the U.S. and Canada) and asking for part number Q56-00005. You need to provide the agent with your SBS product key to validate ownership. To acquire the Entourage CD outside the U.S. and Canada, contact Microsoft's supplemental part fulfillment group.

Several steps need to be completed for Entourage 2004 to be able to communicate with an SBS 2003 server running Exchange 2003.

Verify Proper DNS Resolution to Server

Open a web browser (not Internet Explorer) and go to https://ServerFQDN/exchange using the full internal DNS name, not the server IP address. If you can log in and use OWA, continue to the next section. Otherwise, you will need to review the earlier sections of this chapter to troubleshoot why the connection is failing.

Configure Entourage to Connect to SBS Exchange Using the Setup Assistant

The account settings in Entourage can be configured in two ways. Follow these steps to use the Entourage Setup assistant:

1. Open Entourage 2004.
2. Open the Account Setup screen either in the initial Entourage Setup Assistant or by selecting Tools, Accounts from the menu and clicking New.
3. Enable the My Account Is on an Exchange Server check box.
4. In the E-mail Address field, enter the user's public email address.
5. In the User ID field, enter the logon ID for the user.
6. In the Domain field, enter the domain for the server using either the NetBIOS domain name or the fully qualified internal domain name.
7. In the Password field, enter the user's logon password.
8. Click the right-arrow to continue.
9. Automatic configuration will probably fail, so click the right-arrow again to continue.
10. In the Verify and Complete Settings window, enter the user's full name in the Your Name field.

11. In the Exchange Server field, enter **https://*ServerFQDN*/exchange**, where ServerFQDN is the fully qualified internal domain name for the server.
12. In the LDAP Server field, enter the FQDN of the server (do not include "https://" or "/exchange".
13. Enable the Use SSL for These Servers check box.
14. Click the right-arrow to continue.
15. Click the Verify Settings button. If you have a self-signed certificate on the server, you may get the following error:

    ```
    "Unable to establish a secure connection to [serverFQDN] because the correct
    root certificate is not installed." Click OK to continue.
    ```

16. If the account settings verify, click the right-arrow to continue. Otherwise, click the left-arrow and correct the information that needs to be corrected.
17. Click Finish to close the assistant.

Configure Entourage to Connect to SBS Exchange Using a Manual Configuration

The other method for configuring Entourage to connect to the Exchange server avoids the use of the Setup Wizard and lets you configure the account manually. Follow these steps to accomplish this:

1. Select Tools, Account from the menu and click New.
2. Enable the My Account Is on an Exchange Server check box.
3. Click the Configure My Account Manually button.
4. In the Account ID field, enter the user's logon ID.
5. In the Password field, enter the user's logon password.
6. In the Domain field, enter the domain for the server using either the NetBIOS domain name or the fully qualified domain name.
7. In the Exchange Server field, enter **https://ServerFQDN/exchange**.
8. In the Name field, enter the user's name as it will appear on outgoing messages.
9. In the E-mail Address field, enter the user's public reply-to mail address.
10. Click the Directory tab.
11. In the LDAP Server field, enter the FQDN of the server.
12. Click the Click Here for Advanced Options button.
13. Enable the This Server Requires Me to Log On check box.
14. Enable the Override Default LDAP Port check box and enter **3268** in the field.

15. Click the Advanced tab.
16. In the Public Folder Server field, enter **`https://ServerFQDN/public`**.
17. Select the Synchronize All Items to Server radio button.
18. Enable the DAV Service Requires Secure Connection check box.
19. Click OK.

Configure Local and Remote Access to Exchange 2003 with Entourage 2004

Mobile users with PowerBooks or iBooks face an interesting challenge when trying to use Entourage to read email when in the office or on the road. Using traditional Entourage configuration for connecting to the server while on the local network will not allow a connection while out of the office. Configuring Entourage to use the public name of the server to get it working while out of the office usually causes problems when trying to connect while on the local network.

The answer to this riddle is technically not a Macintosh or even an Entourage solution but is still worth mentioning in this context. For a PowerBook, configure Entourage to use the public URL of the OWA server for connections. Then configure the internal DNS server on SBS to respond with an internal IP address when a lookup for the public URL is made.

To do this, open the DNS Management Console and create a new lookup zone (see Chapter 5, "DNS, DHCP, and Active Directory Integration," for more information on setting up new DNS lookup zones). Give the zone the public domain name for your OWA server. For example, if your OWA server can be reached at `mail.smallbizco.net`, you would set up the lookup zone for `smallbizco.net`. Next, create a Host record for the server in the new lookup zone and point it to the internal IP of the SBS server. In other words, set up `mail` to point to `192.168.16.2` if your public server name is `mail` and your SBS server's internal IP address is `192.168.16.2`. Then, whenever the PowerBook is connected to the local network, it will get the 192.168.16.2 address when it looks up `mail.smallbizco.net` in DNS, and it will get the public IP address for your server when it is connected to the public Internet. Using this single configuration allows the user of the PowerBook to keep a single cache of her Exchange mail data instead of dealing with two profiles.

CAUTION

If you do set up this split DNS zone, you need to populate the internal DNS lookup zone with all addresses for all public names. In other words, you also need to create a www record if you have a public server that responds to `www.smallbizco.net`. Otherwise, when your internal machines do a DNS lookup on `www.smallbizco.net`, the lookup will fail, and the machines will not be able to connect to any sites in the `smallbizco.net` domain.

Remote Connectivity Tools for the Macintosh

In addition to configuring a PowerBook to access Exchange data easily from an onsite or offsite location as described in the previous section, a number of other remote tools can be used from the Macintosh to connect into the internal network from a remote location. This last section of the chapter covers Remote Web Workplace, Remote Desktop Connections, and VPN from the Macintosh perspective.

Remote Web Workplace (RWW)

Contrary to the public rumor mill, the Macintosh platform can use the Remote Web Workplace (RWW) interface provided by SBS, just not all of it. Macintosh users can load the RWW interface and access the Read My Company E-mail and Use My Company's Internal Web Site features (see Figure 17.22 for the standard user's view of RWW).

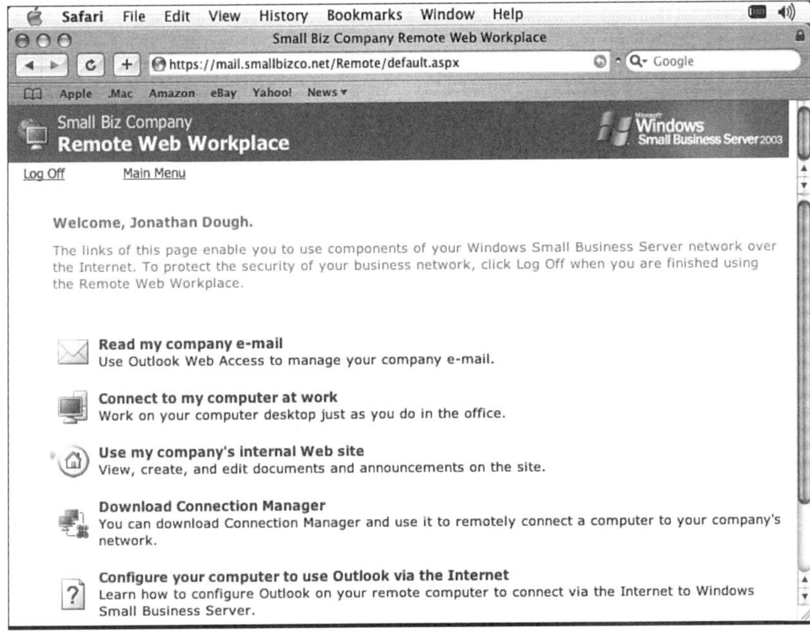

FIGURE 17.22 Safari can load the default user's view in RWW.

Administrators logging in to RWW from a Macintosh can access the Monitor Help Desk, Administer the Company's Internal Web Site, View Server Performance Report, View Server Usage Report, and Use Outlook Web Access links as shown in Figure 17.23.

Some features of RWW cannot be run from the Macintosh, however, such as connecting to client or server desktops, downloading the connection manager, or configuring Outlook via the Internet. All those links require PC-specific applications that are not supported on the Macintosh. Connecting to remote desktops (server or client) is not supported through RWW on the Macintosh because of the ActiveX tool needed to make the remote control connection. However, all these components have workarounds that will be discussed in the next sections.

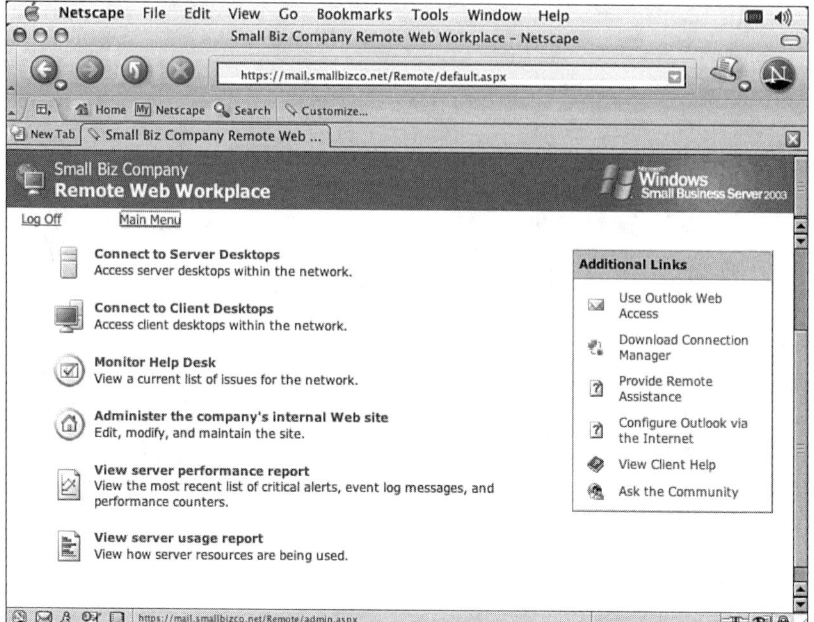

FIGURE 17.23 Netscape can load the default administrator's view in RWW.

A few other issues make accessing RWW more challenging for the Macintosh user. First is the SSL certificate issue that has been discussed earlier in the chapter. If an SBS server is using a self-signed certificate, Internet Explorer for the Macintosh will not be able to connect to RWW, period. Other browsers, such as Safari, Firefox, and Netscape, have ways to handle the unrecognized certificate and can access the main interface.

Second, the Companyweb and monitoring links within RWW use a web authentication mechanism that the early versions of the Safari browser do not process correctly. So Mac users wanting to make as much use of the RWW interface as possible need to rely on Firefox or Netscape or version 2.0 or later of Safari to handle access to those areas of the service.

Third, when accessing email through RWW, the Mac uses the Basic version of OWA as described earlier in this chapter. Otherwise, users on a Macintosh get much of the same functionality from RWW as PC users.

Connecting to the SBS Network Using VPN

If the SBS server has been set up to allow incoming VPN traffic, users running Mac OS X can use the built-in VPN client to remotely access the internal network. The VPN configuration is started with the Internet Connect application, but changes also need to be made in the network configuration to ensure proper VPN access.

Follow these steps to create a new VPN connection and connect to the internal network from the Macintosh:

1. Open the Internet Connect application (select Macintosh HD, Applications, Internet Connect).
2. Select File, New VPN Connection from the menu.
3. Click the PPTP button and then click Continue.
4. Enter the public name or IP address of the server, the username, and the password in the appropriate fields as shown in Figure 17.24.

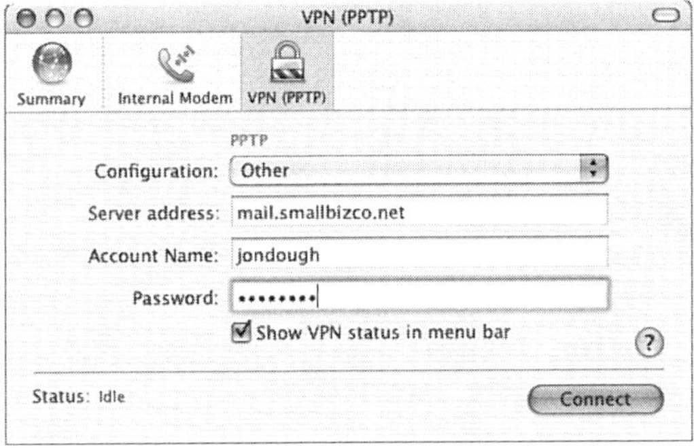

FIGURE 17.24 The server name in the VPN connectoid should be the public Internet name for the SBS server.

5. Click Connect.
6. When the VPN connection is established, quit Internet Connect. Enter a name for the VPN connection when prompted to save the settings.
7. Open System Preferences (select the Apple menu, System Preferences).
8. Click on the VPN (PPTP) section and click Configure.
9. Enter the internal address for the SBS server in the DNS Servers field.
10. Enter the internal domain name in the Search Domains field, as shown in Figure 17.25.
11. Click Apply Now and quit System Preferences.

At this point, you will be able to access resources on the internal network by name. To disconnect the VPN connection, click on the VPN icon in the upper-right of the screen and select Disconnect, as shown in Figure 17.26. To reconnect the VPN session, click the same icon and select Connect.

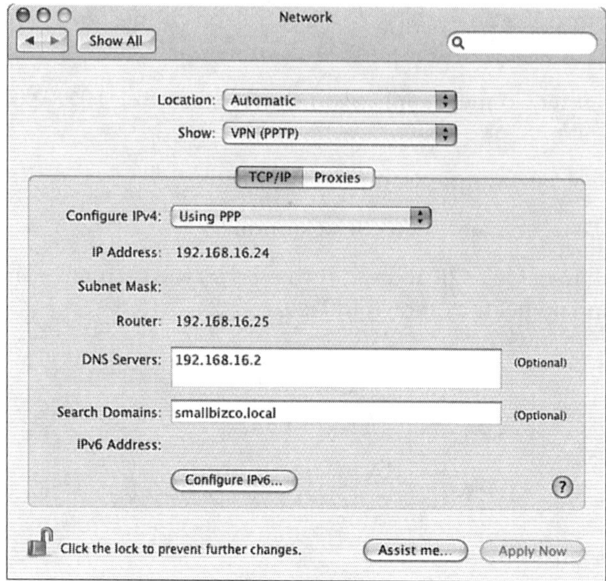

FIGURE 17.25 Adding the DNS server address and domain name allows the Mac to do internal name lookups while connected over VPN.

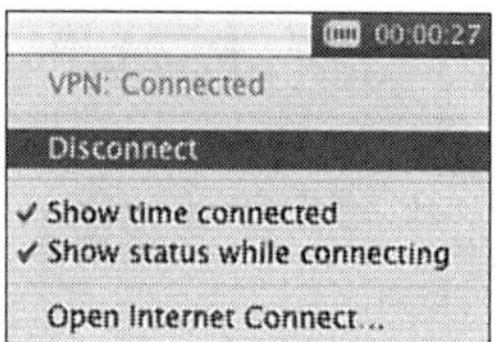

FIGURE 17.26 The VPN icon in the Status Tray allows users to connect and disconnect VPN sessions easily.

Remote Desktop Connection

After the Macintosh has made a VPN connection into the local network, users can use the Remote Desktop Connection (RDC) client from Microsoft to remotely connect to Windows XP workstations or the SBS server. RDC is the Macintosh version of the terminal services client and uses the same services and port number to access remote systems.

The RDC client for Macintosh can be downloaded from the Mactopia site from Microsoft at `http://www.microsoft.com/mac/downloads.aspx#Others`. After the application is launched, the interface is almost exactly like that of the PC version. To help get the best performance out of the RDC connection, some default settings should be modified. Table 17.1 indicates the recommended settings for the RDC client for Macintosh and the tab where those settings are located.

TABLE 17.1 Remote Desktop Connection Performance Will Be Improved Using These Settings

Tab	Recommended Settings
Display	Set colors to Thousands instead of 256.
Local Resources	Select Do Not Play for Remote computer sound.
	Disable the check boxes for Disk Drives and Printers.
Performance	Select Modem (56Kbps) for the connection speed.

The same rules apply to the Macintosh RDC client when connecting to an XP workstation, the SBS server, or a terminal server. Only one connection is allowed on an XP workstation, whether it's a local logon or a remote desktop connection. SBS 2003 allows only Remote Administration connections, not full terminal server support. Otherwise, using the Macintosh RDC client allows the same access as using the PC RDC client.

Summary

This chapter covered the multiple ways that a Macintosh workstation can interact with an SBS 2003 server. Macintosh workstations running any version of the Mac OS can connect to shares on the server via AppleTalk when the server is running Services for Macintosh. Mac OS 10 workstations can also connect to SMB shares on the server after some modifications have been made to the server and the Macintosh. Mac OS 9.2 and Mac OS 10.2/10.3 have trouble with name lookups for internal domains using the `.local` namespace. The workarounds are to use a host file on Mac OS 9.2 and make modifications to the network setup on Mac OS 10.2/10.3. Mac OS 10.4 does not have trouble with the `.local` namespace.

Macintosh workstations can get email from an Exchange server using a variety of methods. OWA provides access to a user's mailbox from inside or outside the local network. Older Macintosh mail clients can use the IMAP protocol to access the mail server, and the Entourage X client uses this protocol by default. For best Exchange server integration, Mac OS 9 machines should use Outlook 2001, and Mac OS X machines should use Entourage 2004.

The Macintosh has some issues working with the self-signed SSL certificate on the SBS websites. Internet Explorer for the Mac will never be able to access secure sites with a self-signed certificate, but Safari, Netscape, and Firefox all have ways to work around the certificate. The self-signed certificate must be installed into the Mac OS certificate store for Safari and Entourage 2004 to access secure SBS websites without warnings.

Macintosh workstations have a number of remote access avenues available as well. Macs can access most of the features of the RWW interface of SBS. The built-in VPN client in Mac OS X can connect with an SBS VPN server easily, and the RDC client allows a Mac to make an RDP connection either to the SBS server or a Windows XP workstation.

Best Practice Summary

- Mac OS should be kept up to date on all systems. When incremental OS releases are made available—for example, from Mac OS 10.3.7 to 10.3.8—those updates should be installed immediately. Major updates, from 10.2 to 10.3 or 10.4, should be tested and planned before installation.
- Services for Macintosh should be installed on the SBS server when there are machines running both Mac OS X and Mac OS 9 and earlier operating systems. This allows the workstations to share files on the server with ease.
- When only Mac OS X-based workstations are on the network, do not use Services for Macintosh. Instead, configure the Mac workstations to connect to the existing SMB shares on the server.
- If you are setting up a new SBS installation, do not use the `.local` top-level domain name. Instead, use `.lan` or `.office` or some other private domain name.
- When configuring email access on the Macintosh platform, use IMAP instead of POP3. This is required for Entourage X Exchange integration and helps cut down on "lost" mail that is common when running multiple POP3 mail clients.
- For tightest Exchange server integration, use Outlook 2001 for the mail client on Mac OS 9 and earlier machines. Entourage 2004 is the best tool to use for Mac OS X.

PART VIII

Administration and Management

IN THIS PART

CHAPTER 18

Backing Up Small Business Server

IN THIS CHAPTER

- Understanding Backup Issues
- Using the SBS Backup Wizard
- Using NTBackup
- Using Third-Party Backup Tools
- Disaster Recovery with SBS Backup Tools
- Troubleshooting Backup Issues

Most people and small businesses take backup seriously only after their first, or sadly even second, disaster. Even then, perhaps, backup doesn't get the respect it deserves given that the data to be backed up may represent the entire intellectual property and value of a business that took years to build. In the time to recover the backed-up data the entire goodwill of the business or its cash flow can be eroded.

Backup is not simple; it needs to be seen in the broader context of business continuity planning and disaster recovery planning. The operative word here is *recovery*, and it is not, as many would see it, merely a case of copying some files to some media or other that may or may not be stored offsite.

Understanding Backup Issues

There are many elements to a backup plan, and these elements need to be considered in terms of the business needs and statutory requirements prior to installation, configuration, and implementation. Disaster recovery planning is a complex undertaking requiring analysis of risk and cost, and the resultant strategy may require more than one type of backup and more than one schedule.

So why do a backup? It may be as insurance against deleted, corrupted, or overwritten data or emails. It may be to provide an audit trail or historic record for legal or taxation purposes. It may also, in the bigger picture, be to provide for the ability to restore the computing system in the event of a catastrophic failure.

File Recovery

SBS 2003 includes the Volume Shadow Copy Service (VSS), which can be scheduled to the requirements of the business and provides not only the capability to recover deleted files and folders but also previous versions of files directly from the desktop. Similarly Exchange Deleted Item Retention (EDIR) provides the capability for the user to recover deleted emails (within the set retention period) directly from Outlook.

VSS and EDIR are far faster and simpler than recovering from backup, where the relevant media has to be located, the restore process initialized, and the relevant file(s) located and then copied back to the system. Scrolling through a large tape can be time consuming, and the process is labor intensive. However, although VSS and EDIR are available, you still need to back up files and data stores as insurance against physical disk loss, damage, or corruption due to application error, viral or malware activity, or even user error.

Archiving

It is often necessary to keep permanent or long-term copies of data for legal, taxation, historic, or auditing purposes. Not only are speed and convenience issues here but also the choice of media. CDs and DVDs are proving not to be good choices for long-term archival storage, and a good deal of data and heritage stored digitally has already been lost.

In addition to the media, consideration must be given to the backup devices and programs. Will the device, drivers, and software be available when the business needs to recover the archived data? It is pointless to have a vault full of backups if there is no way to replay them.

System Recovery

Computers are an enormous boon to small businesses that need to do "more with less." SBS in particular, which hosts many software servers, services, and data on the one piece of hardware, has an immediate appeal. However, SBS does not support clustering or trusts, and can be a single point of failure for all those services and data. There is no failover.

While the server is down, users can be left unproductive. This is an expensive proposition for small and medium-sized businesses where the cost is not spread widely and cannot be absorbed as in large corporates. Without email, Internet, and access to accounting and line-of-business applications, communication with clients and suppliers is often severely disrupted. Should the outage continue for some considerable time, the harm done may be irreparable and may even be a terminal event for the business.

You must consider the needs and type of business and what is an acceptable time period for recovery of the system. The type of disaster and whether the recovery is to be to the same hardware, clone hardware, or different hardware all have a bearing. Restoring an image to the same hardware may go smoothly, but the restored image may be unbootable if restored to new hardware that is significantly different from the original.

Imaging a system before and after applying service packs or making major system changes, however, can be a good practice in providing a restore point for that hardware should critical issues occur due to the changes.

Doing a full system restore of SBS from backup prior to SBS 2003 was nearly impossible even with a System State backup. In SBS 2000 issues with the Short File Name – Long File Name storage and restore meant that the only truly viable option was to rebuild the server from scratch and then restore selective data from backup. The Microsoft developers have worked hard, and with SBS 2003 the full System State backup created by the SBS Backup Wizard allows for a successful full system restore on top of Windows Server.

Hardware and Media

Choice of hardware and media need to be considered in the backup strategy because both the size of the backup and the time taken for the backup/restore can be considerable if the medium is slow. The convenience of the media may also be a factor in the overall success of the backup plan. Although it will be faster to back up to and restore from an external USB HDD, it is also more likely that a backup operator will leave the drive sitting on the server when in a rush than the 2-inch backup tape the operator can pop into her pocket.

Copying files to a floppy disk is a form of backup. In fact many applications, including accounting and line of business applications use copy to floppy as part of their internal backup routine and will prompt the user to do such a backup before closing the application. As long as the data can be successfully retrieved from the floppy disk and utilized, then the aim was met. The relatively limited data storage capacity and unreliability of floppy disks make them of limited use in modern computing. Floppy disks are quickly being replaced by thumb/flash drives, which are a step up in capacity, reliability, speed, and convenience. CDs and DVDs provide inexpensive, convenient storage within the limitations of their storage capacity, but they lack reusability.

Removable or external USB or firewire hard disk drives provide still greater storage capacity, but aside from the laptop drives and enclosures, are magnitudes more cumbersome than tapes and not very tolerant of handling and shock. Concerning price, hard disks are attractive to many small businesses, and this contrasts strongly with tape drives, which, costing thousands of dollars, are something that many small businesses cannot afford. The tapes themselves, however, are small and convenient with good reusability and can be loaded into auto changers when backup volumes are significant or growing.

Online storage at a remote location is another alternative, although bandwidth, reliability of the connection, and possibly the cost, if the ISP charges by the byte, are all issues. Again, depending on the needs of the business, a combination of backups may be the answer—system images burned regularly to DVD combined with online incremental backups, or external HDD backups combined with tape archived data, for example. Backup is not a "one size fits all" endeavor. The solution must be customized to the environment and need.

As the size of the backup and the commensurate time taken to do the backups increases, it is becoming increasingly popular to back up to hard disk first and then to stream to tape or other media at a time more suited to the slower transfer rate. The SBS backup created by the Backup Wizard by using Volume Shadow Copy Services is to an extent using this technique already; however, it all happens on the SBS server, and it would be better if the process was offloaded to a separate backup server.

The Backup Plan

As with all things mission critical and disaster related, there should be built-in redundancy. Even tape autoloaders need to be loaded. Backup media needs to be swapped out and (preferably) taken offsite. Backup logs need to be checked and the right people informed and action taken if a backup (or the system itself) fails.

The backup and restore process requires a detailed and considered plan that should be well documented. The people relevant to the plan should be trained in its implementation, and the plan should be tested, practiced, and revised regularly. Additionally, a current copy of the plan should be stored together with the offsite backup.

In creating the plan, consideration needs to be given to a host of aspects such as:

- What should happen if the backup operator has taken the backups home and goes on vacation to the Bahamas the night before the server crashes?
- Does the shy new girl know what to do if she cannot get the tape out of the tape drive, or does she just not tell anyone?
- What should happen if the backup operator leaves the backups lying on the top of the server because they are too bulky or inconvenient to take offsite for some reason or other?
- Are the backups being regularly tested by doing an actual restore and then verifying the integrity of the files by accessing and manipulating the data?
- Is the backup operator, administrator, or IT person capable of restoring the data? Have they been trained, and are they capable of doing the restore in a timely manner?
- Can the IT person restore the backup (including System State) to new server hardware (new metal)? Has the IT person tested and practiced this and is she therefore critically aware of the issues relating to differing hardware, chipsets, drivers, and so on, the processes involved, and actions required to overcome them?
- Will the recovery be a timely process?
- As the business grows and changes, are the measures still adequate and is the plan still relevant?
- Have the parties involved considered everything relevant to their particular business and statutory needs?

Site and Security

Care and consideration must be given to both the location where the backups are kept and the security surrounding them. As mentioned previously, the backups may be after all the entire intellectual property of the business.

At first glance, a fireproof safe seems like a reasonable place to store backups, but although temperatures inside the safe may not be high enough for papers to spontaneously combust, they may be high enough to utterly destroy the backup media. No one would consider it reasonable for the backup tapes to be left on the dashboard of a car in the searing heat of the parking lot in summer, but it's been done, and by the business owner.

Take this scenario into consideration: A shipping agent's offices burned down. Half the damage was caused by the fire, the other half by the water and the fire fighters. The damage extended to the backup tapes, which were kept onsite. The end result was that the business lost both its paper and electronic records. From memory alone, the business owners had no idea what the full extent of their customer base was nor how to contact their customers. They had no idea where in the world their customer's goods were—which boat, plane, train, dock, warehouse, or bond store they were in—or when they were to be moved or how. Within days, the principals were winding up the business, and within a week fighting off both business and personal lawsuits from customers whose own businesses were in jeopardy due to their reliance on "Just In Time" supply. The business insurance was not sufficient to cover the claims of negligence nor did it provide for new careers and reputations for the principals.

An offsite backup would have preserved the shipping agent's business. To a limited extent, the company could have been up and running in 24–48 hours, but how far offsite is safe? A mile away may be safe if the office burns down, or a lightning strike fries the server, but if the location is susceptible to broad range disasters such as floods, hurricanes, or earthquakes, it may be advisable to have additional backups still farther afield. A remote backup copy would also cover the business if the duration of an event such as a flood or blizzard blocks the client from access to both his own site and that of the offsite backup for an unacceptable period of time.

Not only the site but also the security of the offsite backup is important. Not only should access to the media be protected, but the data bits themselves should be encrypted and the data locked. A USB hard disk backup the boss took home may be isolated from any disaster at the office, but is it safe from little Johnny and his friends when they need somewhere to store their newly found cache of Internet video games? Or, what about the burglar who just happens to be IT savvy and finds all those customer and bank account details on the backup he pocketed? Sadly, far too many business owners come to really consider backup far too late.

Backup Types

Aside from creating a full disk image or just copying a few files, several standard backup types can be run, as discussed in the following sections.

Full Backup

Full backups are the most comprehensive and are self-contained backups. However, the size of the data to be backed up and the time it takes to run a full backup to slow media may make it inappropriate as a regularly scheduled backup. Full backups may be restricted to a weekly or monthly schedule.

Most small businesses that fall within the SBS client base should have no problem doing a full nightly backup as created by the SBS Backup Wizard. If data size does become an issue (for example, multimedia or CAD files), archiving older files or excluding the files from the full backup and running a second data-only incremental or differential backup become options.

The trade-offs of a full backup are that although it provides the fastest restore, the storage space requirement is the highest, and backup and verify time is the longest.

With a full backup, only the previous full backup needs to be stored offsite.

It is also worth noting that each full backup contains an entire copy of the data. If the backup media were to be illegally accessed or stolen, the hacker or thief would then have access to an entire copy of your data.

The SBS 2003 Backup Wizard only creates a full, System State backup, but it does allow for the exclusion of some files and folders. SBS works around the problem of backing up open files by taking a snapshot copy of the drive contents using VSS. A copy of the open file is made by VSS, and the backup process accesses the VSS copy of the file instead of trying to access the open file directly.

Differential Backup

There is a significant distinction between differential backups and incremental backups although they are often confused. *Differential backups* back up all the files that have changed since the last full backup, whereas *incremental backups* back up all the files modified since the last full backup or incremental backup.

The trade-off is that although smaller and subsequently faster than a full backup, a differential backup is slower to restore.

Two backup files are required: the latest full backup and the latest differential backup. The last full backup and the last differential backup are the two backups that you need to store offsite.

Incremental Backup

Incremental backups provide a much faster method of backing up data than either full or incremental backups. An incremental backup backs up only those files that have changed since the most recent full, incremental, or differential backup.

The advantage of lower backup times comes at the price of an increased restore time and the need to safely store more media offsite. When restoring from incremental backup, you need the most recent full backup as well as every incremental backup you've made since the last full backup.

For example, if you did a full backup on Friday and incrementals on Monday, Tuesday, Wednesday, and Thursday, and the server crashes on the next Friday, you would need all five backup files: The Friday full backup and the Monday, Tuesday, Wednesday, and Thursday incrementals.

By comparison, if you had done differential backups on Monday, Tuesday, Wednesday, and Thursday, to restore on the Friday only the previous Friday's full backup plus Thursday's differential backup are required.

NOTE

Windows NTBackup uses the following backup type definitions:

- Normal backup (full)—A normal backup copies all the files you select and marks each file as having been backed up (in other words, the archive attribute is cleared). With normal backups, you only need the most recent copy of the backup file or tape to restore all the files. You usually perform a normal backup the first time you create a backup set.
- Copy backup—A copy backup copies all the files you select but does not mark each file as having been backed up (in other words, the archive attribute is not cleared). Copying is useful if you want to back up files between normal and incremental backups because copying does not affect these other backup operations.
- Daily backup—Daily backup copies all the files you select that have been modified on the day the daily backup is performed. The backed-up files are not marked as having been backed up (in other words, the archive attribute is not cleared). This backup type is generally not used as part of a recovery program because to do a full system restore, you would have to have a normal backup and then a daily backup from each and every day since the normal backup.

Disk Image

Hard disk and partition imaging software takes a snapshot of your hard disk(s) so that you can restore your system at a later time to the exact state the system was in when you imaged the disks or partitions. The image is a sector-by-sector, byte-by-byte copy of the state of the hard disk.

Image utilities often do not allow fine control of what you back up. You can specify the partitions or hard disks to back up, but you usually will not be able to specify which folders to exclude or include. They may also require that the system be offline, although increasingly less so with the newer software.

Although imaging provides a restore form clone capability, the time taken to image the system can be substantial, and verification can be difficult if not impossible without doing a full restore. The full restore, however, can be extremely fast and successful if restoring to the same or substantially similar hardware.

Backup Schedule

In creating the backup plan, it is important to consider the backup schedule in light of the backup type, the time required for the backup to run and verify, the server load, other scheduled events, and the media rotation.

It's assumed, possibly optimistically, that due consideration is being given to the running time required for the backup and verify process as well as other things happening on the server.

Although most operators try to schedule backups during out-of-office hours so as not to impede user performance and minimize open files, it's not uncommon to find the backup/verify process conflicting with such things as virus scans, remote site synchronization (file transfers), the scheduled Exchange Management, or automated software updates (service packs and patches). Site documentation should include an event schedule for the server, and part of regular backup verification should include a check on the running time of the backup/verify process and any potential scheduling conflicts.

> **Best Practice—Managing the Event Scheduler**
>
> Create and maintain a schedule of running events occurring on the server and refer to this prior to installing/running new processes. This should be an integral part of the server/network documentation and its cover sheet.
>
> The running times of processes should be noted regularly, and the schedules and documentation amended as needed. There is more going on than most realize on first thought, and documentation helps tease out the complete picture.

Media Rotation

The media rotation depends on the type of backup, the type of media, the number of media units, and so on. Thought should be given to the fact that data corruption may not be noticed for some time, if the data is not accessed frequently, and it may be necessary to roll back a day, week, month, or even a year.

Table 18.1 shows a typical rotation plan.

TABLE 18.1 Ten-Tape Full Backup Rotation

Period	Day	Time	Type	Media	Offsite	Comments
Weekly	Monday	20:00	Full	D–Monday	✓	Take Offsite–Tuesday Nightly schedule
	Tuesday	20:00	Full	D–Tuesday	✓	Take Offsite–Wednesday Nightly schedule
	Wednesday	20:00	Full	D–Wednesday	✓	Take Offsite–Thursday Nightly schedule
	Thursday	20:00	Full	D–Thursday	✓	Take Offsite–Friday Nightly schedule
	Friday	20:00	Full	D–Friday	✓	Take Offsite–Monday Nightly schedule
					☐	
Week 1	Monday	8:00	Full	W–1	✓	Take Offsite–Monday First thing Monday morning
Week 2	Monday	8:00	Full	W–2	✓	Take Offsite–Monday First thing Monday morning
Week 3	Monday	8:00	Full	W–3	✓	Take Offsite–Monday First thing Monday morning
Week 4	Monday	8:00	Full	W–4	✓ ☐	Take Offsite–Monday First thing Monday morning
Monthly	Last Day	17:00	Full (Data Only)	A–Monthly	✓	Take Offsite–after completion Accounting Backup after Rollover/Commit
					☐	To hold 12 Monthly Backups Tape to Archive Storage Annually

Using the SBS Backup Wizard

The simplest way to create a full System State Exchange aware backup that can be used to restore the SBS in the event of a catastrophic failure and, at the same time, configure shadow copies and Exchange deleted mail retention, is to use the wizard.

The SBS Backup Wizard can be accessed from a number of locations:

- From the To-Do List
- From the To-Do List on the Server Manager
- From the Backup link on the Server Manager

When the wizard launches, click next in the Welcome to Small Business Server Backup Configuration Wizard page to get to the backup location. If the wizard found a compatible tape drive attached to the system, it will enable the Tape Drive option as a recommended default. You may also choose to back up to a location on the hard disk or to a network share.

CAUTION

You cannot back up to optical media such as CD-ROM or DVD-ROM.

After you make your selection, the Backup Data Summary page displays. The SBS Wizard selects all necessary drives and data for a full system backup by default. Should you want to exclude folders or drives, you can do so from this screen by clicking on the Exclude Folders button. From there, you would click the Add Folder button to select the additional folders you want to exclude from the backup.

In the Backup Data Summary page, you can click the Calculate Folder Sizes button to display the size of each item included or excluded from the backup.

Next, in the Define Backup Schedule page, you can set the time and dates you want the backup to run automatically. If you are backing up to tape, the wizard allows you to configure a notification to the tape changer. This sends an email to the person identified as the tape changer, reminding him to change the tape or run a cleaning tape on the drive.

The Storage Allocation for Deleted Files and Emails page appears next, as shown in Figure 18.1. You can set the number of days deleted messages and mailboxes will be retained and allocate space for shadow copies of files and folders.

The last page of the wizard appears showing a summary of the actions that will be taken. When you click Finish, the wizard builds the relevant backup files, scripts, schedules, and alerts and sets the Exchange and Shadow Copy settings while creating a `BackupWizard.log` file (by default located at `C:\Program files\Microsoft Small Business Server\Support`) that can be used for debugging.

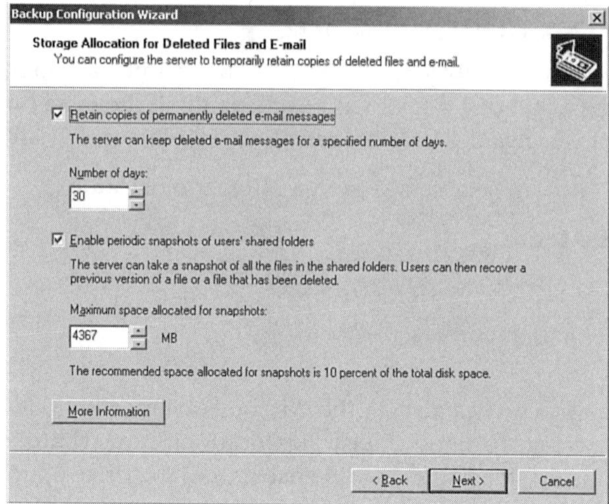

FIGURE 18.1 Storage allocation for deleted files and emails.

Like all the wizards in SBS 2003, the Backup Wizard provides a simple interface to configure many settings scattered about the servers and services. It is often easier to rerun the wizard when these setting need to change than manually configure them and run the risk of misconfiguring them. That is not to say that manual settings aren't possible or even in some cases desirable.

Limitations of the SBS Backup Wizard

Although the wizard provides a wonderful wrapper around NTBackup to vastly simplify the process of creating a full System State backup, it is not a full-fledged backup application in itself, and it has limitations. The wizard is specifically designed to create a backup that can be used to recover the system in the event of a data disaster either in the form of physical failure of the system/hard disk(s) or corruption/deletion of the system files themselves.

The limitations of the SBS Backup Wizard are limitations of both what the wizard is designed to do and what NTBackup itself is designed to do. Although in some instances it may be desirable to have many additional features, those can be found in many of the dedicated and more up-to-date backup software applications and suites.

The SBS Backup Wizard

- Can only create full Exchange aware System State backups
- Is reliant on the VSS for file copy
- Does not use VSS for Exchange backup
- Does not allow for the disabling of the backup verify
- Exclusions work at the drive and folder level only, not the file level

Limitations of NTBackup are as follows:

- Has no remote console
- Does not do software compression
- Cannot do "brick level" (individual mailbox) Exchange backup
- Does not contain a VSS Requestor
- Cannot back up to writable CD-ROM or DVD
- Does not support tape autoloaders/changers
- Cannot create disk images
- Cannot back up network/remote computers System State or Registry
- Has limited error handling and reporting
- Cannot email or print completed job logs
- Cannot eject a tape after a backup
- By design, can only back up directories when using a batch file or through a command prompt
- Has no simple way to write a backup to an arbitrary tape without using the `/um` (unmanaged) option on the command line
- Has no simple way to append backup information to an inserted tape because you must use either the `/t` (tape name) or `/g` (GUID—Globally Unique Identifier) command-line option. Unmanaged mode won't work because you can only append to a specifically named tape.
- Does not have an internal scheduler, so if the backup fails, it will not attempt to rerun until the next scheduled event.

Despite the limitations, within the framework of their stated goal, the wizard and NTBackup fulfill their roles well, and most SBS users do not require any additional functionality or backup software.

Settings Generated by the Wizard

As mentioned previously, in addition to creating a full System State Exchange aware backup of the SBS server, the SBS 2003 Backup Wizard configures several applications external to NTBackup itself that would otherwise need to be manually configured. These are

- Exchange deleted item retention
- Exchange circular logging turned off
- Periodic shadow copy snapshots of shared folders
- The scheduling of the backup action

- Creation of backup reports in SBS Monitoring
- Scheduled email reminders for the backup operator tape changer
- Report generation

Excluding Data from the Backup Wizard

By default, the SBS Backup Wizard backs up all data and system files, including Exchange databases and logs. Drive and folder exclusions must be specifically set during the configuration process. Not all files and folders are backed up, however, as can be seen in Figure 18.2, the Registry key `HKLM\System\CurrentControlSet\control\BackupRestore\FilesNotToBackup`, and in Table 18.2. These files will be automatically re-created by the system itself if required after a restore.

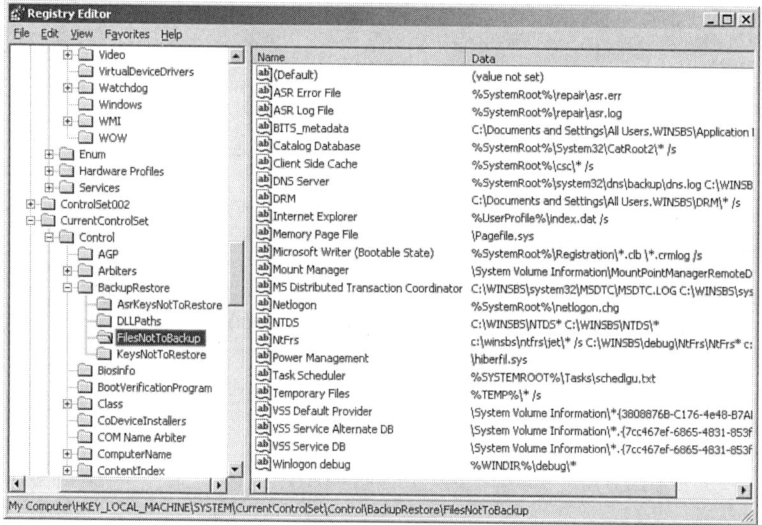

FIGURE 18.2 FilesNotToBackup Registry setting.

TABLE 18.2 Automatic Backup Exclusions

ASR Error File

%SystemRoot%\repair\asr.err

ASR Log File

%SystemRoot%\repair\asr.log

BITS_metadata

C:\Documents and Settings\All Users.WINSBS\Application Data\Microsoft\Network\Downloader*

Catalog Database

%SystemRoot%\System32\CatRoot2* /s

Client Side Cache

%SystemRoot%\csc* /s

TABLE 18.2 Continued

DNS Server

%SystemRoot%\system32\dns\backup\dns.log

C:\WINSBS\system32\dns\dns.log

DRM

C:\Documents and Settings\All Users.WINSBS\DRM* /s

Internet Explorer

%UserProfile%\index.dat /s

Memory Page File

\Pagefile.sys

Microsoft Writer (Bootable State)

%SystemRoot%\Registration*.clb

*.crmlog /s

Mount Manager

\System Volume Information\MountPointManagerRemoteDatabase

MS Distributed Transaction Coordinator

C:\WINSBS\system32\MSDTC\MSDTC.LOG

C:\WINSBS\system32\MSDtc\trace\dtctrace.log

Netlogon

%SystemRoot%\netlogon.chg

NTDS

C:\WINSBS\NTDS*

C:\WINSBS\NTDS*

NtFrs

c:\winsbs\ntfrs\jet* /s

C:\WINSBS\debug\NtFrs\NtFrs*

c:\winsbs\sysvol\domain\DO_NOT_REMOVE_NtFrs_PreInstall_Directory* /s

c:\winsbs\sysvol\domain\NtFrs_PreExisting___See_EventLog* /s

:\winsbs\sysvol\staging\domain\NTFRS_*

Power Management

\hiberfil.sys

Task Scheduler

%SYSTEMROOT%\Tasks\schedlgu.txt

Temporary Files

%TEMP%* /s

VSS Default Provider

\System Volume Information*{3808876B-C176-4e48-B7AE-04046E6CC752} /s

VSS Service Alternate DB

\System Volume Information*.{7cc467ef-6865-4831-853f-2a4817fd1bca}ALT

VSS Service DB

\System Volume Information*.{7cc467ef-6865-4831-853f-2a4817fd1bca}DB

Winlogon debug

%WINDIR%\debug*

Not all files need to be, or should be, backed up. Client application setup files can take up considerable space and are not essential for the restoration of the system. They can be easily copied back to the server from original media after a restore. Excluding these files can significantly reduce both the space required and the duration of the backup/verify and restore processes.

Business data that has been archived but retained on the server may be similarly excluded, as may the contents of antivirus and spam quarantine and backup folders provided that the applications will re-create the folders if they are not present after a restore rather than just fail.

If separate backups are made of line of business applications such as accounts contact management, inventory databases, and the like, these too can be excluded.

Because the SBS Backup Wizard is designed for full system recovery backup, you cannot exclude folders that are part of System folders, which are required for a system restore. Additionally folders within the Program Files directory are also locked from exclusion.

It may be necessary to reinstall or reconfigure some third-party applications if data stores and folders (such as antivirus quarantine files) that are by default stored in the Program Files folder are to be excluded from backup.

Best Practice—Planning the Server File Structure

It is good practice to store all variable data on a separate drive or partition. This makes locating files to be backed up and backup configuration simpler.

Restoration is also both simplified and speeded up because the whole drive/partition can be restored and fragmentation reduced.

SBS 2003 hides the Exchange virtual drive (M); however, if it is visible for any reason, it should be explicitly excluded from the backup.

If backing up to an external hard disk drive or a server disk prior to transferring to other media, the location of the backup must be excluded or the backup process will fail trying to back up its own active backup file.

Best Practice—SQL Databases in Simple Mode

Make sure that SQL Server and MSDE databases are set to Simple mode unless you are excluding them from the backup. SQL Server contains its own backup routine, and this can be configured to back up databases to a folder on the server that can be included in the server backup.

Changing the Backup Notification

The Small Business Backup Script file (by default located at `C:\Program Files\Microsoft Windows Small Business Server\Backup`) does not contain nearly as much information as is actually involved in the wizard process. This is only the `.bks` file that is run by NTBackup. Although the file can be opened and edited in Notepad, it is highly recommended that this not be done, and any changes required be made by rerunning the Backup Wizard. The `.bks` file is actually a Unicode file without the Unicode header bytes.

Best Practice—Change Backup Settings Only with the Wizard

Wherever possible in SBS it is always best to rerun the associated wizard if there is one, instead of making manual adjustments or file edits. This holds true for the Backup Wizard as well. The only way to make sure that the automated backup process runs correctly is to use the Backup Wizard; otherwise, you would have to configure all the backup steps using NTBackup, including scheduling, exclusions, and so on. The wizard is designed to take care of all these steps for you automatically.

To change the Tape Change and Tape Cleaner notification alerts to the backup operator, simply rerun the SBS Backup Wizard.

Using NTBackup

Aside from using the Backup Wizard to create a fully recoverable system backup, it may be a desirable part of the plan to back up individual data structures such as large CAD or multimedia folders, databases, accounting data, CRM, or other line of business applications.

It can also be useful to back up individual structures such as the Exchange databases and log files prior to applying a service pack or patch, or doing other maintenance such as compacting the data stores.

You can access Windows NTBackup via either the Run command (Start, Run, NTBackup) or from the icon shortcut under the System menu.

When NTBackup launches, it starts in Wizard mode. You can click Next to continue with the wizard or click the Advanced Mode link. This section of the chapter covers the Advanced mode interface of NTBackup. In the Backup tab, select the files and folders you want to back up. To back up Exchange Server components, expand Microsoft Exchange Server, *your server name*, and from there you can select Microsoft Information Store to back up the entire Exchange database, or you can drill down into First Storage Group and select either the Mailbox Store or the Public Folder Store.

If you want to save the backup selection to a file, choose Job, Save Selection As from the menu and choose the location and filename for the backup script file.

When you click the Start Backup button, the Backup Job Information dialog appears. From there, you can start the backup immediately, click the Advanced button to select advanced backup options, click the Schedule button to set a schedule for the backup job to follow, or cancel the operation and return to the Backup Selection window.

In the Advanced Backup Options window, you can select the backup type as Normal, Copy, Incremental, Differential, or Daily (these options are described in the "Backup Types" section earlier in the chapter). You can also choose to back up data from Remote Storage (if configured on your server), verify the data after the backup (recommended), compress the backup data (if the device storing the backup supports compression), and back up system protected files with the System State backup (if the System State backup is selected in the backup selection).

When you click the Schedule button, the NT Task Scheduler runs to schedule the backup at regular intervals. The first step in the process is providing the credentials that the task will use to run the backup process. The username and password you provide must be for a user object that is a member of the Backup Operators group.

CAUTION

Although you can use the built-in Administrator account credentials to schedule a backup job, when you change the password for the account, the scheduled backup jobs will start failing. You will need to reenter the credentials for the backup job when you change the administrator password.

Next, you give the scheduled job a name and click the Properties button to set the frequency of the backup job. In the job scheduler, you can schedule the job to run daily, weekly, monthly, once, at system startup, at logon, or when idle. Each of those selections has its own settings. In the Settings tab, you can select other options related to power management, idle time, and even how to handle the job if it hasn't completed within a certain time frame.

Because NTBackup supports running from the command line, it is possible to configure more elaborate backups as part of a broader routine via batch or script commands. Run **`ntbackup /?`** to open the command-line reference help window for NTBackup and see all the command-line options available for NTBackup.

Using Third-Party Backup Tools

Third-party backup tools have been mentioned previously in the chapter. They can add valuable functionality to a disaster recovery plan providing additional features above and beyond those found in SBS Backup.

Examples of such functionality are the capability to create disk images, even bootable disk images that can be used to restore a system from a USB or firewire attached hard disk drive, or restore from a bootable floppy disk.

Brick level backups of Exchange Mailboxes can speed up recovery of individual mailboxes. You would need to use exmerge or the Recovery Storage group to get the same functionality with the default tools. Similarly, they may support full, incremental, or differential SQL Server backups; remote SQL Server backups; and restoration of SQL Server data to an alternate SQL server.

Some third-party backup software solutions allow for network backup, so workstations can be backed up, cloned, and even restored remotely, and many provide remote console control of the server backup and remote view of the running backup process. Some third-party backup solutions also support VSS backup of Microsoft Exchange as they incorporate the VSS Requestor.

To deal with larger backups, third-party applications can do backups cascading to multiple storage devices and support tape changers and optical media such as CD and DVD or even to an FTP device.

At the file level third-party applications can also provide global exclusion filtering and overwrite options such as newer, always, never, and overwrite of Open files. There is also support for file compression.

In many ways these are more up-to-date applications meeting the needs of larger storage, modern hardware and storage media, and both faster and easier recovery. NTBackup is adequate, and with the SBS Backup Wizard wrapper can be a good, inexpensive solution for small businesses.

The right choice of software should be determined by the strategy that best fits the business requirements and the disaster recovery plan.

Disaster Recovery with SBS Backup Tools

The sole reason for a backup's existence is for the data stored on it to be successfully restored at some unforeseen point in time. It is not there to ward off disaster as if by magic.

All backups, be they recent, or archival, should be regularly tested by restoring some or all of the data and ensuring that that data is both readable and usable (can be copied, changed, and so on). At least a partial restore by selecting random files should be done on a monthly basis. This can be done by the backup operators themselves.

Additionally, on a more infrequent and random schedule, a complete "bare metal" system restore to a test server should be done by the responsible IT. A surprise visit to the client to pick up the backup is a good way to check the client's readiness and the efficiency of the backup plan. The test restore also ensures that both the backup operator and the IT are familiar with the process and ready for any contingencies that may present themselves in the event of a real disaster.

On a day-to-day basis, the existence of the shadow copies and of the Exchange deleted item retention, means that users themselves can restore missing data without recourse to the media and backup and all the time and effort entailed in restoring from that.

Restoring a Backup

To do a full system restore of SBS 2003, you must first install the core operating system on the server. In SBS, this means that when you get to the part of installation where the integrated setup starts (see Chapter 4, "Installing SBS 2003 SP1 on a New Server," for more information), you cancel the setup process so that you only have the Windows Server 2003 portion installed but none of the SBS-specific components. Next, you need to install any operating system service packs that were installed when the backup was taken. For example, if you had installed Windows Server 2003 SP1 as part of SBS 2003 SP1 and you reinstall the operating system with pre-SP1 installation media, you will need to install Windows Server 2003 SP1 before you can continue with the restore. Next, you will run NTBackup to restore the data from backup onto the server.

Should the hardware be substantially different from the original, the system may need several reboots into Directory Services Recovery mode for the appropriate drivers to be loaded. This is why it is imperative that the disaster plan be practiced on both similar and dissimilar hardware.

Microsoft recommends that the following items on the new server should be as close as possible a hardware and version match to the original:

- SCSI controller
- Motherboard and chip set
- Number of processors
- Hard disk size
- The drive letter of the boot partition

You can use an IDE controller instead of a SCSI controller. Also, the hard drive on the new computer should have the same number of volumes or partitions, and they should be at least as large as the originals.

If the network cards have changes, you need to rerun the Configure Exchange and Internet Connection Wizard (CEICW) so as to re-create the settings with the new MAC addresses of the network cards (NICs).

You may also need to reregister the server and reinstall additional client licenses.

By rights, disaster recovery deserves a chapter, if not a book of its own. There are a multitude of server configurations, and each one brings its own unique requirement to the recovery process. This is why it cannot be stressed strongly enough that the disaster plan for each business *must* include the testing of recovery to both identical and dissimilar hardware of that business's backup. It cannot be assumed that what worked for business A will work for business B when it comes to disaster recovery.

Best Practice—Backup and Recovery Plan

Create and maintain a backup and recovery plan that contains step-by step instructions that are easy to follow. Get this up to date and store an additional copy together with the offsite backups.

During a disaster there is always confusion and pressure. A clear and concise guide that people can follow will eliminate errors and ensure that the system is successfully restored with the minimum delay and error.

For more information about the backup process on SBS, review the article "How to Back Up and Restore Your Server" from the SmallBizServer site (`http://www.smallbizserver.net/Default.aspx?tabid=144`).

Troubleshooting Backup Issues

Should backups fail, and they do, there are several places to begin the troubleshooting:

- Check the device and the media physically.
- Check the device manager and driver.
- Check the event logs.
- Check the backup log.
- If using tape drives, check the media pools.
- Check the disk space available for storage both on the media and on the server.
- Check the Usenet archives on Google groups.
- Check the Microsoft Knowledge Base if using NTBackup or the vendor site if using third-party backup software.
- Don't forget simple issues like unformatted media, write locks on tapes, and so on.
- Check for conflicting running processes and open files.
- Do a manual backup and watch for error pop-ups.

This is not an exhaustive list but hopefully provides some ideas for where to start. Like all debugging, it is half experience, half luck, and half black art.

Summary

Sometime, somewhere, for some reason, when you least expect it, the system will die. Whether the terminal event for the system becomes a terminal event for the business depends on how good the continuity and disaster planning was in its design and implementation.

The type of backup employed is dependant on many factors and elements, the mix of which may be unique to the site or business. The backup and recovery plan needs to be critically constructed, implemented, tested, practiced, and revised. Given that this has taken place and is taking place, a disaster need not be a catastrophe.

Best Practice Summary

- Managing the Event Scheduler—Maintain a list of scheduled events that run on the server to make sure that there are no conflicts with overlapping tasks.
- Planning the server file structure—Keep data on a separate drive or partition from the system to simplify and streamline data backup and restore processes.
- SQL databases in Simple mode—On SBS Server 2003, ensure that SQL Server and MSDE databases are set to Simple mode unless you are excluding them from the backup.

- Change backup settings only with the wizard—Wherever possible in SBS, it is always best to rerun the associated wizard rather than making manual adjustments or file edits.
- Backup and recovery plan—Create and maintain a backup and recovery plan that contains step-by step instructions that are easy to follow.

CHAPTER 19

Monitoring and Reporting

IN THIS CHAPTER

One of the biggest improvements in Small Business Server 2003 over older versions is the addition of the built-in monitoring and reporting tools. In the past, even a simple task such as sending the backup logs via email could take hours to configure. Today, with just a couple of clicks you can create impressive-looking HTML reports that can be sent automatically via email or retrieved on demand using the company's intranet.

In this chapter you learn how to configure and customize the monitoring, reporting, and alerting tools available in SBS. Also, detailed information on the different sections of each report is presented to give you some insight on the importance of each component.

To Monitor, or Not to Monitor? That Is the Question

It is no secret that the biggest challenge after installing any server is to keep it up-to-date and in top shape. Any business running SBS wants to be certain that it can rely on its server and that if something ever goes wrong you will be right there fixing it.

Monitoring can help you attain that goal by giving you all the information you need to determine the health of any system right at the tip of your fingers. No matter whether you are in charge of one SBS server or two dozen, with proper monitoring your life will be easier.

Any system administrator would appreciate receiving daily emails telling him what's going on with the servers. Many business owners would love to get detailed reports that show how each employee is using the available network resources. Every SMB IT consultant (or anyone who manages multiple SBS servers) will find that receiving reports from each server will help him figure out trends or patterns that occur after certain events. In fact, in some cases even receiving a critical alert via email can help you fix problems before they occur.

Sound amazing? Yes, and fortunately all this and more is available right out of the box with Small Business Server 2003.

Types of Reports and Alerts

As you have probably noticed by now SBS is comprised of numerous components and services that work together. A single SBS server can produce enormous quantities of logs and informational data. Sometimes the logs can be as trivial as the startup of a service or as critical as a system shutdown. With so much information available how do you determine what you need to monitor?

Once again SBS comes to your rescue by giving you preconfigured reports and alerts that contain the most important counters, monitors, and errors. Furthermore, most of these reports/alerts can be further customized to meet your specific monitoring requirements.

The following sections offer a brief overview of what each report/alert is about. (For in-depth information on their contents or how to interpret them, see the "What's Included in Each Report" section later in the chapter.)

Performance Report

This daily report focuses on the overall status of the server. The report includes information on the hardware, uptime, hard disk, memory, and processor(s). It also has a list of the most recent critical errors, status of the last backup, and other miscellaneous information. You can also customize the report to have certain logs attached (for example, backup logs).

The report is sent daily via email to the designated address(es), but it can also be accessed at any time from the server console, via Remote Web Workplace (RWW), or even directly from a web browser inside the LAN.

In general, the information in this report, shown in Figure 19.1, is most useful to the system administrator. Nontechnical users will probably lack the skills to understand the errors and act on them.

BEST PRACTICE—READ THE REPORTS

There is no point in configuring all these reports and alerts if nobody is going to read them. Take time each day to see what happened with your server the day before.

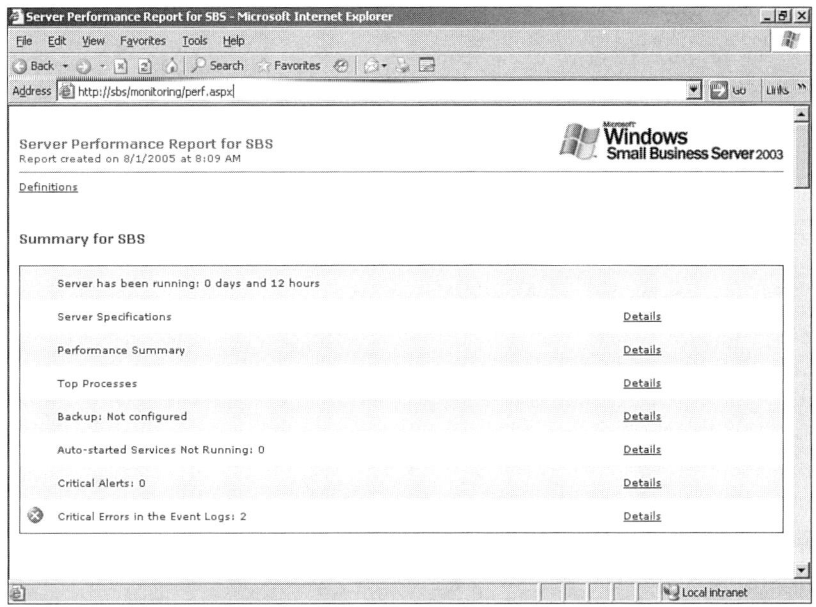

FIGURE 19.1 Sample of a performance report.

Usage Report

This report has specific information about how certain server resources are used or accessed. The report focuses on user details, such as the amount of emails sent and received by each user (as well as totals for the whole company). The report can also include information on Internet usage, individual mailbox growth, and even when and how the server has been accessed remotely.

The report can be sent every other week via email to the designated address(es), but it can also be accessed at any time from the server console, via RWW, or even from a web browser inside the LAN. You can also select the date range for which the report should run.

In general, the information contained in this report, shown in Figure 19.2, is useful not only to the system administrator but to the business owner as well.

BEST PRACTICE—BE PROACTIVE

Whenever you see an error make sure that you have an idea of why it happened and if possible take appropriate action to prevent it in the future. Review the usage reports and note when a user is getting close to her mailbox size limit so that you can take proactive steps to avoid the situation where the user is unable to send email.

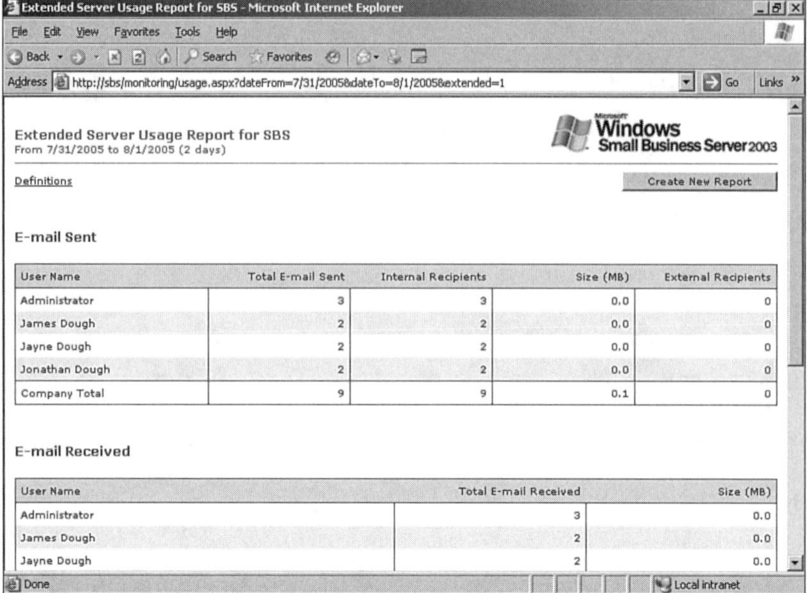

FIGURE 19.2 Sample of a usage report.

Performance Alerts

Alerts are nonregular emails sent whenever a critical event occurs, and they normally require immediate attention. Most alerts indicate that an important service has stopped, the server has restarted, an account has been locked out, or a critical error has occurred. Other alerts are relatively more benign, only indicating that a certain threshold has been exceeded.

In general, due to the technical nature of the alerts they are more useful to the system administrator. Figure 19.3 shows a sample performance alert.

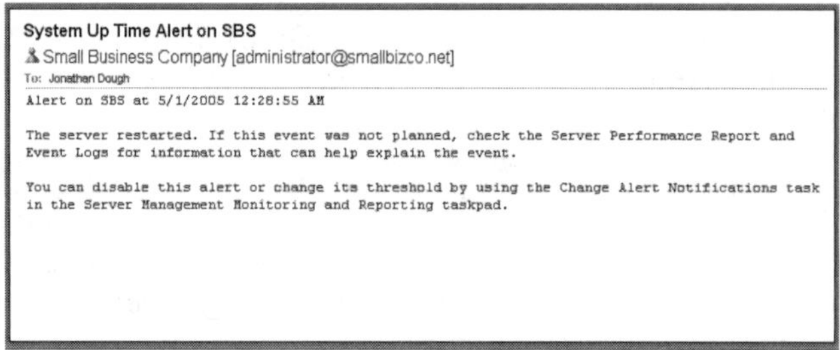

FIGURE 19.3 Sample of a System Up Time alert.

BEST PRACTICE—LOOK AT THE EVENT LOGS

Sometimes just looking at the reports is not enough. If you have a situation where you have multiple instances of the same error you might need to log on to the server and look at the event logs directly. Event log errors can be decrypted by visiting `http://www.eventid.net` (also a great resource for troubleshooting ideas).

Configuring and Using Monitoring and Alerts

If you haven't figured it out already, the SBS world revolves around wizards that make your life simpler, and monitoring is no exception to that paradigm. Can you take a guess where such a wonderful wizard might be? On the To Do list, of course!

Running the Monitoring Configuration Wizard

To configure or modify the monitoring and alert features in SBS use the following steps:

1. Open the Server Management Console. On the left pane expand Standard Management and then select To Do List. Scroll down to Management Tasks and click on Configure Monitoring to open the wizard, as shown in Figure 19.4. Alternatively, you can expand Monitoring and Reporting and click on Set Up Monitoring and Reports.

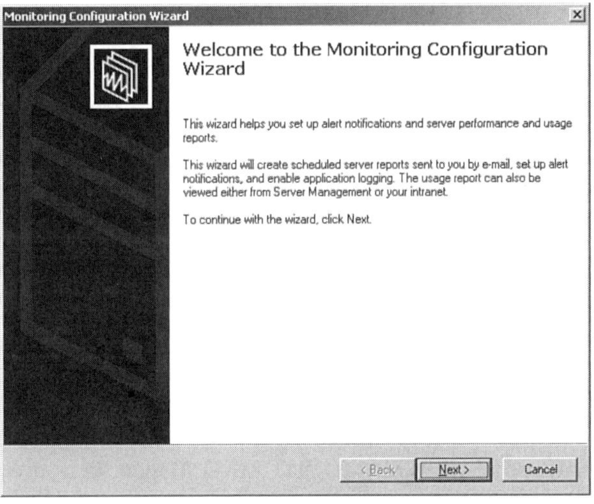

FIGURE 19.4 Monitoring Configuration Wizard welcome screen.

2. On the welcome screen click Next to open the Reporting Options screen (see Figure 19.5). To receive the daily performance reports via email, select the Receive a Daily Performance Report in Email check box.

19

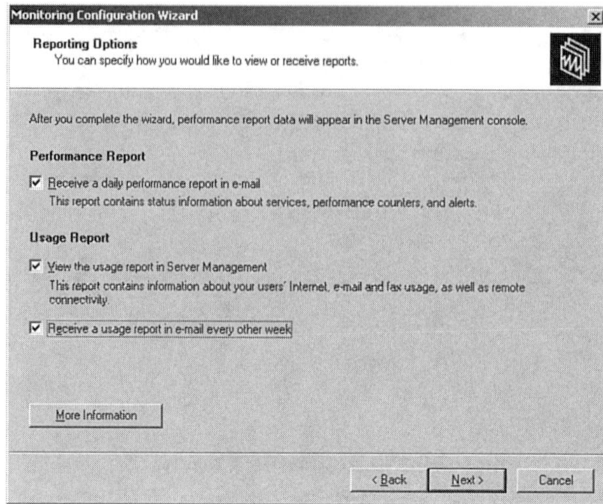

FIGURE 19.5 Reporting Options screen in the Monitoring Configuration Wizard.

3. To be able to see the usage reports in the Server Management Console, select the View the Usage Report in Server Management check box. If you also want to receive the reports every other week via email, select the Receive a Usage Report in Email Every Other Week check box, shown in Figure 19.5. Click Next.

4. Type the email address that you want the reports sent to. If you want to send the report(s) to multiple addresses separate them using a semicolon. Click Next.

   (Remember: Email addresses can be internal, external, or even distribution lists or public folders.)

5. Select the groups that will have access to the usage reports over the intranet. By default only Domain Administrators have access to them. Click Next.

6. To receive alerts via email, select the Send Me Notification of Performance Alerts by Email check box (see Figure 19.6). Type the email address that you want the alerts sent to. If you want to send the report(s) to multiple addresses, separate them using a semicolon. Click Next and finish the wizard.

After you run the wizard for the first time, performance and usage data begins to be collected in a MSDE instance called SBSMONITORING. Depending on what reports you selected you will start receiving them by email soon.

Alternatively, you can access the reports two other ways (if your user account has permissions to see them):

- From inside your network, open Internet Explorer and type **`http://sbs/monitoring/perf.aspx`** (for accessing the performance report) or type **`http://sbs/monitoring`** (for accessing the usage report).

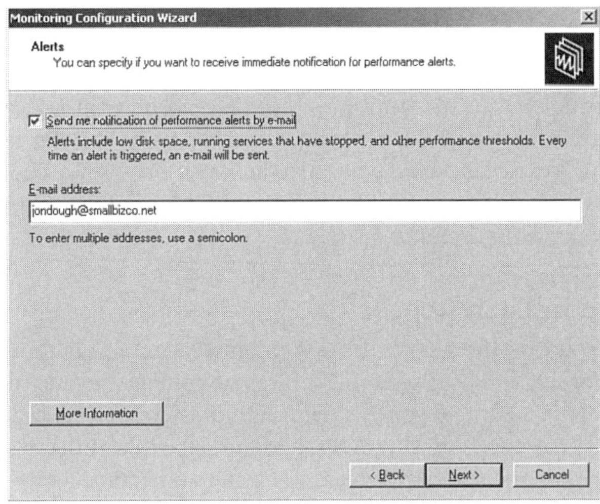

FIGURE 19.6 Alerts screen in the Monitoring Configuration Wizard.

- From outside your network, you can log in to RWW at `http://mail.smallbizco.net/remote`. Click on the last two icons in the main menu to see the reports (see Figure 19.7).

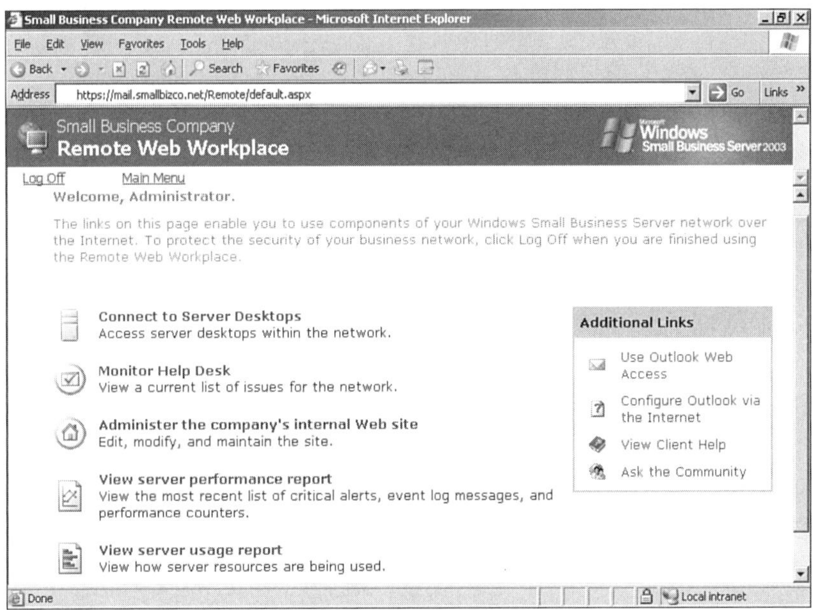

FIGURE 19.7 Monitoring links on Remote Web Workplace.

19

Getting More Out of Monitoring and Alerts

Now that the reports and alerts have been configured you have at your disposal the most relevant information related to the health of your server. The next logical step is to familiarize yourself with each report and alert so that you can quickly determine what is happening with your system and take corrective action if necessary. The next couple of sections show you what to expect in each report or alert and how to customize them so that they become even more useful to you.

What's Included in Each Report

No matter whether you read the reports using your email client or via the company's intranet the HTML format will be the same. Each report contains several sections and subsections that cover different aspects of your server, from service pack level to the status of the last backup. Although most sections on each report are self-explanatory, it's a good idea to print out an actual report and carefully look at every item and consider its significance.

To help you understand each section, from the Configure Monitoring Wizard help files, Tables 19.1 and 19.2 show what to expect on a performance or usage report, respectively.

TABLE 19.1 Server Performance Report Sections

Report Section	Description
Summary information for *ServerName*	The length of time the server has been running since it was last restarted. Links to additional details in the body of the report. Status of Small Business Server 2003 backup. The number of services configured to start automatically that are not running. The number of critical alerts that occurred in the last 24 hours. The number of critical event log errors in the last 24 hours.
Server Specifications	Specifies the operating system and service pack version, processor type and speed, and the amount of RAM installed on the server.
Performance Summary	Lists current values for today and last month and the growth rate percentage for the following performance counters: Memory in use. Free disk space (for each logical disk on the server). Busy disk time (for each physical disk on the server). CPU use.
Top 5 Processes by Memory Usage	Lists the names of the five processes that currently consume the largest percentage of server memory. As a reference, this section also includes the percentage of memory consumed by other processes in the past 24 hours and the total amount of memory installed on the server.
Top 5 Processes by CPU Time	Lists the names of the five processes that currently consume the largest percentage of CPU time.

TABLE 19.1 Continued

Report Section	Description
Backup	Indicates the results from the latest run of Small Business Server 2003 Backup.
Auto-started Services Not Running	Lists services that have been configured to start automatically, but were not running at the time the report was run.
Critical Alerts	Provides detailed information that describes each critical alert that occurred in the last 24 hours.
Critical Errors in Event Logs	Lists critical errors that have occurred in the event logs in the last 24 hours. Details include information about the source of the error, the event ID, the time of the last occurrence, the total number of occurrences, and the associated error message, if any.

TABLE 19.2 Usage Report Sections

Report Section	Description
Internet Activity	Web Activity by Computer—The total and average daily hours a client computer was connected to the Internet during the reporting period. Web Traffic by Hour—The total and average daily number of connections made by all client computers, by hour, during the reporting period. Note: This section is only included if the basic firewall (RRAS) in SBS is enabled. If you have only one network card or are using ISA server, the section will not appear.
E-mail Activity	E-mail Sent—The total number and size of email messages that each user sent to internal and external email addresses. E-mail Received—The total number and size of email messages that each user received from internal and external email addresses. Mailbox Size—The size of each user's mailbox at the beginning and end of the reporting period, and the percentage change in mailbox size.
Outlook Web Access	Outlook Web Access Activity by User—The total and average daily number of visits each user made to an Outlook Web Access site. Outlook Web Access Usage by Hour—The total and average daily number of visits made to an Outlook Web Access site by all users, by hour, during the reporting period.
Remote Connections	Remote Connection Activity by User—The total and average daily number of times each user made a remote connection to the network and the average connection duration in minutes. Remote Connection Activity by Hour—The total and average daily number of remote connections to the network by all users, by hour, during the reporting period.
Fax Activity	Faxes Sent—The total and average daily number of faxes sent to a specific fax number and the average duration and size (in pages) of all faxes sent to that number during the reporting period. Faxes Received—The total and average daily number of faxes received from a specific fax number and the average duration and size (in pages) of all faxes received from that number during the reporting period.

TABLE 19.2 Continued

Report Section	Description
	Faxes Sent by User—The total and average daily number of faxes sent by each user and the average duration and size (in pages) of all faxes sent by that user during the reporting period. Fax Traffic by Hour—The total and average daily number of faxes sent by all users, by hour, during the reporting period.

When Should You Expect an Alert?

When a certain event triggers an alert, you will receive an email almost immediately stating the cause of the alert and the time it occurred. By default, many events can trigger an alert, but they all can be grouped in three main categories:

- Start/stop/restart of a critical service.
- The threshold in a performance counter has been exceeded.
- A critical error occurs that is recorded on the logs.

Normally, alerts in the first and last group require immediate attention. On the other hand, performance alerts might only require attention if they are recurrent.

The truth is that some alerts can be annoying and sometimes even useless, for example, receiving an alert each time a fax fails to send or a printer has an error. Receiving only alerts that are truly critical is a key factor in any monitoring solution, especially if you are managing more than one server.

In the next few of sections you learn how to tweak the alerts so that you only get what you want, but first you should learn what the defaults are. From the Configure Monitoring Wizard help files, Tables 19.3, 19.4, and 19.5 show the preconfigured events that would trigger an alert and what the repercussions might be.

TABLE 19.3 Default Alert Notifications—Services

Service	Description
DHCP Server	Performs TCP/IP configuration for DHCP client computers, including dynamic assignments of IP addresses, specification of the WINS and DNS servers, and connection-specific DNS names. If this service is stopped, the DHCP server will not perform TCP/IP configuration for client computers.
DNS Server	Activates Domain Name System (DNS) client computers to resolve DNS names by answering DNS queries and DNS dynamic update requests. If this service is stopped, DNS name resolution will fail, and DNS updates will not occur. This can prevent users from accessing the server and the Internet.
Error Reporting Service	Collects, stores, and reports unexpected application crashes to Microsoft. If this service is stopped, Error Reporting will occur only for kernel faults and some types of user mode faults.

TABLE 19.3 Continued

Service	Description
Event Log	Activates event log messages issued by Windows-based programs and components to be viewed in Event Viewer.
Fax	Allows users to send and receive faxes, utilizing fax resources available on the computer running Small Business Server 2003. By default, service and performance alerts for Fax are not enabled. If you install and configure a fax modem, you can enable the Fax alerts by using the Alert Notifications configuration tool.
IPSEC Services	Provides end-to-end security between client computers and servers on TCP/IP networks. If this service is stopped, TCP/IP security between client computers and servers on the network will be impaired.
Kerberos Key Distribution Center	Allows users to log on to the network using the Kerberos authentication protocol. If this service is stopped, users will be unable to log on to the network.
Microsoft Exchange Information Store	Manages the Exchange mailbox and public folder stores. If this service is stopped, mailbox stores and public folder stores on the computer running Small Business Server 2003 will be unavailable.
Microsoft Exchange Management	Manages Exchange management information that uses Windows Management Instrumentation (WMI). If this service is stopped, Exchange management information using WMI will be unavailable.
Microsoft Exchange POP3	Provides Post Office Protocol version 3 (POP3) services to client users. If this service is stopped, client computers will be unable to connect to the computer running Small Business Server 2003 by using the POP3 protocol. This alert is disabled by default.
Microsoft Exchange Routing Engine	Provides Exchange routing services using link state information. If this service is stopped, messages will not be routed by the computer running Small Business Server 2003.
Microsoft Exchange System Attendant	Provides monitoring, maintenance, and Active Directory lookup services, such as monitoring of services and connectors, defragmenting the Exchange store, and forwarding Active Directory queries to a Global Catalog server. Most Exchange services depend on the Microsoft Exchange System Attendant service and will stop if this service is stopped. Additionally, if this service is stopped, monitoring, maintenance, and query services will be unavailable.
MSSQL$ SBSMonitoring	This service is required to manage information displayed in server performance reports and usage reports. If this service is stopped, users will be unable to view server performance or usage reports.
MSSQL$ SharePoint	Allows users access to your Windows SharePoint-based intranet site. This service is required for access to your Windows SharePoint-based intranet.
Print Spooler	Manages all local and network print queues and controls all printing jobs. If this service is stopped, printing on the computer running Small Business Server 2003 will be unavailable.

TABLE 19.3 Continued

Service	Description
Routing and Remote Access	Activates virtual private network (VPN) and network address translation (NAT) routing services. If this service is stopped, these services will be unavailable. This service is enabled if you configure router, firewall, or VPN services.
SBCore Service	Provides core server services.
Security Accounts Manager	Signals other services that the Security Accounts Manager (SAM) is ready to accept requests.
Server	Supports file, print, and named-pipe sharing over the network for this computer. If this service is stopped, these functions will be unavailable.
Simple Mail Transfer Protocol (SMTP)	Transports email across the network. If this service is stopped, alert notifications will not be delivered to the recipients.
Terminal Services	Allows multiple users to be connected interactively to the computer running Small Business Server 2003.
Windows Internet Name Service (WINS)	Resolves NetBIOS names for TCP/IP clients by locating network services that use NetBIOS names. If this service is stopped, network NetBIOS services will not function properly.
World Wide Web Publishing	Provides web connectivity and administration through the Internet Information Services snap-in.

TABLE 19.4 Default Alert Notifications—Performance Counters

Alert Name	Performance Counter	Default Threshold
Allocated Memory	Committed Bytes	> 2 gigabytes (GB)
Disk Activity	% Disk Idle Time	< 5%
`inetinfo.exe` private bytes	Process - Private Bytes	> 100 megabytes (MB)
Low Disk Space	Disk Free Megabytes	< 500 MB
lsass.exe private bytes	Process - Private Bytes	> 100 MB
Memory Available	Available Mbytes	< 4 MB
Printing Errors	Print Job Errors	> 1
Processor Activity	% Idle Time	< 5%
Received Fax Failures	Failed Receptions	> 1
Sent Fax Failures	Failed Outgoing Connections	> 1
SMTP Server Remote Queue Length	Remote Queue Length	> 30
`store.exe` private bytes	Process - Private Bytes	> 100 MB
System Up Time	System Up Time	< 600 seconds

TABLE 19.5 Default Alert Notifications—Event Log Errors

Event Log Error	Event ID	Event Log File	Description
Account Lockout	539	Security	An account was locked out due to multiple failed logon attempts that occurred in a short period of time.
Windows Small Business Server Backup failed	5634	Application	One or more components of Windows Small Business Server Backup failed.

Modifying the Default Reports and Alerts

The default reports let you monitor any system with minimal effort and although they are a good start you might feel that you want to monitor other items as well. Fortunately, SBS allows you to customize certain details on the reports so that they become even more useful to you.

BEST PRACTICE—CUSTOMIZE YOUR ALERTS

Adjust the alerts so that they are meaningful to you. Receiving 10 unwarranted alerts each day from a single server can render the whole system useless.

A particularly useful modification is attaching the backup logs to the daily performance report. By default, the Server Performance Report shows you the status of the last backup. However, if the backup has failed for any reason, it just shows an error and issues an alert forcing you to log on to the server and look at the logs directly to determine the cause of the error. Sending the backup logs along the report gives you all the information you need.

BEST PRACTICE—ADD IMPORTANT LOGS TO PERFORMANCE REPORTS

One of the examples presented in the previous section dealt with adding the backup logs to the daily performance report, but you can add whatever you feel is important. For example, if you are using SQL Manager to back up a database to a flat file you might want to add those logs to the report as well.

Follow these steps to attach logs or files to the Server Performance Report:

1. Open the Server Management Console. On the left pane expand Standard Management, click on Monitoring and Reporting to open the Monitoring MMC, and then select Change Server Status Reports Settings.
2. When the Server Status Reports box appears select Server Performance Report and click on Edit. Click on the Content tab and select the logs you want to attach, as shown in Figure 19.8. Click OK to accept the changes and exit the screen.
3. OPTIONAL—If the log you want to attach is not on the list, click Add and select Browse. Then locate the file that you want to attach and give it a meaningful name. Click OK to accept the changes and exit the screen.

Similarly, you can change the frequency of the reports or the time when they are run by opening the Server Status Reports box and changing the settings on the Schedule tab. Remember not to set the daily report so early that the backup job has not finished running by that time.

In general, reports don't require much customization out of the box to be useful. Alerts on the other hand might need a few modifications to get the most out of them. In particular, performance counters usually need to be adjusted to adapt to your situation.

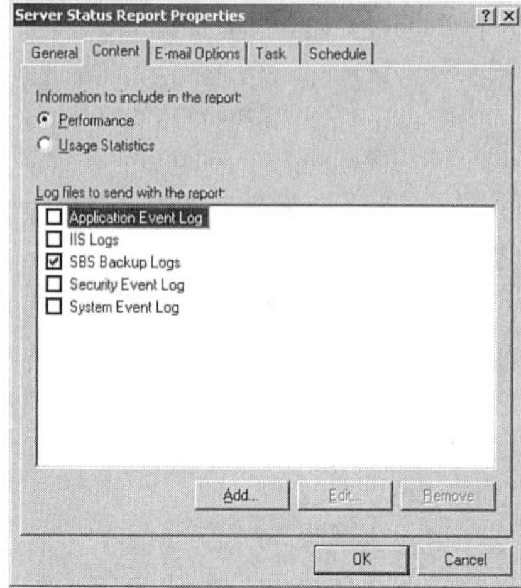

FIGURE 19.8 Adding logs and files to a report.

Follow these steps to modify alert notifications:

1. Open the Server Management Console. On the left pane expand Standard Management, click on Monitoring and Reporting to open the Monitoring MMC, and then select Change Alert Notifications.
2. When the Alert Notifications screen appears click on the Performance Counters tab and select the counter that you want to modify, as shown in Figure 19.9. For example, select Received or Sent Fax Failures and click on Edit. Now modify the threshold to something that is meaningful for you and click OK two times to accept the changes and exit the screen.

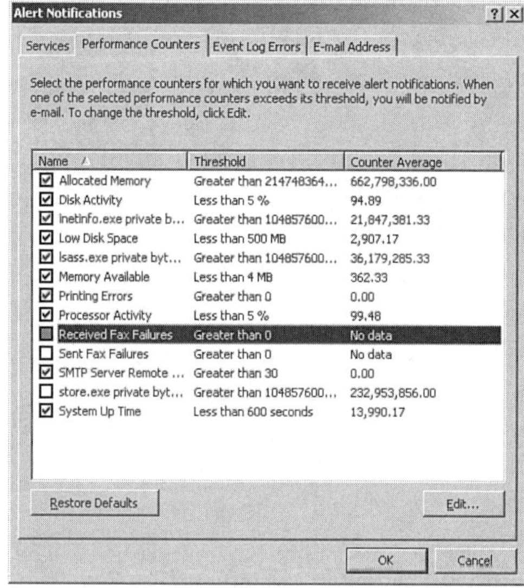

FIGURE 19.9 Perfomance counters in the Alert Notifications screen.

Deciding what values to use as thresholds can be challenging. Use your own judgment to decide what value makes sense to your particular situation. For example, one or two fax failures in 24 hours could just mean that the recipient's fax number was entered incorrectly. In a low fax volume situation four errors could be a symptom that the fax line has been disconnected, but if you are sending 100 faxes every day, four might be an insignificant number.

Remember that in some cases alerts can help you fix problems before they happen. One common scenario is that somebody brings a device (maybe a printer or a scanner) to the network without your knowledge. The device is configured to be a DHCP server, thus SBS senses it and disables its own DHCP service. If you leave it like that, it's possible that the users experience connectivity issues when their DHCP lease expires or their PC is restarted. Fortunately, SBS has sent you an alert telling you that the DHCP service has been stopped. You promptly proceed to check the logs and find out what happened even before the clients notice that the DHCP service is not running. You have saved the day and nobody will ever notice, welcome to world of unsung heroes!

BEST PRACTICE—BE CREATIVE WITH YOUR ALERTS AND REPORTS

If you manage a significant number of servers, creating a rudimentary routing system for the alerts and reports can be useful. You can create special accounts or public folders to store the reports and/or create email rules to forward critical alerts to your phone. The possibilities are truly endless.

Troubleshooting Monitoring and Alerts Issues

The monitoring functions in SBS are normally a set-and-forget kind of service. It might take you a couple of iterations before you can correctly adjust some of the thresholds, but after you find the correct settings you probably won't even have to look at the monitoring settings again. Although there are not many issues related to monitoring the most common ones are presented here.

Reconfiguring and Reinstalling Monitoring and Alerts

If you are having an issue with monitoring or the alerts your first troubleshooting step should be to run the Configure Monitoring Wizard to reset everything back to the default settings. Follow these steps:

1. Open the Server Management Console. On the left pane expand Standard Management, click on Monitoring and Reporting, and select Set Up Monitoring and Reports.
2. On the welcome screen click Next. Select Modify Existing Settings and continue the wizard selecting the options you want.

If the problem is more serious and the preceding steps did not fix it, you might want to reinstall the monitoring features. Follow these steps:

1. Open the Server Management Console. On the left pane expand Standard Management, click on Monitoring and Reporting, and select Set Up Monitoring and Reports.
2. On the welcome screen click Next. Select Reinstall Monitoring Features, click Next, and accept the warning issued. Finish the wizard by selecting the options you want.

Incorrect Name on the Reports

One common problem with reports on SBS 2003 Service Pack 1 is that the sender name and titles of performance and usage reports include the server name instead of the organization name. This is usually not a problem if you manage only one server, but if you receive a dozen of these reports with the same name it can become confusing.

To fix this issue you need to modify the registry. As usual, be very careful when editing the registry and always export the key you will be working on. Follow these steps:

1. Click on Start. Click Run and type **`Regedit`** on the Open box.
2. On the registry editor, drill down to `HKEY_LOCAL_MACHINE\Software\Microsoft\SmallBusinessServer`.
3. Double-click on RegisteredOrganization and enter the name of your organization on the value field. Click OK and close the registry editor.

The next time the report is sent it should have the name of the organization instead of the server name.

IIS Errors When You Try to Access the Intranet Monitoring Pages

Sometimes when you try to access any monitoring page with a web browser you might get an error such as "The Page Cannot be Found" or "Bad Request." This error can occur if the default website in IIS has been assigned a host header value (by default it should be blank). Other causes include problems with the loopback address in IIS if you are using ISA.

To fix this problem you have to remove the host header value from the IIS default website and/or assign the loopback address (127.0.0.1) to it. More details about this error can be found in Microsoft KB article 842693 (`http://support.microsoft.com/kb/842693`).

Summary

SBS 2003 provides excellent reporting and monitoring tools right out of the box. Configuring these reports can be achieved by running the built-in wizards, and the reports can be further customized to include other logs as well.

This chapter focused on the components of each report and alert, providing guidelines for getting more out of them and pointers for troubleshooting common situations that may arise. However, the chapter only scratched the surface in terms of what is possible to configure and monitor in SBS. Furthermore, some applications have their own monitoring functions that do not interact with the one in SBS. The reader is encouraged to further familiarize himself with all the monitoring options found in SBS and even with the ones available from third parties.

Best Practice Summary

- Read the reports—Take time each day to see what happened with your server the day before.
- Be proactive—Whenever you see an error make sure that you have an idea of why it happened and if possible take appropriate action to prevent it in the future.
- Look at the event logs—Sometimes just looking at the reports is not enough.
- Customize your alerts—Adjust the alerts so that they are meaningful to you.
- Add important logs to performance reports—Take advantage of this feature to add other log or data files to the report emails.
- Be creative with your alerts and reports—Customize reports as needed to have a different look and feel or other modification to help easily identify the source of the report.

CHAPTER 20

Group Policy

IN THIS CHAPTER

- Overview of Group Policy
- Working with the Group Policy Management Console
- Working with Group Policy Modeling and Results
- Default SBS Group Policy Objects
- Creating/Modifying SBS Group Policy Objects
- Troubleshooting Group Policy

Those who have been managing networks for any length of time know of the challenges associated with trying to maintain a standard environment across multiple computers. With the ever-important needs to keep antivirus and antispyware tools up-to-date, keep current on software and system updates, and even protect users from their own curiosity, system administrators are constantly working to make sure that software and settings are kept current on all the computers in the network. Fortunately, the implementation of group policy in Active Directory networks helps to automate many of these types of management processes.

Group policy is a complex and powerful component of Active Directory, yet it should not be intimidating to system administrators. This chapter breaks down group policy into its elemental components, describes the default policies created by SBS during setup and configuration, and provides troubleshooting steps to find and resolve group policy problems.

Overview of Group Policy

In a nutshell, group policy allows an administrator to apply settings to users and computers on the network in a managed and granular fashion. Specifically, the tasks listed in Table 20.1 can be managed through group policy.

As Table 20.1 implies, some group policy settings apply to computers, and some apply to users. Logon and logoff scripts would only apply to users when they log on and off the network. Startup and shutdown scripts would only apply to computers. This is only one way that group policy is broken down into logical parts. The next section discusses in more detail the different components that make up group policy.

TABLE 20.1 Tasks That Can Be Managed Through Group Policy

Task	Description
Assign scripts	Group policy can designate different scripts (logon, logoff, startup, shutdown, and so on) to be run.
Redirect folders	Group policy can take standard system folders (My Documents, Application Settings, Desktop, and so on) and point them to locations on the network.
Manage applications	Group policy can assign applications for use by specific users or computers, install updates for applications, or remove unwanted applications.
Modify Registry settings	Group policy can set values for Registry settings for users or computers.

Group Policy Elements

Each user or computer policy has three main sections: Software Settings, Windows Settings, and Administrative Templates. Each individual policy element is stored in one of these three areas in either the user or computer policy group.

Software Settings

Policy elements under this section relate to the installation, update, or removal of software on computers on the network. Software policies enabled in the computer configuration apply to all users who log on to the workstation affected by the policy. This is useful to make an application available to all users of a workstation. Software policies enabled in the user configuration apply to the users identified in the group policy object (GPO) no matter which workstation they use. If a user needs to have an application available to her wherever she logs in, you would set the policy element in the user configuration.

Windows Settings

Policy elements under this section relate to scripts, security settings, folder redirection, and many other settings stored in this area. There is a significant difference in the settings between the computer configuration and user configuration. Table 20.2 lists and describes some of the policy elements and whether they apply to users or computers.

TABLE 20.2 Group Policy Items for Windows Settings

Policy Element	Location	Description
Scripts	Computer Configuration	Startup and shutdown scripts for workstations
Scripts	User Configuration	Logon and logoff scripts for users
Account policies	Computer Configuration	Password and account lockout settings
Folder redirection	User Configuration	Alternate location settings for My Documents, Application Data, and other system folders
Internet Explorer maintenance	User Configuration	Changes to IE defaults, including security zone, favorites, and user interface settings

Administrative Templates

Policy settings in this section generally apply to the environment the user or computer account operates in. Settings applied through Administrative Templates are stored in the computer's Registry: User configuration settings are placed in the HKEY_CURRENT_USER (HKCU) hive, and computer configuration settings are placed in the HKEY_LOCAL_MACHINE (HKLM) hive. Settings in the computer configuration apply to all users who log on to the workstation, and settings in the user configuration apply to the user no matter which workstation in the domain he uses.

Group Policy Scope and Order of Application

One of the most important features of group policy is that more than one policy can be applied depending on the domain configuration. This aids in the management and planning of policy for the entire network while affording a level of granularity not possible prior to Active Directory.

Each group of settings is bundled into a GPO. The GPO contains not only the computer and user policy settings but also the security settings and filters that determine whether the policy gets applied to a specific user or computer.

Specific rules determine the order in which policy elements are applied: local, site, domain, and organizational unit (OU). The following list describes the function of each:

- Local settings—Each computer has a set of local policies applied at boot time before any other policies. Each computer contains only one local policy object.
- Site settings—Each Active Directory site can contain a set of policy objects. Multiple GPOs can be assigned at the site level. A default SBS installation has no site-level GPOs.
- Domain settings—Each domain object in Active Directory can contain another set of GPOs, which are processed after the site settings. A default SBS installation has multiple GPOs defined at the domain level. See the "Default SBS Group Policy Objects" section later in the chapter for more information.
- Organizational unit settings—Organizational units can contain multiple sets of GPOs as well. GPOs associated with OUs are processed last.

NOTE

Group policy can be applied only to organizational units, not containers. This is why the SBS wizards do not place user and computer objects into the Users and Computers containers. When users or computers are added manually in Active Directory and placed into these containers, the only GPOs that will be applied are the Local, Site, and Domain GPOs. No further fine-tuning of group policy can then take place.

If settings conflicts occur between multiple GPOs, the settings in the most recently applied GPO take precedence. Figure 20.1 shows the processing order of GPOs in the SBS environment.

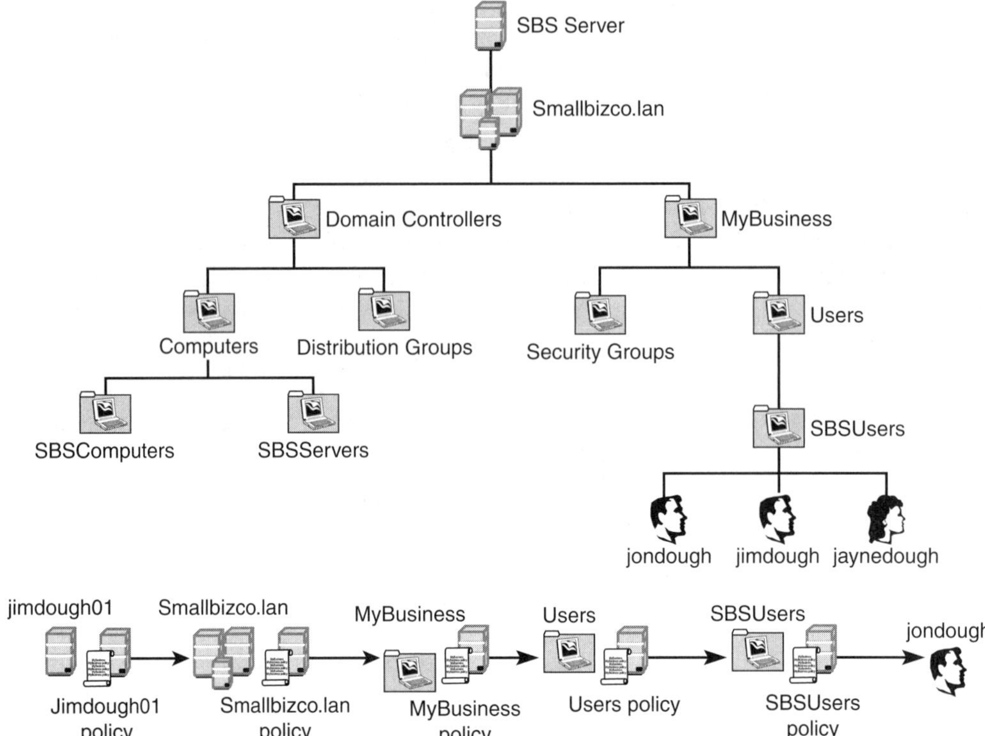

FIGURE 20.1 Group Policy processing order.

Group Policy Filtering

Besides achieving some level of granularity in group policy assignment by assigning policies at different OU levels, you can also further control the application of group policy by security group and Windows Management Instrumentation (WMI) filters. In general, this level of granularity is probably not needed in the SBS environment, but it's nice to know it's available to you should you need it.

> **NOTE**
>
> WMI filtering of group policy was introduced with Windows XP. Windows 2000 workstations do not understand WMI filtering and as a result will not process any policy objects that have a WMI filter attached.

Group Policy Inheritance

Group policy inheritance can be thought of in the same way as NTFS security inheritance. Policies that are set at a higher level in the processing order apply to objects later in the processing order. In some ways, this is really a misnomer because policies set at the domain level aren't really "inherited" by the lower-level objects. If a lower-level object does not override the settings, those settings will remain.

Overriding Group Policy Processing Order

There may be times when you want to have a domain-level policy apply no matter what settings are applied at the OU level. To achieve this, you would need to mark the policy object as Enforced. When a policy object is enforced, no subsequent policy settings can override settings contained in the enforced object.

For example, a system administrator has set a policy in a domain GPO that sets all user desktop backgrounds to be a specific image file. Another administrator creates an OU GPO that sets the desktop background to be a different image file. Because the OU policy processes after the domain policy, the image set in the OU policy is what appears on the desktop of user objects within that OU. If the main administrator wants to have the domain GPO apply no matter what settings are changed in the OU GPO, the administrator can set the domain GPO as Enforced. Then when the OU GPO is processed, if any settings conflict between the OU GPO and the domain GPO, the settings in the domain GPO will still apply.

NOTE

Setting a GPO as Enforced only applies to settings defined in that GPO. A subsequent policy object can change any policy items that are undefined in a GPO that has been set as Enforced.

Working with the Group Policy Management Console

Microsoft significantly improved the tools used to manage Group Policy with the 2003 server series. With the Group Policy Management Console (GPMC), navigating and evaluating policy objects in Active Directory is a much simpler process. In an SBS environment, the GPMC can be used as a standalone console, or you can access it through the Server Management Console.

Navigating the Group Policy Management Console

Figure 20.2 shows the GPMC snap-in in the Server Management Console. The GPMC has been expanded to the domain level so that you can see all the policy objects present at the domain level.

From this view, many of the properties of the policy objects can be seen, including the name of the GPO, whether the GPO is enabled or enforced, any WMI filters applied to the GPO, and the order in which the policy objects are applied. As shown in Figure 20.2, the first policy object processed, the Small Business Server Windows Firewall GPO, has the PostSP2 WMI filter set, meaning that only workstations running Windows XP SP2 or later will process the settings in that GPO. The fourth and fifth policies listed only contain computer configuration settings so the User Configuration settings have been disabled so that those objects will be skipped when the rest of the user settings are applied.

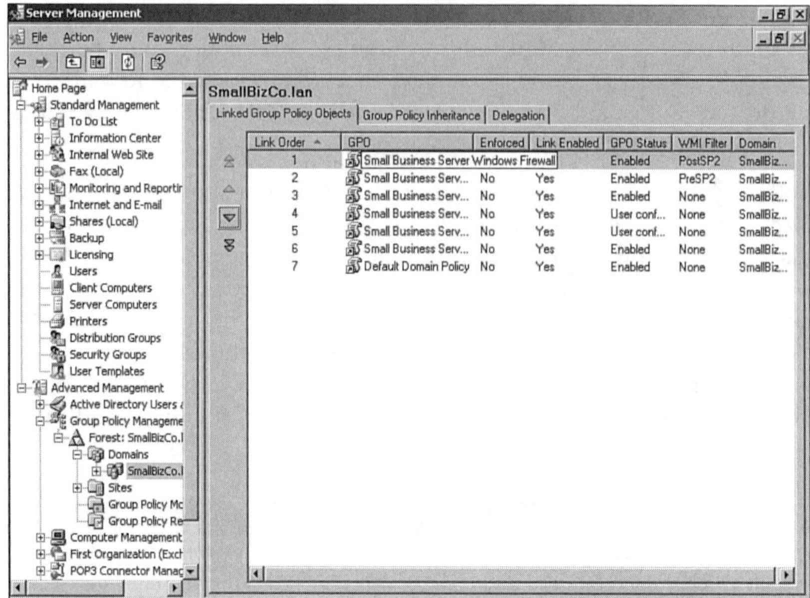

FIGURE 20.2 The Group Policy Management Console snap-in is listed with other snap-ins under the Advanced Management section of the Server Management Console.

NOTE

The Group Policy Management Console can also be run outside the Server Management Console. Simply run `gpmc.msc` at a command prompt or in Start, Run to launch the GPMC.

Figure 20.3 shows that you can browse the Active Directory OU structure to locate additional policies. In this case, Figure 20.3 shows two additional GPOs attached to the Domain Controllers OU.

In addition, navigating the browse tree to the Group Policy Objects folder, shown in Figure 20.4, displays all the GPOs present in the Active Directory structure. Unfortunately, in this view, you cannot immediately tell where in the AD structure the GPOs are tied.

Viewing Group Policy Settings

The Group Policy Management Console provides easy access to view all the settings for each GPO. Those who worked with Group Policy prior to the Windows Server 2003 series remember having to browse to an OU or domain (or suite) in Active Directory Users and Computers and selecting the correct options in the Group Policy tab under the object properties. The GPMC puts all the relevant settings of the GPO in one location for simple review. If you double-click on a GPO object listed in the GPO view shown previously in Figure 20.2, the GPMC displays the settings of the GPO, the details of which are described in the next section.

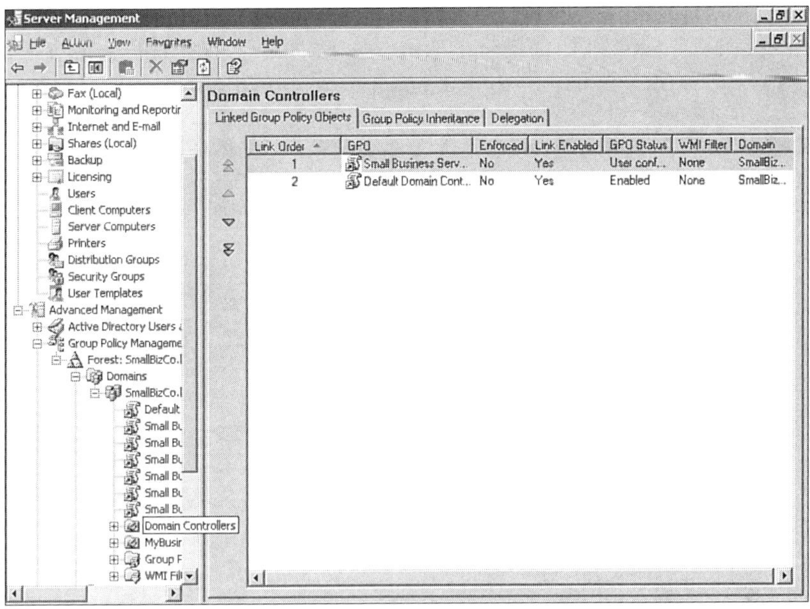

FIGURE 20.3 The browse tree in the left pane allows you to navigate the Active Directory structure to view GPO items.

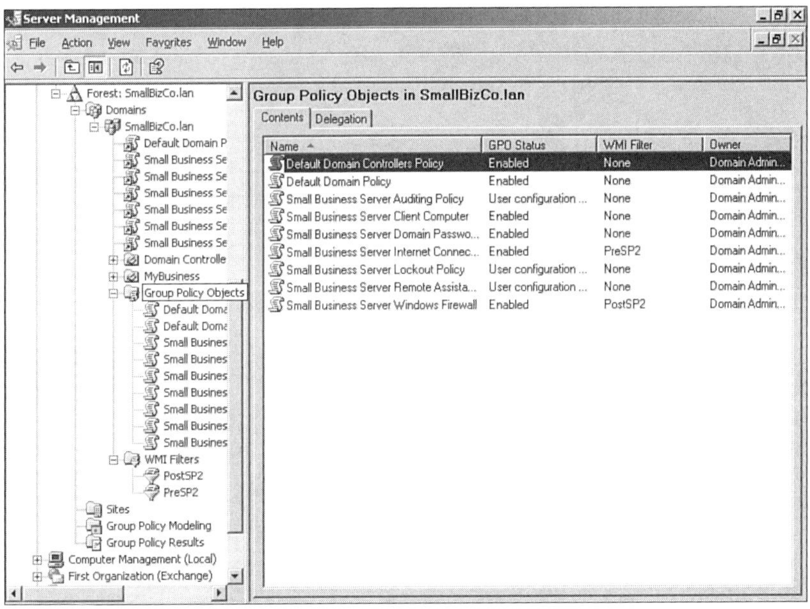

FIGURE 20.4 The Group Policy Objects folder displays all the GPOs that exist in Active Directory.

Group Policy Scope

The initial view of the GPO in the GPMC is shown in Figure 20.5. The Scope tab is initially displayed, which describes the details of how and where the GPO is applied.

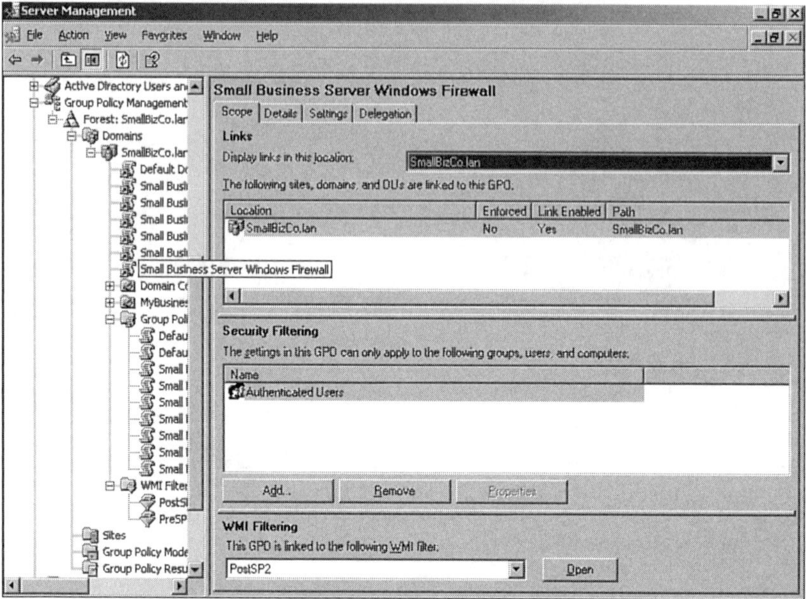

FIGURE 20.5 The Scope tab for each GPO indicates where the GPO is linked, what security filtering is applied, and what WMI filtering is applied, if any.

In Figure 20.5, the Small Business Server Windows Firewall GPO links to the domain, so its settings are applied to every user and computer in the domain. You can also quickly see that the GPO link is enabled but not enforced.

Group Policy Details

When you click on the Details tab, you see the view detailed in Figure 20.6.

In the Details tab, you can see where the GPO is linked (`SmallBizCo.lan`), who owns the GPO (`SMALLBIZCO\Domain Admins`), when it was created and modified, the GUID for the object, and its enabled status. The versions for the user configuration and computer configuration are listed as well. In this example, the User Version shows 0 for AD and 0 for sysvol. This indicates that the user configuration for this GPO has not been modified from the original installation. The Computer Version shows 1 for AD and sysvol, indicating that one set of modifications has been saved to this GPO since it was originally created.

NOTE

If you see different version numbers between AD and sysvol, the GPO files stored on the sysvol share are out of sync with the GPO settings stored in Active Directory. You will not generally see this happen, however, unless an administrator has attempted to edit the GPO files in sysvol by hand.

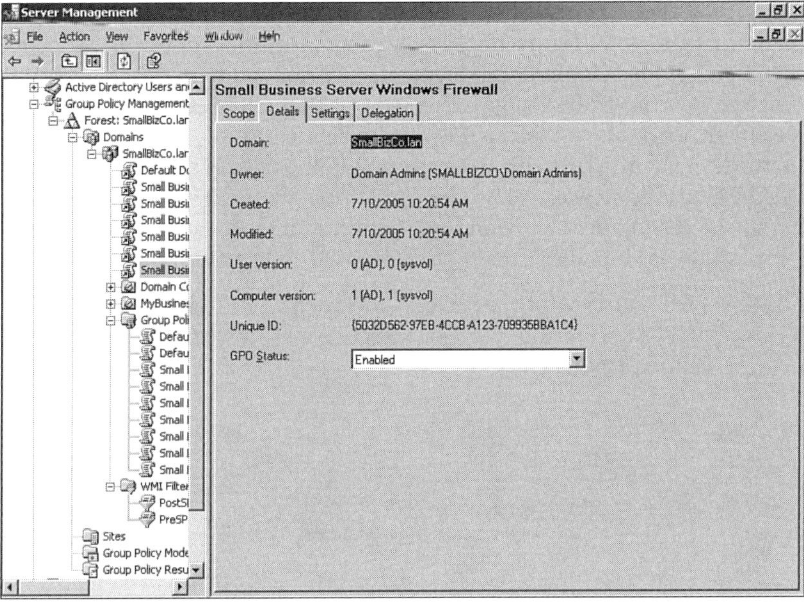

FIGURE 20.6 The Details tab gives technical information about the GPO.

Group Policy Settings

Clicking on the Settings tab displays the view shown in Figure 20.7. This is the view most administrators use when reviewing group policy settings.

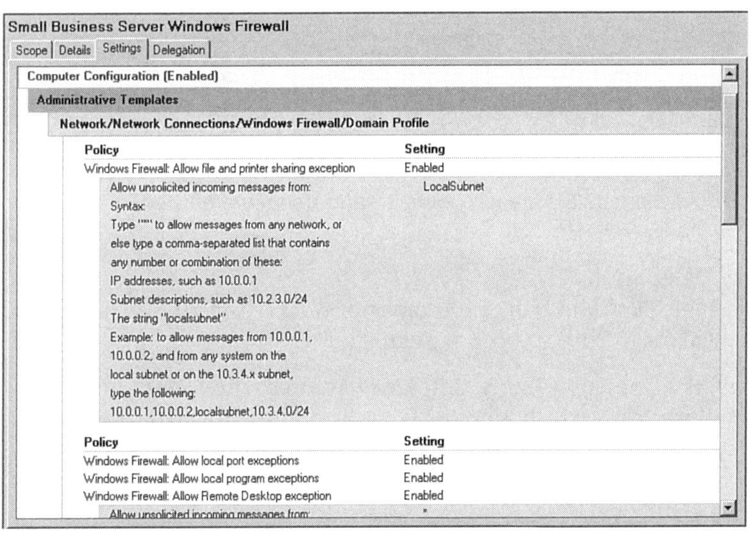

FIGURE 20.7 The Settings tab displays all the active settings in the selected GPO.

When you first select the Settings tab, the GPMC runs a report on the GPO settings to display them in the format shown in Figure 20.7. The settings are broken down into the group elements described in the "Group Policy Elements" section earlier in the chapter. In Figure 20.7, you can see the computer configuration settings start with settings in the Administrative Templates element. This means that no settings are defined in this GPO for the Software or Windows settings elements. The path to the setting in the GPO is also listed so that the first element listed, Windows Firewall: Allow File and Printer Sharing Exception, can be found by navigating the path Computer Configuration, Administrative Templates, Network, Network Connections, Windows Firewall, Domain Profile to find the specific policy.

Figure 20.8 shows a better view of the settings included in the Small Business Server Windows Firewall GPO, specifically the Extra Registry Settings and that no user configuration settings are defined in this GPO.

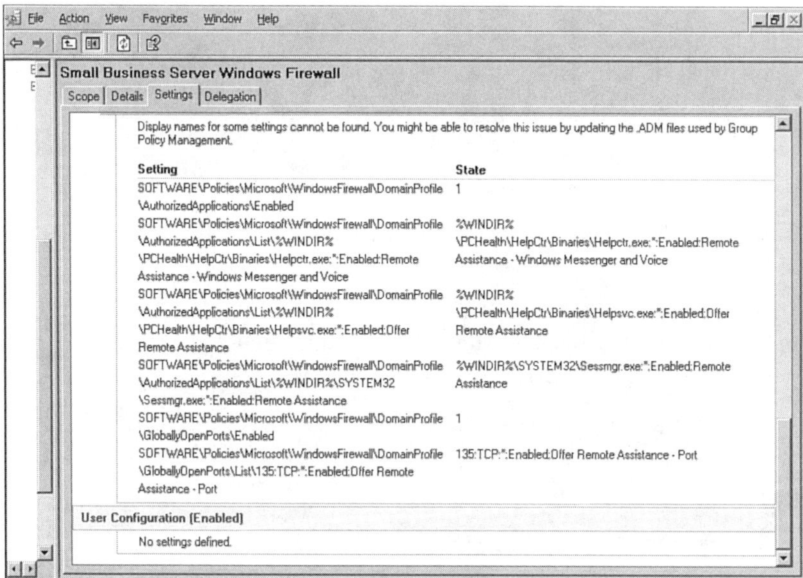

FIGURE 20.8 All the details for each policy setting defined are listed in this view.

Group Policy Delegation

The last tab in this view, the Delegation tab shown in Figure 20.9, lists the permissions on the GPO enabled for the listed security groups.

In Figure 20.9, the Domain Admins, Enterprise Admins, and SYSTEM objects have what amounts to full control over the selected GPO. The Authenticated Users and ENTERPRISE DOMAIN CONTROLLERS objects only have Read permissions on the GPO.

Three levels of access can be assigned to a GPO. Read allows an object to see the contents of the GPO and determine, based on the settings on the GPO, whether the contents should be applied. Edit Settings allows an object to modify the policy settings within the GPO but not to modify the permissions on the GPO or remove it from the domain. Edit Settings, Delete, Modify Security allows the object to perform all actions on the GPO, including removing the object from the domain.

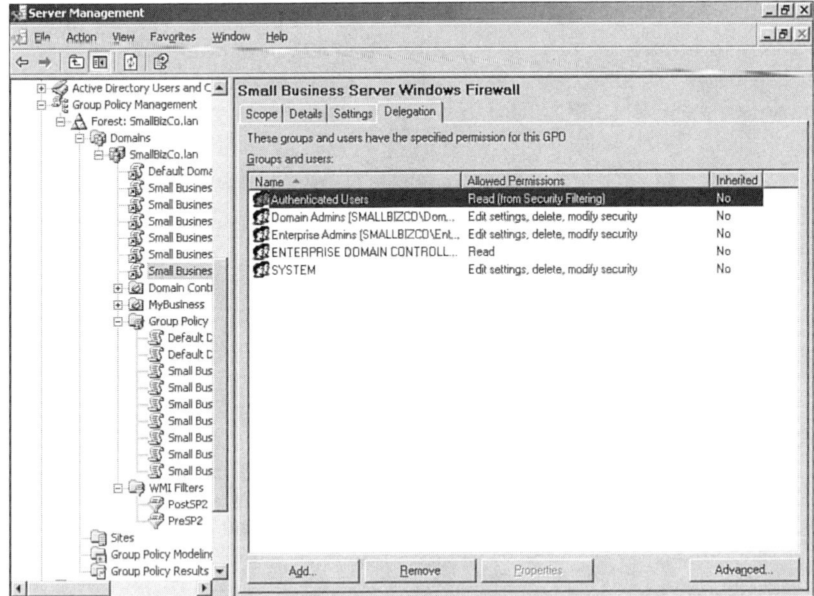

FIGURE 20.9 All the details for each policy setting defined are listed in this view.

Working with Group Policy Modeling and Results

The group policy snap-in for the Server Management Console contains two other elements useful in examining group policy on the SBS network. Group policy modeling gives system administrators a chance to see how group policy would be applied to users and computers under different conditions without having to actually make those changes. Group policy results takes a look at how policy was actually applied to a given user/computer combination given the current policy configuration.

Both tools allow you to view the information in a report similar to the GPO settings screen shown previously in Figure 20.8. The next two sections detail how to generate the modeling and results reports.

Creating the Modeling Report

To create a group policy modeling report, follow these steps:

1. In the Server Management Console, expand Advanced Management, Group Policy Management, and Forest.
2. Right-click on Group Policy Modeling and select Group Policy Modeling Wizard.
3. In the first page of the wizard, click Next.
4. In the Domain Controller Selection page, make sure that the correct domain name is listed; then click Next.

5. In the User and Computer selection page, shown in Figure 20.10, select a user and computer to model, or select the SBSUsers and SBSComputers OUs to model the entire network. Enable the check box next to Skip to the Final Page of This Wizard Without Collecting Additional data and click Next.

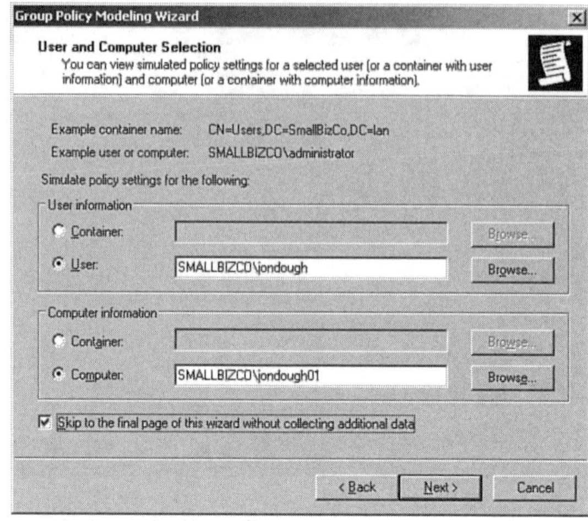

FIGURE 20.10 The Group Policy Modeling Wizard can simulate a single user and computer or groups of users and computers.

6. In the Summary of Selections page, click Next.
7. Click Finish to close the wizard.

Now you can view the report in the console window, shown in Figure 20.11. The upper portion of the report lists the information used to generate the report; then it lists the GPOs that would be applied to this user on this computer and the locations of those GPOs.

When you click on the Settings tab, you can view the policy elements that would be applied and which GPO provided those settings, as shown in Figure 20.12.

Creating the Results Report

The key difference between the Modeling report and the Results report is that the Modeling report is a simulation, but the Results report is based on actual group policy processing and requires the equipment being processed to be active on the network.

NOTE

With Windows XP SP2 defaults, workstations have remote administration blocked in the Windows Firewall by default. For you to use the Group Policy Results Wizard against a Windows XP SP2 computer, you need to enable remote administration through the Windows Firewall. Microsoft KB article 840634 (`http://support.microsoft.com/?id=840634`) has instructions for allowing this exception. Use Method 2 or Method 3 in the article so that you can restrict the IP addresses the firewall will allow to connect. You can also enable this globally on the network through group policy.

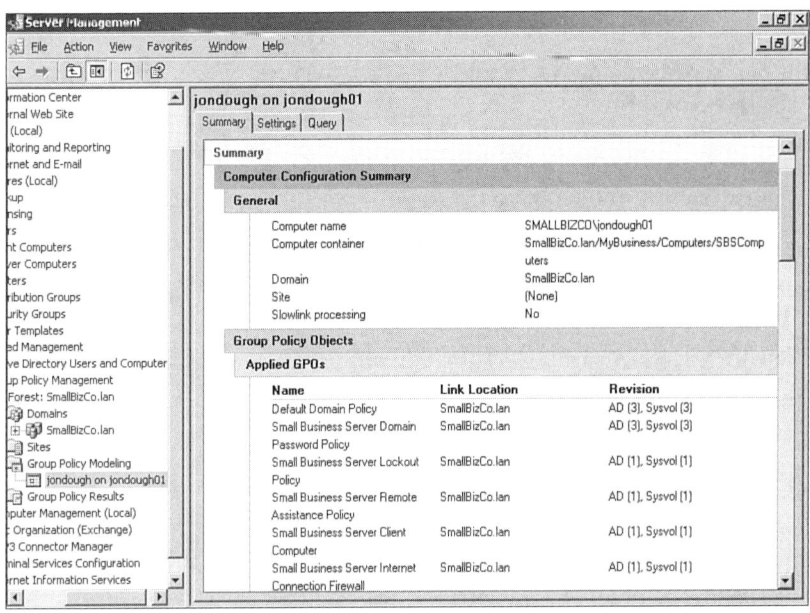

FIGURE 20.11 The group policy modeling report summary shows the GPOs that would be applied to a user and computer.

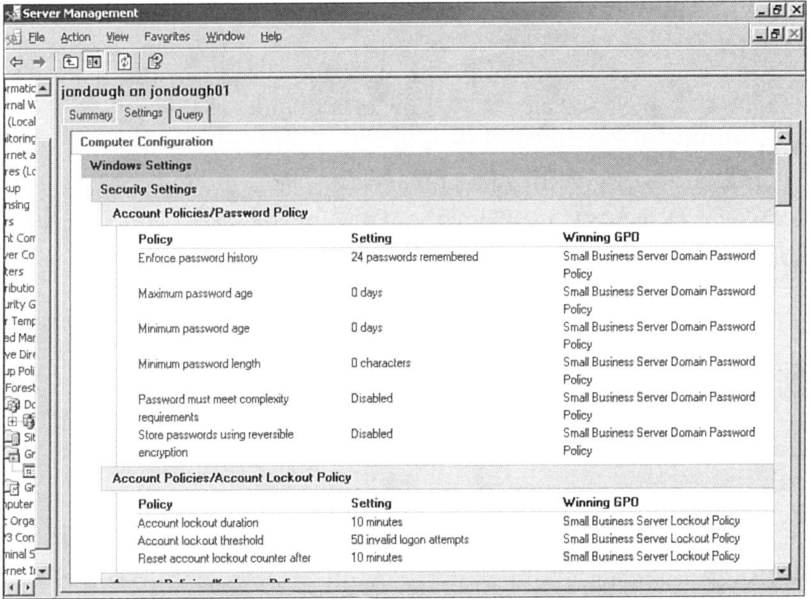

FIGURE 20.12 The group policy modeling report Settings tab shows the policy settings that would get applied.

Follow these steps to create a group policy results report:

1. In the Server Management Console, expand Advanced Management, Group Policy Management, and Forest.
2. Right-click on Group Policy Results and select Group Policy Results Wizard.
3. In the first page of the wizard, click Next.
4. In the Computer Selection page, click the Another Computer radio button and click Browse to select the computer to use for the report. After the computer has been selected, click Next.
5. In the User Selection page, select the domain userid and not the local userid. Click Next.
6. In the Summary of Selections page, click Next.
7. Click Finish to complete the wizard.

The Summary and Settings sections of the report look similar to the Modeling Report sections, with one key difference. The data in the Results report shows the actual settings on the workstation and gives the specific times the settings were applied.

Default SBS Group Policy Objects

This section of the chapter contains the definitions of the default group policy objects created during the setup of SBS 2003 or the installation of SBS 2003 SP1. You can use this section of the chapter as a reference for these objects if you suspect that a default object has been modified. The objects are listed in the default order as well.

Small Business Server Windows Firewall

This GPO contains elements to configure the Windows Firewall in Windows XP SP2, as shown in Table 20.3. This GPO is created when SBS 2003 SP1 is installed, or when SBS 2003 SP1 is applied to an existing SBS 2003 server. This policy has a WMI filter that allows only Windows XP SP2 workstations to process the policy.

TABLE 20.3 Policy Settings for Small Business Server Windows Firewall

Policy Element	Setting
Computer Configuration	
Administrative Templates	
Network | Network Connections |	
Windows Firewall | Domain Profiles	
Windows Firewall: Allow file and printer sharing exception	Enabled—Allow unsolicited incoming messages from: Local Subnet
Windows Firewall: Allow local port exceptions	Enabled
Windows Firewall: Allow local program exceptions	Enabled
Windows Firewall: Allow Remote Desktop exception	Enabled—Allow unsolicited incoming messages from: *

TABLE 20.3 Policy Settings for Small Business Server Windows Firewall

<table>
<tr><th>Policy Element</th><th>Setting</th></tr>
<tr><td>Windows Firewall: Protect all network connections</td><td>Enabled</td></tr>
<tr><td>Network | Network Connections | Windows Firewall | Standard Profile</td><td></td></tr>
<tr><td>Windows Firewall: Allow local port exceptions</td><td>Enabled</td></tr>
<tr><td>Windows Firewall: Allow local program exceptions</td><td>Enabled</td></tr>
<tr><td>Windows Firewall: Protect all network connections</td><td>Enabled</td></tr>
<tr><td>Windows Components | Security Center</td><td></td></tr>
<tr><td>Turn on Security Center (Domain PCs only)</td><td>Enabled</td></tr>
<tr><td>Extra Registry Settings</td><td></td></tr>
<tr><td><code>SOFTWARE\Policies\Microsoft\WindowsFirewall\DomainProfile\AuthorizedApplications\Enabled</code></td><td>1</td></tr>
<tr><td><code>SOFTWARE\Policies\Microsoft\WindowsFirewall\DomainProfile\AuthorizedApplications\List\%WINDIR%\PCHealth\HelpCtr\Binaries\Helpctr.exe:*:Enabled:Remote Assistance -nd- Windows Messenger and Voice</code></td><td><code>%WINDIR%\PCHealth\HelpCtr\Binaries\Helpctr.exe:*:</code>Enabled:Remote Assistance—Windows Messenger and Voice</td></tr>
<tr><td><code>SOFTWARE\Policies\Microsoft\WindowsFirewall\DomainProfiles\AuthorizedApplications\List\%WINDIR%\PCHealth\HelpCtr\Binaries\Helpsvc.exe:*:Enabled:Offer Remote Assistance</code></td><td><code>%WINDIR%\PCHealth\HelpCtr\Binaries\Helpsvc.exe:*:</code>Enabled:Offer Remote Assistance</td></tr>
<tr><td><code>SOFTWARE\Policies\Microsoft\WindowsFirewall\DomainProfile\AuthorizedApplications\List\%WINDIR%\SYSTEM32\Sessmgr.exe:*:Enabled:Remote Assistance</code></td><td><code>%WINDIR%\SYSTEM32\Sessmgr.exe:*:</code>Enabled:Remote Assistance</td></tr>
<tr><td><code>SOFTWARE\Policies\Microsoft\WindowsFirewall\DomainProfile\GloballyOpenPorts\Enabled</code></td><td>1</td></tr>
<tr><td><code>SOFTWARE\Policies\Microsoft\WindowsFirewall\DomainProfile\GloballyOpenPorts\List\135:TCP:*:Enabled:Offer Remote Assistance - Port</code></td><td>135:TCP:*:Enabled:Offer Remote Assistance—Port</td></tr>
</table>

Small Business Server Internet Connection Firewall

This policy governs the Internet Connection firewall included with Windows XP prior to SP1 (see Table 20.4). This policy has the PreSP2 WMI filter applied so that Windows XP SP2 and Windows 2000 clients do not apply this policy.

TABLE 20.4 Policy Settings for Small Business Server Internet Connection Firewall

<table>
<tr><th>Policy</th><th>Setting</th></tr>
<tr><td>Computer Configuration</td><td></td></tr>
<tr><td>Administrative Templates</td><td></td></tr>
<tr><td>Network | Network Connections</td><td></td></tr>
<tr><td>Prohibit use of Internet Connection Firewall on your DNS domain network</td><td>Enabled</td></tr>
</table>

Small Business Server Client Computer

This policy customizes the workstation environment of a computer that has been joined to the domain. Table 20.5 lists the settings for a server client computer.

TABLE 20.5 Policy Settings for Small Business Server Client Computer

Policy	Setting
Computer Configuration	
Administrative Templates	
Network I Network Connections	
Prohibit installation and configuration of Network Bridge on your DNS domain network	Enabled
Prohibit user of Internet Connection Sharing on your DNS domain network	Enabled
System I Logon	
Don't display the Getting Started welcome screen at logon	Enabled
Extra Registry Settings	
`SOFTWARE\Microsoft\WindowsNT\CurrentVersions\WinLogon\SyncForegroundPolicy`	1

Small Business Server Remote Assistance Policy

This policy enables the user of remote assistance through the SBS network. Because these settings exist only in the computer configuration, the user configuration portion of this GPO has been disabled so that it will not get processed with the rest of the User Settings from the other GPOs at logon (see Table 20.6).

TABLE 20.6 Policy Settings for Small Business Server Remote Assistance Policy

Policy	Setting
Computer Configuration	
Administrative Templates	
System I Remote Assistance	
Offer Remote Assistance	Enabled—Helpers: *[domainname]*\Domain Admins

Small Business Server Lockout Policy

This policy establishes the lockout policy for the domain. Again, because these settings appear only in the computer configuration settings, the user configuration settings are disabled (see Table 20.7).

TABLE 20.7 Policy Settings for Small Business Server Remote Assistance Policy

Policy	Setting
Computer Configuration	
Windows Settings	
Security Settings	
Account Policies I Account Lockout Policies	
Account Lockout Duration	10 minutes
Account lockout threshold	50 invalid logon attempts
Reset account lockout counter after	10 minutes

Small Business Server Domain Password Policy

This policy sets the password requirements for the domain. There are two "standard" implementations for this policy. The first settings, listed in Table 20.8, show the settings for the policy before secure password policies are enabled when running the Connect to the Internet Wizard. Table 20.9 shows the policy settings after the secure password policies have been enabled. Again, both tables indicate the defaults. The settings for the domain password policy can be customized in the Configure Password Policies Wizard under the Users node in the Server Management Console.

TABLE 20.8 Policy Settings for Small Business Server Password Policy (Installation Defaults)

Policy	Setting
Computer Configuration	
Windows Settings	
Security Settings	
Account Policies | Password Policy	
Enforce password history	24 passwords remembered
Maximum password age	0 days
Minimum password age	0 days
Minimum password length	0 characters
Password must meet complexity requirements	Disabled
Store passwords using reversible encryption	Disabled

TABLE 20.9 Policy Settings for Small Business Server Password Policy (CEICW Defaults)

Policy	Setting
Computer Configuration	
Windows Settings	
Security Settings	
Account Policies | Password Policy	
Enforce password history	24 passwords remembered
Maximum password age	42 days
Minimum password age	0 days
Minimum password length	7 characters
Password must meet complexity requirements	Enabled
Store passwords using reversible encryption	Disabled

Default Domain Policy

The Default Domain policy contains all the default Windows Server 2003 settings (see Table 20.10). This policy is processed first in order of the SBS domain-level policies so that the basic security and performance structure is established before the SBS-specific policies are processed.

TABLE 20.10 Policy Settings for the Default Domain Policy Object

Policy	Setting
Computer Configuration	
Windows Settings	
Security Settings	
Account Policies | Password Policy	
Enforce password history	24 passwords remembered
Maximum password age	42 days
Minimum password age	1 day
Minimum password length	7 characters
Password must meet complexity requirements	Enabled
Store passwords using reversible encryption	Disabled
Account Policies | Account Lockout Policy	
Account lockout threshold	0 invalid logon attempts
Account Policies | Kerberos Policy	
Enforce user logon restrictions	Enabled
Maximum lifetime for service ticket	600 minutes
Maximum lifetime for user ticket	10 hours
Maximum lifetime for user ticket renewal	7 days
Maximum tolerance for computer clock synchronization	5 minutes
Local Policies | Security Options | Network Security	
Network Security: Force logoff when logon hours expire	Disabled
Public Key Policies | Autoenrollment Settings	
Enroll certificates automatically	Enabled
Renew expired certificates, update pending certificates, and remove revoked certificates	Disabled
Update certificates that use certificate templates	Disabled
Public Key Policies | Encrypting File System | Properties	
Allow users to encrypt files using Encrypting File System (EFS)	Enabled
Public Key Policies | Trusted Root Certification Authorities | Properties	
Allow users to select new root certification authorities (CAs) to trust	Enabled
Client computers can trust the following certificate stores Authorities and Enterprise Root Certification Authorities	Third-Party Root Certification
To perform certificate-based authentication of users and computers, CAs must meet the following criteria	Registered in Active Directory only
Remote Installation Services	
Client Installation Wizard options	
Custom Setup	Disabled
Restart Setup	Disabled
Tools	Disabled

Best Practice—Do Not Modify the Default Domain Policy Objects

Although you may be tempted to change the Default Domain policy object or the Default Domain Controllers policy objects, discussed later, do not make any modifications to either of these policy objects. Follow the example of the SBS development team and create a new policy object or modify another policy object if you need to add policy elements to the SBS network. If you make a change to one of the Default objects and find out that something has gone wrong on the network as a result, it is difficult to "undo" the changes made to a policy object.

The "Troubleshooting Group Policy" section later in the chapter discusses a method for defining, testing, and implementing group policy changes. Follow the guidelines there for correctly implementing group policy changes to the network. Just do not make any changes to the Default policy objects.

Small Business Server Auditing Policy

This policy sets the basic auditing settings for an SBS installation (see Table 20.11). Because there are no user configuration settings related to auditing, the user configuration portion of the policy object is disabled and not processed during the rest of user configuration processing.

TABLE 20.11 Policy Settings for the Small Business Server Auditing Policy

Policy	Setting
Computer Configuration	
Windows Settings	
Security Settings	
Local Policies | Audit Policy	
Audit directory service access	No auditing
Audit logon events	Success, Failure

Default Domain Controllers Policy

The Default Domain Controllers policy is similar to the Default Domain policy in that it establishes the default settings for computers used as domain controllers in the SBS network (see Table 20.12). It is the first GPO processed in the Domain Controllers OU so that the SBS-specific settings in other GPOs in the OU can override the default settings as necessary.

TABLE 20.12 Policy Settings for the Default Domain Controllers Policy

Policy	Setting
Computer Configuration	
Windows Settings	
Security Settings	
Local Policies | Audit Policy	
Audit account logon events	Success
Audit account management	Success
Audit directory service access	Success
Audit logon events	Success
Audit object access	No auditing
Audit policy change	Success
Audit privilege use	No auditing
Audit process tracking	No auditing
Audit system events	Success
Local Policies | User Rights Assignment	
Access this computer from the network	Everyone, *domain*\IUSR_*servername*, *domain*\IWAM_*servername*, BUILTIN\Administrators, NT AUTHORITY\Authenticated Users, NT Authority\ENTERPRISE DOMAIN CONTROLLERS, BUILTIN\Pre-Windows 2000 Compatible Access
Act as part of the operating system	[defined but empty]
Add workstations to domain	NT AUTHORITY\Authenticated Users
Adjust memory quotas for a process	NT AUTHORITY\LOCAL SERVICE, NT AUTHORITY\NETWORK SERVICE, *domain*\IWAM_*servername*, BUILTIN\Administrators
Allow log on locally	*domain*\IUSR_*servername*, BUILTIN\Administrators, BUILTIN\Backup Operators, BUILTIN\Account Operators, BUILTING\Server Operators, BUILTIN\Print Operators
Back up files and directories	BUILTIN\Administrators, BUILTIN\Backup Operators, BUILTIN\Server Operators
Bypass traverse checking	Everyone, BUILTIN\Administrators, NT AUTHORITY\Authenticated Users, BUILTIN\Pre-Windows 2000 Compatible Access
Change the system time	NT AUTHORITY\LOCAL SERVICE, BUILTIN\Administrators, BUILTIN\Server Operators
Create a pagefile	BUILTIN\Administrators
Create a token object	[defined but empty]
Create permanent shared objects	[defined but empty]
Debug Programs	BUILTIN\Administrators
Deny access to this computer from the network	*domain*\SUPPORT_*supportID*
Deny logon as a batch job	[defined but empty]
Deny logon as a service	[defined but empty]

TABLE 20.12 Policy Settings for the Default Domain Controllers Policy

Policy	Setting
Deny logon locally	*domain*\SBS Remote Operators, *domain*\SUPPORT_*supportID*, *domain*\SBS STS Worker
Enable computer and user accounts to be trusted for delegation	BUILTIN\Administrators
Force shutdown from a remote system	BUILTIN\Administrators, BUILTIN\Server Operators
Generate security audits	NT AUTHORITY\LOCAL SERVICE, NT AUTHORITY\NETWORK SERVICE
Increase scheduling priority	BUILTIN\Administrators
Load and unload device drivers	BUILTIN\Administrators, BUILTIN\Print Operators
Lock pages in memory	[defined but empty]
Log on as a batch job	NT AUTHORITY\LOCAL SERVICE, *domain*\IUSR_*servername*, *domain*\IWAM_*servername*, *domain*\IIS_WPG, *domain*\SUPPORT_*supportID*
Log on as a service	NT AUTHORITY\NETWORK SERVICE
Manage auditing and security log	*domain*\Exchange Enterprise Servers, BUILTIN\Administrators
Modify firmware environment values	BUILTIN\Administrators
Profile single process	BUILTIN\Administrators
Profile system performance	BUILTIN\Administrators
Remove computer from docking station	BUILTIN\Administrators
Replace a process level token	NT AUTHORITY\LOCAL SERVICE, NT AUTHORITY\NETWORK SERVICE, *domain*\IWAM_*servername*
Restore files and directories	BUILTIN\Administrators, BUILTIN\Backup Operators, BUILTIN\Server Operators
Shut down the system	BUILTIN\Administrators, BUILTIN\Backup Operators, BUILTIN\Server Operators
Synchronize directory service data	[defined but empty]
Take ownership of files or other objects	BUILTIN\Administrators
Local Policies I Security Options	
Domain controller: LDAP server signing requirements	None
Domain member: Digitally encrypt or sign secure channel data (always)	Enabled
Microsoft network server: Digitally sign communications (always)	Enabled
Microsoft network server: Digitally sign communications (if client agrees)	Enabled
Network Security: LAN Manager authentication level	Send NTLM response only

Creating/Modifying SBS Group Policy Objects

If you need to modify group policy for the network in any way, such as disabling SMB signing for Macintosh file sharing access or configuring workstations to point to the SBS server for WSUS, you need to develop a plan of action for creating, testing, and then deploying the group policy elements on the network. Often, an inexperienced network administrator will find a need to implement a group policy change on the network and charge right in to making the change in a default policy object. There are several problems with this approach, the most significant being that if one of the default policy objects becomes corrupt, the network can quickly become unusable.

Like anything else related to implementation in an SBS environment, a logical approach is in order.

Planning the GPO

Before running headlong into a group policy change, stop and ask a few questions first:

- Does the policy change affect all users or computers on the network?
- If the policy is not universal in scope, will it impact a majority of users or computers on the network, or will it impact only a small number?
- Is the policy change in line with existing policy objects?
- Does policy change conflict with other policies that have been set by previously processed GPOs?
- Could the policy change be overridden by GPOs that are processed after it?

By asking a few simple questions, you can determine up front where the policy object needs to be placed and whether the settings need a separate policy object or can be bundled in with another policy object.

Determining the GPO Location

A new GPO can be placed in several locations in Active Directory: at the site level (which is generally not used in the SBS environment), at the domain level, or at any of the OU levels created by the SBS setup. Alternatively, you can create a new OU in Active Directory and associate the new GPO with that.

Here are a few guidelines for determining where to place the GPO:

- If the policy only impacts a subset of users on the network, place the GPO at an existing OU level or create a new OU.
- If the policy applies to a majority of users or computers across the network, create the GPO at the domain level and use WMI or security group filtering to allow only those accounts that need to process the GPO the ability to access it.
- If the policy applies at the domain level, consider making modifications to one of the existing SBS GPOs instead of creating a new one.

Determining the GPO Scope

In many cases, creating new policy elements in an SBS environment means creating or modifying GPOs at the domain level. A few issues can impact how new policy elements are applied.

A default SBS installation already has several custom GPOs created at the domain level. Before you create or modify a GPO to contain your policy elements, review the existing GPOs to see whether the policy elements you want to change are already defined. If the policy elements are present in an existing SBS GPO (not the Default Domain Policy or Default Domain Controllers Policy GPOs), it may make more sense to change the settings in that GPO than to create a new GPO and make sure that the object is processed in the correct order at the domain level.

If you decide that creating a new GPO at the domain level is the best place to implement the policy changes, you need to determine the correct placement in the GPO processing order for the domain-level GPOs. If the new GPO contains settings that conflict with settings in the Default Domain policy GPO, you need to make sure that the new GPO processes after the Default Domain policy GPO has processed.

Another option to consider for making sure that your policy changes do not get overridden by another policy object is to make the settings on the GPO Enforced. If a policy is marked as Enforced, any subsequent policy objects with conflicting policy settings will not have their changes applied.

Testing the GPO

Before unleashing your policy changes on the network, test the policy settings to make sure that the changes do not adversely impact your normal network environment. There are several ways to create a test environment within your production network so that you can see the results of the policy changes without affecting all users or computers in the environment.

The remainder of this section walks you through the process of creating sample objects in your SBS environment to test the process and give you a real-world example of how to create and implement a GPO test on your network.

Creating a Test OU

The first step to establishing a test environment is to create a Test OU in Active Directory. Follow these steps to create the Test OU:

1. Open Active Directory Users and Computers.
2. Expand the domain; then expand the MyBusiness OU.
3. Right-click on the MyBusiness OU and select New, Organizational Unit.
4. Enter **`Test OU`** in the Name field and click OK.
5. Close Active Directory Users and Computers.

Creating a Test GPO

Next you need a GPO associated with the Test OU. Follow these steps to create the GPO:

1. In the Server Management Console, expand Advanced Management, Group Policy Management, Forest, Domains, *your internal domain*, and MyBusiness. Select Test OU.
2. Right-click on Test OU and select Create and Link a GPO Here.
3. Enter the GPO name as Test GPO and click OK.

Now that the GPO exists, you need to edit the settings in the GPO. As an example, follow these steps to create an easily identifiable policy setting in the new GPO:

1. Right-click on Test GPO and select Edit.
2. Under User Configuration, expand Windows Settings, Internet Explorer Maintenance and click on Browser User Interface.
3. Double-click on Browser Title and enter **`GPO Testing`** in Title Bar Text.
4. Click OK and close the Group Policy Object Editor.

Running a Group Policy Modeling Report

Now that the Test OU and Test GPO have been created and modified, you can run a modeling report to make sure that the settings get applied properly. Follow these steps to run the group policy modeling report and use the new Test OU for results:

1. Right-click on Group Policy Modeling in the Group Policy Management Console and select Group Policy Modeling Wizard.
2. Click Next.
3. In the Domain Controller Selection page, click Next.
4. In the User and Computer Selection page, select a user and computer from the network; then click Next. Do not enable the check box next to *Skip To the Final Page of This Wizard Without Collecting Additional Data.*
5. In the Advanced Simulation Options page, click Next.
6. In the Alternate Active Directory Paths page, click the Browse button next to User Location and browse to the Test OU created earlier. Enable the check box next to Skip to the Final Page of This Wizard Without Collecting Additional Data, as shown in Figure 20.13. Click Next when finished.

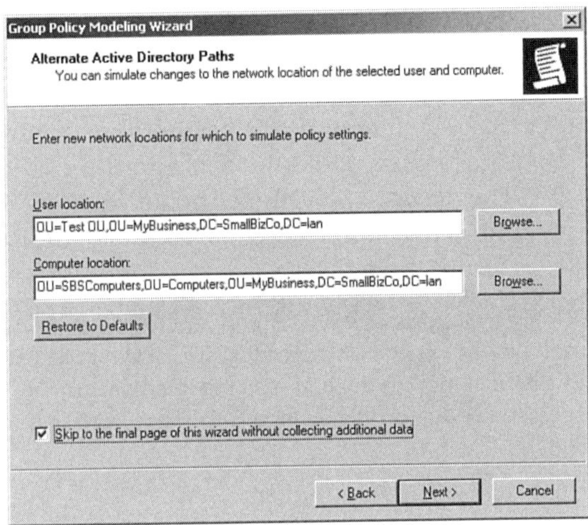

FIGURE 20.13 Specify an alternate Active Directory location to test the settings in the Test GPO.

7. In the Summary of Selections page, click Next.
8. Click Finish to close the wizard.

Now you can browse through the report and see in the Summary page that the Test GPO was applied under the User Configuration Summary section. You can also see in the Settings page, as shown in Figure 20.14, that the phrase "GPO Testing" was applied to the Internet Explorer title bar by the Test GPO.

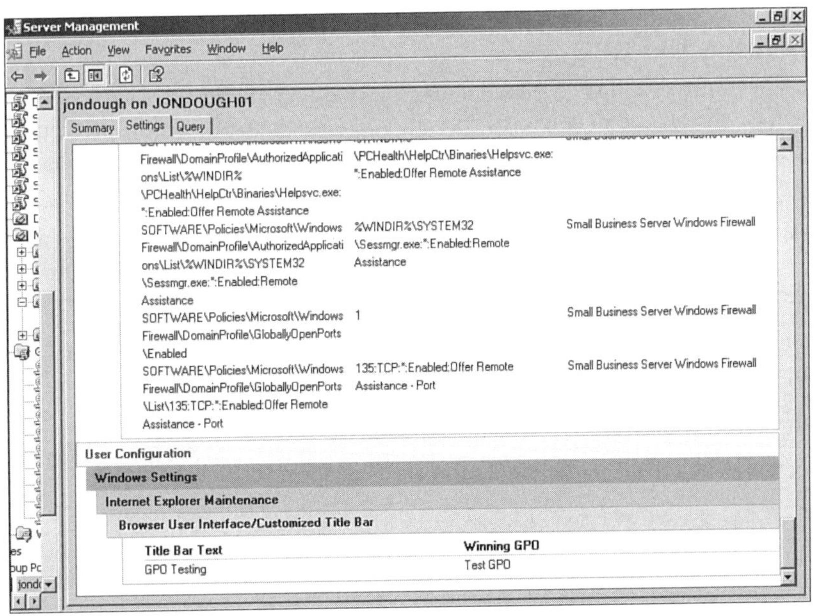

FIGURE 20.14 The winning GPO is listed in the Settings of the group policy monitoring report.

Running a Live Test

After you have verified that the policy settings are processed in the modeling report, you should now test the settings on a live box. There are two basic methods for doing this. The first is to move either the computer or user object for the accounts you want to test into the Test OU. The next time the computer reboots and the user logs in, it picks up the settings from the Test OU. The drawback of this method is that you have to remember to move the user or computer object back to its original location after you complete the test.

> **CAUTION**
>
> If you have a more complex group policy scheme that has GPOs applied at multiple OUs, you would need to make sure that moving the user or computer object to the Test OU would not remove it from the processing path for the existing GPO structure. If that happens, you will not have a valid test result.

The other method for testing is to attach the Test GPO to the OU or Domain object where it will reside in production and filter access to the Test GPO through security group settings. This would involve creating a security group, possibly called GPO Testers, in Active Directory and giving only that group read access to the policy object. When you are ready to test, add the desired users or computers to that security group and reboot the workstation to have the Test GPO apply. Again, you would need to remove the members of that security group after the GPO has been implemented successfully on the network.

No matter which method you choose, try to test with several user and computer accounts to make sure that there are no unexpected behaviors resulting from the changes you made to group policy.

Implementing the GPO

After you have fully tested the policy changes and are satisfied that you have not created any new problems on the network as a result, you can go ahead and implement the changes on the network. How you do this depends on how you created the test environment.

If you created a test policy object and linked it to a test OU, rename the GPO, unlink it from the test OU, and link it to the OU or domain element where you want it to go. To link an existing policy object to an Active Directory object, follow these steps:

1. Locate the object where you want the GPO to apply in the Group Policy Management Console.
2. Right-click on the object and select Link an Existing GPO.
3. Select the GPO from the list and click OK.

If you linked the test GPO to the desired domain element and restricted access to it with security group or other filters, remove the filters.

Best Practice—Adding Additional Group Policy Objects

Be careful when adding group policies to the SBS server. A default installation can have seven or eight GPOs already defined. Adding more GPOs can significantly slow down the logon process. Although you generally should not modify the default SBS policies created, you should also avoid creating a separate GPO for each policy element you want to customize.

Chapter 17, "Integrating the Macintosh into a Small Business Server 2003 Environment," discusses creating a GPO named Disable SMB Signing to allow Macintosh workstations to connect to the SBS server via SMB shares. This object is created as a separate, standalone GPO because it has one specific single purpose.

If you have multiple policy elements that make sense to bundle together, consider placing these elements in the same GPO. Likewise, if you have policy elements in line with existing GPOs, modify the SBS GPOs to include your policy elements.

Finally, make sure that your GPO is disabled while you are building it. If you are unable to complete editing a GPO in one sitting, you do not want a partially completed GPO active on the network with the potential to wreak havoc on users.

Troubleshooting Group Policy

With a standard SBS setup, there will generally be few group policy issues to troubleshoot. Clients may encounter errors showing up in the event logs on servers and workstations indicating that there were problems applying group policy settings. These errors, usually UserEnv 1030 and 1058 errors, actually indicate a communications problem between the workstation and the server or a misconfiguration of network settings, not actually a problem with the group policies themselves.

Group policy issues often appear as anything but group policy problems. The issues that appear depend largely on the types of changes made in group policy. In most cases, when group policy is applied and not fully tested, a policy change will have an impact on another aspect of the network, and the only clue the system administrator has that group policy might be the culprit is that the problems started appearing around the time that a change was made in group policy.

Group Policy Testing Tools

This chapter has already covered the Group Policy Modeling and Group Policy Reporting Wizards, but they deserve mention yet again because of their importance in determining not only what *should* happen with group policy but also what actually *does* happen.

Other tools that are useful in troubleshooting group policy problems are the command-line tools `gpresult` and `gpupdate`.

Using Group Policy Modeling and Results

Both the Modeling and Results Wizards are good first-step tools to aid in troubleshooting. If you suspect problems with group policy try the following steps:

1. Run a group policy Modeling report for a workstation or user experiencing a problem.
2. Review the report and make sure that the policy settings you are expecting to be there are actually showing up in the model.
3. Run a group policy results report against the same user and/or machine and compare the results to the modeling report. If the settings between the two reports do not match, drill down into where the differences appear and try to determine why the policy is not being applied in the same way.

Using `gpresult` and `gpupdate`

Another way to determine what policies have been applied on a workstation is through the `gpresult` command. This tool, which only runs in a command prompt, generates text data that matches the graphical output of the group policy results report. This tool is run directly on the workstation and can be used to collect results data when the Windows XP SP2 firewall blocks RPC requests from the server.

To get the most information out of `gpresult`, run `gpresult /v` at the command prompt and redirect the output to a text file. You can then review the command output by opening the file in Notepad or another text-editing tool.

As you can see from the listing, you get access to the same data present in the Group Policy Results report. Some administrators find this output more difficult to work with, but it can always be generated at the workstation, especially when the Group Policy Results Wizard cannot contact the workstation to collect the data remotely.

The `gpupdate` command replaces the `secedit` command from Windows 2000. The most common use of `gpupdate` in troubleshooting policy issues is to force policy to be reapplied on demand either at the server or a workstation. Normally, group policy is applied on a regularly scheduled basis at both the server and workstation level. When you are troubleshooting a group policy problem, you want to avoid any unnecessary delays when you can, and `gpupdate` can help cut down on those delays.

To force the server to immediately update changes made in GPOs across the entire network, run `gpupdate /force` from a command prompt on the server. This forces the server to process and apply all group policy objects defined in Active Directory. When workstations are connected correctly to the domain, this also triggers an update to occur on the workstations as well.

If needed, `gpupdate /force` can be run on a workstation to ensure that it has pulled the latest policies from the server and applied them locally.

Group Policy Disaster Recovery

Before making any changes to group policy, you should use the tools in the Group Policy Management Console to back up the GPO first. You can also back up the entire set of GPOs on the server through the tool as well. In the Group Policy Management Console, expand Forest, Domains, *domainname*, and right-click on the Group Policy Objects folder.

One of the options in the pop-up menu is Back Up All. When you select this option, you can save all the GPO configurations to a single location on the server. This location should be a secure location so that normal users cannot access and/or modify the settings files. Alternatively, you can right-click on each individual GPO and select the Back Up option to save the settings for just that object. Ideally, you should do this immediately after setting up the server so that you have a set of default settings to recover should something happen to the group policy configuration.

The only other tool for performing a disaster recovery on group policy mishaps is the system state backup. Because the system state backup contains security and policy information as well as system files and configuration data, if group policy becomes corrupt to the point that the network is unusable, you could restore from a recent system state backup to recover the policy elements as a whole. Of course, for this to actually work, you must be collecting a system state backup as part of your regular backup regimen.

Best Practice—Do Not Use `dcgpofix` to Recover from Group Policy Problems

`dcgpofix` should only be used on an SBS server as an absolute last resort. This tool restores group policy on a server back to the point immediately before the server was promoted to Domain Controller status. In other words, all the customization of security and group policy performed by the SBS setup process is lost. Use this tool only when there is absolutely no other way to get control back on a server.

If you do have to run `dcgpofix` to regain access to a server, you need to restore a system state from backup to get the SBS customizations back on the system. If a system state backup is not available for restore, you can look at rerunning the SBS installation process. At a bare minimum, you need to re-create the SBS policies by hand to restore at least some of the security and configuration to the server. If you run `dcgpofix` to recover access to your server, do not assume that it is safe to let your server go back to its regular routine.

Summary

Group policy gives a network administrator incredible power over the settings on the network. With group policy, applications can be installed and removed from workstations, Registry entries can be modified, scripts can be assigned and run, and folders can be redirected to alternate locations. The settings that control these network features are collected into group policy objects that are linked to objects in Active Directory that determine how the policy will be applied. Policies are always applied in the same order: Local, Site, Domain, and OU. If multiple OUs are present between the user or computer object, policies attached to the OUs closest to the Domain object are processed first, and those attached closest to the user or computer objects are processed last. When different GPOs have conflicting settings, the settings from the last GPO processed are the ones that apply. GPOs can be filtered by WMI filters and security group filters to give greater granular control over where policy elements are applied.

SBS provides several tools in the Server Management Console to help you manage group policy. The Group Policy Management Console snap-in appears under the Advanced

Management node in Server Management. In this console, you can quickly view the properties of each GPO, including the settings contained within. GPOs are edited with the Group Policy Object Editor, which is invoked by right-clicking on a GPO and selecting Edit. The GPMC also contains the Group Policy Modeling and Results Wizards, which can help you plan and troubleshoot group policy in the network.

Troubleshooting group policy is most effectively done with the Group Policy Modeling and Results Wizards. The `gpresult` and `gpupdate` command-line tools can also be used to help diagnose group policy problems.

Best Practice Summary

- Do not modify the Default Domain policy objects—Changes made to the default policies are difficult to test and undo if problems are encountered.
- Adding additional group policy objects—Even though you should create separate GPOs to contain unique policy groups, having too many GPOs in Active Directory significantly slows down logon times for users.
- Do not use `dcgpofix` to recover from group policy problems—`dcgpofix` should only be used as a last resort because it does not "fix" SBS-specific policies when it runs.

CHAPTER 21

Managing Workstations Through Group Policy

IN THIS CHAPTER

Managing any group of computers can be a daunting task. Even a small network with just five workstations can quickly become complicated to manage whenever you have to make individual changes to each computer.

Group policy is a powerful administration tool that will help you apply a vast array of settings across dozens of computers with just a few mouse clicks. Basically, that's what group policy is all about: allowing you to work more efficiently by centralizing the way settings and policies are established. It also brings a certain degree of standardization to your workstations and servers because you can exert a great of control on what's allowed.

In this chapter you learn the basics of using group policy to manage workstations from the comfort of your server. Suggestions also are provided on how to implement policies that increase the security of your network by blocking users from unnecessary meddling with their computers.

Why Manage Workstations?

In the past it might have been possible to leave workstations at the mercy of their users without much risk. In those days, many people didn't know much about computers, and security threats came from few vectors.

Unfortunately, the average user today is much more tech savvy and has enough computer knowledge to be dangerous. Keep in mind that these are the same users who will install peer-to-peer file sharing software (for example, Kazaa) in a business network and have their workstations full of spyware and malware.

Because of that, sometimes you have to protect your network from its own users. The damage can be accidental or not, but the important thing is that you analyze what you need to do to prevent it. Group policy can help you accomplish a portion of this task by greatly reducing what the user is allowed to do (or even see).

From a social standpoint, group policy is probably not going to make you the most popular person around the office. Let's face it: People don't like to feel restricted at all. You might want to work closely with the HR department to create policies that are backed by the company's employee policies.

Although thousands of settings are available in group policy, it is important to keep everything in perspective. Albert Einstein once said "Make everything as simple as possible, but not simpler," and this applies perfectly to group policy. My advice is to cover all your bases, but do not try to control everything. Controlling too much can become an administrative nightmare.

The next couple of sections show the most common uses for group policy and how to implement them.

BEST PRACTICE—DO MORE WITH GROUP POLICY

After you have gone through the material in this chapter and in Chapter 20, "Group Policy," you should be well-equipped to start increasing your management efficiency by developing and implementing group policy on your network. Many technologies, including WSUS (Windows Software Update Services) rely on the correct application of group policy to work correctly, so the more you know about and are comfortable with group policy, the better off you will be.

As with any technology, practice makes perfect. Set up a test network and begin working with group policy and see what improvements you can make to your management tasks by relying on group policy.

Folder Redirection and Offline Files

Folder redirection is an impressive feature that transparently forces users to store almost everything on the server (as opposed to each individual workstation). As you probably know, in Windows each user has its own My Documents folder as well as a Desktop, My Pictures, and so on, which are stored as part of the user's profile on each particular machine.

Most people store everything on their My Documents folder or their desktops, and even when they have a network share to store their data they simply forget to use it. This creates a problem for administrators because normally backups are not performed at the workstation level. Backing up every workstation is uncommon and unpractical.

Folder redirection can help you attain two goals:

- Store everything on your server—Always have a backup of everybody's data.
- Create a Work Anywhere environment—No matter where any user logs on, he will have access to his files and settings.

With folder redirection end users save their data to their own My Documents or Desktop folders, but Windows automatically redirects those locations to a share on the server. This way all their data and some settings, too, can be stored on the server where they will be backed up along with all the other network data.

Additionally, with the proper group policy settings, establishing a Work Anywhere environment is possible. If a workstation hard disk dies suddenly, you can easily relocate the user to another machine without any significant data loss. This also makes upgrades much easier because you can assign a new computer to an existing user, and the only thing you really need to do is install any third-party programs.

Another advantage of using folder redirection is that you can operate multiple devices simultaneously and still get a similar experience across all of them.

NOTE

Do not confuse folder redirection with roaming profiles. Although their purpose sounds similar, they are very different features that can even be used concurrently.

The following link provides information on both features and how they can complement each other: `http://www.microsoft.com/resources/documentation/Windows/2000/server/reskit/en-us/prork/prdc_mcc_tqht.asp`.

On the other hand, using folder redirection has its drawbacks. For example, the Recycle Bin no longer keeps the deleted files in these folders because they are no longer located on the computer. This particular problem is mitigated by using Volume Shadow Copy on the volume used to store the data. In fact, using Shadow Copy in conjunction of folder redirection has the additional benefit of being able to revert back to a previous version even if the file has been overwritten (the Recycle Bin can't handle this).

You might be thinking what happens if the server goes offline. Is the computer unusable? Also, what happens to laptops when they are not connected to the domain?

Folder redirection can work in combination with another feature called Offline Files to overcome these issues. By configuring Offline Files the computer keeps a cached copy of your data on your computer in case your network is not accessible. This is particularly important for laptops, because your users probably want to keep working on their documents even when they are outside the office.

Offline Files can keep users working seamlessly without the server. Most importantly, as soon as they are back online the device will synchronize its date with the server (where it is again safely backed up).

Configuring Folder Redirection

The process of setting up folder redirection consists of three steps: setting up a share, giving it the appropriate permissions, and configuring group policy.

For the purpose of this example we are going to redirect My Documents and the Desktop to a share named `\\SBS\UserData\` with the username and redirection type as subdirectories. For example, the desktop for Jon Dough will be located at `\\SBS\UserData\JonDough\Desktop`. Follow these steps:

1. Use Windows Explorer to open the volume that should have the data stored and create a folder named User Data. Right-click on the newly created folder, select Properties, click on the Sharing tab, and select Share this Folder. On Share name type **`UserData`** and set the permissions so that the Everyone group has Full Control. Click OK.

> **NOTE**
>
> We are *not* giving everybody full control of every user's data. The NTFS security permissions (that will be configured later) grant access only to the appropriate individuals; these are simply share level (SMB) permissions.

2. Go to the Security tab, click on the Advanced button, and uncheck the Allow Inheritable Permissions box. When prompted, select Remove All Previous Permission Entries.

3. Click Add to add the Creator Owner group and assign it Full Control to Subfolders and Files Only. Repeat the procedure for domain users giving them List Folder/Read Data and Create Folders/Append Data permissions to This Folder Only. Finally, give Local System Full Control to This Folder, Subfolders and Files. Figure 21.1 shows how the permissions should look after you add every group.

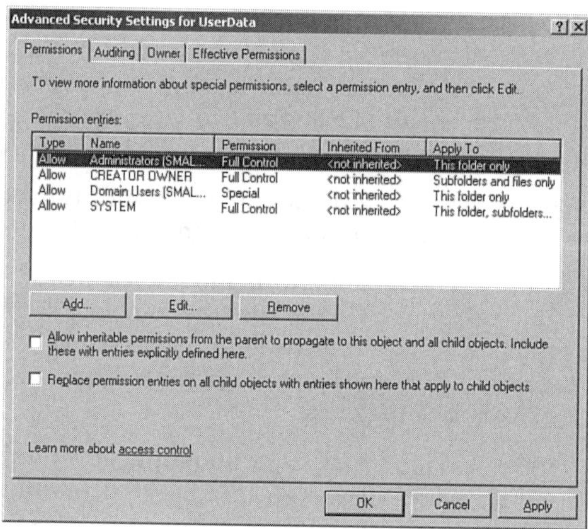

FIGURE 21.1 Advanced NTFS Permissions screen.

4. Open the Group Policy Management Console (GPMC) from Server Management. Expand the domain, right-click Group Policy Objects, select New, and name it Folder Redirection Policy.

5. On the right pane, right-click the Folder Redirection Policy and select Edit to open the Group Policy Editor. From there expand User Configuration, Windows Settings to reach Folder Redirection.

6. On the Folder Redirection screen right-click on Desktop and select Properties (see Figure 21.2). On the Setting drop-down box, select Basic and make sure that you select Create a Folder for Each User Under the Root Path; then type **`\\SBS\UserData`** on the Root Path box. Look carefully at the bottom so that you can see whether the proposed file structure matches what you want.

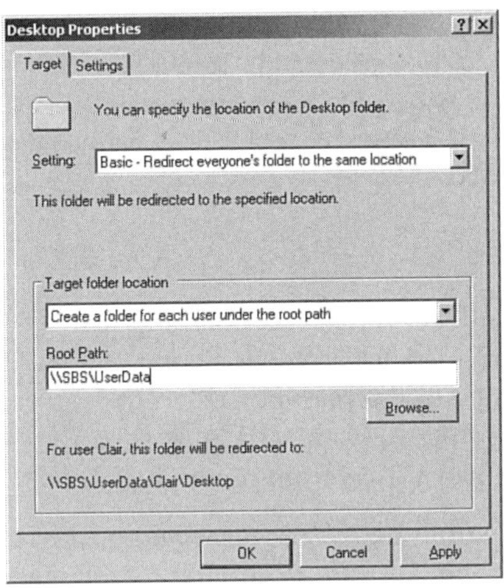

FIGURE 21.2 Desktop Folder Redirection screen.

7. Close the Group Policy Editor and proceed to linking the folder redirection policy to the domain or the appropriate Organizational Unit. Open the GPMC and right-click on the domain, select Link an Existing GPO, and select the Folder Redirection Policy from the list. Workstations will be configured to use folder redirection at next logon.
8. To redirect the other special folders just repeat step 6 for My Documents, Application Data, and/or Start Menu.

In a typical SBS installation basic folder redirection should suffice, but there are cases where using Advanced is necessary. For example, if you have multiple sites (possibly connected using a VPN link), you might want to use advanced to be able to redirect each set of users to the appropriate server located in their site.

> **NOTE**
>
> If you are interested in folder redirection only for My Documents, the wizards in SBS provide a simpler way to configure it. Just follow steps 1 and 2 in the preceding list and then open the Server Management Console, expand users, and click on Configure My Documents Redirection.
>
> Using group policy directly gives you a greater number of options (not to mention other types of folder redirection).

Best Practice—Set Up Folder Redirection

Whether it's through the SBS My Documents Folder Direction task or through setting up group policies to redirect the Desktop and other folders, you should enable folder redirection for the workstations on your network to help protect the data that would otherwise reside on the workstation. Users have become accustomed to saving data into their My Documents folder over the years, and now that many Microsoft applications default to saving new files into the My Documents folder, redirecting the My Documents folder to the server gets the user data off the workstation and onto the server where it can be backed up.

Additionally, consider redirecting the Desktop folder to the server as well. Many users still save data to the desktop because it's easier for them to find it later. This can be done only through custom group policy objects.

Configuring Offline Files

As previously mentioned Offline Files provides a complementary service to folder redirection by keeping a cached copy of the files located on the server. By default, all redirected folders are made available offline. However, in some situations you might want to modify the default settings or even block users from modifying the settings you have established.

Offline Files is a bit more complicated than folder redirection, especially because most of the settings appear on both the User and Computer Configuration sections. In most cases, settings placed on Computer Configuration take precedence over User Configuration, but in other cases they are combined. My preference is using Computer Configuration because usually the behavior of Offline Files should be dictated by the type of computer (desktop versus laptop), and this way you can create policies that affect these groups separately.

This example blocks users from modifying the existing Offline Files settings and adds this policy to the existing folder redirection policy (created on the previous section). Although you could create a new policy for this, it is recommended to place all related group policies together because doing so can greatly improve the processing speed. Follow these steps:

1. Open the Group Policy Management Console (GPMC) from Server Management. Expand the domain and Group Policy Objects. On the right pane right-click the folder redirection Policy and select Edit to open the Group Policy Editor. From there expand Computer Configuration, Administrative Templates, Network, Offline Files.
2. On the Offline Files folder screen right-click on Prohibit User Configuration of Offline Files and select Properties. Select Enable to keep Offline Files working, but the user will not be able to modify its behavior. Click OK and close the Group Policy Editor.

Table 21.1 shows some of the other Offline Files settings that you can set using group policy. Use the same procedure to add them as outlined previously. For more details on each of these settings, open the Explain tab on the setting's properties.

TABLE 21.1 Selected Computer Configuration Group Policy Settings for Offline Files

Policy Setting	Description
Prohibit user configuration of Offline Files	Prevents users from enabling, disabling, or changing the configuration of Offline Files.
Synchronize all Offline Files when logging on	Determines whether offline files are fully synchronized when users log on.
Synchronize all Offline Files before logging off	Determines whether offline files are fully synchronized when users log off. Note: This and the preceding option can significantly increase your network traffic.
Action on server disconnect	Determines whether network files remain available if the computer is suddenly disconnected from the server hosting the files.
Remove "Make Available Offline"	Prevents users from making network files and folders available offline.
Prevent use of Offline Files folder	Disables the Offline Files folder.
Administratively assigned offline files	Lists network files and folders that are always available for offline use. Note: This setting is useful when you have shares that need to be available offline to everyone.
Turn off reminder balloons	Hides or displays reminder balloons and prevents users from changing the setting.
Reminder balloon frequency	Determines how often reminder balloon updates appear.
Initial reminder balloon lifetime	Determines how long the first reminder balloon for a network status change is displayed.
Reminder balloon lifetime	Determines how long updated reminder balloons are displayed.
Event logging level	Determines which events the Offline Files feature records in the event log.
Prohibit "Make Available Offline" for these files and folders	Prohibits specific network files and folders from being made available for offline use.
Do not automatically make redirected folders available offline	Disables automatic caching of redirected shell folders, such as My Documents, Desktop, Start Menu, and Application Data. Note: If you enabled folder redirection, you should not enable this unless the computer does not need to be offline.
At logoff, delete local copy of user's offline files	Deletes local copies of the user's offline files when the user logs off.
Subfolders always available offline parent folder is made available offline.	Makes subfolders available offline whenever their
Encrypt the Offline Files cache	Determines whether offline files are encrypted. Note: Very important setting for computers (especially laptops) that contain sensitive data.
Configure Slow link speed	Configures the threshold value at which Offline Files considers a network connection to be slow.

Managing Workstation Access

Besides controlling where files and folders are stored, group policy can also be used to control access to workstations and other network resources.

Logon Restrictions

Group policy can be used to enforce the logon time restrictions that you apply to a user or a group of them using Active Directory.

This can not only help you prevent unauthorized access after-hours from employees, but it also protects your network from being vulnerable through an user's account by creating a specific time window where logons can occur.

To configure logon restrictions, follow these steps:

1. Open the Group Policy Management Console (GPMC) from Server Management. Expand `smallbizco.local`, right-click Group Policy Objects, select New, and name it Logon Restrictions.
2. On the right pane, right-click the Logon Restriction Policy and select Edit to open the Group Policy Editor. From there expand Computer Configuration, Windows Settings, Security Settings, Local Policies, and then click Security Options.
3. On the right pane of the Security Options screen right-click Microsoft Network Server: Disconnect Clients When Logon Hours Expire and select Properties.
4. Select the Define This Policy box and set it to Enabled. Click OK and close the editor.

Alternatively, you could add this item to an existing policy instead of creating a new one (this reduces network overhead by not having to process many separate group policies).

Locking Down Users

With thousands of group policy settings and numerous administrative templates, sometimes it's difficult to find the specific settings that will enhance the security of your network.

Fortunately, several guidelines are available to help administrators use group policy to lock down users depending on how much control you need or want to give to the user. This section highlights some of policies that you should consider configuring if you want to greatly reduce the ability of your users to modify the settings in Windows.

Tables 21.2 and 21.3 show some of the most common user configuration and computer configuration group policies used to manage workstations. All the values provided are suggestions, and some of these policies might not even apply in your case. Consider which policies are really required and modify them.

TABLE 21.2 User Configuration Group Policy Settings for Managed Workstations

Policy	Setting
User Configuration, Administrative Templates, Control Panel	
Prohibit access to the Control Panel	Enabled
Control Panel, Add or Remove Programs	
Remove Add or Remove Programs	Enabled
Control Panel, Display	
Remove Display in Control Panel	Enabled
Control Panel, Printers	
Prevent addition of printers	Enabled
Prevent deletion of printers	Enabled
Desktop	
Don't save settings at exit	Enabled
Prevent adding, dragging, dropping, and closing the Taskbar's toolbars	Enabled
Prohibit user from changing My Documents path	Enabled
Desktop, Active Desktop	
Disable Active Desktop	Enabled
Network, Network Connections	
Ability to Enable/Disable a LAN connection	Disabled
Prohibit access to properties of a LAN connection	Enabled
Prohibit access to the New Connection Wizard	Enabled
Prohibit TCP/IP advanced configuration	Enabled
Start Menu and Taskbar	
Gray unavailable Windows Installer programs Start Menu shortcuts	Enabled
Prevent changes to Taskbar and Start Menu Settings	Enabled
Remove access to the context menus for the taskbar	Enabled
Remove Drag-and-drop context menus on the Start Menu	Enabled
Remove links and access to Windows Update	Enabled
Remove Network Connections from Start Menu	Enabled
Remove programs on Settings menu	Enabled
Remove Run menu from Start Menu	Enabled
System	
Prevent access to Registry editing tools	Enabled
Prevent access to the command prompt	Enabled
Disable the command prompt script processing also?	No
Turn off Autoplay	Enabled
Turn off Autoplay on:	CD-ROM drives
System, Ctrl+Alt+Del Options	
Remove Task Manager	Enabled
Windows Components, Internet Explorer	
Disable changing Advanced page settings	Enabled
Disable changing Automatic Configuration settings	Enabled
Disable changing certificate settings	Enabled
Disable changing connection settings	Enabled
Disable changing proxy settings	Enabled
Disable changing ratings settings	Enabled

TABLE 21.2 User Configuration Group Policy Settings for Managed Workstations

Policy	Setting
Windows Components, Internet Explorer	
Disable external branding of Internet Explorer	Enabled
Disable Internet Connection Wizard	Enabled
Windows Components, Internet Explorer, Browser Menus	
Disable Save this program to disk option	Enabled
Windows Components, Internet Explorer, Internet Control Panel	
Disable the Advanced page	Enabled
Disable the Connections page	Enabled
Disable the Programs page	Enabled
Disable the Security page	Enabled
Windows Components, Microsoft Management Console	
Restrict the user from entering author mode	Enabled
Restrict users to the explicitly permitted list of snap-ins	Enabled
Windows Components, Task Scheduler	
Hide Advanced Properties Checkbox in Add Scheduled Task Wizard	Enabled
Hide Property Pages	Enabled
Prevent Task Run or End	Enabled
Prohibit Browse	Enabled
Prohibit Drag-and-Drop	Enabled
Prohibit New Task Creation	Enabled
Prohibit Task Deletion	Enabled
Windows Components, Windows Explorer	
Allow only per user or approved shell extensions	Enabled
Do not request alternate credentials	Enabled
Hide these specified drives in My Computer	Enabled
Pick one of the following combinations	Restrict all drives
Hides the Manage item on the Windows Explorer context menu	Enabled
No "Computers Near Me" in My Network Places	Enabled
No "Entire Network" in My Network Places	Enabled
Prevent access to drives from My Computer	Enabled
Pick one of the following combinations	Restrict all drives
Remove "Map Network Drive" and "Disconnect Network Drive"	Enabled
Remove DFS tab	Enabled
Remove File menu from Windows Explorer	Enabled
Remove Hardware tab	Enabled
Remove Search button from Windows Explorer	Enabled
Remove UI to change menu animation setting	Enabled
Remove Windows Explorer's default context menu	Enabled
Removes the Folder Options menu item from the Tools menu	Enabled
Windows Components, Windows Explorer, Common Open File Dialog	
Hide the common dialog places bar	Enabled
Windows Components, Windows Installer	
Prevent removable media source for any install	Enabled

TABLE 21.3 Computer Configuration Group Policy Settings for Managed Workstations

Policy	Setting
Computer Configuration, Windows Settings, Security Settings, Local Policies, Security Options	
Accounts: Rename administrator account	"!%Admin%!"
Accounts: Rename guest account	"!%Guest%!"
Devices: Allowed to format and eject removable media	Administrators
Devices: Prevent users from installing printer drivers	Enabled
Devices: Restrict CD-ROM access to locally logged-on user only	Enabled
Devices: Restrict floppy access to locally logged-on user only	Enabled
Devices: Unsigned driver installation behavior	Do not allow installation
Interactive logon: Do not display last username	Enabled
Interactive logon: Do not require CTRL+ALT+DEL	Disabled
Interactive logon: Number of previous logons to cache (in case domain controller is not available)	10 logons
Interactive logon: Prompt user to change password before expiration	14 days
Interactive logon: Smart card removal behavior	Lock Workstation
Microsoft network server: Disconnect clients when logon hours expire	Enabled
Network access: Do not allow anonymous enumeration of SAM accounts and shares	Enabled
Recovery console: Allow automatic administrative logon	Disabled
Recovery console: Allow floppy copy and access to all drives and all folders	Disabled
Shutdown: Allow system to be shut down without having to log on	Disabled
Shutdown: Clear virtual memory pagefile	Enabled
Event Log	
Maximum application log size	10240 kilobytes
Maximum security log size	10240 kilobytes
Maximum system log size	10240 kilobytes
Prevent local guests group from accessing application log	Enabled
Prevent local guests group from accessing security log	Enabled
Prevent local guests group from accessing system log	Enabled
Administrative Templates, Network, Network Connections	
Prohibit use of Internet Connection Sharing on your DNS domain network	Enabled
System	
Turn off Autoplay	Enabled
Turn off Autoplay on:	CD-ROM drives
System, Logon	
Don't display the Getting Started welcome screen at logon	Enabled
Run these programs at user logon	Disabled
Windows Components, Internet Explorer	
Disable Automatic Install of Internet Explorer components	Enabled
Disable Periodic Check for Internet Explorer software updates	Enabled
Disable showing the splash screen	Enabled
Disable software update shell notifications on program launch	Enabled
Security Zones: Do not allow users to add/delete sites	Enabled
Security Zones: Do not allow users to change policies	Enabled

TABLE 21.3 Computer Configuration Group Policy Settings for Managed Workstations

Policy	Setting
Windows Components, Internet Explorer	
Windows Components, NetMeeting	
Disable remote Desktop Sharing	Enabled
Windows Components, Task Scheduler	
Hide Advanced Properties Checkbox in Add Scheduled Task Wizard	Enabled
Hide Property Pages	Enabled
Prevent Task Run or End	Enabled
Prohibit Browse	Enabled
Prohibit Drag-and-Drop	Enabled
Prohibit New Task Creation	Enabled
Prohibit Task Deletion	Enabled
Windows Components, Windows Installer	
Remove browse dialog box for new source	Enabled

For more in-depth information about each policy setting and an extended list of templates for managing workstations using group policy download the following installation package: `http://www.microsoft.com/downloads/details.aspx?familyid=354B9F45-8AA6-4775-9208-C681A7043292&displaylang=en`

In most cases Terminal Servers (due to their nature) require extensive use of group policy to limit user activities. Although locking down Terminal Servers is outside the scope of this book, the principles are the essentially same as locking down a workstation, and there are several good resources on the Internet on how to accomplish this task. The following link provides a starting point:

`http://www.microsoft.com/downloads/details.aspx?FamilyID=7f272fff-9a6e-40c7-b64e-7920e6ae6a0d&DisplayLang=en`

Best Practice—Lock Down Users

The SBS community at large recognizes that the single most significant threat to network security is not a compromise at your network gateway. Instead, the greatest area of concern for system administrators is the user desktop. Chapter 10, "Workstation Security," addresses some aspects of securing the user desktop. Many of those steps can be accomplished through group policy.

If you are merely beginning to look into locking down users, the most important thing you can do early on is, when choosing a user template, choose only the minimum rights and roles that person needs to perform her job.

Other Group Policy Uses

The settings showed in this chapter are only the tip of the iceberg in terms of the number of settings available to configure using group policy. In fact, there are many more settings than the ones shown in the Group Policy Editor by default. The capabilities of group policy can be expanded by using additional administrative templates (ADM), which normally contain settings specific to a program.

One of the most used sets of administrative templates comes with the Office 2003 Policy Template Files and Deployment Planning Tools. You can download them here: `http://office.microsoft.com/en-us/assistance/HA011513711033.aspx`.

This kit includes 11 administrative templates that control everything from the behavior opening unsafe macros to showing full menus when you click on them. Similarly, numerous templates are available for other applications. In some cases, if you can't find what you are looking for creating your own ADM templates is a possibility (KB article #323639 gives you an overview of the process).

Another use of group policy includes deploying software automatically to workstations. Although SBS has its own system of distributing software (select Server Management, Client Computers, Assign Applications to Client Computers), using group policy is much more versatile and doesn't require user interaction.

More information on deploying software using group policy can be found at `http://www.microsoft.com/technet/prodtechnol/windowsserver2003/library/DepKit/3ddda5bf-cf67-4408-b68c-7e1fcb5e47ee.mspx`.

If all your workstations are running Windows XP (or Windows 2003 Terminal Servers), you can even enable Software Restriction Policies. This feature allows you to identify and block certain programs from running in your domain. (You could use this to block those pesky P2P programs from running at all!)

More information of software restriction policies can be found at `http://www.microsoft.com/technet/prodtechnol/windowsserver2003/library/TechRef/ad3b6293-4a22-46a5-a95b-7c50ca1fd1fb.mspx`.

Troubleshooting Group Policy Issues

Troubleshooting group policy can be a complex task. The vast amount of settings configurable using group policy and the fact that it depends on other technologies such as DNS and Active Directory don't make it any easier.

The best practice when creating a new group policy is to restrict it to a test group before implementing it in a production environment (see Chapter 20, "Group Policy," for more information). Unfortunately, sometimes even when taking every precaution things do not go as planned and the end result is not what you expected. Do not fear; help is here! The next few sections go over fixing the most common problems and even preventing them in some cases.

Backing Up and Documenting Group Policy Changes

Group policy is backed up as part of the System State, which the SBS Backup Wizard includes automatically. However, restoring a whole server due to a group policy issue is not an attractive proposition.

Although using the GPMC has improved the manageability of Group Policies, it is still possible to find yourself in a situation where you can't roll back to your original configuration. One practice that can save you a lot of headaches consists of documenting and individually backing up any changes you make to group policy.

The simplest approach (and one that can potentially save you hours of troubleshooting) is to keep a copy of the group policy report before and after you make the changes. The steps are presented here:

1. Open the Group Policy Management Console (GPMC) from Server Management. Expand `smallbizco.local`, right-click Group Policy Objects, and select the policy you want to print.
2. On the right pane, click on the Settings tab, and you should obtain a report on all the settings configured on that policy (see Figure 21.3).

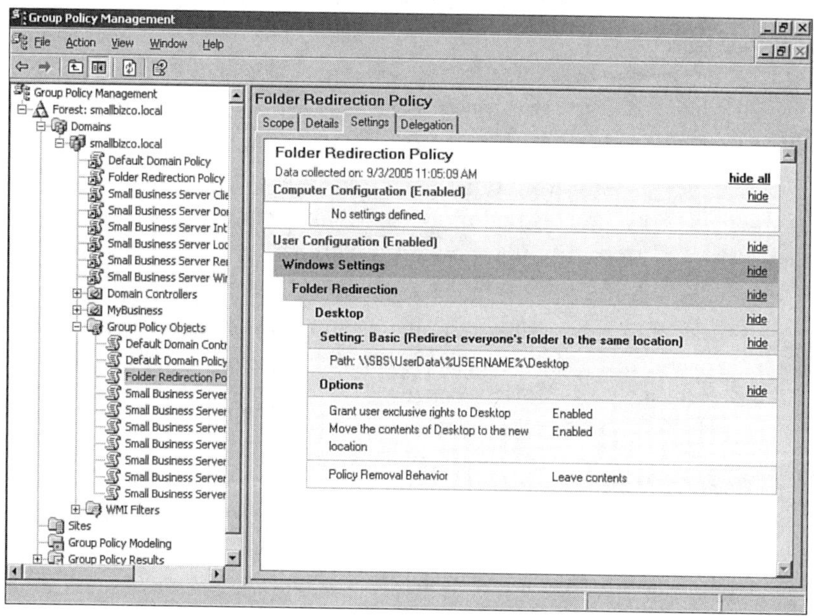

FIGURE 21.3 Group Policy Management Console report.

3. Right-click anywhere on the report and select Print or Save Report (as an HTML file).

Additionally, before modifying anything on the Group Policy Management Console, it's always a good idea to make a backup of your existing settings in case you need to roll back to them.

To back up group policy objects on the Small Business Server domain, follow these steps:

1. Open the Group Policy Management Console (GPMC) from Server Management. Expand `smallbizco.local`, right-click Group Policy Objects, and select Back Up All. Type in the location, description, and click OK.

2. Alternatively, right-click on the policy you want to save and select Back Up. Type in the location and the description.

Follow these steps to restore a group policy object:

1. Open the Group Policy Management Console (GPMC) from Server Management. Expand `smallbizco.local`, right-click Group Policy Objects, select the policy you want to restore, and click Restore From Backup.
2. Follow the Restore Group Policy Object Wizard by selecting the location of the backup file, click Next, and the Finish.

Best Practice—Document Group Policy Changes

Before you walk away from the terminal where you just modified group policy settings, make sure that you document the changes that were made. Use any method convenient for you, but note what modifications were put into place so that you can go back and undo changes if they cause a problem, or you can rebuild the changes in case of a disaster on the server.

General Troubleshooting Guidelines

If you just applied a group policy and you are not seeing the results you expected, the first thing you should remember is that changes made via group policy are not immediate, and some even require a logoff or even a reboot.

By default, computers have a 90-minute group policy refresh interval while Domain Controllers have only 5 minutes. However, to prevent network degradation due to a group of computers requesting group policy updates at the same time, there is a random offset time that can vary from plus or minus 30 minutes. In other words, when you change group policy settings, it can take up to 120 minutes before it is actually applied.

If you want changes to occur immediately, you can open a command prompt on the client and run GPUPDATE, which refreshes the group policy settings.

If you need to determine whether a group policy is being applied to a specific user and/or machine, you can open a command prompt and run GPRESULT on the affected device. You get a short report with the name of each policy (divided on User or Machine policies) and information on whether it is applied. Also, remember that several of the built-in GPOs found in SBS have their User or Machine settings disabled to speed up the loading process. If you modify the existing policies, make sure that you are doing it on the right location.

There is also a server-side tool called the Group Policy Results Wizard that can be used to determine which GPOs are applied and the resultant set of policy. You can access this tool by opening the GPMC and right-clicking on Group Policy Results to bring up the wizard (see Figure 21.4). Follow the wizard to select the computer and the user you want to probe, and you will obtain a report detailing everything applicable to that user/machine combination.

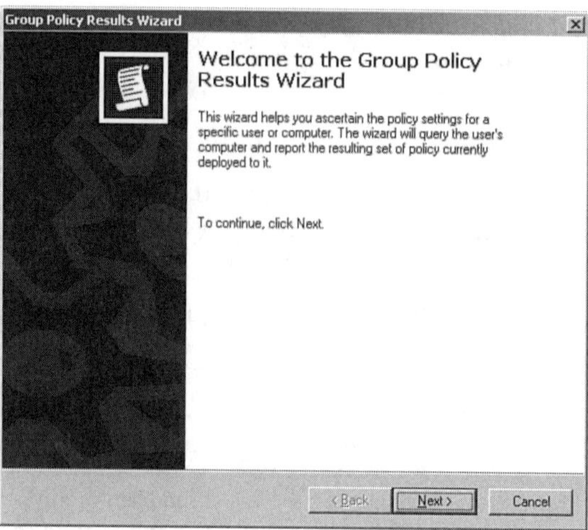

FIGURE 21.4 The Group Policy Results Wizard.

Finally, another common source of errors in group policy is incorrect DNS configuration. Group policy depends heavily on Active Directory and DNS. You must make sure that your server and every workstation are set to use the SBS DNS server. Your ISP DNS servers must *never* be used to resolve DNS queries inside the SBS domain because unpredictable results might occur and group policies might not even load.

If you are still experiencing issues with group policy the following whitepaper outlines additional troubleshooting steps and techniques used to determine the cause of the problem: `http://www.microsoft.com/downloads/ details.aspx?FamilyId=B24BF2D5-0D7A-4FC5-A14D-E91D211C21B2&displaylang=en`.

Troubleshooting Folder Redirection

Most folder redirection problems are normally caused by incorrect NTFS permissions issues rather than group policy problems. If you have asserted that the folder redirection policy is being applied to the users and still it's not working, you might be experiencing a permissions issue.

Reopen the share root folder that has each user's redirected folders and verify that the NTFS permissions are correct. Of particular importance is that the Creator Owner group has Full Control over Subfolders and Files only and that the user (as a member of the Domain Users security group) must have Create Folders/Append Data permissions to the root folder.

Remember that the user-redirected folders will be created automatically when the folder redirection group policy is applied. In that process, the NTFS permissions are set so that each user is the owner of his own folder. Also, permission inheritance is blocked, and only the user and the Local System account have Full Control access over those folders. However, to create those folders, the user must have enough permissions on the root of the share.

NOTE

One important side effect of automatically creating the user redirected folders on the network share is that the administrator (or anybody else for that matter) no longer has access to each user's files and settings.

Although this is certainly desired in some environments, there might be situations where the administrator (or other users, such as a manager) should have access to those folders. You can find more information in the following Microsoft KB article:
`http://support.microsoft.com/default.aspx?scid=kb;en-us;Q288991`.

Summary

Using group policy with SBS 2003 can help you manage groups of computers from a central location without manual intervention. Group policy provides a vast array of settings that help you accomplish simple tasks, such as setting a default home page in Internet Explorer, as well as complex ones, such as blocking access to certain programs.

This chapter focused on the use of group policy for managing workstations, allowing administrators to make changes to a group of computers with just a few mouse clicks. Although the most common uses were presented, many aspects of group policy were not covered. Because having a highly managed environment can significantly reduce your administrative costs, it pays to learn more about group policy.

Best Practice Summary

- Do more with group policies—Although it might seem intimidating at first, using group policy is definitely the best approach to managing many aspects of a group of computers. Group policy is used for much more than what is outlined in this chapter (such as forcing WSUS to clients), so you will need to use it at some point or another.
- Set up folder redirection—Using folder redirection of My Documents (and in most cases also the desktop) is a must. Important data should always reside on the server where it is properly backed up and not on the workstations.
- Lock down users—Do not downplay the threat that your own users pose. Invest time learning how to lock down users as much as needed. Use the templates provided to create a highly managed workstation environment.
- Document any changes—Each time you modify a setting from its default value you should document it. Don't rely on your memory because it is likely that three months later you will not remember what exactly you blocked to prevent some user from performing a certain task.

CHAPTER 22

Security Patches and Hotfixes

IN THIS CHAPTER

- The Composition of a Patch and the Notification Process
- The Patch Testing and Risk Analysis Process
- Resources for Security Patches and Vulnerabilities
- Implementing WSUS with SBS
- WSUS on OEM Systems
- Troubleshooting Security Patch Issues

On September 9, 1945 the first software debugging event occurred. Then Lieutenant Grace Hopper found a moth trapped inside a computer system being tested (`http://www.history.navy.mil/photos/pers-us/uspers-h/g-hoppr.htm`). From that point forward, *debugging* computer programs has been standard practice. These *fixes* have taken on new significance in the era of security patches. No longer are patches needed to remove software *bugs* or defects to ensure the proper operation and stability of the software. These days the issue of ensuring that your systems have all the latest updates can mean the difference between a protected and secure system and one that is insecure and possibly infected by viruses, slowed down by spyware, and worst of all, under the subversive control of someone else. Contact a security professional in charge of a network, and she will say a foundation of basics is needed to keep a system secure. A firewall, antivirus software and antispyware on the desktops, and software patching in place are the minimum requirements you need for proper security.

This chapter assumes that you have a server and workstations that have assets that you need to protect. There is data on that machine of importance; the goal is to protect that data from threats. Today, the threats to those electronic assets range from the secretary who downloads the virus-laden email, to the "script kiddie" who unleashes a worm on the Internet, to groups using phishing attacks to trick your users to get remote control software and keystroke loggers, but tomorrow those threats will be different. Software can never be 100% bug free. The favorite line of Michael Howard, Senior Security Program Manager, Secure Engineering Group, Microsoft Corporation, is "One person's feature is another's exploit." Most of the time in an SBS network, after patch management tools are in place, it's easier to deploy patches than to mitigate the exposure to the flaw. However, there might be times when, due to a line of business applications that do not support a patch, you will be unable to deploy patches. In those cases, you can use specific resources to mitigate until you can patch.

Make no mistake, the best defensive posture you can make to ensure that you are protected from threats both internally and externally is not just patching systems. To be proactive, you should ensure that you have basic antivirus and antispyware software, firewalls on the inside and outside of your network, proper restrictions on user and workstations rights so that each user and computer system gets only the minimal amount of access to resources it needs, and last but not least a good dose of common sense on the part of you your end users. Patching is merely one piece of the puzzle that you must have in place.

Today's threats are not just dependent on your patch status but rather are blended threats. The attackers are preying on vulnerability in one piece of software on your system for which there is no fix, typically a web browser, combined with a third-party attack tool, typically a website, that is unpatched as well. The website, although having a patch available to patch its vulnerability, has not deployed the patch. Thus the combination of the delay in patching combined with your lack of patch availability, works together. As a result, there will be times that patching isn't enough. Defense in depth will be your key.

This chapter includes a variety of patch management tools, processes, and procedures, but keep in mind that after you set these up in your network, the greatest amount of your time will not be spent ensuring that your clients' computers are up to date, but that systems maintain a level of usability after the patches are applied.

The Composition of a Patch and the Notification Process

Before beginning the discussion of tools used to deploy patches and service packs, a discussion of the foundation of what is included in a security patch and a service pack in the Windows 2003 operating system must be given.

Microsoft Knowledge Base article 824684 (Description of the standard terminology that is used to describe Microsoft software updates: `http://support.microsoft.com/default.aspx?kbid=824684`) defines a Security Update as a "broadly released fix for a product-specific, security-related vulnerability. Security vulnerabilities are rated based on their severity. The severity rating is indicated in the Microsoft security bulletin as critical, important, moderate or low." Security patches are needed when a bug that has security implications has an issue. Included in these patches for the Windows 2003 platform are several bundles of code (Description of the contents of Windows XP Service Pack 2 and Windows Server 2003 software update packages: `http://support.microsoft.com/default.aspx?scid=kb;en-us;824994`]).

For server patches you will see the following codes in the patches that let you know which version you have:

- Srv03_rtm.—Indicates that the file came from the original release to manufacturing version of the file and has not been updated
- Srv03_gdr.—Indicates that the file is from a security update, critical update, and so on, and has not been updated by a hotfix
- Srv03_spx.—Indicates that the file has been updated from a service pack
- Srv03_qfe.—Indicates that the file on your system is from a hotfix

The security patch process normally begins when a researcher contacts the software vendor and indicates that there is a software flaw or vulnerability (Microsoft TechNet Security: Definition of a Security Vulnerability: `http://www.microsoft.com/technet/archive/community/columns/security/essays/vulnrbl.mspx`), or the vendor discovers it on his own. Historically, many of these flaws were of a type called *buffer overflows*. In this type of flaw a part of the code expects a certain data input, and the container is purposely overflowed with data causing the system to break and "dump" the attacker in a position usually enough to take over the system remotely. Recently, more patches have been needed for types of files, such as various types of image files.

After an update to the software program is coded, tested, and prepared for release in the number of language versions supported by the particular software, the vendor notifies those affected by the software fix. This coding and testing process can be as short as several weeks to as long as several months depending on the underlying affected code and the dependencies of other software on that code. And then the patch is deployed and all is good, right? Unfortunately, if it was as easy as that, this chapter would be one page long. The reality is that you are introducing new code into an established system. Although the code has been tested by Microsoft to meet a certain standard, it has not been tested for your specific environment. Furthermore for small firms, it is difficult to make a duplicate, identical system. Although Microsoft has increased its patch testing process to include outside partners and independent software vendors to increase the reliability and dependability of patches, the probability is that Microsoft has not tested your clients' line of business applications.

Many ask whether the world will get to a day when patching is not needed. In general, most experts say that we are getting to the day when it's less needed, but given that human beings write code, and other human beings review the code and make it do things the original authors and developers never intended, we will always have security flaws. The analogy is always to bridge designers and software developers. The bridge designer knows the design constraints she is up against—gravity, weather, and so on—and these constraints remain basically constant. Now look at software. Computers use as their foundation for communication a software design model that was assumed to be on a trusted network. Browsers were designed to offload computing power to desktops to help ease the load on web servers. Yet one could argue that your desktops that browse are one of your riskiest attack positions in an SBS network, and thus you should perform a risk analysis of your need for timing of patching based on the surfing habits of the end users and historical security incidents.

Service packs are bundles of cumulative packages of hotfixes, security updates, critical updates, and improvements. A service pack undergoes both internal and external testing. Many in the security industry believe that you should apply service packs, but only apply those security patches that you deem necessary for your environment under the theory of reducing the amount of new code in your network that you need to be concerned with. (Microsoft TechNet Security: Why Service Packs Are Better Than Patches: `http://www.microsoft.com/technet/archive/community/columns/security/essays/srvpatch.mspx`.) They believe that you should review the patches, prioritize the risks, identify the attack vectors, review exactly how the attack would be done, examine the security vulnerability listserves to see which ones have active exploit code, and prioritize patching accordingly. Most small business specialists would argue in the SBS environment that there are just not enough resources to perform this type of analysis, nor does one see enough issues with patches to make this sort of blanket statement. Either the consultant patches everything, or he secures as best as he can and deploys in a delayed fashion. The customer of the small business consultant will not see the value in the deployment of a patch when it breaks things.

Best Practice—Understanding Service Packs Versus Security Patches

Service packs are more tested and are expected to be fully supported by Microsoft partners on the day they come out (especially large vendors that rely on Microsoft platforms for revenue streams).

Security patches go through much less rigorous testing, and vendors do not obtain patches before releasing to test.

Your clients may have a specific line of business application that requires you to perform additional analysis or may not support the application of patches. Be aware of this Catch 22. For many line of business applications in healthcare, banking, and accounting, have your client review the patch supportability on the key line of business applications. Consultants typically find that vendors only certify applying service packs and only some security patches. Therefore, if necessary, discuss the patching strategy with your customer. Discuss the risks of not patching with that of supportability. Help to guide your customers into asking vendors to support patching if they do not already do so.

The Patch Testing and Risk Analysis Process

Before Windows Update, Microsoft Update, or Windows Software Update Services are ever deployed in the network, you should decide on a patch testing and deployment strategy with your client. Most would strongly argue that if you have Windows XP with Office 2003, you should not spend your time or your client's dollars doing any sort of testing for that interaction. Patch issues typically occur with third-party products. If you historically have not seen issues with desktops and patches in your client base, it will probably be acceptable to turn on automatic updating on the workstations either via Windows Update or Microsoft Update or Windows Software Update Services. If, however, you have seen issues on certain desktops or certain applications, or your client prefers more granular control, when you set up Windows Server Update Services, you can easily set up *patch zones* and determine which machines get updates and when.

The patch testing process in a small firm environment differs greatly from a large enterprise deployment. Large firms typically have a lab setting of identical hardware and similar or identical data. One would think that the best test lab would be identical databases, but in reality, when patching or updating databases, it actually may be more beneficial to set up a batch of test data that can have many more alternatives and variations to test out all sorts of possibilities. Obviously, if your small business client has this type of budget so that you can set up a lab like this, count yourself lucky.

Patch testing process number two includes breaking a mirror of the drive and patching the original drive, ensuring that all is well and then resyncing the mirror. Again this is testing on a real live system with real life data with somewhat of a reasonable quick restore process.

Patch testing process number three is typically used in a small business environment. In this procedure a few key users obtain the patches earlier than others in the office, and they report any issues seen. The people obtaining these patches first should be those individuals in the office that are your "expert users."

Patch testing process number four is referred to as "watching for dead bodies." There are several resources that you can review for issues with patches. In this process someone patches before you and reports any issues. Invariably this process includes someone deploying something as "small" and "innocuous" as a service pack during a lunch hour and expecting it to have no issues. Resources for this process include

- The patch management listserve at `www.patchmanagement.org` where system administrators report patch issues
- The Community newsgroups for SBS hosted on the Microsoft news server
- The Community listserves for SBS at `sbs2k-subscribe@yahoogroups.com` or `mssmallbiz-subscribe@yahoogroups.com`
- Finding a local SBS user group in your area to share information (review the ever-increasing SBS user groups listed at `http://www.smbnation.com`)

This patch testing process relies on not only you obtaining information from these resources but also relating your experiences. Never assume that just because you administrate a number of small business networks that you cannot find unique patch issues that are later seen in larger networks. Time and time again, issues in smaller networks are found sooner and reported earlier than other places. Later in this chapter the resources for troubleshooting patch issues are discussed, but in general remember that any issue with a security patch is a free call to Microsoft Product Support Services.

There is a variation of a patch testing method that many SBS consultants could consider as part of consulting toolkit. That is the process of *virtualization*, whereby you can use virtual server tools to "snap" an image of the drive and test the patches. Vendors such as Vmware have software that transforms a physical machine to a virtual one. P2V software as it's called, `https://www.vmware.com/products/vtools/p2v_features.html`, could be used to "snap" an image of a system, patch the image, review log files for proper application, and then patch the real machine. Interactions between hardware and software patches will not be caught with this method but issues with key software may be.

When deciding what tool you will use to patch, you first need to determine the risks in your network. In a typical small business network, the desktops are running with administrative rights such that the user can install anything, the user can browse anywhere, and phishing and browser hijacks attacks can occur often. Thus in a network like this, patching something such as Internet Explorer would be a high priority on the desktops. Conversely, patching Internet Explorer on a server where you are not using the Internet and surfing is not a high priority if the underlying vulnerability has an attack vector of merely surfing. Discuss the end users' computer use with the business owner to best set your patching strategy. Ensure that the firm has an acceptable use policy that forbids such activities as downloading music, downloading unapproved software, or other activities that increase the risk at the firm. Resources for setting up security policies can be found on the SANS.org website at `http://www.sans.org/resources/policies/`.

In a perfect world, you should be able to read the security bulletins and determine mitigations and workaround techniques listed in each bulletin. You then deploy that mitigation technique and wait for the service pack. In the small business world, it's typically easier to deploy the patch than it is to deploy the recommended mitigation. Consultants need to fully understand the network ports they have open to the outside world to better understand how quickly they need to patch.

In each security bulletin is a section that discusses mitigation options. This also gives you the information about the risk of attack and infection based on the listed rating as deemed by Microsoft, as shown in Figure 22.1. Microsoft's rating system may not always match your rating. For each of your clients, you will build an idea of their risk and risk tolerance based on your interaction with them.

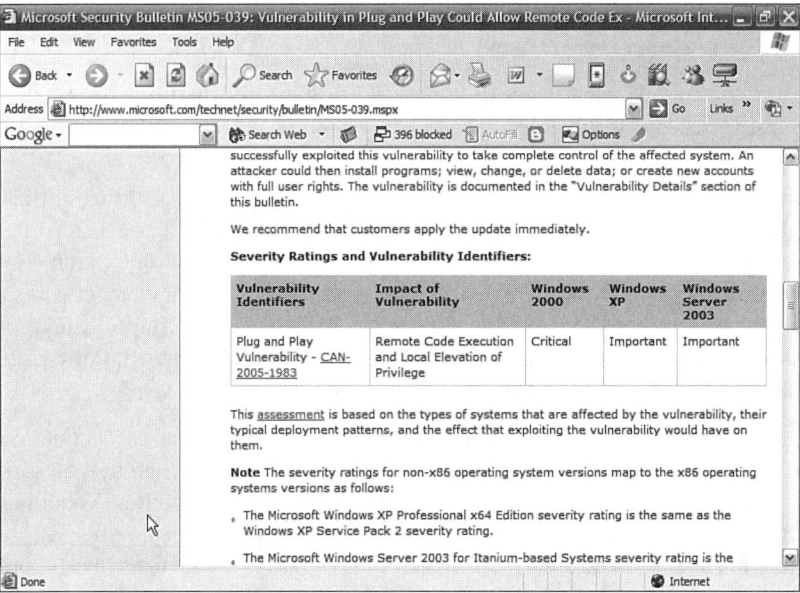

FIGURE 22.1 Severity rating and vulnerability identifiers in each security bulletin—sample from MS 05-039.

Security bulletins have ratings to let you know whether the issue is Critical, Important, Moderate, or Low, as shown in Figure 22.2, (Microsoft Security Response Center Security Bulletin Severity Rating System: `http://www.microsoft.com/technet/security/bulletin/rating.mspx`).

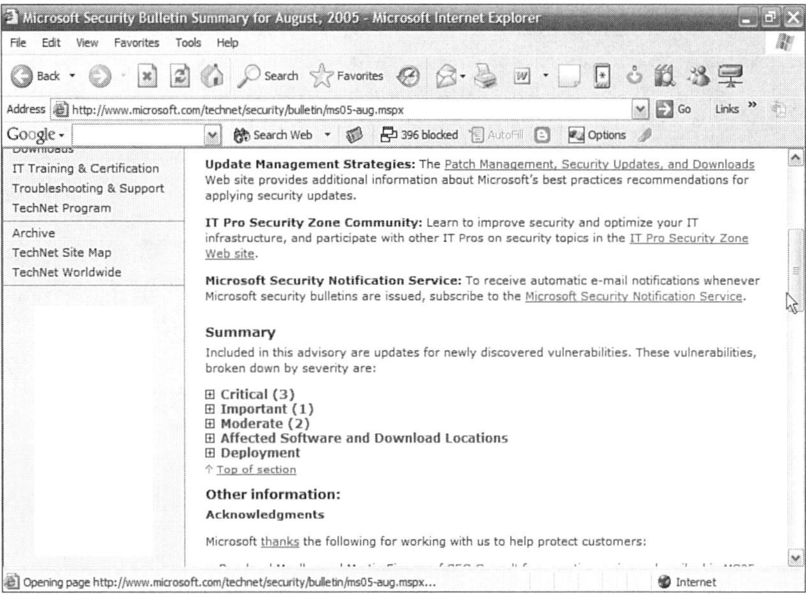

FIGURE 22.2 Summary bulletin for August showing severity ratings.

Critical typically means that the items is *wormable* meaning that little or no end user interaction is needed for this vulnerability to affect you. This can be a risk for you if the port is open on your outside firewall, or, as in the case of Blaster and Slammer, these two worms were brought inside the network on infected VPN client connections and because (at that time) workstations typically were not running host-based firewalls and thus were able to be easily infected behind the firewall and inside the network.

For many companies, a security patch with a rating of Critical is placed on a fast track for patching. However, keep in mind that although a patch may need to be critical for workstations, it may not be critical for servers.

Key words to look for in reading these bulletins for impact of vulnerability are as follows:

- Remote code execution—This means that the vulnerability can come from outside an organization and affect you.
- Elevation of privilege—A user may be able to increase the rights on his or her system and thus into the network with this vulnerability.
- Information disclosure—Private information about network infrastructure or confidential information may be leaked.
- Spoofing—What you think you are "talking to" may not be what you are really talking to.

Arguably the remote code and elevation of privilege are the ones to patch the quickest for.

The Open Firm

Many small businesses are in the category of what can be called the *open firm*. The use of local administrator on the desktop is used extensively in the office, email attachments are needed by all, all employees are allowed to surf without limitations, downloads can be performed, and perhaps employees are even allowed to utilize file swapping sites inside the firm. Most consultants would see this firm as one they would spend time cleaning out malware on a regular basis. For this firm, patching needs to be done quickly and may not be enough to keep the firm clean and secure. In all these sample scenarios, we will assume that antivirus and antispyware are fully installed on the workstations. They may not have data on their network that is regulated, or their network contains highly sensitive data. If they do have on their network sensitive data such as *PII* or *personal identity information*, you need to advise them to move to what one would deem category two.

The Moderately Secure Firm

The moderately secure firm still has to maintain full administrator rights on its systems for line of business applications but has begun the process of stripping email attachments. Thus for this firm, an immediate deployment of patches may not be needed, nor warranted. This firm may have data inside its network that is regulated or requires special handling.

The Paranoid Firm

The firm that is paranoid has locked down the workstations so that the end users do not have rights to install software. This firm has properly placed user restrictions such that only those people who need to get into any particular directory or application have rights to that area of the network. For this firm, you will probably gain the most time before you are required to patch.

Resources for Security Patches and Vulnerabilities

At a minimum, you should sign up for the Microsoft Security Bulletin notifications Comprehensive edition. This gives you an email on the second Tuesday of every month listing exactly what patches have been released. In addition, it gives you a heads-up email on the Thursday before and security advisories as shown in Figure 22.3.

Best Practice—Signing Up for Security Patch Information

If you sign up for no other security notification, make sure that you sign up for the Microsoft Advanced Security notifications at

`http://www.microsoft.com/technet/security/bulletin/notify.mspx`.

Patches are announced the first Thursday of the month and released the second Tuesday of the month (unless there is a vulnerability in the wild and the patch is deemed of high priority to be released "out of band").

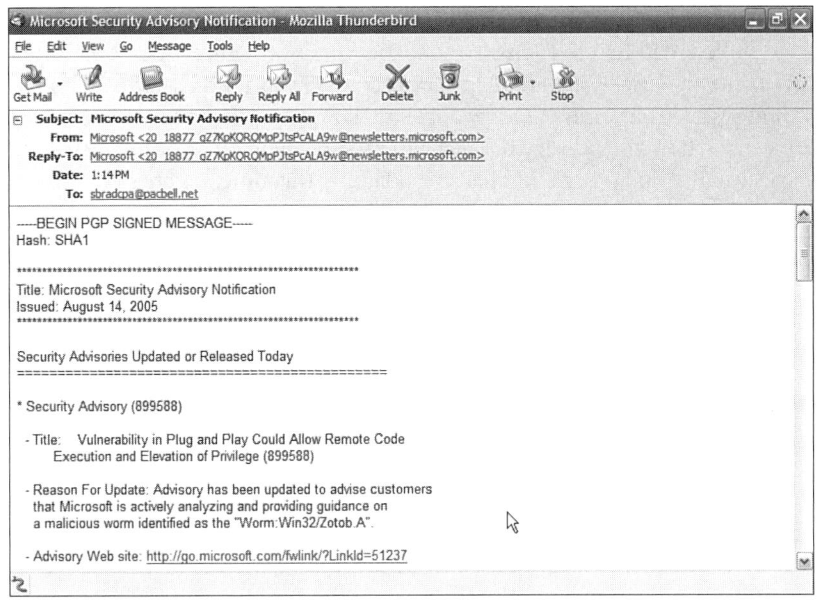

FIGURE 22.3 Sample security advisory from Microsoft warning customers of the release of Worm.

If you want additional resources for not only patched but unpatched vulnerabilities, your resources include the following (also see Appendix A, "SBS Resources," for more):

- Microsoft Security Advisories—`http://www.microsoft.com/technet/security/advisory/default.mspx`
- Secunia—`http://secunia.com/` RSS feed on the right
- MSRC blog—`http://blogs.technet.com/msrc/`

The important point that you should not overlook is that generally small businesses are not specifically targeted, unlike the larger firms, so the resources you need to spend looking at unpatched vulnerabilities (with one exception discussed next) should not be as much as those in large corporations. You could argue strongly that your client's risks are not the same as those running the web servers at amazon.com or Microsoft.com. The one exception is random drive-by attacks on browsers (this includes all web browsers such as Internet Explorer, Firefox, Opera, and so on). Due to the foundational way that the Internet was built, such that processing of pages was intended to be offloaded to local computers, we run a risk when our machines run as local administrator rights on the workstation. Thus, make sure that you have antispyware protecting you on all workstations.

Windows Update and Automatic Updates

Once upon a time, the only automatic tool you had to update the systems in an SBS network was a tool built into workstations and servers called Windows Update. The only problem with this tool was that it only patched Windows security issues. Thus for your workstations with Office installed, you had to then also visit the Microsoft Office Update website to perform an update of Office software. Furthermore, there was (and is) software included in your operating system that even Windows Update did not patch. Today the recommendation is, for every workstation and server, that you flip each of these over to the Microsoft Update if you are on supported platforms. Microsoft Update, at this time, patches both Windows and Office patches, thus eliminating the need to manually go to the Office Update site.

Furthermore for the server platform, Microsoft Update covers Exchange and SQL and will cover ISA server in the future. Thus to ensure that you are up to date on the basics of Microsoft patches, you are strongly encouraged to use Microsoft Update and not Windows Update.

For workstations, however, there is one caveat that you need to be aware of: On workstations not running Office 2003 where the caching the installation files have been left behind (Microsoft Office Assistance: Distributing Office 2003 Product Updates: `http://office.microsoft.com/en-us/assistance/HA011402381033.aspx`), or for earlier versions of Office, you many times have to point to the original install source. Thus in these earlier versions, many consultants have used a little trick to ensure that they didn't have to dig around and find where the firm stored the original OEM CD-ROM of that Office installation. On workstations with large hard drives, they would copy the entire OEM CD-ROM of Office to the local workstation and either reinstall the application from there, or repoint the patch dialog box to the copied CD-ROM files. This eliminated the need for scotch taping the media to the side of the computer or other unusual ways to ensure that the original media was kept near the machine needing patching.

Before being able to use Microsoft Update, two ActiveX files are installed on your system:

- MUWebControl Class
- WUWebControl Class

These files will automatically be deployed the first time you visit Microsoft Update, but you will need to allow them to be installed on XP SP2 systems by clicking on XP SP2's ActiveX block toolbar. Additional downloads may be required such as updated background installers and other tools as follows:

- Windows Genuine Advantage control
- Windows Installer 3.1
- Background Intelligent Transfer Service (BITS) update

After this first visit is completed you are then able to receive downloads and automatic updates for both Windows and Office from the same site. Although you can return to Windows Update by going to the Change Settings options and selecting to opt out of Microsoft Update, most would strongly recommend that if you have Windows 2000 and Windows XP clients that you stay on Microsoft Update. (Comparing MBSA, MU, WSUS, and SMS 2003: `http://www.microsoft.com/windowsserversystem/updateservices/evaluation/compare.mspx`.)

For many small firms, although you would not want to set up automatic updates on a server, it is perfectly acceptable to do so on the workstations. You have your choice of ways to deploy patches even through the automatic method (see Figure 22.4):

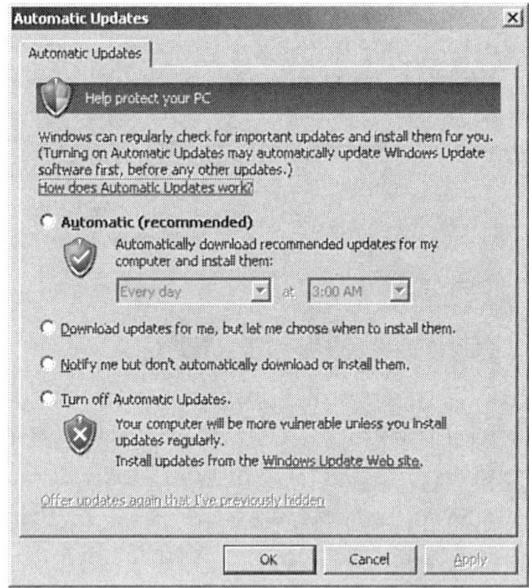

FIGURE 22.4 The Automatic update screen showing the different patch deployment options.

- Automatic (Recommended)—Automatic reboot: This method is the most autocratic of the three. You set up your systems to deploy patches and reboot. You can set them up to deploy in the middle of the night, but you need to make sure that the system is turned on. Keep in mind that this method even deploys patches to a system that is running in Restricted User mode, so you may consider this if your firm has locked-down desktops.
- Download Updates for Me, But Let Me Choose to Install Them—This option is for those firms that want to give their end users a bit of flexibility but still mandate patching as soon as the automatic updates pick up the patching. Choosing this option also offers up the ability on Windows XP SP2 machines to download patches on shutdown or to delay them until the next time the user is on the system. This is recommended for laptops in particular as a deployment methodology.
- Notify Me But Don't Automatically Download or Install Them—This is an identification and scan only option whereby the "bubble" shows up in the bottom-right corner when the patches are downloaded. In a small firm this would not be recommended because the users may tune out messages in the system tray.
- Turn off Automatic Updates—This option is not recommended unless you know you have a third-party solution in place, or you have assured yourself that you will be manually monitoring the patching of that machine.

For all these options, if you are seeing issues with installing patches, review the log file located typically under the `C:\Windows` directory. There are two files you are looking for:

- `WindowsUpdate.log` is the newer log file for the V.5 and above series of Windows Update, which includes Microsoft Update.
- `Windows Update.log` is the older log file for the V.4 and below updates.

Review the last entries in these log files and then inside the Microsoft Update interface, click on Help and Support and then click on Try Solving Your Problem with the Troubleshooter. Many typical errors seen with Microsoft Update and Windows Update are documented there.

Microsoft Baseline Security Analyzer (MBSA)

For a more automated approach of scanning your network for both missing patches and security issues, MBSA is the tool for you. Combine this with Visio, and you can even diagram the risks in your environment. There are currently two versions of MBSA, and they scan different systems, so you may need to install and run both in a firm. MBSA 2.0 obviously covers only the newer operating systems and newer Office packages, thus it would be wise to begin to move your clients to where it's easier for both you and them to protect their assets.

MBSA 2.0 covers users who primarily have:

- Windows 2000+ SP3 and later
- Office XP+ and later
- Exchange 2000+ and later
- SQL Server 2000 SP4+

MBSA 1.2.1 covers the following:

- All of the above and
- Office 2000
- Exchange 5.0 and 5.5
- Other products supported by MBSA 1.2.1 and not Microsoft update as identified in Knowledge Base article 895660 (`http://support.microsoft.com/?scid=kb;en-us;895660`)

For a network where the XP SP2 firewalls are enabled inside the network, which is the recommended way, and the default way that SBS 2003 sets up its networks, you will need an additional patch to allow the workstations to be scanned from the server. Microsoft Knowledge Base 895200 must be obtained and deployed to your Windows XP workstations to be able to remotely scan (Availability of Windows XP COM+ Hotfix Rollup Package 9: `http://support.microsoft.com/default.aspx?scid=kb;en-us;895200`).

Merely call the Microsoft Product Support Services and request the free hotfix for this issue.

Keep in mind that although this tool is primarily for scanning of patches, it is much more than that and includes guidance for passwords, running services, and lack of firewalls. This additional information can be a bit confusing in the typical SBS network. For example, the tool will scan to see whether a firewall is present on the server. For both SBS 2003 Standard (with the RRAS firewall) and Premium (with the ISA firewall) it will say that there is no firewall because it is not configured or is not available on this operating system. In reality because MBSA does not understand the RRAS or ISA firewall, it cannot report on these.

Then in addition, if you have set up the Backup Wizard on the SBS server it will complain about the SBSbackup user not having secure settings for Internet Explorer. Disregard both of these notifications and review the documentation and guidance in the MBSA literature where these issues are discussed in greater detail.

Another tool you may want to download and use to scan your system for keeping it healthy is the Microsoft Exchange Best Practices Analyzer tool, which can be found at `http://www.microsoft.com/exchange/downloads/2003/exbpa/default.mspx`. It gives you guidance on settings as well as the condition of the server.

SBS Downloads Site

At times, the SBS 2003 platform has patches unique only to it. Future plans for patching on the SBS 2003 platform include those software fixes unique to the SBS platform, but in the meantime, bookmark the following web page, and when you are patching for security patches, also review this website as well:
`http://www.microsoft.com/windowsserver2003/sbs/downloads/default.mspx`.

Best Practice—Minimum Patching Recommendations

In a recent book, and in numerous talks around the world, Microsoft Security guru, Dr. Jesper Johansson, states that one of the best ways to get yourself hacked is to not deploy patches. Although the opinion is that servers and workstations in small businesses are not targeted by hackers, they can be hurt by collateral damage in larger attacks on the Internet. Thus keeping up to date on patching is a key security element for any size firm. This should include at least these items:

- Ensure that you are on SBS 2003 sp1 (latest service pack at the time of this writing).
- Make sure that the server and workstations are connected to Microsoft Update rather than Windows Update because this ensures that the server and workstations are patched for the majority of needed software patches.
- Review the SBS specific patches page at `http://www.microsoft.com/windowsserver2003/sbs/downloads/default.mspx`.
- The "best" best practice that you should attempt to perform at each client, in each network, in each customer base you install is to follow a best practice step out of the large enterprise space. The more you standardize the servers and the workstations, the easier your life will be, both in terms of identifying patterns but also in assisting you in streamlining the patch process. Typically small businesses have a copy of nearly every Microsoft operating system starting with Windows 95 all the way to Windows XP, and these days even potentially beta versions of unreleased software. Your life will be easier if you only need to worry about security patch issues for the latest versions of desktop and server operating systems as well as Office platforms.

- Office 2003 no longer requires the original CD-ROM media to apply security patches, thus making it much easier to keep this version up to date with patches as compared to the prior versions (Microsoft Office Assistance: Local Source Makes Patching Easier: `http://office.microsoft.com/en-us/assistance/HA011402371033.aspx`).
- Windows XP Service Pack 2 with the firewall enabled inside the network has additional resiliency to attack vectors and includes Data Execution Prevention (Changes to Functionality in Microsoft Windows XP Service Pack 2: Part 1: Introduction: `http://www.microsoft.com/technet/prodtechnol/winxppro/maintain/sp2chngs.mspx#XSLTsection129121120120`).
- Windows 2003 Service Pack 1 also includes the Data Execution Prevention and enhancements to Internet Explorer that blocks ActiveX scripting and thus many times reducing the criticality of the security bulletin on the server. A new technology called *hotpatching* reduces the amount of needed rebooting of the server. (A detailed description of the Data Execution Prevention (DEP) feature in Windows XP Service Pack 2, Windows XP Tablet PC Edition 2005, and Windows Server 2003: `http://support.microsoft.com/kb/875352`.)
- Internet Explorer 7 when released on Windows Vista will include additional protection for phishing, surfing, and overall more security (`http://www.microsoft.com/downloads/details.aspx?familyid=718e9b3a-64fe-4a4c-9ddf-57af0472ead2&displaylang=en`).
- Internet Explorer 7 on Windows XP increases security (but not as much as on Windows Vista).
- Consider the use of patch deployment and reporting tools, discussed later in this chapter.

The lesson to be learned here is that being on the newest versions means that you are on more protected versions and, I would argue, versions that obtain much more testing resources for patch quality purposes. Windows 98 and Windows ME only get critical patches, and one patch for that platform took until April of 2005, two months after the other platforms (Windows 2000, Windows XP), which were patched in early February for the same issue. Your clients may indicate that they cannot afford to upgrade from Windows 98, but I would strongly argue to the contrary. The ability to remotely manage Windows 2000 and XP using the server, the ability to remotely patch, and, as pointed out, the overall lack of support resources for Windows 98 and Windows ME means that these platforms just do not make economic and, especially, security sense anymore. Neither platform has a security foundation, and each was written for a much more innocent time on the Internet.

Shavlik HFNetChk Pro

There is actually a slightly easier way to patch systems than using Microsoft Update and MBSA, and that is to use patch tools. As the old saying goes, you get what you pay for, and HFNetChk Pro, although not a free tool, is a reliable way to ensure that the workstations and servers in your network are kept up-to-date for updates on Windows, Office, Exchange, SQL, and ISA server, and also patches unique to SBS 2003 as well as third-party software such as Adobe, Firefox, and Real Player.

The list of software supported as of the time of this writing includes Windows software as well as many third-party programs.

Given the reasonable price tag of Shavlik's Basic and HFNetChk5 editions, you might be wise to review and examine the flexibility of this patch tool given its lengthy listing of supported software. It is a *push* technology and not a pull, and thus you can launch the console, scan the computers, push out patches, force a reboot, and then when completed, rescan again to ensure compliance. The streamlining of *push* patch technology versus *pull* technology (which is what WSUS offers) should be considered when making your decision. Typically you can be up and installing with this tool in less than 30 minutes, and it can be deployed at the server or at a workstation to be used as a patch deployment method.

Best Practice—Taking a Page from the Enterprise Folks

Some of the best practices can be learned from the enterprise folks. When deploying a new workstation, even if it's an OEM preinstalled machine, either take the time to uninstall all the annoying "phone home" unneeded software, or reinstall it from scratch installing only those pieces of software you need. The less additional software that you need to worry about updating, the better off you are. These days Real Audio, Adobe, Instant Messengers, and even our own antivirus software have been found to have vulnerabilities. Have a listing of software deployed in a firm so that you know what you need to update.

Consider preparing *slipstreamed* installs to assist you in quickly and easily deploying patches. The document entitled Techniques for Patching New Computers, `http://www.microsoft.com/technet/desktopdeployment/articles/080305tn.mspx`, includes information about how to easily bring a system up-to-date before installing it in a network.

In general, the wise thing to do is always build new machines behind a firewall router device to ensure that even while the system is being built it is protected.

Implementing WSUS with SBS

When SBS 2003 was released in October 2003 at the Worldwide Partner Conference in New Orleans, Steve Ballmer also announced the next version of a free patch management tool. Two years later, and almost at the same time as Service Pack 1 for SBS, it finally was released. Windows Software Update Services (WSUS) or *Wah-Suhs* as we call it, basically puts the Microsoft Update website on your own server where you can control the patches. It is perfectly safe to place WSUS on the SBS 2003 box itself.

There are two ways to set up a WSUS deployment scenario for a consultant. First, you can merely remote into your client's server, approve patches, and automate the deployment.

Second, you can, as a consultant, be the remote patch tool for your clients themselves, whereby you are the master WSUS patch engine, and their servers will point to your system as the master patch engine. However, you need to ensure that a few items are in place: You either need to be a Microsoft Certified Partner or a Microsoft Registered Partner, and you must have a Service Line Agreement in place.

WSUS provides the consultant with a way to deploy and manage patches from a single console per network, or, with additional complexity, all of his networks from a single console.

There are some items of legal note to be aware of when you take the responsibility of patch management for your client:

- Do not attempt to guarantee quality of patches for your client. Even with all the testing tools at your disposal, you are guaranteed to miss something—hardware issues, deep buried software issues. It is a guarantee that you will not be able to find all issues ahead of time.
- Do not attempt to test Office and Windows patches. Microsoft has a patch testing process that includes external testers, OEMs, and ISVs. Microsoft ensures that its flagship products', Office and Windows, patches are tested. Performing testing on the interaction of Windows XP and Office is a waste of your time.
- Do begin to build a database of prior patch issues with your client base. SBS networks were affected with file locking issues with Office 2003 and Windows XP on SBS 2000 networks due to SMB signing issues. Make note of patches that affect core functionality and watch for issues. Document the files included in those patches that caused issues in the past and look for those files in future patches, thus keeping an eye out for patches that may need additional testing procedures.
- Understand the best ways to have you or your client test patches. Review what the patch is fixing and make sure that you look for issues in what is being patched. Make sure that VPNs connect, Remote Web Workplace is functional, printing functions work, and network devices connect.
- Remember that in some cases you are accepting EULAs on behalf of your client and thus you may want to specifically have in writing the understanding of the level of responsibility between yourself and your client on patching. Do not attempt to guarantee patches.
- Set up a managed monitoring service for your clients and consider including security patches in this monthly service, but do not include service packs in this plan. Service packs tend to need more planning for a small firm than security patches.
- If your client is not ready for the "managed plan" yet, prepare recommended improvements based on your review of the client's issues.

The process for installing WSUS on a SBS server is fairly straightforward. Although there are step-by-step whitepapers for installation on the Windows 2003 platform, the installation for SBS 2003 has been a bit streamlined. You can choose to deploy WSUS on the SBS server itself, or if you have a member server that merely does file and print sharing, you can deploy the WSUS on the member server. If the member server is a Terminal Services and application sharing box, you will want to deploy WSUS on the SBS box itself.

Given that this book's emphasis is on SBS 2003 with the application of Service Pack 1, we will assume that you have a server either installed or via OEM channels that already has the Service Pack 1 installed, or you have deployed it. If you do not have SP1 already installed, it's recommended that you do that first because it will place on your system the needed files such as the needed .NET SP1 and Background Intelligent Transfer System

(BITS). Although you can install WSUS on a box without Service Pack 1, it's generally recommended to do so first.

Generally, it's wise to be on later platforms, and WSUS will only patch and support Windows 2000 Professional with Service Pack 3 or 4, Windows 2000 Server with Service Pack 3 or 4, Windows XP Professional, Gold (no sp), Service Packs 1 and 2, and Windows 2003 (all versions).

Because SBS already has several websites competing for the default website location of port 80, the port of 8530 is chosen instead. The installation takes up to about 8GB if you plan on storing the security patches locally, so be sure to choose a location preferably not on the `C:` drive to install the patch location.

When setting up the group policy to have the WSUS patch server location be seen by the workstations, make sure that you have `http://servername:8530` listed. In addition, there have been several reported issues with the clients not "checking in" with the console, thus you should review the up-to-date release notes at the time you install as well as review late-breaking tech notes on the WSUS wiki (`http://www.wsuswiki.com/`) and the WSUS blog (`http://blogs.technet.com/wsus`)—two online resources that have late-breaking issues. For many SBS installations, it is recommended that you place a domain name in Client Side Targeting to force the clients to check in to the server. Otherwise, the workstations may not show up in the console to then allow you to move them into the patch zones. Alternatively, you can set up your WSUS strictly on a group policy basis, which is documented fully at the `Smallbizserver.net` website at `http://www.smallbizserver.net/Default.aspx?tabid=159`.

Using either method, the key element here is when you set up the zones you identify your risk tolerance. Remember our lengthy discussion of thinking about the risk and threats to your client's network? This is the time to bring that back into focus. Workstations have different risk than servers, than do servers with line of business applications, than do laptops. Place each type of risk asset into the appropriate patch category and then assign how it will be patched. Automatic approval? Manual approval? This is your call on how the network responds when a security patch is to be deployed.

Resources on the Microsoft website include

- `http://www.microsoft.com/downloads/details.aspx?FamilyId=E99C9D13-63E0-41CE-A646-EB36F1D3E987&displaylang=en`
- `http://www.microsoft.com/windowsserversystem/updateservices/techinfo/default.mspx`

Installing WSUS

In addition to the recommended prerequisite of the SBS 2003 Service Pack 1, preferably the server you are installing WSUS on will be at least a 750 megahertz (MHz) processor and have 1GB of RAM memory or more. The SBS platform already has the necessary .NET and IIS services running.

To begin the process, you first go to the WSUS download site, register using Microsoft Passport, answer all necessary questions, and download the installer. Unlike other

Microsoft software, you need to answer some questions about you and the firm you are deploying this on (see Figure 22.5). However, the form is only built for one company, and you should review the choices for opting out of the marketing and notification options. It appears that the intent of the form is to gather information for each client; however, the use of Passport technology ties it to the individual consultant's information.

> **NOTE**
>
> There has been some discussion of whether you can install WSUS on one server and forklift the entire database of synchronized patches onto another server; however, given the need for individual firm sign-up on the registration form, it is unclear whether this is allowed. This registration process is a bit unusual. At this time, it is the only free software on the Microsoft website that requires this level of questions and responses. Answer the questions based on your normal client deployment.

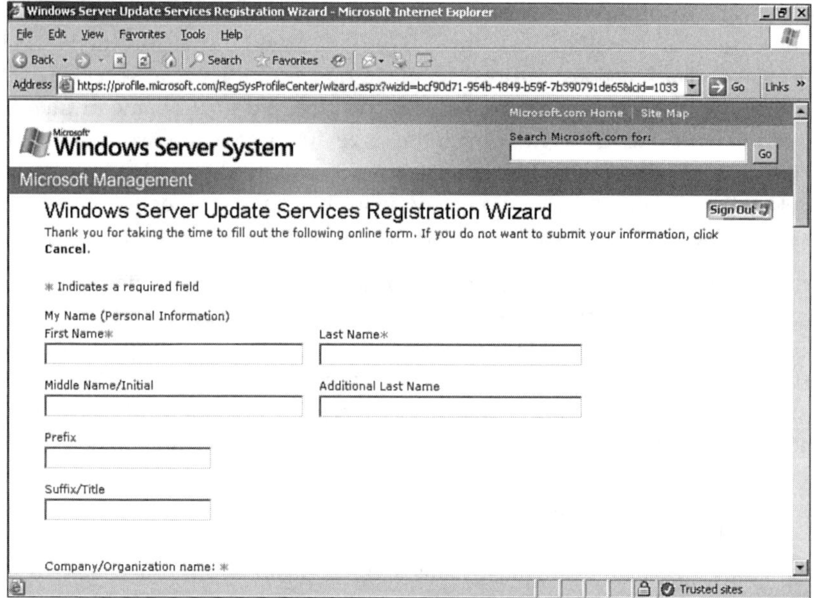

FIGURE 22.5 Registration for WSUS, including firm information.

Before beginning the installation, review your drive space locations. You will not want to install the patches, which have a reserved space of 6GB minimum, on the root drive. Although the WSUS documents state that it could be as large as 30GB of patches, if you set up the WSUS to ensure that you only download for your language, you should minimize the patch storage size. Make sure that you are logged in as the domain administrator and double-click the installer file `WSUSSetup.exe` to begin the process by saving it to your computer.

The latest version of `WSUSSetup.exe` is available on the Microsoft website for Windows Server Update Services at `http://go.microsoft.com/fwlink/?LinkId=47374`. After you download the installer, launch it and follow these steps to complete the installation:

1. On the Welcome page of the wizard, click Next.
2. Review the EULA and accept the terms of the agreement.
3. On the Select Update Source page (see Figure 22.6), take the default of `C:\WSUS` or choose to move the installation to another partition if you don't have enough space on the main partition.

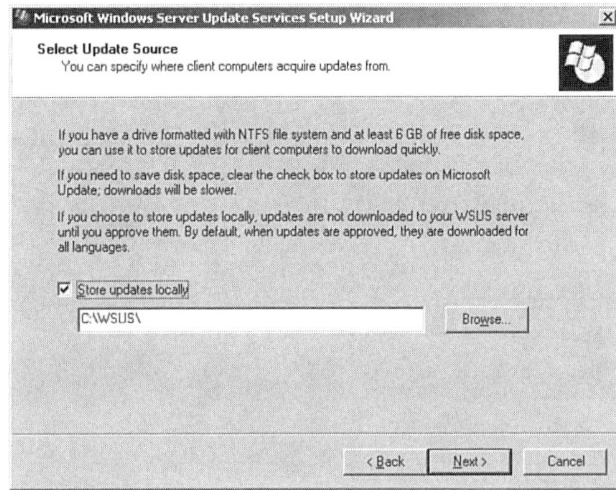

FIGURE 22.6 Although the default for WSUS prompts you to load this on `C:`, consultants recommend an alternative location.

4. On the Database Options page, install WMSDE if the computer you are installing to runs Windows Server 2003. (At this point, you will need 2GB more; again, the recommendation is to not place this on your root drive.)

Best Practice—Selecting the Best Location for WSUS Databases

When deploying WSUS on your server you have two choices: WMSDE and SQL Server. For a consultant deploying WSUS remotely, installing with a WMSDE database is fully self-contained and can be done entirely from a remote location. If using SQL server, the install needs to be done at the site to deploy the necessary media.

- You can choose to store patches locally, or if you do not, the clients will connect to Microsoft Update directly to get approved updates, and the server will just be a conduit for an approval process. Remember that this reserves 6GB of storage, so it's wise to not use the default of `C:\WSUS`, which is offered to you, and instead place it on a `D:` or other location. Although in general, it's recommended to keep the default options, given that the defaults place everything on `C:`, it is recommended to review and change if hard drive locations are tight on space, and click Next. Most consultants recommend that this go on a partition other than your main root drive.
- To reduce traffic to the Internet by having each workstation pull updates from the Microsoft servers every time an update is installed, configure WSUS to store the update data on the local SBS server. To keep the full catalog of update information stored locally, you will need 6–8GB of space on the server. You will also want to store the update data on a drive other than the system drive. (WMSDE is the default storage database for

WSUS, but you can use SQL to store the patches. If you are interested in SQL as a deployment storage option, more information is in the WSUS whitepaper.)

- Remember that WMSDE is the larger expanded version of the SQL lite desktop application that does not have a 2GB database limit. So although the 2GB is indicated in the wizard, plan accordingly and choose database locations that will not later cause size problems on your system.
- If you cannot use WMSDE, a SQL Server instance must be provided for WSUS to use, by clicking Use an Existing Database Server on This Computer and typing the instance name in the SQL Instance Name box. For more information about database software options besides WMSDE, see the "Deploying Microsoft Windows Server Update Services" whitepaper. This must be installed prior to the WSUS installation if you prefer a SQL database. For consultants installing WSUS over a remote connection, remember that the WMSDE install can be done totally remotely, whereas a SQL install needs someone to find and insert the Premium CD-ROM when prompted. The recommendation for SBS installs is to use the default WMSDE.

5. Keep the default options or choose an alternative partition for the WMSDE, and click Next.
6. WSUS on SBS 2003 deploys on port 8530 rather than port 80, and the software now installs on your system (see Figure 22.7).

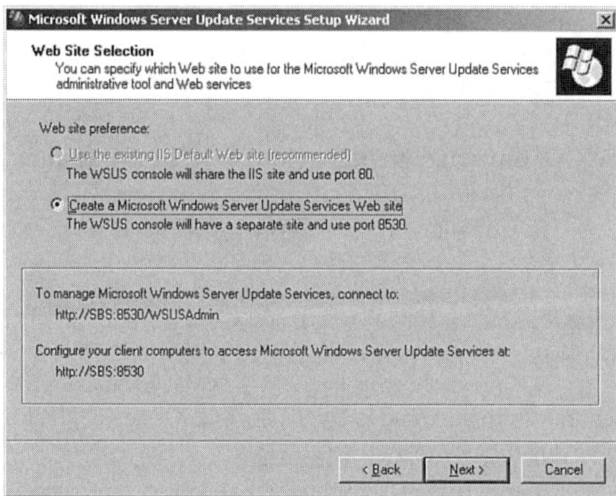

FIGURE 22.7 Selection of the default port that WSUS uses for purposes of deployment to workstations.

Best Practice—Setting Up a Mirror WSUS Server

For consultants who want to set up a mirror server and be the centralized patch approver for all their clients, it's recommended that you review the documents in the "Deploying Microsoft Windows Server Update Services" whitepaper located at `http://www.microsoft.com/downloads/details.aspx?FamilyId=E99C9D13-63E0-41CE-A646-EB36F1D3E987&displaylang=en`. Keep in mind that you will need to be a Microsoft Certified Partner or a Microsoft Registered Partner with an SPLA agreement in place. It also is recommended to ensure that an SSL configuration is set up between your clients and your deployment server. More information on this can be found at `http://go.microsoft.com/fwlink/?LinkID=41777`.

From that document there are certain things to keep in mind: Securing your WSUS deployment with SSL increases the workload of the server. You should plan for about a 10% loss of performance because of the additional cost of encrypting all metadata sent over the wire. If you are using remote SQL, the connection between the WSUS server and the server running the database is not secured with SSL. If the database connection must be secured, consider the following recommendations:

- Put the database on the WSUS server (the default WSUS configuration).
- Put the remote SQL Server and the WSUS server on a private network.
- Deploy IPsec on your network to secure network traffic. For information about how to deploy IPsec in your environment, see "Overview of IPSec Deployment" (`http://www.microsoft.com/`).

Again, be aware of the additional requirements and legal issues that you may face in being the master deployment center.

When you are finished, you are prompted to launch the WSUS administration site at `http://servername:8530/WSUSAdmin/`.

Synchronization for the First Time

On completion of the installation, you set the synchronization and proxy settings. To administer WSUS, go to http://servername:8530/WSUSAdmin/ to begin the process. The key here is that it is only through synchronization with the Microsoft servers that you pick up the patches. Although you can set a manual synchronization, be aware that the process does take time, thus it's recommended to enable an automatic synchronization. Follow these steps to complete the initial synchronization:

1. On the WSUS console toolbar, click Options, and then click Synchronization Options. Your initial view of WSUS should look like the information in Figure 22.8.
2. If you are using ISA server, or are behind a hardware firewall, you need to include proxy information. In the Proxy Server box, select the Use a Proxy Server When Synchronizing check box, and then type the proxy server name and port number (port 80 by default) in the corresponding boxes.
3. If you want to connect to the proxy server by using specific user credentials, select the Use User Credentials to Connect to the Proxy Server check box, and then type the username, domain, and password of the user in the corresponding boxes. If you want to enable basic authentication for the user connecting to the proxy server, select the Allow Basic Authentication (Password in Clear Text) check box.
4. Under Tasks, click Save Settings, and then click OK in the confirmation dialog box.
5. You must manually synchronize one time to see the additional software options beyond Windows such as Office, Exchange, and SQL. Carefully review as well the additional software offerings such as drivers and security rollups (see Figure 22.9).

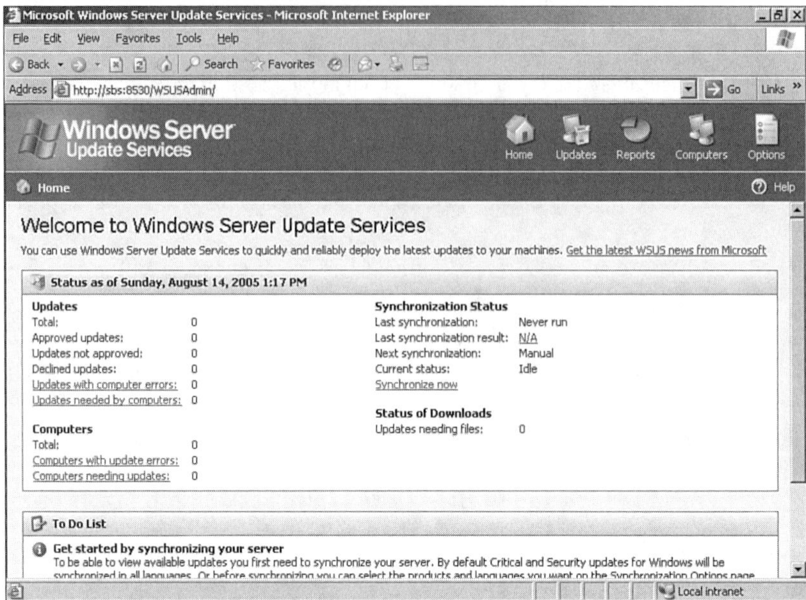

FIGURE 22.8 Status screen showing the initial view of a deployed WSUS console on SBS.

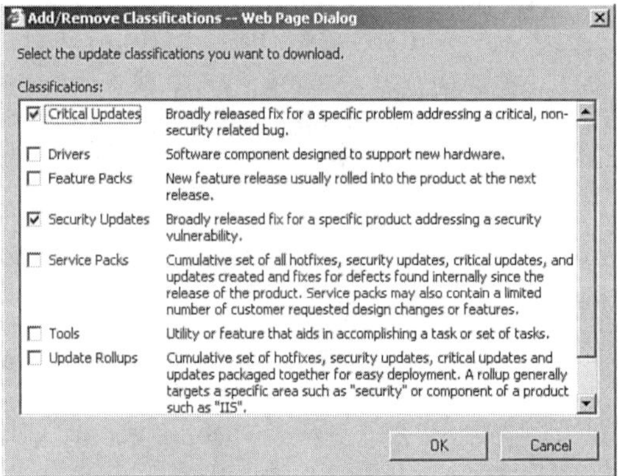

FIGURE 22.9 Review the synchronization options for additional software such as drivers, feature packs, and so on.

6. Make sure that you change the option in the Advanced Synchronization Options Web Page Dialog window to download only those patches that match the locale of the server. This ensures that you are not downloading unnecessary security patches on your network when they are not needed (see Figure 22.10).

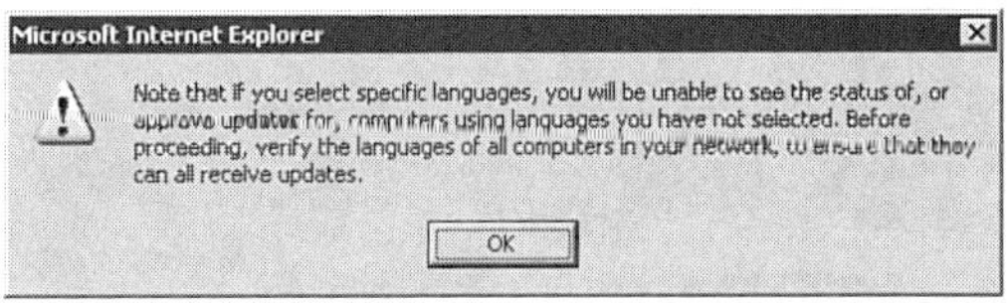

FIGURE 22.10 Selection of language of patches to ensure the minimal install of patches over the Internet connection.

Setting Up Group Policy for WSUS on Your Server

Follow these steps to create a new group policy object for WSUS on the SBS server. For more information about group policy on SBS, see Chapter 21, "Group Policy."

1. In the Server Management Console, expand Advanced Management, Group Policy Management, Forest, Domains, and then click your SBS domain. Right-click on the domain and select Create and Link a GPO Here.
2. Name your policy something descriptive. Click OK.
3. Right-click on the new policy object and select Edit. Then expand Computer Configuration, Administrative Templates, Windows Components, and then click Windows Update.
4. In the details pane, double-click Specify Intranet Microsoft Update Service Location. Type the HTTP URL of the same WSUS server in both Set the Intranet Update Service for Detecting Updates and Set the Intranet Statistics Server. For example, type **`http://`*`servername`*`:8530`** in both text boxes, where *`servername`* is the name of your WSUS server, as shown in Figure 22.11. Click OK when finished.

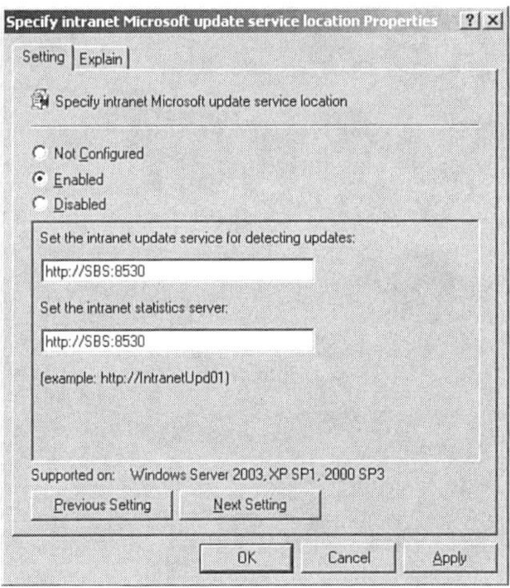

FIGURE 22.11 Specification of Intranet Microsoft Update Server location in Group Policy Console.

5. Double-click on Configure Automatic Updates. Select the appropriate setting under Configure Automatic Updating based on your previously determined risk level, as shown in Figure 22.12. Click OK when finished.

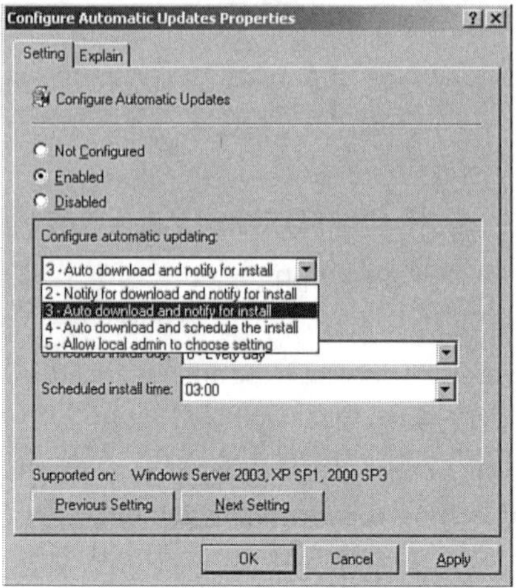

FIGURE 22.12 Specifying behavior of automatic updates (see previous discussion of automatic update selection impact in Figure 22.4).

6. Double-click on Enable Client-Side Targeting and enter the name of the SBS server, as shown in Figure 22.13. This ensures that the workstations check in with the server appropriately. Click OK when finished.

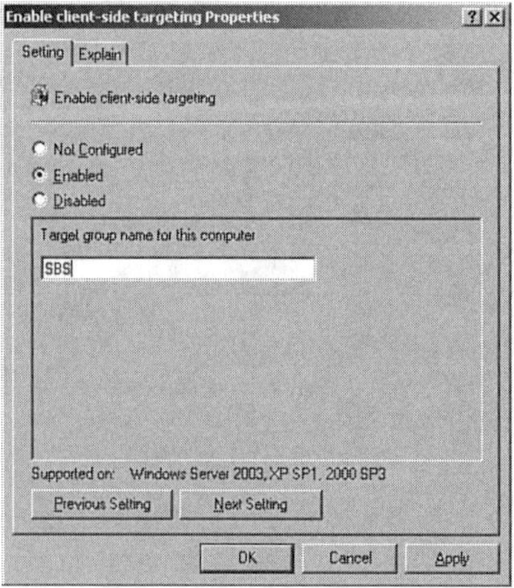

FIGURE 22.13 Specifying a name for client-side targeting to ensure that workstations check in with the server.

NOTE

There is a known issue with some workstations not reporting in to the server; either use this as a workaround or obtain this hotfix for the server—FIX: IIS 6.0 may send an "HTTP 100 Continue" response in the middle of the response stream when you send a POST request: `http://support.microsoft.com/?id=898708`.

7. Double-click on No Auto Restart for Scheduled Automatic Update Installations. Click on the Enabled radio button to ensure that clients will not be abruptly restarted. Click OK when finished.

After you have finished, review the settings in the Group Policy Settings window. This should look similar to Figure 22.14.

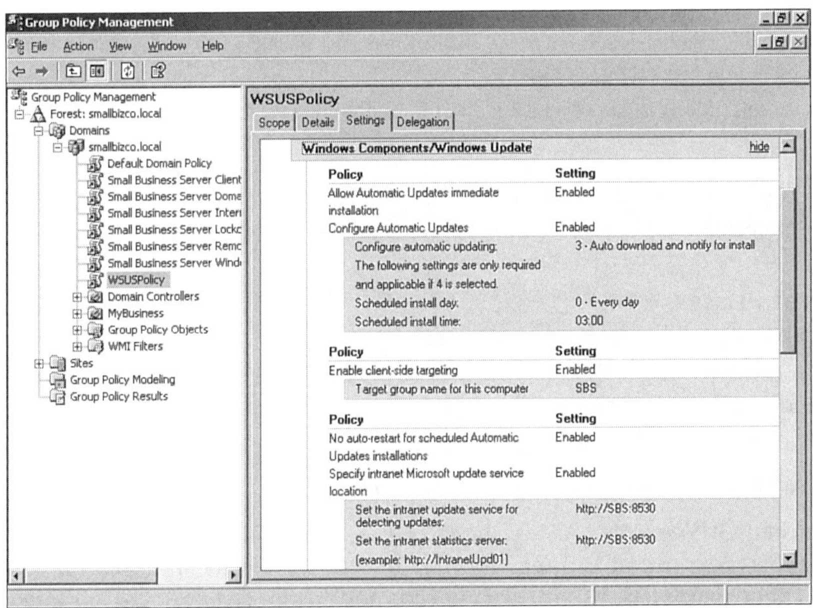

FIGURE 22.14 Review the group policy settings.

At a command prompt on the server type in **`gpupdate /force`** to speed up the process of the deployment of the group policy settings and the checking in of the workstations. After the workstations have checked in to the server, you can set up groupings and use the Move Computer tool in the console to move them into your patching groups.

Preferably you should have at a minimum three zones:

- Server zone—This ensures that patches will be manually approved for the servers and deployed only when the consultant wants the servers to be patched. Remember that many times in an SBS network, the server may be the device that needs less immediate patching due to its use of the enhanced IE lockdown, ports closed, and the use of XP SP2 firewalls on workstations.

- Workstation zone—In most small business firms, this is your "risk" zone. Because workstations install with local administrator rights, these machines need quick patching.
- Laptop zone—You may need to set up different patch needs for your mobile devices.
- Line of business application—Additional zones that you may need to set up include different patch needs for your workstations or servers that have key line-of-business applications.

Best Practice—Establishing Patch Zones and Risk Zones

Now you as the consultant get to prove your worth. This is where the earlier discussion of risks meets group policy. What have been historical issues with patching in the past? Do some workstations and applications have no issues? Is there one application only deployed on a few workstations that is troublesome? Identify those systems that can have patches automatically pushed to them and those applications that cannot. Set up zones for users who will be your main patch testers and communicate to them (via email) when their machine has been patched so that they can notify you when they see issues.

Discuss this process ahead of time and use this opportunity to define when you can patch.

In the Computer Groups screen, manually type in your patch zones, and as the workstations and server(s) check in you can reassign them to the particular zone.

Approval Process

After you perform this initial synchronization, you are ready to begin the process of setting up the approval. Although you can set up your zones to patch automatically, it's generally recommended to manually approve servers after appropriate testing or review of community patch issues have been done.

For manual approvals perform the following steps:

1. On the WSUS console toolbar, click Updates. By default, the list of updates is filtered to show only Critical and Security Updates that have been approved for detection on client computers. Use the default filter for this procedure.
2. On the list of updates, select the updates you want to approve for installation. Information about a selected update is available on the Details tab. To select multiple contiguous updates, press and hold down the Shift key while selecting; to select multiple noncontiguous updates, press and hold down the Ctrl key while selecting.
3. Under Update Tasks, click Change approval. The Approve Updates dialog box appears (see Figure 22.15).
4. In the Group Approval Settings for the Selected Updates list, click Install from the list in the Approval column for the Test group, and then click OK.

You can change your patch zone or group settings to be automatically deployed if you want. Again, this may be recommended for some workstations but not for all computers.

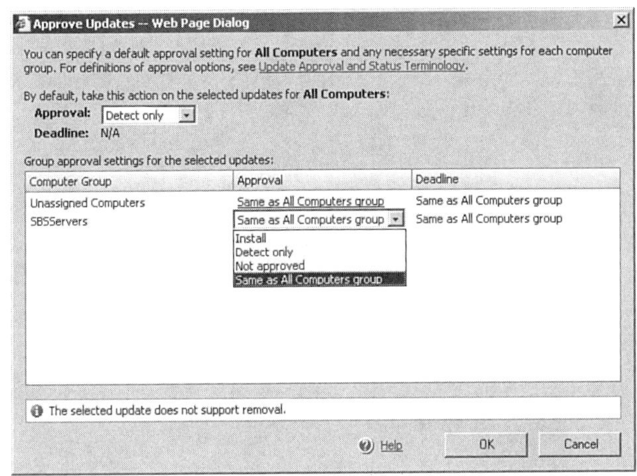

FIGURE 22.15 Approval process for patching.

For additional resources on scripting WSUS for faster deployment of patches, review the following resources: Microsoft TechNet column: "Tales from the Script—July 2005: I'll Get You, My Pretty...And We'll Manage Windows Update, Too!": `http://www.microsoft.com/technet/community/columns/scripts/default.mspx` and `http://uphold2001.brinkster.net/vbshf/forum/forums/thread-view.asp?tid=199&posts=1`.

An automatic synchronization should be set up and then you need to decide which machines are automatically updated, and which machines are manually updated. In general, we recommend that servers be manually updated, and thus you need to set the automatic deployment method for the Server group to always be manual But for workstations and member servers, you can decide based on your prior risk and patching analysis. You may want them to be set for automatic deployment of patches, and you may even consider an automatic reboot at an unused time of the day. Remember that a forced unattended reboot in the middle of the night can also be done on workstations using restricted user mode. They do not need local administrator rights for patch deployment if the patch policy is set to a mandatory reboot process.

Remember that because WSUS relies on the same technology as Windows Update and Microsoft Update, any issues on a workstation with those mechanisms affect WSUS as well. Therefore, the same recommended log file and troubleshooting tools are recommended. You may need to delete the catroot2 folder, reregister DLL files, or perform any of the other techniques described inside the Microsoft Update troubleshooting tool.

For more resources on using and streamlining WSUS, we recommend signing up for the WSUS listserve on the website `www.patchmanagement.org` and following the WSUS blog at `http://blogs.technet.com/wsus/` and the WSUS wiki at `http://www.wsuswiki.com/`. On a regular basis, administrators discuss issues they have seen with particular patches not deploying properly and the solutions they have had with that particular patch. In general, most issues are on the client side requiring registering of DLLs or other client-side issues.

WSUS on OEM Systems

For those consultants who have clientele with servers installed with an image from an Original Equipment Manufacturer (OEM), an issue with the installation of WSUS on these original installed images has been identified. Note that this does not occur on machines that have been reinstalled from scratch using OEM media, merely those that use the original image from the manufacturer. If you go to install WSUS on an OEM machine, if the installation is still the original manufacturer image, the install will fail and you will have to manually install (see Figure 22.16). (It is expected that this issue will ultimately be resolved; however, if you come upon one of these servers that have this issue there is a relatively pain free workaround.)

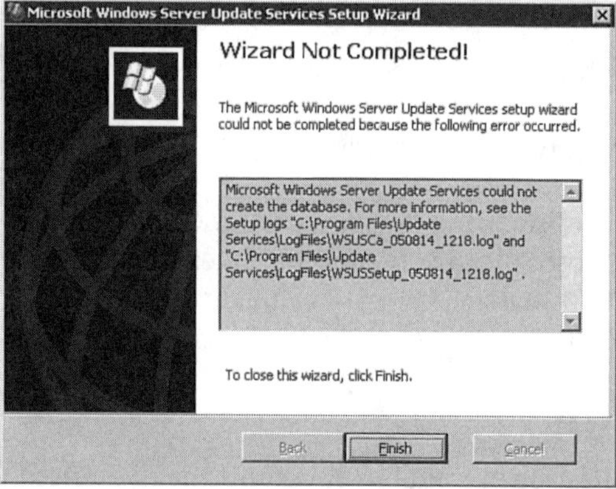

FIGURE 22.16 Installing WSUS on an OEM preinstalled machine with failure.

The steps are similar to those performed on the normal WSUS install with one change. The WMSDE database is manually deployed first:

1. Download the WSUS installer to your computer.
2. On the SBS server, create a folder called `C:\WSUSFiles` (or other drive letter where you have temporary room).
3. Download `http://www.microsoft.com/windowsserversystem/updateservices/downloads/WSUS.mspx` Windows Software Update Services from the website, clicking through Passport and answering questions as noted.
4. Save the file to the `C:\WSUSFiles` directory.
5. Extract the WSUS setup files using the command **`WSUSSetup.exe /X`**.
6. Change to the newly existing directory at `C:\WSUSFiles\wmsde`.
7. Type the following command line:

```
Sqlrun03.msi INSTANCENAME=WSUS BLANKSAPWD=1 REBOOT=ReallySuppress
➥DISABLENETWORKPROTOCOLS=1 DISABLEAGENTSTARTUP=1 DISABLETHROTTLE=1
```

NOTE

As a reminder for those interested in the security of databases, this sets up a blank password for the WMSDE database. When the final version of WSUS is installed, a randomly generated password is set.

You can also at this step move the database to another partition by adding `Targetdir=D:\WSUS` (`D:` meaning an alternative drive letter) to the command script.

8. Open the `services.msc` snap-in, right-click the MSSQL$WSUS, and choose Start. If you do not see the service, run the command line again, repeating step 7.
9. Install WSUS as outlined in the "Installing WSUS" section earlier in the chapter.
10. Launch `c:\WSUSFiles\WSUSSetup.exe` and follow the onscreen instructions, ensuring that you place the patch or data files on a drive that can hold the files. (If you planned to install the WMSDE on an alternative drive, during the install, make sure that you change the defaults from `C:\` to the drive letter to which you manually installed WMSDE earlier.)
11. When the setup is complete, you can delete the `C:\WSUSSetup` folder. If you configured WSUS to store the update files in `C:\WSUS`, make sure that you do not delete that folder.

Troubleshooting Security Patch Issues

Deployingi security patches introduces new code into your network. Some of these patches can have an impact on how your existing systems operate. So how can you best deal with the issues? Check with your fellow small business consultant. On a regular basis in listserves, newsgroups, and user groups, consultants report on issues in their networks and the resolutions. Before deploying patches on systems where you know you have fellow consultants who are supporting similar systems, ask whether someone has tested the patches or had experience.

Although each security bulletin contains a listing of "known issues," it may not include all the unusual line of business applications that your client uses. Some recommended resources for checking issues with security patches include

- Patch management listserve located at `www.patchmanagement.org`
- SBS newsgroups
- SBS listserves
- SBS partner/user groups in your area

For more information, see Appendix A, "SBS Resources."

Don't forget that any issue with a security patch or service pack is a free support call to Microsoft. Don't be hesitant to reach out and use the community resources you have to determine how best to keep your client patched and protected.

Best Practice—Understanding Your Patch Resources

Issues with a security patch or service pack are a free call to Microsoft Product Support Services. See `www.microsoft.com/support` for the phone number for your area. For Microsoft partners, review your additional support resources. Review patch issues with your personal patch community (preferably with similar consultants that use similar software). Install a patch tool to make patching and reporting easier. If possible, review mitigation options for alternatives when you cannot patch due to line of business applications.

The key element in troubleshooting is ensuring that you review when the issue occurred and trace that back to the date the system was patched. If you are unsure, the best way to troubleshoot is to back off the patches one by one, and then manually install them, one by one. Review the monthly security bulletin, noting the Knowledge Base article numbers, and go into Add/Remove and manually uninstall each one that came out that month, going into safe mode if need be to remove the patches. Reboot the affected system and then see whether the symptoms disappear. Now one by one apply the security patches to see which one is the culprit. If the issue is a mere cosmetic annoyance, most consultants will typically leave the patch on. If, however, the issue is more business disruptive, most will remove the patch, determine the threat vectors of going without that patch (seeing whether exploits are in the wild from reading security vulnerability listserves), and then call Microsoft Product Support Services.

If reading vulnerability postings from Full Disclosure security bulletins just is not how you want to spend your day, again, reach out to your community resources and ask. Invariably you will find someone like me who does like to keep track of such things who will let you know the risk you are taking by leaving something temporarily unpatched. Always review the security bulletin for the patch you removed for additional mitigation procedures that you may be able to perform and wait for a remedy without worrying about any risk to your client.

This process will protect your client the most, instead of removing all the patches or using the roll back method on Windows XP. Ensuring that you've reviewed the bulletins before beginning the patching process will provide the best patch experience.

The next troubleshooting that you will do is primarily that of the installation of the patches. As stated earlier, one particular log file needs to be reviewed. `WindowsUpdate.log` is the newer log file for the V.5 and above series of Windows Update, which includes Microsoft Update.

Review the last entries in these log files and then inside the Microsoft Update interface, click on Help and Support, and then click on Try Solving Your Problem with the Troubleshooter.

A sample error log file is as follows:

```
005-06-01 18:31:12 992 158 Misc WARNING: SendRequest failed with hr =
➥80072efd. Proxy List used: <(null)> Bypass List used : <(null)> Auth
➥Schemes used : <(null);>
```

Some of the resources for troubleshooting Microsoft Update issues include the following Knowledge Base articles:

- `http://support.microsoft.com/default.aspx?scid=kb;en-us;836941`
- `http://support.microsoft.com/default.aspx?scid=kb;en-us;836940`
- `http://support.microsoft.com/default.aspx?scid=kb;en-us;883821`
- `http://support.microsoft.com/default.aspx?scid=kb;en-us;836962`
- `http://support.microsoft.com/default.aspx?scid=kb;en-us;883822`

More resources can be found at the following search location:

```
http://search.microsoft.com/search/results.aspx?View=en-
us&p=2&c=10&st=b&qu=Microsoft+Update+web+site&na=31&cm=512
```


Summary

The process of deploying and applying security patches is arguably the easy part. As Microsoft has moved to a monthly patch cycle and provided additional patch quality testing procedures, the issues impacting SBS 2003 have gone down. If you as a consultant plan to perform any third-party testing of patches for your client, very carefully word your engagement letter. It is guaranteed that you cannot test adequately enough to replicate the use of a piece of software that your client depends on for her business needs. You cannot adequately build test data to ensure that variations of data will not be affected by patching. The best you can do is to not deploy patches the first day, read the known caveats included in each security bulletin, and, by all means, don't deploy service packs at a lunch hour on a Wednesday afternoon. You are introducing change into your client's business process—plan accordingly.

Keep machines fully patched, and that's one less thing to worry about. These days the process of keeping computers patched is getting easier every day. Make it easier on yourself by arming yourself with tools to make the deployment easier.

Best Practice Summary

- Understanding service packs versus security patches—Security patches are usually quick fixes that go through limited testing before release. Service packs are heavily tested and may contain product improvements in addition to fixes.
- Signing up for security patch information—Sign up to receive regular updates from the Microsoft Technet Security Bulletin.
- Minimum patching recommendations—Update SBS 2003 to Service Pack 1 as soon as possible, start running updates through Microsoft Update instead of Windows Update, and check the SBS downloads page for any SBS-specific updates not advertised through Microsoft or Windows Update.

- Taking a page from the enterprise folks—Don't settle for OEM installs of servers and workstations; rebuild them from scratch. Build slipstream install media for service packs.
- Selecting the best location for WSUS databases—You can opt to use WMSDE or SQL for your WSUS database. The data needed for WSUS will be at least 8GB, so make sure that you have a drive or partition with plenty of space to store the current data and allow for future growth.
- Setting up a mirror WSUS server—Be aware of potential legal ramifications if you choose to host WSUS data for your clients at an offsite location.
- Establishing patch zones and risk zones—Create different zones in WSUS to accommodate for testing and other deployment factors.
- Understanding your patch resources—Identify and develop your patch resources to help ease the pain of testing and applying patches.

PART IX

Premium Technologies

IN THIS PART

CHAPTER **23**

Internet Security and Acceleration Server 2004 Basics

IN THIS CHAPTER

- New Features in ISA 2004
- ISA Concepts

Internet Security and Acceleration Server 2004 (ISA) is an advanced firewall designed specifically with the protection of Microsoft products in mind. Exchange, Microsoft Office, Outlook Web Access, SharePoint, Internet Information Server, Routing and Remote Access, Active Directory, Outlook Mobile Access, Remote Web Workplace, and Outlook over the Internet (http over RDP) are all protected best by Microsoft's own firewall. Because of the unique position of having all these applications running on a single server, using the best firewall protection is imperative. Although you'll get some push back from "hardware" firewall aficionados, when the talk turns to protecting Active Directory, using Exchange RDP, and inspecting SSL and VPN tunnels, the "hardware is better" guys quickly fall silent, unless they've spent many thousands of dollars acquiring and properly configuring a high-end enterprise firewall. ISA allows the SBS administrator to protect the network using sophisticated inspection and detection technologies at a fraction of the cost and administrative effort.

ISA Firewall Appliances

Hardware firewalls are really just firewall appliances. Although new on the market and not reviewed in this book, ISA Server firewall appliances are now available. So if you'd like to run an ISA Server separate from your SBS server, an ISA Server appliance is an option. Operating on a prehardened, embedded Windows operating system, the ISA Server firewall appliances may look like "hardware" firewalls, but they offer the superior protection afforded only by ISA Server.

NOTE

Making sure that your SBS network is secure is an ongoing process, and it doesn't stop with ISA Server. No discussion on any security topic can be complete without a mention of keeping client PC operating systems and applications fully patched; spyware, adware, malware, and viruses off your network; and wireless networks secure.

By any measure ISA isn't an easy product to master. Just as other components of SBS, such as Exchange Server, warrant an investment in training on your part, so does ISA. Enterprise IT administrators spend their whole careers mastering Exchange *or* ISA. If you're an SBS admin, you're expected to know both and more, so it's best to admit right from the get go that you probably won't have all the information that you need at all times already in your skill set or stored in your brain for ready access. Fortunately, some excellent free resources are available for troubleshooting, configuring, and learning ISA 2004. (See the sidebar "Free Resources for ISA Learning.") Handy built-in templates and wizards also are available, which we'll point out along the way and show a few tweaks you may want to make. This chapter focuses on things in ISA specific to or at least significant in the default configuration of SBS.

Free Resources for ISA Learning

Microsoft Technet Virtual Lab

`http://www.microsoft.com/technet/traincert/virtuallab/isa.mspx`

Tools Repository

`http://www.isatools.org/`

Microsoft Newsgroups

`http://www.microsoft.com/technet/community/newsgroups/server/isa.mspx`

Technet

`http://www.microsoft.com/technet/prodtechnol/isa/default.mspx`

On-Demand Webcasts

`http://www.microsoft.com/events/AdvSearch.mspx`

SBS Specific Blog

`http://isainsbs.blogspot.com`

Microsoft Knowledgebase

`http://support.microsoft.com/ph/2108`

New Features in ISA 2004

ISA 2004 is as different from ISA 2000 as ISA 2000 was from Proxy 2.0. ISA 2004 offers many new features, all of which are well documented on Microsoft's website. This section highlights a few new features that SBS administrators will appreciate the most.

ISA Management MMC

The face-lift of the ISA Management MMC is the first thing that you'll notice (see Figure 23.1). It's now organized into three vertical panels. On the left is the navigation panel, in the center is the display of the item you've selected, and on the right is the task pad or toolbox. Getting around is easy, and the MMC is well organized.

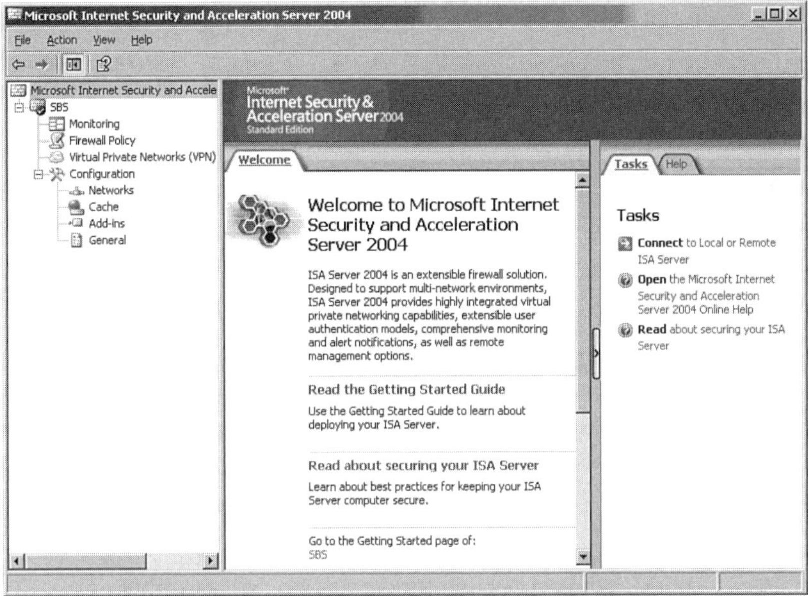

FIGURE 23.1 The new MMC for Internet Security and Acceleration Server 2004.

ISA Networks

Arguably the most important new feature of ISA 2004 is that it no longer trusts the internal network. Stateful inspection will be performed on all traffic in your network regardless of the source or destination. ISA 2000 only knew two networks, internal and external, and it completely trusted the internal network. In ISA 2004 you'll notice that by default SBS recognizes five networks: internal, external, LocalHost, VPN clients, and VPN quarantined clients, and it doesn't trust any of them. Having removed the LAT (Local Area Table), ISA is now free to handle unique relationships between the various networks.

Each network that you specify can have a unique set of policies to handle the traffic for that network. One policy can be applied to several networks, or the policy can be applied to only one network. A couple of examples can be seen in the default configuration of the Firewall Policy (see Figure 23.2).

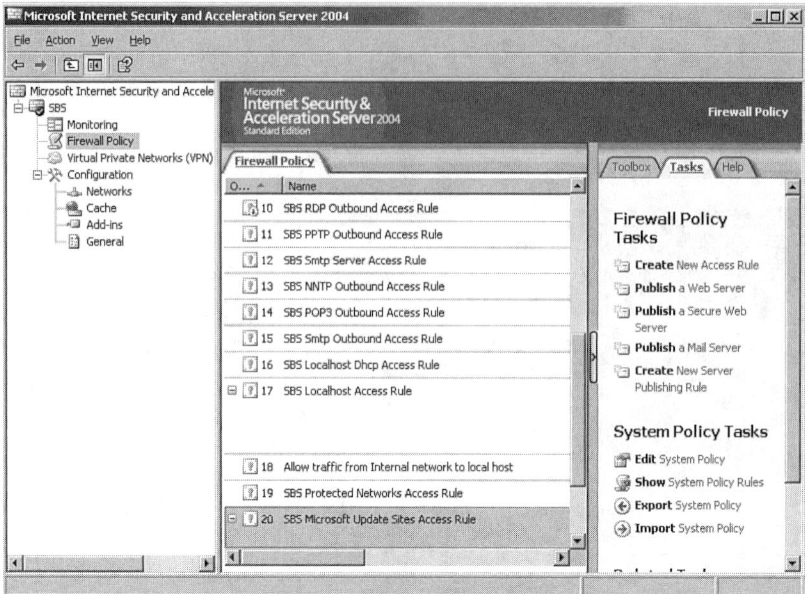

FIGURE 23.2 The Firewall Policy rules are numbered. Policy is applied from the top down.

Policy Ordering

When you create a new policy you'll notice that if you haven't previously specified where to place that policy it is placed at the end of the list. Policies are processed from the top down. This means that it will take longer for your server to get to processing rules at the bottom of this list than at the top. It also means that you need to be careful at which position you place your new rule.

The policy Traffic Vetween VPN Client and Internal Networks allows VPN clients to access the internal network. If you look at the From and To columns, you'll notice that this policy applies to both the internal network and the VPN client network. Looking down the column you'll see other examples. Take particular notice of the network types All Protected Networks and All Networks (and LocalHost). These are known as *network sets*. Network sets represent more than one network and are there to simplify administration by grouping networks, much like groups in Active Directory. Two network sets are created by default. The ISA 2004 Help file describes them as follows:

- All Networks (and LocalHost)—This network set includes all networks defined for ISA Server. When you create a new network, the new network is automatically included in this network set. All Networks is the same as Anywhere. Every IP address is included in both Anywhere and in All Networks.
- All Protected Networks—This network set includes all networks except the built-in external network. When you create a new network, the new network is automatically included in this network set.

Remember one important thing about these preconfigured groups: *Any new network you create will automatically be added to them.* For this reason, use them with caution. For example, if you create a new network object called Wireless Network, it will automatically become part of the All Networks (and LocalHost) network set. Is this what you really want? Maybe, but maybe not. Say that you have traveling consultants come to your office with laptops, and they need Internet access. You only want the Wireless Network to get out to the Internet but not have access to anything on the internal network. If you have used the network set All Networks (and LocalHost) in a moment of laziness when you created a rule for access to your SQL Server or NAS device, you've also just allowed Wireless Network users to access those things too.

VPN Quarantine

Another new feature is VPN Quarantine. ISA 2004 is fully integrated with the Windows Server 2003 VPN Quarantine feature. This allows you to create a sandbox for your VPN users to sit in while they are checked for a match with your VPN security policy. Your VPN security policy can require patches and virus protection, but beware that Microsoft hasn't provided much for the small business consultant to work with here. There are no wizards, no templates, just a development platform waiting for scripts that you'll have to write by hand. In sum, it's ugly at this point but still worth noting.

As if just to tempt you, Microsoft has made it easy to enable VPN Quarantine even if you don't yet have the VPN security policy set up.

You can enable VPN Quarantine, and all your VPN clients will be Quarantined and then disconnected when the time to comply with your VPN security times out. Figure 23.3 shows the VPN Quarantine Clients Properties configuration options. VPN Quarantine is a wonderful idea whose time is near. Many small businesses have sales staff working from hotels, cars, and home on PCs that are out of their direct control, but vendors have yet to step up and create the add-ins necessary for small business to use this feature easily.

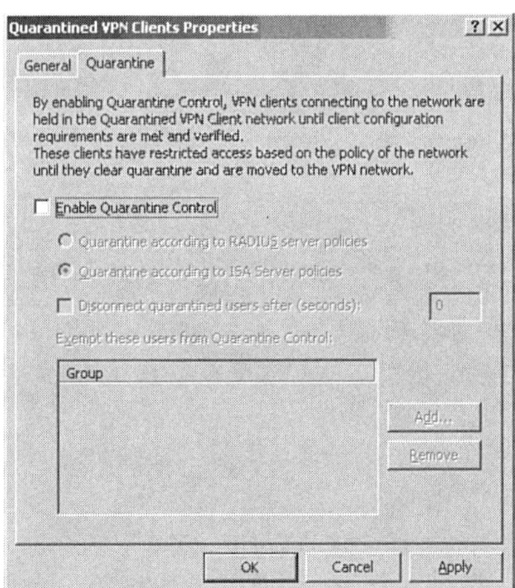

FIGURE 23.3 VPN quarantine settings.

Apply or Discard?

After you get started customizing the configuration of ISA 2004 Server, you'll quickly notice the presence of Apply and Discard buttons at the top of the ISA Management screen as shown in Figure 23.4. Even though you have made your changes and selected OK at the end of the change, you still have options. Doing nothing lets the changes remain dormant until you reboot or make a decision. Clicking Apply will apply your changes to new sessions only. Clicking Discard will undo your changes.

NOTE

To have your changes apply to all sessions immediately you'll need to restart the Firewall Service or disconnect the sessions in the Sessions tab in Monitoring.

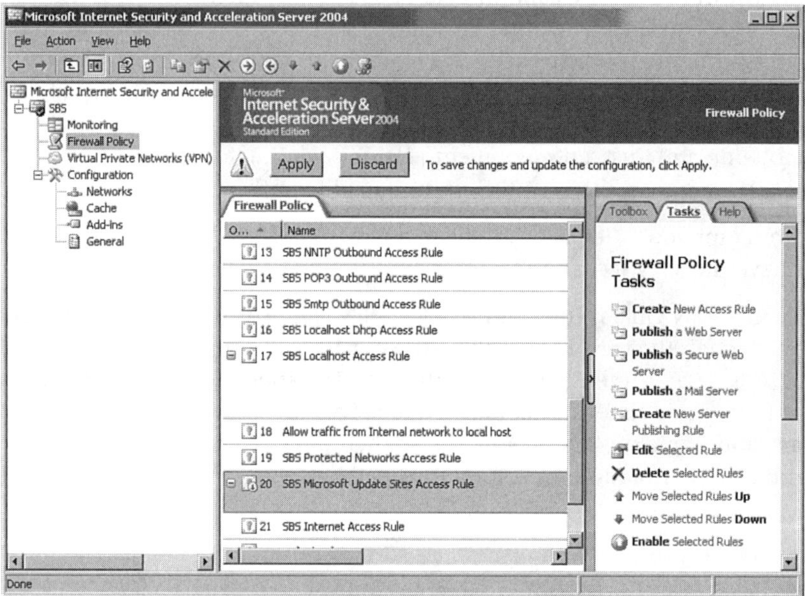

FIGURE 23.4 Click the Apply button for your changes to take effect. Click Discard to cancel your changes.

Best Practice—Apply Changes One at a Time

Although it is tempting to make all your changes now and apply them later, it might not be a good habit to get into. Making several changes and then applying them all at once will likely result in a troubleshooting nightmare if things don't go as planned.

To avoid this, apply each change you make one at a time and test to make sure that it is doing what you intended before moving on to the next step.

Administration Delegation

Another new feature is administration delegation, which is found under Configuration, General. You are now able to offer the business owner or other interested individual monitoring access to the ISA Server without running the risk that he will reconfigure something. ISA 2004 recognizes three different levels of admin: ISA Server Basic Monitoring, ISA Server Extended Monitoring, and ISA Server Full Administrator.

From the ISA Server Help file, Table 23.1 shows what each level of delegation authorizes.

TABLE 23.1 Administration Delegation Roles in ISA 2004

Activity	ISA Server Basic Monitoring	ISA Server Extended Monitoring	ISA Server Full Administrator
View Dashboard, alerts, connectivity, sessions, services	X	X	X
Acknowledge alerts	X	X	X
View log information		X	X
Create alert definitions		X	X
Create reports		X	X
Stop and start sessions and services		X	X
View firewall policy		X	X
Configure firewall policy			X
Configure cache			X
Configure VPN			X

Administrators who have Extended Monitoring role permissions can configure all report properties with the following exceptions:

- Cannot configure a different user account when publishing reports
- Cannot customize report contents

Best Practice—Teach Monitoring Skills

A bit of training may be necessary to make sure that the person doing the monitoring knows what she is looking at and has an idea of how to spot a problem. In both of the monitoring delegations, Acknowledge Alerts is allowed. If a person isn't aware what the alert really means, she may panic when she sees it and start calling IT support when it really isn't necessary; some normal alerts occur to let you know that ISA is doing its job preventing unintended access to your network. Or worse yet, the would-be administrator may just acknowledge an alert without recognizing its seriousness. In either case, alert acknowledgement is best left to a qualified professional.

Most business owners, if they are interested in what the firewall is doing, are going to want to run reports from ISA 2004. Perform the steps in the following sections to set up administration delegation for extended monitoring and install the remote administration client on the person's desktop.

Assign Administrator Delegation

1. In the ISA 2004 Management MMC in the left pane, expand Configuration and then select General.
2. In the center pane select Administration Delegation. Click Next. Click the Add button on the Delegate Control page. Click Browse and then enter the name of the person or group that you want to delegate to. Click Check Name and then click OK.
3. On this same page, under Roles you have a drop-down menu. Select ISA Server Extended Monitoring and click OK. You should now see your selection Users/Roles box under Domain/Administrator and BUILTIN/administrators. Click Next.
4. Review your changes; they should look similar to Figure 23.5. If correct, click Finish. Click Apply at the top of the page to apply this change now.

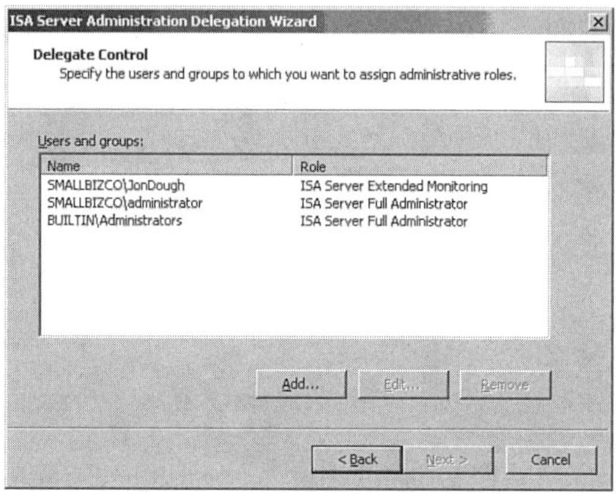

FIGURE 23.5 Review your list of whom administration of your ISA is delegated to and which role each person is playing before clicking Next.

Install the Remote Administration Client

Now that you've designated who can monitor ISA you'll want to install the Management tool on the workstation that the admin will be using. Follow these steps:

1. Insert SBS 2003 SP1 disk 3 into the workstation.
2. Browse the CD to the `X:\ISA2004\` directory and run `ISAAUTORUN.exe`. Follow the installation wizard and enter your SBS 2003 license code for the ISA 2004 license code.
3. You'll be warned that ISA Server can't be installed on your operating system. That's OK; you're only going to install the management client. Your list of items to be installed should match those in Figure 23.6. Click Next. Then click Install.

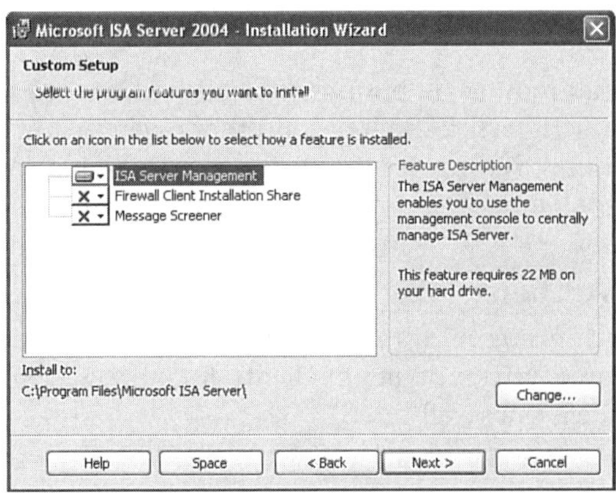

FIGURE 23.6 The list of ISA Server components to be installed on your workstation should only indicate ISA Server Management.

4. When the installation is finished, an Internet Explorer window pops up letting you know that the installation was successful. Close this window.
5. To Run ISA Management on the workstation, click Start, Programs, Microsoft ISA Server and select ISA Server Management.
6. In ISA Server Management, in the left pane, right-click on Microsoft Internet Security and Acceleration Server 2004 and select Connect To.
7. In the Connect To dialog box the radio buttons Another Computer (Remote Management) and Connect Using the Credentials of the Logged-On User should be selected. Enter the name of your SBS server in the box (see Figure 23.7) and click OK. You should now be connected to your server.

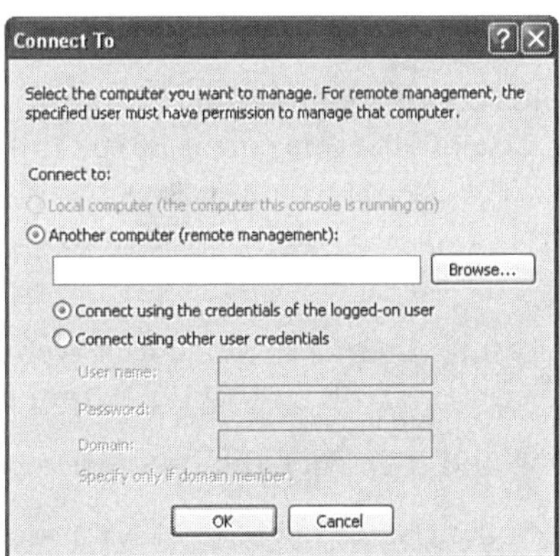

FIGURE 23.7 Enter the name of your ISA Server or click the Browse button.

ISA Concepts

ISA is different than what most small business consultants are used to seeing. It is an enterprise class firewall with features well beyond those seen in any other firewall deployed in a small business setting. It is necessary to understand some basic concepts before attempting to troubleshoot or customize the configuration.

Understanding ISA Client Types

Probably one of most confusing things about ISA server for new administrators is client types. ISA recognizes three different types of clients: SecureNat, Web Proxy, and Firewall. Windows-based computers can be all three.

The SecureNat Client

A SecureNat client is one that is configured with its gateway address pointing at the internal IP address of the SBS server. Servers on your network are configured as SecureNat clients as will be non-Microsoft operating systems. The SecureNat client can only access protocols that are in the protocol list and don't require any secondary connections. This is also the only client type that can use non-TCP or UDP connections such as ICMP (ping). A typical workstation in an SBS network running a Windows operating system such as Windows XP will access the ISA server as a SecureNat client only when using non-tcp or udp connections.

To configure a non-Microsoft operating system computer or a server as a SecureNat client simply configure the gateway address in your TCP/IP settings with the internal IP address of your SBS server.

In the ISA logs, traffic being sent from SecureNat clients is logged with the originating IP address only because there is no mechanism for passing the username and password along to ISA. This limits your ability to control Internet access for these clients.

The Web Proxy Client

A Web Proxy client is one that is configured to send requests to ISA's web proxy feature using a particular port. In the case of SBS, this port is 8080. This client type supports only http, https and ftp downloads. The username and password are passed from Windows to the ISA Server for access control purposes. Follow these steps to configure a Web Proxy client:

1. To configure a computer using Internet Explorer as a Web Proxy client, open Internet Explorer and select Tools, Internet Options from the menu.
2. Click the Connections tab and then click the LAN Settings button.
3. Under Proxy Server, check the Use a Proxy Server for Your LAN box. In the Address box type the name of your server. In the Port box type, **8080**. Check Bypass Proxy Server for Local Address. Your settings should look like those in Figure 23.8. Click OK. Click OK again to exit Internet Options. You must close your browser for the settings to take effect.

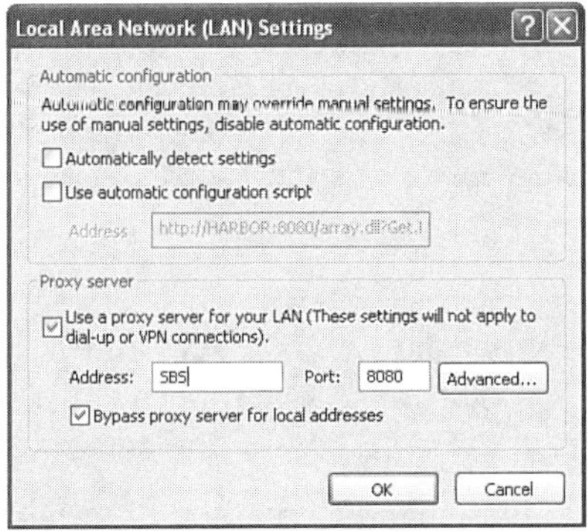

FIGURE 23.8 These settings allow Internet Explorer to use ISA's proxy capabilities.

The Firewall Client

A Firewall Client is one in which the ISA Firewall Client software has been installed, configured, and enabled. The Firewall Client is a powerful tool and should be installed wherever possible. The Firewall Client does not require that a protocol definition be defined on the ISA Server for the client to use that protocol. It can send username and password credentials from Windows and from any Winsock-enabled application to the ISA Server. Installing the Firewall Client often eliminates any problems that users are having accessing a particular website or using a web-enabled application. When installed the Firewall Client intercepts any tcp or udp traffic and sends it on to the proxy with credentials included. Further, this information is sent as encrypted data using Kerberos, thwarting the sniffing of username and passwords of web-enabled applications. Considering that many small businesses use web applications for payroll, 401k management and deposits, and online banking, encrypting the transmission is an excellent idea.

Best Practice—Always Install the Firewall Client

The ISA Firewall Client is such a powerful tool both for ease of access to the Internet and for Internet management purposes that every permanent Windows workstation on your network should have it installed.

The Firewall Client software is found on your SBS server under `c:\program files\Microsoft ISA Server\clients`. The firewall client folder is shared by default as `mspclnt`. To install the Firewall Client run `Setup.exe` from this folder. The installer walks you through the installation process. It is a straightforward process. When the installation is complete, a reboot is recommended, and you'll notice the Firewall Client icon in the system tray.

NOTE

You need to be logged in with local administrator rights to perform the installation of the Firewall Client.

NOTE

If you are upgrading from ISA 2000 and your clients have the Firewall Client already installed, you'll need to uninstall the ISA 2000 Firewall Client before installing the ISA 2004 Firewall Client. Fortunately, the icons in the system are different so you'll be able to easily spot whether a particular workstation has been updated.

By default ISA Server accepts either the ISA 2000 Firewall Client or the new ISA 2004 Firewall Client. However, if you want to be sure that the data sent via Firewall Client is always encrypted data, you can set ISA to require the new client.

1. Open ISA Management and Expand Configuration. Click on General. In the right pane click Define Firewall Client Settings.
2. In the dialog box that opens uncheck Allow Non-Encrypted Firewall Client Connections as in Figure 23.9.

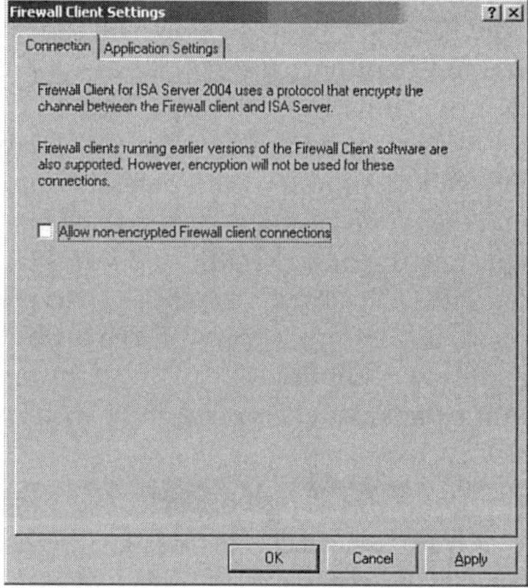

FIGURE 23.9 If this box is checked ISA allows ISA 2000 and proxy clients to connect; unchecked, only clients using the client capable of encryption, ISA 2004 Firewall Client, is allowed.

Unless you have already set up automatic configuration for your Firewall Client application, you'll need to specify the name of your SBS server in the Configuration tab of the client on each computer. Follow these steps to configure the Firewall Client on each workstation:

1. Right-click on the Firewall Client icon in the system tray of the workstation and select Configure. Verify that the Enable Microsoft Firewall Client for ISA 2004 Server is checked.
2. Click Manually Select ISA Server (see Figure 23.10). Enter the name of your SBS server in the box and click the Test Server button. You should see a pop-up window indicating that the server was found, and it replied. Both boxes should report the same server name.

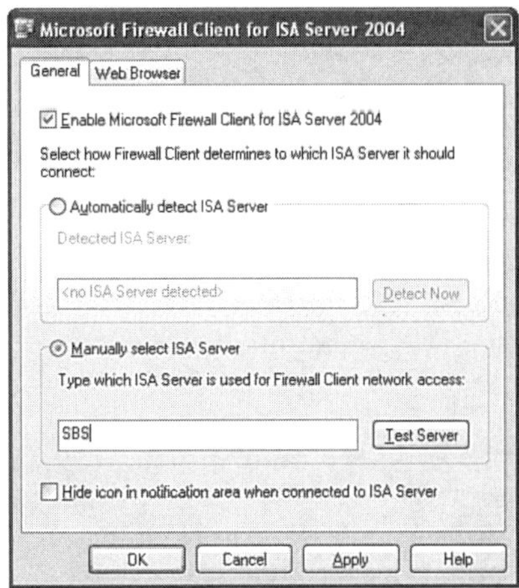

FIGURE 23.10 The Firewall Client can be manually configured to connect to your ISA Server.

3. Close the pop-up windows and then click OK to accept your Firewall Client configuration changes.

To see the various clients in action on your network, open the ISA Management MMC. Follow these steps:

1. Expand your Server Name and Click on Monitoring. Click on the Logging tab.
2. Click Start Query to launch the predefined traffic Query. It takes a moment to launch and then you are treated to a live look at the traffic on your network. Here you can see the source IP, protocol being used, whether the client is the authenticated type, and much more.

Follow these steps to assign the Firewall Client to client computers:

1. Open Server Management. Click Computers and then click the Set Up Client Applications link.
2. On the Available Applications page, click Add.
3. In the Application Name box, type **`Firewall Client`**; then in the Location of Setup Executable for This Application box, type **`\\SBS\Mspclnt\Setup.exe /v"SBS=ServerName ENABLE_AUTO_DETECT=0 REFRESH_WEB_PROXY=1 /qn"`** where `SBS` is the name of your server. Click Finish.
4. Choose Yes when prompted to assign the application to client computer to open the Assign Applications Wizard.

As Figure 23.11 demonstrates, when you are finished, the Firewall Client is listed as an application that can be assigned to your client computers.

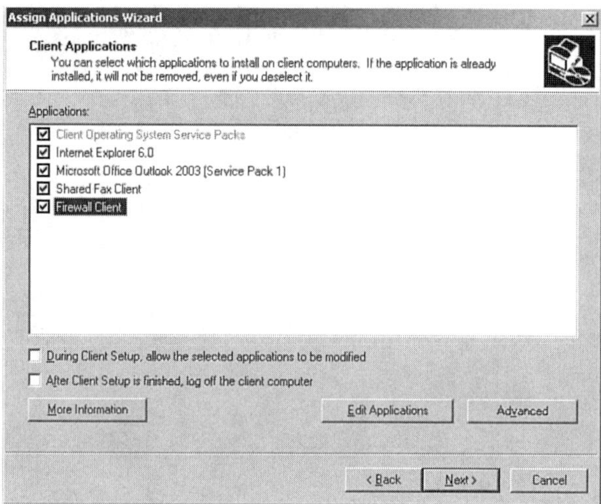

FIGURE 23.11 The Firewall Client is not configured for automatic deployment to the client computers by default but can be added.

Managing Log Information

ISA logs a lot of information. When you are attempting to troubleshoot a problem and watching for traffic of a particular type you'll quickly realize that there is a lot of NETBIOS-related traffic diverting your attention.

Best Practice—Use Logs for Troubleshooting

By default every rule in the Firewall Policy will be logged. For monitoring purposes this is great because it gives you a full and complete picture of what's going on. However, for troubleshooting this means that the log will contain a lot of information that you don't need to see. You'll want to stop logging for some rules to make it easier to see the problem area. The procedure described here applies to logging for any rule.

In particular, the rule Allow Access from Trusted Computers to the Firewall Client Installation Share on ISA Server generates a huge number of log events. This rule is a system rule and can't be altered except through system policy, but you can turn off logging for this rule in the Firewall Policy. Doing so not only makes your log easier to read but also reduces the space requirements for log storage and the RAM that the SQL Server instance for ISA logging requires.

To turn off logging for this rule you first have to be able to select it in Firewall Policy. By default all the System Policy rules are hidden from view. At the top of the page, click the View menu and select Show System Policy Rules (see Figure 23.12). This exposes the System Policy rules in the Firewall Policy window. These rules are created by the predefined SBS security template applied during installation.

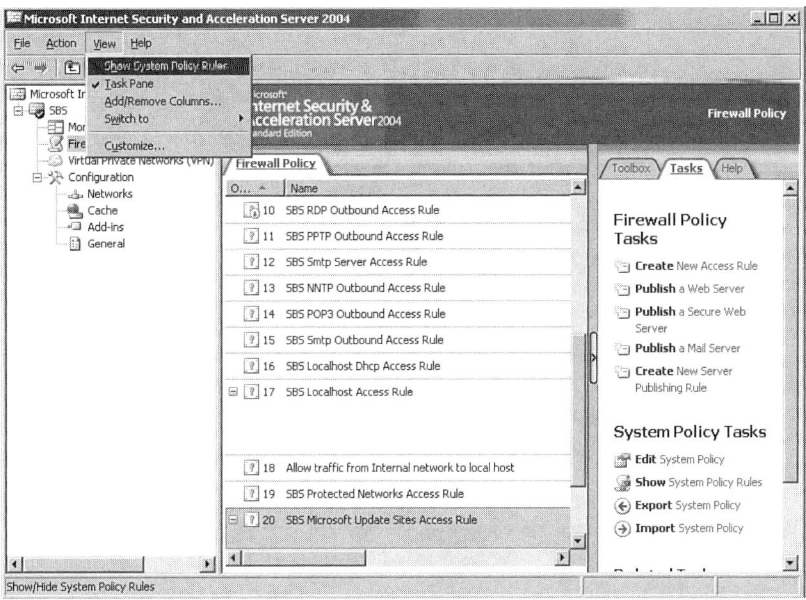

FIGURE 23.12 The Show System Policy Rules option is found under View and also as a button in the Task list.

To disable logging for a particular rule, follow these steps:

1. In the center pane scroll down to the rule, Allow Access from Trusted Computers to the Firewall Client Installation Share on ISA Server. Right-click on this rule and select Properties.
2. Move to the Action tab. Uncheck the Log Requests Matching this Rule box as shown in Figure 23.13. Click Apply and click OK.
3. Click Apply at the top of the Firewall Policy window, and this rule takes effect immediately for new sessions.

> **NOTE**
>
> If you would rather not disable logging for this policy but want to reduce the amount of RAM that the log generation uses, there is another option: You can reduce the amount of RAM that the SQL Server instance is allowed to use for firewall logging. For a good tutorial on this, see `http://www.smallbizserver.net/Default.aspx?tabid=247`.

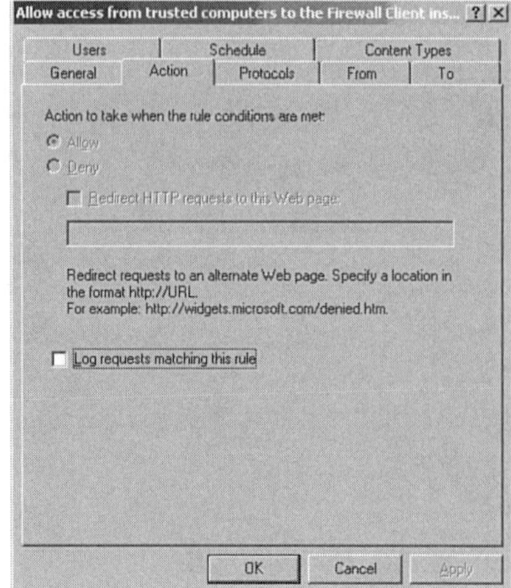

FIGURE 23.13 Unchecking this box stops ISA from logging requests for this rule.

Maintaining ISA Log Files

By default ISA keeps up to 16GB of log files on your server. Storage space on SBS servers is almost always at a premium, and small businesses would probably rather use that 16GB for something other than ISA Server logs. Fortunately, ISA has a log maintenance feature buried under the Monitoring section of ISA Management where you can change not only how much space the logs take up but also where the logs are stored, and you can force them to leave some free space on the drive. To adjust the amount of space that logs may potentially take up on your server follow these steps:

1. In ISA Management click on Monitoring. Then select the Logging tab. On the Task pad click Configure Firewall Logging. The Firewall Logging Properties box opens.
2. Click the Options button. Figure 23.14 displays the Options screen where a number of log settings can be modified.
3. To move the firewall logs to another folder or drive, select the This Folder (Enter Full Path) radio button and enter the path where you want the logs stored. It would be a good idea to keep the logs off the system partition. It's better to store them on a data partition.
4. To limit the size of log files make sure that the Limit Total Size of Log Files box is checked and enter a number in gigabytes. The smallest ISA allows is 4GB.
5. To make sure that some free space is maintained on the drive where the logs are stored, make sure that the Maintain Free Disk Space box is checked and enter a number in megabytes. The default, 512MB, is probably sufficient.
6. Click OK when finished with your selections.
7. Follow the same procedure for taming the logs for the web proxy and SMTP message screener.

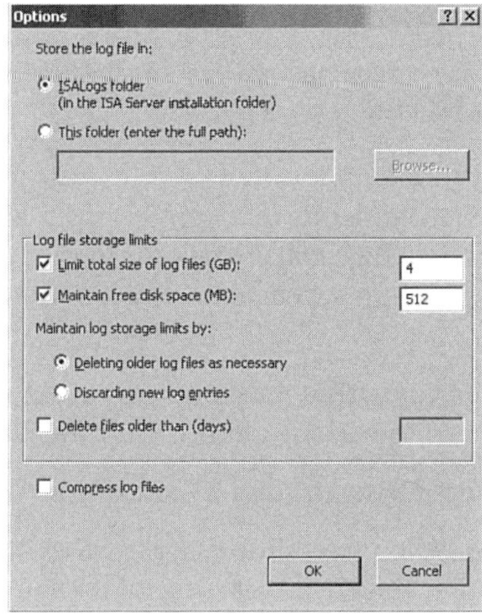

FIGURE 23.14 The log size limits are tucked away under the Options button.

NOTE

The SMTP message filter is disabled by default in SBS, so unless you've enabled it, it isn't really necessary to modify the log settings here.

Best Practice—Reduce the Space That ISA Logs Use

By default ISA uses up to 16GB of space on your hard drive before starting to overwrite logs. For the small business this represents a large time span. Limiting the space that ISA uses for log storage is reasonable for small businesses.

ISA Lockdown Mode

SBS 2003 SP1 comes prehardened, so in general there is no need to make changes typical of hardening, such as stopping services or moving them from automatic to manual. This has already been done for you. However, you may want to implement safeguard: an alert that puts ISA Server into Lockdown mode if the firewall fails to log events.

ISA 2004 Server Firewall Service fails closed. This means that if the Firewall Service stops, the ISA Server launches into Lockdown mode. Lockdown mode leaves the ISA Server isolated but still connected to the Internet. You'll want to review the Help file for a complete list of exactly what happens when your server enters Lockdown mode, but in summary: ping from internal is allowed, outgoing web requests are allowed, remote management is allowed, no incoming web requests are allowed, and VPN connections are not allowed. This combination allows an administrator to access the server, review the logs for troubleshooting and/or investigative work, and restart the Firewall Service when the problem is resolved.

> **NOTE**
>
> While in Lockdown mode any changes that you make to the Firewall Policy do not take effect until the Firewall Service is restarted.

Microsoft's hardening guide recommends that you set up an alert if your ISA Server is unable to log events. A failure to log events would mean that in the event of an intrusion you'd be flying blind in your attempts to determine when the intrusion occurred and by what means.

In SBS the Logging alert is already set up for you. If you want to have this alert trigger Lockdown mode, you will need to edit the alert. To edit the alert, follow these steps:

1. In ISA Monitoring, select Alerts. In the Taskpad choose Configure Alert Definitions.
2. In the Alerts Properties dialog box, shown in Figure 23.15, scroll down to Log Failure, select Log Failure, and click Edit.

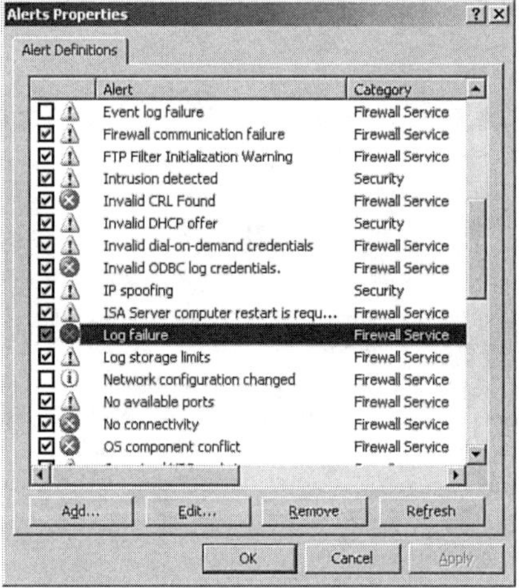

FIGURE 23.15 The Alerts Properties box lists all the currently configured alerts, and each can be edited from here.

3. Move to the Action tab, check the Stop Selected Service box, and click the Select button.
4. In the Select ISA Server Services dialog box, shown in Figure 23.16, check Microsoft Firewall and click OK. Click OK two more times until you are back at the Monitoring screen; then click the Apply button when you are ready to have the policy change take effect.

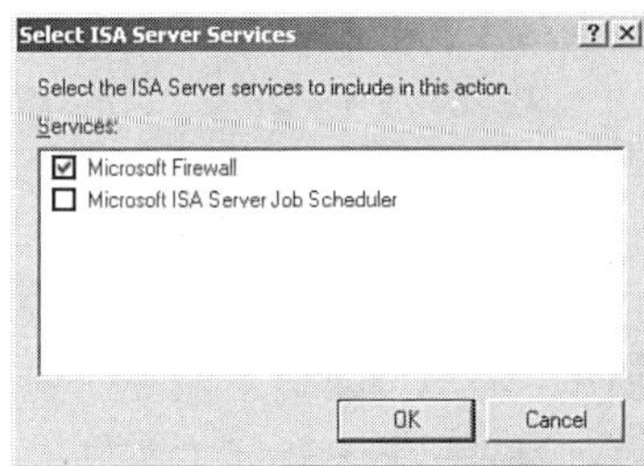

FIGURE 23.16 With this configuration a failure of the ISA Server to log activities results in the firewall service shutting down.

CAUTION

Should the drive that ISA is logging to fill or ISA become unable to reach its location, this alert will be triggered. Therefore, make sure that your logs have plenty of room, and choose a local drive if possible.

Client Connections

ISA 2004 can be installed on your server as an upgrade from ISA 2000 or as a new install. As of this writing, few differences have been noticed. The upgrade option actually exports your settings, translates them to ISA 2004, and imports the settings leaving you with an identically functioning network. One difference that has caught the attention of locations that use secure websites extensively is client connections.

Client connections are limited to 160 in a new installation of ISA 2004 and 40 in an upgrade from ISA 2000. The purpose of limiting client connections is to prevent a single workstation from flooding the network. Speaking from experience, having a Trojan-infected computer show up on your network, in this case a roaming laptop, and take up all the bandwidth to the Internet by generating thousands of connections is a bad thing. It brings your network to its knees, and it's difficult to track without a high-quality firewall such as ISA 2004. The company in question went through several different consulting companies and spent thousands of dollars before getting the problem resolved. If the company had had an ISA 2004 server, it would not have even had a problem; the infected laptop would have been identified in the logs as having exceeded its connection allotment. Having as few client connections as your clients need to work is a good thing. When the client connections are exceeded, that client won't be able to open any additional connections, and an alert will be triggered.

Best Practice—Limit Client Connections

Keep the limit on client connections as low as possible for good network performance. This number varies depending on which sites and Internet applications you use. Limiting client connections prevents network flooding in the event of a Trojan or similar type of attack.

If you have performed an upgrade of ISA 2000 to ISA 2004, you may find that you need to increase the number of client connections. To increase the number of connections allowed per client, follow these steps:

1. In ISA Management, under Configuration click General. Then select Define Connection Limits. Figure 23.17 shows this window.
2. In the Connection Limit Per Client (TCP and non-TCP) item, select a number between 40 and 160. When a client exceeds the number that you have selected, it will not be able to create any new TCP connections and in the case of non-TCP connections the oldest ones will be dropped. From users' perspective, they'll notice that they are unable to do everything that they are attempting on the Internet and may be unable to reach websites.
3. Click OK and then click Apply when you are ready to have the changes take effect.

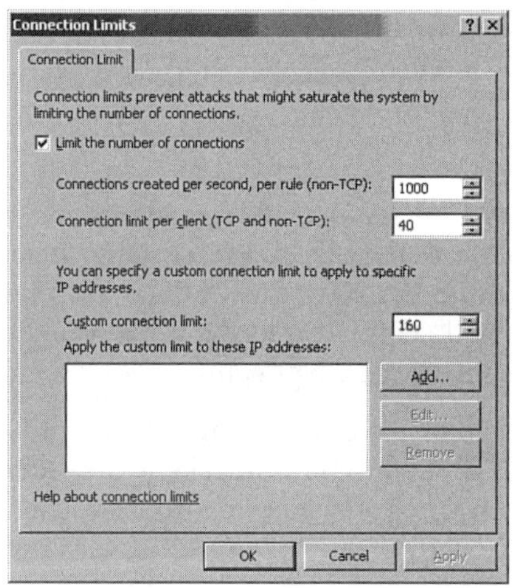

FIGURE 23.17 The Connection Limit per Client is set unusually low after upgrading from ISA 2000.

Internet Acceleration

Acceleration of the Internet is a big part of the name of ISA Server, but in reality it's a small part of what it does. It's kind of funny really, because one of the criticisms of ISA by those who haven't investigated it, since its forerunner Proxy 1.0 came out, is that it's just a cache server.

Small businesses are enjoying greater bandwidth than ever. Not that long ago T1 speeds were reserved for those with big budgets, but thanks to advances in DSL and cable Internet technologies even the smallest business can afford the Internet at high speed. Even so, the use of the Internet by employees at small businesses demands efficient use of the bandwidth. This is what caching does for your business; it makes efficient use of your bandwidth.

The default cache size is set at 100MB on the drive that ISA is installed. This is the minimum recommended setting. An additional .5MB for each web proxy client is recommended. Because Microsoft doesn't know how many clients you have at the time of installation, this configuration item is left for you to do. To adjust the cache settings, follow these steps:

1. In ISA Management, Expand Configuration and click on Cache.
2. On the Tasks pane click Define Cache Drives (Enable Cache). The Define Cache Drives window opens as in Figure 23.18.

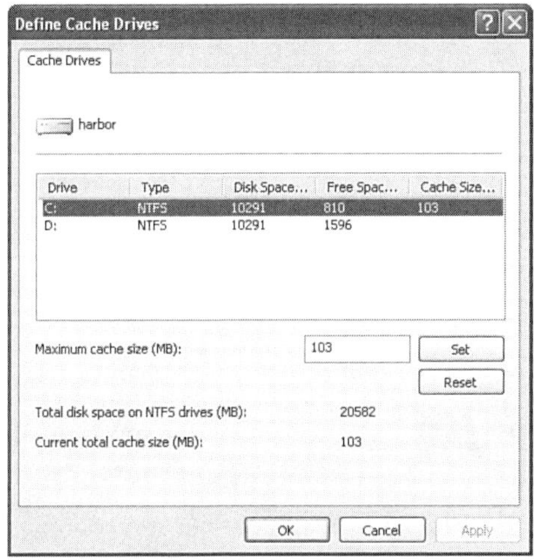

FIGURE 23.18 The cache is set at the recommended minimum by default.

3. In the Define Cache Drives windows, increase the number in the Maximum Cache Size (MB) by .5MB for each web proxy client on your network; then round up to the nearest whole number.
4. Click the Set button. Notice that you may also move where the cache is stored. Click OK when finished.

Best Practice—When to Set an Even Larger Cache

Depending on the type of business, you may find that a large cache yields benefits. Real estate and travel agencies are but two of many possible examples where Internet usage is intense. Users at these types of businesses would appreciate a larger cache size. A 500MB cache for a small business of this type would not be out of line. However, the Microsoft recommended cache size is 100MB + 0.5MB per web proxy client computer.

Controlling Cache Free Memory Use

ISA can get carried away and use up more free memory than would be best considering all the applications that your SBS server has to run simultaneously. To adjust the amount of free memory that ISA uses for caching, follow these steps:

1. In the same cache Task pane, click Configure Cache Settings. In the Cache Settings window click the Advanced tab.
2. As Figure 23.19 shows, in the Percentage of Free Memory to Use for Caching box you are given the option of changing the amount of free memory allocated for caching purposes. The default configuration is 50%.

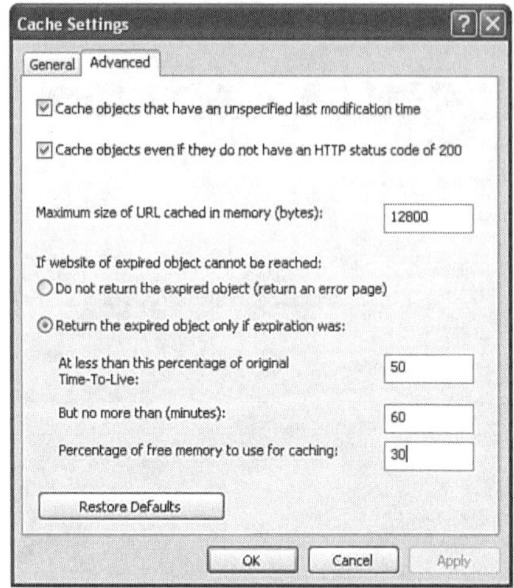

FIGURE 23.19 Depending on the capabilities of your server you may need to force ISA to use less free memory for caching.

3. Taking into consideration how much memory you have on your server and the amount of Internet usage you are expecting, you may modify this number down to save memory for other applications. Enter the percentage and click OK. Then Click Apply when you are ready to have the change take effect.
4. You are prompted to restart the Firewall Service either now or later.

Summary

SBS 2003 SP1 users are fortunate to have a firewall of such capability. Even though this product is complex, it can be easily managed through the use of the ISA Management MMC. The new features in ISA 2004 are easily discovered, managed, and tweaked. After you have a basic understanding of what ISA does and how the MMC is organized, the flow of traffic through the Firewall Policy from the top down becomes clearer.

This chapter only touched on the basics of ISA management. Remember, as mentioned at the beginning of the chapter, enterprise administrators make a whole career out of managing ISA. SBS administrators are extraordinary and require knowledge of many server products to make an SBS network function smoothly. The resources listed at the beginning of this chapter should be entered in your favorites list. As your knowledge grows, so too will your question list, and these resources can provide the answers for you.

The ISA 2004 server is pretty well set up and ready to go thanks to the SBS integration team. This leaves the SBS administrator with the task of customizing the server for his particular business needs. After you've completed your logging tweaks, delegation of some administrative tasks, adjusting the client connections, installing the Firewall Client on your client computers as appropriate, increasing the cache, and changing the amount of memory and drive space allocated for various ISA tasks you're ready to tackle some customization and learn how to create new rules.

Your ISA server is ready for action and prepared to handle common and complex hack attempts and Trojan infections all the while providing faster Internet access and securing your communications.

Best Practice Summary

- Apply changes one at a time—Applying changes individually allows for testing and verifying the proper operation of each change.
- Teach monitoring skills—Train individuals who will be acknowledging ISA alerts to know what to look for and to respond appropriately.
- Always install the Firewall Client—Use the Firewall Client on client workstations to enable logging and advanced firewall access settings.
- Use logs for troubleshooting—The information tracked in the ISA logs quickly points you to the element that may be causing access problems.
- Reduce the space that ISA logs use—Because the log information collected by ISA for smaller organizations will be small, setting the maximum log size to a smaller value can save disk space needed for other server tools.
- Limit client connections—Reducing the number of outbound client connections in ISA can help prevent network flooding and the spread of some Trojans.
- When to set an even larger cache—In organizations where users rely on a great deal of static web information, increasing the size of the cache may result in better performance.

CHAPTER 24

Internet Security and Acceleration Server 2004 Advanced Administration

IN THIS CHAPTER

In Small Business Server a number of compromises are necessarily made to get everything working together in a friendly and efficient way. ISA is configured to protect each component of SBS but not in the textbook manner where ISA resides on its own separate server. Instead ISA uses a combination of access rules, application filters, web filters, server publishing, and intrusion detection to reach a level of security that small businesses can't enjoy otherwise.

Each small business using SBS is unique. Each has specific applications, business partners, security needs, and network configurations that require customizing which filters are active and how ISA helps you manage your network and keep it secure. Because these needs change over time, as the business grows, applications change, and security needs grow, it is important to have a good enough foundation in configuring ISA that the lessons learned can be applied to situations that will occur in the future.

If one thing can be said of the Internet, it's that security needs continue to increase as our dependence on the Internet increases. Fortunately for ISA users, when issues like the release of MSBlast occurred, ISA networks were not endangered. ISA was and is smart enough to tell the difference between a legitimately formatted RDP request and a dangerous one. This was due to the powerful filtering combinations it is capable of. Of course we still had to patch our workstations, but it wasn't because our firewall was going to let the worm through, it was only to prevent our workstations from getting infected by a visiting infected laptop. Patching in this manner is a much less panic-driven affair and could be handled by the normal workstation patching process. Given the large bull's eye that ISA wears by virtue of being Microsoft's flagship security product, ISA's excellent track record of never having been breached when configured properly is impressive.

The first section of this chapter points out some additional features and customizations that can be made for more efficient network management and explains the various types of filters and filter elements. The second section presents a few scenarios for allowing or preventing various types of network traffic and Internet privileges for users. These are meant to be generic enough examples that the lessons learned can be applied to other situations that may arise on a small business network.

Managing ISA

Managing ISA Server is as simple as clicking down through the ISA Management Console and seeing what's there. However, each network, even in an SBS environment, is unique, and therefore your management needs may vary from the standard configuration. This section describes some of the changes you may want to implement.

Customize the Dashboard

The Dashboard can be customized to a limited extent. The Dashboard, shown in Figure 24.1, consists of informational displays for the Connectivity Verifier, Services, Alerts, Sessions, and Performance. Most small businesses won't create Connectivity Verifiers because they don't have remote server connections. If you are not using this particular feature, roll up the Connectivity Verifier and leave room on the Dashboard to unroll the more interesting Performance Monitor, as shown in Figure 24.1.

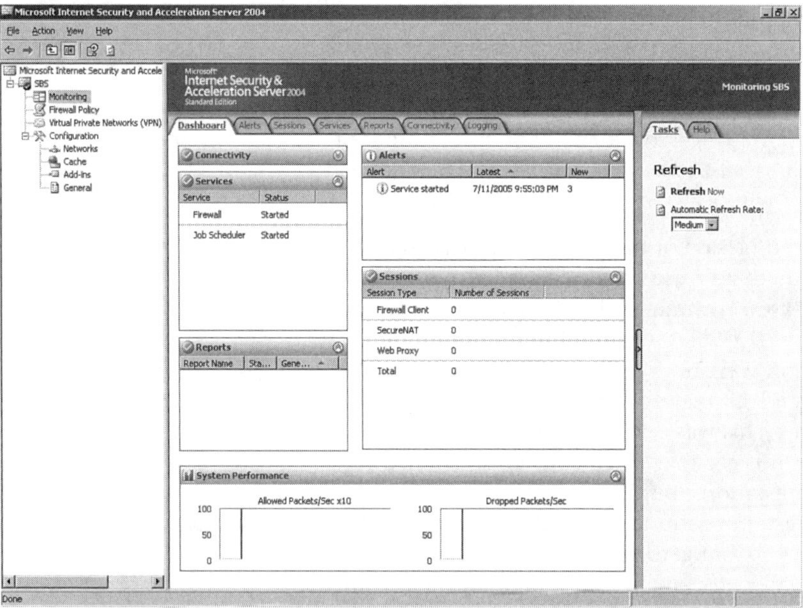

FIGURE 24.1 ISA Dashboard with rolled-up Connectivity Verifier.

To roll up or unroll an item on the Dashboard, click on the arrow on the right of each section.

Acknowledging Alerts

In Chapter 23, "Internet Security and Acceleration Server 2004 Basics," in the "Administration Delegation," section the acknowledgment of alerts was left to administrators. When an alert occurs the administrator needs experience to know whether the alert is significant to the business and if so, how to react to it. There are two options for handling alerts: Reset the alert, which makes it go away entirely, or acknowledge it (or them). Resetting the alert removes the alert. Acknowledging the alert changes the status to acknowledged, removes the alert from the Dashboard, but leaves the alert on the Alerts tab for your reference. Acknowledging the alert is the more conservative action to take. An acknowledged alert can be referenced while a solution is being sought. After you are finished troubleshooting the acknowledged alert, reset it.

To acknowledge an alert from the Dashboard, right-click on the alert and click Acknowledge All Instances, as shown in Figure 24.2.

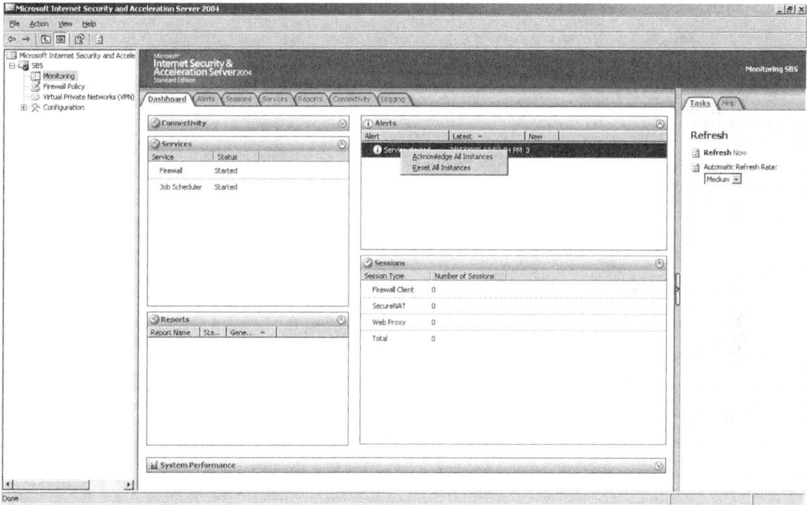

FIGURE 24.2 From the Dashboard, alerts can be reset or acknowledged.

To reset an alert from the Dashboard, right-click on the alert and click Reset. Or if you have previously acknowledged an alert and are now ready to reset that alert, go to the Alerts tab, right-click on the alert, and click Reset, as Figure 24.3 shows.

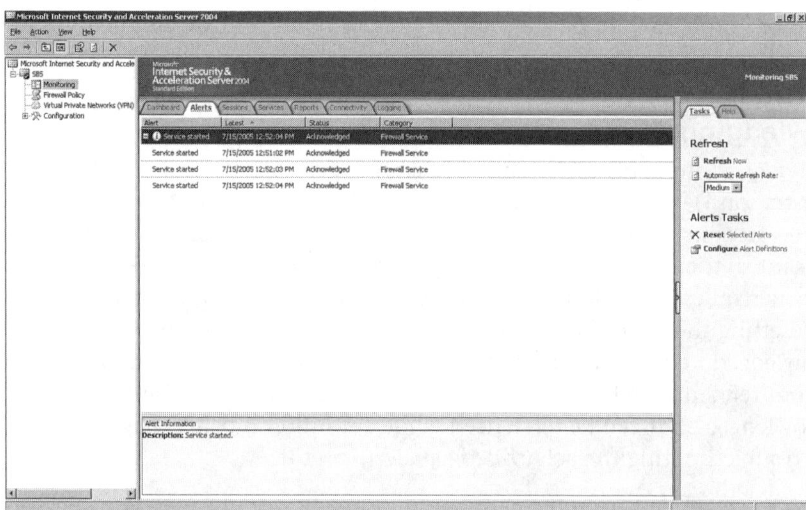

FIGURE 24.3 Once acknowledged from the Dashboard the status of the alert also changes on the Alerts tab.

DHCP Spoof Detection

Using a static IP address on all interfaces on the SBS server is preferable. However, many small business owners do not feel that they can afford the extra cost that the ISP charges for Internet service with a static IP address, and so they use DHCP on the external network card. The danger is that your SBS server can be spoofed into accepting an IP address that isn't offered from your ISP but rather from someone attempting to hack your network. DHCP spoofing is a technique whereby a "fake" DHCP server offers SBS an IP address that it will accept if not for DHCP spoof detection. In DHCP spoof detection, ISA keeps note of the network from which it received a DHCP address. If during the renewal process ISA is offered an address outside the previous network, it will reject the offer. Many commonly used inexpensive PPPOE DSL networks that small businesses use provide addresses from a wide range of networks. So the DHCP spoof detection may cause ISA to reject a legitimate offer. To let ISA accept any DHCP offer, simply reset the network card. This can be done in the Alerts task pane after you select the Invalid DHCP Offer alert.

Configure a Wireless Access Point

Setting up a wireless access point for employee laptops is a breeze in ISA 2004. With the ISA Server set up and functioning on your network, all the rules governing internal client access to the network apply to your employee laptops as well so long as you connect the wireless access point to the internal side of your server and set up the access point to allow the DHCP server on SBS to assign IP addresses to the clients. This simple wireless network configuration results in your laptops becoming members of the Internal Network group in ISA, and they receive all the access rights associated with that network.

The exact setup instructions vary according to brand of wireless router that you are using, so this chapter describes the procedure in general terms. During the initial set up of most wireless routers, you have the option of choosing Access Point or Wireless Gateway. Choosing Access Point allows the wireless router to provide wireless access to your network from the internal NIC of your server. Client computers connected in this manner have the same access to your network as those using an Ethernet cable. Connect an Ethernet cable to one of the LAN ports on the wireless router and connect the other end of the cable to your network switch or hub. The port that you connected each end to should light up.

Wireless Network Security

When using a wireless access point remember that any wireless adapter within reach may attempt to access your network. Set up strong security for your wireless network. Use the strongest security that your client computers will support with the longest most complex key available. When configuring a WEP access code use a complex password as the security key. To be sure that your laptops enjoy the same user experience as "hard-wired" computers on the network, join all laptops to the domain.

If you do not want your laptop computer users to have the same privileges as other computers in your DHCP server you'll need to create reservations so that your laptop computers are always assigned the same IP address. The next step is to create a Wireless Network network in ISA and assign your laptops to this network. This network can then be added to any ISA Firewall Policy rule allowing the administrator to control which resources the laptops can access.

Enabling Intrusion Detection

Intrusion detection is one of the things that businesses expect their firewall to do. It is somehow gratifying (and a little frightening) to see the Event Viewer filled with blocked attack attempts. Although no one likes the idea that someone is trying to get in, those events are evidence that ISA really is protecting your network. By default, however, intrusion detection is not enabled.

ISA groups attacks into two major categories: common and DNS. Click on General and then under Additional Security Policy click on Enable Intrusion Detection; then click on DNS Attack tab. Each of the listed attacks is well described by clicking on the question mark in the upper right corner of this dialog box. To enable intrusion detection, move to the Common Attacks tab and check the Enable Intrusion Detection box. As shown in Figure 24.4, check each of the common attack types. When you select Port Scan, the option to select the number of well-known ports scanned and the number of total ports scanned before the alert is triggered becomes active. The defaults are a good place to start. Finally check the Log Dropped Packets box.

NOTE

False positive all-port scans are known to occur. The most common reason for false all-port scan alerts is a rudely reset session on the remote end. This results in ISA not receiving an acknowledgement that the session has ended, and trailing packets from that session trigger the all-port scan alert. These can be identified by seeing whether there is normal traffic coming from the same IP address earlier in the logs. If so, the alert can be safely discarded.

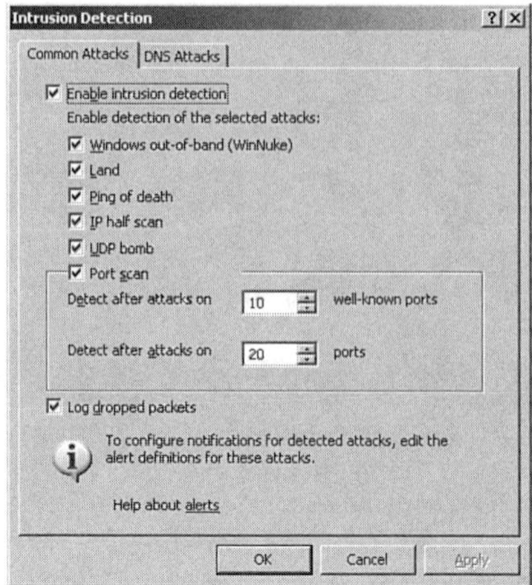

FIGURE 24.4 ISA intrusion detection common attack types.

Select the DNS Attacks tab, as shown in Figure 24.5. Check Enable Detection and Filtering of DNS Attacks. Check all attack types except DNS Zone Transfer. The DNS server on your SBS server does not allow zone transfers. The Zone Transfer attack is therefore prevented by the SBS DNS configuration, so it is not necessary to have ISA also look out for this type of attack. The other types of DNS attacks are buffer overflow attacks and could create a denial of service condition. Click OK.

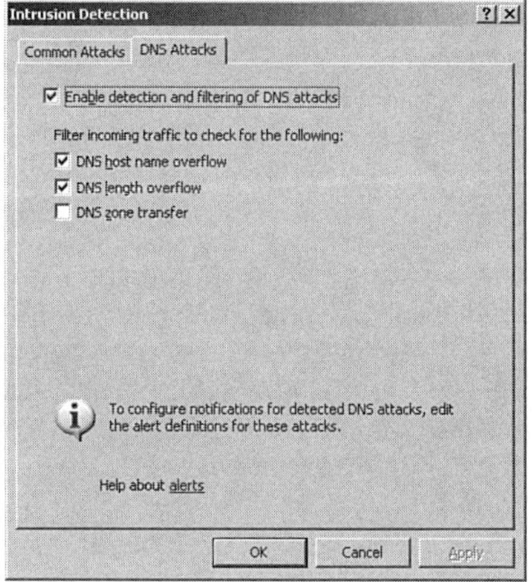

FIGURE 24.5 ISA intrusion detection of DNS attacks.

In this same section you'll also notice an item called Define IP Preferences, also shown in Figure 24.6. In general, these settings should not be changed. Although they at first appear to be additional security settings waiting to be selected, doing so could result in unintended consequences. Filtering IP fragments may interfere with IPSec and L2TP VPN clients, or streaming multimedia. Routing IP traffic causes the entire packet to be sent to the requested resource, whereas leaving it unchecked causes ISA to send only the data portion of the packet. Although enterprise networks with high volume may choose to modify the default settings, in general SBS networks should have no need to do so.

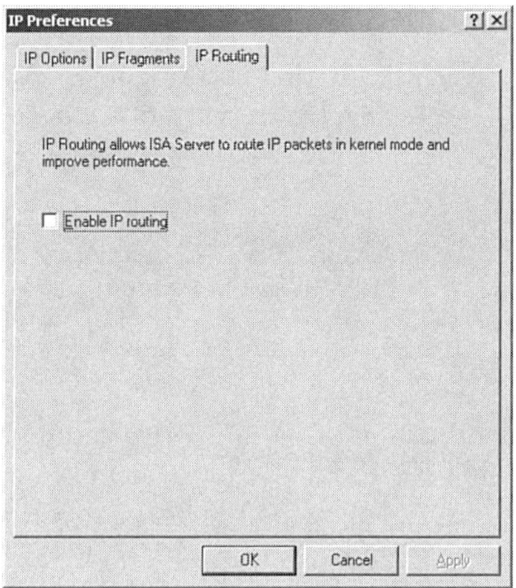

FIGURE 24.6 IP filtering options, in general, should not be changed.

Best Practice—Intrusion Detection Effect on Event Logs

Intrusion detection is probably the one thing that people think of when they think about what a firewall is going to do for them. Intrusion detection can be enabled on ISA server and the resulting blocked packets logged in the Event Viewer. Doing so may give the administrator a heads-up on potential problems, but it also increases the length of your event logs because the most common attacks now happen frequently.

So configure your event log size accordingly. By default, the setting is 16MB per log. The blocked packet entries appears in the application event log, so the log retention size should be doubled to make sure that you aren't overwriting events too quickly.

Setting Up Automatic Detection for the Firewall Client

The Firewall Client can be set up to automatically detect the ISA Server. Doing so resolves the problem with laptop computers that roam between networks and enables them to automatically detect whether they should use the ISA Server. This saves laptop users from having to reconfigure their Internet access when they switch between networks. It also saves the administrator from having to touch each client computer to manually enter the name of the ISA Server into the Configuration tab on the Firewall Client. Configuring automatic detection for the Firewall Client depends on the Firewall Client being able to access information in your DNS server, IIS, and ISA. The configuration for this is significantly different on SBS servers than on other implementations of ISA.

The heart of the automatic detection is a file called `WPAD.dat`. This file contains the Firewall Client configuration data. WPAD stands for Web Proxy Auto Discovery. When the Firewall Client configuration is set for Automatically Detect the ISA Server, the Firewall Client asks DNS for the location of the WPAD information. DNS points it to the IIS location—`http://SBS/wpad.dat`. The information in this file configures the Firewall Client.

The first step is to obtain a `WPAD.dat` file that is configured for SBS. This can be found at `http://isatools.org/sbs_wpad_2.zip`. Download the file onto your SBS server and expand it. This gives you two files, `wpad.dat` and `sbs_wpad.txt`.

CAUTION

The `sbs_wpad` files are currently in beta. Use caution and test your configuration before deploying the files on a production SBS server.

Instructions and current beta status information is also contained in the `sbs_wpad.txt` file. Read it thoroughly before beginning your implementation because the directions may change as the beta progresses. Following the beta period, the file and instructions will be moved to the Microsoft Downloads page for ISA at `http://www.microsoft.com/isaserver/downloads/2004/default.mspx`.

Modifying ISA

ISA comes preconfigured with all the necessary settings to operate a generic installation of SBS 2003. However, because many businesses don't fit exactly into the generic model, modifying ISA's configuration is necessary.

Understanding Application and Web Filters

It is not an understatement to say that application filters are the real strength of ISA. Back in the day, router/firewall administrators were accused of not caring about anything above layer 3 in the OSI model, where packets are routed. Application filters allow ISA to inspect packets at layer 7 where the data resides. Being able to inspect the contents is a huge advantage giving ISA the capability to prevent a wide range of attacks by filtering out contents that don't adhere to standards. Most attacks count on the fact that firewalls in place today aren't intelligent. All they know is open or closed. ISA on the other hand checks the packet to see whether it matches the expected configuration and also whether this type of data is allowed on your network at all.

To see the application filters, expand Configuration and then click on Add-ins. There are no configuration options in the filters themselves except to enable or disable them. By default all the filters are enabled except the H.323 and the SMTP filters (see Figure 24.7). The configuration of each of these filters actually comes in the specific rule definition as is described later in this chapter in the section "Allowing FTP Upload and Download to External Servers."

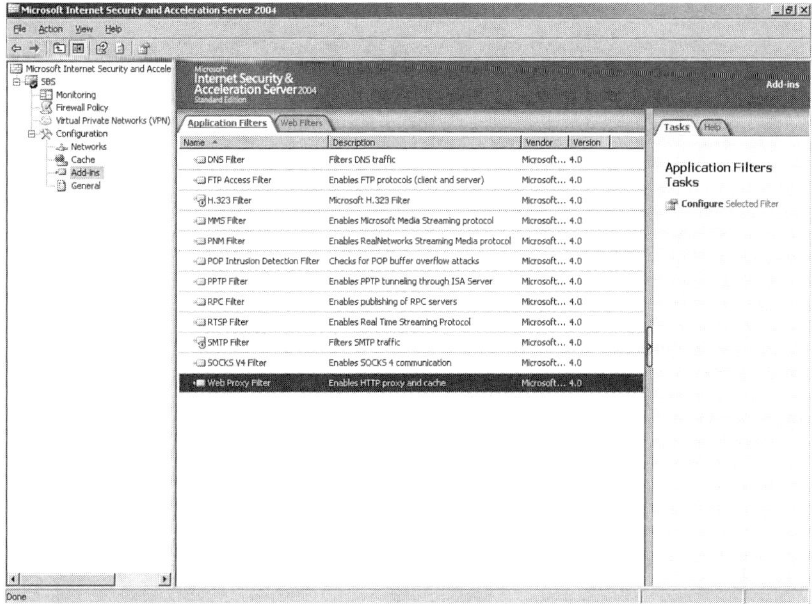

FIGURE 24.7 ISA application filters

Web filters are similar to application filters in that they are simply enabled or disabled in this section. Web and application filters allow advanced security configurations of the features that they control and both application and web filters can be extended by third-party developers.

Anatomy of a Firewall Policy

The Firewall Policy in ISA 2004 Server is made up of both System Policies and user-specified policies called Firewall Policy Rules. There are about an equal number of each in the default configuration. Both types of policies are required for ISA to work for SBS and are created for you when you run the Connect to the Internet Wizard.

System Policies can be changed only through the System Policy editor, whereas Firewall Policy Rules can be edited directly. During day-to-day administration, you will most often deal with Firewall Policy Rules and not the System Policy.

Firewall Policy Rules are made up of several components: access rules, protocol definitions, user set, schedule, domain name set, URL sets, and content filters. (see Figure 24.8) You can pick and choose which of these components are needed for your new rule. The best way to learn how to create a new policy is to look at the existing policies. To facilitate this, ISA 2004 has a new feature that allows you to copy a rule. To copy a rule, right-click on the rule that you want to copy and select Copy, then right-click and select Paste to paste the copied rule into the Firewall Policy. The copied rule is called *Rule Name* (1), where *Rule Name* is the name of the original rule. Rename the copy and then begin your configuration changes. This feature can be a real time-saver.

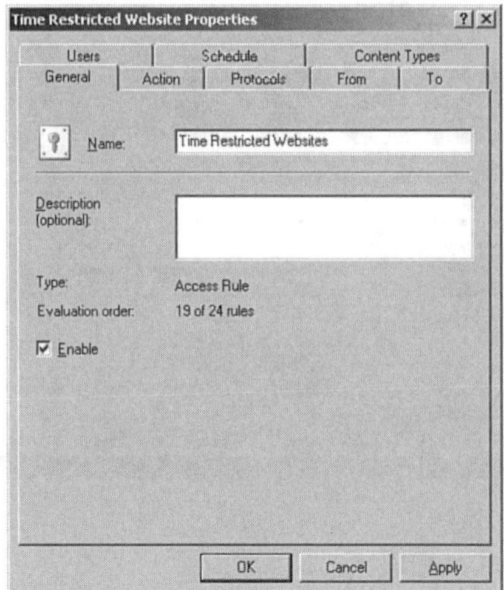

FIGURE 24.8 There are many options for refining a Firewall Policy Rule. Each tab contains options for fine tuning.

If you have created rules in ISA 2000, you'll notice that you can now define each component as you configure the rule instead of configuring each item individually and then creating the rule last. This feature is also a great timesaver.

Opening a Port

Opening a port is an antiquated term that really has no place in ISA management. In pinhole type firewalls/routers there are buttons that allow you to open or close ports. Sometimes they allow you to specify which protocol the port will be used for, but often this is predefined too. The problem with this type of security is that it is nondiscriminate. If the port is open, data is welcome to come in or leave from your network through this hole. If the port is closed, it isn't. ISA rules are concerned with the port as well but go much further in keeping the keys to your network. ISA checks to see whether the proper protocol is being used, who is welcome and who isn't, which direction the data is flowing, what kind of data it is, whether it is the right time of day to allow this, and so on. In short, there is no opening of ports. ISA administrators configure Firewall Policy Rules.

Components of a Firewall Policy Rule

Understanding firewall policy isn't rocket science. At first it appears intimidating because there are so many options. In reality, the options allow the administrator an unprecedented amount of flexibility and control. A brief description of each component follows.

- Access rules—The simplest definition of an access rule is that it allows clients on the source network to access a destination network. Together access rules make up Firewall Policy, and they can be seen listed in order in the Firewall Policy. Access rules are processed in order from 1 on up. Keeping your access rules in order is important from two standpoints: security and performance. Obviously, the closer to the top an access rule is in the list the faster the response time will be. From a security standpoint, when ISA gets to an access rule that allows your request, it is granted, even if another rule farther down the list would have prevented it.

- Protocol definitions—Protocol definitions define how ISA should handle traffic from particular protocols. ISA management contains many predefined protocols. You can also add your own.
- User set—User sets are groups of users to which a rule applies. ISA is Active Directory aware so a user set can consist of Active Directory users.
- Schedule—Schedules let you determine when a rule will be in force.
- Content filter—A content filter specifies which types of files the rule applies to.
- Domain name and URL sets—A domain name set is similar to a URL set. Whereas a URL set contains a group of dissimilar URLs, a domain name set specifies an entire domain. Rules can be applied against either of these sets.

Creating New Firewall Policy Rules

Two common requests for new rules are to create a rule to restrict certain websites during business hours and always deny access to certain websites. Mangers often want to deny these sites to particular users as well. We'll use the components discussed previously to create both of these rules.

Restrict Access to Certain Websites by Time of Day and Username

To create a rule to deny access to particular websites during business hours, except the lunch hour, in Firewall Policy, follow these steps:

1. Highlight the SBS Internet Access Rule and in the Tasks pane click on Create New Access Rule. This opens the New Access Rule Wizard. Enter a descriptive name for the rule such as Restricted Websites; then click Next.
2. Make sure that Deny is selected then click Next.
3. Make sure that All Outbound Traffic is selected and click Next.
4. On the Access Rules Sources page, click the Add button. A pop-up box called Add Network entities opens. Expand Network and select Internal; then click Close and click Next.
5. In the Access Rule Destinations screen, click the Add button. In the Add Network Entities pop-up window, click New and select URL Set. Enter a descriptive name into the Name box such as Restricted URLs. Then click the New button and enter the URL of the website that you want to restrict access to. Click New again to add additional sites to the list. When your list is complete, click OK.
6. The URL set that you just created is now listed under URL Sets. Select it and click the Add button. Click Close. The URL set now is listed in the This Rule Applies to Traffic Sent to These Destinations box. Click Next.

7. In the This Rule Applies to Requests from the Following User Sets, either click Add to restrict access to these sites to only a few people or click Next.
8. If you want to restrict these sites to only a few people, click the Add button, and in the Add Users pop-up window click New and select User Set. (see Figure 24.9) A user set is like an Active Directory group, and you assign users to this group. Enter a name for your user group, such as Internet Restricted Users, and click Next. Click the Add button and select Windows Users and Groups from the list. This opens the familiar Select Users or Groups from Active Directory in a pop-up window. Enter the first username in the box and click the Check Name button. Click OK to add this name to your group. Repeat this procedure until all the users you want to restrict Internet access for are members of the group and click Next. Click Finish to save the user set. The new user set will be listed in the available user sets. Select it and click the Add button. Click Close to continue with the wizard. Highlight All Users and click Remove if you do not want to restrict access for all users. Click Next and then click Finish.
9. Right-click on the Restrict Websites rule and select Properties. Move to the Schedule tab. Click the New button to create a new schedule for this rule. (see Figure 24.10) Type a descriptive name for the schedule, such as When Internet Restrictions are in effect, into the Name box. In the Schedule box all blue areas represent when the rule is in effect and therefore certain websites are restricted. All white areas represent when the rule is not in effect and users will be able to access the websites. The blue, Rule in Effect, areas are already selected for you. Click and drag to highlight the times when you do not want this rule in effect—for example, before and after office hours and during lunch. When finished creating the schedule, click OK. In the Schedule drop-down box, select the schedule you just created and click OK. Click Apply when you are ready to have the rule take effect.

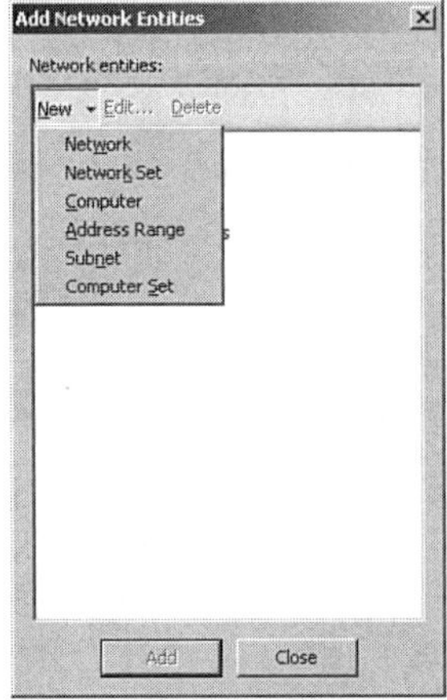

FIGURE 24.9 New user sets or URL sets can be created during the configuration of the rule.

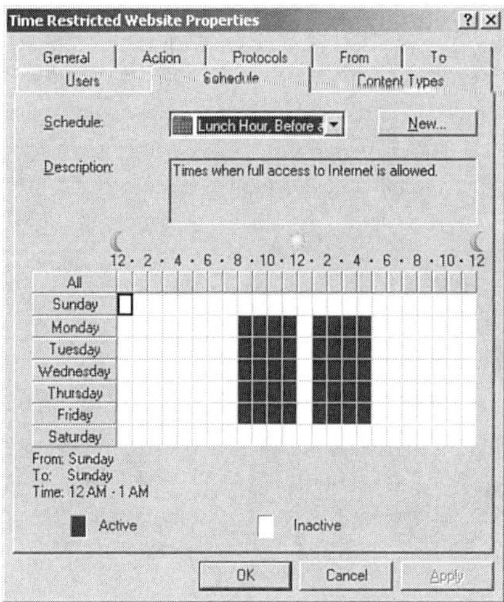

FIGURE 24.10 A schedule can be created and assigned to a rule, which will turn the rule on and off at designated times.

Create a Rule to Always Deny Particular Websites

If you also have a list of websites that you never want any of your users visiting. The same procedure used to create the rule to restrict sites based on time of day and username can be followed. Only this time there is no need to create a user set because by default all users are denied access to these websites and there is no need to modify the schedule because by default the rule is always active. To configure a rule to always deny access to certain websites, follow these steps:

1. In Firewall Policy highlight the SBS Internet Access Rule and then select Create New Access Rule from the Tasks pane. Give the rule a descriptive name such as Websites Never to Be Visited and click Next.
2. Make sure that Deny is selected and click Next.
3. Make sure that All Outbound Traffic is selected and click Next.
4. Click the Add button, expand Networks, select Internal, and click Add. Click Close to return to the wizard and click Next.
5. Click Add; then click New and select URL Set. In the Name box enter a descriptive name, such as Never Allow These URLs. Click New to add a URL. Repeat until your list is complete. Then click OK to return to the wizard.
6. Select the URL set you just created from the list and click Add. Click Close to return to the wizard. Click Next.
7. Click Next and click Finish. Click Apply when you are ready to have this rule take effect.

Best Practice—Using Scripts for Blocking Sites

If you have a long list of websites that you want to restrict, it's time to employ scripts. Some industrious people have made a hobby of collecting lists of advertising websites, pornography, and other plagues of the Internet. Several companies have as well, and these lists can be purchased from them. Two good sources for software add-ons both free and for fee are `http://www.isaserver.org/software/` and `http://isatools.org`.

Configure Websites for Direct Access

Occasionally you run into a website that requires a helper application that isn't proxy aware. In these cases you'll be denied access to the site. Often the support staff for these websites doesn't have a clue how to help you. They'll simply say that they don't support client computers behind a proxy. If you need to access a website where this is the case, you'll need to enable the site for direct access.

Direct access enables the client computer to access only the specified site directly, whereas all other sites continue to be accessed more securely from behind the proxy. To enable a site for direct access, follow these steps:

1. Expand Configuration; then click on Networks.
2. Right-click on Internal and select Properties.
3. Move to the Web Browser tab. Bypass Proxy for Web Servers in This Network and Directly Access Computers Specified in the Domains Tab should both be checked.
4. In the Directly Access These Servers or Domains box, (see Figure 24.11) you see the Internet IP address of your SBS server. Click the Add button and enter the IP address of the site that you need to directly access in the From and To box; if the support staff has given you a range, enter the beginning of the range in the From box and the end of the range in the To box. The support staff should be able to give you this information. If all you have available is the URL for the site, select the Domain or Computer radio button and click Browse, or enter the URL. Click OK to finish and click Apply.
5. If you want to have this policy change take place immediately, you'll need to update the Firewall Client manually. To do this, at the workstation right-click on the Firewall Client and select Configure.
6. Move to the Web Browser tab, check the Enable Web Browser Automatic Configuration box and click the Configure Now button. You get a Web Browser Settings Update pop-up box indicating that the web browser settings were successfully configured. Click OK to close it. Then click OK to close the Microsoft Firewall Client for ISA Server 2004 configuration screen.

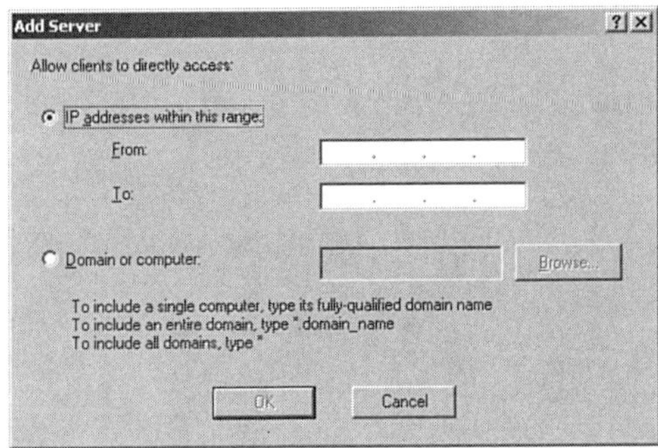

FIGURE 24.11 Websites that require direct access can be specified by IP address or name.

Direct Access Required = Nonconforming Website

One of the most frustrating things about having to configure direct access to certain websites is that it would be completely unnecessary if those websites would conform to industry standards or understood that more and more businesses are using sophisticated firewalls that won't tolerate nonauthenticated network use or poor coding. The only solution is to complain to the company with the problematic website and then allow direct access to it. Recognize that this is a compromise in your security that you have to make to accommodate this website.

Add SSL Tunnel Ports

Https websites are used by many banks and other financial institutions to provide secure transmission of data. By default the only SSL port that is allowed is 443. This means that ISA only allows secure socket layer communications to happen on this port. This is the standard port used by https websites. Some administrators have varied from the standard port and are using other ports for secured communication. If you find that you are unable to access an https website, the first step is to call the administrator of the website and ask which port is being using for SSL. For the purposes of our example we'll say that the website requires port 5443.

The SSL port designations held in the Registry are a little difficult to modify directly. Fortunately, the website `http://isatools.org`, which is known for housing many useful ISA scripts, has one that makes adding, removing, and displaying your SSL ports easy. The script can be downloaded at `http://isatoools.org/ISA_tpr.js`.

After you have downloaded the script, simply double-clicking on it causes it to display which SSL ports are currently installed on your server. However, running it from the command prompt is where the power is. Enter **`/?`** After the filename and press Enter to view the available switches and syntax for this script.

To allow SSL communications on port 5443 enter the following at the command prompt after navigating to the folder where you have saved the script. We'll call the port bankport5443. Type **`Isa_tpr.js /add bankport5443 5443`** and press Enter. (see Figure 24.12) After the command has processed, a Windows Script Host box pops up and reminds you to restart the Web Proxy service; click OK. Another series of script boxes appear that display the new port information.

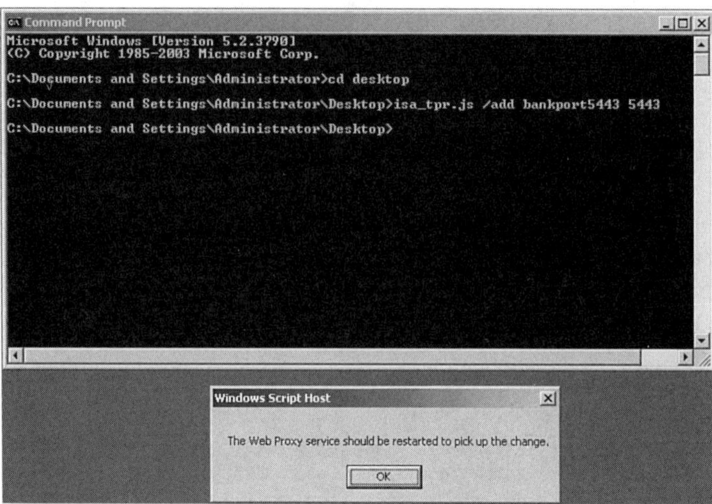

FIGURE 24.12 Using the script to create a new port for SSL also confirms that it was successful.

Nonstandard SSL Ports

Many financial institutions and ecommerce stores use SSL to secure data transmissions. The standard port for these communications is 443, but some locations use other ports, sometimes for security by obscurity reasons, sometimes for other internal reasons. ISA restricts SSL communications to port 443. SSL communications are encrypted, and many firewalls cannot determine what is contained within the packet. If you are hosting an SSL website, ISA has the capability to look into the packet, inspect the contents, encrypt it again, and let it continue on its way. ISA uses SSL Bridging to achieve this. In this way, Trojans, viruses, or other malformed contents can't make their way into the network simply because they are in an SSL tunnel. When adding an SSL port to ISA the same protection is afforded to these additional ports.

Allowing FTP Upload and Download to External Servers

The initial setup of ISA 2004 in SBS does not enable FTP Outbound access. However, many small businesses need to be able to use FTP. Small manufacturing firms FTP download CAD files of parts to be manufactured, whereas architecture firms often upload finished drawings to clients or builders. In both cases, files might go back and forth between a small business and its client several times before the product is finished.

NOTE

FTP Inbound isn't enabled by default either but can be set up using the Connect to the Internet Wizard in the SBS Management MMC.

FTP is one of the oldest protocols and as such wasn't developed with security in mind. Because of this, consider your FTP needs carefully, and only allow as much access as necessary. The first step is to note which users are going to need FTP access and whether they need to both upload and download FTP. Finally the type of ISA client that your computers are will tell you which rule you need to modify.

To enable FTP downloads for clients other than Firewall Clients, follow these steps:

1. Click Firewall Policy; then right-click SBS FTP Access and select Properties.
2. Click the Users tab, click the Add button, and then click New. The New User Set Wizard opens. Click Next to move to the next page.
3. Click Add and from the pop-up menu select Windows Users and Groups as shown in Figure 24.13. Add your users, click Next, and then click Finish.
4. Your user set is now listed in the Users window. Select the group you just created and click the Add button; then click Close. The FTP user group now is listed in the Users tab.
5. Select the General tab and check Enable; then click OK.
6. If you also want to enable the uploading of files via FTP to remote servers go back into the properties of the SBS FTP access rule and move to the Protocols tab. Click the Filtering button and select Configure FTP. Uncheck the Read Only box to allow the uploading of FTP files; then click OK.

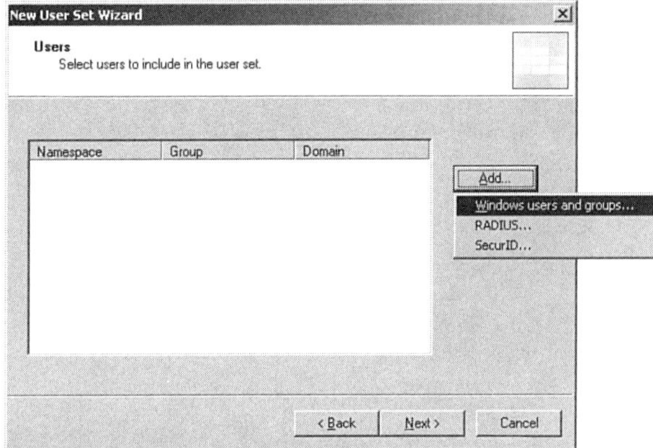

FIGURE 24.13 A new user group consisting of Active Directory users can be configured during the editing of the SBS FTP access policy.

Firewall Clients don't need the FTP Outbound access rule, which is why it is disabled by default. The Firewall Client can negotiate the use of a port through the SBS Internet access rule. But because the FTP application filter is set to read only for the SBS Internet access rule, these clients won't be able to upload files out of the network. To change this you'll need to configure the FTP filter for the SBS Internet access rule. Follow these steps:

1. Right-click on the SBS Internet access rule, select Configure FTP, and uncheck the Read Only box (see Figure 24.14).

2. Click OK; then click Apply when you are ready for the new rule to take effect.

You've just created a rule that allows members of the FTP Users group to upload and download files.

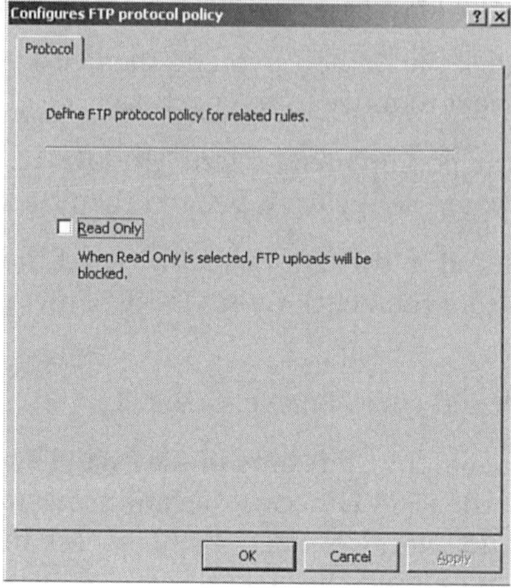

FIGURE 24.14 Unchecking Read Only in the FTP filter configuration allows FTP files to be uploaded out of the network.

Best Practice—FTP Application Filter

FTP is one of the oldest protocols. In the Internet's humble beginning security was not the issue that it is today; therefore, the FTP protocol wasn't designed to secure transmissions. The FTP application filter is designed to assist you in controlling who has the ability to upload or download using FTP. If FTP access is required, the best practice is to allow FTP access only for downloads to your network but not allow users to FTP data out of your network. If FTP out is also required, creating a user group whose members require FTP uploads is recommended.

Publish a Web Server

You have three choices for publishing a website. You can let your ISP or another hosting service do it for you. (Most small businesses do.) You can host the website on your SBS server, in which case the Connect to the Internet Wizard configures the necessary ISA server components for you. Or you can add a second server to your network and host the website there, in which case you'll need to configure ISA to direct the web requests to that server. Because this chapter is only about ISA, the chapter assumes that your IIS server is already configured and that your website is ready. The chapter also assumes that you've selected port 81 as the port that the website will be accessed on. Follow these steps to publish a website housed on a second server:

NOTE

Because port 80 is already in use on SBS, to avoid any potential conflicts you should publish your website on an alternate port.

1. In Firewall Policy, select Publish a Web Server from the Task pane. Give your policy a descriptive name representing your website. In this example we'll use Project Status Website and assume that it's a website where clients can go to check the status of the prototype development for the widget that they designed. Click Next.
2. The wizard has already selected Allow on this page, so click Next. In the Computer Name or IP Address box, enter the full name of the web server or its IP address. In the Path box enter `/*` if this is the only website on your server; otherwise, enter `/folder name` where *folder name* is the name of the folder that contains your website as shown in Figure 24.15. Click Next.
3. The Accept Requests For box should already have selected This Domain Name (enter below). In the Public Name box enter the URL for your website, `projectstatus.smallbizco.com`. In the Path box enter the same path as before, `/*`. Click Next.
4. In the Web Listener drop-down menu list, select SBS Web Listener. Click Next.
5. Because you want all clients to be able to access the website, All Users is the appropriate choice. Click Next and then click Finished.
6. Your rule is now listed in the Firewall Policy. Right-click on the rule you just created and move to the Bridging tab. Check Redirect Requests to HTTP Port and enter the alternate port number that you used in IIS when you set up the website. Click OK to save the changes.

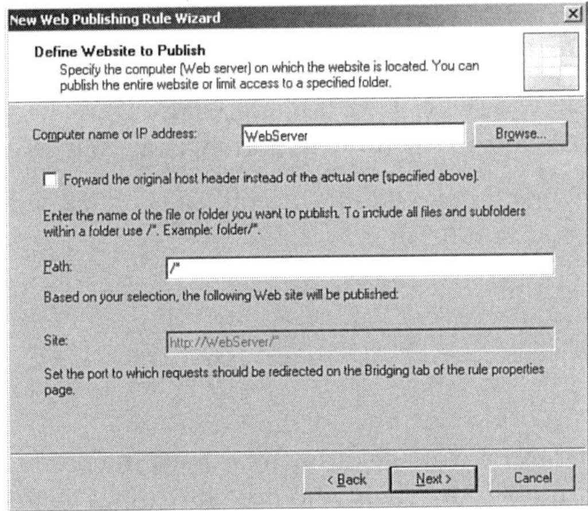

FIGURE 24.15 When configuring your web publishing rule, a subfolder can be specified if more than one website resides on your server.

Best Practice—Making the Web Hosting Decision

Making the decision on whether to host your website on SBS, buy an additional server, or let an offsite company host your website for you is one that should be carefully considered from a security standpoint. Assuming that you have the in-house talent to design and set up web hosting, the next decision is whether you also have the in-house talent to make sure that your website and the server that it runs on is secure and will remain that way through website revisions.

Many capable small and large website hosting services are available that are reasonably priced. The question to ask them is not whether their web servers are secure but how often they are patched and which web server software they are running. All software requires patching. It only takes a moment to find out what the latest patch level is and compare this to what the web host you are considering is running. If they pass this test and have a good customer support reputation, you may well be better off letting these professionals host the website for you.

Troubleshooting

Two things about troubleshooting are important to keep in mind. First, you want to try to avoid it. Second, if you've not managed to avoid the problem, you need to start at the top and work your way down in order of complexity. Here's a list of troubleshooting tips beginning with those that help you avoid pitfalls:

- Never click the Apply button until you have reviewed the changes you just made.
- Always apply one change at a time; then test that change.
- Always run the Firewall Client. If a particular workstation is having a problem but no others are, start by checking IP configuration and that the Firewall Client is connected on the workstation.
- Make sure that the workstations are not infected with spyware and aren't running another firewall software on the workstation before you begin troubleshooting.
- If a website cannot be viewed, it might be a DNS issue. Verify your DNS settings on both the server and the workstation.
- If an SSL website cannot be viewed, it might be using an alternative SSL port. Add the appropriate SSL port to the tunnel port range on your server.
- If a web application will not connect, it is probably an authentication issue. Configure the application for direct access.
- Use the logs to determine at what point the client request is being denied.

Summary

Using ISA to protect an SBS network gives small business the power to allow access where and when necessary to those individuals who need it without compromising security in other areas. Out-of-the-box ISA and the SBS wizards configure all the default settings that allow the components of the server to get along securely on a single server. But because all small businesses have unique needs, understanding how to configure ISA to allow access specific to your needs is imperative. If it is possible to boil down ISA configuration it would be in the creation of Firewall Policy Rules. Many components make up a Firewall Policy Rule, and those components can be combined in various ways to achieve the desired result. In addition to Firewall Policy Rules, small businesses may add additional servers to the network that require Internet access. Publishing rules are used to control access to other servers on the network. After ISA is configured, the administrator spends most of his time simply monitoring ISA, watching for intruders or Internet activities from internal users that may place the small business in a compromising situation or reduce productivity. ISA displays all this information in the Dashboard and Monitoring sections of the ISA Management MMC.

Although ISA can at first seem complex, taking the time to learn how it works yields benefits that no other firewall within budgetary reach of small businesses can provide. Although ISA was designed primarily for the large enterprise, where IT staff make their whole careers managing the firewall, the management of an ISA Server for the small business is not that difficult or time consuming. The results of a little effort will reward themselves many times over, just as soon as the next outbreak aimed at perceived security flaws occurs while your network is still humming along protected by ISA.

Best Practice Summary

- Intrusion detection effect on event logs—Because an unchecked event log can fill up a server hard drive, the level of logging allowed for intrusion detection should be configured to ensure that the log will not grow too large.
- Using scripts for blocking sites—If you have a large list of sites you want to block from your users, look at using scripts to configure ISA blocking for those sites instead of entering the sites manually.
- The FTP application filter—It can assist you in controlling who has the ability to upload or download using FTP. If FTP access is required, allow FTP access only for downloads to your network, but do not allow users to FTP data out of your network. If FTP out is also required, create a group whose members require FTP uploads and only assign permission to that group.
- Making the web hosting decision—For a variety of reasons, most small businesses decide to let someone else host their website. Because the data on that website is being entrusted to someone else, you need to find out whether their servers are fully patched, what their patching policy is, what the backup policy is, and how good their customer service is.

PART X

Appendix

IN THIS PART

APPENDIX A

SBS Resources

IN THIS APPENDIX

- Microsoft Community Resources
- Small Business Community Resources
- Exchange Resources
- Macintosh Resources
- Outlook Resources
- Outlook Web Access Resources
- ActiveSync/PocketPC Resources
- SBS Monitoring and Reporting Resources
- Group Policy Resources
- RRAS, VPN, and Firewall Resources
- Terminal Server Resources
- Workstation Security Resources
- Security and Patching Resources

The following is a list of online resources for materials presented in the book.

Microsoft Community Resources

These resources are hosted and/or developed by Microsoft.

Websites and RSS Feeds

- Microsoft Windows Small Business Server 2003—`http://www.microsoft.com/windowsserver2003/sbs/default.mspx`
- Microsoft Windows Small Business Server 2003 Downloads—`http://www.microsoft.com/windowsserver2003/sbs/downloads/default.mspx`
- Windows Small Business Server 2003 Recent KBs—`http://support.microsoft.com/common/rss.aspx?rssid=3208&ln=en-us`
- Windows Server 2003 Recent KBs—`http://support.microsoft.com/common/rss.aspx?rssid=3198&ln=en-us`
- Complete Microsoft Product RSS Feeds—`http://support.microsoft.com/selectindex/?target=rss`
- Troubleshooting Windows Small Business Server 2003—`http://download.microsoft.com/download/5/6/1/561c9fd7-0e27-4525-94ec-4d2d38f61aa3/TSHT_SBS.htm`
- MSDN RSS Feeds – Website—`http://msdn.microsoft.com/aboutmsdn/rss/`
- Microsoft Small Business Community—`http://www.mssmallbiz.com/`

Newsgroups

- SBS 2003 Public Newsgroup—`microsoft.public.windows.server.sbs` `http://support.microsoft.com/newsgroups/default.aspx?NewsGroup=microsoft.public.windows.server.sbs`
- SBS 2003 Private Partner Newsgroup (for Microsoft Partners, password needed for access)—`microsoft.private.directaccess.smallbizserver2003`

Web Logs (Blogs)

- Windows Small Business Server Documentation—`http://blogs.msdn.com/sbsdocsteam/`
- The Official SBS Support Blog—`http://blogs.technet.com/sbs/`
- Charlie Anthe—`http://blogs.msdn.com/canthe/`

Small Business Community Resources

The following non-Microsoft resources pertain to the small business market as a whole.

Websites/Blogs

- SmallBizServer.net—`http://www.smallbizserver.net`
- Amy Babinchak—`http://isainsbs.blogspot.com/`
- Tim Barrett—`http://timothybarrett.blogspot.com/`
- Susan Bradley [SBS-MVP]—`http://www.sbsdiva.com/`
- Dean Calvert [SBS-MVP]—`http://msmvps.com/calvert/`
- Sean Daniel—`http://seanda.blogspot.com/`
- Steve Downs—`http://www.stevereno.net/sbs/sbs.php`
- Javier Gomez [SBS-MVP]—`http://msmvps.com/javier/`
- Chad Gross [SBS-MVP]—`http://www.msmvps.com/cgross/`
- Jeff Louck [SBS-MVP]—`http://www.msmvps.com/sbs/`
- Vlad Mazek—`http://www.vladville.com/`
- Eriq Oliver Neale—`http://simultaneouspancakes.com/Lessons/` `http://www.eonconsulting.net/OnQ/`
- Mad Blogger (Paul)—`http://blog.flaphead.dns2go.com/`
- Tavis Patterson—`http://www.taznetworks.com/rss/webblog.html`
- Wayne Small [SBS-MVP]—`http://www.msmvps.com/sbsfaq/`

- Anne Stanton [CRM-MVP]—http://thenorwichgroup.blogs.com/
- Gavin Steiner—http://interprom.blogspot.com/
- Bill Vogel—http://sbsbill.blogspot.com/
- Kevin Weilbacher—http://www.msmvps.com/kwsupport/
- Nick Whittome [SBS-MVP]—http://msmvps.com/thenakedmvp/
- Small Business Trends—http://www.smallbusinesses.blogspot.com/
- Small Business CEO—http://smallbusinessceo.blogspot.com/
- *Windows IT Pro magazine*—http://www.windowsitpro.com/

Mailing Lists

- SBS2k Yahoo Group, Microsoft SBS 4.5, 2000, and 2003 Support—
  http://groups.yahoo.com/group/sbs2k/
  Sbs2k@yahoogroups.com
- SmallBizIT Yahoo Group, Small Business IT Consultants—
  http://groups.yahoo.com/group/smallbizIT/
  smallbizit@yahoogroups.com
- SBS Group Leads Yahoo Group, International SBS IT Professional Groups, Leader's Group—http://groups.yahoo.com/group/newSBSgroups/
  SBSgroupLEADS@yahoogroups.com
- MSSmallbiz—http://groups.yahoo.com/group/mssmallbiz/

Exchange Resources

- Technical Resources for Exchange Server—http://www.microsoft.com/exchange/techinfo/default.mspx
- Microsoft Exchange Server TechCenter, Part of Microsoft TechNet—
  http://www.microsoft.com/technet/prodtechnol/exchange/default.mspx
- Exchange Server 2003 Technical Documentation Library, Part of Microsoft TechNet—http://www.microsoft.com/technet/prodtechnol/exchange/2003/library/default.mspx
- MSExchange.org—Microsoft Exchange Server Resource Site
  http://www.msexchange.org/

Macintosh Resources

Web Pages and RSS Feeds

- MacWindows – Integrating Macintosh and Windows—http://www.macwindows.com/
- MacFixIt – Troubleshooting Solutions for the Macintosh—http://www.macfixit.com/
- Macintosh News Network—http://macnn.com
- Apple Discussion Forums—http://discussions.info.apple.com/
- MacInTouch Home Page—http://www.macintouch.com/
- Mac OS X Hints—http://www.macosxhints.com/
- MacForumz—http://www.macforumz.com/

Newsgroups

- Microsoft Entourage Newsgroup—
  microsoft.public.mac.office.entourage
  http://support.microsoft.com/newsgroups/default.aspx?NewsGroup=microsoft.public.mac.office.entourage
- Microsoft Remote Desktop Client for Macintosh Newsgroup—
  microsoft.public.mac.rdc
  http://support.microsoft.com/newsgroups/default.aspx?NewsGroup=microsoft.public.mac.rdc
- Microsoft Newsgroup for Other Mac Products—
  microsoft.public.mac.otherproducts
  http://support.microsoft.com/newsgroups/default.aspx?NewsGroup=microsoft.public.mac.otherproducts
- alt.mac
- comp.sys.mac

Mailing Lists

- MacProfessionals Yahoo Group—
  http://groups.yahoo.com/group/MacProfessionals/
- AllMacs Yahoo Group—http://groups.yahoo.com/group/allmacs/

Outlook Resources

- Business Contact Manager Update for Outlook—Allows licensed users of Outlook 2003 to share customer information and sales opportunities. Also integrates with

Microsoft Office Small Business Accounting 2006. http://www.microsoft.com/office/outlook/contactmanager/prodinfo/update.mspx

- Outlook 2003 with Business Contact Manager Update Add-in: Business Contacts for Pocket PC—Synchronize Outlook 2003 with Business Contact Manager Update with a Pocket PC. Note: Not compatible with SmartPhones, only with Pocket PCs. http://www.microsoft.com/downloads/details.aspx?FamilyId=F3BC2918-C310-4599-81D1-558CF385ED88&displaylang=en
- Enabling a Superior Client Experience with Outlook 2003—This whitepaper describes the new features and improvements for Outlook 2003, and explains improvements in bandwidth and synchronization optimization. http://www.microsoft.com/office/outlook/prodinfo/enabling.mspx
- LookOut —Add-on allows lightning fast searches inside Outlook. http://www.lookoutsoft.com/Lookout/lookoutinfo.html
- Using General Purpose Public Folder Trees in Exchange 2003—Tutorial for creating public folders for use in Outlook to share contacts companywide. http://www.msexchange.org/tutorials/General-Purpose-Public-Folder-Trees-Exchange2003.html

Outlook Web Access Resources

- Exchange 2003: Outlook Web Access Web Administration—Administration with a web-based user interface that allows tuning of the Outlook Web Access settings. http://www.microsoft.com/downloads/details.aspx?FamilyID=4BBE7065-A04E-43CA-8220-859212411E10&displaylang=en
- Xbox Theme for Outlook Web Access—Custom theme to dress up Outlook Web Access to have an Xbox look and feel. http://www.microsoft.com/ downloads/details.aspx?FamilyID=aeca9fe8-e8fc-455a-9d65-468d194e866b&DisplayLang=en
- Creating and Deploying Outlook Web Access Themes—Get detailed information on installing the Xbox OWA theme, or create and install your own themes. http://www.microsoft.com/technet/prodtechnol/exchange/2003/library/owathemes.mspx

ActiveSync/PocketPC Resources

- Windows Mobile Downloads—Links for PocketPC devices, including the latest version of ActiveSync. http://www.microsoft.com/windowsmobile/downloads/
- Windows Mobile 5.0—The new operating system for Pocket PCs and SmartPhones. Includes a mobile version of Windows Media Player 10. http://www.microsoft.com/windowsmobile/5/default.mspx

- Microsoft Global Contact Access—Use this plug-in to access information in the Global Address List (GAL) on your Exchange server, such as contacts and coworkers free/busy information. Available for SmartPhones and Pocket PC Phone Edition. `http://www.microsoft.com/windowsmobile/downloads/global/default.mspx`

SBS Monitoring and Reporting Resources

- How to Create and Configure Performance Alerts in Windows Server 2003—Provides an overview on the customizable performance alerts that exist in Windows Server 2003, which can be integrated with the Small Business monitoring tools. `http://support.microsoft.com/?kbid=324752`
- SBS Visual Guide (To Do List, Configure Monitoring)—Step-by-step visual guide on running the Configure Monitoring Wizard. Site also provides excellent information on every aspect of the To Do List. `http://www.sbs-rocks.com/sbs2k3/sbs2k3-m4.htm`
- Performance Logs and Alerts interface – Technet—Provides in-depth information on the customizable performance alerts that exist in Windows Server 2003. Excellent resource for those who need to extract much more information than what SBS shows by default. `http://www.microsoft.com/technet/prodtechnol/windowsserver2003/library/ServerHelp/2bdb5fda-ac0c-4d6a-af26-933dac49e85b.mspx`

Group Policy Resources

- Group Policy - Microsoft—Contains webcasts, whitepapers, and links about using/configuring group policy. `http://www.microsoft.com/technet/prodtechnol/windowsserver2003/technologies/featured/gp/default.mspx`
- Managing Terminal Servers Using Group Policy—Provides in-depth information and suggestions for locking down Terminal servers using group policy. `http://www.microsoft.com/windowsserver2003/techinfo/overview/lockdown.mspx`
- Group Policy Administrative Templates – Technet—Information on how to create your own administrative templates from scratch. `http://windows.microsoft.com/windows2000/en/server/help/default.asp?url=/windows2000/en/server/help/ADM.htm`
- Managing Office 2003 with Group Policy—Brief article on how to use and obtain Microsoft's administrative templates for Office 2003. Excellent resource to manage Office settings across multiple computers. `http://office.microsoft.com/en-us/assistance/HA011402401033.aspx`

RRAS, VPN, and Firewall Resources

- SBS 2003 Standard with UPnP Router—Visual guide on configuring the RRAS firewall and UPnP routers. http://www.smallbizserver.net/Default.aspx?tabid=156
- Configuring Remote Access in SBS—Visual guide to configuring PPTP virtual private networks with SBS 2003. Includes troubleshooting steps. http://www.smallbizserver.net/Default.aspx?tabid=133
- Connecting Clients to the Server via VPN—Visual guide on configuring Windows XP for PPTP VPN connections manually. http://www.smallbizserver.net/Default.aspx?tabid=92
- Remote Workstations and Small Business Server—Step-by-step instructions for joining remote workstations to an SBS domain using virtual private networks. http://www.smallbizserver.net/Default.aspx?tabid=146

Terminal Server Resources

- LabMice.net Collection of Terminal Server Resources—http://labmice.techtarget.com/windows2003/TerminalServices/default.htm
- Deploying Office 2003 in a Windows Terminal Services Environment—http://office.microsoft.com/en-us/assistance/HA011402071033.aspx
- Guidelines for Deploying Terminal Server—http://www.microsoft.com/windowsserver2003/techinfo/overview/quickstart.mspx
- Remote Desktop Client for the Macintosh—http://www.microsoft.com/mac/otherproducts/otherproducts.aspx?pid=remotedesktopclient

Workstation Security Resources

Antivirus Tools

Free Online Scanning Tools

- Authentium Command on Demand—http://www.commandondemand.com/
- WindowsSecurity.com Trojan Scanner—http://www.windowsecurity.com/trojanscan/
- Panda ActiveScan—http://www.pandasoftware.com/activescan/com/default.asp?language=2
- TrendMicro HouseCall—http://housecall.trendmicro.com/
- RavAntivirus—http://www.ravantivirus.com/scan/indexie.php
- Symantec Security Check—http://security.symantec.com/
- McAfee freescan—http://us.mcafee.com/root/mfs/default.asp

Free Antivirus Programs (Includes Evaluation Versions and Cleanup Tools for Specific Outbreaks)

- Sophos Evaluation Version—http://www.sophos.com/products/eval/
- Antidote SuperLite (scanner only)—http://www.vintage-solutions.com/English/Antivirus/Super/index.html
- AntiVir Personal Edition Classic—http://www.free-av.com/antivirus/allinonen.html
- AVG Anti-Virus Free Edition—http://www.grisoft.com/doc/289/lng/us/tpl/tpl01
- F-Prot Anti-Virus for Windows Trial Version—http://www.f-prot.com/download/corporate/trial/
- NOD32 Trial Version—http://www.nod32.com/download/trial.htm
- McAfee Stinger—http://vil.nai.com/vil/stinger/

Security Response Toolkit

- NetCat—http://netcat.sourceforge.net/http://www.securityfocus.com/tools/139
- SysInternals AccessEnum—http://www.sysinternals.com/Utilities/AccessEnum.html
- SysInternals AutoRuns—http://www.sysinternals.com/utilities/autoruns.html
- SysInternals Contig—http://www.sysinternals.com/utilities/contig.html
- SysInternals DiskView—http://www.sysinternals.com/utilities/diskview.html
- SysInternals FileMon—http://www.sysinternals.com/utilities/filemon.html
- SysInternals ListDLLs—http://www.sysinternals.com/utilities/listdlls.html
- SysInternals Page Defrag—http://www.sysinternals.com/utilities/pagedefrag.html
- SysInternals ProcessExplorer—http://www.sysinternals.com/utilities/processexplorer.html
- SysInternals PS Tools—http://www.sysinternals.com/utilities/pstools.html
- SysInternals RegMon—http://www.sysinternals.com/utilities/regmon.html
- SysInternals Rootkit Revealer—http://www.sysinternals.com/utilities/rootkitrevealer.html
- SysInternals Sdelete—http://www.sysinternals.com/utilities/sdelete.html
- SysInternals ShareEnum—http://www.sysinternals.com/utilities/shareenum.html

- SysInternals Sync—http://www.sysinternals.com/utilities/sync.html
- SysInternals TCPView—http://www.sysinternals.com/utilities/tcpview.html
- Heysoft LADS—http://www.heysoft.de/Frames/f_sw_la_en.htm
- myNetWatchman SecCheck—http://www.mynetwatchman.com/tools/sc/
- Inetcat.org NBTScan—http://www.inetcat.org/software/nbtscan.html
- FoundStone BinText—http://www.foundstone.com/index.htm?subnav=resources/navigation.htm&subcontent=/resources/freetools.htm
- WinPcap—http://www.winpcap.org/install/default.htm
- WinDump—http://www.winpcap.org/windump/
- Ethereal Installer—http://www.ethereal.com/download.html
- Nmap—http://www.insecure.org/nmap/
- Tigerteam.se SBD (encrypted netcat)—http://tigerteam.se/dl/sbd/
- BlackIce PC Protection—http://www.digitalriver.com/ dr/v2/ec_dynamic.main?SP=1&PN=10&sid=26412
- CPU-Z—http://www.cpuid.com/cpuz.php
- ISCAlert—http://www.labreatechnologies.com/

Security and Patching Resources

General Security Information

- Microsoft Security Advisories—http://www.microsoft.com/technet/security/advisory/default.mspx
- MSRC blog—http://blogs.technet.com/msrc/
- Full Disclosure—https://lists.grok.org.uk/mailman/listinfo/full-disclosure
- Daily Dave—https://lists.immunitysec.com/mailman/listinfo/dailydave
- Metasploit RSS feed—http://www.metasploit.com/
- OSVDB mailing list—http://www.osvdb.org/mailing-lists.php
- Ntbugtraq—http://www.ntbugtraq.com/
- SecuriTeam—http://www.securiteam.com/mailinglist.html
- SecurityFocus Mailing Lists—http://www.securityfocus.com/archive

WSUS Resources

- WSUS listserver—http://www.patchmanagement.org
- WSUS community forum—http://www.wsus.info/default.asp
- WSUS wiki—http://www.wsuswiki.com/
- WSUS download—http://www.microsoft.com/windowsserversystem/updateservices/default.mspx
- WSUS blog—http://blogs.technet.com/wsus/
- WSUS MVP blog—http://msmvps.com/athif/

Index

Numbers

A

B

C

D

E

F

G

H

J

K-L

M

N

O

- OWA (Outlook Web Access), 116, 235-238
  - Administration Kit, 241-243
  - accessing with RWW (Remote Web Workplace), 360
  - enabling, 236-238
  - Macintosh platforms, 428
  - Outlook Web Access Administration Kit, 241-243
  - OWA Basic, 238-239
  - OWA Premium, 239
  - OWA Premium with ActiveX, 240
  - Private Computer security configuration, 244
  - Public or Shared Computer security configuration, 244
  - resources, 613
  - spell checking, 239
  - troubleshooting, 252

P

Q-R

S

How can we make this index more useful? Email us at indexes@samspublishing.com

T

W

X-Y-Z